INTERNATIONAL RELATIONS

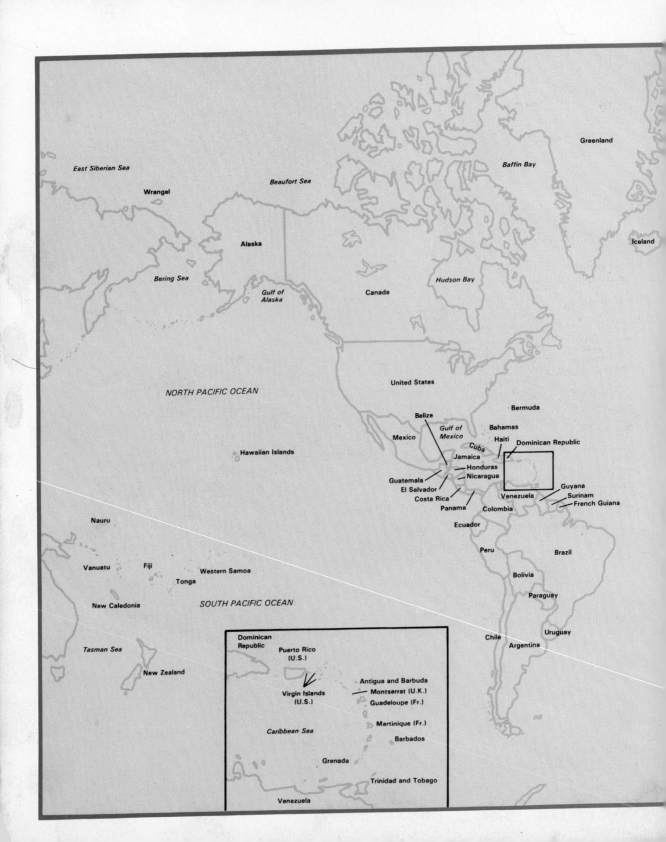

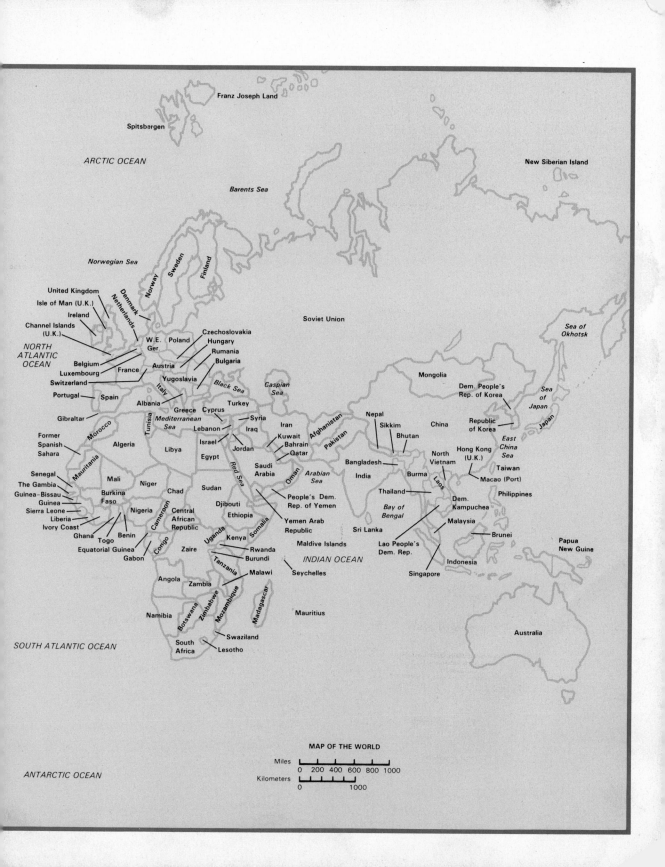

MAP OF THE WORLD

INTERNATIONAL RELATIONS

The Global Condition in the Late Twentieth Century

SECOND EDITION

Frederic S. Pearson

J. Martin Rochester

Both of the University of Missouri–St. Louis

RANDOM HOUSE   NEW YORK

For Melvadean and Ruth, experts in the fine
art of conflict resolution, and for Stephen, Sean, Nathaniel,
Helen, and Emma and all those for whom the global condition
will be a way of life

Second Edition

Copyright © 1984, 1988 by Newbery Award Records, Inc.

Library of Congress Cataloging-in-Publication Data

Pearson, Frederic S.
  International relations.

  Includes bibliographies and index.
  1. International relations. I. Rochester, J. Martin. II. Title.
JX1391.P4 1988   327   87–23363
ISBN 0–394–36877–0

Text design: Suzanne Bennett
Cover design: Nadja-Furlan-Lorbek

Manufactured in the United States of America

Copyright acknowledgments and photo and illustration credits appear at the back of the book.

Preface

When we began this project, the immediate question we faced was: Does the world really need another international relations textbook, given the many books already available on this subject? We answered in the affirmative, convinced that we could write a book that would be somewhat distinctive in content as well as style. In particular, we were seeking to write a book that would somehow appeal to beginning students—its primary audience—as well as to more knowledgeable readers, a book that would combine in a balanced fashion the traditional as well as the new approaches to the study of international relations. We believe we succeeded in this goal, but we will let the reader be the judge. This second edition follows the same orientation as the first, but includes considerable updating of information, major revision of certain sections, and some reorganization of topics, all designed to improve upon the initial version.

In terms of *content*, we have tried to give comprehensive coverage to the major topics in the field. The general theme of the book can be summarized as the need for scholars, policymakers, and laymen to take into account the complex variety of relationships that exist today—among more than 5 billion people, 160 countries (nation–states), and 3000 international organizations—in order to understand the "global condition" in the late twentieth century and to make intelligent judgments about international affairs. Although nation-states remain the key actors in the drama of world politics, and national security the fundamental concern, other actors and issues are competing for attention, with these forces containing the seeds of both increased conflict and increased cooperation among peoples. The organization of the text carefully reflects this theme. Part I introduces international relations as a field of study and provides *historical* background for contemporary world politics. Part II focuses on *states* as actors and examines the determinants of foreign policy, international bargaining and diplomacy, and war. Part III focuses on *international institutions*, including international law and international organizations. Part IV examines the congeries of forces involved in *global problem solving*, with separate chapters devoted to arms races, terrorism, coordination of the world economy, economic development, and the management of renewable and nonrenewable resources. Part V contains a concluding chapter that looks to the *future*—the year 2000 and beyond—and offers an analysis of alternative world order models.

In terms of *style*, we have sought to combine high scholarly standards with readability. The text discusses the latest theoretical ideas and research findings in a lively, readable manner—complete with photographs, cartoons, tables, graphs, case studies, and vignettes. We feel that these "supplementary" materials have not in any way compromised academic integrity but instead have added another dimension to the text. For the beginning student, we have employed several pedagogical aids, including a summary of important points and suggested readings at the end of each chapter, and a glossary of terms. For the more scholarly reader, a notes section is provided at the end of the book.

Admittedly, it is often difficult to find a lighter side to a world in which several million people lack access to drinkable water, and in which the stockpile of nuclear weapons amounts to roughly fifteen tons of TNT for every man, woman, and child on earth. Notwithstanding the cartoons and sidelights, the reader will find that the authors consider international relations a deadly serious subject—a subject where the ability to develop and communicate sound knowledge will have much bearing on the prospect of humanity's surviving into the next century. We hope this book makes at least some small contribution in this regard.

As with any project that has consumed several years of effort, we are indebted to many people. At the very top, we must acknowledge the special contribution of Professor Edwin Fedder, who as Director of the Center for International Studies at the University of Missouri-St. Louis provided the kind of personal, intellectual, and material support for this project that was indispensable. We wish to thank the Center for International Studies itself, including staff members Robert Baumann, Mary Hines, and Shirley Watts, who provided a myriad of services too numerous to mention, as well as Jan Frantzen, Lana Sink, and Pamela Vierdag of the Political Science Department staff, and Rebecca Thompson. We greatly appreciate the cooperation of the many publishers who granted us permission to use copyrighted material. We also owe considerable thanks to the many reviewers who offered helpful critiques of the manuscript. A long-standing intellectual debt must be acknowledged to our "mentors," William Coplin at Syracuse University and J. David Singer at the University of Michigan, both of whom in their own way taught us the importance of sound scholarship in collecting evidence and of sound pedagogy in presenting it. Finally our acknowledgments would be incomplete without expressing gratitude to Bert Lummus, our editor, and to his superb staff at Random House—particularly project editor Beena Kamlani and assistant editor Pat Plunkett—who all contributed greatly to the final product.

For our families who have had to live with us for the past several years, amidst the conflict that always attends collaboration, we reserve a well-earned dedication.

F.S.P.

J.M.R.

Contents

PART II

National Actors and International Interactions   99

PART III

International Institutions 287

PART IV

The Global Condition:
The Politics of Global Problem Solving   353

PART V

Conclusion   523

PART
I

Introduction

An introduction to the study of international relations in our time is an introduction to the art and science of the survival of mankind.

KARL W. DEUTSCH, *The Analysis of International Relations*

This is a book about contemporary international relations. The quotation from Deutsch suggests both the importance of studying international relations and the immensity of the task. Albert Einstein was once asked, "Why is it that when the mind of man has stretched so far as to discover the structure of the atom we have been unable to devise the political means to keep the atom from destroying us?" Einstein reputedly responded, "That is simple, my friend, because politics is more difficult than physics."

The moral of this story, of course, is not that introductory physics courses are the easy courses at universities, only that getting a handle on international relations phenomena and bringing them under control can in some ways be more vexing than conquering the mysteries of the physical universe. In exploring a wide range of international relations phenomena in this book, we will be attempting to show the complexity of the world today at the same time that we are trying to unravel that complexity.

Before this exploration can begin, it is necessary first to provide some intellectual and substantive background for the study of contemporary international relations. Hence, in Part I we will discuss the development of international relations as a field of study, the various approaches that students of international relations have used through the years, and the differing concerns of scholars, policymakers, and laymen (Chapter 1). We will also present a brief *historical* look at the evolution of international relations over the last three centuries (Chapter 2) as well as a bird's-eye view of the planet *today*, comparing the environment of contemporary international relations with that of the past (Chapter 3).

CHAPTER

1

The Study of International Relations, or Getting a Handle on the World

On a hot muggy evening on August 25, 1980, if you happened to be in St. Louis, Missouri, in mid-America, sitting in front of a television set viewing the world, national, and local news, you would have received the following bits of information:

Zimbabwe becomes a member of the United Nations as Prime Minister Robert Mugabe addresses the General Assembly in New York City. . . . Iranian militants holding U.S. embassy personnel warn against any further attempts to rescue the hostages. . . . Memorial service for James S. McDonnell, founder and chairman of McDonnell-Douglas Aircraft Corporation, to be held Saturday at Washington University. . . . Polish workers in Gdansk continue their strike in quest of free trade unions. . . . International Longshoremen's Association in U.S. boycotts ships carrying Polish goods, refusing to unload cargo in American ports. . . . Buildup of Soviet troops reported along East German border. . . . President urges new jobs program to combat recession and unemployment, especially the hard-hit auto and steel industries. . . . Anheuser-Busch, the St. Louis-based brewery, reports record sales during the second quarter of this year. . . . Bethlehem Steel admits bribing shipowners in Colombia to purchase equipment from its shipbuilding division. . . . Ferguson Jenkins, pitcher for the Texas Rangers, arrested in Toronto on charges of possessing cocaine. . . . Police investigate four weekend killings in St. Louis. . . . Dow Jones Industrial Average down, with slow trading on the New York Stock Exchange. . . . Beijing says Reagan's call for official government relations with Taiwan threatens U.S.-China relationship. . . . Congressman accused of accepting payment to speed up immigration procedures for Arab sheik. . . . Public hearing held to discuss federal and state roles in solving Missouri's environmental problems. . . . Weather continues hot and muggy.[1]

From Poughkeepsie to Peoria to Portland: The Relevance of International Relations

This same scene could have been played out, with some local variations, in Poughkeepsie, New York or Peoria, Illinois or Portland, Oregon—or, for that matter, in West Berlin or Tokyo or Montreal. The date, too, is incidental, since similar topics of discussion could have been grist for any news program on almost any evening within recent memory. The events reported above seem fairly typical of the happenings of our time, of life in the late twentieth century (at least as seen through the eyes of the mass media).

While the specific events will vary from place to place and moment to moment, one basic thread can be found among the daily occurrences reported in the news: Although they might appear to be removed in various degrees from the immediate concerns of the average man or woman on the street (or student in the classroom), all such events have some interrelatedness and potential implications for each of us. In the case of the St. Louis newscast, at first glance some events seem to fall neatly into the category normally labeled "international" (involving foreign concerns), while others seem to fall equally neatly into the category normally labeled "domestic" (involving national or local concerns). However, the fact is that almost all the events have elements of both. The "international" events are not so far removed from a locality like St. Louis, and the "domestic" events even of a local nature are not unconnected with world affairs.

LINKAGES IN AN INTERDEPENDENT WORLD

Using the newscast as an illustration, any number of linkages can be cited. For example, one of the most important domestic concerns in the United States is the high crime rate. It has been well documented that a considerable amount of crime occurring in cities like St. Louis is related to drug usage and can be traced to the international drug traffic from other countries.[2] Most heroin consumed in the United States comes from opium production in Southwest Asia (including Iran and Afghanistan), Southeast Asia (including Burma, Laos, and Thailand), and Mexico. Colombia, in Latin America, is the chief supplier of marijuana and cocaine—and would likely have been the source of the drugs that Ferguson Jenkins allegedly took with him across the U.S. border into Canada. (Jenkins was an interesting story in his own right— a Canadian citizen and one of the most successful pitchers in the history of U.S. major league baseball, which by the way includes two "foreign" teams, Toronto in the American League and Montreal in the National League.)

The Polish workers' strike not only caused the Soviet troop mobilization in Eastern Europe but had effects in the United States as well—the threat of bottlenecks in U.S. ports due to the longshoremen's boycott in support of the workers and, also, the anxious concern of thousands of Polish-Americans with family ties in Poland. Even more intimately touched by international events was the Sickmann family of Krakow, Missouri, whose son Rocky was among the Americans held captive in Iran by militant students. Along with the families of other hostages, the Sickmanns conducted their own brand of international "diplomacy," sending messages to the Iranian government and pleading for release of the hostages. The actions of the International Longshoremen's Association and the Sickmann family are just two examples among countless others that illustrate not only the link between international and local happenings but also the role of private individuals and groups as actors seeking to shape events in an area commonly considered the preserve of policymakers, diplomats, and soldiers.

SIDELIGHT

A STUDY IN INTERDEPENDENCE

If you drive a Ford Escort, chances are that your transmission was made in Japan, your wiring in Taiwan, your door lift assembly in Mexico, your shock absorber struts in Spain, your rear brake assembly in Brazil, your steering gears in Britain, and assorted other parts elsewhere. Since 1980, when the article below trumpeted the arrival of a "world car," increased numbers of American car owners have been motoring around in automobiles—not only the Ford Escort but also the Chevrolet Nova, the Pontiac Sunbird, and many others—containing parts from all over the world.

A Dodge dealer in Mount Kisco, New York, offers an unusual optional extra: A bumper sticker that proclaims, "This vehicle built in America by Americans for Americans." On a similar nationalistic note, the United Auto Workers union is advertising in newspapers and on radio for Americans to buy American cars. And at least twelve states have adopted regulations requiring state agencies to do just that.

It is getting harder, however, to buy a car that is not only assembled in America but made entirely with American-made parts. Dodge, despite the bumper sticker, is a striking example. Almost 15 percent of the Dodge Omni and its twin, the Plymouth Horizon, is manufactured abroad.

The new Ford Escort is being assembled in three countries and the American version contains parts from nine foreign countries. Conversely, the European version of the Escort contains parts manufactured in the United States.

Even the death of James S. McDonnell was not just a local story. "Mr. Mac" was the head of McDonnell-Douglas, one of the two largest defense contractors in the United States (the other being General Dynamics, also headquartered in St. Louis). Aside from being the biggest single employer in the state of Missouri and absolutely vital to the local economy, the company's influence stretched far beyond into other areas. Their F–4 and F–15 aircraft were among the most popular fighter planes in the world, purchased by countries such as Iran, Saudi Arabia, and Israel. And it was McDonnell's company that had been instrumental in making the United States the largest "arms merchant" in the world, with U.S. sales totaling $123 billion between 1971 and 1980 and continuing at a brisk pace in the 1980s.[3]

The economic well-being of communities like St. Louis can be affected substantially by international developments ranging from increases or de-

Only a few months ago the talk in the auto industry was about the world or global car, the economical small car of standardized design capable of being assembled with components produced around the world and suitable for American highways, European city streets and African trails. The world car is on its way—the emblem of the new Ford Escort, for example, depicts a globe—but today the most noticeable trend is toward global car parts, in which components from individual countries are going into increasing numbers of cars built by American auto manufacturers and their foreign competitors.

South Korea and Taiwan, for example, provide everything from ignition wires to intake valves, while Brazil manufactures entire auto and truck engines. "And the trend is going to continue," said Frank Armbruster, director of interdisciplinary studies at the Hudson Institute. "If you can make an equivalent car for $2,000 or $3,000 less, you do it. And in the current economy, the pressure to do so will remain."

But Mr. Armbruster thinks it may be a mixed blessing. "What does it do to a country's military mobility if, for example, it no longer has people to make engines?" he asked. "During World War II we depended on civilian skills to support us in a conventional war. We shifted people from making sewing machines to making machine guns. What if you no longer have those skills?" Moreover, he said, "What about a small country that specializes in making certain auto parts to supply the U.S. or Japanese market if the bottom drops out of the auto market? It could have a devastating effect on such countries."

This is a dramatic turnabout from not too long ago, when almost all the equipment in a car originated in the country of manufacture.

Source: Excerpted from Edwin McDowell, "Made in U.S.A.—with Foreign Parts," *New York Times* (November 9, 1980). Copyright © 1980 by The New York Times Company. Reprinted by permission.

creases in the incidence of war to increases or decreases in tariff barriers. For example, the problems of the American automobile industry reported in the newscast had been building for some time and could be traced partly to the flood of foreign imports—led by the Japanese—that would claim over 25 percent of the domestic car market in the United States by the late 1980s. The President's announcement regarding a jobs program was especially good news for the St. Louis metropolitan area, the second largest auto-manufacturing center in the United States (outside of Detroit) and a major victim of car-plant closings and layoffs. (One is tempted to posit a relationship between the economic problems experienced in Missouri and elsewhere in the United States at the time and the record beer sales reported by Anheuser-Busch of St. Louis, with people perhaps being driven to drink by economic adversity; it should be added, though, that part of the company's success could be attributed to its expanded foreign operations, such as the marketing of Budweiser beer in Europe under agreement with a Czech firm.)

Even the local and national weather has international dimensions. The record heat wave that struck St. Louis and much of the United States during the summer of 1980 could be seen as part of a larger global climatic pattern of extreme temperature fluctuation in recent years. Some experts trace the erratic weather conditions to environmental factors such as the "greenhouse effect" (the accumulation of carbon dioxide in the atmosphere caused by the burning of coal and other fossil fuels) and the "aerosol effect" (the suspension of trillions of dust and smoke particles in the atmosphere, which block the sun's rays), with the former factor tending to produce an increase in the earth's temperature and the latter factor having the exact opposite result.[4] While climatologists remain uncertain about the long-term consequences of all this pollution, there is no question that the problem is a global one that spills over national boundaries. Missouri's environmental policy decisions have potential consequences not only for neighboring Cairo, Illinois but—in combination with thousands of similar decisions made in other localities—for Cairo, Egypt, and other parts of the globe as well.

This entire discussion thus far simply illustrates a growing reality that we are living in an interdependent world. The fact that the term **interdependence** has become a cliché does not make it any less real a phenomenon. One can debate the exact definition of the term and the extent to which interdependence has actually increased—for example, whether it has reached the point where one can consider the world a "global village" as Marshall McLuhan has suggested or "Spaceship Earth" as Barbara Ward Jackson has suggested—but it is hard to dispute the essential validity of the following observation: "We live in a world in which rebellion in Chile can cause an assassination in Vienna, in which Turkish poppies can produce muggings in Montreal, in which industrial effluents in Detroit can cause cancer in Windsor, Ontario, Canada. . . ."[5] This is not mere "globaloney," as some would say. The most dramatic aspect of interdependence, of course, is the fact that global annihilation can occur today in a matter of minutes through the use of thermonuclear weapons.

MAKING THE PUBLIC MORE WORLDLY

Judging from the results of numerous public opinion surveys taken in the United States, it would appear that the average American is not very aware of the relevance of the outside world. For example, just as the great national energy debate was heating up in the United States in the late 1970s, at a time when the United States imported almost 50 percent of its oil needs from abroad, half of the American people did not know that the United States imported *any* foreign oil.[6] At the height of the Vietnam War, in March of 1966, more than 80 percent of the American public could not correctly identify the Viet Cong, the communist insurgents against whom American troops were fighting in South Vietnam.[7] Showing a similar ignorance of conditions on the other side of the globe, over half the Americans interviewed in more recent polls in the 1980s were not sure whether it was the United States or the Soviet Union which was a member of the North Atlantic Treaty Organization (NATO) alliance, or whether the United States was on the side of the government or rebels in the Nicaraguan and Salvadoran civil wars occurring in Central America.[8]

Numerous other examples of the American public's lack of information about international affairs, past and present, can be cited.[9] Although the public in other countries, particularly in Western Europe, often seems to be better informed than the American public, there is much evidence to suggest that even in these countries a sizable segment of the population has only marginal interest in and knowledge about international affairs despite the implications of interdependence.[10] In all countries, many people seem to adopt the attitude of the student who was asked, "Which is worse, ignorance or apathy?" The response: "I don't know and I don't care!"

Even those individuals who are interested in international affairs and do attempt to become informed often find it difficult to comprehend the myriad events that are reported daily and to fit these events into any kind of coherent framework. How are U.S.-Colombian relations affected by the actions of American-based multinational corporations that do business in Colombia, or U.S.-Iranian relations affected by the giant multinational oil companies operating in the Middle East? In a showdown with the Soviet Union over Poland or over any other issue, is it possible that the United States has the capability to kill every Russian twenty-seven times but can still "lose" a nuclear war? Can the sale of the U.S. government's most sophisticated military aircraft to Israel and Saudi Arabia, mutual enemies, be expected to promote peace in the Middle East, or war? In the United Nations, why is Zimbabwe (formerly Rhodesia) entitled to the same voting power as the United States in the General Assembly, when the United States is thirty times bigger in population and pays a thousand times more money into the UN budget? And to what extent do American (or French or Soviet) foreign policy makers, while pondering the potential consequences of their decisions for the nation and the world, ask the question: "How will it play in Peoria (or Marseilles or Vladivostok)?"

The basic purpose of this book, aside from generating increased *interest* in international relations, is to contribute to some *understanding* of a broad range of contemporary international phenomena and what could be called the "global condition" in the late twentieth century. In other words, we shall attempt to make sense out of what may at times appear to be chaos.

THE CONVENTIONAL WISDOM: A SAMPLER

A key objective of this book is to give students a more sophisticated understanding of international relations phenomena. The following quotations are representative of a number of ideas about international relations that have rolled off the tongues of practitioners and the pens of philosophers over the years. Do *you* accept the validity of the propositions embodied in these statements, or do they appear somewhat simplistic?

On the types of countries that are war-prone:

"A tyrant . . . is always stirring up some war or other, in order that the people may require a leader."—Plato, *The Republic*, 4th century, B.C.

"Of all nations, those most fond of peace are democratic nations. . . ."—Alexis de Tocqueville, *Democracy in America*, 1835

On the prevention of war:

"To be prepared for war is one of the most effectual means of preserving peace."—George Washington, first annual address to Congress, January 8, 1790

". . . only when our arms are sufficient beyond doubt can we be certain beyond doubt that they will never be employed."—John F. Kennedy, inaugural address, January 20, 1961

"History has shown us all too well that weakness promotes aggression and war, whereas strength preserves the peace."—Ronald Reagan, paid political announcement, 1980 presidential election campaign

"I've often wondered what would have happened if we [the U.S., Japan, and Germany] had the same bonds of trade and commerce before 1939 or before 1941 [as we have today]. That's why I'm such a staunch advocate of global commerce."—Jimmy Carter, Twenty-sixth World Conference of the International Chamber of Commerce, October 1, 1978

On winning wars:

"It is said that God is always for the biggest battalions."—Voltaire, quoting Frederick the Great, in a letter to M. Riche, February 6, 1770

On the virtues of the "carrot" (nice guy) versus the "stick" (tough guy) approach to exercising influence in international affairs:

"Speak softly and carry a big stick; you will go far."—Theodore Roosevelt, Minnesota State Fair, September 2, 1901

"If the adversary feels that you are unpredictable, even rash, he will be deterred from pressing you too far."—Richard M. Nixon, *The Real War*, 1980

The "What" Question: Defining International Relations

As a starting point, let us try to define as precisely as possible what we mean by the term **international relations.** Trying to define international relations reminds one of the judge in the obscenity case who said, "I can't define it, but I know it when I see it." A dictionary provides us with some guidance, defining international relations as "a branch of *political science* concerned with relations between political units of *national* rank and dealing primarily with *foreign policies*, the organization and function of government agencies concerned with foreign policy, and the factors (as geography and economics) underlying foreign policies [italics ours]."[11]

DEFINITIONAL PROBLEMS

That seems to be a reasonable enough definition of international relations—except for at least three problems that arise immediately. First, where does the International Longshoremen's Association fit in, with its veiled threats to selectively boycott international shipping? What about multinational corporations, or the Palestine Liberation Organization (PLO)? None of these are "national political units" or "governments," nor are they entirely subsumed by the latter; they seemingly are excluded from the dictionary definition, yet they are not exactly irrelevant to relations between nations. Second, in an interdependent world, is it as easy as the dictionary definition suggests to separate "foreign" policy decisions from "domestic" policy decisions? A decision by the U.S. government to legalize certain drugs may be a purely domestic matter, but it is likely to be accompanied by changes in U.S. foreign policy regarding international narcotics control as well. Likewise, arms control may be purely a foreign policy concern, but such decisions can have important domestic fallout. The blurring of domestic and foreign policy concerns becomes all the more problematical in other areas, such as energy, economic, and agricultural policy. Third, although the dictionary cites international relations as a "branch of political science," the field clearly encompasses not only political but also economic and other relations, being multidisciplinary in scope.

We are not arguing here that the field of international relations has no boundaries, only that the boundaries are perhaps harder to identify than in other fields of study. However, if one is to develop an understanding of international relations, then clearly there is a need to establish *some* boundaries at the outset, granted that "the effort to draw them with any great precision is at best arbitrary and at worst futile."[12] Over the years the "boundary" question in the international relations field has occasioned almost as much conflict among academics as other sorts of boundary questions have caused among nations.[13] We have no desire here to add to this great debate about the essence of international relations. We want only to make sure that students have a grasp of what the field is all about.

As an alternative to the dictionary definition, consider for a moment a second, much broader definition of international relations: the study of all human interactions across national borders and the factors that affect those interactions. Figure 1.1 indicates the various kinds of interactions that are possible.

Examples of the first type of interaction (line A) would be a meeting between the Prime Minister of Zimbabwe and the President of the United States, or a communication from the Soviet government warning the U.S. government not to meddle in any future civil strife in Poland, or U.S.-Japanese negotiations regarding the imposition of tariff barriers and quotas against Japanese cars imported into the United States. What do all of these situations have in common? They all involve interactions between *national governments*—more specifically, between official representatives of national political units we call **nation-states.**

Examples of the second type of interaction (line B) would include talks between the Oil Minister of Saudi Arabia and the representatives of a multinational oil company, or a raid by Israeli troops against PLO commando bases in Lebanon, or a visit by an out-of-office but aspiring U.S. presidential candidate to Beijing (Peking) to discuss politics with Chinese government officials. **Nonstate actors** like multinational corporations or the PLO may initiate international interactions or they may be the targets of them, but in either case their activities are a part of international relations.[14]

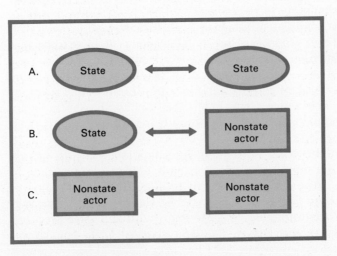

Figure 1.1
KINDS OF INTERNATIONAL INTERACTIONS

Examples of the <u>third type</u> of interaction (line C) could conceivably include the Texas Rangers playing the Toronto Bluejays in Toronto, a meeting of trade union representatives from a variety of countries, or an exchange of letters between pen pals in England and Outer Mongolia. Although many of these kinds of interactions are quite far removed from the weighty concerns of statesmen, even the travels of Ping-Pong teams between New York and Beijing (the much-publicized U.S.-China "Ping-Pong diplomacy" of 1971) can on occasion be an important form of international relations.

Broadly speaking, all of the above interactions constitute international relations. Obviously though, not all of these lines of interaction are equally important and deserve equal treatment. It is safe to say that when most people think of international relations, they think in dictionary terms of relations between national governments that act on behalf of nation-states, as typified by the first set of examples. This preoccupation is justified, since it is true that only national governments are in a position to make foreign policy and only national governments ultimately have the legal authority to control all interactions across national boundaries. In this book, we, too, will primarily be concerned with relations between national governments. But we will also be concerned with the other two types of interactions and the role of nonstate actors, particularly insofar as they affect the relations between governments and have an impact on world affairs.

THE SUBSTANCE OF INTERNATIONAL RELATIONS

What are we finally left with, then, as a definition of international relations? The working definition that we have decided to adopt in this book is one that is borrowed from political science and reflects the authors' primary concern with the political dimension of international relations. Hence, we will be using the terms international *relations* and international *politics* interchangeably and examining economic and other relations in their political context. If "politics" is "the study of who gets what, when, and how,"[15] then <u>international politics is the study of who gets what, when, and how in the international arena.</u> This is a somewhat narrower and more focused definition than the one offered initially as an alternative to the dictionary definition, but it seems to capture better what the field of international relations—and this book—are most about.

As this definition suggests, politics has to do with the way in which a group of people living together govern their affairs. In the case of international politics, we are interested in how over 5 billion human inhabitants of the planet do so. To the extent that one can think of the world's roughly 5 billion people as constituting a single political entity, the most striking and fundamental feature of this polity is that it is a highly *decentralized* one, with the members organized in over 160 territorially based units—nation-states—recognizing no higher authority than their own individual governments. As we have noted, notwithstanding the existence of nonstate actors, the nation-state remains the primary form of political organization and locus of authority in the world. In other words, international politics occurs in an arena in which there is no set of central authoritative institutions (no world government) to regulate the behavior of the members, in contrast with *intra*national politics, which is regulated to some extent by courts, legislatures, and other authoritative bodies. The United Nations is at best a primitive attempt at creating a world government out of a system of formally independent states.

The decentralized nature of the international polity, in the eyes of many observers, makes the body politic inherently prone to disorder and violence, so that its members tend to be obsessed with feelings of insecurity and the need to arm themselves, if only for self-protection. Although many national societies experience similar problems of violence and instability in the form of civil wars, it is true that such problems seem built-in and endemic to international society because of the very structure of relationships among the constituent units. Nonetheless, the international community is not eternally at war; humanity has often been able to overcome these deficiencies and achieve some peace and order in international relations even without authoritative institutions. *Cooperation* occurs amidst *conflict*. As John Stoessinger has expressed it: there is in international relations an "ever-present tension between the struggle for power and the struggle for order,"[16] the drive for more national resources being tempered by the mutually felt need for at least some modicum of stability.

This central concern of international relations is not new; it has existed as long as there have been nation-states. However, it has taken on greater urgency today not only because humankind has the capability for total global destruction but also because of the emergence of a truly global society in which the proliferation of economic, social, and other transactions across national boundaries is straining the capacities of national governments to regulate these relations.[17] While some see the "shrinking and linking" of the world as marking progress toward fulfillment of the historic dream of a harmonious world community,[18] others see it as sowing the seeds for possibly even greater conflicts among nations and people than in previous eras.[19] The mere three-and-one-half-hour time span it now takes to travel from London to New York aboard the Concorde airliner is exceeded in earthbound travel efficiency only by the thirty-minute ride that can be taken by a nuclear warhead aboard an intercontinental ballistic missile between Moscow and New York.

It is, indeed, somewhat paradoxical that at the same time that humanity has the potential for unparalleled conflict, there is also the potential for unprecedented cooperation. There have been more international agreements signed since 1945 than were negotiated in the previous 2000 years. The growth of international organizations in recent years and the ongoing attempts to formulate "regimes" or "rules" in various problem areas[20]—nuclear weapons proliferation, control of the oceans, management of the international economy, and other areas—represent the latest, most ambitious efforts yet to deal with the age-old concern of maintaining order in the absence of a world government. Increasingly, too, there is a call not only for order but for a *just* order based on an equitable distribution of resources. One can see in all this a "political system" at work, with global problem-solving processes operating, albeit in a decentralized fashion.

It should be added that international relations can be studied at several levels, with some concerns directly involving only a few countries or a single geographical region, although ultimately all international relations can be fitted into a larger global context. A recurrent theme of this book is that a variety of actors and a complicated network of relationships must be taken into account in any attempt to fully understand contemporary international politics.

The "How" Question: Alternative Approaches

Just as the "what" question has produced much debate within the international relations field, so also has the "how" question. How should one go about studying international relations in terms of the various approaches that might be used? Actually the "what" and "how" questions have never been completely distinguishable, as will be seen in the following discussion, which briefly traces the development of international relations as a field of study. We will examine two aspects of the "how" question: (1) the various *paradigms* that have guided theory and research in the field over the years and (2) the various *methodologies* that have been utilized.

ALTERNATIVE PARADIGMS

A **paradigm** is an intellectual framework that structures one's thinking about a set of phenomena.[21] Paradigms are nothing more than "cognitive maps" that help to organize reality and to make some sense out of the multitude of events that occur in the world each day.[22] Different paradigms offer different models of reality or views of the world, and thus have the effect of focusing attention toward some things and away from others. There are four major paradigms that have structured thinking about international relations in this century: (1) the *idealist* paradigm, (2) the *realist* paradigm, (3) the *globalist* paradigm, and (4) the *Marxist* paradigm.

The **idealist paradigm** can trace its roots at least as far back as Dante, the Italian poet of the fourteenth century who wrote of the "universality of man" and envisioned a unified world-state.[23] In the twentieth century this paradigm has been most closely associated with Woodrow Wilson and other thinkers

SIDELIGHT

THE SHRINKING AND LINKING OF THE GLOBE

The following excerpt from Alvin Toffler's *Future Shock* illustrates the shrinking of the world in terms of travel speed. One might add to his list of figures that during the Apollo 15 moon shot that carried the first men to the moon, the astronauts traveled at a rate of 24,000 miles per hour.

The acceleration [in the pace of change] is frequently dramatized by a thumbnail account of the progress in transportation. It has been pointed out, for example, that in 6000 B.C. the fastest transportation available to man over long distances was the camel caravan, averaging eight miles per hour. It was not until about 1600 B.C. when the chariot was invented that the maximum speed was raised to roughly twenty miles per hour.

So impressive was this invention, so difficult was it to exceed this speed limit, that nearly 3500 years later, when the first mail coach began operating in England in 1784, it averaged a mere ten miles per hour. The first steam locomotive, introduced in 1825, could muster a top speed of only thirteen mph, and the great sailing ships of the time labored along at less than half that speed. It was probably not until the 1880s that man, with the help of a more advanced steam locomotive, managed to reach a speed of one hundred miles per hour. It took the human race millions of years to attain that record.

It took only fifty-eight years, however, to quadruple the limit, so that by 1938 airborne man was cracking the 400-m.p.h. line. It took a mere twenty-year flick of time to double the limit again. And by the 1960s rocket planes approached speeds of 4000 miles per hour, and men in capsules were circling the earth at 18,000 miles per hour. Plotted on a graph, the line representing progress in the past generation would leap vertically off the page.

From Alvin Toffler, *Future Shock* (New York: Random House, 1970), p. 26. Copyright © 1970 by Alvin Toffler. Reprinted by permission of Random House, Inc.

around the time of World War I, when international relations was just emerging as a distinct academic field in the United States.[24] The idealists were prominent in the interwar period—between the end of World War I in 1918 and the beginning of World War II in 1939—and are still an active school of international relations as represented by the World Federalists and similar groups. Like many observers of international affairs, idealists are attracted to the challenge of minimizing conflict and maximizing cooperation among nations. What distinguishes the idealists, however, is their tendency to focus attention on legal-formal aspects of international relations, such as international law and international organization, and on moral concerns such as human rights. It was out of the ashes of World War I that idealists claimed to have learned certain lessons about the workings of international relations and what had to be done to prevent another catastrophe like that war. In their minds, a new world order had to be constructed based on a respect for law, the acceptance of shared universal values, and the development of international organizations like the League of Nations.

Idealists tend to be most interested in how the world *ought* to be, not necessarily in how it actually *is*. The idealist would argue that the reality of the moment is not the only possible reality. The idealist mode of thinking is perhaps best captured in the statement by President Wilson when questioned by his advisers about the practicality of his League of Nations idea: "If it won't work, it must be made to work."[25]

It was the very failure of the idealists to anticipate and prevent World War II that gave rise to the dominance of the **realist paradigm** in the immediate postwar period after 1945. While the idealists argued that their ideas had not been fully implemented in the interwar period and hence had not been fairly tested, realists like E.H. Carr contended that they *had* been tested but could not stand up against armies marching across Europe and halfway around the world.[26] Hans Morgenthau, in his classic work *Politics Among Nations*, became identified as the "father" of realism, even though Carr had been writing a few years earlier and the roots of realist thought could in fact be traced as far back as the sixteenth century to Machiavelli's *The Prince*.[27] Realists are just as interested as idealists in the problem of conflict management, but they are less optimistic about the effectiveness of international law and organization and about the extent of international cooperation that is possible. Realists view international relations almost exclusively as a "struggle for power" (rather than as a "struggle for order") among nation-states. To the realist, the ultimate goal of all countries is security in a hostile, anarchic environment. Their policies are determined by power calculations in pursuit of national security. Countries that are satisfied with their situation are inclined to pursue *status quo* foreign policies, while countries that are dissatisfied are inclined to pursue expansionist foreign policies. Alliances are made and broken, old friends are rejected and old enemies embraced, all depending on the requirements of "realpolitik."

It is not surprising that realists have tended to focus on such topics as military strategy, the elements of national power, diplomacy and other instruments of statecraft, and the nature of national interests rather than such subjects as international law and organization. The realists claimed to have learned their own lessons from World War II, namely that the way to prevent future wars was to rely not on formal-legal institutions or moral precepts but on a "balance of power" capable of deterring would-be aggressors, or on a "concert of powers" willing to police the world. The realist paradigm has dominated the thinking of an entire generation of international relations observers in the postwar era—scholars, practitioners, and laymen alike—and continues to exert a powerful hold on many. Contemporary realists incorporate more economic analysis into their writings and are often referred to as "neorealists."[28]

The third paradigm, the **globalist paradigm** (sometimes called the transnationalist or modernist paradigm), has only recently gained attention and approaches the study of international relations from a somewhat different perspective than either the idealist or realist paradigms.[29] Led in 1971 by a groundbreaking volume edited by Robert Keohane and Joseph Nye and entitled *Transnational Relations and World Politics*, the globalists have focused their attack on the realist paradigm in particular, arguing that the latter has never entirely corresponded with reality and is especially inadequate in comprehending contemporary events in an age of interdependence.[30] Most globalists have not rejected the realist paradigm totally but have sought to refine and amplify it, their premise being that the dealings between national governments are only one strand in the great web of human interactions. Rather than viewing international relations through realist lenses as simply a contest between national units driven by the single concern of national security, the globalists perceive a more complex set of relationships between not only national governments but also nonstate actors, involved not only in war and peace issues but in other more narrow issue-areas as well (for example, in the air safety issue-area, the role of such entities as the International Civil Aviation Organization, the International Air Transport Association, the International Federation of Airline Pilots Associations, and the airline interests within various countries).[31] Whereas the world of the realist is populated primarily by soldiers, diplomats, and foreign policy makers, the world of the globalist includes multinational corporation executives, transnational labor union

"Real politik"

leaders, and skyjackers. In short, globalists choose to consider a much wider range of actors and concerns than do realists in their study of international relations.

Somewhat related to but distinct from the globalist paradigm is the **Marxist paradigm.** Marxists trace their intellectual roots to Karl Marx, the nineteenth-century German philosopher who wrote *Das Kapital* and (with Friedrich Engels) *The Communist Manifesto.* Marx argued that **capitalist** economic systems, which stressed private property and the accumulation of private wealth, produced a "bourgeois" ruling class that exploited a "proletarian" working class. He indicated that once class distinctions and private property were eliminated in a worldwide workers' revolution, there would be no further need for national governments and nation-states. A harmonious global **communist** society would result, with each person receiving wealth according to need rather than privilege.

Latter-day Marxists have added some new wrinkles to these theories, since capitalism has proved to have more staying power than Marx predicted. In particular, Marxists maintain that capitalist states have been able to relieve their inner class tensions by exploiting other, less developed countries—utilizing cheap foreign labor and captive foreign markets to avoid economic collapse. The Marxists, like the globalists, point to the spreading tentacles of multinational businesses and transnational coalitions of elite groups but find much more harmful effects of such actors than do globalists. Military and business leaders of developed capitalist states are supposedly linked up with counterparts in less developed states. It is claimed that even the average laborer in capitalist states has lost class consciousness and has been co-opted into the ranks of the "bourgeoisie" by purchasing the products of exploited workers in less developed states. Marxists, then, view international relations more as a struggle between rich and poor classes than as a contest between national governments or nation-states. What is needed, according to this view, is for leaderships to emerge that are capable of replacing "laissez-faire" (free market) capitalist economies with more mass-oriented, centrally planned and managed economies which will supposedly result in more harmonious social relations both domestically and internationally.

We shall draw on all these different perspectives in this book. They represent very general orientations toward international affairs. Few people are in actuality pure realists or pure idealists, although many lean heavily in one direction or the other. Keeping in mind the role of paradigms in structuring one's view of the world, it is important to understand that there are often conflicting interpretations of international relations because different peoples and cultures, based on their historical and recent experiences, often have different lenses through which they see things. For example, many people in Africa and Asia who have experienced colonialism start with a somewhat different set of assumptions about the world than, say, Americans. While many Americans are inclined to interpret international affairs in terms of the realist or perhaps the idealist paradigm, many observers in less developed countries might be more inclined to view events in the context of the Marxist paradigm.

ALTERNATIVE METHODOLOGIES

The second aspect of the "how" question has to do with methodologies. Although there is some overlap between the methodological debate and the paradigm debate, somewhat different issues are involved in each. The great debate in the area of methodology has boiled down to the "traditionalists" versus the "behavioralists."[32] Until the 1960s, the international relations field was dominated methodologically by the **traditionalists,** for whom knowledge was something that could be arrived at only through firsthand participant observation and practical experience or secondhand immersion in the great works of diplomatic history and related library resources. In addition to diplomatic histories, the literature consisted largely of statesmen's memoirs, international law treatises, and philosophical writings.

During the 1960s,[33] traditionalists were challenged by an increasing number of **behavioralists** like Karl Deutsch, J. David Singer, and James Rosenau who sought to make the international relations field more *scientific*. Hence, their goal was to build a cumulative body of knowledge based on more sophisticated and rigorous methods borrowed from the biological and physical sciences.[34] The tools of the trade for the behavioralists were aggregate data, quantitative analysis techniques, and computers.[35] The behavioralist literature consisted of writings that emphasized the systematic development and testing of *theories* that could *explain* the dynamics of international relations.

Today, traditionalists and behavioralists remain divided over various methodological issues and the extent to which the international relations field can approach the scientific level of the biological and physical sciences. Each side is interested in many of the same questions: Under what circumstances do wars tend to occur? What is the impact of domestic politics on foreign policy? Under what conditions is deterrence likely to succeed, or to fail? What is the relationship between foreign aid and political influence? What effect does increased interdependence between nations have on relations between governments?[36] And so forth. While behavioralists believe their methods will ultimately enable them to answer such questions with a high degree of precision and confidence, even to the point of being able to predict various international occurrences, the traditionalists argue that the complexities of the international environment and the limits of quantification are such that reasonably educated guesses (along the lines of the local weather forecaster rather than the nuclear physicist) are the most we can ever hope for. Actually, most behavioralists would be willing to settle for the predictive powers of meteorologists, who deal in probabilities and tendencies and whose only certainties are that mistakes will occur; as Charles McClelland has said, "the goal is not to foretell exactly what events will take place in China [in 1997]" but rather "to develop skill in showing 'which way the wind is blowing' and, therefore, what might well happen under stated circumstances."[37]

Despite continued disagreement among traditionalists and behavioralists, an uneasy truce has been declared between the two camps in the last several years. The discipline is now in the "post-behavioral" era, with both sides recognizing that neither has a monopoly on wisdom (or knowledge) in this field and that the "science" of international relations is still in its infancy. In the same spirit of humility, we will refrain from taking methodological sides in this book and we will make use of both traditional and quantitative research in our study of international relations.

The Concerns of
Policymakers, Scholars, and Laymen

All of us—policymakers, scholars, and laymen alike—have some need for knowledge about international relations, although not all of us have exactly the same needs. All of us want to have a handle on the world, although some of us are content with a looser grip than others. The scholar would generally like to know everything there is to know; the policymaker, whatever it takes to keep the country going from one day to the next (or, if you are President of the United States, from one four-year term to the next); and most laymen, only whatever it takes to enable them to make at least roughly informed judgments about how well the policymakers have been doing. Let us look first at the relationship between policymakers and scholars, and then relate their concerns to those of the average person.

QUESTIONS FOR SCHOLARS AND POLICYMAKERS

Thinkers and writers from the times of Plato and Machiavelli to the present have always sought to influence the actions of policymakers.[38] Indeed, some have gone beyond mere influence to actual policy-*making*. Henry Kissinger and Jeane Kirkpatrick are two contemporary examples. For the most part, however, international relations scholars do not have as much influence as they would like.

The world of the scholar is somewhat different from the world of the practitioner. The scholar tends to be more concerned about long-term trends, hypothetical relationships, and general patterns ("theory") while the practitioner tends to deal more with specific cases and immediate situations that seem to have unique characteristics ("practice").[39] As you recall from our discussion of methodology, scholars are interested in the following kinds of theoretical questions: Under what circumstances do wars tend to occur? What is the impact of domestic politics on foreign policy? Under what conditions is deterrence likely to succeed, or to fail? What is the relationship between foreign aid and political influence? What effect does increased interdependence between nations have on relations between governments? In contrast, although policymakers may have some intellectual curiosity about theoretical questions, they tend to be preoccupied with more concrete matters: Will the sale of several sophisticated military aircraft to Saudi Arabia aggravate hostilities in the Middle East? What is the impact of radical left-wing groups on foreign policy in, say, the Philippines? What conditions are necessary to deter a Soviet nuclear strike against the United States? Can a $150 million economic aid package buy Indian friendship toward the United States? How will the imposition of a 2 percent higher quota on Japanese car imports into the United States affect U.S.-Japanese relations? Scholars, too, may address these questions, but only as slices of a broader set of phenomena to be investigated.

Notwithstanding these differences, scholars and policymakers do share one common goal: to understand how the world operates. Plato himself suggested that each had something to offer the other and that the ideal ruler was a combination thinker and doer, a "philosopher-king." There is nothing more practical than a good theory that can order reality for policymakers and help them to anticipate the possible consequences of their decisions.

QUESTIONS FOR LAYMEN

To the extent that laymen are interested in international relations, they tend to be more intrigued by the concrete questions that preoccupy policymakers than by the abstract, theoretical ones that concern scholars. Yet laymen, just like policymakers, can benefit from answers to the theoretical questions. The same general knowledge that can help policymakers deal more intelligently with the problems that cross their desks can also help laymen in their roles as citizens more intelligently evaluate the soundness of the decisions made by their government. Although policymakers and laymen are inclined to dismiss theoretical concerns, it should be noted that they cannot escape them entirely. Even if they are not fully conscious of it, their judgments are ultimately based to some degree on "theories"—a variety of personal assumptions about how the world works—however undeveloped (and unfounded) those theories may be. In order to see how the concerns of policymakers, scholars, and laymen intertwine, let us briefly examine the different *modes of analysis* that people engage in when they think about social phenomena in general and international relations phenomena in particular.

Modes of Analysis

At least four modes of analysis can be identified: (1) description, (2) explanation, (3) normative analysis, and (4) prescription.[40] *Description* is the most basic type of analysis: One simply tells what reality looks like or has looked like. When one indicates how many wars have occurred in the world in the last twenty years and whether dictatorships have been more war-prone than democracies, one is making descriptive statements, which may be true or false. *Explanation,* though based on description, requires one to go beyond merely reporting a fact and to account for its existence. The ability to explain some past or present set of phenomena can imply the ability to predict the future as well, although not necessarily. *Normative analysis* entails making value (moral) judgments about some reality thought to exist or thought to be possible. When one laments the fact that the United States has no greater voting power than Zimbabwe in the United Nations, despite contributing a much larger share of the UN budget, one is making a normative statement that is cast in "good-bad" rather than "true-false" terms. Finally, *prescription* involves offering recommendations as to a future course of action or policy, given some goal to be achieved (which itself may involve prior value judgments). One engages in prescriptive analysis when trying to solve the world's problems—for example, when purporting to have a solution to the conflict between the Israelis and the Arabs. Although these four modes of analysis constitute distinct intellectual tasks reflecting different purposes of inquiry, they are all somewhat interrelated.

The relationship between these modes of analysis—and how policymakers, scholars, and laymen use them—can best be illustrated by a single example. Suppose you are interested in the distribution of wealth in the world. An example of a descriptive statement would be the following: One half of the world's people live in countries with a per capita gross national product (PGNP) of under $500, roughly one quarter live in countries with a PGNP between $500 and $2000, and roughly another one quarter live in countries with a PGNP above $2000.[41] This statement, which happens to be true, simply indicates what the world looks like. It says nothing about why it looks this way, nor does it assume any moral judgments about whether this is good or bad, nor does it suggest what if anything might be done to deal with this situation. If you were to inquire why this condition exists—because of climatic differences (since most of the poorer countries are located in the Southern Hemisphere) or technological differences (since most of the poorer countries are underdeveloped technologically) or racial differences (since most people in the poorer countries have black, brown, or yellow skin) or colonial heritage (since most of the poorer countries have only recently gained independence), or whatever—you would be shifting from description to explanation and would be engaged essentially in what we have called theoretical pursuits. If you decide that, regardless of causes, the existing distribution of wealth is bad in terms of being unethical and also fostering resentment and international conflict, then you would be engaging in normative analysis. And if you were to seek to alter this situation and were to recommend economic development strategies aimed at redistributing wealth in the world, then you would be playing problem-solver and engaging in prescription.

The reader may recognize that many people engage in all of these modes of analysis, often all at once. There is a tendency to make a "mesh" of things, blending the four types together without being fully aware that what passes for factual description may only be wishful thinking and what passes for an explanation may be merely a rationalization for policies one is already predisposed toward. Most of us prefer to concentrate on normative and prescriptive analysis more than the other two modes, since debating the great moral issues of the day and solving the world's problems seem inherently more interesting than examining a set of tables and graphs. Applying knowledge somehow seems more fun than acquiring it in the first place. For policymakers, normative and prescriptive analysis is their main job; for the layman, they lend themselves more easily to discussion over a glass of beer after a hard day's work.

However, the trouble is that one cannot properly perform normative and prescriptive analysis *until* one has done serious descriptive and explanatory analysis, that is, until one has as accurate a picture as possible of what the world looks like and why it is the way it is. Without a handle on the world, moralizing is reduced to pontification and prescriptions are doomed to failure. As we suggested earlier, practitioners and laymen often act on the basis of a certain set of assumptions about the world that are not very well spelled out or tested out, leading at times to unforeseen and disastrous results. It is only fair to add that professors can be equally guilty of not doing their "homework." (The box on page 10 lists a few samples of some popularly held notions about international relations that have been found by researchers to be of questionable validity or for which the evidence is at best mixed.)

The reason we have bothered to devote space to these rather abstract matters is to alert readers at the outset that they will be disappointed if they expect to find in the pages that follow a solution to conflicts in the Middle East and other problems in the world or a polemical attack on the evildoers responsible for these problems. The emphasis in this book is on basic description and explanation—with important bits of information provided along with a conceptual framework for digesting them—which is in keeping with our stated purpose of contributing to some *understanding* of international phenomena in the late twentieth century. In the process of imparting a better understanding, we hope to arouse further curiosity about international relations. We also hope to sharpen the reader's ability to analyze problems and, ultimately, to propose or evaluate remedies for them. A careful diagnosis of the "global condition" is necessary before one can ascertain what cures might be applied.

The Plan of This Book

In the remaining chapters in Part I, we will further set the stage for the study of international relations by briefly examining the historical development of the international system up to the present. We will trace the roots of the global condition and provide an overview of the environment in which contemporary international relations occur, going beyond our initial observations and sketching in greater detail some of the trends mentioned in Chapter 1. In Part II we will focus on nation-states and national governments as actors in world politics, examining their foreign policy behavior and official interactions and the kinds of phenomena (such as the use of economic and military power) that many consider the "real stuff" of international relations. This section of the book will thus tend to deal with some of the more conflictual aspects of international politics. In Part III we will shift our attention to attempts to develop international institutions, including international organizations and international law, which are designed to facilitate the routine flow of economic and other transactions across national boundaries and to provide conflict-management mechanisms when disagreements occur; we will focus here more on the cooperative impulse in international politics and the search for some degree of order in a decentralized world. Then, after having exposed students to the rudiments of world politics in the previous sections, in Part IV we will pull things together by treating the international system as a global polity in which there is at work a political process consisting of (1) a number of issues or problems on the agenda, (2) a number of different demands made by a variety of actors (both state and nonstate) in these issue-areas, and (3) a series of outcomes or outputs ("regimes") produced by the interactions of these actors in the different issue-areas; by focusing on the congeries of forces at work in five selected issue-areas—arms control, terrorism, coordination of the international economy, economic development, and the management of resources—we hope to illustrate in a holistic fashion the rich dynamics of contemporary international relations and how the current generation of *Homo sapiens* is coping with the historic tension between order and disorder. In a concluding chapter, in Part V, we look ahead toward the year 2000 and beyond.

SUMMARY

1. Today we are living in an interdependent world. The well-being of all communities can be substantially affected by international developments ranging from increases or decreases in the number of wars to increases or decreases in tariff barriers.

2. International politics can be defined as the study of who gets what, when, and how in the international arena.

3. Unlike domestic politics, international politics occurs in a decentralized fashion, with no world legislature or other central authoritative institutions to regulate the members of the international community—the more than 160 nation-states in which people are organized around the world.

4. Although there is potential for unparalleled conflict today, represented by nuclear weapons, there is also potential for unprecedented cooperation, represented by the growth of international organizations.

5. The idealist school is one of the four major paradigms that have structured thinking about international relations in this century. This school emphasizes the importance of international law and organization, as well as moral concerns such as human rights, in the hope of maximizing cooperation between states.

6. The realists are less optimistic about the potential for international cooperation, viewing international relations primarily as a power struggle between nation-states in the pursuit of national security. Realists focus on military strategy, the elements of national power, and the nature of national interests rather than international law and organization.

7. The globalist paradigm views international relations in more complex terms, as consisting not only of war and peace issues but also of economic and other narrower issue-areas and involving not only national governments but multinational corporations and other nonstate actors.

8. The Marxist paradigm views international relations as a class struggle between the world's rich and poor rather than a contest between nation-states.

9. There are two general methodological approaches to the study of international relations. Traditionalists seek knowledge through participant observation, practical experience, and the careful understanding of diplomatic history. Behavioralists take a more scientific approach, using aggregate data, quantitative analysis techniques, and computers to systematically develop and test theories that could explain the dynamics of international relations.

10. Despite differing orientations, scholars, policymakers, and laymen all share an interest in understanding how the world works. There is nothing more practical than a good theory.

11. At least four modes of analysis are used in examining international relations: (a) description, which simply declares what reality looks like; (b) explanation, which accounts for the existence of that reality; (c) normative analysis, which makes ethical or value judgments; and (d) prescription, which offers recommendations as to a future course of action or policy. Although these various modes constitute distinct intellectual tasks reflecting different purposes of inquiry, they are all interrelated.

SUGGESTIONS FOR FURTHER READING AND STUDY

Much has been written in recent years about interdependence. See the works cited in Note 17, especially the excellent piece by Edward Morse entitled "Interdependence in

World Affairs," in *World Politics,* ed. by James N. Rosenau, Kenneth W. Thompson, and Gavin Boyd (New York: Free Press, 1976), pp. 660–681, which summarizes the empirical and normative issues treated in the literature.

For an excellent discussion of the "what" question, see Patrick M. Morgan, *Theories and Approaches to International Politics,* 4th ed. (New Brunswick, N.J.: Transaction Books, 1986), ch. 1. The author examines the boundary question as well as other problems in studying international relations, including the so-called "levels of analysis" problem. For the distinction between domestic policy and foreign policy, see James N. Rosenau, "Foreign Policy as an Issue-Area," *The Scientific Study of Foreign Policy,* 2nd ed. (London: Nichols, 1980), pp. 461–500; and Eugene J. Meehan, "The Concept 'Foreign Policy,' " in Wolfran F. Hanrieder, ed., *Comparative Foreign Policy* (New York: David McKay, 1971), pp. 265–294. The nature of nation-states and the nation-state system is treated in Barry Buzan's *People, States, and Fear* (Chapel Hill: University of North Carolina Press, 1983).

For the "how" question, see James E. Dougherty and Robert L. Pfaltzgraff, *Contending Theories of International Relations,* 2nd ed. (New York: Harper & Row, 1981); and Klaus Knorr and James N. Rosenau, eds., *Contending Approaches to International Politics* (Princeton, N.J.: Princeton University Press, 1969); the former offers a wide-ranging examination of both paradigm and methodological concerns while the latter focuses more on methodological issues. A comparison of the idealist and realist paradigms can be found in John A. Vasquez, ed., *Classics of International Relations* (Englewood Cliffs, N.J.: Prentice-Hall, 1986), chs. 1 and 2; the globalist and realist paradigms are critiqued in Ray Maghroori and Bennett Ramberg, eds., *Globalism Versus Realism: International Relations' Third Debate* (Boulder, Colo.: Westview Press, 1982). Among the classic realist works are E. H. Carr, *The Twenty Years' Crisis, 1919–1939* (London: Macmillan, 1939), and Hans J. Morgenthau, *Politics Among Nations* (New York: Knopf, 1948). In addition to Woodrow Wilson's writings, idealist thought can be found in such works as Bertrand Russell, *Which Way to Peace?* (London: M. Joseph, 1936), and Grenville Clark and Louis B. Sohn, *World Peace Through World Law: Two Alternative Plans,* 3rd ed. (Cambridge, Mass.: Harvard University Press, 1966). Among recent works that exemplify the globalist perspective, in addition to the ones cited in Note 29, are Richard W. Mansbach and John A. Vasquez, *In Search of Theory: A New Paradigm for Global Politics* (New York: Columbia University Press, 1981), and Dennis Pirages, *The New Context for International Relations: Global Ecopolitics* (North Scituate, Mass.: Duxbury Press, 1978). A concise treatment of the Marxist world view can be found in Keith L. Nelson and Spencer C. Olin, *Why War?* (Berkeley: University of California Press, 1979), pp. 69–74. For examples of specific studies that use quantitative techniques to examine international relations phenomena, see J. David Singer, ed., *Quantitative International Politics: Insights and Evidence* (New York: Free Press, 1968), and John E. Mueller, ed., *Approaches to Measurement in International Relations* (New York: Appleton-Century-Crofts, 1969).

An extensive discussion of the various modes of analysis and the role of theory in the international relations field is furnished by David Edwards, *International Political Analysis* (New York: Holt, Rinehart and Winston, 1969); also, see Alexander L. George, "Theory for Policy in International Relations," *Policy Sciences,* 4 (December 1973), pp. 387–413. Regarding the relationship between the scholar and the policymaker, see the Whiting article mentioned in Note 39, as well as Robert L. Rothstein, *Planning,*

Prediction, and Policymaking in Foreign Affairs (Boston: Little, Brown, 1972). Two articles that examine a variety of themes discussed in Chapter 1 are Norman Palmer's "The Study of International Relations in the United States: Perspectives of Half a Century," *International Studies Quarterly*, 24 (September 1980), pp. 343–363; and William Olson's "Growing Pains of a Discipline: Its Phases, Ideals, and Debates," in Olson *et al.*, eds., *The Theory and Practice of International Relations*, 6th ed. (Englewood Cliffs, N.J.: Prentice-Hall, 1983), pp. 391–401.

There are two resources which are invaluable to the beginning student in the international relations field. One is Jack C. Plano and Roy Olton, *The International Relations Dictionary*, 4th ed. (Santa Barbara: ABC-CLIO, 1988), which gives concise definitions of several hundred commonly used terms in the international relations field. The other is Merry Coplin's *Handbook for Library Research in International Relations* (New York: Learning Resources in International Studies, 1972), which is a guide to the use of books, periodicals, governmental documents and other library resources in the international relations field.

2

A Glimpse Into the Past: The Historical Development of the International System

In examining the evolution of international relations over the years, some observers are struck by the degree of *change* that has occurred while others are struck by the degree of *continuity*. The former lean toward the *sui generis* school of history, which argues that history never repeats itself since each historical event is unique ("one of a kind"); the latter lean toward the *déjà vu* school of history, which argues that the more things change the more they stay the same ("I've seen it all before").

Representative of the first view are the following statements, one by Barbara Tuchman, a historian, and one by Alvin Toffler, a futurologist. Consider the comments by Tuchman, comparing the circumstances surrounding the Soviet invasion of Afghanistan in 1979 with those existing on the eve of World War I in 1914:

> Events in history do not—I would venture to say cannot—repeat themselves; nor can they be acted out in the same pattern as before because circumstances are never the same as before. They alter as the years pass, and the longer the elapsed time, the more new factors enter the situation. When the pace of change, as in the twentieth century, is rapid, the change can be immense.[1]

Similarly, consider Toffler's comments on the futility of comparing the present with the past, whether with regard to international relations or any other phenomena:

> The final, qualitative difference between this and all previous lifetimes is the one most easily overlooked. For we have not merely extended the scope and scale of change, we have radically altered its pace. We have in our time released a totally new social force—a stream of change so accelerated that it influences our sense of time, revolutionizes the tempo of daily life, and affects the very way we "feel" the world around us. We no longer "feel" life as men did in the past. And this is the ultimate difference, the distinction that separates the truly contemporary man from all others. For this acceleration lies behind the impermanence ... radically affecting the way we relate to other people, to things, to the entire universe of ideas, art and values. ... [2]

In contrast, consider the remarks of Kenneth Waltz, one of the more prominent members of the second school:

> International politics is sometimes described as the realm of accident and upheaval, of rapid and unpredictable change. Although changes abound, continuities are as impressive, or more so. ... In the two world wars of this century [for example] ... the same principal countries lined up against each other, despite the domestic political upheavals that took place in the interwar period. The texture of international politics remains highly constant, patterns recur, and events repeat themselves endlessly. The relations that prevail internationally seldom shift rapidly in type or in quality.[3]

Perhaps the most well-known and oft-quoted statement reflecting the *déjà vu* school of history belongs to the philosopher George Santayana, who cautioned that "those who cannot remember the past are condemned to repeat it."[4]

Change and Continuity in International Relations: Sui Generis *or* Déjà Vu?

Are international relations characterized mostly by change, or by continuity? As suggested in Chapter 1, the authors would argue that elements of both change *and* continuity can be identified in international relations, that the truth lies somewhere between the *sui generis* view of history and the *déjà vu* view.

SUI GENERIS

On the one hand, it is obvious that, strictly speaking, events never repeat themselves exactly in the same manner; as the ancient Greek philosopher Heraclitus noted, one can never step in the same stream twice. At the very least, the particular personalities involved in shaping events change. More importantly, it is also obvious that the environment in which international relations are conducted itself undergoes change. Clearly, there have been countless developments in international relations over the years that would make today's world unrecognizable at first glance to the statesman of the eighteenth or nineteenth century or even the early twentieth century—the invention of weapons of mass destruction capable of leveling entire countries, the negotiation of a treaty to avoid a shoot-out in outer space, energy crises and population explosions, skyjackings by revolutionaries, the "Coca-Colaization" of the world, instantaneous satellite communication of happenings in one corner of the globe to the opposite corner, the growth of multinational corporations, to name but a few developments.

DÉJÀ VU

On the other hand, even though the particular personalities and conditions surrounding various international events may change over the years, some commonalities and parallels can still be found throughout different periods of international relations history. While events may never repeat themselves exactly, they may nonetheless share some rough similarities. Indeed, it is the assumption that individual events are not wholly unique and that there are identifiable patterns of international behavior which enables us to develop useful knowledge about international relations; otherwise, there would be no lessons to be learned from the study of international relations and no perspective to be derived from history.

Wars continue to be fought, even if the nature of the weapons changes drastically. The process of diplomacy goes on, even if the territory being negotiated happens to be in outer space. Pressures caused by population pushing against resources have regularly been a source of friction in international relations, even though they may now be of a different kind and magnitude than in the past. If skyjackings are a fairly recent phenomenon, international terrorism is not. Societies have always experienced "cultural diffusion" of ideas and tastes across national boundaries—whether in the form of Coca-Cola or beer or more revolutionary innovations, despite frequent attempts by governments to limit "foreign" influences. In this sense, interdependence is not altogether new today—only more intricate, more accelerated, and more difficult to prevent or undo. Nations and peoples still manage to misunderstand and misperceive each other's actions even as advanced communications technology provides greater and faster information about the world than ever before. And new forms of human organization may develop, but old ones—such as nation-states—persist alongside them.

In short, some features of international relations are more enduring and less given to change than other features. Change is not as all-pervasive as the *sui generis* school might suggest, nor is it as insignificant and superficial as it might be depicted by the *déjà vu* school. There are important *continuities* to be observed in international relations, but there are also important *changes* as well. "New generations take up the story, the grass grows again over concentration camp and battlefield, new divisions spring up between old wartime comrades while scars of conflict heal and the children of enemies marry and produce new generations with their own affinities and differences, loves and hates."[5]

THE INTERNATIONAL SYSTEM IN FLUX

It is this history that we wish to trace in this chapter. In discussing the evolution of international relations, our concern is not to provide a detailed chronology of events but rather, in the space of a few pages, to provide some sense of how certain essential aspects of international relations have changed significantly over the years while others have remained relatively constant. Such historical perspective can enable us to understand better the *current* global condition.

In order to furnish a thumbnail sketch of several hundred years of history in a single chapter, it is helpful to utilize the concept of **international system,** which can be defined as the general pattern of political, economic, social, geographical, and technological relationships that govern world affairs or, more simply, as the general setting in which international relations occur at any point in time. At times, the basic fabric of international relations seems to change so much, not necessarily in all its parts but in many key elements, that one can say the international system has been "transformed." There is considerable disagreement among scholars as to how often international system transformation has occurred and one distinct era of international politics has given way to another era.[6]

For purposes of discussion, we will divide the last several centuries of international relations history into four periods: (1) the Classical International System (1648–1789), (2) the Transitional International System (1789–1945), (3) the Post–World War II International System (1945–1973), and (4) the Contemporary International System. These correspond roughly to the international systems identified by Coplin, Holsti and a number of other scholars in the field.[7] Some observers might take exception to this compartmentalization of history, especially to the significance of 1973 as a watershed date denoting the end of the post–World War II era. However, these chronological boundaries are not offered as the definitive mileposts in the life of the international system but only as rough markers that can serve as a basis for organizing our historical discussion and comparing the past with the present. We will examine the first three systems in this chapter and leave the contemporary international system for closer scrutiny in Chapter 3.

In order to compare different eras of international politics, it is necessary to identify those elements of the international system that are potentially subject to change and that seem to be most worthy of comparison. An examination of the scholarly literature suggests that among the most important characteristics ("variables") of the international system are the following: (1) the nature of the *actors* (nation-states and nonstate actors); (2) the *distribution of power* (equilibrium among several major actors or dominance by one or two actors); (3) the *distribution of wealth* (the extent of the "rich-poor gap" between actors); (4) the *degree of polarization* (flexibility or rigidity of alignment); (5) the *objectives* of the actors (preoccupation with territorial acquisition or some other objective); (6) the *means* available to actors for pursuing their objectives (the nature of weapons technology, for example); and (7) the *degree of interdependence* (in terms of both "interconnectedness"— the raw volume of goods and services, people, and communications flowing across national boundaries—and "mutual sensitivity and vulnerability"—the potential effects of one country's actions on other countries).[8] We now examine how and to what extent these features of international relations have changed over the years.

The Classical International System (1648–1789)

By most accounts, the "story" of international relations begins in 1648, with the **Peace of Westphalia** ending the Thirty Years' War. This date is widely accepted as marking the origin of the international system because it was only in the mid-seventeenth century that the world began to witness the emergence of actors called *nation-states*, cited in Chapter 1 as the primary units of political organization on the globe. That is to say, it was only then that there appeared on the scene certain entities having the following characteristics: (1) a single *central government* exercising **sovereignty** over (2) a relatively fixed *population* within (3) a relatively well-defined *territory.* Such entities were said to be "sovereign" in terms of there being a government that had supreme decision-making authority within the boundaries of the territorial unit and that acknowledged no higher authority outside those boundaries. Sovereignty did not mean that the state was necessarily able to control all the actions of its members at all times, only that internally it could claim a monopoly on the legitimate use of physical force as a possible tool in seeking to compel their obedience and externally it could claim a monopoly right to act on their behalf vis-à-vis other states. (See the box on pages 35–37 for a discussion of definitional problems surrounding such terms as **state, nation**, and **nation-state**. These terms are worth examining in some detail, since they are essential to the study of international relations and can be a source of much confusion.)

THE BIRTH OF THE NATION-STATE

It is important to keep in mind that from a long-term historical perspective, the nation-state is a relatively young institution in human affairs. It is not even 400 years old—which is not very old when compared to at least 5000 years of recorded history and thousands more in the prehistoric period. Human beings had been on the earth for roughly two million years prior to the mid-seventeenth century. However, they had been organized in other kinds of political units, such as tribes, city-states, and empires, rather than nation-states. One can read Thucydides' accounts of the city-state system of ancient Greece (which lasted from 800 B.C. to 322 B.C.), Kautilya's writings on the ancient Hindu state system under the Mauryan Empire (325 B.C.–183 B.C.), and Machiavelli's accounts of the city-state system of Renaissance Italy (during the fifteenth century). The history of humanity could be read as the search for the optimal political unit, with the pendulum seemingly swinging between two extremes: almost a single universal political order (e.g., the world empires of Rome and Alexander the Great) and a set of much smaller, highly fragmented polities (e.g., the series of walled cities and other entities that typified the Middle Ages).[9]

In Europe, for example, even as late as 1600, there were elements of both fragmentation (manifested by the semi-sovereign political jurisdictions presided over by various feudal lords and princes) and universalism (manifested by the Pope and the Holy Roman Emperor who claimed supreme spiritual and secular authority). In short, the political landscape of Europe consisted of a

NATIONS, STATES, AND NATION-STATES: SOME PROBLEMS IN DEFINING TERMS

In everyday conversation, people tend to use a number of terms interchangeably—"nations," "states," "countries"—to refer to those entities that are distinguished by thick boundary lines on world maps. Although one might casually interchange these terms, they are not exactly synonymous. Technically speaking, "state" refers to a *legal-political* entity, "nation" refers to a *cultural* or social entity, and "country" refers to a *geographical* entity. In defining "state" and "nation," the distinction is not merely technical; it has real importance for international relations scholars as well as policymakers and lawyers.

When we say that "state" refers to a legal-political entity, we mean an entity that has a sovereign government exercising supreme authority over a relatively fixed population within well-defined territorial boundaries and acknowledging no higher authority outside those boundaries. Today, there are well over 160 such territorial units considered by most observers to be states. Such entities have "international legal status," which enables them to enter into treaties, join intergovernmental organizations like the United Nations, exchange ambassadors, and engage in other "official" international activities. In short, whether one uses the term or not, "states" are the main reference points one sees on a world map. Some states, like the United States and the Soviet Union, are obviously well known, but other states, like Lesotho and Nauru, are less so. No matter how tiny or inconspicuous a state is, its sovereignty gives it at least formal equality with all other states.

A "nation," on the other hand, is conceptually and legally different. When we say "nation" refers to a cultural or social entity, we mean a group of people having some sense of shared historical experience (generally rooted in a common language or other cultural characteristics) as well as shared destiny. A nation may comprise part of a state (e.g., the Timorese constituting a distinct cultural group within the state of Indonesia), may be coterminous with the state (e.g., the American people and the United States), or may spill over several different states (e.g., the Palestinians in Israel, Lebanon, Jordan, and several other states). As one can imagine, there are many more "nations" than "states" in the world.

These distinctions are not always clear-cut. In the case of the United States, the society is composed of many nationality groups claiming different national origins (Irish-Americans, Polish-Americans, and other "hyphenated Americans"); but because these groups over time have for the most part become assimilated into American society and have come to identify themselves as "Americans," one can say that the state and nation are practically one in the United States. The oneness of the state and nation is also the case in many other established states such as France and Italy. Although various groups in Italy quarrel vociferously, sometimes violently, over the political institutions of the state, they nonetheless consider themselves "Italians" and do not speak of seceding to form a new state. In contrast, the Timorese in Indonesia tend not to consider themselves Indonesians; the Palestinians in Israel, Jordan, and Lebanon tend not to think of themselves as Israelis, Jordanians, or Lebanese; the Kurds in Iran and Iraq tend not to identify themselves as Iranians or Iraqis. In all the latter cases, the states in question are plagued by culturally diverse populations that include separatist movements intent on establishing their own independent statehood. Even in the case of the Soviet Union, while many think of "Russians" and "Soviets" as being synonymous, the fact is that the Russians are a distinct nationality group that happens to dominate the Soviet state but is feeling increasingly threatened by other nationality groups in the Central Asian part of the country that do not identify nearly as much with the state.

It has often been noted that in the early development of the international system, during the seventeenth and eighteenth centuries, it was the state that created the nation. That is, the states were ones in which the central political authorities gradually managed to forge a sense of national identity among a group of people who happened to find themselves living within the same set of borders but who had not previously thought of themselves as "French" or "English." In the nineteenth and early twentieth century, however, the nation often created the state. Groups sharing common linguistic and other cultural bonds eventually united into single states, with the prime examples being the loose confederation of German-speaking territories forming Germany in 1870 and the various Italian-speaking territories forming Italy around the same time. The pattern in the latter part of the twentieth century has been more like that in the seventeenth and eighteenth centuries insofar as many of the societies in Africa and Asia that achieved independence from colonial powers after World War II became states whose borders did not correspond to any natural cultural groupings but were the artificial product of imperialist rivalries and colonial mapmaking: hence, in countries like Indonesia and Uganda, the leaders who had led the independence movement were faced with the problem of getting diverse and often historically hostile tribal units to identify with the new state in which they were situated. An important aspect of world politics over the years has been this search by culturally distinct nations for statehood and by polyglot states for nationhood.

In the course of this book we will follow the literary convention of using various terms—states, nations, countries—interchangeably; unless otherwise specified, we will be using these terms to refer to the political-legal entities known as "states." There is one other term, which we have already mentioned, that requires some explanation, namely "nation-state." This term is used by scholars as a synonym for "state," not to add confusion to an already confusing terminology but rather to connote the fact that over the last three centuries there has been a persistent impulse to achieve some congruence between state and national boundaries, to make the state and nation one in the minds and hearts of its people.

crazy-quilt pattern of duchies, independent cities, feudal manors, kingdoms, ecclesiastical territories, and assorted other units tied together in a complicated hierarchy. While kings and queens sat on thrones in England and France, their authority was contested by both local princes and papal powers in Rome.[10] However, as 1648 approached, the political landscape was changing. Gunpowder was making the walled cities of the past no longer viable as units of political organization capable of protecting their populations. The small but rising bourgeois commercial middle class began casting their lot with kings and queens against the prerogatives of the landed nobility. And the authority of the Pope and Holy Roman Emperor, always existing more in theory than in reality, became even more marginal. The feudal order was dying.[11]

These trends culminated in the Peace of Westphalia in 1648, symbolizing a fundamentally new set of political arrangements based upon the sovereignty of the nation-state. In consolidating their power against local princes and repudiating any allegiance to higher religious or other authorities outside their territory, national monarchs seemed to be rejecting the forces of both fragmentation and universalism that had characterized previous eras. As we will see, the development of nation-states has been an uneven phenomenon, with the first ones appearing in the seventeenth century, others (such as Germany and Italy) not materializing until the mid-nineteenth century, and still others (such as many societies in Africa and Asia) appearing only in the mid-twentieth century. As we will also see, the nation-state has managed to survive despite both centrifugal forces (tending toward fragmentation) and centripetal forces (tending toward universalism). But that is getting ahead of the story.

ACTORS IN THE CLASSICAL SYSTEM

When one examines the international system that existed in the seventeenth and eighteenth centuries, commonly referred to as the "classical" era of international relations, one finds a relatively small number of actors involved in international politics—namely, the heads of royal families of England, France, and other European nation-states along with their aristocratic elites. The claim by King Louis XIV of France that *"l'état c'est moi"* ("I am the state") was applicable to his fellow monarchs as well, and derived from the "divine right of kings" or some other such rationale. Only toward the very end of the eighteenth century was *dynastic nationalism* to give way to *democratic nationalism* whereby sovereignty derived from the will of the people who inhabited the state. Indeed, throughout much of this period, the average peasant in the village still did not identify wholeheartedly with the state and was not inclined to respond emotionally to flag-waving and other national symbols. (It was hard for Louis XIV to wave the banner of French nationalism when his wife was Spanish, his chief adviser was from the Italian peninsula, and his army consisted largely of foreign mercenaries.) Patriotism had not yet become a major impulse in the affairs of state.

POWER AND WEALTH

Although there existed independent entities outside of Europe, such as China and Japan, and later the United States, international politics in this period was essentially *European* politics. Power (in terms of military capability and related factors) was distributed roughly evenly among several dominant European states, including England, France, Austria, Sweden, Spain, Turkey, and (as the era progressed) Prussia and Russia. (**Power** is as important a concept in the study of international relations as the concepts state and nation, and can be just as much a source of confusion. See the box on pages 39–41 for a focused look at problems in assessing national power, both historically and in contemporary times.) The European states were similar not only in power but also in wealth. At a time when the Industrial Revolution was not yet fully underway, all states had similar sources of wealth and the differences between them were not nearly as great as the disparities that were to develop later.

There was always the possibility that a given state might not be satisfied with its power or wealth position and might threaten the sovereignty of other states and upset the equilibrium by engaging in empire-building. In the absence of any centralized political authority in the international system, order among states was to be maintained primarily through the so-called **balance of power**. Any aggressively minded states intent on hegemony would, it was hoped, be deterred by the prospect of coming up against a coalition of states having equal or superior power; if deterrence failed and an attack occurred, the latter coalition could be expected to fight to defeat the aggressor. Throughout much of the classical era, France was viewed as the major threat to the stability of the system, with England assuming the chief "balancer" role, even though the latter's own hegemonic ambitions were somewhat suspect as well.

DEGREE OF POLARIZATION

In order for the balance of power to operate as intended, it required a low level of polarization, i.e., a high degree of alignment flexibility, whereby

POWER: SOME PROBLEMS OF DEFINITION AND MEASUREMENT

Power has been variously defined—by Hans Morgenthau as "man's control over the minds and actions of other men," by Karl Deutsch as "the ability to prevail in conflict and overcome obstacles," and by Robert Dahl as the ability of one actor "to get [another actor] to do something that [the latter] would not otherwise do."*

The concept of power has taken on different meanings in international relations, depending on the context in which the term has been used. In the context of national actors, it normally refers to a country's existing strength (a commodity a state possesses in some amount) or a goal (something a state wants more of). In the context of interactions between states, it normally refers to their relative capabilities and the manner in which one state seeks to control the behavior of another state, i.e., the economic, military, or other tools of influence used. In the context of the international system, as treated in this chapter, it normally refers to the stratification pattern formed by the global power distribution among states.

It is one thing to define power; it is another thing to try to measure it so that one can make accurate statements about which states are powerful and which states are not so powerful. One encounters measurement problems no matter what the context within which one is analyzing power. In regard to the actor context, many classic works have attempted to identify the "bases" of national power—certain national attributes upon which a state's capacity to influence others presumably depends. Almost invariably the list includes geography (territorial size, location, and natural resources), population (size, homogeneity, and level of education), economic capability (gross national product and degree of industrialization), and military capability (quantity and quality of weaponry and troops). Countries possessing a sizable land area and population, economic and military capability, and natural resource endowment, along with a high level of economic and technological development, have traditionally been considered "powerful" by definition, whether or not they take advantage of these assets.

Aside from the measurement problem of deciding what weight to assign each of these factors, there is always some analyst who argues that some attribute has been erroneously omitted from the list, so that the list can become endless. Also, there are analysts who argue for the inclusion of such "soft" and less measurable factors as national character and morale. Others have noted, too, that the importance of these factors can vary from one historical period to another. For example, territorial features such as a large land mass or insular location or mountainous topography may have conferred power (at least in terms of invulnerability to attack) in the eighteenth century but may be somewhat less significant in an age of intercontinental ballistic missiles. Similarly, a large population may have been the *sine qua non* needed in the nineteenth and early twentieth centuries to produce tons of weapons and bodies for the armed forces but may be somewhat less crucial in an age of automated industry and warfare. One could argue differently, though, that a rough terrain and large population can still pose formidable obstacles to a would-be aggressor even in modern times, as in the case of guerrilla warfare.

Although a country's power may be closely associated with its human and material resource base, power and resources are not exactly the same. Here is where the interaction context must be taken into account. As in other areas of life, the "underdog" sometimes wins in international relations since the country in a seemingly favored position is unable to translate its resources into domination of another country. The "paper tiger" is a well-known phenomenon in international relations. Also related to the interaction context, the exercise of power can take many different forms, ranging from moral suasion to economic coercion to the threatened or actual use of military force. Certain national attributes may be relevant to certain modes of statecraft but not to others. And certain modes of statecraft may be common to some historical eras more than to others.

In regard to the systemic context, scholars have tended to characterize the global distribution of power in terms of either equilibrium among several major powers or hegemony by only one or two, depending on the historical era. Often the major powers are referred to as "poles" toward which other lesser states gravitate for protection. Further distinctions are made between "great powers," "middle powers," and "small powers," usually based on possession of the aforementioned national attributes assumed to be associated with power. However, countries designated as "powerful" do not necessarily act powerfully at all times. It is often difficult to determine where to draw the line between, say, a "middle power" and a "small power" and which states belong in which categories.

One is on much safer ground attempting to ascertain the general power structure of the international system rather than attempting to identify an exact ranking of states. Indeed, despite all the measurement problems and disagreements cited here, a fairly broad scholarly consensus exists on the nature of the power structure in the three international systems discussed in this chapter.

Our point in making these comments is to emphasize that power is a more complex concept than is sometimes suggested by the way the term is bandied about in everyday discourse. The kinds of problems noted here not only complicate efforts by scholars to analyze power but also complicate the power calculations of policymakers as well. As we will see in Chapter 3, power is especially difficult to assess with precision in contemporary international relations.

* Hans J. Morgenthau, *Politics Among Nations,* 5th ed. (New York: Knopf, 1973), p. 28; Karl W. Deutsch, "On the Concepts of Politics and Power," *Journal of International Affairs,* 21 (1967), p. 334; Robert A. Dahl, "The Concept of Power," *Behavioral Science,* 2 (July 1957), p. 203.

countries could shift their power quickly from one side to another as a counterweight against would-be aggressors. The international system in this period was, indeed, flexible, in the sense that the European powers and other actors in the system did not fall into rigid armed camps at opposite poles poised against each other but rather were amenable to making and breaking alliances frequently as the situation warranted. Although there was enormous palace intrigue, wheeling and dealing, and military maneuvering associated with the balance of power at this time, the classical system worked fairly effectively, if imperfectly, as at least a crude vehicle for maintaining stability in the international system—not necessarily out of any conscious attempt by states to keep order but out of their mutual security concerns.[12]

Two factors, in particular, contributed to the flexibility of the system and the operation of the balance of power mechanism. One was the concentration of decision-making competence in the hands of a few rulers, so that decisions about alliance-making and breaking could be taken swiftly without need for consultation or popular approval. The second was the absence of any major ideological cleavages among the main actors. Had such differences existed, certain potential alliance partners might have been somewhat incompatible, which might have inhibited the shifting of alliances called for by the balance of power calculus. Not only were the leaders of European states all conservative monarchs steeped in similar cultural traditions, but in many instances they were also related by marriage. The combination of multiple power centers together with flexibility of alignments made for an international system that scholars have labeled **multipolar.**[13]

OBJECTIVES AND MEANS

The European monarchs spoke the same "language" in more ways than one. In particular, they shared to some extent a common understanding of the "rules of the game" surrounding international politics at the time: (1) not to interfere in the internal affairs of another country in any way that might destabilize monarchical institutions and (2) not to allow any one state to achieve dominant power in the system (unless it happened to be one's own state). The objectives of states in the classical era were not so much national objectives as personal objectives of the various rulers, namely to enhance dynastic wealth, power, and prestige.

While the royal houses of Europe shared common bloodlines and values, they also had conflicts of interests. All rulers experienced the "security dilemma" that statesmen in later generations were to experience as well— the felt need for more national power in order to increase national security, although the quest for power merely tended to increase feelings of insecurity. Although some rulers may have harbored hegemonic aspirations, the objectives they usually sought were relatively limited, partly because the available means for pursuing national objectives were also relatively limited. The stakes over which wars were fought consisted mostly of a few patches of real estate— Alsace or some other province—several of which changed hands frequently without their inhabitants having much opportunity to develop a clear national identity. The classical era, then, was not known as an era of peace, but rather one in which the violent international conflicts that occurred were fairly small affairs between monarchs, resembling blood feuds or gentlemanly rivalries in contrast to the total wars among whole societies which were to be waged in subsequent eras.

As much as one national leader might wish to crush and eliminate another, the niceties of palace etiquette and the realities of limited military power tended to dictate otherwise. For firepower, monarchs relied on small expensive professional armies, often consisting of foreign mercenaries whose loyalty was questionable and whose desertion rate was high. The military technology they were armed with—muskets and cannon loaded with gunpowder—was deadly enough but relatively crude and applicable only on a small scale compared with the state of the art that was to be developed in the nineteenth and, of course, the twentieth century. The masses were largely innocent bystanders during wartime, being raped, plundered, and pillaged but not having any vested interests in the outcome of most conflicts; their political and economic lot was not likely to change very much no matter what the fate of their sovereign was or even who their sovereign happened to be.

DEGREE OF INTERDEPENDENCE

All of this made for an international system that had a curious blend of parochialism and cosmopolitanism. While the elites of Europe traveled and conversed freely across national boundaries, the masses knew little of the world outside their towns and villages, much less outside their national borders. While monarchs were reliant to some extent on gold and other resources from the New World beyond the oceans to help finance their professional armies, nation-states in this period were still fairly self-contained and self-sufficient economic units only minimally dependent on international commerce. While diseases could have contagious effects spreading across national boundaries, cultural and other kinds of diffusion processes occurred slowly; the still primitive communications technology kept one corner of the globe insulated from developments in another corner, so that there was little likelihood of revolutions and terrorist activities becoming immediate world-wide epidemics. While balance of power considerations created mutual concerns in the military sphere, the primitive nature of weapons technology meant that—in contrast to later periods—allies were not linked together by any need for coordinated military planning and training, and enemies did not share the common bond of knowing that a fatal decision by one side could mean annihilation for both. In short, the classical international system was characterized by a relatively low degree of interdependence among states, both in terms of "interconnectedness" (the raw volume of transactions across national boundaries) as well as "mutual sensitivity and vulnerability" (the potential effects of one country's actions on other countries).

However, many of these conditions were already starting to change toward the end of the eighteenth century. The French Revolution that occurred in 1789 not only ushered out the monarchy in France but also set in motion certain forces that were to usher in a new era of international politics.

The Transitional International System (1789–1945)

Although the French Revolution was preceded a decade earlier by the American Revolution, the "shot heard around the world" that started the thirteen colonies' revolt against the British was neither as loud as the storming of the Bastille in Paris nor as revolutionary a turning point in the development of the international system. The reason was simply that France was an integral part of the European state system that dominated world politics at the time, while the fledgling United States remained on the periphery. The distinctiveness of the "transitional" international system that emerged at the end of the eighteenth century and was to last until 1945 lay precisely in the fact that it constituted a bridge between the classical and post–World War II eras, retaining certain features of the former while also introducing new features presaging the latter. The transitional era was like a "prism" through which passed certain elements of the past that were refined and reshaped and out of which emerged a new ambience—a new environment—surrounding international relations.[14]

ACTORS

With the French Revolution that ultimately brought Napoleon Bonaparte to power, an age of **nationalism** began that was to carry over into the late twentieth century. The new nationalism was based on a firmer relationship between the central government of the state and the people over which it presided, particularly a greater emotional bond between the two created by the greater involvement of the masses in the political life of the country. It was the new nationalism that enabled Napoleon—posing as a man of the people while wearing emperor's clothing—to recruit a mass citizen army through nationwide conscription of young Frenchmen and to mobilize the French *nation* in support of France's military activities abroad. French nationalism had the unintended effect of provoking nationalism in other states that felt threatened. If the rise of mass democracy meant that leaders might have to become more sensitive to public opinion in formulating foreign policy, it also meant that they potentially could count on the total military and economic capabilities that their societies had to offer in international politics. Although full-scale democratic institutions developed only gradually and unevenly in Europe and elsewhere during the transitional era, rulers could increasingly claim to be acting on behalf of a mass, nationalistic following in a way that their predecessors in the classical period could not.[15]

Nationalistic impulses led to the appearance of new states on the map. Some gained their independence from colonial masters (e.g., the Latin American states in the early nineteenth century revolting against Spain), and others emerged through the political unification of culturally similar groups that had previously been only loosely affiliated (e.g., the confederations of German-speaking and Italian-speaking peoples forming the modern states of Germany and Italy in the mid-nineteenth century). Although nationalistic impulses led to the liberation of some peoples, such as the independence of the Romanians from Turkish rule in 1878, the same impulses touched off a new wave of European imperialism that resulted in the subjugation of other peoples in Africa and elsewhere. Pressures for national "self-determination" grew stronger, especially following World War I when Poland and Hungary became independent along with several other states. Although a considerable increase in the number of independent national actors occurred during the transitional era, with over fifty nation-states existing in the world by 1945, this was only the prelude to a much more explosive proliferation of nation-states that was to take place in the subsequent era, particularly in Africa and Asia. (See Fig. 2.1 for historical trends in the growth of nation-states, which shows the pivotal character of the transitional era.)

Aside from the proliferation of nation-states, the transitional era also witnessed the proliferation of other kinds of actors as well, notably *individual human beings*. It was during this time, in 1830, that world population reached 1 billion, with the second billion coming only 100 years later in 1930. Through most of this period the world population boom was caused primarily by lower death rates in Europe and North America, which was the result of major medical and health care advances that accompanied industrialization in the northern part of the globe. However, just as the proliferation of nation-states was to be even more explosive in the post–World War II period and was to be

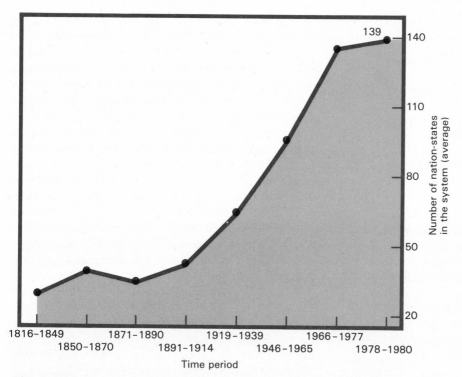

Figure 2.1
THE GROWTH OF NATION-STATES IN THE INTERNATIONAL SYSTEM
The numbers represent "average system size" for a given time period. For the periods from 1816 to 1919, "nation-states" were defined as territorial units having at least 500,000 population and recognized as states by England and France; for the periods from 1919 to the present, they were defined as territorial units having at least 500,000 population and recognized by any two major powers or holding membership in the League of Nations or United Nations. Because of the 500,000 population threshold, roughly thirty "mini-states"—most of which entered the system in the last two decades—are not counted here.

concentrated in the southern part of the globe, so also was humanity to multiply in even greater numbers after World War II—reaching the 4 billion mark by 1975 and 5 billion a decade later—largely as a result of the transfer of medical technology to the peoples of Africa, Asia, and Latin America. (See Fig. 2.2 for world population trends, which also shows the pivotal character of the transitional era.)

POWER AND WEALTH

The increased industrialization that occurred in Europe and America in the nineteenth and early twentieth centuries contributed to a growing disparity

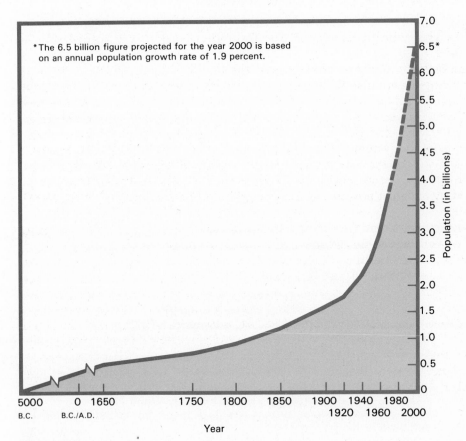

*The 6.5 billion figure projected for the year 2000 is based on an annual population growth rate of 1.9 percent.

Figure 2.2
THE GROWTH OF WORLD POPULATION

in wealth between societies in the Northern Hemisphere and those in the Southern Hemisphere. While a "rich-poor gap" had historically always existed *within* societies, the gap that started to form *between* them during the transitional era was virtually unprecedented. In the past, the masses in one national society were roughly as well off as their counterparts in any other society. The Industrial Revolution was to spread far from Europe but it bypassed the southern half of the globe, thus leaving some societies with rapid income growth and markedly improved living standards for their rich and poor citizens alike, while other societies were practically untouched. Countries such as Britain and France saw their per capita gross national product jump from roughly $250 in 1815 to over $1000 by the mid-twentieth century. The widening rich-poor gap, which had produced a 2 to 1 ratio between incomes in industrial and nonindustrial societies by 1850, was to become even more accentuated in the post–World War II system (increasing to 10 to 1 in 1950 and 20 to 1 by 1970), leading to eventual confrontation between the peoples in the economically developed North and the economically underdeveloped South.[16]

Industrialization not only skewed the distribution of wealth in favor of certain states but also further skewed the distribution of power in their favor as well, since the new economic technology was readily convertible into military advantage. As in the classical system, power throughout the transitional era was distributed fairly evenly among several states that dominated the rest of the system, although Great Britain was considered the "first among equals" during the nineteenth century and the identity of the other "great powers" changed in some cases between the two centuries. (See Table 2.1 for a listing of "great powers" from the classical system to the post-World War II system.)[17]

In particular, the transitional era witnessed the emergence of two highly industrialized non-European states as major world powers by the beginning of the twentieth century—the United States (with the defeat of Spain in 1898) and Japan (with the defeat of Russia in 1905). Russia, itself a semi-European state (straddling Eurasia) and a semi-powerful member of the international system throughout the nineteenth century, was to take on special significance as a world actor after the Bolshevik Revolution of 1917 created the Soviet Union. Indeed, it was the gradual passing of European domination of the state system that was perhaps the most salient feature of the transitional era. As historian Geoffrey Barraclough observed, the year 1900 represented both the peak of the European-centered world and the beginning of its decline: "[While]

Table 2.1

GREAT POWERS IN THE INTERNATIONAL SYSTEM, 1799–1945

	1700	1800	1875	1910	1935	1945
Turkey	X					
Sweden	X					
Netherlands	X					
Spain	X					
Austria (Austria-Hungary)	X	X	X	X		
France	X	X	X	X	X	
England (Great Britain)	X	X	X	X	X	
Prussia (Germany)		X	X	X	X	
Russia (Soviet Union)		X	X	X	X	X
Italy			X	X	X	
Japan				X	X	
United States				X	X	X

Source: Kenneth Waltz, *Theory of International Politics,* Table 8.1. © 1979, Addison-Wesley, Reading, Mass. Reprinted by permission of Random House, Inc. Adapted, with permission, from Quincy Wright, *The Study of War,* Appendix 20, Table 43, 1965, University of Chicago Press.

by 1900 European civilization overshadowed the Earth," the period between 1900 and 1945 was "a period of utmost confusion in which a new system was struggling to be born and the old system fighting hard for its life."[18] By the end of the transitional era, not only had Britain and the continental European states been eclipsed by the United States and the Soviet Union,[19] but other non-European power centers such as China were already looming on the horizon as well.

DEGREE OF POLARIZATION

In addition to bringing non-European powers to the fore in world politics, the transitional era injected **ideological** conflict—the competition between rival political philosophies—into international relations for the first time and portended the extreme polarization that was to occur in the post–World War II period. It was in the mid-nineteenth century that Karl Marx wrote his treatises urging the working classes of the world to unite under the banner of **communism** against their "bourgeois" rulers. Although Marx envisioned ultimately a single classless and stateless world society, history ran counter to his predictions. Combined with the forces of nationalism, the forces of ideology created some further hardening of relations among states. At the beginning of the transitional era, the international system was polarized between Napoleon's armies seeking to export the French Revolution across Europe and the armies of the conservative European monarchs seeking to stem the revolutionary tide. Toward the end of the era, the United States under Woodrow Wilson and the Soviet Union under Lenin exchanged diatribes on the relative merits of democratic capitalism as opposed to communism, followed by Benito Mussolini in Italy and Adolf Hitler in Germany lecturing both Wilson's and Lenin's successors about the supremacy of **fascism** and **national socialism.**

Throughout most of the transitional era, however, alignments in the international system were still fairly flexible, as neither newly developed national rivalries nor ideological differences prevented states from keeping their options open as to prospective alliance partners. In other words, the system was still multipolar in terms of both power and alignment. Although ideological conflict occurred within countries between liberal democratic and conservative monarchical forces, it was not fought out on the international plane. The battle lines in the few wars that were waged in the period were not drawn clearly along ideological lines (e.g., the democracies of Britain, France, and the United States joining arch-conservative Russia against other conservative countries like Germany and Austria in World War I). Indeed, the jockeying for position by the European states on the eve of World War I in 1914 resembled the balance of power machinations engaged in by European monarchs in the classical system, except that the advent of mass democracy and modern military technology had partially lessened decision-making flexibility in the transitional era.[20]

OBJECTIVES AND MEANS

The one hundred years between the Congress of Vienna, which ended the Napoleonic Wars in 1815, and the beginning of World War I in 1914 have been recorded as a period of relative peace in international relations, with several minor but no major wars occurring in the interval. Although the nationalistic fervor of the time threatened to unleash violent conflict, the major powers were usually able to avoid direct military confrontation partly by sublimating chauvinistic energies through a collective carving up of territory in Africa and elsewhere. **Imperialism** was a response to a dual need to pacify a restless public at home and to ensure access to raw materials and markets associated with growing industrialization in the late nineteenth century. The objectives of the major powers—consisting primarily of territorial land-grabbing—were not unlike those pursued in the classical era, although more highly expansionist and defined more in terms of the greater glory and well-being of the nation rather than any individual ruler. Imperialist objectives could be accommodated without major conflict as long as there was enough colonial territory to go around, a condition that had evaporated by 1914.

Not only had available territory disappeared by 1914, but so also had the memory of the horrors of the Napoleonic Wars, during which the involvement of the entire French nation in the war effort had resulted in the death of massive numbers of French citizens. New generations were more impressed by the swift and painless fruits of victory won by the Prussians in their seven-week war with Austria in 1866. However, the "century of peace" between 1815 and 1914—including the "cheap" Prussian victory achieved through the innovative use of the railroad, telegraph, and breechloading rifle—disguised the growing and more deadly military arsenals that were increasingly available to states as potential means for pursuing foreign policy.[21] The mobilization of mass armies combined with the application of science and technology to warfare ultimately produced an unparalleled world war, which was to end formally in 1918—four autumns after the German Kaiser had promised that his troops would be back home "before the leaves fall."[22]

The *total* war that World War I became—fought with poison gas, machine guns, submarines, and biplanes in addition to rifles and bayonets—was to pale in comparison with World War II less than a generation later. It lasted six autumns, from 1939 until 1945.[23] Although the horror of World War I had failed to leave a lasting imprint on the minds of the leaders of the day, the globe-encircling weapons of World War II were to leave a somewhat more indelible impression. A historical era that began with the new importance of the mass foot soldier was giving way to the atomic age. (See Fig. 2.3 for trends in the range and destructiveness of weaponry.)[24]

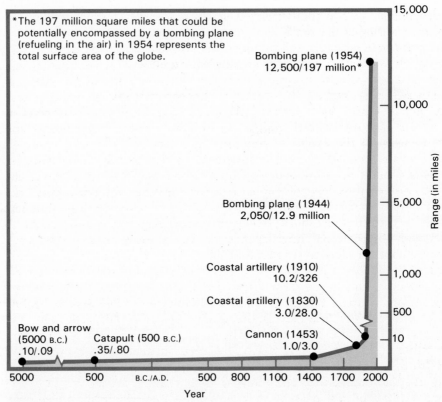

*The 197 million square miles that could be potentially encompassed by a bombing plane (refueling in the air) in 1954 represents the total surface area of the globe.

Bombing plane (1954)
12,500/197 million*

Bombing plane (1944)
2,050/12.9 million

Coastal artillery (1910)
10.2/326

Coastal artillery (1830)
3.0/28.0

Bow and arrow
(5000 B.C.)
.10/.09

Catapult (500 B.C.)
.35/.80

Cannon (1453)
1.0/3.0

Range (in miles)

15,000
10,000
5,000
1,000
500
10

5000   500   B.C./A.D.   500   800   1100   1400 1700   2000

Year

Figure 2.3
TRENDS IN RANGE AND DESTRUCTIVENESS OF WEAPONS DELIVERY VEHICLES
The first number indicated beneath each weapon on the graph represents its maximum range in miles; the second number represents the "killing area" (in square miles)—the maximum area within which lives and property may be destroyed by such projectiles.

DEGREE OF INTERDEPENDENCE

While the transitional era saw the arrival of total war, it also saw the arrival of increasing interdependence among states, particularly in the economic sphere—a development that was to be interrupted by the two world wars but was to be resumed in the post–World War II era. The emergence of total war alongside economic interdependence seemed a paradoxical phenomenon at first, but the two proved they could exist together in the same system. Although trade interdependence among European states had become so great by the end of the nineteenth century that many observers at the time assumed war between them unthinkable lest it totally disrupt their economies, World War I demonstrated that political impulses could be stronger than economic imperatives. In the interwar interval between 1919 and 1939, the very economic interdependence of the industrialized states made the Great Depression a global one, adding to the tensions that resulted in World War II.

The point here is that interdependence is not something that appeared just yesterday. It was rather a process already well underway at the turn of this century and was already having uncertain implications for world order. As Kenneth Waltz has argued, in some respects economic interdependence was greater before World War I (particularly if one uses "exports plus imports as a percentage of gross national product" as an indicator of interdependence and if one focuses on the extent of economic ties among the major powers).[25] Some analysts even called the late nineteenth and early twentieth centuries "the *belle époque* [beautiful epoch] of interdependence"[26] while others at the time recognized interdependence as a mixed blessing, observing that "the world is, more than ever before, one great unit in which everything interacts and affects everything else, but in which also everything collides and clashes."[27]

Although international interdependence was growing in the nineteenth century, it is misleading to suggest that the phenomenon peaked in the years preceding World War I and went downhill thereafter. Quite to the contrary, in many ways it was only the tip of the iceberg. For one thing, while it is true that in most countries foreign trade as a percentage of GNP was to decline from record pre–World War I levels, the *total volume* of world trade in absolute terms was to expand enormously in the twentieth century, increasing from $15.6 billion in 1880 to over $2 trillion by 1980.[28] In addition, regarding many other dimensions of "interconnectedness," such as flows of people and mail across national boundaries, one likewise finds that the trends begun in the transitional era did not peak in that period but instead foreshadowed even greater interdependence that was to follow after World War II.[29] As for other, more fundamental aspects of interdependence—such as "mutual sensitivity and vulnerability" regarding military-strategic and ecological concerns—the conclusion appears even more inescapable that the transitional era marked the historic but only bare beginning of a truly interdependent world.

THE RISE OF NONSTATE ACTORS: INTERNATIONAL ORGANIZATIONS

Finally, one other phenomenon, closely related to interdependence, developed significantly during the transitional era and was to become an even more important feature of the international system after World War II. This was the growth of **international organizations** as nonstate actors in world politics. In particular, *intergovernmental organizations* (IGOs) appeared on the scene, ranging from the modest creation of the Central Commission for the Navigation of the Rhine in 1815 to the Universal Postal Union and International Telegraph Union in the mid-nineteenth century to the League of Nations and ultimately the United Nations in the twentieth century. A variety of such organizations were to be established on both a regional and global basis by member governments in response to problems that transcended national boundaries and seemed to call for institutional responses.

SIDELIGHT

THE "COCA-COLAIZATION" OF THE WORLD:
A HISTORY LESSON

Long before American culture had given the world Coca-Cola, Americans themselves had been touched by all sorts of foreign influences. Ralph Linton's classic piece on "cultural diffusion" clears up any illusions Americans might have that interdependence is a wholly new phenomenon and that the United States has been the engine behind it.

Our solid American Citizen awakens in a bed built on a pattern which originated in the Near East . . . He throws back covers made from cotton, domesticated in India, or linen, domesticated in the Near East, or wool from sheep, also domesticated in the Near East, or silk, the use of which was discovered in China . . . He slips into his moccasins, invented by the Indians of the Eastern woodlands, and goes to the bathroom, whose fixtures are a mixture of European and American inventions, both of recent date. He takes his pajamas off, a garment invented in India, and washes with soap invented by the ancient Gauls. He then shaves, a masochistic rite which seems to have been derived from either Sumer or ancient Egypt.

Returning to the bedroom he removes his clothes from a chair of southern European type and proceeds to dress. He puts on garments whose form originally derived from the skin clothing of the nomads of the Asiatic steppes, puts on shoes made from skins tanned by a process invented in ancient Egypt . . . and ties around his neck a strip of bright-colored cloth which is a vestigial survival of the shoulder shawls worn by the seventeenth-century Croatians. Before going out for breakfast, he glances through the

Additionally, there was the growth of another type of nonstate actor, nongovernmental organizations (NGOs), formed among private groups of individuals sharing specialized interests across national borders, also on both a regional and global basis. While a few such organizations had existed from the beginnings of the nation-state system (e.g., the Rosicrucian Order in the seventeenth century), they were to proliferate in the transitional era (e.g., the International Red Cross and the Salvation Army in the 1860s) and—as with IGOs—increase even more dramatically after World War II. A special sub-category of NGO, the multinational corporation (MNC) was to become especially significant as an actor in world affairs.[30] (See Figs. 2.4 and 2.5 for trends in the growth of IGOs and NGOs.)[31] Thus, just as total war existed alongside interdependence, the age of nationalism was accompanied by the rise of "transnationalism" as nonstate actors were becoming more organized across national boundaries.

window, made of glass invented in Egypt, and if it is raining puts on overshoes made of rubber discovered by the Central American Indians and takes an umbrella, invented in Southeastern Asia . . .

On his way to breakfast, he stops to buy a paper, paying for it with coins, an ancient Lydian invention. At the restaurant a whole new series of borrowed elements confronts him. His plate is made of a form of pottery invented in China. His knife is of steel, an alloy first made in Southern India, his fork a medieval Italian invention, and his spoon a derivative of a Roman original. He begins breakfast with an orange, from the Eastern Mediterranean, a canteloupe from Persia, or perhaps a piece of African watermelon. With this he has coffee, an Abyssinian plant, with cream and sugar. Both the domestication of cows and the idea of milking them originated in the Near East, while sugar was first made in India. After his fruit and first coffee he goes on to waffles, cakes made by a Scandinavian technique from wheat domesticated in Asia Minor. Over these he pours maple syrup, invented by the Indians of the Eastern woodlands . . .

When our friend has finished eating he settles back to smoke, an American Indian habit, consuming a plant domesticated in Brazil in either a pipe, derived from the Indians of Virginia, or a cigarette, derived from Mexico. If he is hardy enough he may even attempt a cigar, transmitted to us from the Antilles by way of Spain. While smoking he reads the news of the day, imprinted in characters invented by the ancient Semites upon a material invented in China by a process invented in Germany. As he absorbs the accounts of foreign troubles he will, if he is a good conservative citizen, thank a Hebrew deity in an Indo-European language that he is 100 percent American.

Source: Ralph Linton, *The Study of Man: An Introduction,* © 1936, renewed 1964, pp. 326–327. Adapted by permission of Prentice-Hall, Inc., Englewood Cliffs, N.J.

To summarize, a metamorphosis in international relations occurred between 1789 and 1945. Out of the shadows of the transitional system, the outlines of contemporary international relations were coming more into focus. Most notably, an international system that at the beginning of the era was essentially a European state system had gradually expanded to become a European-centered world by the late nineteenth century and a global system no longer anchored to Europe by the end of the era.[32] It was still a "lopsided" world,[33] in the sense that three-fourths of the sovereign states were located in Europe or the Western Hemisphere. Moreover, patterns of interdependence and international organization membership were very uneven, with the rich industrialized states being far more enmeshed in these processes than the poor less-developed states. As we will see, the uneven nature of such phenomena was to continue after World War II, as the roots of the "global condition" of the late twentieth century were becoming ever more noticeable.

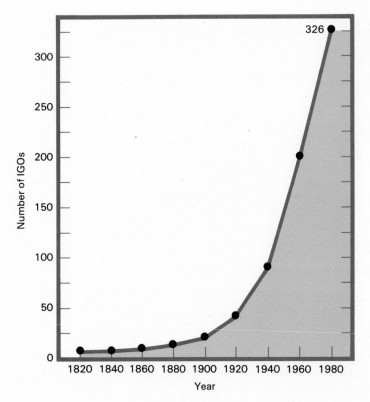

Figure 2.4
**TRENDS IN THE GROWTH OF
INTERGOVERNMENTAL
ORGANIZATIONS (IGOs) IN THE
INTERNATIONAL SYSTEM**

The Post–World War II International System (1945–1973)

There is almost total agreement among scholars that the two atomic bombs that were dropped by the United States on Hiroshima and Nagasaki in 1945 marked the beginning of a new era of international politics that, though foreshadowed by the previous era, was distinctive in many ways. There is less consensus, however, on whether this international system that emerged out of the cauldron of World War II still persists today in its main features, or has itself become so changed in recent years that yet another, newer international system can be said to exist in the contemporary period. Our view is that although the "postwar" system has persisted into the late twentieth century in certain respects, some of the most distinctive features of that system started breaking down and a new environment started taking shape by at least the early 1970s. In our discussion of the postwar system, we will not treat actors, power and wealth, and other variables as separate subtopics but will examine more general developments during this era.

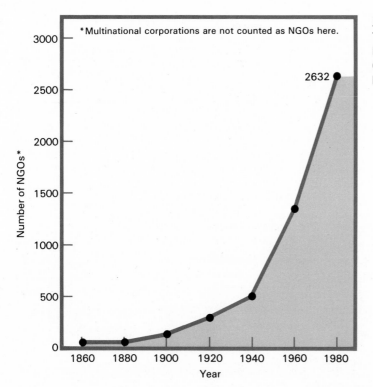

*Multinational corporations are not counted as NGOs here.

2632

DISTINCTIVE FEATURES OF THE POSTWAR SYSTEM: SUPERPOWERS AND BIPOLARITY

The arrival of the atomic age and weapons of mass destruction in 1945 was an occurrence that from the start had profound consequences for world politics.[34] Initially, it fostered two related developments that were virtually unprecedented in international politics and that, more than anything else, distinguished the post–World War II system from previous international systems. One of these developments was the emergence of only two states as the dominant powers in the international system—the United States and the Soviet Union. The two were labeled "superpowers" to distinguish them from the second tier of powers (including Britain and France, which had experienced economic devastation in World War II, Germany and Japan, which had experienced military defeat, and China, which had yet to industrialize) and the bottom tier of states. What particularly separated the United States and the Soviet Union from all the rest were the enormous nuclear arsenals the two states built after World War II, although the Soviet Union was not to achieve full nuclear parity with the United States until the 1970s.[35] Of the two giants, the United States was "first among equals," accounting in 1950 for 50 percent of the world's military spending and financial reserves as well as two thirds of the world's industrial production.[36]

The second related development was the emergence of a highly polarized system in terms of alignment configurations, i.e., the appearance of the **East-West conflict** and "Cold War" waged between two cohesive blocs organized around competing ideologies and led by the two superpowers. One bloc, the so-called "First World" (or the "West"), consisted of the United States along with the economically developed capitalist democracies of Western Europe, Japan, Canada, Australia, and New Zealand. The other bloc, the "Second World" (or the "East"), consisted of the Soviet Union along with the relatively developed Communist states of Eastern Europe as well as Communist China.[37] Accusing each other of seeking global hegemony, the Americans and Soviets organized the two blocs into opposing alliances, with the members within each bloc becoming closely linked not only militarily but also economically. Dependent on the United States and the Soviet Union for both military and economic support, the members of the respective coalitions adhered rigidly to the policies established by the bloc leaders, at least initially. The other states in the system tended, also, to gravitate toward the two "poles." This system was labeled **bipolar**, to refer to both the power and alignment structure.

FISSURES IN THE POSTWAR SYSTEM

In the early postwar period, there were few parts of the globe that were not tied to one or the other bloc. Much of Asia and Africa remained Western-controlled colonial possessions in the first decade after World War II, while the Latin American countries became part of the U.S. alliance network and the Soviets brought a few other states outside Europe into their orbit. Hence, only a handful of states, notably Yugoslavia and India, occupied the middle ground between Eastern and Western camps in the late forties and early fifties. However, as the postwar era progressed, "bipolarity" gave way to "tripolarity" in terms of alignment patterns, with the middle ground becoming more crowded by the proliferation of newly independent nation-states in Africa and Asia, many of which tended to adopt a "nonaligned" stance in the East-West conflict. Strictly speaking, these countries did not constitute a third "pole" or rival "bloc" in the system—no alliance was formed among them—but they did represent a third element to be reckoned with in world politics. The so-called **Third World**, consisting of less developed countries found mostly in the Southern Hemisphere, was not to become a major force in world politics until later; but it had already started materializing as a distinct entity when twenty-nine Afro-Asian nations met in Bandung, Indonesia, in April of 1955 to call for an end to all colonialism.[38]

The "decolonialization" process itself, which introduced unparalleled cultural diversity into the international system, was a major development in the postwar era. Between 1945 and 1973, the number of nation-state actors more than doubled from roughly 60 to over 130. Whereas in 1945, almost a quarter of the world's people and its land area remained under colonial rule, by 1973 less than one percent of the world's population and territory were still without self-government. In the span of a single generation, some one billion people and eighty nations achieved independence—a dramatic revolution in human affairs.

While both the United States and the Soviet Union sought to recruit the new nations into their respective blocs, their efforts were only mildly successful, not only because the two giants tended to neutralize each other in many areas but also because the new Third World nationalism placed limits on what even superpowers could do to cajole or coerce even tiny states into line. In particular, because of the widespread aversion to foreign rule, the two superpowers—more than "great powers" in the past—were inhibited from expanding their influence in the world through direct territorial annexation or occupation.[39] Instead of acquiring territory, the object of superpower competition was to gain *influence* over the foreign policies of individual Third World states. The time-honored balance of power "game" continued to be played but in a somewhat different manner than in the past. If the world map had previously resembled a gigantic "Monopoly" board on which the players competed for property, the map in the post–World War II era looked more like a chessboard on which two players attempted to manipulate a set of "pawns" for maximum advantage. Third World leaders increasingly learned to play both superpowers off against each other in this game.

LARGER CRACKS IN THE POSTWAR SYSTEM

The development of an independent, "nonaligned" Third World movement in the late fifties and sixties was symptomatic of a larger phenomenon that was becoming apparent yet not fully appreciated at the time—namely, the growing fragmentation of both the power structure and the alliance structure of the postwar international system. The very factor that had fostered a world of dual superpowers and bipolarity at the outset of the postwar era—the advent of nuclear weaponry—was, along with other factors, increasingly contributing to a diffusion of power and alliance disintegration as the postwar system wore on.

Regarding the disintegrative tendencies within the Western and Eastern blocs, what were initially minor disagreements eventually became major ones. On the Western side, for example, the Suez crisis of 1956 saw the United States essentially siding with the Soviet Union against America's own allies, admonishing the British and French for their military aggression against Egypt and pressing for their withdrawal from Egyptian territory. The "Atlantic alliance" survived, but the incident left its members with strained feelings and lingering suspicions about the worth of American alliance commitments.[40] Almost at the same moment in time, on the Eastern side, the Hungarian

Revolution occurred and threatened to remove a Communist satellite from the Soviet orbit; while the revolt was frustrated and Hungary was forced back into the Soviet sphere, the episode left a legacy of doubts among members of the "Communist commonwealth" regarding the true nature of Soviet fraternal feelings toward them.[41] Finally, also in 1956, the Soviet leadership—mindful of the mutual devastation that could be caused by the escalation of conflict into nuclear war between the United States and Soviet Union—called for "peaceful coexistence" between the two superpowers.

By the 1960s, some observers were already prophesying "the end of alliance," due to the uncertainty of superpower defense guarantees in an age of intercontinental ballistic missiles and the difficulty of maintaining bloc cohesion in the face of what seemed to be lessening tensions and security threats accompanying a partial "thaw" in the Cold War.[42] The Europeans, in particular, were growing less concerned about military aggression and, also, less confident of superpower assistance should such aggression somehow arise. The result was a gradual loosening of unity within both blocs, with the French under Charles de Gaulle becoming the main mavericks in the Western bloc and the Romanians under Nicolae Ceausescu, along with the Chinese under Mao Tsetung, becoming the chief mavericks in the Eastern bloc. Just as de Gaulle was proclaiming that "France has no permanent friends, only permanent interests," Ceausescu and other Communist party leaders in Europe and elsewhere were urging "polycentrism" in place of a single party line emanating from Moscow.[43] Indeed, at times—for example, when Greece and Turkey, two members of the Western alliance, went to war over Cyprus in the late sixties and early seventies—there appeared to be more fighting going on *within* the blocs than between them.

The fragmentation of the alliance structure in the postwar system tended to coincide with the fragmentation of the power structure. Not only had the "nuclear club" expanded to six members by the early 1970s,[44] but more importantly, nuclear arsenals that were once thought to confer superpower status were increasingly proving to be nonusable and of questionable relevance to the day-to-day exercise of power in international relations. If anything, the existence of nuclear weapons and the fear of escalation seemed to make military giants like the United States and the Soviet Union more gun-shy and less inclined to use the full array of armed force that had historically been the traditional tool of influence relied on by "great powers." The "superpower" label itself was becoming something of a misnomer as the United States experienced humiliation at the hands of two small Asian countries—North Korea during the *Pueblo* incident of 1968[45] and Vietnam during the disastrous Indochina war that ended in 1972—while Soviet advisers were being rudely evicted from Egypt in 1972.[46] Insofar as the United States and the Soviet Union remained powerful actors, it was their *economic* prowess—the ability to provide or withdraw foreign aid and trade benefits—as much as military

SIDELIGHT

HISTORICAL FACTS

- *The total world population in* A.D. 1:
  Approximately 250 million people

- *The longest reign of a major European monarch:*
  Louis XIV of France, who ascended the throne in 1643 at age four and reigned until his death seventy-two years later in 1715

- *The longest tenure in office by a democratically elected head of government:*
  Tage Erlander, Swedish Prime Minister for twenty-three years between 1946 and 1969

- *The first resident embassy established abroad:*
  Accredited to the court of Cosimo de Medici by the Duke of Milan in 1450 (in the Italian city-state system)

- *The first intergovernmental international organization:*
  The Central Commission for the Navigation of the Rhine, created in 1815

- *The inventor of dynamite:*
  Alfred Nobel (initiator of the Nobel Peace Prize), in 1866

- *The first tank used in battle:*
  "Mother," produced by the British and used at the Battle of Flers in 1916, during World War I

- *The first air force:*
  Created in 1794 by the French government, which used balloons for reconnaissance purposes during the Napoleonic Wars

prowess that gave them leverage in world politics. Other states, including economically revived West Germany and Japan and even some less developed countries, were also learning how to use economic resources as instruments of influence.

Conclusion

We have seen how the international system has undergone some profound changes over the centuries, but also how there have been some basic continuities. Continuity and change mark world politics even today.

We have noted that by the 1970s the post–World War II international system seemed to be in ferment. It was in a state of flux in terms of its most distinctive feature, the alignment and power structure that had dominated world politics since 1945. Although the postwar order had not collapsed completely—the U.S. and USSR, after all, remained the most visible actors as the East-West competition remained among the most visible aspects of world politics—it was nonetheless under various stresses and strains. These stresses and strains could be seen most strikingly in the Arab oil embargo of 1973. One must be careful not to exaggerate the importance of any single event, particularly one like the oil embargo whose significance has been widely disputed. Clearly, the embargo was not in itself a pivotal event that restructured international affairs. However, this episode seemed to accentuate many important developments that had been brewing for some time—not only the growing diffusion of power and flexibility of alignments beneath the surface of a bipolar world but also the further proliferation of nonstate actors and ever more intricate patterns of interdependence. In a sense, the oil embargo, combined with the American defeat in Vietnam and several other occurrences in the seventies, signified the passage of the "postwar" era into the "contemporary" era. Scholars could debate whether or not the postwar system had been transformed into an entirely different system, but in any case the environment surrounding international relations had taken on a new and much greater complexity, one that will be delineated in the next chapter as we move on to an examination of the *contemporary* international system.

SUMMARY

1. One can identify elements of both change and continuity in international relations over the years.

2. International relations as we know it today can trace its roots to the Peace of Westphalia in 1648, when in place of the walled cities of the feudal era there emerged political units called nation-states that had central governments exercising sovereignty over a fixed territory and population.

3. International relations history since 1648 can be divided into four periods: (a) the classical system, (b) the transitional system, (c) the post–World War II system, and (d) the contemporary system. These systems differ in a number of ways, including the nature of the actors, the distribution of power and wealth, the degree of polarization, the objectives of the actors and the means available to them, and the degree of interdependence.

4. The classical international system (1648–1789) was characterized by a fairly even distribution of power and wealth among several European states ruled by monarchs who shared common values and understandings of the "rules of the game." These actors dominated the state system. Other features of the system included a high degree of alliance flexibility, limited objectives and means, and a relatively low level of interdependence.

5. The transitional international system (1789–1945) constituted a bridge between the classical and the post–World War II eras, in that it saw the beginning of (a) a world population boom; (b) a proliferation in the number of nation-states, brought on by increased nationalism; (c) a rich-poor gap between states, brought on by the Industrial Revolution that spread throughout the North but bypassed the South; (d) ideological conflict in international politics; (e) total war and weapons of mass destruction; (f) an economically and otherwise interdependent world; and (g) international organizations, both IGOs and NGOs, as nonstate actors in world politics.

6. Power continued to be distributed fairly evenly among several states in the transitional era, with Britain "first among equals." However, it was this era that saw the gradual passing of European dominance of the state system and the emergence of the United States, the Soviet Union, and Japan as world powers.

7. Despite ideological cleavages between states, there remained a high degree of alliance flexibility and states of all types engaged in imperialism.

8. Imperialist objectives could be accommodated without major conflict as long as there was enough colonial territory to go around. This condition had evaporated by 1914, by which time the world powers had also acquired the military means to fight total wars.

9. The post–World War II international system (1945–1973) has been called a bipolar system because, unlike the previous eras that featured multiple power centers and flexible alignments, this era was mostly characterized by two relatively rigid blocs of states organized around competing ideologies and led by two dominant "superpowers." The Western bloc, led by the United States and its nuclear arsenal, consisted of the economically developed capitalist democracies. The Eastern bloc, led by the Soviet Union and its nuclear arsenal, consisted of the developed communist states.

10. Bipolarity loosened somewhat with the emergence of the Third World, consisting of the less developed countries, which tended to adopt a nonaligned stance in the East-West conflict. The proliferation of newly independent Third World countries in the 1950s and 1960s reflected the growing fragmentation of both the power structure and the alliance structure of the postwar international system.

11. By the 1970s, power had become more diffuse, alliances less unified, interdependence ever more intricate and complicated. The postwar pattern of international relations was in flux, with a new and more complex environment marking the contemporary era of international relations.

SUGGESTIONS FOR FURTHER READING AND STUDY

For a general discussion on the utility of history in the study of international relations, see Raymond Aron, "Evidence and Inference in History," *Daedalus*, 87 (Fall 1958), pp. 11–39, and Arthur N. Gilbert, "International Relations and the Relevance of History,"

International Studies Quarterly, 12 (December 1968), pp. 351–359. The term "system" is used widely in many disciplines, including political science and international relations. A good general discussion of the concept can be found in Oran R. Young, *Systems of Political Science* (Englewood Cliffs, N.J.: Prentice-Hall, 1986). Regarding the application of "systems" analysis to international relations, see Charles A. McClelland, "On the Fourth Wave: Past and Future in the Study of International Systems," in James N. Rosenau *et al.*, eds., *The Analysis of International Politics* (New York: Free Press, 1972), pp. 15–37. As discussed in Note 6, many scholars have attempted to demarcate distinct international systems that have existed at various points in history, an approach that has been called "historical sociology." A major exponent of this approach is Stanley Hoffmann, who has identified three international systems similar to those discussed in this chapter; see "International Systems and International Law," *World Politics*, 14 (October 1961), pp. 205–237.

There are a number of excellent narrative histories that provide detailed chronologies and analyses of events in various historical periods. For the classical period, see Leo Gershoy, *From Despotism to Revolution, 1763–1789* (New York: Macmillan, 1944). For the nineteenth and early twentieth centuries, see Edward V. Gulick, *Europe's Classical Balance of Power* (Ithaca, N.Y.: Cornell University Press, 1955); A. J. P. Taylor, *The Struggle for Mastery in Europe, 1848–1941* (Oxford: Clarendon Press, 1954); and F. S. Northedge and M. J. Grieve, *A Hundred Years of International Relations* (New York: Praeger, 1971). For the post–World War II era, see Charles L. Robertson, *International Politics Since World War II: A Short History*, 2nd ed. (New York: John Wiley, 1975); and Peter Calvacoressi, *World Politics Since 1945*, 5th ed. (New York: Longman, 1987). In chs. 1 and 2 of *Gulliver's Troubles, or The Setting of American Foreign Policy* (New York: McGraw-Hill, 1968), Stanley Hoffmann discusses developments in the late 1960s that started to change the postwar pattern of international relations.

A number of writings can be cited that focus on specific aspects of international politics discussed in this chapter. On the historical development of nationalism, see C. J. H. Hayes, *The Historical Evolution of Modern Nationalism* (New York: Macmillan, 1945), as well as Rupert Emerson, *From Empire to Nation* (Cambridge, Mass.: Harvard University Press, 1960). On the concept of "nation-state," see Alan James, *Sovereign Statehood* (London: Allen and Unwin, 1986), and Mostafa Rejal and Cynthia H. Enloe, "Nation-States and State-Nations," *International Studies Quarterly*, 13 (June 1969), pp. 140–158. On the historical operation of the balance of power (along with a conceptual treatment), see Inis Claude, *Power and International Relations* (New York: Random House, 1962). On the history of weapons technology and military strategy, see George H. Quester, *Offense and Defense in the International System* (New York: John Wiley, 1977), and Jack S. Levy, "The Offensive/Defensive Balance of Military Technology: A Theoretical and Historical Analysis," *International Studies Quarterly*, 28 (June 1984), pp. 230–235. On the development of economic inequalities, see W. Ashworth, *A Short History of the International Economy Since 1850* (New York: Longman, 1975), and Simon Kuznets, *Economic Growth and Structure* (New York: W. W. Norton, 1965). On the historical development of both intergovernmental and nongovernmental international organizations, see Harold K. Jacobson, *Networks of Interdependence*, 2nd ed. (New York: Knopf, 1984), chs. 2 and 3. On historical trends relating to interdependence, see James A. Field, "Transnationalism and the New Tribe," in Robert O. Keohane and Joseph S. Nye, eds., *Transnational Relations and World Politics* (Cambridge, Mass.: Harvard University Press, 1971), pp. 3–22; Peter J. Katzenstein, "International Interdependence: Some Long-Term Trends and Recent Changes," *International Organization*, 29 (Autumn 1975), pp. 1021–1034; and Richard Rosecrance et al., "Whither Interdependence?" *International Organization*, 31 (Summer 1977), pp. 425–472.

On the general theme of "continuity and change" in the international system, see a fresh perspective provided in "World System Debates," a special volume of *International Studies Quarterly*, 25 (March 1981).

A Bird's-Eye View of the Present: The Contemporary International System

Our purpose in this chapter is to give an overview of the general setting in which contemporary international relations occur. Before providing this "bird's-eye view" of the contemporary international system, we first will look briefly at the oil embargo of 1973. The significance of the oil embargo episode will be seen below, as we relate its various elements to the more general features of the contemporary international system. Even if it was not truly a seminal historical event in the same class as the dropping of the first atomic bomb, it makes a useful case study for demonstrating the growing complexity of international politics in the late twentieth century.

The Oil Embargo of 1973

BACKGROUND

The oil embargo of 1973 was fueled by rising tension in the Middle East over two different sets of issues that had been simmering for some time. One set of issues involved territorial disputes between Israel and its Arab neighbors, which had originated with the creation of the state of Israel in 1948 and which had been the cause of three different wars—the War of Independence in 1948, the Suez conflict of 1956, and the Six Day War of 1967—prior to the Yom Kippur War that began in October of 1973. In addition to continuing the quest for a national homeland for the Palestinian refugees who had been uprooted from their homes during the 1948 and 1967 wars, a number of Arab states sought in 1973 to redress their own particular territorial grievances against Israel that had accumulated after their defeat in the 1967 war. Egypt sought to recover the Sinai Peninsula, Syria sought to recover the Golan Heights, and Jordan sought to recover the West Bank of the Jordan River including Jerusalem.[1] The ongoing Middle East conflict had long been viewed as a "sideshow" to the central East-West axis of conflict in the postwar period. Middle East politics involved issues that were largely extraneous to the Cold War, although Western countries had tended to side with Israel and the Eastern countries had tended to side with the Arabs.[2]

The second set of issues surrounding the oil embargo involved economic disputes between the major oil-consuming states and the oil-producing states of the Third World. The latter had created the **Organization of Petroleum Exporting Countries (OPEC)** in 1960, hoping to strengthen their position through collective action. In particular, the governments of oil-producing countries in the Third World had long been seeking to acquire greater control over their own oil resources from the multinational corporations and the governments of oil-consuming industrialized countries. The OPEC goal was to gain direct ownership and to determine both price and production levels. It was not until 1973, with the rapid growth in world energy consumption and the increasing reliance on petroleum that had developed over the previous decade, that OPEC members found themselves in a commanding bargaining position.[3]

The less developed countries had increasingly become key sources of world crude oil production, with Middle East countries in particular accounting for 41 percent of the world total by 1972. At the same time, the major industrialized countries, particularly in Western Europe and Japan, had become increasingly dependent on oil imports to meet not only their oil consumption needs but their overall energy requirements, with Middle East oil alone filling almost half (47 percent) of Western Europe's aggregate energy needs and over half (57 percent) of Japan's aggregate energy needs by 1972. The most glaring statistics were the Western European and Japanese dependence on imports for 99 percent of their total oil consumption, mostly supplied by the Middle East, a condition that had existed for some time but had been exacerbated by their growing use of petroleum as an energy substitute for coal.[4] The United States, while less vulnerable due to its own indigenous oil production capabilities and more varied energy alternatives, nonetheless had seen its share of world crude oil production decline considerably by 1972, at the same time that its demand for oil and reliance on foreign sources had increased steadily. Between 1962 and 1972, U.S. oil imports had increased from 2 million barrels to 5 million barrels a day, with the import share of total U.S. oil consumption jumping from roughly 20 percent to 30 percent; on the eve of the oil embargo, in October of 1973, this figure had reached close to 35 percent, although oil imports still represented only about 13 percent of overall energy consumption and were derived mostly from sources outside the Middle East.

By 1973, OPEC had grown into an organization consisting of governmental representatives from thirteen countries spanning four continents. The majority were Arab states in the Middle East (Algeria, Iraq, Kuwait, Libya, Qatar, Saudi Arabia, and the United Arab Emirates); one was a non-Arab Middle Eastern state (Iran); two were African (Nigeria and Gabon, the latter an associate member); one was Asian (Indonesia); and two were Latin American (Ecuador and Venezuela). What they all had in common was the fact that they were all underdeveloped countries, and they together accounted for over 85 percent of world oil exports and were seeking to use the oil "weapon" to promote their economic development. (Figure 3.1 shows the geography of oil in the Middle East, the cockpit of OPEC "petropolitics" and the scene of the 1973 oil embargo.)

THE SEQUENCE OF EVENTS

On October 6, 1973—on Yom Kippur, Judaism's holiest day of the year—war broke out in the Middle East, pitting Israel against Egypt and Syria assisted by Jordan. OPEC members were not uniformly sympathetic to the Arab cause; many members were interested only in using the oil weapon to extract

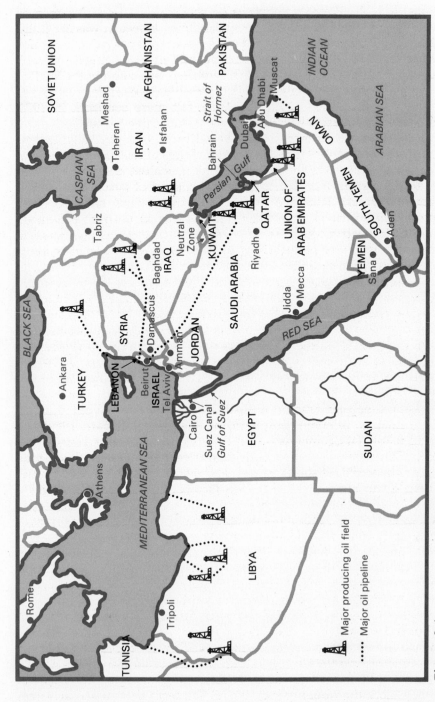

Figure 3.1
OIL IN THE MIDDLE EAST—1973

concessions from the Western countries on economic issues rather than on political issues involving Middle East boundary lines. Indeed, it was not OPEC but OAPEC (the Organization of Arab Petroleum Exporting Countries, which consisted of the Arab OPEC group plus Egypt and Syria) that launched the oil embargo.[5] Arab oil ministers had tried the embargo tactic during the Six Day War in 1967 but could not apply sufficient pressure on Western countries to convert them to the Arab cause. The Arabs felt more confident in 1973, however, given the industrialized world's increasing thirst for oil.

Two weeks after the outbreak of the Yom Kippur War, OAPEC members cut off all oil exports from Arab states to the United States, in retaliation for American arms shipments to Israel; shortly thereafter, the embargo was extended to the Netherlands due to its strong support of Israel,[6] and later in November to Portugal, Rhodesia, and South Africa, which had also taken strong pro-Israeli positions. In addition to imposing an outright ban on oil exports against the latter countries, the Arab oil ministers (Iraq dissenting) in early November announced a cutback of oil production by 25 percent, a freeze on exports to "friendly" countries at the September level, and a plan to allocate the rest among other countries. The "friendly" countries to be accorded preferential treatment were Britain, France, and Spain, which at the time had adopted a less blatantly pro-Israel official posture than other Western states. The threat of further production cutbacks caused the European Community, then composed of nine Western European states, to issue on November 6 a resolution calling for Israeli withdrawal to its pre-1967 borders and Israeli concessions on the Palestinian question. Japan followed suit, likewise toning down its previously unequivocal support for Israel.

At the same time that Arab oil ministers were planning and executing an OAPEC oil embargo in connection with the Arab-Israeli dispute, they were also joining fellow OPEC members in a confrontation against the major oil-consuming countries in connection with larger economic issues. OPEC took advantage of the world oil shortages to *quadruple* the posted price of a barrel of oil—from \$3 to almost \$12—between October and December. It was a virtually unprecedented exercise of power by a group of less developed countries. In many ways, this act of defiance was a more significant aspect of the 1973 oil crisis than the embargo itself.

The winding down of the Yom Kippur War in early 1974 with the help of the United Nations, combined with Arab satisfaction over economic victories and over Western European and Japanese revision of their Middle East policies, led OAPEC to lift the oil embargo against the United States in March and against the Netherlands in July and to restore production levels. In terms of Arab political demands, the oil weapon ultimately worked more effectively against Great Britain, France, West Germany, and Japan—the most vulnerable countries—than against the United States, which never did abandon its support of Israel. In the case of the countries that submitted to Arab political demands, it was really more the *threat* of massive oil shortages than actual shortages that accounted for their tilt toward the Arabs.[7] The combination of various factors—a sixty- to ninety-day emergency oil reserve supply, government-influenced energy conservation, and the failure of OAPEC members to induce other OPEC members to collaborate—limited the economic chaos and damage that could actually be inflicted on Western Europe and Japan by the Arab oil ministers.

The effort to embargo some countries and grant preferential treatment to others was difficult to enforce, not only because oil-producing countries like Iraq and the Soviet Union ignored Arab requests for cooperation, but also because the Arabs still had to rely on the major multinational oil companies to distribute the oil among their industrialized customers. The so-called "Seven Sisters" (Exxon, Chevron, Mobil, Texaco, Gulf, Shell, and British Petroleum) controlled the flow of two thirds of Western Europe's and Japan's oil supply and ultimately were in a position to allocate oil to various countries according to their own economic criteria rather than Arab political criteria. As a result, the Netherlands (headquarters of Shell Oil) along with the United States were not damaged any more than nonembargoed states; indeed, few industrialized states suffered seriously. The main suffering was to come not from the embargo and production cutbacks but from the economic effects of oil price increases imposed by OPEC.

While the Arabs derived more mileage out of a general atmosphere of panic and *perceived* economic deprivation in the West than out of any actual damage incurred, there was little question that they had the capability to disrupt economies in the industrialized world if they chose to make full use of the oil weapon, especially when backed by fellow OPEC members. At the very least, the petroleum price increases sent a shock wave through the world (the industrialized and nonindustrialized parts alike), even if the embargo did not. The whole episode, as noted, occasioned a rethinking of Middle East policy in much of Western Europe and Japan.

POSTSCRIPT

As a postscript, it should be added that after 1973 even the United States started to shift its Middle East policy slightly, and in 1978 for the first time approved the sale of sixty sophisticated F–15 jet fighters to Saudi Arabia on the grounds that they were needed to balance the sale of ninety F–15s and F–16s to Israel. However, the Arab oil "weapon" remained an uncertain one, and indeed diminished in importance along with OPEC in the 1980s. Following a second price surge in 1979, the combination of increased energy conservation efforts in the Western industrialized states, increased petroleum supplies from non-OPEC sources (including newly opened British oil fields in the North Sea as well as expanded Mexican and Soviet exports), and overproduction by many OPEC members themselves in violation of OPEC production quotas (to generate revenue to support their economic development needs or, in the case of Iran and Iraq, to support a costly war) all resulted in a world oil glut in the 1980s and a rollback in prices that seemed to signal to most observers the decline of OPEC.[8] The price of oil dropped from a high of $34 per barrel in 1981 to $29 in 1984, to $15 in 1986, with only a modest recovery thereafter.

Still, one could not help wondering whether a changing world energy picture in the future might yet restore OPEC in general and the Persian Gulf oil-producing states in particular to world prominence in international politics. The Western industrialized world in the 1980s was still directly dependent on OPEC for several million barrels of oil a day, with the Persian Gulf states of the Middle East being key suppliers (and Saudi Arabia being the most influential because of its unparalleled oil reserves). If demand for oil were to rise steadily due to economic growth, or disruptions were to occur in OPEC supplies due to Middle East turmoil, there remained the distinct possibility that the events of 1973 could recur.

Characteristics of the Contemporary International System

The oil embargo episode symbolized the "new international politics." The new international politics was actually not altogether new since some of its features were an extension of long-term trends that had simply become more pronounced (for example, the growing role of nonstate actors and interdependence in affecting relations between countries). Other features, however, represented a clearer break with the patterns that had characterized much of post–World War II international relations (for example, the increased fluidity of alignments and decreased meaningfulness of any "pecking order" among world powers).

DISTRIBUTION OF POWER

The ability of the OPEC nations in 1973 to quadruple the price of oil and of the OAPEC nations to bend the Middle East policies of Western Europe and Japan raised questions about whether any pecking order still existed among the countries of the world in terms of power rankings. In particular, a group of underdeveloped countries, many of which were tiny "statelets" (e.g., Kuwait, Qatar, and the United Arab Emirates, each with less than a million people) and all of which were devoid of the assets traditionally associated with power, seemed to demonstrate that power had become extremely diffuse and ambiguous in world affairs. It is difficult to imagine how such states could have possibly succeeded against the likes of France, Britain, and Germany in the nineteenth century or even the early twentieth century.

It is true that the oil embargo did not really test the two so-called "superpowers" since the United States was not nearly as vulnerable as its allies, and since the Soviet Union was never even targeted (and even if it had been, as the world's leading oil producer it would not have been very vulnerable either). It is also true that if the United States and the Soviet Union had conspired together to cut off weapons supplies to their respective Israeli and Arab clients in the Middle East, it is possible they could have dictated an immediate end to the fighting or greatly affected the outcome.

While the United States and the Soviet Union continue to exercise substantial power today, their "superpower" status nonetheless has been repeatedly called into question in recent years by a variety of factors. The United States, in particular, between 1950 and the late 1970s, saw its share of world military spending decline from 50 percent to 25 percent, its share of world monetary reserves drop from 50 percent to less than 7 percent, and its share of world industrial output fall from two thirds to less than one third.[9] It has been a case of other countries partially catching up to what was after World War II an extraordinary lead enjoyed by the United States in several areas.

Although both the United States and the Soviet Union today remain among the most self-sufficient nations on earth, each has become increasingly dependent on selective resources from the outside world. For example, the United States since 1973 has become dependent on imports for over half of its consumption requirements in nine basic raw materials vital to industry.[10]

"And as a last resort in hand-to-hand combat, you can always strike the enemy with your wallet."

Dunagin's People by Ralph Dunagin. © 1975 Field Enterprises, Inc., courtesy of Field Newspaper Syndicate.

Petropower: Is it in decline?

The Soviet Union has become increasingly dependent on other countries to meet its food requirements, becoming a large importer of grain in recent years, despite being among the biggest wheat producers in the world.[11] Many of the suppliers of these imports to both countries are themselves dependent to some extent on U.S. or Soviet exports (e.g., Arab dependence on U.S. technology), so that the United States and the Soviet Union are often able to exercise counterpressures against countries seeking to exploit dependencies. Still, insofar as dependencies exist, they undermine the "superpower" status of both the United States and the Soviet Union.

What is especially striking about the contemporary era, as exemplified by the oil politics of 1973, is that countries find themselves in possession of certain economic and other resources that in the past did not translate directly into power but which today can provide considerable leverage in world politics. At the same time that such resources as oil and grain have become a part of the currency of power, traditional military resources have become somewhat devalued.[12] While American leaders made veiled threats to occupy the oil fields if pressed too far by OAPEC in 1973, the prospect that the wells would be set ablaze first by the Arabs lessened the impact of such a threat. The decline of OPEC in the 1980s owed more to economic realities than to political-military realities.

One cannot discount military power, as we will note in Chapter 7 when examining the relative effectiveness of economic and military power. It is true, for example, that after 1973, around the time the Soviet Union attained full nuclear parity with the United States, the Soviets became somewhat more ambitious in their global reach. However, American and Soviet military might has been less readily usable than the military prowess enjoyed by great powers in the past, due mostly to mutual American and Soviet fear of escalation and nuclear holocaust. The huge nuclear arsenals of both countries are the shadow that hovers over the entire international system and seemingly grants these states ultimate control over the fate of humanity. But it is only a shadow—always lingering in the background though not coming directly into play. One cannot say for certain that these arsenals will never be used in the future, only that there are enormous constraints on their use.

Moreover, many other countries are gradually developing this "life and death" power. At least twenty other states—including several less developed ones—are reportedly on the brink of joining the "nuclear club," which presently consists of the United States and the Soviet Union along with its "lesser" members, China, Britain, France, and India.[13] However modest a country's nuclear capability, it cannot be lightly dismissed given the destructive potential of even a single atomic weapon.

Despite the increased diffusion and ambiguity of power in the contemporary world, observers of international relations continue to engage in one of the favorite pastimes of the field—rank-ordering states according to their power and fitting them into a neat pecking order. Many observers still speak of the two "superpowers" at the top, trailed at a great distance by all the rest.[14] Others have noted the emergence of five world power centers—the United States, the Soviet Union, the European Community (which had grown to twelve Western European members by the late 1980s, led by France, Britain, and West Germany), Japan, and China.[15] Still others attempt to list "middle powers" and "small powers." One such listing, offered by James Dougherty as a rough intuitive portrait of world power relationships, appears in the box below. (One could obviously add as "middle powers" the likes of India and Israel.)

As noted earlier, most attempts to construct such pecking orders assume that there are certain national attributes that constitute "elements" or "bases" of national power and that, when added together, provide a summary index of a given state's power. *Size*—in terms of population, land area, gross national product, or military resources—has been traditionally considered an important determinant of power. Dougherty's listing of power centers and middle powers, for example, generally conforms to the traditional notion of power as related to size. Most of the countries listed are relatively large on several or all the size dimensions just mentioned.

A SUGGESTED PECKING ORDER IN WORLD POLITICS

World power centers

United States	European Community (notably France,	Japan
Soviet Union	Britain, and West Germany)	China

Middle powers

Argentina	East Germany	Netherlands	Spain
Australia	Egypt	North Korea	Sweden
Belgium	Greece	Pakistan	Turkey
Brazil	Indonesia	Poland	Venezuela
Canada	Iran	Saudi Arabia	Vietnam
Cuba	Italy	South Africa	Yugoslavia
Czechoslovakia	Mexico	South Korea	

Small powers and mini-states

All the other states in the system

Source: From James E. Dougherty, "The Configuration of the Global System," in Gavin Boyd and Charles Pentland, eds., *Issues in Global Politics* (New York: Free Press, 1981), pp. 12–19.

If size were the only important determinant of power, then it would not be difficult to produce an accurate power ranking. Certainly, there are vast disparities among countries in the contemporary system in terms of size, differences that are likely to become even more accentuated as more and more "mini-states" or "micro-states" enter the community of nations as the decolonization process winds down. As one writer notes, "Thirty-two countries, one fifth of the membership of the contemporary international community, have less than 1 million people, and half of these—the microstates—are under 300,000" while "half of [all] the members of the family of nations are less populous than the state of North Carolina."[16] The sovereign equality of nations cannot disguise the fact that they come in many different sizes and shapes, as indicated in Table 3.1.

While Table 3.1 shows the wide differences between countries in size characteristics, it also illustrates the limited utility of trying to construct a meaningful power ranking of countries based on size criteria alone. Bangladesh and Pakistan are among the most populous countries in the world (the eighth and the tenth largest, to be exact); yet it is questionable whether their ability to affect international relations is necessarily greater than that of some tiny oil-rich Arab states, such as Kuwait and the United Arab Emirates, with a million or less people. Realizing the simplistic nature of looking only at size features, many analysts also try to take into account *qualitative* elements of national power—such as level of economic and technological development—which may confer added stature upon some smaller states like Israel. In one recent study, for example, power is defined as the capacity of a state to both exercise influence and to resist influence attempts. Therefore it is said to depend on factors such as a state's geographical position, political organization and governmental legitimacy, and leadership competence, as well as material capabilities. The latter capabilities then are classified along three "dimensions": demographic capabilities (represented by an educated urban population); industrial capabilities (reflected in the society's consumption of energy supplies); and military capabilities (indicated by the size of its armed forces).[17]

Although these national attributes are measurable and countries can be ranked by them, the utility of pecking order exercises remains questionable for a variety of reasons, many of which were alluded to in our initial discussion of power in the previous chapter. One problem is that today so many societal variables are relevant to the exercise of power that it is difficult to obtain agreement on a single set of criteria, much less on what weight should be assigned to each individual criterion. Some observers have suggested, for example, that the kind of "high-tech" technological prowess possessed by the Japanese today may be more crucial to exercising power in the future than the more traditional economic bases of power such as coal and steel production. A second problem is that power may be based as much on intangibles such as *will* as it is on paper counts of tons of steel or numbers of rifles and riflemen. The latter may be more measurable but not necessarily more

Table 3.1
SIZE CHARACTERISTICS OF SELECTED COUNTRIES

Country	Population (in millions)	Land Area (in sq. miles)	Gross National Product (U.S. $ millions)	Total Armed Forces
Bangladesh	98.0	55,585	12,360	91,000
Barbados	0.3	166	1,100	No Army
Brazil	132.6	3,285,620	227,280	276,000
Canada	25.2	3,830,840	330,870	83,000
Egypt	46.2	386,095	33,340	445,000
Gambia	0.7	4,125	180	No Army[a]
Haiti	5.4	10,710	1,710	7,000
Indonesia	158.9	740,905	85,400	278,000
Israel	4.2	8,015	21,290	142,000[b]
Japan	120.1	142,705	1,248,090	243,000
Kuwait	1.8	9,370	27,570	12,000
Malta	0.4	122	1,210	800
Nigeria	96.8	356,605	74,120	94,000
Pakistan	92.4	310,320	35,420	483,000
People's Republic of China	1,030.2	3,704,440	318,310	3,900,000
Saudi Arabia	10.8	926,745	116,380	63,000
Seychelles	.064	156	110	1,200
Soviet Union	275.0	8,646,400	1,563,000	5,300,000[c]
Sri Lanka	15.6	325	5,660	21,000
Sweden	8.3	173,620	99,060	66,000[d]
Switzerland	6.6	15,935	105,060	20,000[e]
Turkey	48.3	300,870	57,810	630,000
United Kingdom	56.3	94,475	480,680	327,000
United States	237.0	3,614,170	3,670,490	2,152,000
Yugoslavia	23.0	98,740	48,690	241,000

[a]560 police; signed and ratified a Confederation Pact with Senegal in 1981, calling for a joint army in the future.
[b]Armed forces mobilizable to 400,000 in 24 hours.
[c]Includes 1.3 million railroad construction, labor, and general support troops.
[d]Armed forces mobilizable to 800,000 in 72 hours.
[e]Armed forces mobilizable to 1 million in 48 hours.

Source: Population and GNP data are for 1984 and were obtained from *World Bank Atlas, 1986* (Washington, D.C.: World Bank, 1986). Data on armed forces are for 1985 and were obtained from *The Military Balance, 1985–86* (London: Institute for Strategic Studies, 1986) and supplemented from *World Military Expenditures and Arms Transfers, 1985* (Washington, D.C.: U.S. Arms Control and Disarmament Agency, 1985). Data on land size are for 1985 and were obtained from *The Times Atlas of the World* (London: Times Books Limited, 1985).

important.[18] While all the will in the world cannot compensate for a lack of resources, all the resources in the world may be meaningless without the will to use them.

The example that is commonly cited to illustrate the role of "will" was the unwillingness of the United States during the early seventies to use more than a small fraction of its military arsenal against North Vietnam, a country which managed to win the Vietnam War even though it was far inferior to the United States on almost any conventional measure of power. One could argue that the United States lacked the necessary resources to achieve its goals 10,000 miles away from home. In any case, what was thought by some to be "the greatest power in the world" was unable to defeat a "band of night-riders in black pajamas."[19]

Even if one can somehow overcome the above analytical problems, the notion of an international pecking order makes sense only if one thinks of power as some gross societal capability or set of resources that can be hypothetically mobilized and employed. However, today especially it is more helpful to think of power as an influence *relationship* in which the capacity of one country to exert influence on another ultimately depends not only on the sum of their respective potential resources ("raw" factors), but also on several relative factors: (1) whether a country actually has the right resources to apply to the particular situation, (2) whether a country attaches the same importance or salience to the situation as an adversary country, and (3) how many other demands are being made on a country's resources at that moment. In short, power is best viewed as *situation-specific* or *issue-specific*.[20]

The OPEC countries are still potentially powerful in affecting world energy politics, but much less so in other issue-areas. Japan is a major actor in the international economy but, with a smaller army than Indonesia, plays a relatively minor role in the area of arms control and other military-strategic concerns. Canada, whose vast real estate dwarfs its population, contains valuable raw materials that make the country influential in global mineral politics. Malta, with its 800-strong army, has played a key role in the politics of the law of the sea; this is beyond anything one would expect from a quick glance at its resource base and more prominent than any role it has played in any other issue-area. The Vatican City State, the smallest state in the world in both population (1000) and territory (.17 square mile) and without any army divisions, has exercised far more influence on the politics surrounding the world population issue than most states considerably larger in size, although it has had little effect in persuading states to abide by its "commandments" in areas other than birth control.

We do not wish to imply that all countries are equal in power today and that power is now so elusive a concept that it is just as reasonable to rank the United States as number 160 and Malta as number 1 as the other way around in the international hierarchy. The contemporary international system *is* stratified in terms of power, but the stratification does not lend itself to predicting "winners" and "losers" quite so easily as in the past. Some countries like The Gambia—"mini-states" without any vital natural or other resources that can currently be used as bargaining chips—can be safely assigned to the bottom of the international ladder; other countries like the United States and the Soviet Union—states that potentially can project power over a wide geographical area and over a wide range of issues—can be safely placed toward the top of the ladder. A pecking order of sorts may be said to exist but it is one that is given to frequent collapse. If one must be careful not to underestimate the power of the United States and the Soviet Union today, one must also be careful not to exaggerate it.

DISTRIBUTION OF WEALTH

The contemporary international system is stratified in terms of not only power but also *wealth*, although here, too, the stratification pattern is complicated. One of the side effects of the OPEC price decisions in 1973 was the further widening of the rich-poor gap among countries. While the gap after 1973 was closed somewhat between the rich developed states and a few less developed states (a handful of OPEC members), the gap became even more accentuated between the developed states and many other less developed ones (the poorest ones that could least afford to absorb the oil price shocks). The result was the creation of a **Fourth World** of countries that have been pejoratively referred to as international "basket cases," sinking to new depths of poverty.

The "less developed countries" (LDCs) today include a wide assortment of states—the "nouveau riche" but still in many ways underdeveloped OPEC nations like Saudi Arabia and Kuwait; a growing group of so-called "newly industrializing countries" (NICs) that have developed some industrial infrastructure and are "upper middle income" states, including Brazil, South Korea, Singapore, Taiwan, Mexico, and Argentina; the "Fourth World" countries like Bangladesh and The Gambia (in addition to over thirty other states that are listed by the World Bank as low income economies and have been designated by the United Nations as "least developed countries"); and others which do not quite fit any of these categories. The "developed" countries themselves range from the most highly developed and wealthiest market economies like the United States, Japan, and most members of the European Community to the less wealthy, centrally planned economies of Eastern Europe.

As noted in Chapter 1, one half of the world's people live in fifty countries with a per capita gross national product (PGNP) under $500; roughly one quarter live in fifty countries with PGNP between $500 and $2000; and roughly another one quarter live in sixty countries with PGNP over $2000.[21] Table 3.2 indicates how wealth, population, and nation-states are distributed in the world according to region.

As this table shows, both population and poverty (defined in terms of PGNP, the most commonly used indicator of standard of living and level of economic development) tend to be concentrated in the Southern part of the globe. This fact is made even plainer when one adds that of the twenty-seven countries with PGNP greater than $6000, all are far above the equator except for Australia and New Zealand and a handful of oil-rich states. We live in a world in which per capita gross national product ranges from an average of $280 per year in Fourth World countries (located primarily in sub-Saharan Africa and

Table 3.2

DISTRIBUTION OF WEALTH, POPULATION AND NATION-STATES BY REGION

Region	Population (in millions)	Number of Countries with PGNP less than $500	Number of Countries with PGNP $500–$2000	Number of Countries with PGNP greater than $2000
Sub-Saharan Africa	398	30	12	3
Middle East	215	2	11	10
Asia	2,635	12	7	5
Latin America	398	3	17	10
Oceania	23	3	2	3
Western Europe	401	0	0	18
Eastern Europe (including Soviet Union)	411	0	1	9
North America	260	0	0	2
TOTAL	4,741	50	50	60

Source: Adapted from *World Bank Atlas, 1986* (Washington, D.C.: World Bank, 1986). Data are for 1984.

Asia) to more than $11,000 per year in developed states with market economies.[22]

One can perhaps see the differences between states more vividly if one examines the developmental characteristics of some selected countries. Table 3.3 shows that the poorer countries in PGNP terms tend to have relatively low literacy rates, high infant mortality rates, and short life expectancies. However, the pattern is complicated by the fact that low PGNP does not always correlate exactly with such characteristics. In particular, it is clear that a number of countries that on paper appear to be very rich, based on a high PGNP produced suddenly by an oil bonanza or some other good fortune, have in fact not yet attained a level of economic development commensurate with their PGNP. Other countries that on paper appear to be poor still manage through imaginative government planning and societal resourcefulness to stretch their resources to produce what seems to be a surprisingly high standard of living.

Saudi Arabia, for example, is one of the "richest" countries in the world yet has a literacy rate of 30 percent and life expectancy of fifty-five years; Sri Lanka, one of the "poorest" countries in the world, has a literacy rate of 87 percent and life expectancy of sixty-five years. There are many factors that account for these discrepancies. One that is especially significant is the inability of societies, even those blessed with the huge financial resources of some Arab oil sheikdoms, to modernize overnight and to produce all the benefits associated with a high level of economic development—sophisticated transportation, health care, and educational systems. Hence, some analysts

Table 3.3

THE RICH-POOR GAP AMONG SELECTED COUNTRIES

Country	PGNP (U.S. $)	Literacy (%)	Infant Mortality (per 1000 Live Births)	Life Expectancy at Birth (Years)
Bangladesh	130	33	132	50
Barbados	4,340	99	23	72
Brazil	1,710	78	70	64
Canada	13,140	98	9	75
Egypt	720	45	102	58
Gambia	260	25	191	36
Haiti	320	38	107	54
Indonesia	540	75	101	54
Israel	5,100	95	14	74
Japan	10,390	99	7	77
Kuwait	16,200	70	29	71
Malta	3,370	85	21	73
Nigeria	770	43	113	49
Pakistan	380	30	119	50
People's Republic of China	300	70	38	67
Saudi Arabia	10,740	30	101	55
Seychelles	2,430	58	27	70
Soviet Union	5,200	99	36	69
Sri Lanka	300	87	40	65
Sweden	11,880	99	8	78
Switzerland	15,990	99	8	79
Turkey	1,200	75	82	63
United Kingdom	8,530	99	10	74
United States	15,490	99	11	75
Yugoslavia	2,120	91	32	69

Source: Data on PGNP are for 1984 and were obtained from *World Bank Atlas, 1986* (Washington, D.C.: World Bank, 1986). Data on literacy rates, based on percent of population fifteen years of age or older able to read and write, are the latest available estimates as of 1987 and were obtained from *UNESCO Statistical Yearbook, 1985* (Paris, UNESCO, 1985). Data on infant mortality rates and life expectancy are the latest available estimates as of 1987 and were obtained from *World Bank Atlas, 1986* (Washington, D.C.: World Bank, 1986); and Ruth Leger Sivard, *World Military and Social Expenditures, 1985* (Washington, D.C.: World Priorities, 1985).

have argued that PGNP is a misleading indicator of national wealth and they have suggested another measure—the physical quality of life index (PQLI), which combines literacy rate, infant mortality rate, and life expectancy.[23]

Regardless of what indicators are used, it is clear that the contemporary international system is divided into "haves" and "have-nots." Some countries rank high on almost every measure of national well-being while some rank uniformly low and others show uneven developmental characteristics. Even in the case of oil-rich countries like Nigeria and Indonesia, efforts to develop an improved standard of living are hampered by their having to distribute wealth among huge populations and by the unpredictability of oil revenues. A large population may often be an asset in terms of power, but it can be a liability in terms of economic development. As less developed countries have gained greater access to advanced medical technologies, life expectancy has been increasing somewhat, in the process contributing to the enormous population growth that has outstripped economic growth in many cases. We will discuss these problems and the politics associated with them in Chapter 14.

DEGREE OF POLARIZATION

The 1973 oil crisis illustrated a number of ways in which the international system had drifted away from extreme polarization toward greater flexibility in terms of alignment patterns. Within the Western bloc, there was disarray as the European and Japanese allies for the most part abandoned their traditional support of the American position on Israel; even within the European Community, there was dissension, with the Dutch isolated from the other members on Middle East policy. Although the Eastern bloc had little involvement with the events of 1973, Rumania continued to demonstrate its nonconformist tendencies by maintaining friendly relations with Israel, a posture contrary to that of the other Eastern European states. The United States and the Soviet Union themselves were hardly polarized on the Middle East question, gradually realizing that it was in their mutual interest to call on the United Nations to facilitate a cease-fire before the conflict escalated too far. (While the Soviets paid lip service to the Arab embargo, they proceeded to take advantage of the high oil prices on the world market to peddle petroleum to the West.)

Although it can be argued that the Middle East conflict was not a true test of "bipolarity" since the conflict did not involve strictly East-West issues and the alliances were still left intact, this would seem to miss the point. The point is that the whole concept of a bipolar world, as understood by policy-makers and scholars after World War II, assumed not only the existence of two superpowers but also that East-West issues were *the* all-consuming issues in international politics. At the very least, the events of 1973 showed how other sets of issues could vie for attention and how fluid and complicated alignments could be on such issues.

The East-West axis of conflict did not disappear after 1973. It clearly remained an important element of international politics as the Cold War continued to blow hot and cold. However, it was joined by other axes of conflict, most notably the **North-South** confrontation, which took on increasing importance as the success of OPEC states emboldened other Third World countries to make more strident demands for a "New International Economic Order." It was on May 1, 1974—less than two months after the end of the oil embargo against the United States—that a majority of Third World states in the UN General Assembly pushed through a "Declaration on the Establishment of a New International Economic Order" and a "Programme of Action," followed in December by a "Charter on the Economic Rights and Duties of States."

Whereas the East-West conflict pitted the non-communists against the communists, the North-South conflict pitted the rich against the poor. Although both the United States and the Soviet Union variously posed as the champion of the poor and the oppressed, neither could hide the fact that they were located far above the equator and, more importantly, shared some interests in common (as developed industrialized states) that were somewhat at odds with the interests of the less developed states. The United States, however, because of its greater role in the international economy, along with its role as leader of a bloc of former colonial powers, became the more frequent target of Southern hostility and demands. Although a depressed world economy put calls for a New International Economic Order on hold in the 1980s, as Third World confidence and militancy were dampened, the North-South conflict continued to fester and seemed likely to remain a major source of international tensions for the foreseeable future.

The East-West and North-South conflicts may indeed be, in the words of one commentator, "the two dominant struggles of our time."[24] However, it is important to keep in mind not only that many issues do arise that are unrelated to these "struggles," but also that even on these two axes of conflict one does not find totally cohesive blocs.

With regard to the East-West axis, the "Western alliance" remains a fragile collection of countries whose only commonality is that they are industrialized democracies; on the Eastern side, Soviet coercion tends to make the "Communist commonwealth" more cohesive, but fragile nonetheless. Within each bloc, intricate economic ties create some closeness but also some conflicts of interest. From time to time, Soviet and American mutual interests have jointly been pursued to the exclusion of their allies' interests (e.g., restraints on the transfer of nuclear weapons technology to other states).

With regard to the North-South axis, although the "South" gives the appearance of solidarity,[25] it is also a somewhat fragile bloc of countries representing considerable variety and potential conflicts of interest. Although the South has managed to maintain a remarkable degree of cohesion on a broad range of economic issues, many rivalries exist and togetherness breaks down frequently. For example, as noted earlier, even within a small subset of the South—OPEC—unity has been undermined by disagreements over oil pricing and production policies (between big states like Iran, which need more oil revenue to satisfy large economic development needs, and small states like Kuwait, which can manage with less revenue), by religious conflicts (between Sunni Muslims dominant in Saudi Arabia and Shiite Muslims dominant in Iran), and by territorial disputes (between Iran and Iraq, which have fought a war against each other in the 1980s).

There are, indeed, many different sources of conflict and many cross-cutting cleavages in world politics today. The contemporary international system has been called a "revolutionary" system, in terms of the upheavals relating to issues of religion, ethnicity, and social-economic change in places as diverse as the Philippines and Iran. Many of these tensions spill over national boundaries and result in international conflicts which cannot always be placed on East-West or North-South axes.

The formation of shifting coalitions of actors across various issues has become more and more prevalent. The battle lines in contemporary international politics are not as clear-cut as bipolar imagery suggests, with the lines often quite tangled.

> One graphic illustration of the entangling economic relationships that now cross ideological lines is the pipeline system for the flow of oil and natural gas. In the early 1960s the Soviets began to build a pipeline network of their own. The first pipeline was to Czechoslovakia, and the next, the Friendship Pipeline, linked Soviet oil fields to East Germany and the Baltic seaports. In the 1970s the Soviets . . . extended the Czech pipeline to make it possible to supply oil and natural gas to Western Europe. (Since the pipeline [was] entirely inside Czechoslovakia, East Germany [did] not have to be consulted about sales to West Germany.) . . . For many years Soviet oil sales to West Europe through the pipeline system and the use of tankers have become increasingly important for the West Europe economy.[26]

It should be added that in the 1980s Western European allies of the United States rejected American pleas to limit their energy imports from the Soviet Union, and instead collaborated with Moscow in providing the Soviets cheap loans and advanced technology to build a natural gas pipeline connecting the rich fields of Siberia with the heart of Western Europe.

The complicated nature of coalition-building in world politics is clearly exemplified by the seemingly "strange" coalitions that materialized in response to the U.S. attempt to organize a worldwide boycott of the 1980 Olympic Games in Moscow as punishment for the Soviet invasion of Afghanistan that year. (See the sidelight on page 84 for a list of participants and nonparticipants.) It is getting so that one needs a scorecard to keep track of such issues, not only because there are so many new "players" (i.e., new mini-states joining the community of nations) but also because the "teams" (i.e., coalitions) change so often.

One must remember, though, that alignments in the contemporary system are not totally flexible. There are still rigidities, notably the ideological differences that persist between East and West and limit the realm of alignment possibilities to some extent. Insofar as there is still bipolarity left in the

SIDELIGHT

KEEPING SCORE AT THE 1980 OLYMPIC GAMES: THE INTERNATIONAL POLITICS OF SPORT

The Olympic Games that were held in Moscow in July of 1980 initially threatened to be a "no show" Olympics as the United States urged a total boycott of the games by all nations to protest the Soviet invasion of Afghanistan earlier in the year. Ultimately, eighty-one nations participated, with sixty-five "no shows." The United States met unexpected resistance in some quarters and picked up unexpected support in other places. Among those countries that sent athletes to Moscow were several U.S. allies (noted below in italics under "participants"). Among those countries that joined the United States in the Olympic boycott (listed below as "nonparticipants") were a number of countries that ordinarily would not be found holding hands with each other, including Taiwan and China, Pakistan and Bangladesh, and Israel and a few Arab states. The most incongruous U.S. "ally" on this issue was Iran, which at the time was locked in a bitter struggle with the United States over the fate of fifty-two American hostages who had been seized at gunpoint from the U.S. Embassy in Tehran several months earlier. The most unlikely U.S. "adversary" was Puerto Rico, which fielded a team despite Puerto Rico's close ties (including common citizenship) with the United States. In the case of Iran and the Arab states, they were motivated primarily by the desire to protest the invasion of a fellow Muslim state rather than by any natural affinity toward the United States or deep-seated aversion toward the Soviet Union. Some countries, like Burma, decided to boycott simply

international system, it is sufficiently loose that the contemporary system can more appropriately be called **bimultipolar**[27]—a term that characterizes very well the complexity of alignment patterns along with power configurations today.

OBJECTIVES AND MEANS

As the oil embargo and Olympic boycott episodes suggest, different countries tend to see different sides of issues. Some countries viewed these situations as "national security" problems while others treated them as more narrow and less menacing economics and sports concerns. Many observers have noted that in the contemporary international system "national security" has become a more ambiguous concern than in the past. Although it may remain the overriding concern of nation-states, it has become more difficult to define and to separate from other matters.

As Patrick Morgan suggests, instead of thinking of the international system as a *single* "game table," we should think of it as "a *series of game tables* with different games for varying stakes. Every player participates in one or due to lack of world-class athletes and money. In perusing the list below, one is hard-pressed to discern any East-West or North-South alignment patterns, even over an issue so seemingly central to world politics that an American president labeled it "the greatest threat to world peace since World War II."

Participants

Afghanistan, Algeria, Angola, *Australia*, Austria, *Belgium*, Benin, Botswana, Brazil, *Britain*, Bulgaria, Cameroon, Colombia, Congo, Costa Rica, Cuba, Cyprus, Czechoslovakia, *Denmark*, East Germany, Ecuador, Ethiopia, Finland, *France*, *Greece*, Grenada, Guatemala, Guinea, Guyana, Hungary, *Iceland*, India, Iraq, Ireland, *Italy*, Jamaica, Jordan, Kuwait, Laos, Lebanon, Lesotho, Libya, *Luxembourg*, Madagascar, Mali, Malta, Mexico, Mongolia, Mozambique, Nepal, *Netherlands*, Netherlands Antilles, *New Zealand*, Nicaragua, Nigeria, North Korea, Panama, Peru, Poland, *Portugal*, Puerto Rico, Rumania, San Marino, Senegal, Seychelles, Soviet Union, Spain, Sri Lanka, Sweden, Switzerland, Syria, Tanzania, Togo, Trinidad and Tobago, Uganda, Venezuela, Vietnam, Yugoslavia, Zambia, Zimbabwe.

Nonparticipants

Argentina, Albania, Antigua, Bahrain, Bahamas, Bangladesh, Barbados, Belize, Bermuda, Bolivia, Burma, Canada, Cayman Islands, Central Africa, Chad, China, Chile, El Salvador, Egypt, Fiji, Gambia, Haiti, Honduras, Hong Kong, Indonesia, Iran, Israel, Japan, Kenya, Liberia, Liechtenstein, Malawi, Malaysia, Mauritania, Mauritius, Monaco, Morocco, Norway, Pakistan, Papua New Guinea, Paraguay, the Philippines, Qatar, Saudi Arabia, Singapore, Somalia, South Korea, Sudan, Swaziland, Taiwan, Thailand, Turkey, United States, Upper Volta, Uruguay, Virgin Islands, West Germany, Zaire.

two but some play in a great many simultaneously. Many of the games are interdependent, so that play in one game often influences play in another [italics ours]."[28] Likewise, Stanley Hoffmann states that we have witnessed

> the move from a world dominated by a single chessboard—the strategic-diplomatic one (which either eclipsed or controlled all others)—to a world dispersed into a variety of chessboards. This is partly the result of the nuclear stalemate (which has somewhat neutralized the strategic chessboard and reduced, if not its fundamental importance, at least its daily saliency), partly the product of economic and social processes and scientific invention in a world obsessed by the quest for economic growth.[29]

Both Morgan and Hoffmann are referring to the fact that the traditional notion of international relations as a "balance of power" struggle waged primarily in military terms no longer seems completely applicable to the contemporary international system. Even an inveterate realist like Henry Kissinger, while U.S. Secretary of State, felt compelled to acknowledge a new reality—the existence of a new agenda of issues (energy, environment, population, the uses of space and the oceans, and other concerns) "whose benefits and burdens transcend national boundaries."[30]

Such concerns raise questions about where to draw the line between "national security" and "international security," between the pursuit of national objectives and the pursuit of "global welfare management" objectives.[31] If it no longer makes sense to conceive of international relations simply as a "balance of power struggle among nation-states," does one then conceive of it as "a system of relationships among interdependent, earth-related communities that share with one another an increasingly crowded planet that offers finite . . . quantities of basic essentials of human well-being . . ."?[32]

In our view, both these conceptions are inadequate representations of the contemporary international system. On the one hand, one must be careful not to get too carried away by the rhetoric of "interdependence." As Robert Paarlberg notes, the "old issues of sovereignty and security continue to receive far more attention than any new agenda of global welfare management issues."[33] Similarly, Klaus Knorr has pointed out that, although there has been some decline in the actual use of force by states in recent years, there has also been an increase in military expenditures, military manpower, and arms imports.[34] On the other hand, there is much evidence today of interdependence, with at least as many pressures for cooperation as conflict.

DEGREE OF INTERDEPENDENCE

The oil politics and economics of 1973, probably more than any other single episode, popularized the notion that the world had become highly interdependent. There was a good deal of hard evidence to back up this general feeling. Based on an extensive study of international transaction trends in such areas as trade, investment, tourism, and mail and phone communications, Alex Inkeles concluded that over

> a wide range of systems of exchange we find evidence for rapid acceleration in the development of ties linking nations, their institutional components, and the individuals who populate them. The abundance and complexity of the networks which interconnect the world's population are, and have been for some time, growing at a phenomenal rate. With some variation according to the specific indicator used, recent decades reveal a general tendency for many forms of human interconnectedness across national boundaries to be doubling every ten years.[35]

Despite the attempts by some national governments to set up barriers to international flows of goods (through tariffs and quotas), people (through immigration and travel restrictions), and ideas (through jamming radio signals), modern communications and travel technology has made borders extremely "permeable."[36]

One needs to keep interdependence in proper perspective, however. For example, even though the number of university students studying abroad has been increasing in recent years by 7 percent per year, 98 percent of the world's total student body remains at home to receive schooling.[37] One must remember that international transactions are still merely a tiny fraction of all human interactions in relative terms. Then, too, the growth of international transactions is only one aspect of the interdependence phenomenon. Increasing human interconnectedness across national boundaries may or may not affect a second, more important aspect of interdependence—the mutual sensitivity and vulnerability nation-states and national governments experience with regard to each other's actions. The fact that more and more people around the world may be watching "Sesame Street" while drinking Coca-Cola is not necessarily relevant to world politics. Some kinds of international flows (e.g., trade) obviously have the potential to create greater sensitivities and vulnerabilities than other types of flows (e.g., pen pal correspondence).

Interdependence is a very *uneven* phenomenon, both in terms of patterns of interconnectedness and patterns of sensitivity and vulnerability. Regarding interconnectedness, it is clear that goods and services, people, and communications do not flow evenly around the world. The bulk of world trade, for example, occurs among developed capitalist countries, with considerable trade also occurring between the latter and the less developed countries (including OPEC) and among developed Communist countries. In the 1980s, 71 percent of the exports of developed capitalist countries went to other developed capitalist countries, with only 23 percent going to less developed countries and 5 percent to the developed Communist states. Less developed countries participate in the international trade arena primarily through interactions with the developed capitalist countries, rather than with fellow less developed countries or with the developed Communist states. Developed Communist states tend to trade mostly among themselves, with East-West trade accounting for only 33 percent of their total trade in 1980, their trade with the less developed countries being only 18 percent, and the remainder occurring within the Eastern bloc.[38]

Very similar patterns can be found with regard to the flow of foreign investment funds, tourists, and communications, leading some observers to speak of an interdependent First World, an interdependent Second World, and a Third World whose parts do not interact very much except for coalition-building in the United Nations and in selective relations like OPEC membership. The industrialized democracies, in particular, account for well over half of all memberships in the more than 3000 international nongovernmental organizations (NGOs) today and are headquarters for almost 90 percent of all these organizations;[39] they likewise account for well over half of all memberships in the roughly 300 intergovernmental organizations (IGOs).[40]

Not only are interconnectedness patterns uneven in the contemporary international system, but so also are sensitivity and vulnerability patterns. If by "sensitivity" and "vulnerability" one means the general tendency today for many problems, like pollution and inflation, to spill over national frontiers and defy unilateral national solutions, then it is true that all states are interdependent. Certainly, on *some* dimensions of interdependence (e.g., ecological concerns relating to pollution and climatic change), it would seem that everybody has an equal stake in the matter. However, on other dimensions (e.g., economic), some countries are less sensitive and vulnerable to external actions than are other countries.

The oil embargo of 1973 showed very clearly that all countries were not mutually interdependent with regard to petroleum. The Arab states along with the Soviet Union were wholly self-sufficient in energy, and the United States was moderately self-sufficient; Japan and Western Europe were heavily dependent at the time on Middle East oil. The energy situation made the United States *sensitive* to the use of the oil weapon but not nearly as *vulnerable* as its allies.

Much interdependence is *asymmetrical* in nature, with dependencies being one-sided. As noted earlier, the United States and the Soviet Union are among the most self-sufficient nations on earth. Most relationships that the United States (or the Soviet Union) enters into with another country tend to be asymmetrical, i.e., the United States (or the Soviet Union) tends to attach less importance to the relationship than does its counterpart. For example, to the extent that the United States and Zaire are interdependent, it is Zaire that "needs" the United States more than the United States "needs" Zaire. However, even here, the United States has some dependency, since Zaire is a chief source of cobalt, a mineral that is found practically nowhere in the United States and is essential for making certain communications equipment as well as aircraft engines.[42] If no substitute could be found for cobalt, if no alternative suppliers were available, and if Zaire were able to reduce its own import and export dependence on the United States, then the United States indeed would not only be "sensitive" but "vulnerable" in this area.[43]

Countries can try to minimize their dependence on other countries by reducing their permeability and erecting various barriers, although "undoing" interdependence can be extremely difficult and costly. Among the countries that have felt especially "penetrated" and have made special efforts in recent years to lessen this condition—with modest results—are Albania, Burma, Canada, Iran, and Tanzania.[44] Suffice it to say that interdependence is very real but also very complicated.

Some Further Complications

If the reader does not find the contemporary international system complicated enough, there are a few other complications that might be noted that have only been hinted at in our discussion up to now. In particular, in offering a bird's-eye view of the international system, we have been looking at the world essentially through global and state-centric lenses. That is, we have examined such things as the distribution of power and wealth, degree of polarization, and interdependence largely in the context of (1) the world as a whole and (2) relationships between nation-states. Our picture of contemporary international relations would be incomplete, however, if we did not add two other perspectives: (1) the *regionalization* of world politics and (2) the role of *nonstate actors* in world politics.

REGIONALIZATION

This book is about the "global condition" and, as such, assumes that all international relations ultimately fit into a global context. At the same time, the richness and complexity of international politics can be lost sight of if one fails to note that below the global level lies a series of *regional subsystems.* Each regional subsystem, although touched by global concerns such as the East-West and North-South conflicts, exhibits a life of its own in certain respects. One can, for example, talk about the politics of the Middle East or Latin America or Sub-Saharan Africa or Western Europe or Eastern Europe or North America or Asia. (Depending on how complicated one wants to get, one can distinguish between East Asian, South Asian, and West Asian subsystems within Asia.)

Although the rivalry between Pakistan and India, say, may not be particularly visible at the global level, it may reveal more about and have greater bearing on the politics of South Asia than the larger East-West or North-South conflicts do. It may also be of greater interest to the average Indian or Pakistani. Even the Middle East, while central to global energy politics, can be treated in some respects as a distinct subsystem, with its own peculiar dynamics based on local or regional issues and rivalries.[45] Numerous other examples of "discontinuities" in the international system can be cited that illustrate the oversimplifications that are necessarily made when one attempts to treat the international system as a coherent whole.[46] The point here is that in a general discussion of international relations—which this book is—one can rightly treat the international system in a global context, but one should also keep in mind that an even greater complexity exists beneath the surface.

NONSTATE ACTORS

An additional complexity is introduced when one acknowledges the fact that nation-states, acting through national governments, are not the only actors in international relations and that *nonstate* actors—such as intergovernmental and nongovernmental organizations and multinational corporations—have some effect on international relations. We noted earlier that these kinds of actors have existed on the world scene for a long time and that they proliferated in the twentieth century, particularly after World War II. However, we have not discussed their importance in international relations. Nonstate actors are worth examining only if one can demonstrate that they are to some extent autonomous agents in international politics—that they have their own distinct objectives apart from national governments, that they actively pursue these objectives in the international arena, and that they have some impact on world politics and relations among states.

For example, one cannot fully understand the dynamics of the oil embargo episode of 1973 unless one takes into account the variety of nonstate actors involved. This would include the multinational oil companies, which were in a position to help reinforce or frustrate the Arab oil embargo through their independent allocation policies; nongovernmental organizations such as the Palestine Liberation Organization, whose demands for a homeland contributed to tensions and hostilities in the Middle East; intergovernmental organizations such as OAPEC and the European Economic Community, which attempted to coordinate policy between Arab oil-producing nations and Western European oil-consuming nations respectively; and the United Nations, which helped to defuse the Yom Kippur War by providing a peacekeeping force of 7000 to monitor the disengagement agreement between Israel and Egypt.

State-centric analysts might well argue that if "push had come to shove" the economic clout of the oil companies would have proved no match for the power of governments, that OAPEC and the EEC were little more than fragile collections of Arab and Western European states, that the Yom Kippur War between Israel and the Arab states would probably have started with or without the PLO, and that the UN action could not have been taken without the blessing of both the United States and the Soviet Union. Our point, though, is not that nonstate actors played the dominant role in 1973, only that they were a not insignificant part of the equation that produced a quadrupling of the price of oil along with other important results at the time.

Many other examples can be cited of nonstate actors, organized either *subnationally* (within national boundaries) or *transnationally* (across national boundaries), competing with national governments in affecting world politics. World politics can be seen as a series of issue-areas in which outcomes are determined by congeries of forces including both state and nonstate actors. Recent case studies have suggested the relevance of nonstate actors to many different sets of issues.[47] Even in the war-peace area, traditionally considered to be the exclusive domain of national governments, one may choose to ignore the role of nonstate actors like the United Nations and the International Red Cross, but one cannot ignore the substantial capacity of actors like the Irish Republican Army and the PLO to generate violence in the international system.

Many observers have associated the nonstate actor phenomenon with what they perceive to be the decline of the nation-state as a political, economic,

The new patriotism?

and social unit. One noted scholar, reflecting upon the growth of multinational corporations in particular, has observed that "the state is about through as an economic unit."[48] Another observer, formerly a high-level U.S. policymaker, has said that "the nation-state is a very old-fashioned idea and badly adapted to serve the needs of our present complex world."[49] Still another observer, who has had his feet in both the academic and policymaking sectors, has commented as follows:

> A new pattern of international politics is emerging. The world is ceasing to be an arena in which relatively self-sustained, "sovereign," and homogeneous nations interact, collaborate, clash, or make war. . . . Transnational ties are gaining in importance, while the claims of nationalism, though still intense, are nevertheless becoming diluted. This change, naturally, has gone further in the most advanced countries, but no country is now immune to it. The consequence is a new era—an era of the global political process.[50]

There is some disagreement among those who envision the possible demise of the nation-state as to whether the primary threat to its viability comes from *disintegrative* tendencies from *within* (i.e., the revival of ethnic conflict and separatist movements on the part of minorities)[51] or *integrative* tendencies from *without* (i.e., the transnational links referred to above) or both. Some analysts go so far as to speak of a "new feudalism" (see box on page 92).

THE "NEW FEUDALISM"

It has been said that the nation-state came into being largely because the previous unit of human organization—the walled city or moated castle of the feudal era—no longer could provide for the protection and security of its population in an age of gunpowder. Some scholars have argued that the nation-state today likewise can no longer perform the security function and is as much an anachronism as the walled fortress of yore, given the ease with which national boundaries can be penetrated by nuclear weapons. In the excerpt below, James Nathan suggests that the security function of the nation-state has broken down not only in terms of vulnerability to nuclear attack but also in regard to another form of violence—international terrorism. He sees recent developments in this area as a throwback to feudal times, drawing an analogy between the relationship of lord and vassal in the Middle Ages and the relationship of multinational corporation executives and private security firms today. Whether or not one agrees about the obsolescence of the nation-state, Nathan's discussion raises some interesting questions about the role (or non-role) of national governments and armed forces in this area and how this phenomenon can be fitted into the traditional "state-centric" framework.

A Texas-based company called Oil Field Security Consultants recently notified potential corporate clients that it had its "own SWAT team of professionals who can be deployed on location to anywhere in the world within twenty-four hours." Another company, based in London, wired the major U.S. oil companies that "we stand ready . . . [as] a last resort . . . [to] conduct 'search and destroy' missions," against those who would harm company property, lives, or operations.

The business of countering terrorists has never been better. Approximately forty counter-terrorist firms offer an impressive panoply of services. Some provide protection through chauffeur training and electronic perimeter defenses. Firms may also supply information on specific terrorists and even negotiate with terrorists for the release of kidnaped company personnel.

Large overseas corporations that deal with counter-terrorist businesses should be aware of the extraordinary implications of this commerce. If the international corporate sector seeks protection by private counter-terrorist security firms, a medieval situation may emerge in which the security function of the state is usurped by private contractors. To the extent that this trade prospers, it may be a portent of a new kind of feudalism.

There have been about 7000 overseas terrorist incidents since 1970. During that same decade, multinational corporations paid $150 to $250 million in ransom. U.S. corporations have been the target of many of these attacks, suffering 25 percent of all kidnapings, explosions, and bombing incidents in 1979. . . . Since the success rate for terrorist efforts is extraordinarily high—more than 70 percent of the time ransom is paid or political prisoners released or both—terrorism appears to be a growth industry.

Yet if a multinational business does negotiate with terrorists and ransoms a kidnaped employee, it may be subject to other penalties. In March 1980, five years after Exxon Corporation paid $14.2 million to Argentine terrorists in return for the release of an abducted executive, a stockholder lawsuit was filed demanding that officials responsible for the payment reimburse the company for a decision taken "beyond the lawful powers and the authority of Exxon."

Source: Excerpted from James A. Nathan, "The New Feudalism." Reprinted with permission from *Foreign Policy* #42 (Spring 1981). Copyright 1982 by the Carnegie Endowment for International Peace.

Others speak of just the opposite, an emergent "global village." In either case, if these observers are correct, the world is presently witnessing the most significant and sweeping change the international system has experienced in the last 400 years, namely the transformation of the very structures in which human beings are organized and around which their political life revolves.

However, it needs to be emphasized that for every observer who sees the imminent demise of the nation-state, there are at least three other observers who argue that the nation-state is alive and well. The latter are quick to remind the former that the twentieth century has been the century of "the state"—that is, the seemingly universal tendency in all modern societies, democracies and nondemocracies alike, is for national governments to become bigger and more heavily involved in the lives of their citizens. If the nation-state is withering away, someone has forgotten to tell the leaders in Washington and Moscow and other national capitals. In nondemocratic societies especially, which include two thirds of the world's people,[52] not only has government become increasingly pervasive internally, but there still remain severe constraints on the amount of transnational activity in which citizens can engage outside national boundaries. If anything, the 1980s have witnessed increased rather than decreased state control. Given these countertrends, prognostications about the demise of the nation-state do seem quite premature.

We would argue that there is a "global political process" at work today, but that nation-states remain at the core of this process. They remain the key actors in the drama of contemporary world politics, although they are being buffeted by both centrifugal and centripetal forces, which in the short run may undermine the ability of national governments to control events fully in international relations and in the long run may even pose challenges to their very existence. In terms of world order, these forces contain the seeds of both increased conflict and increased cooperation. In the latter part of this book, we will explore the relationships that exist between the various nation-states and nonstate actors in the global political process.

Conclusion

The international system today remains a decentralized system, even if, as some say, some sort of "central guidance" mechanism is needed more than at any time previously. Nation-states are still legally and formally sovereign—independent—but are behaviorally interdependent to a greater degree than in the past. Nationalism persists alongside transnationalism, regionalism alongside globalism. National governments are bigger than ever but less able by themselves to deal with problems that spill over national boundaries. "National security" continues to be a paramount concern but is juxtaposed with the problem of "international security." The international system remains stratified in terms of power and wealth, although the patterns are complex, with so-called "superpowers" often frustrated by "mini-states" and with the enormous wealth of advanced industrialized states exceeded (on paper at least) only by the riches of a few desert kingdoms. East-West and North-South conflicts exist, but so do East-East, West-West, and various other permutations of conflicts. As noted, the system is best labeled "bimultipolar." And if communications and travel technology has produced a "shrinking and linking" of the world and a nascent "world society," it has also made individuals in some cases even more aware of the *differences* that exist between peoples within that global society.

We have attempted in this chapter to provide an overview of the general setting in which international relations occur in the late twentieth century. We obviously live in complicated and tumultuous times, although the world has never been an uncomplicated place. Having provided a broad-brush portrait of the contemporary international system, we are now ready to examine it in greater detail and in more dynamic perspective. In later chapters we will focus on specific elements of the international system and will see how the interactions of over 5 billion people, 160 nation-states, and 3000 international organizations are determining "who gets what, when, and how" in the global polity.

SUMMARY

1. The oil embargo of 1973 illustrated the growing complexity of international relations in the late twentieth century. As reflected by the oil embargo episode, the contemporary international system is characterized by (a) increased ambiguity in the measurement and exercise of power, (b) decreased cohesion of alliances and blocs, (c) complicated patterns of interdependence, and (d) the growing role of nonstate actors in world politics.

2. Regarding the distribution of power in the contemporary system, it is more difficult to identify a meaningful "pecking order" among states today than in the past. "Superpowers" are often frustrated by "mini-states."

3. Whereas in the past power could be measured mostly in military terms, today such factors as economic resources can be at least as important in influencing international relations, as demonstrated in 1973 by a handful of small oil sheikdoms. Although military power clearly cannot be discounted, the nuclear weaponry concentrated in the hands of the United States and the Soviet Union is less readily usable than the more conventional military prowess enjoyed by the great powers of the past.

4. There are vast differences between states today in terms of size. However, power is based on a wide variety of societal variables, not only raw size but also many qualitative or intangible factors, and it can best be viewed as situation-specific or issue-specific.

5. Regarding the distribution of wealth, the oil price hikes of 1973 contributed to many less developed countries—the oil importers—becoming even poorer, while other less developed countries—the oil producers—joined the ranks of the rich (at least in PGNP terms). The Third World, then, includes a great variety of states characterized by different levels of development. Some countries in the world rank high on almost every measure of national well-being, others rank low on almost every measure, whereas others have uneven developmental characteristics.

6. The international system has become somewhat less polarized and more flexible in terms of alignment patterns. The East-West conflict between the Communists and the non-Communists still exists, but other important axes of conflict such as the North-South struggle between rich and poor states also exist. One's enemies on one axis of conflict might be allies on some other axis, as coalitions shift across various issues. In short, the international system might more appropriately be called bimultipolar rather than bipolar.

7. Traditional military-security issues, while remaining the highest priority of states, now have to compete for attention with other newer concerns that have been added to the international agenda (energy, food, etc.).

8. The oil embargo popularized the notion that the world had become highly interdependent. However, interdependence is very uneven, both in terms of interconnectedness and patterns of sensitivity and vulnerability. Some countries are relatively independent and others relatively dependent.

9. Below the level of the global system are several regional subsystems, each of which exhibits to some extent a life of its own apart from global concerns. These forces of regionalism must be kept in mind when dealing with the international system.

10. International relations are further influenced by nonstate actors, such as IGOs and NGOs and multinational corporations. These groups can pursue objectives apart from national governments and compete with the latter in affecting world politics. The more autonomous these actors are, the more they tend to undermine the

sovereignty of national governments. Although transnationalism is an important force in contemporary world politics, it is premature to speak of the demise of the nation-state, given the continued attachment to nationalism felt throughout the world.

SUGGESTIONS FOR FURTHER READING AND STUDY

Among the many works dealing with the oil embargo of 1973, *The Oil Crisis*, by Raymond Vernon, ed. (New York: W.W. Norton, 1976), is especially useful in examining the role of different state and nonstate actors in this episode.

On the distribution of power and wealth in contemporary world politics, see Klaus Knorr, *Power and Wealth* (New York: Basic Books, 1973). On power alone, see Ray S. Cline, *World Power Assessment: A Calculus of Strategic Drift* (Washington, D.C.: Georgetown University Center for Strategic and International Studies, 1975), and Saul B. Cohen, "A New Map of Global Geopolitical Equilibrium: A Developmental Approach," *Political Geography Quarterly*, 1 (July 1982), pp. 223–241. Three excellent articles which point out the complexity of power in the contemporary international system and the difficulty in constructing "pecking orders" are David Baldwin, "Power Analysis and World Politics: New Trends vs. Old Tendencies," *World Politics*, 31 (January 1979), pp. 161–194; Stanley Hoffmann, "Notes on the Elusiveness of Modern Power," *International Journal*, 30 (Spring 1975), pp. 183–206; and Robert O. Keohane, "Theory of World Politics: Structural Realism and Beyond," in Ada W. Finifter, ed., *Political Science: The State of the Discipline* (Washington, D.C.: American Political Science Association, 1983), esp. pp. 522–526. On the distribution of wealth in the contemporary international system, see Lester R. Brown, *The Twenty-ninth Day* (New York: Norton, 1978), ch. 8, and David Morawetz, *Twenty-five Years of Economic Development, 1950–1975* (Washington, D.C.: World Bank, 1977), ch. 2. For a discussion of some problems in measuring wealth, see Morris D. Morris, *Measuring the Condition of the World's Poor* (New York: Pergamon Press, 1979). A good discussion of a variety of trends in contemporary world politics, including alignment patterns in the East-West and North-South conflicts, can be found in Seyom Brown's *New Forces in World Politics* (Washington, D.C.: Brookings Institution, 1974).

For a discussion of the growing tension between national security and international security and a call to rethink the traditional objectives and means of state action—especially from the perspective of U.S. foreign policy—see Stanley Hoffmann, *Primacy or World Order* (New York: McGraw-Hill, 1978), and Robert J. Johansen, *The National Interest and the Human Interest* (Princeton, N.J.: Princeton University Press, 1980). A good overview of the interdependence phenomenon is provided by George A. Lopez, *Dependence and Interdependence in the International System* (New York: Learning Resources in International Studies, 1978); a counterpoint is offered by David Fromkin, *The Independence of Nations* (New York: Praeger, 1981). On the role of nonstate actors in contemporary world politics, see Phillip Taylor, *Nonstate Actors in International Politics* (Boulder, Colo.: Westview Press, 1984). A discussion of "global policies and policy processes" can be found in Marvin S. Soroos, *Beyond Sovereignty: The Challenge of Global Policy* (Columbia, S.C.: University of South Carolina Press, 1986).

The somewhat paradoxical trends and countertrends relating to nationalism and transnationalism and the disintegration and integration of nation-states are elucidated in K. J. Holsti, "Change in the International System: Interdependence, Integration, and Fragmentation," in Ole R. Holsti *et al.*, eds., *Change in the International System* (Boulder, Colo.: Westview Press, 1980), pp. 23–53; and R. Harrison Wagner, "Dissolving the State: Three Recent Perspectives in International Relations," *International Organization*, 28 (Summer 1974), pp. 435–466.

PART
II

National Actors and
International Interactions

I only regret that I have but one life to lose for my country.
NATHAN HALE, UTTERED ON THE GALLOWS, SEPTEMBER 22, 1776

*Our country: in her intercourse with foreign nations may she always be in
the right; but our country, right or wrong.*
STEPHEN DECATUR, A TOAST OFFERED IN APRIL OF 1816

Nationalism is an infantile disease. It is the measles of mankind.
ALBERT EINSTEIN

For better or worse, nationalism has been a powerful force in world affairs. It continues to be so today, even though it is being diluted somewhat by a variety of other forces. There is hardly a place on the planet other than the high seas and the airspace above them that does not fall within the sovereign jurisdiction of some nation-state. Even if one adopts what we have called a "globalist" perspective—acknowledging the existence of a variety of actors in world politics—it is hard to dispute the assertion that "the starting point of international relations is the existence of states, of independent political communities."[1]

Part II focuses on *nation-states* as actors in world politics, i.e., the formulation and conduct of foreign policy by national governments and the dynamics of their interactions. One manifestation of the decentralized nature of the international system is the absence of any single, universally recognized, definitive list of nation-states in the world. Some policymakers and scholars would include such places as the Vatican City, Puerto Rico, Monaco, Taiwan, and Bophuthatswana, while others might omit these, depending on the political and analytical criteria being employed.[2] Allowing for some disagreement, there are well over 160 entities today that are widely viewed as nation-states.

In this section we will examine the kinds of foreign policy behavior that countries in general and four countries in particular (the United States, the Soviet Union, China, and India) display (Chapter 4). We will also investigate the different sets of factors that affect such behavior (Chapter 5), including a look inside the foreign policy decision-making process itself (Chapter 6). Hence, our discussion of foreign policy is aimed at both description and explanation. In addition, we will examine how countries interact with each other, and how international relations can be treated as a "game" (or a series of "games") in which nations seek to influence each other through various modes of statecraft (Chapter 7). Finally, we will discuss the occasional breakdowns in the "game" of international politics and examine the circumstances under which violence occurs and the different forms it can take (Chapter 8).

4

Describing Foreign Policy Behavior: What Is It Nation-States Do?

In November of 1933, sixteen years after the Bolshevik Revolution in Russia, the United States agreed to formal diplomatic recognition of the Soviet Union. In 1979, thirty years after the Communist Revolution in China, the United States agreed to formal diplomatic recognition of the People's Republic of China (PRC). In 1950, just one year after the latter revolution, American leaders had ignored India's warnings that China would fight if U.S. troops came too close to China's borders during the Korean War. In 1962, Indian leaders, who had strongly supported the PRC's recognition and membership in the United Nations and who had rightly predicted the American-Chinese confrontation over Korea, were themselves shocked by a large-scale Chinese invasion of their Himalayan frontier. This record indicates persistent problems experienced in relations among the four most populous states on earth.

In this chapter we will examine the foreign policy behavior of nation-states. We will focus particularly on the United States, the Soviet Union, China, and India, not simply because they are the biggest states—smaller states can have important impacts in world politics, as already noted—but because their contrasting historical experiences have produced certain distinctive behavior patterns the study of which can provide interesting and useful insights into the conduct of foreign policy generally. In many ways their behavior illustrates the range of options open to all countries in international relations. Although some states may enjoy wider latitude of maneuver than others, all face similar kinds of decisions about how to act on the world stage.

The Nature of Foreign Policy

U.S. recognition of the People's Republic of China was so delayed that jokes about American eyesight problems became standard through much of the post–World War II era; it seemed that Washington had somehow overlooked at least 800 million people on the Asian mainland. When the Nixon administration attempted to ease relations with the Communist regime in Beijing (Peking) in 1971, reflected in a series of exchanges and tours involving American and Chinese table tennis teams, Beijing insisted that such "Ping-Pong diplomacy" could not produce fuller diplomatic relations until the United States withdrew its recognition of the rival Chinese government on the island of Taiwan. Ultimately the Chinese and American leaders settled on a compromise that saw the PRC recognized as China's official representative while the U.S. continued "unofficial" relations with Taiwan.

Although recognition of new governments by other states is normally a routine, legal formality, at times it is used as a political tool to reward or punish certain behavior. Countries can communicate with each other without such recognition, for example by using third parties to transmit messages, but diplomatic recognition is of high symbolic value, especially when granted or withheld by major powers. On the eve of recognition by Washington, the Soviets in the 1930s and the Chinese in the 1970s had not suddenly changed from untrustworthy enemies to loyal friends of the United States. Instead, Washington, Moscow, and Beijing discovered they needed each other. The U.S. and USSR were brought together by growing concern over Japanese power in the Pacific, and the U.S. and PRC found common ground at the end of the Vietnam War in mutual anxiety about the USSR.

Establishing diplomatic relations is one type of foreign policy behavior. Other types include the threatened or actual use of force, the formation of alliances, the giving of foreign aid, voting in international organizations, and countless other acts. **Foreign policy behavior,** then, refers to the actions states take toward each other. It is important to note that these actions usually are not taken as ends in themselves but are tied in some way to larger purposes—from long-run aspirations to more immediate aims—that national leaders hope to achieve in their dealings with other countries. **Foreign policy,** then, refers to the set of decisions made by national leaders which are intended to serve as broad guidelines for choosing among various courses of action in specific situations in international affairs. For example, the PRC's *policy* toward the United States was to find a potential counterweight to Soviet power in Asia at a time when the U.S., stung by defeat in Vietnam, might withdraw from the region. Its *behavior*, reflecting that policy, was to accept cultural exchanges and diplomatic relations with the U.S. When one talks about states' foreign policies and behaviors, in other words, one means both the *goals* that national governments pursue in the international arena as well as the *instruments*—the political, diplomatic, economic, and military tools—that they employ to achieve these goals. We will discuss the various factors that shape nation-state policies and behaviors in Chapters 5 and 6. Before we can investigate what makes nation-states "tick," however, we must first see what it is they do.

Patterns of Foreign Policy Behavior

The nature of foreign policy is such that one can expect to find double standards and inconsistencies in the records of all countries. It is not easy to label countries as simply "peace-loving" or "warlike" or to use other such categorizations. Nevertheless, patterns of foreign policy behavior can be identified. Arnold Wolfers, an astute observer of international relations, suggested that all foreign policy behavior ultimately boils down to three possible patterns: (1) self-preservation (maintaining the status quo); (2) self-extension (revising the status quo in one's own favor); and much more rarely, (3) self-abnegation (revising the status quo in someone else's favor).[1] Although all international relations may boil down to this, one can do a little more to describe foreign policy behavior. That is, one can attempt to classify a nation-state's foreign policy behavior along a number of specific dimensions, keeping in mind that behavior can change over time and with different sets of leaders and conditions.

ALIGNMENT

One can first speak of *alignment* tendencies, in particular whether national leaders choose to ally with certain countries or to remain neutral. Our focus here is not on the alignment configurations in the international system as a whole (i.e., bipolarity and multipolarity as discussed in Chapters 2 and 3) but the alignment decisions of individual countries. A country's alignment behavior can vary from time to time during its history in response to changing circumstances and can influence the probability of its survival. For example, partly because neutrality had failed to shield Holland from Germany's attack and occupation in 1940, the Dutch government joined the North Atlantic Treaty Organization alliance soon after World War II. The shifting nature of alignments is vividly recalled in the World War II coalition of the U.S., Britain, USSR, and China against three of America's current allies—Germany, Italy, and Japan.

Alliances are formal agreements to provide mutual military assistance; as such, they carry certain benefits as well as risks.[2] Allied countries can pool their military resources, acquire access to foreign bases, and stake out territories that enemies are on notice will be denied them by force if necessary. Yet an allied state also risks interference by allies in its domestic affairs, the possibility of being dragged into another ally's quarrels, and the ultimate possibility of a sell-out if war begins. Table 4.1 indicates the general likelihood of such sell-outs, as well as trends in the formation of alliances and other types of alignment agreements. Although the historical record suggests a high degree of alliance fidelity, many observers have questioned the reliability of alliance guarantees in the contemporary nuclear age.

Neutrality is a stance of formal nonpartisanship in world affairs. By keeping a low profile, neutrals may avoid some of the problems associated with alliances, particularly the generating of potential enemies and counteralliances.[3] However, neutrals must also be aware that if war clouds gather, there may be no one committed to providing a protective military umbrella. Switzerland is one country that has carried neutrality to an extreme, even refusing membership in the United Nations lest it involve the Swiss in controversial "collective security" military or economic sanctions against states accused of violating the UN Charter.[4]

While the term "alignment" as used above refers to formal agreements on alliance or neutrality, it can also describe the general affective orientation of

Table 4.1
ALIGNMENT TENDENCIES

Nineteenth-century alliances were mainly military pacts with allies promising to help defend each other, while in the twentieth century, states have opted more often for promises not to attack each other. Pacts formed during years in which major wars were occurring were mainly mutual defense agreements. During years of peace a wider variety of alignment pacts were formed. The threat of war seems to lead to more explicit promises of mutual defense. Alliances and other alignment pacts were honored most of the time in both the nineteenth and twentieth centuries, and the threat of war occurring in the year of alignment generally increases only slightly the probability that the pact will be honored.

Type of Alignment	Historical Era		Formed in Year of War or Peace	
	1815–1919	1919–1945	War	Peace
Military pacts[a]	38 (60%)	18 (27%)	32 (54%)	24 (34%)
Nonaggression pacts[b]	8 (13%)	37 (56%)	20 (34%)	26 (37%)
Ententes[c]	17 (27%)	11 (17%)	7 (12%)	21 (30%)
Effectiveness of Pacts	1815–1919	1919–1945	War	Peace
Invoked and honored	33 (89%)	9 (82%)	24 (92%)	18 (82%)
Invoked and not honored	4 (11%)	2 (18%)	2 (8%)	4 (18%)

[a] Military pact—Promise to intervene with force on behalf of allies (what we here include as an "alliance").

[b] Nonaggression pact—Promise not to intervene with force against a state or states involved in war that are parties to the pact.

[c] Entente—Promise to consult together in time of threat (what we here include as an "alliance").

Source: Ole R. Holsti, P. Terrence Hopmann, and John D. Sullivan, *Unity and Disintegration in International Alliances: Comparative Studies,* Tables 12 and 14. © 1973. Adapted with permission from John Wiley and Sons, Inc.

a country, i.e., which nation or nations it tends to side with on key issues. Countries can tilt toward one side or another in a conflict without necessarily becoming part of a formal alliance. For example, Israel, which is *not* a U.S. ally, has sided with the United States on many issues; France, which *is* a U.S. ally, has frequently disputed U.S. policy. As noted previously, since the 1950s there has existed a group of Third World countries taking a stance of **nonalignment**—siding with the United States on some issues and with the Soviet Union on other issues but refusing to become locked into either camp in the East-West conflict. In the contemporary era in particular, countries often have to make alignment decisions with regard to not one but several axes of conflict (e.g., not only the East-West conflict but also the North-South conflict).

SCOPE

A second foreign policy dimension is the *scope* of a country's activities and interests. Some countries have extensive, far-reaching international contacts, while other countries have more limited activities abroad. A country's scope of contacts can affect the outcome of disputes and crises, for instance, if worldwide connections are needed (as they were during the oil embargo of 1973), or if regional influence is needed (as it was in quieting Lebanon's civil war in the 1970s). Major powers in international relations have historically been those that have defined their interests in **global** terms, interacting regularly with countries in nearly every region of the world. While so-called "great" or "super" powers can fail in their attempts to influence or control events, what distinguishes them from other countries is the scope of their interests and the panoply of means available to them to pursue those interests even at a distance.

Most countries in the world are essentially **regional** actors, interacting primarily with neighboring states in the same geographical area except for contacts, frequently concerning economic issues such as trade, with major actors like the United States and the Soviet Union outside their region. For example, Guatemala in Latin America does not interact much with Malawi in Africa. Admittedly, the foreign policy scope of some states defies easy categorization. Even poor or militarily weak states can have a few important extra-regional interests (e.g., Cuban military adventures in Africa or world-wide petroleum contacts maintained by the Dutch through the Shell Oil Corporation). Indeed, in an age of interdependence all countries are to some extent concerned about the politics of both their neighbors and distant regions. However, states such as the United States and the Soviet Union can more accurately be labeled global actors because of the comprehensive nature of their concerns and contacts—political, economic, military, and diplomatic. For example, Washington and Moscow maintain embassies in almost every country in the world, while most other states can afford embassies in only a few countries and so rely on the United Nations and international organizations for the bulk of their formal diplomatic contacts. Roughly two thirds of the nations of the world maintain diplomatic missions in fewer than sixty countries, with the most diplomatically pervasive countries being located in North America and Europe.

At some moments in history, certain factors, such as key weaknesses or geographic remoteness, may cause the scope of a country's foreign policy to become so narrow that **isolationism** results. This was the case with Burma in the 1960s and 1970s.[5] Few countries have ever been totally cut off from the outside world, and in an age of interdependence, isolationism becomes an increasingly less viable foreign policy orientation. As we will see, the United States, the Soviet Union, and the People's Republic of China all have passed through periods of relative isolationism and of mainly regional interests, ultimately branching out into global concerns.

MODUS OPERANDI

In addition to the alignment and scope dimensions of a nation's foreign policy, we can speak of foreign policy "m.o." (*modus operandi*, or method of operation). Just as police have noted recurrent patterns in the behavior of criminals and have used such patterns to identify suspects, states also evidence characteristic behavior patterns and favored methods of pursuing goals. We do not mean to imply that international relations resemble crime (though there are those who would make the argument), only that the notion of *modus operandi* can be useful in describing foreign policy behavior. Such patterns can change over time, sometimes quite quickly with dramatic leadership changes; as we have cautioned, it is not easy to fit multifaceted foreign policies into neat pigeon-holes. Yet certain actors leave characteristic imprints, and we can classify these along at least two dimensions: (1) degree of *multilateralism* and (2) degree of *activism*.

The more **multilateralist** a state, the greater its tendency to seek joint solutions to problems through diplomatic forums in which several states participate—such as the United Nations—rather than utilizing purely **bilateral** (country to country) approaches. The 40 Nation Committee on Disarmament (which includes the United States and the Soviet Union) is an example of the multilateral approach to arms control, while the Strategic Arms Limitation Treaty (SALT) talks between the United States and the Soviet Union are an example of the bilateral approach. As these examples indicate, countries do not rely exclusively on one or the other mode of diplomacy. However, some states seem to devote considerably more resources and energies than other states to international organizations and multilateral action. China is one state that has especially downplayed multilateralism. As of 1980, it had ratified only six out of some 190 UN multilateral treaties—far fewer than the United States or the Soviet Union and most other states—and belonged to only five international organizations in the UN system, compared to 17 for the United States and 12 for the Soviet Union.[6] Although more recently China has increased its participation in the UN system, the PRC still belongs to relatively few international organizations. Table 4.2 lists the states with the highest number of intergovernmental organization (IGO) memberships in the world, with Scandinavian states occupying three of the top four positions. Among less developed states, India ranks first.

In the area of foreign aid, in particular, Canada and the Scandinavian states have channeled a large percentage of their contributions (roughly half) through international organizations such as the World Bank. In so doing, these countries give up some control over the ultimate disbursement of the funds. In contrast,

Table 4.2

STATES WITH THE HIGHEST NUMBER OF IGO MEMBERSHIPS

Rank Order	State	Full and Associate Memberships in All Categories of IGOs
1	Denmark	164
2	France	155
3	Norway	154
4	Sweden	153
5	United Kingdom	140
6	Finland	139
7	Federal Republic of Germany	135
8	The Netherlands	131
9	Belgium	127
10	Italy	124
11	United States	122
12	Spain	113
13	Canada	110
14	Japan	106
15	Iceland	105
16.5	Australia	104
16.5	Soviet Union	104
18	India	102
19	Brazil	100
20	Poland	99
21	Algeria	96
22.5	Austria	95
22.5	Yugoslavia	95
25	Egypt	94
25	Mexico	94
25	Switzerland	94

Source: Harold K. Jacobson, William M. Reisinger, and Todd Mathers, "National Entanglements in International Governmental Organizations," *American Political Science Review,* 80 (March 1986), p. 149. Based on the *Yearbook of International Organizations* (Union of International Associations, 1981). Data are for 1981. Used by permission of the American Political Science Association.

the United States, West Germany, France, and many other countries, evidently more protective of their purse strings, have traditionally provided the bulk of their foreign aid in bilateral form through their own governmental agencies. Although the amount of foreign aid given multilaterally by the United States through the UN has been substantial, it has been proportionally lower than that supplied by the Scandinavians and many other countries, especially in terms of ability to pay (i.e., foreign aid as a percentage of gross national product).

The more *active* a state, the more likely it is to initiate actions in international relations or to resist initiatives taken by others. Acts of resistance can range from protests, threats, and warnings to the actual use of force. This dimension is partly related to scope and alignment. For example, it has been suggested that certain leaders define their country's role in world affairs as "bastions of revolution," as "defenders of the faith," and as "regional leaders or protectors" or "active independents," while others have styled themselves as "isolates," as "protectees," or as "faithful allies."[7] We should not assume that leaders always act on these perceptions, but certain governments' foreign policies have been more dynamic and less *passive* than others. For example, the Third World nonaligned movement was launched by ambitious and assertive leaders such as Nehru of India, Nasser of Egypt, Tito of Yugoslavia, Sukarno of Indonesia, and Nkrumah of Ghana—all interested in taking strong stands on issues such as anticolonialism and economic development.

One important aspect of activism is the extent to which governments are accommodative with regard to vital interests, particularly in terms of *willingness or unwillingness to use armed force*. Like the other dimensions, this one can be difficult to measure since leaders may be accommodative on one issue and strongly resistant on another. Furthermore, accommodation—coming to terms with an opponent—may be a passive or even cowardly policy in one situation but a prudent and shrewd compromise in another context. Nevertheless, certain countries have historically been noted for fanatical resistance to foreign threats, while others have compromised or given up more readily. Despite possessing a formidable army in 1938, the government of Czechoslovakia chose not to resist forcibly a German invasion; without reliable allies to aid them, they evidently deemed last-ditch resistance futile.[8] Similarly, Czech leaders did not call upon the army to resist the Soviet invasion in 1968, which ended the brief period of liberalization known as the "Prague Spring." Yet in nearby Poland, the army fought a futile two-week war against the Nazi invaders in 1939, with haunting scenes of Polish horse cavalry charging German tank divisions in suicidal resistance. There are those who argue that a Soviet invasion of Poland today, to suppress religious or democratic forces, would be met with similar fanaticism. We cannot assume that one group of people is invariably braver or more prudent than another. Perhaps if the Czechs had known the extent of Nazi crimes to come, they would have resisted more fanatically; and perhaps if the Poles were convinced that resistance to the Soviets would bring no outside help and would totally destroy the country, they, too, might conclude that "discretion is the better part of valor." Yet in understanding foreign policy behavior, we, as well as leaders contemplating invasions, such as Iraq's leaders upon attacking Iran in 1980, should realize that the influence of religion or ethnic hatred as well as other factors can make one country resist more fiercely than another.

Another aspect of activism is a country's tendencies toward **intervention** in the internal affairs of other countries. Interventions can be military (e.g., sending troops across a border), economic (e.g., sending financial aid to an opposition group that might overthrow a government), or diplomatic (e.g., advising a government on how to deal with a rebellion). Interventionism is not a new phenomenon; interventionist behavior can be found at least as far back as the Napoleonic era when Napoleon sought to export the French Revolution to other countries, while the conservative monarchs of Europe responded by attempting to suppress liberal-democratic uprisings in Greece, Spain, and elsewhere. Although interventionism is not new, it has become an increasingly prevalent form of foreign policy behavior in the twentieth century and is an especially visible feature of contemporary international relations. There are many conditions that promote interventionism today: the existence of advanced communications and related technology that render national boundaries increasingly permeable to external propaganda and other outside influences; the existence of many states created during the decolonialization process that are politically unstable due to serious economic problems and multiethnic populations and that therefore provide inviting targets for foreign subversion in collusion with disenchanted domestic groups; and the existence of nuclear weapons, which—especially for countries like the United States and the Soviet Union—make interventionism in its economic, diplomatic, or even low-level military forms a less risky mode of pursuing interests than the kind of direct large-scale use of armed force that could possibly escalate to all-out war.

Some states resort more often than others to interventionism. Many states are content to influence the foreign policies of other states without necessarily seeking to shape the nature of their governments and internal politics. The post–World War II record of instances of the direct use of military force (short of war) by one country inside another provides a conspicuous example: the U.S., Soviet Union, Britain, and France intervened in other countries more than seventy times between 1946 and 1980, with Britain alone responsible for nearly half of the total.[9] If one takes into account a country's economic capabilities (measured in GNP) when ranking states on interventionism, then smaller states such as Israel, Syria, Iraq, Libya, Vietnam, South Africa, and Cuba are highly interventionist also, given their capabilities. Table 4.3 lists the interveners in major civil wars of the 1970s, based on a study that examined various forms of military intervention, including not only the direct use of armed force but also supply of equipment, training, advisers, and financial support to factions in foreign disputes.

Four Case Studies

We have identified several dimensions of foreign policy that we consider suggestive, although certainly not exhaustive, of the kinds of behavior patterns

Table 4.3
INTERVENERS IN THE CIVIL WARS OF THE 1970s

Civil War[a]	Interveners[b]
Angola	Congo, Cuba, Soviet Union / France, China, United States, South Africa, Zaire
Burundi	Zaire
Guatemala	None
Iran	United States
Jordan	Israel / Egypt, Libya, Syria
Kampuchea	North Vietnam, China / Australia, Laos, France, South Vietnam, Thailand, United States
Lebanon	Israel, Saudi Arabia, Syria / Iraq, Libya, Syria, Egypt
Nicaragua	Costa Rica, Cuba / Honduras
Pakistan	India / Jordan, North Korea, China, Saudi Arabia, United States
The Philippines	United States
Rhodesia	South Africa / Angola, Cuba, East Germany, Mozambique, China, Soviet Union, Tanzania, Zambia
Sri Lanka	Britain, India, Soviet Union

[a] Civil wars beginning and ending during the 1970s.
[b] A slash separates interveners on opposing sides.

Source: Bertil Dunér, *Military Intervention in Civil Wars: the 1970s* (London: Gower, 1985), p. 140. Used by permission of Gower Publishing Company Limited.

nation-states manifest. We have also noted that foreign policy often appears "schizophrenic"; i.e., there are notable disparities between the officially proclaimed principles of some countries and their actual behavior. This dualism is evident in the history of U.S., Soviet, Chinese, and Indian foreign affairs, a history we will review in the remainder of this chapter. An examination of these four states provides a concrete portrait of the workings of international politics at the global and regional levels, and the manner in which foreign policy behavior can vary in terms of alignment, scope, methods of operation, and other features.

American Foreign Policy: A Profile

America has been called the world's first "new nation."[10] Refugees and adventurers from the "Old World," Americans from the beginning reacted against the outside world and particularly the world of traditional European powers. With great commercial zeal, America's founders envisioned a unique society practicing a different form of relations with other countries. They would not reestablish monarchy and engage in foreign conquests but would concentrate on exploiting the advantages of a practically private continent. Although there would be the need to dispose of a few obstacles on the continent posed by native American Indian tribes and foreign empires, and although slavery would underwrite the southern economic system, the new nation generally saw itself behaving in a nobler fashion than the already established states.

To protect and nurture the young republic, early American foreign policy was neutral in terms of alignment tendencies and mainly regional in scope. Americans also came to see themselves as somewhat isolationist—insulated from European affairs by vast oceans and preoccupied with taming the frontier. Indeed, after alliance with France during the Revolutionary War, the United States, on George Washington's advice in his Farewell Address in 1796, chose to avoid such "entangling alliances" over the next two centuries until the signing of several security pacts following World War II. But even in the early nineteenth century, America's aloofness from the world was not complete, as traders, adventurers, and religious missionaries traveled far and wide. While Congress passed high tariffs to protect infant industries from foreign competition, fast Yankee clippers plied the seas in search of trade. While promising not to interfere in European affairs, American leaders called on Europeans not to meddle in the Western Hemisphere. The **Monroe Doctrine** officially established the United States as an aspiring regional power with an activist "protector" role, although its behavior was frequently more accommodative than its rhetoric might have suggested. The initial confinement of American interests and the concern of early presidents about hostile European empires were at least partly dictated by the nation's relatively limited military power.

As a dynamic new republic with the "manifest destiny" to fill a continent—interrupted momentarily by a civil war in mid-century—the United States was unlikely to cease its westward push to the Pacific coast. Few Americans wanted to build an Old World–style empire, but many wanted to find wealth and influence in places controlled by foreign powers, places as far away as China.[11] On the continent itself, Texas and California were "liberated" in the mid-nineteenth century through war against Mexico, a conflict largely provoked by Presidents Tyler and Polk. In a similar vein overseas, Spanish possessions ranging from Puerto Rico to the Philippines were garnered in a war at the turn of the century. Without a formal empire, the United States obtained dependencies, bases, and considerable prestige as a growing—if seemingly reluctant—world power.[12]

In the process of nineteenth-century expansion, U.S. policy reflected a characteristic dualism. As a fresh new state free of the taint of empire, Americans could speak of high principles, of promoting democracy abroad, of favoring revolutionaries in Latin America and the Philippines while seeking to overthrow Spanish "despots." Americans could denounce exclusive spheres of influence in Asia, which benefited the rich European powers. Yet in defending such noble causes, American leaders were also serving the interests of various domestic groups in the United States such as those wishing a share of the China trade (hence, the famous "Open Door" Notes on China in 1900). The pursuit of U.S. influence was reflected, for example, in President Theodore Roosevelt's turn-of-the-century "gunboat diplomacy" in Asia and "big stick" policy in Latin America, and his dispatch of the U.S. Navy on an around-the-world excursion to "show the flag."

The need to apply moral sugarcoating to self-interested actions has been a frequent and recurring feature of the U.S. foreign policy style. Although not unique in this, American leaders have tended to couch their actions in terms of morality more than most leaders.[13] This is different from the mere manipulation of rhetoric and propaganda so familiar in world politics and reflects a tendency to treat international relations as a morality play—the struggle of the good against the bad. While idealistic tendencies can be refreshing, they can also lead to policy confusion and charges of hypocrisy when morality loses out, as it so often does, to concrete interests.

The mix of principles and interests was especially evident in U.S. participation in World War I. The U.S. government insisted at the outset that its neutral status entitled it to freedom of the seas. Neutrality was difficult, however, as Germany and England sought to blockade each other. Pro-British sentiment in the United States increased with German attacks on American shipping, and when the United States finally entered the war, President Woodrow Wilson justified the cause with statements about a war "to end war" and to "make the world safe for democracy." He was concerned as well about Europe coming under the domination of a single empire centered in Berlin. While none of the conservative blood-related European monarchies resembled what we think of today as totalitarian despotisms, raising issues of democracy and national self-determination could help sell the war at home and distinguish the American cause from the sordid balance of power deals that characterized Europe.

At the Versailles Peace Conference following World War I, Wilson took the lead in urging the creation of the League of Nations and a new world order based on law and democratic principles. Although Wilson's foreign policy seemed to represent high ideals, a number of historians have noted that those ideals also happened to conform with many elements of American self-interest and that Wilson was at least partly motivated by a desire to expand American influence, including the promotion of freer international trade.[14]

America had grown economically and militarily powerful by the early twentieth century, but was slow to take on all the responsibilities of a great power; the myth of uniqueness persisted. In the postwar period, Americans sought a "return to normalcy," rejecting Wilson's multilateralist plea for League of Nations membership and leaving European powers to their own unsuccessful balancing act. U.S. leaders did try in the 1920s to preserve commercial order and relieve the great financial burdens on Germany. But when the Great Depression hit, Presidents Herbert Hoover and Franklin

Roosevelt turned protectionist, greatly restricting U.S. trade in a short-term effort to protect jobs. With the world's greatest trading nation withdrawing, total world trade dried up and unemployment spread, contributing to the rise of fascism and militarism in Europe and Japan.

Once again the dualism of American policy was exhibited in dealing with China and Japan during the 1930s. Japan invaded northern China in 1931, setting up a puppet state of Manchukuo. Secretary of State Stimson, concerned about China and potential threats to the Philippines, announced that the United States would not diplomatically recognize new states created by conquest. However, the nonrecognition policy, a policy without teeth, merely inflamed U.S.-Japanese relations without ousting Japan from China and without settling U.S.-Japanese differences in the Pacific. Many historians trace the road to Pearl Harbor from this 1931 decision.[15]

When in the late 1930s it again seemed that Berlin was intent on dominating Europe, this time with Adolf Hitler at the controls, President Roosevelt tried to ease a war-shy America toward a firmer commitment to England. While promising to keep America out of war, Roosevelt pressed successfully for suspension of neutrality legislation on trade and for massive aid to Britain and the Soviet Union once World War II began in Europe. With public opinion running against involvement, it was the shock of Japan's attack on Pearl Harbor in December of 1941 that finally brought the United States into the war, and showed that when pushed, Americans seemed to be more resistant than accommodative.

A generation of American leaders grew to political maturity with the "lessons" of World War II fresh in their minds. These impressions were to affect strongly the scope, alignment, and *modus operandi* of U.S. policy after 1945. Emerging from the war as the world's leading military and economic power, challenged only by the Soviet Union, the United States would never again sit by and allow "aggressors" to go unchecked. The luxury of isolationism (as we have seen in discussion of the nineteenth century, always more a myth than a reality in U.S. policy) could no longer be afforded. America became a chief architect and key member of the League of Nations' successor, the United Nations. But more fundamentally there was national consensus that the United States would have to play a permanent role in world power balancing to prevent states hostile to U.S. interests from dominating whole continents.[16]

It may have been inevitable that the two most powerful wartime allies, the United States and the Soviet Union, surviving a grueling conflict with Germany and emerging relatively intact, would turn suspicious eyes on each other in 1945 as they surveyed the postwar wreckage. From the Soviet point of view, it was necessary and legitimate for Moscow to have friendly regimes along the potential invasion routes into Russia, especially in Poland and Czechoslovakia.[17] Many Americans, on the other hand, had been struck by the memory of the **Munich Pact** of 1938, when Britain and France abandoned their Czech

The Japanese attack on Pearl Harbor, Hawaii, on December 7, 1941. In the foreground is the USS *West Virginia* **and in the background the USS** *Tennessee.*

allies and appeased Hitler's territorial demands. For Americans, it was easy to perceive any Soviet moves toward increased control in Eastern Europe or the Mediterranean as analogous to German drives in 1938. U.S. leaders interpreted civil wars and local disputes involving Communist parties as part of a global challenge spearheaded by the regime of Josef Stalin in Moscow, even though in Greece, for instance, the Russians held back from fully supporting the Communist cause, partly out of deference to prior agreements with Britain.[18]

The Cold War was ushered in in March of 1946, with Winston Churchill's "Iron Curtain" speech, in which he warned of the wall that Moscow was building around Eastern Europe.[19] This was followed by two actions in the spring of 1947—the enunciation of the **Truman Doctrine** warning the Soviets against aggression in Greece and Turkey, and the launching of the **Marshall Plan** to rebuild the war-torn economies of Western Europe. It was hoped that revived prosperity would keep Communist parties from victory at the polls in France and surrounding countries and would reconstitute markets for the vigorous U.S. economy. By the time the Soviets absorbed Czechoslovakia as a Communist satellite in 1948, U.S. diplomat George Kennan had already written his famous *Foreign Affairs* article under the pseudonym "Mr. X," urging the **containment** of communism that was to become the major theme running through American policy after World War II.[20] For the first time since the nation's early days, the United States in 1949 entered into a peacetime military alliance—the **North Atlantic Treaty Organization** (NATO)—and agreed to station troops overseas.[21] It was hoped that the U.S. policy of alliance commitments backed by American nuclear superiority would contain further Communist advances outside Eastern Europe.

Moves to demobilize the U.S. army were reversed by new challenges, such as North Korea's attempt in 1950 to reunify Korea by force. Korea, an area not previously included in descriptions of U.S. security interests, suddenly seemed crucial to the defense of the newly pro-Western Japan and hence seemed to require broadening the scope of American military commitments. U.S. leaders, viewing North Korea as a Soviet puppet, came to the defense of South Korea. Although the Truman administration did not wish to become involved in a land war against neighboring China, the Korean War brought U.S. troops to China's doorstep. Mao Tse-tung's Communist government had achieved control of the Chinese mainland only in 1949, pushing Chiang Kai-shek's Nationalist forces onto the small island of Taiwan. Communist Chinese leaders were very sensitive to potentially anti-Communist forces on their border. After repeated warnings to the Americans, Chinese troops entered the Korean War, inflicting heavy losses on U.S. forces that had approached the Yalu River while battling the North Koreans. Thus, American neutrality in the Chinese civil war gave way to defense commitments to both South Korea and Taiwan.

Other challenges confronting American leaders included a series of crises over Berlin and the future of Germany, which had been divided into eastern and western occupation zones after World War II. The Soviet Union, stung by Hitler's invasion, wanted a permanently weakened Germany, while the Western allies opted to rebuild an economically viable Germany that would not require permanent occupation. When the West went ahead with currency reform in 1948 over Soviet objections, the Soviets blockaded land and canal access to Berlin, a city 100 miles inside the Russian occupation zone (now East Germany) but within which the Allies had occupation rights. However, Stalin left air routes open, and thus Truman was able to supply West Berlin for a year by air.

In the 1950s, trouble brewed again in divided Germany as the Soviets sought unsuccessfully to discourage the United States from including West Germany in NATO. Premier Nikita Khrushchev, Stalin's successor, attempted to force the Western powers to recognize the East German state or be forced out of Berlin. During the summer of 1961, NATO nations were shocked to find the Russians and East Germans building a fortified wall in Berlin to separate East from West and stem the outflow of skilled workers fleeing to the West.

President Kennedy accepted that wall and, many feel, paved the way for the ultimate agreement on the status quo in Germany, which was to come a decade later when East and West Germany were officially recognized as sovereign states.[22]

In the 1950s the Soviet Union and the United States also began to compete for influence in the newly emerging less developed countries of Asia, Africa, and Latin America—the "Third World." Washington had great difficulty coming to grips with Third World nationalism as more and more countries achieved independence from colonial rulers. Leaders like Secretary of State John Foster Dulles during the Eisenhower administration wanted allies to resist communism. However, Third World leaders, such as Jawaharlal Nehru of India, saw colonial rule and economic backwardness as greater problems than communism. Hence, Dulles's appeals for alliance were resisted in much of the Third World. Instead, a neutralist movement developed among Third World countries representing a variety of political and economic systems.

Since the United States and the Soviet Union were both armed with vast nuclear and conventional arsenals, certain "rules" were developed to regulate their competition in the Third World. These included a tacit understanding that direct confrontation between Soviet and American forces was to be avoided. As noted earlier, the object of the competition was not to acquire territory but to gain influence over the foreign policies of Third World states, entailing at times intervention in their internal affairs to determine the makeup of their governments.

For the most part, the "battle" for the Third World—a competition still ongoing today—was not fought with direct military intervention by the Americans and the Soviets. The Soviets were to commit their *own* troops to major military action in the Third World only once—not until Afghanistan in 1979; the Soviets did, however, participate in lesser military actions, such as in Egypt's "war of attrition" against Israel along the Suez Canal in 1970, and in assisting Cuba's African interventions in the 1970s and 1980s. The Americans also had only one major direct military engagement in the Third World after 1960—the Vietnam conflict in the decade between 1962 and 1972—although U.S. forces were directly involved in several lesser interventions such as landings in Lebanon in 1958 and 1983, in the Dominican Republic in 1965, and Grenada in 1983.

In addition to direct military intervention, the two superpowers relied frequently on more subtle forms of intervention, including supplying arms to local forces, feeding propaganda, and plotting rebellions or assassinations. The United States, for example, undermined left-wing or revolutionary regimes in Iran in 1953, in Guatemala in 1954, and in Chile in 1973. The Soviets helped unseat right-wing regimes in Peru in 1968, Somalia in 1969, and Nicaragua in 1979, and opposed pro-Western factions in the Angola and Mozambique civil wars of the 1970s. The regimes that one side tried to topple, the other side generally tried to prop up. As it turned out, both the U.S. and Soviet interventionist efforts produced mixed results in terms of successes and failures.

Nothing reflected U.S. frustrations in the Third World more than the Vietnam War. John Kennedy had assumed the presidency in 1961, urging democratic reform. But Kennedy also stated that he would opt for right-wing dictatorship in preference to left-wing dictatorship along the lines of Fidel Castro's Cuba. Kennedy's advisers developed doctrines of "nation-building," which called for development of Third World economies to win peasants' loyalty to pro-Western leaders while keeping Communist insurgents at bay with U.S. Green Berets and other special counterinsurgency forces. Theories about nation-building were tested in the laboratory of Vietnam and were found wanting. Unfortunately, in the words of journalist I. F. Stone, it proved difficult to win a war in a "peasant society on the side of the landlords."[23] What was at first a modest American counterinsurgency force had become an army of 500,000 by the mid-sixties after Lyndon Johnson succeeded Kennedy. President Johnson struggled for the "hearts and minds" of the Vietnamese people; but the bombings, defoliations, and search and destroy missions of the Johnson administration, and later the Nixon administration, failed to win America's longest war.

The immediate "lessons" of Vietnam caused President Nixon and Secretary of State Kissinger to conclude that the United States could no longer police the world alone, and resulted in a somewhat different pattern of behavior through much of the 1970s. The mission of maintaining U.S. influence in distant regions remained the same, but the techniques were changed with the **Nixon Doctrine,** which stressed "self-help" by pro-American regional powers in the Third World. Washington would supply the weapons and advice to enable these powers to resist revolutionaries and preserve regional stability, especially in areas such as the Middle East where vital resources were at stake. The classic example of such a regional power was Iran under the Shah, to whom Washington sold almost unlimited military supplies. Ultimately, however, even with the most advanced weapons in the world, the Shah and his army were unable to suppress a popular revolution which swirled around a militant religious leader, the Ayatollah Khomeini.

Kissinger also sought to contain communism and Soviet influence through a basically pragmatic, less ideological approach toward the Soviet Union, for example offering Moscow trade benefits in return for Soviet restraint in the Third World. The result was a relaxation in American-Soviet tensions that came to be known as **détente.** Actually, there had been previous moments of détente in the post–World War II era, including Khrushchev's "peaceful coexistence" speech in 1956 and the aftermath of the Cuban missile crisis in 1962,[24] when the cooling of tensions had been accompanied by a series of important arms control agreements. However, American-Soviet relations had always exhibited a roller coaster pattern, with periods of détente interrupted by episodes of hostility. Kissinger hoped to establish a "permanent structure of peace" based on recognition of the fact that the Soviets had finally achieved true nuclear parity with the United States, as reflected in the Strategic Arms Limitation Agreement of 1972 (SALT I),[25] and that both sides had a vested interest in world stability. Despite Kissinger's efforts, disagreements persisted in the Middle East and elsewhere.[26]

During the Nixon administration, America's economic predominance in the global economy began to erode visibly. The Vietnam years and resulting inflation, together with higher oil prices and stiff overseas competition from Europe and Japan, took their toll on U.S. trade. Throughout the 1970s, Washington had to wrestle with its commitments to international free trade and investment at a time when exports were declining, imports increasing, and domestic industries beginning to shut down. As in the 1930s, considerable domestic political support developed for trade protectionism in the form of tariffs and other barriers against foreign imports, pressure that was to mount with each succeeding year.

Following the Kissinger era in the Nixon and Ford administrations, Jimmy Carter arrived in Washington in 1977 and attempted to revise certain central elements of U.S. foreign policy, playing down the necessity for Soviet "containment," for U.S. interventionism and support of leaders with poor human rights records, and for an expanding nuclear arms race and global arms trade.[27] Instead, President Carter initially proposed significant nuclear arms reductions, arms trade restrictions, and greater stress on conflict settlements—as in the Middle East. Perhaps his greatest achievement was the Camp David settlement which he mediated between Israel and Egypt.

The dual concerns of morality and interests, and the tensions that can exist between them, were especially evident in the Carter administration foreign policy. While raising the human rights issue to global prominence, Carter's human rights policy, like most Carter reforms, was unevenly applied and progressively abandoned, especially with the shock of events such as the Soviet invasion of Afghanistan in 1979. Human rights violations, such as those by China, South Korea, and Pakistan, were ignored in order to improve relations with those regionally influential anti-Soviet powers. The imperatives of American influence, oil supplies, and trade in the Middle East seemed to require vastly increased arms exports to Israel, Egypt, and Saudi Arabia.[28] Although continuing to show restraint in foreign interventionism, as in Zaire, Ethiopia, and El Salvador, the administration sometimes waffled on the question of what role the U.S. should play, as in the Iranian and Nicaraguan civil wars.

Carter's foreign policy posed special problems in U.S.-Soviet relations. Whereas Kissinger generally had not stressed human rights concerns, and had developed a rapport with Soviet leaders that some say improved the situation for Soviet Jews and dissidents, Carter's stress on human rights resulted in Soviet complaints about U.S. meddling in internal affairs. Détente had already begun to erode during Kissinger's tenure in office, but it crumbled completely during the Carter years and was buried during the Soviet invasion of Afghanistan. In response to the invasion, the United States reduced agricultural trade with the Soviet Union, boycotted the 1980 Olympic Games in Moscow, and with congressional support already waning, shelved a signed but unratified SALT II nuclear arms control treaty. In view of deteriorating American-Soviet relations, Carter decided in January of 1979 that it was finally time to recognize the People's Republic of China as the government of the Chinese people, even if it meant ending the thirty-year commitment to the rival Chinese regime in Taiwan.

When the Reagan administration assumed office in 1981, it sought to downplay the human rights issue and to disassociate itself from Carter initiatives. In the process it threatened to return to the policy of containment with all the rhetoric that had accompanied that policy in earlier years. The Soviets were accused of terrorism, of involvement in El Salvador and Africa, and of seeking nuclear superiority in the arms race. When Nixon's "regional policeman" concept for the Persian Gulf failed in Iran, Carter had resorted to developing U.S. conventional force readiness, including a rapid deployment force. With a multi-year, multi-billion-dollar defense budget increase, the Reagan administration followed suit, seeking to restore American military power that had been maligned since Vietnam.

President Reagan also moved toward an expanded interventionism in foreign policy, enunciating a **Reagan Doctrine** which argued for weakening and undermining Third World Soviet clients, such as Angola, Libya, Vietnam, and Nicaragua. Yet a characteristic American dualism continued to prevail. Clients where the Soviets had established firm interests and commitments, such as Syria, generally were not challenged. No direct major confrontations with the Soviets were undertaken. Military action was mounted only against militarily weak opponents, such as Grenada and Libya. Ill-fated Marine landings in Lebanon were meant somehow to renew the Camp David peace process by involving Jordan. In a search for popular anti-Communist leaders in countries of strategic importance to the United States, President Reagan even withdrew support from the pro-Western but corrupt Marcos and Duvalier regimes in the Philippines and Haiti—a tactic similar to that of the Carter administration in Latin America. A call for Strategic Arms Reduction talks (START) was substituted for SALT; yet the Reagan administration as well as the Soviet Union continued for several years to abide by most provisions of the unratified SALT II treaty. Alongside moralistic pronouncements about the Soviet "evil empire" were pragmatic decisions to renew agricultural sales to Moscow.

Throughout the postwar era, America's allies have complained about Washington's lack of consultation. While this may be a natural result of alliances among militarily unequal states, American diplomatic style, especially during the Nixon-Kissinger years as well as the Carter and Reagan administrations, reflected a special penchant for the "Lone Ranger" approach to defense matters.[29] European allies complained bitterly about arbitrary Carter decisions on new missile systems and Persian Gulf defense pledges, and about Reagan economic policies that were deemed to harm trade and build anti-Western hostility in the Third World. Americans themselves were frustrated at Europe's less moralistic and more accommodative perspective on Soviet interventionism. In the 1980s, some U.S. leaders began to stress a Pacific as opposed to an Atlantic outlook on foreign policy and called for greater European self-reliance in defense policy. Yet traditionalists still stressed the importance of NATO and Europe to American security. The Japanese and Americans had trade and strategic differences as well. While Europeans, Japanese, and Americans debated global problems and the merits of radical or reactionary regimes in such places as Libya, Iran, Angola, Nicaragua, and South Africa, international corporate executives, traders, and bankers from both sides of the Atlantic and Pacific attempted to carry on as "business as usual" with all these parties.

Soviet Foreign Policy: A Profile

We have touched upon the record of Soviet behavior in reviewing American foreign policy, as the two giants have increasingly become preoccupied with each other. Soviet leaders can look back to American participation in the Allied invasion of their country soon after the Communists seized power in the Bolshevik Revolution of 1917, following the fall of the Czar. In those days Russia's primary concern was Germany. Russians continue to worry about the prospect of a reunited and fully rearmed Germany on their border, even though the United States is the major Soviet competitor today.

Soviet foreign policy has become increasingly global in scope over the past seventy years. Following an early history of relative isolation, the Soviet Union was to claim leadership of the Communist bloc of nations and to champion Marxist struggles against Western capitalism. Yet Soviet behavior has remained essentially pragmatic despite the revolutionary tone of its oratory. Indeed, many observers have pointed out that a good deal of Soviet behavior, such as heavy military spending, reflects traditional Russian foreign policy concerns inherited from the czars. As in the American record, there has frequently been a gap between the Soviet Union's articulated ideals and practical policies. As we will see, the Soviet Union has been both accommodative and resistant during key crises.

Pragmatism was evident even in the early years of the Russian Revolution. During World War I, Soviet leaders appeased Germany, signing the Treaty of Brest Litovsk, which involved significant concessions in return for promises of peace. Revolutionary leaders, facing internal opposition and a war-ravaged economy, had to make good on their promises of peace and bread. Vladimir Lenin, the father of the Bolshevik Revolution, while hoping to inspire revolutions elsewhere, knew that accepting the high price of peace would allow his regime to consolidate control in at least the heartland of Russia and the Ukraine. He pushed forcefully when he thought he could get away with it, as in an early war against Poland, but was always ready to take one or two steps backward if necessary. Revolutionary action was put on the back burner, in much the same way that U.S. leaders frequently downplayed democracy and human rights when such concerns conflicted with more practical matters.[30] (See the box below.)

While the Soviet regime in the 1920s was preoccupied with civil war in Russia, the idea of revolution against capitalist governments nevertheless started to catch on in certain parts of the world. In a way, Moscow offered an alternative to Woodrow Wilson's advocacy of national self-determination for the European states that acquired independence from the German and Austrian empires. Wilson had little to offer leaders in other regions who wanted

---

LENIN'S VIEWS OF PRAGMATISM IN A REVOLUTIONARY FOREIGN POLICY

The importance of ideology—an organized belief system—as an element in Soviet foreign policy behavior has long been debated. Some have maintained that pragmatic interests, reflecting Russian nationalism, are more important. The evidence seems strongly to favor pragmatism, but a state that predicates its educational, cultural, and political life on doctrines enunciated by a single party is bound to have its views of the world conditioned by ideology to a degree. How, then, do class-conscious Soviet leaders, believing that capitalism oppresses the masses and alienates individuals from their collective interests, justify pragmatic cooperation with non-Socialist states? Lenin gives an indication:

> Tactics must be based on a sober and strictly objective appraisal of *all* the class forces in a particular state (and of the states that surround it, and of all states the world over) as well as of the experience of revolutionary movements. . . . To carry on a war for the overthrow of the international bourgeosie, a war which is a hundred times more difficult, protracted and complex than the most stubborn of ordinary wars between states, and to renounce in advance any change of tack, or any utilisation of a conflict of interests (even if temporary) among one's enemies, or any conciliation or compromise with possible allies (even if they are temporary, unstable, vacillating, or conditional allies)—is that not ridiculous in the extreme?*

* V. I. Lenin, *Leftwing Communism, An Infantile Disorder: A Popular Essay in Marxian Strategy and Tactics* (Moscow: Progress Publishers, 1968, first published in 1920), pp. 47 and 53. Reprinted by permission of Progress Publishers.

independence from the British and French empires. One such aspiring leader was the young Vietnamese Ho Chi Minh, whose country was refused independence by the French in 1919 at the Versailles Peace Conference. Wilson could not force his allies to dismantle their empires, so young Ho, who remained a strong Vietnamese nationalist, turned to Moscow for guidance and training. It was the beginning of a fifty-five-year struggle for the Vietnamese, and foretold the appeal that the Soviet Union was to have in some parts of the Third World.

Even though Ho was not alone in his conversion to communism in the early part of the twentieth century, Soviet leaders at the time continued to behave quite conservatively, not wanting to risk their newly established state in foreign wars and not fully trusting national liberation leaders in Asia and elsewhere. In its early days the Soviet Union was relatively isolated from world affairs. It did not take up membership originally in the League of Nations, nor did it even enjoy diplomatic recognition from many countries. This isolation eased somewhat in 1922 with the signing of the Rapallo treaty for commercial and diplomatic relations with Germany. Both Germany and Russia could play each other off against Britain and France and did so frequently during the 1930s.[31]

As we have noted, power considerations have been a primary Soviet concern, even at the expense of ideology. When Stalin succeeded Lenin in the 1920s, his primary concern was to restore Soviet industry and build the military. He justified the sacrifices that were extracted from the Russian people by articulating an ideology that emphasized the happiness of future generations at home as long as outside threats and "capitalist encirclement" could be withstood. Socialism had to be built first and protected in one country. The interests of Communist parties around the world had to bow to Russian interests as interpreted by Moscow. Ideology was tailored to fit the interests of the moment. Stalin, like Lenin, was a realist-opportunist, but with an added element of paranoia. He purged or executed thousands of political opponents (over six million by some estimates) and exiled leaders like Trotsky who favored the interests of the international Communist movement over Soviet national interests.

The limited role of ideology is perhaps best illustrated by Soviet reactions to Mao Tse-tung's attempted revolution in China during the 1930s. Seeing Mao as both an uncontrollable Communist upstart and as too weak to win, Moscow continued to recognize non-Communist Chiang Kai-shek's government. In many ways the seeds of the Sino-Soviet split were sown well before Mao assumed power in China; the split could even be traced to traditional rivalries that predated the advent of the Russian Revolution itself.[32]

In August of 1939, dedicated revolutionaries throughout the world were shocked to learn that Hitler and Stalin, Europe's archenemies, had signed a nonaggression pact. Each country had agreed not to oppose the other in war; in fact, secret understandings allowed them to share in an attack on Poland.

Disillusioned Communists in Europe and America left the Party, bewildered at such an unlikely turn of events. Stalin, interested above all in the survival of the Soviet state in a sea of hostile powers, had witnessed the weak British-French response to Hitler at Munich and concluded that if Britain and France would not protect an ally in Czechoslovakia, they could hardly be expected to fight against Nazi Germany to protect a Communist regime in Moscow. A time-saving nonaggression pact with Hitler seemed the best alternative. Confident that the Allies would still fight to save Poland and perhaps overestimating British and French firepower, Stalin assumed that Germany might at least be turned away from Poland, the doorstep to the Soviet Union,[33] while the Soviet Union consolidated territory in Poland and Finland.

For all his calculations, Stalin could not change Hitler's unlimited and unreasonable goals. In June of 1941, German troops came smashing into the Soviet Union, and none of the time or goodwill Stalin had tried to buy kept the Germans from reaching the gates of Stalingrad and Moscow. The Soviet army, relying on slogans of Russian nationalism rather than Communism and aided with military equipment from Great Britain and the United States, fought a bitter rearguard resistance. In all, an estimated twenty million Russian soldiers and civilians died in a war the Soviet government labeled the "Great Patriotic War."[34] The trauma of such losses was to have profound effects on Soviet foreign policy after the war.

On the one hand, the Russians could argue that they experienced the reality of total war far more than American citizens and knew far better the suffering and destruction it entailed. On the other hand, the experience hardened the Russians, perhaps moving them a bit further toward the resistance end of the accommodation-resistance spectrum. Determined that they would never again allow such an invasion, Soviet leaders took advantage of the Red Army's position to occupy territories immediately bordering the Soviet Union. The Western powers agreed to the general terms since it would have been extremely difficult to oust the Russians from their points of strength. Moreover, Roosevelt and others evidently believed that the Soviets were entitled to certain fruits of victory and that Japan's defeat and world peace depended on some type of U.S.-British-Soviet cooperation.[35] Only then could the newly established United Nations work to police world trouble spots and avoid a paralyzing veto from one of the great powers in the organization.

Those hopes were dashed in the early days of the Cold War. As discussed earlier, Soviet attempts to expand their influence were met by increasing Western resistance. Hindered by an inferior Soviet atomic arsenal, Stalin's successor, Nikita Khrushchev, was careful to repudiate Stalin's doctrine on the "inevitability of war" between Communist and capitalist camps and to substitute "peaceful coexistence" in its place. Khrushchev called for economic and political competition rather than military confrontation.

Through the 1950s and 1960s, Soviet leaders concentrated primarily on controlling as much of the immediate border area as possible in Europe, South

Asia, and East Asia. In what they perceived to be their own sphere of influence, particularly in Eastern Europe, the Soviets showed a willingness to act ruthlessly to maintain their influence, which included direct military intervention in East Germany in 1953, Hungary in 1956, and Czechoslovakia in 1968, when domestic political uprisings threatened to move those satellites out of the Soviet orbit. In the latter two cases, the Soviets tried to justify their behavior by claiming they were fulfilling obligations toward fellow members of the **Warsaw Pact,** an alliance formed in 1955 by the Soviets and their satellites following West Germany's entry into NATO.[36]

Only gradually did Soviet leaders become actively interested in distant Third World struggles. For example, they distrusted early postwar Arab leaders as "tools of Britain," since many Arab monarchs owed their thrones to the British. Oddly enough (in view of today's politics), the Soviet Union was one of the first states to recognize and supply arms to Israel in 1948, viewing the Jewish state as a potential British and Arab opponent. Only in the mid-fifties, with the emergence of Egyptian President Nasser's opposition to Western and particularly British influence, did Soviet leaders begin to see the usefulness of Third World leaders in the East-West conflict. Moscow frequently put aside ideology to aid such leaders, looking the other way, for example, while Nasser jailed Egyptian Communists.

In the 1960s, the United States and the Soviet Union established certain cooperation despite their rivalry. It has been said that the two became allies against "mutual nonexistence."[37] Although the Soviet Union remained behind in military power, the existence of U.S. and Soviet nuclear weapons gave pause to leaders on both sides, especially after the harrowing confrontation over Cuba in 1962.

The Cuban missile crisis was spawned partly by Khrushchev's desire to deploy offensive nuclear missiles ninety miles from U.S. shores as a counterweight to overall American strategic superiority and threats to Fidel Castro's Cuba. President Kennedy's response to the discovery of the missiles was to institute a naval blockade of Cuba to force Soviet withdrawal of the missiles. The crisis proved a disaster for Soviet foreign policy, even if it was not as great a success for the Americans as the press claimed. Confronted with U.S. naval superiority in the Caribbean, Khrushchev had to back down. Khrushchev's recklessness opened him to such ridicule inside and outside the Kremlin that, at least partly as a result, in 1964 he was quietly removed from his leadership position in favor of Leonid Brezhnev and Aleksei Kosygin, with the former emerging as the new head of the Soviet Communist Party.

The Cuban missile crisis had a major effect on American-Soviet relations. Several agreements were reached, including the establishment of a "hot line" to improve communications in future crises. At the same time, assessing their own naval and nuclear inferiority, the Soviets embarked on a crash armaments program that was to produce virtual parity with the United States in many defense areas by the mid-1970s. While U.S. military officials expressed alarm in the 1970s at the great Soviet buildup, its roots can be traced at least partly to the Cuban missile crisis.

While the U.S.-Soviet competition continued in the Third World, tensions eased somewhat in Europe during the Kissinger era of détente. Agreements were signed in the early seventies recognizing German and Polish borders that had been disputed since World War II, regularizing access to Berlin, and acknowledging the status quo in Eastern Europe and the Soviet-supported regimes there. In the so-called Helsinki Agreements, the Soviet Union also committed itself to allowing freer communication of ideas and respect for human rights, which it has always preferred to define as economic rather than political rights. The Soviet Union interpreted these agreements as a recognition of its zone of influence and security. However, NATO members came to voice increasing support for political dissidents in Eastern Europe and increasing concern about growing Soviet military power. Although Western European states built up economic interests in the East, including the Euro-Soviet natural gas pipeline and agricultural sales, East-West trade did not expand as much as the Soviets had hoped due to persistent tensions between the blocs and especially the efforts of the U.S. to restrict Moscow's access to advanced technology and trade credits.

As its military power grew, so did Soviet assertiveness in areas distant from Moscow. Soviet forces engaged in military support operations in the Middle East and Africa for the first time in the 1970s. In the 1970s and 1980s, as previously, Soviet intervention was characterized by failure as well as success, with the greatest gains coming in relatively small and weak states. (See the "balance sheet" in Table 4.4. Depending on how one defined success and failure, in terms of increased or decreased influence, other states could possibly be added as "gains" or "losses" in the 1980s.)

The Egyptian-Israeli and Ethiopian-Somalian conflicts not only exemplified increased Soviet involvement in the Third World, but also showed just how quickly alignments can change in international relations and how difficult it is for the Soviet Union or any other country to control events. The battle lines were especially muddled in the latter case, as the Israelis and Soviets—ordinarily archenemies—found themselves simultaneously supporting Ethiopia in the late 1970s against a Somalian government backed by the United States and several Arab countries (the Soviets viewing Ethiopia as a more reliable client than Somalia on the Horn of Africa and the Israelis fearing Arab control of both sides of the Red Sea). Just a few years previously, Ethiopia had been counted in the pro-U.S. column and Somalia was considered a vital Soviet base in Africa. In regard to the ongoing Middle East conflict, just two years after Soviet pilots had assisted Egyptian President Anwar Sadat in air battles along the Suez Canal, Sadat ordered Soviet advisers expelled from Egypt. He then utilized the Russians again to advise in the successful crossing of the Canal in the 1973 war and then re-expelled them while cultivating friendly relations with the United States and eventually Israel.

In 1979, 80,000 Soviet troops moved into Afghanistan, creating what

President Carter dramatically called "the greatest threat to peace since World War II." Employing helicopter gunships, widespread bombing, and harsh mobile military tactics, Soviet forces became bogged down in a "counterinsurgency" conflict with Afghan rebels that could not help but conjure up comparisons with the American experience in Vietnam. Some interpreted the invasion as a possible prelude to Soviet moves toward the Persian Gulf oil routes or warm-water ports, although Afghanistan had no such ports. Others attributed the invasion simply to the need by the Soviets to maintain dominant influence in a neighboring country where Muslim tribal forces were attempting, with outside aid from the United States, China, and Pakistan, to topple a pro-Soviet regime. For China, the Soviet occupation of Afghanistan, which grew to over 100,000 troops, was the latest of a series of grievances, including lingering border disputes and Soviet patronage of Vietnam. Dissent about the war's length, casualty rates, and effects on military morale could even be heard on the streets of Moscow as the war continued during the 1980s, leading to increased efforts at a UN-mediated settlement.

Leonid Brezhnev's death in 1982 brought to power the physically infirm Yuri Andropov, who died within two years and was succeeded by Konstantin Chernenko, another infirm leader who had an even briefer tenure of office. The subject of ridicule about their aging leadership, the Soviets attempted to project a more youthful and vigorous international image with the appointment of Mikhail Gorbachev as General Secretary of the USSR Communist Party in 1985. Soviet influence had declined in the Middle East since 1970, and President Reagan had succeeded in convincing NATO members to deploy new U.S. cruise and Pershing missiles to counter the Soviet arsenal aimed at Western Europe. Gorbachev attempted to regain the initiative by exploring the possibility of renewed diplomatic relations with Israel and a comprehensive Middle East peace conference. On the arms race issue, he offered to freeze both medium- and long-range nuclear weapons levels, halt all nuclear weapons tests, and substantially reduce conventional forces in central Europe. In response to Reagan's proposed Strategic Defense Initiative (SDI, or "Star Wars") antimissile system, Gorbachev further proposed to eliminate all nuclear weapons in stages by 1995. A war of words occurred over whether the Soviets or the Americans were being more sincere about arms control, and eventually some agreements emerged on the status of medium- and short-range nuclear weapons.

Soviet foreign policy behavior, like that of the United States, defies simple pigeonholing. Moscow has displayed a variety of behavior modes over the years, some "dovish" and some "hawkish." At times Soviet leaders have operated out of what appeared to be defensive instincts, and at other times they have seemed to act on more opportunistic impulses. Highly secretive and fearful of the outside world, the Soviet Union has been embarrassed by incidents such as the questionable downing of a Korean civilian airliner over sensitive Soviet military installations in 1984, and the failure of Soviet authorities to alert neighboring countries to radioactive fallout from the

Table 4.4

KEEPING SCORE IN THE COLD WAR: THE SOVIET BALANCE SHEET

Gains and losses for the Soviet Union between 1945 and 1986. "Gains" do not mean total Soviet domination of these countries, and "losses" do not necessarily mean total estrangement. Rather the categories represent gains or losses of diplomatic influence (in terms of "pro-Soviet" orientation).

	Mongolia	Albania Bulgaria East Germany Poland Romania Yugoslavia	North Korea	Hungary
Gains		1945	1946	1947
Losses				
Gains	1952	1953	1954	1955
Losses				
			Yemen (Sana)	Algeria
	Ghana Mali			
Gains	1960	1961	1962	1963
Losses	China	Albania Guinea	Indonesia	Iraq
	Congo Iraq	Cuba Somalia Sudan		Guinea India
Gains	1968	1969	1970	1971
Losses	Mali	North Korea Yemen (Sana)		Sudan
		Ethiopia	Afghanistan Yemen (Aden)	Cambodia
Gains	1976	1977	1978	1979
Losses		Guinea India Somalia	Iraq	

Source: Adapted from *The Defense Monitor,* XV, no. 5 (1986), p. 7, with the permission of the Center for Defense Information, Washington, D.C.

Table 4.4 (Continued)

KEEPING SCORE IN THE COLD WAR: THE SOVIET BALANCE SHEET

Gains and losses for the Soviet Union between 1945 and 1986. "Gains" do not mean total Soviet domination of these countries, and "losses" do not necessarily mean total estrangement. Rather the categories represent gains or losses of diplomatic influence (in terms of "pro-Soviet" orientation).

Czechoslovakia	China		
1948	1949	1950	1951
Yugoslavia			
Syria		Indonesia Iraq	Guinea
1956	1957	1958	1959
		Syria	
	Vietnam	Syria	Egypt
1964	1965	1966	1967
	Algeria	Ghana	
			Angola Laos Mozambique
Bangladesh		Libya	
1972	1973	1974	1975
Egypt			Bangladesh
1980	1981–1986		
Congo			

leaking Chernobyl nuclear power plant in the Ukraine in 1986 (causing widespread contamination in both Western and Eastern Europe). While they have backed wars of "national liberation," they also have cooperated with "reactionary" regimes when they have deemed it necessary. With far-flung interests to protect and an increasing need to modernize and gain advanced technologies, the Soviet Union is hardly a radical state blindly favoring world revolution.

The Soviets pay close attention to what they refer to as the "correlation of forces," gauging carefully the forces likely to prevail in a given dispute or confrontation. For example, in 1983, Soviet leaders and their Syrian clients did not vigorously oppose Israel's occupation of Lebanon, for fear of escalation and a widening war.[38] Revolutions are supported where they might weaken the West, but are resisted or suppressed where they might threaten Moscow's influence, open a region to chaos, or result in a direct military confrontation with the U.S. Despite the global scope of Soviet foreign policy, Soviet leaders, like their American counterparts, continue to reserve their firmest security commitments for "core" European allies rather than for Third World states.

Chinese Foreign Policy: A Profile

We have seen that certain American moves since World War II have been conditioned by Soviet moves, and that the Soviets have responded in complex ways to the Americans. At the same time, both have cast nervous glances at China, alternating between anxiety over the prospect of having the Oriental behemoth as an enemy and euphoria over the prospect of having it as an ally. Both have sought to use China in their own favor but have found the Chinese to be independently minded and not easily exploitable.

As with the United States and the Soviet Union, a dualism is apparent in Chinese foreign policy. China is both an ancient society and a new state.[39] The Chinese people can point to a civilization that has flourished and has absorbed invaders and conquerors for thousands of years (see Figure 4.1). Outsiders were, and in some ways still are, considered barbarians; this was natural for a society that in its early days encountered no dynamic civilizations and considered itself the "Middle Kingdom" around which the rest of the world was organized.

It has always been difficult to identify the boundaries separating China's foreign and domestic policies. Traditionally, the Chinese considered themselves more a civilization than a state or nation as known in the West. The Empire included surrounding peoples from whom the Emperor, the Son of Heaven, was prepared to receive tribute and commerce. The tributary states, which for the Chinese included even England and Holland at one time, were

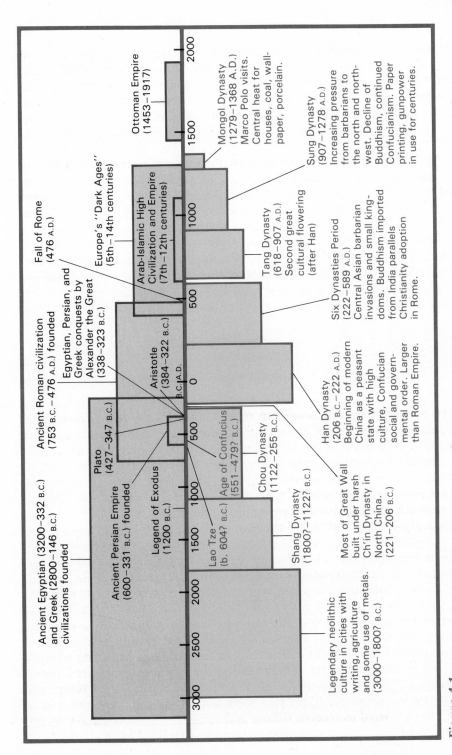

Figure 4.1
HISTORICAL DEVELOPMENT OF CHINESE AND WESTERN CIVILIZATIONS

expected to conform to civilized Chinese behavior and to accept the harmony and hierarchies of Chinese life. China dominated nearby lands, but the Koreans, the Indochinese in Southeast Asia, the Japanese, and others generally ruled themselves within the accepted standards. On the whole, the self-contained Chinese civilization had little need for and was expected to have little to do with foreigners; it was isolated and yet sublimely confident.

When Westerners arrived, therefore, the Chinese were slow to react to a potential threat, since the barbarians were expected to conform and adjust to Chinese civilization.[40] Although Marco Polo had shown great deference to the Khan during his visit in 1275 and was dutifully impressed by the use of paper money and the burning of coal, later generations of Westerners were not to be intimidated. By the mid-nineteenth century, the British had already introduced the opium trade and in the Opium War forced the Chinese to continue opium imports. Other major powers, including Russia and the United States, joined in efforts to carve out exclusive trade concessions and territory. Frustration over foreign domination led to the Boxer Rebellion in 1900, which saw the storming of foreign embassies in Peking by Chinese militants. The Boxers were crushed by the combined forces of the "civilized" nations of the West and Japan. However, the Boxer Rebellion shook China out of its complacent Middle Kingdom mentality and forced the Chinese to recognize the need for some change.

Following the democratic-minded Nationalist Revolution led by Sun Yat-sen in 1911, marking the end of the Manchu Empire, the fight for the succession to Chinese power raged between one of Sun's Nationalist disciples, Chiang Kai-shek, and a young Communist named Mao Tse-tung. It resembled the feuds that had been fought among warlords in ancient Chinese history, except that there was need for some degree of accommodation between the two factions in order to deal collectively with the Japanese invasion. Once the long struggle against the Japanese ended with the termination of World War II, Chiang and Mao concentrated on the unfinished business of determining who would govern the Chinese people. The United States attempted a mediating role in the civil war initially but bowed out after failing to achieve peace. Mao ultimately achieved victory in 1949, Chiang fled to the island of Taiwan with the remnants of his army, and the Truman administration was saddled with blame for the "loss of China" even though it was never Truman's to lose.

Mao faced an enormous rebuilding task in a country that remained a largely rural peasant society. A history of foreign exploitation also made the Beijing leadership highly suspicious of and resistant to foreign powers. China's identification with the Third World was partly a function of its underdeveloped status and partly a function of its need for ideological justification in its opposition to potentially harmful world powers. In signing a security treaty with the Soviets in 1950, Beijing entered into an uneasy relationship with Moscow.

The Chinese began to press long-standing grievances over "unfair and unequal" nineteenth-century treaties. While reluctant to risk military action far from their territory, Chinese leaders were quite willing to use force closer to home, to keep foreign powers away from the borders, and to incorporate parts of "ancient China." Tibet was invaded and subdued in the 1950s; China risked a war in Korea, despite American atomic weapons, in order to push U.S. forces away from the Chinese border; China attacked and routed Indian forces to quiet Indian border claims along the Himalayan frontier; and Beijing harassed the Taiwan government when it appeared that Chiang Kai-shek might launch an attack against the mainland, and reminded the United States that Taiwan was part of a single Chinese state. (Indeed, the Communists and Nationalists agreed that Taiwan, Tibet, and the border areas were rightfully part of "one China"; they simply disagreed on who should rule China.)

When it came to promoting revolution and pursuing ambitions in the far reaches of the Third World, the Chinese leadership exercised caution, relying mostly on rhetoric and moral support. Even when the Chinese developed nuclear weapons in the 1960s, they were not in a very good position to help Third World countries materially, either in military or economic terms. Although they undertook certain projects, such as building railroads in Tanzania and other black African states, the Chinese Communists, like their predecessors, remained reluctant to involve China too deeply in world affairs. During the Vietnam War the Chinese condemned U.S. imperialism and called for peasant uprisings against capitalist societies; but Mao's regime became too preoccupied in the late sixties and early seventies with its own internal upheaval—the so-called **Cultural Revolution**—to cultivate revolutions elsewhere.

During the Cultural Revolution, Mao attempted to instill revolutionary fervor in a generation of Chinese that had not experienced the "Long March" that had enabled the Communists to survive the civil war in the thirties. The Red Book containing Chairman Mao's sayings became the bible of Chinese society—a dramatically transformed society in which schools and universities were closed for several years, people were removed from positions of authority and forced, often by groups of zealous youths, to repent their past "sins," and highly trained scientists and professionals were made to work among peasants on farms and in villages. This severely damaged the Chinese economy. As for its international relations in this period, China virtually withdrew from world affairs—retaining only *one* ambassador in a single foreign country (Egypt). This episode in Chinese history called to mind an order in the ancient Chinese Book of Rites that "the officials of the Empire shall have no intercourse with foreigners."[41]

The Cultural Revolution had been at least partly motivated by Mao's desire to distinguish the Chinese model of communism from the Soviet model, which had resulted in a rather rigid government with a central bureaucracy, inflexible planning, and privileged party and professional elites. Mao argued that a classless society along Marxist lines could never be achieved through a Soviet-style system. He also observed that the Soviets had become "bourgeois" themselves and had acted in no less an imperialistic fashion than the United States in the Third World, thereby relinquishing their leadership role in the international Communist movement.

On the surface the Sino-Soviet split became evident only in the mid-sixties and seemed to be only a battle over ideological purity—but in fact the split could be traced to long-standing concerns of security and prestige. Mao's deep-seated hostility toward the Soviets was based on historical rivalries over territorial and other issues, together with Stalin's initial indifference to the Chinese Communist revolution. The Soviets likewise harbored deep-seated animosity toward the Chinese—the potential "yellow peril" represented by almost a billion "peasants" poised along their 4500-mile border.[42] The Soviets had denied Chinese access to nuclear secrets in 1958, a harbinger of the withdrawal of Soviet technicians and equipment in 1961. Mao countered with blistering criticism of the Soviet backdown in the Cuban missile crisis. The 1950 security treaty became a dead letter and the Sino-Soviet relationship deteriorated rapidly, despite periodic attempts at reconciliation.

China's successful nuclear explosions in 1964, together with the unpredictable, almost self-destructive tendencies of the Cultural Revolution and growing friction over border questions, alarmed the Soviet leadership in the late 1960s. Moscow responded by building up its forces along the Chinese border, so much so that rumors circulated about planned Soviet attacks on the nuclear test grounds in Xinjiang Province. The Chinese condemned the **Brezhnev Doctrine,** articulated by the Soviet leader in the wake of the Russian invasion of Czechoslovakia in 1968. According to Brezhnev, Communist countries could intervene in those states where "capitalist circles" threatened to topple an established Communist government. This was little more than a restatement of similar rationalizations Khrushchev had directed toward Eastern Europe when sending tanks to Hungary in 1956. Nevertheless, Beijing enlarged its border forces, and what had been mainly a political propaganda fight became a military confrontation.

In 1969, two clashes occurred along the Ussuri River, scene of Sino-Russian skirmishes even at the turn of the century. In some instances Mao's forces initiated the fighting and taunted the Russians, trying to show they could defend their country. Meanwhile, China's overall foreign policy began to shift. Previously, Beijing had condemned the schemes for world domination by the *two* "imperialist" powers operating out of Washington and Moscow, citing such joint American-Soviet proposals as the nuclear nonproliferation treaty as being self-serving. Increasingly in the 1970s, however, Chinese leaders concentrated their criticism on the Soviet threat.

It seemed imperative that Beijing respond to American initiatives and improve relations with Russia's opponents in Washington. With the Vietnam War fading from memory, and after the deaths of Chou En-lai in 1975 and

Mao in 1976, the new Communist Chinese regime headed by Deng Xiaoping stepped up its wooing of Washington, looking not only for military support against the Soviets but advanced technology for modernizing a Chinese economy that had been set back at least a decade by the Cultural Revolution. The Chinese Communists showed they could be as pragmatic as their Soviet counterparts.

Under Deng, the Chinese pursued "four modernizations" in agriculture, industry, science, and defense. Putting aside traditional aversion to Western influences, Beijing actively sought to apply Western technological innovations to Chinese society through expanded trade. The prospect of breaking into a market of almost a billion people made American business interests highly supportive of the opening to China; the manufacturers of farm machinery and computers were especially intrigued by the size of the market, not to mention the makers of soft drinks and deodorants. The only possible hitch was the questionable ability of the Chinese to finance their purchases. In a whirlwind public relations tour of the United States, between munching hot dogs and watching Wild West rodeos, Deng called Russia the greatest threat to world peace and predicted a Soviet-instigated World War III. China also finally came out of the UN "closet" in July of 1978, casting a vote in the UN Security Council in favor of a Western-sponsored proposal for a peacekeeping force in Namibia (South-West Africa); Beijing had been recorded as "not participating" ever since it assumed UN membership in place of Taiwan in 1971. China began to take a more active role both inside and outside the UN. Chinese forces briefly invaded Soviet-backed Vietnam in 1979, attempting unsuccessfully to end the latter's occupation of Kampuchea and to test the Chinese People's Liberation Army under fire. Some of China's neighbors, such as Thailand and Singapore, which had feared Chinese revolutionary expansionism in the 1960s, now turned a more suspicious eye on the Soviet Union. Other neighbors, such as the Indonesian and Malaysian governments, still feared Chinese dominance through links with sizable overseas Chinese communities living throughout Southeast Asia. Concern about Soviet ambitions also led China to become one of NATO's staunchest nonmember supporters.

Most observers watched the Sino-American rapprochement—symbolized by the U.S. diplomatic recognition of the PRC in 1979—with cautious eyes, mindful of how quickly it could dissipate if the Chinese reverted to previous form under a less pragmatic regime that might succeed the octogenarian Deng, or if stirrings of support for Taiwan materialized in the administration of Ronald Reagan or his successor. China's opening to the West did not produce great immediate dividends in the 1980s; some in Beijing lamented increased corruption and crime and the problem of distributing goods through overburdened Chinese ports. There were grumblings about the limits of Western reliability and willingness to transfer the latest technologies. Western traders also were somewhat disillusioned by Chinese tendencies to purchase a few items and then try to manufacture copies themselves. China was able, however, to agree with Britain about the eventual return of Hong Kong to Chinese rule—with a degree of economic autonomy—at the turn of the century, and to expand trade and joint business ventures with Japan and other capitalist states. Although offering increased sales of modern military equipment to Beijing, many Western countries still held back from too cozy a strategic partnership for fear of overly alarming Moscow.

While the United States and the Soviet Union qualify for superpower status on the basis of their huge military arsenals and worldwide interests, China remains a marginal world power, beset by a largely preindustrial domestic economy, capital and foreign currency shortages, and an underequipped military establishment. Yet China represents at the very least a formidable regional power in Asia, and continues to maintain involvement in other regions as well, for instance as one of the primary suppliers of arms to Iran during the Iran-Iraq war of the 1980s.[43] Although China's nuclear forces remain dwarfed by those of the United States and the Soviet Union, they constitute a growing capability to strike at opponents even at considerable distances. China continues to claim the singular distinction of speaking for more than one-fifth of humanity.

Indian Foreign Policy: A Profile

Once called the "jewel in the crown" of the British Empire, the vast Indian subcontinent remains of major strategic interest to the United States, the Soviet Union, and China, as well as to smaller states of the region. When British colonial rule ended in 1947, the subcontinent was divided along religious lines into independent Indian and Pakistani states, the former mainly Hindu and the latter mainly Muslim. The bloody religious and ethnic conflict that attended the creation of these two states presaged subsequent outbreaks of violence and discord that were to occur within and between India and Pakistan throughout the postwar period. The assassination of Prime Minister Indira Gandhi in 1984 by Sikh separatists in the Punjab was yet another example of intense religious conflict in the area. Yet, paradoxically, India is the center of a vigorous nonviolence movement, based mainly on Hindu and Buddhist precepts. Thus, in Indian foreign policy behavior, as in the three previous case studies, we can discern a tension between word and deed, between principles and practice.

Such tensions extend far back into the ancient history of Indian civilization, a history nearly as old as China's. India is named for the civilization that flourished more than 4000 years ago along the banks of the Indus River; today the three major rivers of the Himalayan basin—the Indus, the Ganges, and the Brahmaputra—form the lifeblood of three separate states: India, Pakistan, and Bangladesh (formed out of the eastern part of Pakistan by an Indian-

Standing around Mrs. Indira Gandhi's funeral pyre are her family (from left to right): Rahul Gandhi, Prime Minister Rajiv Gandhi's son; Rajiv Gandhi, Prime Minister of India, his Italian wife Sonia, and their daughter, Priyanka.

supported civil war in 1971). From the ancient Indian civilizations came remarkable culture and art, but also somewhat conflicting political philosophies related to foreign affairs.

India historically has been buffeted by foreign influences, since the subcontinent was the object of trade expeditions and the scene of frequent waves of invasion by people either fleeing other conquerors or engaged in their own conquests: the Aryans (from southern Russia, the forerunners of Indo-European language groups) around 1500 B.C.; the Persians in 500 B.C.; the Greeks, led by Alexander the Great, in 326 B.C. (which led Indians to form their own unified northern empire under the Mauryan Dynasty); further Persian and central Asian invasions during the Mauryan fragmentation until A.D. 320; Arabs, bringing the Islamic faith in the eighth century (which resulted in Muslim ruling dynasties later); twelfth-century Turkish-Afghan tribes; the fierce Mongols of the fourteenth century; Timur and Lame's (Tamerlane's) central Asian armies in 1398; Western European powers led by Portugal from 1498 to the eighteenth century; and the Islamic Mughal invaders who consolidated power in India in 1556, finally to lose it to the British. In the process, India experienced harsh and strong imperial leaders and a complex mixture of ethnic, religious, and social elements.[44]

There is a contradiction in Indian tradition between "realist" views of the type enunciated by the fourth century B.C. Mauryan adviser Kautilya, who said that states should seek to expand power and territory, and "idealist" doctrines of the type enunciated by the third century B.C. Mauryan emperor Ashoka, who said that states should refrain from violence and war. Following his own rather ruthless consolidation of power, Ashoka went on to advocate an enlightened policy of peace and nonviolence. Similarly, in the twentieth century, Indian leaders Mohandas Gandhi and Jawaharlal Nehru found the time ripe for nonviolent resistance to British rule. (On Gandhi and nonviolence, see the box on page 139.) Nehru, India's first Prime Minister, wove nonviolence into Indian doctrine, becoming a strong advocate of peaceful settlement of international disputes, such as those in Korea and Indochina in the 1950s. However, utilizing Kautilyan approaches on matters closer to home, his government also fought militarily against Pakistan and later China and Portugal to consolidate the new Indian state. The concept of power itself in Indian usage can entail both military and nonmilitary, forceful and yet more subtle psychological forms of dominance, manipulation, and patronage.

India's military interventionism, like China's, has been confined mainly to its immediate geographical area. India has dominated the foreign policies of small neighboring dependencies such as Bhutan, Sikkim, and Nepal, even intervening militarily at times, and has campaigned for the rights of and attempted to mediate the disputes of Indian ethnic minorities in Sri Lanka (formerly Ceylon). Indian forces ousted the Portuguese from their colonial outpost in Goa in 1961, and have fought three wars against Pakistan, the first two (1947 and 1965) mainly for control of the still divided territory of Jammu and Kashmir, and the third, in 1971, between West and East Pakistan, which led to the formation of Bangladesh. China's invasions of Tibet in 1950 and 1959 and of the disputed northeastern Indian frontier in 1962 created further tensions between India's avowed commitment to pacific settlement of conflicts and its felt need to maintain military strength. A major Indian military buildup resulted, including development of the capability to produce and deliver nuclear weapons. India's military buildup, noticed by Pakistan and China, fueled a South Asian arms race which still continues (with Pakistan rumored to have a crash nuclear program of its own).

Indian philosophy, more than Western philosophy, allows for inconsistencies such as those between violence and nonviolence in politics. Indians tend to doubt universal solutions to every human problem. Therefore, they are not surprised by the contradictory ideologies, intergroup conflict, or shifting alignments so familiar in international politics. In fact, Indian leaders have pioneered the concept of nonalignment in this century, which has been called a strategy of "selective and plural, rather than permanent bloc agreement."[45]

THE GANDHIAN VIEW OF NONVIOLENCE
IN INTERNATIONAL RELATIONS

Gandhi offered the following views on nonviolence in international affairs:

> It is open to the great powers to take . . . up [nonviolence] any day and cover themselves with glory and earn the eternal gratitude of posterity. If they or any of them could shed the fear of destruction, if they disarmed themselves, they will automatically help the rest to regain their sanity. But then these great powers have to give up imperialistic ambitions and exploitation of the so-called uncivilized or semi-civilized nations of the earth and revise their mode of life. It means a complete revolution. Great nations can hardly be expected in the ordinary course to move spontaneously in a direction the reverse of the one they have followed, and, according to their notion of value, from victory to victory. But miracles have happened before and may happen even in this very prosaic age. Who can dare limit God's power of undoing wrong? One thing is certain. If the mad race for armaments continues, it is bound to result in a slaughter such as has never occurred in history. If there is a victor left the very victory will be a living death for the nation that emerges victorious. There is no escape from the impending doom save through a bold unconditional acceptance of the non-violent method with all its glorious implications.

—M. Gandhi, "Harijan," November 12, 1938 (seven years before the explosion of the first atomic bomb); cited in *The Collected Works of Mahatma Gandhi*, vol. 68 (New Delhi: Government of India, 1977), p. 94.

Yet Gandhi, as an Indian nationalist, also recognized the following realities of human nature:

—Modern states are based on force, and cannot necessarily non-violently resist internal disorders and external aggression;
—States have the right to wage defensive as well as just wars;
—Military training and service are duties for citizens of independent states;
—Those who are disloyal to their states can be shot, since disloyalty is a grave crime.

—M. Gandhi, *Delhi Diary* (Ahmedabad: Navajivan, 1948), pp. 25, 37, 259.

The scope of Indian foreign policy since independence has broadened through membership in the Commonwealth, a consultative group of former British colonies, and involvement in the nonaligned movement, formed in 1955 as a diplomatic counterweight to the Western and Eastern blocs. Nonaligned states see themselves as not taking permanent sides in international disputes; unlike more traditional and retiring neutrals, such as Switzerland and Sweden, they are inclined to speak out strongly on issues of concern to the Third World and to align themselves temporarily with various powers if necessary to achieve goals of self-determination, security, or economic development. This can include playing one bloc off against another in order to increase influence and the amount of aid received. The nonaligned movement became fragmented and lost momentum with the death of early pioneers such as Nehru, but still constitutes the basic stance of most Third World states.

The politics of the Indian subcontinent illustrate the way superpower global concerns mix with priorities of regional powers. The major powers brought their Cold War competition to South Asia in the 1950s, particularly with U.S. and British alliance offers, India resisted, but archrival Pakistan signed on as a Western ally, joining both the Southeast Asian Treaty Organization (SEATO) and the Central Treaty Organization (CENTO), thereby posing potential conflicts of interest between India and the West. Yet Pakistan soon learned the limits of U.S. commitments, which were designed to contain communism, not India.

China's 1962 Himalayan attack affected India's pattern of shifting alignment in the 1960s by bringing about a close relationship with the United States during the Kennedy years. India, the world's largest parliamentary democracy, was portrayed by Washington as an alternative model of Third World development to compete with Mao's brand of radicalism. Despite significant foreign aid, however, American-Indian relations soured later in the decade because of the further shocks of the 1965 Indian-Pakistani war and, to an extent, the Vietnam War. When India and Pakistan went to war, both the United States and Britain (also a SEATO and CENTO member) suffered conflicting loyalties, and ultimately cut off the supply of weapons and spare parts to the combatants in 1965. This brought the fighting to an inconclusive halt, but embittered both India and Pakistan, the former turning increasingly thereafter to the Soviet Union, and the latter to China, for military assistance.

When Indian-Pakistani warfare again erupted in late 1971 over Bangladesh, the Soviet Union backed New Delhi's efforts to foster Bangladeshi independence. Soviet support of attacks on Pakistan, a U.S. ally in SEATO, infuriated American leaders during the era of U.S.-Soviet détente. American aid to India was suspended and U.S. warships were dispatched near the Bay of Bengal, probably as a signal of displeasure to Moscow and the assertive Indian leader Indira Gandhi (Nehru's daughter, but no relation to the "Mahatma"). Just prior to the war, Mrs. Gandhi had signed a twenty-year Pact of Friendship with the Soviet Union that included a mutual nonaggression pledge and a promise by each to consult the other in the event either were under attack by a third party. The Nixon administration viewed the pact with alarm, even though it was likely aimed at China. Having tried to reassure Washington of India's nonhostile intentions, Mrs. Gandhi deeply resented the American naval intrusion.[46]

A complicated chess match has resulted in South Asia, with India and the Soviet Union aligned against a Chinese-Pakistani axis, and the United States increasingly involved on the latter side since the Soviet intervention in Afghanistan. While generally supporting Soviet initiatives, Mrs. Gandhi, and her son Rajiv, who succeeded to power following her assassination in 1984, also felt some misgivings about increased superpower involvements near the subcontinent. India has tried to foster a negotiated settlement in Afghanistan, including nonintervention provisions on all sides, the establishment of an Asian security system, and the formation of a South Asian Association for Regional Cooperation to facilitate scientific, cultural, and other exchanges. While India generally has not minded having its chief regional rival, Pakistan, distracted by the Afghan fighting—Pakistan has been partially drawn into the conflict in support of fellow Muslim Afghan rebels—superpower confrontations and chaos near Indian borders have given New Delhi pause. The dangers of a spiraling regional arms race also have led to occasional Indian-Pakistani consultations about agreements for peaceful coexistence.

India and Pakistan both have sought to interest the major powers in providing aid and supporting their regional struggles. The shift in U.S.-Chinese-Soviet relations after Vietnam gave both India and Pakistan new options. India and the Soviet Union gravitated together, as New Delhi became Moscow's most strategically important Third World "client," while Pakistan accepted vastly increased American military aid. However, none of the Asian regional powers can count on unconditional superpower backing, and neither super-power can expect an unconditional welcome to the subcontinent from the regional powers.

India retains ambitions for regional leadership, based on the size and technical skills of her population, which is said to include the largest number of trained scientists in the Third World.[47] New Delhi is determined to exercise more influence in the Indian Ocean area and to become more self-reliant in the field of high technology. Yet, always a land of contrasts, India is beset by internal problems; the grinding poverty of her rural villages and urban slums and the recurrent communal warfare among her ethnic and religious groups (for example, between Hindus and Sikhs) slow the pace of her development and restrict her foreign policy influence.

Conclusion

China, the Soviet Union, and the United States have each journeyed through periods of relative isolation, regional preoccupation, and globalism; of alliance, neutrality between warring sides, of foreign war and intervention; and of civil war and revolutionary upheaval. In contrast, India has refrained from alliance membership through its relatively short history as an independent nation-

Table 4.5
FOREIGN POLICY PROFILES

Country	Alignment	Scope	*Modus Operandi*
United States	Neutrality between 1800 and 1945, with exception of U.S. involvement in World Wars I and II. Alliance network after 1945 as Western bloc leader.	Mainly regional preoccupation in nineteenth century. Scope expanded throughout nineteenth and twentieth centuries and became global by 1945.	Mainly bilateralist, though willing to use multilateral diplomacy and institutions when serving U.S. purposes. Active regional intervener in nineteenth and early twentieth centuries and global intervener after 1945.
Soviet Union	Shifting informal alignments with major powers, but no alliances until 1939 and World War II. East bloc alliance leader after World War II.	Mainly Eurasian regional from 1917 to 1955. Third World competitive and increasingly global after 1955, mainly on political-military, rather than economic issues.	Mainly bilateralist, though increasingly willing to use multilateral organizations as Western dominance in them decreases. Regionally interventionist in Eurasia, and increasingly in Middle East, with use of clients for intervention at greater distances, especially since 1970.
People's Republic of China	After 1949, alliance with USSR. Alliance lapsed, with move toward U.S. and NATO in 1970s.	Mainly Asian regional; increasing Third World contacts after 1955, though with lapse during Cultural Revolution. Increasing contact with North America, Japan, and Western Europe after 1972.	Almost exclusively bilateralist, until late 1970s. Regionally interventionist in Asia. Active aspirant for Third World leadership and leadership of world communism.
India	Member of British Commonwealth, but committed to neutralism. Informal alignment with USSR since 1971, but no alliance.	Mainly Asian regional, but with global concerns related to anticolonialism and economic development.	Multilateralist, particularly on issues outside South Asia. Regionally interventionist in South Asia. Active aspirant for Third World, and particularly Indian Ocean, leadership.

state and has primarily confined itself to pursuing regional interests, although it has also experienced severe civil violence, foreign war, and military intervention. In their foreign relations, they have employed varying and sometimes similar tactics: trade restrictions as well as trade concessions; diplomatic nonrecognition and recognition; Olympic boycotts and table-tennis competitions; covert intelligence and propaganda activities along with cultural exchanges; and the threatened or actual use of armed force along with ringing support for the peaceful settlement of disputes. In Table 4.5 we summarize the main aspects of the foreign policy behavior of the four countries.

In the space of a single chapter we have tried to describe the foreign policy record of four countries. Our synopses, of course, cannot possibly do complete justice to the subject. Although our analysis might suggest that nation-states are driven by fairly simple motives, a closer look at the *determinants* of foreign policy behavior in the next chapter will indicate otherwise. We have seen some of the things nation-states do. We now turn to a fuller consideration of *why* they do them.

SUMMARY

1. Foreign policy is a set of priorities and guides for action in certain circumstances which underlies a country's behavior toward other states, and includes both the basic goals a national government seeks to pursue in the international arena and the instruments used to achieve these goals.

2. Foreign policy behavior can generally be classified along three dimensions: (a) alignment, (b) scope, and (c) *modus operandi.* Countries have different alignment tendencies, with some choosing to ally with other countries and others remaining neutral.

3. Major powers have historically defined the scope of their interests in global terms, whereas most other countries are essentially regional actors, and a few even isolationist.

4. Countries also demonstrate a characteristic *modus operandi.* Some countries tend to operate multilaterally, whereas others use primarily bilateral approaches. Similarly, some states are more active and willing to use force than others in world affairs.

5. Like most countries, the United States, the Soviet Union, China, and India demonstrate significant disparities between their officially proclaimed principles and their actual behavior. These countries have also gone through significant changes or fluctuations in alignment, scope, and methods of operation and have utilized a variety of political, economic, and military tools of foreign policy.

6. The United States in its early history maintained a foreign policy that was neutral in terms of alignment behavior and mainly regional in scope. By the turn of the twentieth century, however, the United States had become a world power with

global interests. A recurring feature of U.S. foreign policy has been the need to find moral justification for self-interested actions.

7. The containment of communism became a major theme in American foreign policy after World War II, with the United States organizing a global alliance network against the Soviet Union. Relations between the two countries have alternated between periods of détente and episodes of hostility. Both countries have actively intervened in the internal affairs of Third World countries, but they have avoided direct military confrontation with each other.

8. Following an early history of relative isolation, Soviet foreign policy has become increasingly global in scope. Like the United States, the Soviet Union has frequently shown a gap between its rhetoric and its practical policies; it has been both accommodative and resistant during key crises. Power considerations have been a primary concern even at the expense of ideology.

9. Throughout much of its early history, the self-contained Chinese civilization had little to do with foreigners, remaining relatively isolated. Under Mao Tse-tung, China was expansionist at the regional level and challenged the Soviet Union for leadership of the world Communist movement. The post-1949 alliance between Communist China and Communist Russia was uneasy. China's overall foreign policy began to shift in the 1970s, as Chinese leaders began to criticize the Soviet threat and to improve relations with the United States. China and India have also experienced tensions, primarily due to their competition for regional dominance as well as China's links to Pakistan.

10. India's ancient foreign policy doctrines have given the young Indian state room for contradiction between neutralism and shifting alignments. Indian subcontinent politics have involved the superpowers in regional disputes and have also exposed regional actors to dangers of superpower confrontation. On a broader plane, India, like China, has been a major voice in the Third World.

SUGGESTIONS FOR FURTHER READING AND STUDY

In addition to the sources on U.S., Soviet, Chinese, and Indian foreign policy cited in the notes for this chapter, those interested in profiling a country's foreign policy can make use of the following types of information sources: (1) major national and international newspapers and news periodicals, such as the *Jerusalem Post*, *Times* (London), *Current Digest of the Soviet Press*, *Peking Review*, *Times of India*, *Wall Street Journal*, *Manchester Guardian Weekly*, *Le Monde*, *Christian Science Monitor*, and *German Tribune*; (2) regional journals, such as *African Affairs*, *Journal of Modern African Studies*, *Africa Today*, *Africa Report*, *Asian Survey*, *Asian Studies*, *Journal of Asian Studies*, *Journal of Latin American Studies*, *Latin American Research Review*, *Middle East Economic Digest*, and *Middle East Monitor*; (3) chronologies and news compilations, such as *Facts on File*, *Deadline Data on World Affairs*, *Keesing's Contemporary Archives*, and *New York Times Index*; (4) statistical abstracts and yearbooks, such as the *Yearbook of World Affairs*, *Europa Yearbook*, *Whitaker's Almanack*, and *Statesman's Yearbook*; and (5) scholarly indexes such as the *International Political Science Abstracts*.

In addition, good comparative studies of foreign policy can be found in Charles W. Kegley and Patrick McGowan, eds., *Foreign Policy: USA/USSR* (Beverly Hills: Sage International Yearbook of Foreign Policy Studies, vol. 7, 1982); Dan Caldwell, ed., *Soviet International Behavior and U.S. Policy Options* (Lexington, Mass.: Lexington Books, 1985); Raymond Garthoff, *Détente and Confrontation: American and Soviet Relations from Nixon to Reagan* (Washington, D.C.: Brookings, 1985); Roy C. Macridis, ed., *Foreign Policy in World Politics,* 6th ed. (Englewood Cliffs, N.J.: Prentice-Hall, 1985); Wolfram F. Hanrieder and Graeme P. Auton, *The Foreign Policies of West Germany, France, and Britain* (Englewood Cliffs, N.J.: Prentice-Hall, 1980); Christopher Clapham, ed., *Foreign Policy Making in Developing States* (London: Saxon House, 1977); Robert A. Mortimer, *The Third World Coalition in International Politics,* 2nd ed. (Boulder, Colo.: Westview Press, 1984); Mohammed Ayoob, ed., *Conflict and Intervention in the Third World* (New York: St. Martin's Press, 1980); J. J. Stremlau, *The Foreign Policy Priorities of Third World States* (Boulder, Colo.: Westview Press, 1982); Carsten Holbraad, *Middle Powers and International Politics* (New York: St. Martin's Press, 1984), and *Superpowers and International Conflict* (New York: Macmillan, 1979); and Marshall D. Shulman, ed., *East-West Tensions in the Third World* (New York: Norton, 1986).

CHAPTER

5

Explaining Foreign Policy Behavior: Why Do Nation-States Do What They Do?

We have seen that it is possible, at least in general terms, to describe patterns of foreign policy behavior. Not all countries act in the same manner. The next question is *why?* Why do some countries seek global or regional influence, while others are relatively isolationist? Why do countries ally with or intervene inside other countries? Why are some countries more inclined to use force or multilateral diplomacy in certain circumstances than other states?

These and similar questions have perplexed policymakers as well as scholars and laymen. For example, Winston Churchill, as British Prime Minister, grappled with the same sorts of questions and offered his own answer concerning Soviet behavior: "I cannot forecast to you the action of Russia. It is a riddle wrapped in a mystery inside an enigma; but perhaps there is a key. That key is Russian national interest."[1]

It is impossible to know all the "why's" of international relations. Leaders themselves often are not fully conscious of precisely which pressures exert the greatest influence on their own behavior. However, when we hear on the evening news that Egypt's President Anwar Sadat kissed Israeli Prime Minister Golda Meir while spurning Palestinian leader Yassir Arafat (in the mid-1970s), or when we see films of Jordan's King Hussein hugging Sadat's predecessor, Gamal Nasser, at a Cairo summit conference after barely escaping the poisoned nose drops supposedly arranged for him by pro-Egyptian agents (in the mid-1960s), one would hope that political scientists can do better than *National Enquirer* or *Parade* gossip columnists in deciphering affairs of state. As we saw in the last chapter, seemingly perplexing behavior, such as a trip by one of America's foremost anti-Communists, Richard Nixon, to meet with one of the world's most dedicated revolutionaries, Mao Tse-tung, can have a certain underlying logic.

In fact, a serious body of scholarly research on the causes of foreign policy behavior does exist. This body of research, often referred to as **comparative foreign policy analysis**, has provided us with a better understanding of the forces that shape nation-state behavior. We will examine a number of comparative foreign policy theories and research findings in this chapter as we explore the "why" question. As we will see, differences in the foreign policy behavior of countries, as well as changes in any single country's behavior over time, can be attributed to a variety of influences found both within and outside national boundaries.

Determinants of Foreign Policy Behavior: An Explanatory Framework

THE CONCEPT OF NATIONAL INTERESTS

Many people, "realists" in particular, would argue that international relations is not nearly as complicated as we are making it sound, that *all* foreign policy behavior of any importance can be traced simply to what Winston Churchill referred to as **national interests.** According to this view, national leaders basically seek to maximize their country's advantages vis-à-vis other states, either in cooperation with or at the expense of such states. The concept of national interests is worth examining since it has been the basis for much speculation about the motives behind state actions. We engaged in such speculation ourselves indirectly in the previous chapter, suggesting that American, Soviet, Chinese, and Indian foreign policy behavior over the years has conformed more to self-interest than to ideological or moral principles. The question remains, however, whether this in itself constitutes a complete explanation of foreign policy behavior.

There are at least three fundamental interests that all nation-states are said to have: (1) ensuring the physical survival of the homeland itself, which includes protecting the lives of its citizens and maintaining the territorial integrity of its borders; (2) promoting the economic well-being of its people; and (3) preserving national self-determination regarding the nature of the country's governmental system and the conduct of its internal affairs. All of these together can be considered a nation's core values or most basic foreign policy goals.[2]

Several problems, however, are associated with the term "national interests." They partly explain why countries can share similar goals yet behave quite differently. First, the term itself is extremely vague and provides few clues for policymakers to follow in their decision making. For example, does a nation's economic well-being entail economic self-sufficiency, i.e., nonreliance on the outside world for any crucial resources? And does that goal then require territorial expansion beyond one's existing borders?

Second, related to the first problem, not all states and leaders employ the same criteria for determining when national defense and economic needs are being satisfied; some countries and some leaders have shorter yardsticks and are satisfied with less than others. As happens frequently, for example in the Middle East, what are felt to be purely self-defense policies by one country can be construed as blatant aggression by another country.

Third, the three goals of national defense, economic prosperity, and self-determination can often be incompatible, necessitating trade-off decisions of the "guns or butter" and "better red than dead" variety. Not all national leaders rank all goals equally.

Fourth, "national interests," as interpreted by a government, may benefit the nation as a whole, or may benefit only privileged segments of the nation. Even if everyone has a collective stake, certain working definitions of "national interests" tend to coincide with the interests of some groups more than other groups (e.g., a $300 billion U.S. Defense Department budget would seem to benefit an individual on the welfare rolls less than it would benefit, say, a McDonnell-Douglas Aircraft Company employee).

Fifth, some governments are not content just to articulate and pursue the three basic goals noted above. Additional goals can be identified, such as commanding prestige, which may be only peripherally related to the other three.

The final problem, which we mentioned earlier in our discussion of the contemporary international system, is a question that runs through all these concerns: Where do "national interests" end and "international interests" (the interests of the world community) begin, and how does one separate the two? Although few if any foreign policy makers would agree, some people argue that if the chief national goal is the physical safety of one's citizens, nothing short of dismemberment of the nation-state and its replacement by a world government will spare the human race from annihilation in the nuclear age. Peace, however, has often taken a backseat to the other needs of nations. Moreover, even when it is accorded the highest priority as a foreign policy goal, peace can be pursued in quite different ways: by building a strong military deterrent, or by arms control, or by both. (One can see the complexities of peace in the case of the McDonnell-Douglas company, which has given its employees paid holidays on NATO *and* United Nations anniversary dates, celebrating the creation of both a military alliance and a world peace organization.)

Given the problems we have cited, the concept of national interests would seem to raise as many questions as it resolves. Important as it may be, the concept is a highly ambiguous one both as a guide to action for policymakers seeking to conduct foreign policy and as an explanatory variable for scholars seeking to account for international phenomena. Governments do seek to achieve basic goals, but reality is too complicated to be explained by a single factor. It is necessary, then, to go beyond an explanation based only on national interests and to look more systematically at the welter of factors affecting nation-state behavior.

AN EXPLANATORY FRAMEWORK

It is helpful to have some framework for classifying the various determinants of foreign policy behavior and for organizing a discussion of them. We shall categorize the determinants of nation-state behavior as follows: (1) **systemic factors**—conditions external to the state that are present in the international system surrounding it; (2) **national attribute factors**—characteristics of the nation-state itself; and (3) **idiosyncratic factors**—characteristics of individual national leaders and groups of decision makers.

This list of factors corresponds essentially to other lists developed by scholars engaging in comparative foreign policy analysis. Some observers adopt a simpler scheme, noting that one can view states as actors in world politics from just two vantage points—either from "inside out," i.e., looking at how foreign policy is shaped by factors internal to the state, or from "outside in," i.e., looking at how foreign policy is shaped by factors external to the state.

By permission of Johnny Hart and Field Enterprises, Inc.

The survival of the homeland

Others adopt a more elaborate scheme, examining variables that operate at as many as six or more "levels of analysis," including the individual, role, governmental, societal, bilateral or interstate, and global levels. The three levels of analysis that we have identified above embrace all of these elements. Whatever scheme one uses to explain foreign policy behavior, one must take into account not only the nature of the individual decision makers but also the nature of their domestic and external environments, which create opportunities as well as constraints. These three levels of analysis—systemic, national, and individual—are discussed separately below.[3]

The Role of Systemic Factors

Systemic factors are closely related to "national interest" explanations of foreign policy behavior, since leaders often define their country's interests in terms of the problems or opportunities in the world around them. Leaders do not have nearly as much control over their external environment as they do over their domestic environment, and hence foreign policy makers often find themselves reacting to, rather than shaping, unforeseen events or intractable conditions. Among the factors in a country's external environment that can affect its foreign policy are (1) geography, (2) international interactions and links, and (3) the structure of the international system.

In Chapters 2 and 3, we defined an international system as a broad set of relationships among interacting states, and noted that one can talk about the international system as a whole (the global system) or about regional subsystems. We saw in the last chapter, for example, that South Asia has several interacting states, some large and some small, and that outside powers—the USSR, China, and the United States—impinge upon this regional system as well. Actions by one state in such a system can have momentous implications for the others. The importance of systemic factors in explaining foreign policy, and particularly in accounting for *alignment* behavior, will become apparent in this discussion.

GEOGRAPHY

Among the more crucial geographical features that can affect foreign policy are, first, conditions along a nation's borders and, second, distances that must be traversed to reach key points of strategic interest. The German resort to armed force in World War I and World War II can be explained at least partly as a response to being geographically sandwiched between France (and conceivably Great Britain) on the one side and Russia on the other. German tactics were similar in both wars, even though the German government was led by a traditional autocratic monarch in 1914 and by a modern totalitarian dictator in 1939. In both cases German leaders felt obliged to attack France in a lightning swing from the north to knock the French out of the war quickly. In 1914 the Germans tried to eliminate France so they could turn attention to prolonged warfare with the gigantic Russian army to the east. In 1939 Hitler had concluded a nonaggression pact neutralizing the Russian threat for the time being, but he too wanted no prolonged war in the west that could have left Germany vulnerable to Moscow in the east.

The Germans' reaction to their geographical landscape was not unique and typifies concerns about "two-front" wars in other countries, such as Israel and the Soviet Union. A persistent tendency of "sandwiched" states is to strike first in threatening situations with preemptive attacks in order to avoid prolonged two-front warfare. Israel's 1967 strategy reflected these concerns, and the 1978 Camp David accords with Egypt are better understood when one notes the fact that the Egyptian front was effectively neutralized. Israeli Prime Minister Begin told an election rally during the Lebanese missile crisis of 1981 that "if we did not have the peace treaty with Egypt today, we would already have mobilized the reserves . . . because of the dispute with Syria!"[4]

Some geographical factors, such as the possession of vital natural resources, are basically national attributes and will be discussed in the next section. Here we are mainly interested in those geographical factors that are systemic in nature, such as location, the number of borders to be defended, and the degree of access to various points on the globe.[5] Geography can confer upon a country certain advantages or disadvantages that can affect its foreign policy behavior in a variety of ways, including the scope of its interests as well as the degree of conflict or cooperation experienced. Among possible advantages a country might enjoy are control of strategic waterways (for example, Turkey's position along the Dardanelles) or remoteness from warring powers (for example, American insulation from Europe in its early history). By the same token, geographical disadvantages can include landlocked territory, a problem faced by some thirty states in the world that lack coastlines, or extreme proximity to warring powers (Poland's historic position in the cockpit of Europe).

It is important to realize, however, that advantages at one moment can soon turn to disadvantages. Control of waterways can attract foreign envy, resentment, or attack. Insulation can mean that long distances must be traversed to reach key world regions (witness America's difficulties in reaching the Persian Gulf or its 10,000-mile supply line to Vietnam). Advantages can also be quickly erased by technological and other circumstances; for example, the Panama Canal and the Suez Canal, while still significant waterways, have diminished in importance somewhat as they have been hard-pressed to compete economically with other shipping routes and unable to accommodate super-tankers and giant aircraft carriers.

Just as advantages can evaporate due to technological changes, so also can technology be employed to overcome disadvantages. At least as far back as Hannibal's elephantine crossing of the Alps, leaders have devised ingenious ways of circumventing geographical barriers. In the contemporary age in particular, technology can neutralize geographic factors to some extent; the development of intercontinental and intermediate-range missiles, for example, has lessened the value of neighboring territories as protective buffers, although countries still squabble over ownership of mountaintop fortresses and other geographical assets.

Borders continue to be of utmost importance to leaders of nation-states. Chinese sensitivity to the approach of American forces during the Korean War, American sensitivity to the placement of Soviet offensive missiles in Cuba in 1962, and Soviet sensitivity over the intrusion of the ill-fated Korean airliner KAL 007 into Soviet airspace in 1984 all testify to the nearly universal concern states have about border security. While all states share such concerns, varying geographical locations can ease the degree of anxiety. As seen in our four case studies, the United States has not been confronted by major nearby hostile powers as have the Soviet Union, China, and India. (Table 5.1 shows the great variation among states in terms of the number of borders that must be defended.)

The Netherlands exemplifies how geography can affect the foreign policy behavior of a small country. Located at the mouths of three major European rivers and facing the sea, Holland has always been a transportation center, with canals designed to carry goods into the heart of Europe, and especially into Germany. The location of the Netherlands has meant that throughout history Britain, France, and Germany have all been vitally interested in who exercises control over Dutch territory. The Netherlands has oscillated in policy between neutrality and alliance with these powers in order to preserve independence and prevent attack. Until World War II, tiny Holland also attempted to maintain a worldwide empire of 100 million people in the Pacific (what is now Indonesia) and Latin America (Surinam). Long a maritime power, the Dutch found it increasingly difficult to reach those distant possessions

Table 5.1

THE NUMBER OF NEIGHBORS OF SELECTED COUNTRIES

Number of countries within 1000 km		Number of contiguous countries			
Soviet Union	28	Soviet Union	12	Pakistan	4
Poland	25	China	12	Nigeria	4
France	24	Brazil	10	Italy	4
Italy	23	West Germany	9	Mexico	3
Turkey	22	Zaire	9	Indonesia	3
		Sudan	8	Vietnam	3
Japan	4	Saudi Arabia	7	United States	2
Australia	2	India	6	Bangladesh	2
Canada	1	Algeria	6	Canada	1
Sri Lanka	1	Libya	6	United Kingdom	1
New Zealand	0	Argentina	5	Australia	0
		Iran	5	Japan	0

Source: J. P. Cole, *Geography of World Affairs,* 6th ed. (London: Butterworths, 1983), Table 3.2. Used with permission of Butterworths.

and defend them. More and more the Dutch had to rely on the British and Americans for protection against the Japanese, but this cooperation embarrassed the Netherlands before World War II, since Holland was supposedly neutral in the German-British disputes of the 1930s.[6]

It should be evident not only that geography brings about certain policies but also that already established policies define the importance of geography. As long as the Dutch attempted to maintain an empire, their geographical remoteness from the Pacific was a problem; when they dismantled the empire, Pacific access receded in importance. Today, a number of countries worry about the Persian Gulf because of the importance they have attached to industrial development through petroleum-based fuels. Given different fuel policies and lower fuel prices, the Middle East loses some of its "intrinsic" importance.

International relations research has revealed some uncertainty about the overall importance of geography in predicting conflict or cooperation among countries. Traditional philosophers such as Kautilya and Machiavelli argued that states that border each other tend to be natural rivals. Some contemporary analysts have also concluded that geographical proximity increases *conflict*,[7] while others argue that it increases various forms of interstate *cooperation*, from trade and tourist traffic to diplomatic contacts.[8] The equivocal role of geographical proximity in promoting conflict or cooperation is exemplified by two cases: on the one hand, the 5500-mile undefended frontier between the United States and Canada (each being the other's major trading partner) and, on the other hand, the 4500-mile Sino-Soviet border manned on each side by one million troops.

INTERNATIONAL INTERACTIONS AND LINKS

Some writers have argued that countries can be close or far apart not only in a geographical sense but in other ways as well. There is evidence that the degree of similarity or difference between countries—the "distance" between them in terms of political, economic, cultural, and other characteristics—can be a key to the volume and kinds of transactions between them. Generally speaking, the more similar countries are in political, economic, and cultural features, the greater the level of trade, communications, and other forms of interaction likely to occur between them.[9]

However, countries that are dissimilar in many respects can also develop intense interactions and become linked together in a kind of social system. Such a social system can be defined as a set of closely and continuously interacting entities. Such continuous interaction affects the entities themselves, engaging most of their energies in the system. For example, because the Americans and Soviets, the Indians and Pakistanis, or the Arabs and Israelis have been continuous competitors for four decades, they now rivet their attention on each other in what might be called ongoing conflict systems; they mimic each other's defense strategies and budgets; their societies rely increasingly on the military; and in a sense their politics reflect each other. Such systems have profound effects on those caught in them, and even mortal enemies can come to depend on each other in bizarre ways; even conflict systems contain elements of cooperation.

One such system described in the previous chapter is the U.S.-Soviet-Chinese triangle. These three states have been connected by complex conflictual and cooperative ties, ranging from border and naval skirmishes to trade and cultural exchanges. The moves of any two are of immediate concern to the third. Basic social forces are at work in such systems, forces common to love triangles, business dealings, party politics, and international relations. Rules affecting such systems include the old maxim, "My enemy's enemy is my friend."

Interdependencies also can influence foreign policy. Foreign aid to and investment in a country can increase or diminish its foreign policy options, depending on the number of strings attached to the money. Countries heavily in debt to foreign powers often lack the finances needed to undertake important projects and can be pressured by their creditors for repayment. Creditors and powerful states are also somewhat bound by interdependencies. West Germany has more than once had to bail out faltering Italian and Turkish economies in order to preserve the Western European trading system and the viability of NATO's southern flank. Once countries such as West Germany or the United States enter organizations such as the European Economic Community (EEC) or NATO, they have a stake in the survival of those organizations, and therefore lose a degree of policy flexibility. They could let fellow EEC or NATO members go bankrupt or fall victim to domestic disturbance, but there would be a price to pay in terms of the survival of those organizations.

(a)

(b)

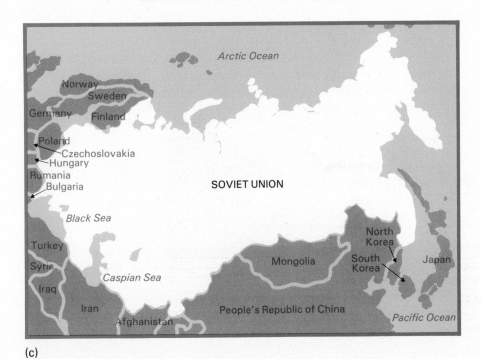

(c)

Figure 5.1
THE "TWO-FRONT" PROBLEM: GERMANY, ISRAEL, AND THE SOVIET UNION
(a) Germany on the eve of World War I; (b) Israel on the eve of the Six Day War;
(c) the Soviet Union today.

Interdependence has affected the Soviet Union as well. As Polish trade unions agitated for more freedom in the 1980s, the Soviets were tempted to intervene, perhaps with troops, to preserve the Polish Communist system. Poland's room to maneuver was narrow. Yet leaders in the Kremlin also had to calculate costs, not only the cost of possible Polish resistance but at least two other factors: first, the likelihood that West Germany would withdraw its financial investments and support of the shaky Polish economy, thus leaving the Soviet Union to pay Poland's mounting bills, and second, the likelihood that the last vestiges of détente would evaporate and a new cold war would arise in Europe. None of these costs precluded a Soviet intervention; they merely made it likely that Moscow would explore a variety of less costly options before resorting to extreme remedies.

INTERNATIONAL SYSTEM STRUCTURE

There is considerable debate about how the structure of the global system affects the behavior of the actors, and especially how unipolarity, bipolarity, and multipolarity affect conflict and war. Certain writers argue that with *one* dominant world power or center of alignment, other states are kept in order and few wars occur.[10] Others maintain that with *two* major powers balancing each other, world war is unlikely since neither will have the incentive to confront the other directly, although small-scale fighting between less powerful states can still occur.[11] Still others maintain that the balancing of *several* powerful states in a multipolar system diverts the attention of every power; hostilities cannot be focused in one place very long and war is minimized.[12] Obviously these theories can become quite complex and contradictory. Much research has gone into testing the rival claims, without any consensus emerging except for the general conclusion that the overall system structure limits the options of both major and minor powers.[13]

The role of system structure in foreign policy can be examined at the *regional* as well as the global level. In the Middle East a traditional rivalry dating to biblical times exists between three great civilizations based in the cities of Baghdad, Damascus, and Cairo. The struggle among these three power centers for regional dominance is reflected historically in the eighth- to eleventh-century movement of the capital of the Islamic "caliphate," or empire, from Arabia to Damascus to Baghdad, and finally to Cairo. Outside powers, such as Persia (now Iran) and the Ottoman Empire (now Turkey), also intervened at times in this Arab system. Rivalries persist today in new form and over new issues, with Iraq, Syria, Egypt, and Iran still contending for Middle Eastern leadership. The competition has spawned wars, assassinations, summit meetings, and intrigues—as well as gestures of Arab and Islamic unity.[14]

Global power hierarchies and regional disputes together can complicate the choices leaders must make. If a region is in the "sphere of influence" of a major power, that power's government might insist on approving the important policy moves of less powerful states in its sphere. Although we have noted a certain slippage in superpower control in recent years, the Soviet Union clearly exercises a veto on most initiatives taken by Eastern European states in dealing with Western Europe, and the United States traditionally has tried to control certain Latin American initiatives through such means as the armed landings in the Dominican Republic in 1965 and Grenada in 1983, and support for anti-government "contra" rebels in Nicaragua in the 1980s. In Western Europe, however, Washington has allies who are not client states but are relatively strong and able to resist U.S. pressures; as the nineteenth-century German leader Bismarck observed, an alliance is like horseback riding—the struggle is over who must be the horse.

Freedom of action for minor powers can be somewhat greater in areas that are not clearly in the geopolitical sphere of one power, as in the case of Africa or the Middle East. For example, it was easier for President Sadat to demand and achieve the removal of Soviet forces and advisers from Egypt in 1974 than it would be for Polish leaders to accomplish the same feat, despite the fact that Poland might be technically more powerful than Egypt in terms of industrial or military strength. Poland finds itself in a very undesirable geopolitical position, and historically has had to defer to both Russia and Germany. Egypt too has been victimized by major powers historically and has been unable to attract enough aid to support its growing population; yet Egypt has had greater freedom to make international connections since it is not in the backyard of any power.

Clearly, a country's external environment can affect behavior ranging from war involvement to commercial activity. The direction of international trade, the channeling of international communications, the exchange of diplomatic visits, and the formation and collapse of alliances all reflect to some extent the ebb and flow of systemic forces. For example, as long as the Soviet Union is viewed as posing a major threat to the Western industrialized democracies, one can expect unity among NATO members, relatively little East-West trade, and few other transactions between the blocs; when the Soviet threat subsides and a period of détente occurs, as has happened periodically since World War II, alliance unity tends to decline and greater inter-bloc "fraternization" can occur. Regional or global polarity patterns can put some states in a position to dominate their neighbors, as with India and China in Asia. Leaders of weaker states may seek to play such powers off against each other, or to align closely with other states to bolster their mutual security, as in the case of the small oil-rich kingdom of Kuwait, which due to spillover attacks during the Iran-Iraq war in the 1980s moved to defend itself not only through expensive weapons purchases but also by joining its neighbors in a Gulf Cooperation Council Pact. The box on page 160 summarizes some research findings on the role of systemic factors.

ASSUMPTIONS AND RESEARCH FINDINGS
ON SYSTEMIC FACTORS

Some common assumptions about the effects of systemic factors on foreign policy behavior:

1. The more two states depend on each other economically and otherwise, the more peaceful their relations will tend to be.

2. The more often different peoples and cultures interact, the greater the tendency for understanding and friendship to increase between their governments.

3. The more balanced two states are in terms of power, the less likely they are to go to war with each other.

4. The greater the external threat confronting the members of a group, such as an alliance, the more cohesion there will be within the group.

Some research findings related to the above assumptions:*

1. There is no clear relationship between the level of economic, communications, and other transactions between states and their tendency to experience violent conflict with each other (Rummel, 1968); if anything, such contacts may even increase the probability of conflict (Wright; Russett), although beneficial trade links have been found to decrease conflict (Gasiorowski).

2. The less geographic distance between states, the more interactions between them (Cobb and Elder; Brams); although geographic proximity may increase trade and other cooperative transactions, it is also correlated with interstate wars (Singer).

3. The more borders a country has with other countries, the more violent conflicts in which it tends to become involved; the farther away a crisis is from the country it affects, the less likely that country is to use force to deal with the crisis (Weede, 1970; Wright; Richardson).

4. Former colonial ties tend to promote trade, foreign aid, and other interactions between states (Brams; Wittkopf).

5. There is no clear connection between the degree of power parity (equality) between two states and their propensity to go to war with each other (Rummel, 1966; Sullivan); wars of various types occur between equals as well as unequals; if anything, power parity slightly increases the chances of a long, severe war (Ferris).

6. A bipolar power distribution tends to limit the magnitude of wars in the international system, although bipolarity of alliance blocs somewhat increases the risk that war will break out in the system (Wayman).

7. Alliance cohesion tends to increase as the outside threat increases; wartime alliances tend to disintegrate once war has ended; although common ideology among allies can contribute to alliance cohesion, the establishment and maintenance of alliances is based primarily on security concerns (Holsti *et al.*).

* Full citations for the specific studies noted in parentheses appear at the end of this chapter. Research findings can depend on the measurements used to test relationships. The findings noted here should be treated as suggestive rather than as the last word on the subject.

The Role of National Attributes

The presence or absence of various national attributes also can strongly affect a country's foreign policy behavior, particularly in terms of *scope* and *modus operandi*. For instance, in the 1930s, Japan, a rapidly industrializing country with very limited natural resources, embarked on an expansionist foreign policy to dominate Asian markets and resources. Such ambitions made the Japanese even more dependent on foreign raw materials. When, by 1941, the United States had cut its trade with Japan and worked to deny Tokyo access to the rich oil and rubber fields of the Dutch East Indies (as punishment for the Japanese occupation of China), Japanese leaders saw little alternative to an attack on U.S. naval facilities at Pearl Harbor. With merely a few months' oil supply left, Japan attempted to eliminate the American presence from the Western Pacific, even though its leaders knew that they could not win a long war against the United States.[15]

The Japanese example illustrates what some researchers have labeled a "lateral pressure," or tea-kettle effect in foreign policy. It is argued that as a nation-state grows, either in population or economic output, it experiences new demands for raw materials and other resources, only some of which can be satisfied through domestic sources. The result is similar to pressure building inside a steam kettle; the expanding pressure can lead to expansionist foreign policy behavior designed to obtain the needed resources from other countries— presumably by peaceful means if possible, but by force if necessary. In this way national attribute scarcities interact with the international system, as the expanding state comes up against resistance from other expanding or declining states.[16]

Clearly, Japan would not have been sensitive to U.S. pressure in 1941, or to Arab pressure concerning petroleum supplies in 1973, if its islands sat atop vast oil deposits. It should be noted, though, that it is not always easy to predict the precise policy a state suffering scarcities will adopt; in 1941 Japan forcibly resisted U.S. demands for its withdrawal from China, while in 1973 Tokyo modified its previous pro-Israeli line and began to acknowledge the rights of Palestinians. In the first instance Japan was highly resistant to pressure, in the second instance highly accommodative.

Such variations in foreign policy would appear to be traceable not merely to a country's sheer population size or resource base but also to its other national attributes, including its economic and population growth rates, the technology available to it to exploit or create substitutes for resources, the extent of its internal political instability, the ethnic and other societal divisions within it, and the readiness of its armed forces, together with the nature of its governmental system and public attitudes about the use of force and other tools of foreign policy. As a shorthand way of grouping these characteristics, we will speak of (1) demographic, (2) economic, (3) military, and (4) governmental attributes.[17] Many of these attributes relate to aspects of national power that we discussed earlier in Chapters 2 and 3. If one thinks of power as the capability to *act* (and especially to *influence* others) in international relations, one can readily understand how certain national attributes can contribute to or limit a state's capabilities and, hence, vitally shape its foreign policy behavior.

DEMOGRAPHIC ATTRIBUTES

The size, motivation, skills, and homogeneity of a country's population help determine the foreign policy levers available to its government. Therefore they affect foreign policy scope and *modus operandi*, such as the degree of a country's assertiveness and its success in influencing others. Population size is an important facet of national power mainly because a large population provides personnel for armed forces and industry. Military force and industrial output allow a government to threaten punishments or offer rewards to other states. A country such as Canada, with its vast territorial size and wealth of natural resources, fails to rival either the United States or the Soviet Union for international influence partly because it has a population of only 25 million. Large populations, however, can be mixed blessings, especially if the state in question lacks resources necessary to feed, educate, and employ the multitudes. On the basis of population alone, India should be a major world power; yet it wrestles with developmental problems in trying to support a huge populace with scarce resources and must devote most of its productive capacity to meeting basic needs.

A society's ethnic divisions can also put its foreign policy makers under pressure. Enemy states might be tempted to support dissident groups in order to overthrow a rival state's government, and opposition groups within a state might oppose their country's government and its foreign policies if they feel threatened by those policies. Iran and Iraq have long disputed such issues as control of the Shatt-al-Arab, the waterway that marks their border. Each has tried to take advantage of Kurdish and religious minorities residing within its rival's borders in order to weaken its enemy's position. Both have supported the Kurds in their struggles for national independence in the *other* state. Iraq's Sunni-Muslim-dominated government has been sensitive to the possibility that Shiite-Muslim Iran might try to arouse the large Shiite Iraqi population; and Iran has had similar fears about Iraq's effects on the Sunni-Muslim Arabs living in Iran's oil-rich Abadan province.[18]

The mixing of demographic characteristics and international systemic factors can be seen clearly in the tragic events of the Lebanese civil war of the 1970s and 1980s. Lebanon and, to a lesser extent, Syria have diverse ethnic and religious minorities that are frequently at each other's throats. Syria traditionally has sought to dominate Lebanese politics, and has taken an interest in the struggles of diverse Lebanese Islamic and Druse religious groups against each other and against Lebanon's diverse Christian communities. Yet because Israel also has sought to control sections of Lebanon, and has backed Christian and even some Islamic groups in efforts to weaken militant Palestinians operating from Lebanese territory, Syria has had to play a tricky balancing act for fear of war with Israel and lost influence in Lebanon. Damascus has sided first with one and then with another rival Lebanese faction in order to keep any one of them from becoming too strong and autonomous. In the process, with the added impact of Israeli and Palestinian intrusions, Lebanese society has been torn further apart and innocent civilians on all sides have been massacred.

ECONOMIC ATTRIBUTES

A state's demography is closely related to its economy. A skilled and technologically advanced population can enable a country to achieve high living standards, to enjoy trade advantages in the international market, and to dominate or assist other states. On the other hand, countries that are overpopulated relative to technological skills and available resources are likely to have unstable economies and governments, to be vulnerable to penetration by outside powers, to suffer recurring famine and chronic poverty, and therefore to orient their foreign policies toward the pursuit of foreign aid and military protection.[19]

Essentially three types of economic characteristics affect a state's foreign policy behavior, especially the scope and *modus operandi* dimensions: the size and growth rate of a nation's economy, its degree of wealth, and the nature of its economic system (capitalist, socialist, or communist). Economic size and rates of growth are generally measured in gross national product

(GNP)—the estimated total value of goods and services produced in a year. Industrialization tends to boost GNP, but some predominantly agricultural countries such as India also have relatively large GNPs. A large economy generally increases a country's interests in and means of influencing events abroad. Large industrialized countries, however, can have economic weaknesses that affect foreign policy. For example, because of its dependence on foreign trade, Britain has found it difficult to support United Nations resolutions calling for trade sanctions against South Africa aimed at ending that country's system of racial discrimination toward blacks (known as **apartheid**).

Besides economic size, a country's overall wealth (the total amount of income available per person, usually measured as GNP per capita) also influences foreign policy. Rich countries can better afford the expense of participating in international organizations and maintaining embassies abroad than poor countries, for example. In one study of intergovernmental organization membership, it was found that among the twenty states having the most IGO memberships, fifteen were wealthy, developed countries of various sizes (a pattern that could be discerned in Table 4.2 in the preceding chapter).[20] Poor states not only belong to fewer IGOs, they also have fewer overseas embassies and, hence, will be even more reliant on multilateral diplomatic contacts (particularly through the UN) than rich states. The wealth of a country obviously is also the main determinant of whether it is a donor or a recipient of foreign aid. Clearly, it is the sheer size of the U.S. economy and its wealth that has provided the resources necessary for the United States to play a global role in world politics in the postwar era.

In addition, the type of economic system is often thought to bear heavily on a country's foreign policy. *Capitalist* economies (those emphasizing private ownership of wealth and capital) tend to spawn powerful interest groups that seek foreign trade and investment. In protecting overseas assets, capitalist states frequently try to resist or to overthrow governments advocating the expropriation of property and radical redistribution of wealth. Lenin predicted early in this century that capitalist states would fall into warfare among themselves over the resources and markets of less developed societies, which capitalists supposedly had to exploit in order to sustain their economies. World War I could conceivably be interpreted in this light but hardly World War II, which involved the Soviet Union and the capitalists on the same side.[21]

There is no evidence that *communist* states (those advocating state ownership of wealth and capital and a dictatorship by an elite revolutionary vanguard) are less war-prone than capitalist states. Indeed, imperialism and war predated the rise of both capitalism and communism, so that type of economic system would not appear to account for such phenomena. Communist states are generally less involved in foreign trade and investment activities, however, given their tendency to adopt autarkic (self-sufficiency) policies designed to shield their planned economies from the vagaries of the international economy.

Finally, *socialist* or social democratic states (those having some measure of state ownership of wealth but without dictatorship) have attempted to coordinate their foreign policies through frequent international meetings. In recent years states such as Sweden, Denmark, Norway, and the Netherlands, which have strong Socialist parties, have been quite supportive of the positions of Third World countries on the issues of economic development and racism (especially on South African apartheid). Naturally this support is also influenced by interests in trade with the Third World (especially oil), and tempered in some cases by the need for cooperation with the United States as well.

Economic concerns of states generally are outweighed by security concerns. The American grain embargo of 1979 did not result in a Soviet decision to remove Russian troops from Afghanistan, despite quite pressing Soviet agricultural shortages that were relieved only by turning to other suppliers. Yet, in terms of the day-to-day conduct of foreign policy, foreign ministries probably spend more time considering economic issues than security issues. Economic issues are becoming of increasing importance in foreign policy, as we will see in later chapters. States experiencing trade and international debt problems, undergoing inflation or recession, suffering diminished productivity, or judged undesirable for foreign investment clearly are at a foreign policy disadvantage that can be remedied only with great difficulty.

MILITARY ATTRIBUTES

A country's readiness for war can interact with the factors already discussed, especially with geographic factors, to produce more or less assertive and interventionist foreign policies. A country can be dissatisfied about conditions at home or in the international system, but if it lacks the military capability to change the situation, it is likely to remain relatively passive and to confine itself to diplomacy rather than force. In the case of a well-armed Japan, desperate for the nearby oil supplies in the Pacific in 1941, the use of force seemed feasible and productive, at least in the short run, when diplomatic negotiations with the United States broke down. Conversely, a Japan that in 1973 had based its considerable world influence almost exclusively on economic rather than military might found diplomatic solutions more attractive than force in dealing with a problem in the distant Persian Gulf.

Although ratings of military power are important in predicting relations among states (see Table 5.2), such rankings must be interpreted with care. Some countries excel according to some military criteria and fall short on others. Countries can be ranked according to size of armed forces, number of weapons of various types, skill levels, research and development efforts, amount of military expenditures, and military expenditures as a percentage of GNP or per person. The Arab states have more raw weaponry and larger armed forces than the Israelis, but Israel has enjoyed superior technology and skill levels, the potential of total mobilization, and high motivation. In the

Table 5.2
MILITARY RANKINGS OF THE WORLD'S "TOP TWENTY"

	1983 Defense Expenditures ($ millions)[1]	1983 Defense Expenditures as % of GDP/GNP[2]	1983 Regular Armed Forces (thousands)
1. United States	239,400	7.4%	2,152
2. Soviet Union	235,000[3]	12–17%[3]	5,300[4]
3. China	34,500[5]	8.6%[5]	3,900[6]
4. United Kingdom	24,469	5.5%	327
5. West Germany	22,375	3.4%	478
6. Saudi Arabia	21,813	18.2%	63
7. France	21,654	4.2%	464
8. Iran	17,370	13.3%	305
9. Argentina	12,778[7]	8.9%	108
10. Japan	11,654	1.0%	243
11. Iraq	10,293	33.7%	520
12. Italy	9,698	2.8%	385
13. East Germany	8,685	5.7%	174
14. Canada	6,767	2.1%	83
15. India	6,476	3.4%	1,260
16. Poland	5,766	2.7%	319
17. Australia	5,199	3.2%	70
18. Israel	4,981	29.8%	142[8]
19. Czechoslovakia	4,618	3.8%	203
20. South Korea	4,387	5.7%	598

[1] The figures are current U.S. dollars.
[2] GDP = Gross domestic product, i.e., the value of domestically traded goods and services only. The values are in local currencies, with GNP used when GDP unavailable, and estimated where official figures unavailable.
[3] U.S. CIA estimate. Soviet expenditures are subject to extensive debate and disagreement; the USSR does not categorize defense budgets as in the West, and reports its own figure of $21.3 billion. It is difficult to price the value of products in a Communist economy, and the CIA's own estimates have been reduced since 1983.
[4] Including 1.3 million railroad construction, labor, and general support troops.
[5] U.S. Arms Control and Disarmament Agency estimate.
[6] Being reduced by up to 25%.
[7] Increased after Falklands (Malvinas) war in 1982.
[8] Israel's armed forces can be quickly expanded to over 500,000 by total mobilization.

Source: Compiled from The Military Balance, 1985–86 (London: The International Institute for Strategic Studies, 1985), pp. 168–173; supplemented from World Military Expenditures and Arms Transfers, 1985 (Washington, D.C.: U.S. Arms Control and Disarmament Agency, 1985), Table I.

Arab-Israeli conflict as well as other conflicts in the region, Middle Eastern states have reached beyond their own independent military capabilities and depended heavily on imported weapons from major powers. Middle Eastern states generally have experienced intense economic strain in maintaining their arms competitions, despite the oil wealth of some states, as evidenced in Table 5.2 by the large percentage of the gross domestic or national product devoted to defense by Iraq, Iran, Saudi Arabia, and Israel. In Iran's case, heavy defense spending under the Shah failed to produce a military capable of keeping him in power—indeed, helped spawn the resentment and revolution that toppled him in 1979—and failed to deter Iraq from launching a war to regain territory from Iran during the political chaos that accompanied the revolution. Since the revolution, Iran has continued to allocate vast funds to its military establishment as a result of its ongoing war with Iraq. In this conflict, Iran

SIDELIGHT

NATIONAL ATTRIBUTES

The following rankings of national attributes are based on 1986 figures.

■ *The country with the largest Muslim population in the world:*
Indonesia (approximately 150 million Muslims)

■ *The country with the largest Catholic population in the world:*
Brazil (approximately 120 million Catholics)

■ *The richest country in the world among countries with over one million people (based on per capita GNP):*
Kuwait (approximately $17,000)

■ *The country with the second largest land area in the world (after the Soviet Union, which spans eleven time zones):*
Canada (3.9 million square miles)

■ *The country that devotes the largest percentage of its GNP to military expenditures:*
Iraq and Israel (each approximately 30 percent)

■ *The country with the largest armed forces in the world:*
Soviet Union (approximately 4.5 million)

■ *The country with the greatest population density among countries with over 1000 square miles of territory:*
Bangladesh (approximately 1,500 people per square mile)

■ *The largest wheat producer in the world:*
United States, Soviet Union, and China (each accounting for approximately 20 percent of total world production)

■ *The largest crude oil producer in the world:*
Soviet Union (approximately 20 percent of total world production)

■ *The country whose people enjoy the longest life expectancy at birth:*
Switzerland (79 years)

sometimes has employed "human wave" assaults, relying on a combination of fundamentalist Islamic fervor and Iranian nationalism to motivate young foot-soldiers to attack Iraqi tank brigades and minefields and to carry the Gulf war to Iraqi territory. With Iran resorting to such "intangibles" and Iraq resorting to advanced military hardware, including chemical weapons, the war has produced a virtual stalemate. In examining the military attributes of the two countries and the impact such traits have had on their foreign policy behavior, one must keep in mind that their national military capabilities have been augmented not only by arms imports from other countries but also by the financial backing of other states that has facilitated the arms purchases. (Financial support has come from, among others, Libya in the case of Iran and Saudi Arabia in the case of Iraq.)

In comparing U.S. and Soviet military capabilities as well, one needs to take into account the attributes of allies, such as Britain, West and East Germany, Italy, Poland, Japan, and France. Though allied unity in war cannot be assumed, the aggregate strength of blocs of states necessarily figures into defense and foreign policy planning. Other factors to be considered include the relative quality of personnel and weaponry and the number of threats against which one's armed forces are directed. U.S. forces evidently are more mobile for longer distances than Soviet forces, although the latter have improved in this respect in recent years. U.S. weapons systems are more electronically sophisticated, though this can present problems since high-technology systems require more maintenance and more sophisticated operators. Also, because of their relatively smaller conventional armed forces, the NATO countries have continued to rely on the deployment of nuclear weapons to discourage any Warsaw Pact attack in Europe. Recently there have been calls for expanded and improved NATO conventional armaments to lessen the need to resort to nuclear weapons.[22]

The level of a country's or bloc's military preparedness is monitored by other interested governments in planning their foreign policies. In the late 1930s, many of the smaller Western European countries that might have relied on Britain and France for protection against an expansionist Germany accurately assessed the lack of British-French military readiness and deduced from this that the Western allies were not reliable protectors.[23] It is sometimes a mistake to read too much into the state of a nation's readiness at any particular moment. The side with the largest battalions does not inevitably win all confrontations. As American experience in Vietnam showed, certain types of military power are sometimes unsuited to a specific situation or to a government's political goals. It can also be a mistake to equate a state's military capabilities with its intentions necessarily to use them to launch a war. Finally, a country might be ill-prepared at the start of a crisis but able to gear up later, as was the case with the United States after Pearl Harbor, when it became the "arsenal of democracy."

GOVERNMENTAL ATTRIBUTES

One view of world politics is that it does not much matter whether states are **democracies** or **dictatorships** ("open" or "closed" political systems), because the pressures of the international system or other national attributes largely determine foreign policy. One could predict a hostile response by a major power that just discovered enemy troops encamped near its borders regardless of whether its leaders were elected or self-appointed. Those taking this position argue that national interests are interpreted by an elite professional foreign policy establishment, with domestic politics and mass public opinion playing relatively minor roles.

Others, however, argue that domestic politics and the nature of a country's political system do affect interpretations of national interests and foreign policy. Perhaps exaggerating a bit, one noted observer has commented as follows about American foreign policy:

> One of the most consistent and incurable traits of American statesmanship [is] . . . its neurotic self-consciousness and introversion, the tendency to make statements and take actions with regard not to their effect on the international scene to which they are ostensibly addressed but rather to their effects on those echelons of American opinion, congressional opinion first and foremost, to which the respective statesmen are anxious to appeal.[24]

A continuing debate exists in the international relations literature about the importance of governmental variables in shaping foreign policy. It has been hypothesized that type of government system (democracy/dictatorship) is related to (1) propensity to fight wars, (2) policy flexibility, and (3) efficiency and discretion.

For extreme views on the question of war involvement, one can recall, on the one hand, Woodrow Wilson's claim that democracy and self-determination could eliminate the occurrence of war, and on the other hand, George Kennan's comparison of democracies to a gigantic, pinheaded prehistoric monster wallowing in the mud unaware of the environment until some enemy finally whacks his tail off: "Once he grasps this, he lays about with such blind determination that he not only destroys his adversary but largely wrecks his native habitat."[25] Democracies are often seen as slow to act but, once aroused, very susceptible to emotionalism and difficult to restrain. The evidence on war-proneness is mixed, with most studies showing little overall connection between type of regime and number of war involvements.

Kennan has also argued that democracies have special problems fighting protracted "limited wars," such as Vietnam, since there will be a tendency for a restless public to demand a conclusive outcome: "Win or get out." Hence, democracies are seen as following relatively inflexible, "all or nothing" types of policies. Dictatorships are supposedly more able to switch policies when necessary. Yet we must note that the Soviet Union failed to reappraise its policy of backing Egypt after the latter's defeat in the 1967 Six Day War against Israel, a failure that cost millions of rubles in burned-out Soviet-supplied equipment. The Soviets immediately poured millions more into rearming Egypt, an obviously poor risk, only to be eventually expelled from the country after the 1973 fighting. By the same token, the democratic United States managed to end its security treaty with Taiwan when relations with Beijing seemed more important in the 1970s.

Policy flexibility and change are not unknown in democracies, while dictatorships can display their own brand of rigidity. In fact, like many dictators, both Stalin and Hitler reportedly severely punished advisers who disagreed with their policies. Therefore advisers started to think twice about suggesting policy changes which, had they occurred, might have averted disasters suffered by both Russia and Germany in World War II.[26] Interestingly, Lyndon Johnson displayed somewhat similar vindictiveness toward dissenters in his Vietnam-plagued administration.[27] As we will discuss later, the reasons for such inflexibility can have more to do with decision-making dynamics common to all political systems than with the type of political system itself.

Dictatorships are also seen by some as more efficient and decisive than democracies in conducting foreign policy. Without democratic checks and balances, an authoritarian leader is supposedly freer to act in world affairs. However, examples can be found of decisive leadership exercised in democracies, such as the case of Golda Meir. Secretary of State Kissinger evidently valued such decisiveness, longing for the kind of ironfisted control enjoyed by Prime Minister Meir over her cabinet and over Israeli politics as an elder stateswoman. When confronted by a cabinet of ambitious rivals under Prime Minister Rabin (Meir's successor) during Middle Eastern peace talks in 1975, Kissinger was reminded that when Golda spoke, it was a commitment.[28] One could argue, also, that the greater potential for careful deliberation, debate, and scrutiny of foreign policy decisions in a democracy gives the latter an advantage over dictatorships in some respects.

Critics of democratic foreign policy processes note that the strong roles of the legislature and the press can jeopardize the discretion and state secrecy that are often essential to the conduct of foreign policy. Those heading the Nixon administration were extremely concerned about information "leaks," and even authorized burglaries by "plumbers" to stop the leaks. Yet discretion is a matter of law, ethics, and competent administration as much as a product of strict control. President Nixon himself taped supposedly confidential conversations with foreign leaders in the Oval Office; confidence in U.S. discretion had to be shaken when these leaders found out about the tapes during the Watergate hearings, and the ability of the American government to carry on frank diplomacy had to be impaired. In fact, journalists have long claimed that most leaks are planted by government officials themselves for political impact. In other words, it is not so much the intrusion of press or parliaments that limits confidential diplomacy, but the actions of executive leaders and agencies. Differences between political systems in maintaining secrecy should not be overdrawn. Despite Nazi totalitarianism, Hitler's entire strategy for the 1939 invasion of Western Europe was leaked in advance to disbelieving foreign officials by a high-ranking informant in the German army.[29] Conversely, detailed government information on the destination and value of arms sales to other countries is kept from the public and even from parliamentary bodies in many Western democracies.

We are not arguing that type of governmental system is an irrelevant factor in world politics, only that its importance is sometimes exaggerated. All leaders, whether presiding in open or closed political systems, are concerned to some extent about their domestic political environment. Admittedly, in democratic countries there are greater domestic pressures due to a wider circle of relevant actors, some controlling the purse strings, others seeking out news stories, others evaluating the proper strategy for the next election campaign, and still others complaining about how their taxes are spent or whether their children will be drafted. However, even in nondemocratic countries various groups inside and outside the government might dissent on foreign policy and must be placated or satisfied. Soviet Premier and Communist Party Chairman Khrushchev lost his job in 1964 at least partly because of foreign policy mistakes, including the fiasco of his Cuban missile policy in 1962.

One set of domestic political pressures, in particular, that can be found in democratic and nondemocratic systems alike are the demands made by various agencies within the government itself. Examples of such *bureaucratic* pressures are the battles that have been fought over the years between the U.S. Army, Navy, and Air Force over slices of the defense budget pie; decisions on new weapons systems can sometimes be based more on political pressures by certain military services than on battlefield needs.[30] For example, bureaucratic battles within the Reagan administration, especially between the State and Defense departments, reportedly affected such actions as the 1982 intervention in Lebanon and the 1986 decision to scrap the SALT II treaty understandings.[31]

In addition to bureaucratic pressures, *societal interest groups* can have an impact on foreign policy, especially in democracies, where they are freer to organize and operate. Among the kinds of interest groups that can exert influence are ethnic groups (e.g., the reputed role of the "Jewish lobby" in the U.S. in affecting American policy on the Middle East), ideological groups (e.g., the pacifist groups in many Western European countries opposing placement of long-range nuclear missiles by the United States within their borders), and economic groups (e.g., munitions manufacturers seeking to promote increased arms sales abroad or farmers protesting grain embargoes that limit their export earnings). Interest groups clearly have more impact on domestic policy than on foreign policy; within the domain of foreign policy, they are likely to have more impact on foreign economic issues than on military-security issues. However, in an age of interdependence, as the domestic and foreign policy arenas along with economic and security concerns become increasingly blurred, it is possible that interest groups may come to play a larger role in foreign policy.

Public opinion also can limit a leader's freedom of action in foreign policy, especially in democracies (at election time in particular), although leaders in both open and closed political systems can manipulate public opinion to some extent by taking advantage of the public's generally low level of concern and information about foreign policy. In democracies, public opinion backlash is likely to be greater and more politically costly than in dictatorships if policies fail to produce promised results. Despite indications to the American electorate in 1964 that American boys would not be sent to do the fighting that Asian boys should be doing, President Johnson was able to escalate U.S. military involvement in Vietnam for four years, manipulating both public and congressional opinion to support his policies.[32] However, as casualties increased, as middle-class youths were drafted in ever greater numbers, and as the news media brought horrible war scenes and accounts of American failures to family dinner tables each night, public pressures opposing the war mounted among diverse groups—some demanding quick victory, others compromise with the North Vietnamese, and others immediate withdrawal. In such circumstances the President seemed caught in a game of musical chairs; the object was not to be the President when Vietnam fell. Therefore, U.S. bombing targets were sometimes widened, battlefield casualty figures were sometimes doctored, and peace overtures were sometimes offered—all three frequently in combination—at least partly in an effort to convince the public that those in charge knew how to bring peace to Southeast Asia. Arguments were even heard in the Johnson administration, as well as the Nixon administration that followed, that American public opinion was Hanoi's best weapon since dissension supposedly encouraged North Vietnam to fight on.[33] Public opinion did not cause an American defeat in Vietnam, however; it merely reflected the concern caused by increasingly bleak events, and it raised the political cost of the war.

Finally, there is one other political factor sometimes thought to affect foreign policy behavior: the amount of domestic political instability experienced by a regime. Internal political instability can diminish the credibility of a country's foreign policy and affect its degree of activism. If a national government is fighting a civil war, its promises to pay its bills, to preserve order for foreign investors, to participate effectively in alliances, and to undertake other commitments all become suspect. Some theorists have also speculated that regimes pressured by internal conflict are likely to trump up external conflicts against foreign "scapegoats" in order to divert public attention from domestic problems and to unify the country. Individual cases can be cited that seem to support this hypothesis, such as the Argentine invasion of the Falkland (Malvinas) Islands against the British in 1982, at a time of mounting domestic unrest and deteriorating economic conditions in Argentina. Britain's forceful response to this South Atlantic invasion also was seen in some quarters as an opportunity for Prime Minister Margaret Thatcher's government to regain popularity lost in a time of soaring unemployment. However, while foreign policy moves sometimes pay dividends in domestic politics, the overall evidence is that leaders seldom tailor foreign policy primarily for domestic effects. Governments seem to be reluctant to risk foreign confrontations in most cases when their own population, and perhaps more importantly their armed forces, are not unified and reliable. If anything, war involvements have historically eroded public unity, especially if the wars are long and costly; foreign conflict involvement can worsen or cause domestic conflict. Domestic conflict may induce foreign conflict, however, if enemy states are tempted to intervene in the unstable state to take advantage of political disruption and gain territory or other concessions. See the box on page 174 for a summary of research findings related to the **scapegoat hypothesis** and other hypotheses dealing with national attributes.

The Role of Idiosyncratic Factors

Until now we have discussed mainly objective factors that affect foreign policy. In this section we will examine subjective factors that can have an impact. Those who might be called "environmental determinists" would argue that at least 90 percent of the decisions made by national governments and the results of these decisions would have occurred regardless of the identity of the specific individuals in decision-making positions. Especially in the case of "big" events, it is argued that the objective constraints and historical forces at work are larger than any single individual. For example, environmental determinists would contend that a harsh peace treaty in 1919 and the subsequent economic depression in Germany would have produced a German desire for revenge no matter what leader had come to power in Berlin; in other words, Adolf Hitler did not "cause" World War II.

In contrast, others argue that single individuals ("devils" or "saints") are indeed capable of shaping great events. Those who rely on the **great man (or woman) theory**, or other explanations of foreign policy that focus on individual decision makers, emphasize the role of *idiosyncratic* factors. Here we find the assumption that Charles de Gaulle's presence in the Élysée Palace in Paris, or Stalin's in the Kremlin, or Churchill's in Whitehall, or Mao's in Beijing has materially changed the course of history. Idiosyncratic accounts have ranged from Pascal's perhaps overstated musings that if Cleopatra's nose had been only slightly shorter, the face of the world would have been changed, to Robert Kennedy's equally dramatic and perhaps overstated observation that if six of the fourteen men in the "Ex Com" decision group formed during the Cuban missile crisis had been President of the United States, the world would probably have blown up.[34] How different are these approaches from the perspective of a balance of power systems theorist!

ASSUMPTIONS AND RESEARCH FINDINGS ON NATIONAL ATTRIBUTES

Some common assumptions about the effects of national attributes on foreign policy behavior:

1. Countries with large populations are more war-prone than countries with small populations, in terms of requiring more lebensraum ("living space") and/or having more manpower and economic resources with which to undertake foreign military activity.

2. Large, economically developed countries have a higher level and broader scope of international interactions than small, less developed countries.

3. Economically developed countries belong to more international organizations than less developed countries.

4. The level of economic development of a country is closely related to its voting behavior in the United Nations, especially on North-South questions.

5. Democracies are less warlike than dictatorships.

6. Countries experiencing domestic turmoil are especially likely to become involved in foreign conflict, either in terms of engaging in aggressive behavior against external "scapegoats" or being vulnerable to military intervention.

Some research findings related to the above assumptions:*

1. Big countries tend to become involved in more wars than small countries (Modelski; Wright; Small and Singer) and tend to initiate more conflictual acts (warnings, threats, etc.) in general (Weede, 1970).

2. Although large, developed countries tend to engage in more conflictual acts than small, less developed countries, this is at least partly a function of the former's greater activity in general. Large, developed countries not only engage in more conflictual actions than small, less developed states but also more cooperative actions as well. Economic development seems to lead to a slightly higher percentge of cooperative as opposed to conflictual acts (Salmore and Hermann; Duval and Thompson).

3. Economically developed countries tend to belong to more intergovernmental organizations than less developed countries (Jacobson), tend to be more negative in their attitudes toward the

United Nations (Vincent, 1968), and tend to utilize the International Court of Justice more (Coplin and Rochester).

4. Level of economic development is a strong predictor of UN voting behavior, especially on North-South issues, with less developed countries tending to vote together in support of increased multi-lateral aid, decolonization, and other issues (Alker and Russett; Vincent, 1971).

5. There is little relationship between type of governmental system and war involvement (Rummel, 1968; Luard); open states are only slightly less war-prone and less conflictual in behavior than closed states, although there is a link in recent years between a state's evolution toward political freedom and less war involvement (Haas; Salmore and Hermann; Weede, 1984; Chan).

6. The domestic and foreign conflict behavior of nations are generally unrelated, although states in certain regions and with certain forms of government engage in foreign and domestic conflicts simultaneously more often than other states. When domestic conflict becomes intense, states tend to retreat from foreign involvements to resolve the situation at home. Severe domestic conflict can tempt other states to intervene (Tanter; Rummel, 1963; Wilkenfeld; Pearson).

* Full citations for the specific studies noted in parentheses appear at the end of this chapter. Research findings can depend on the measurements used to test relationships. The findings noted here should be treated as suggestive rather than as the last word on the subject.

The fact is that both objective conditions *and* idiosyncratic factors must be taken into account in seeking a full understanding of foreign policy. Adopting what might be called an "environmental possibilism" approach, we would argue that a decision maker's domestic and international environments (i.e., national attribute and systemic factors) impose limits on the capacity to act, but that individuals can and do exercise some element of free will and do make a difference. It took a Hitler to take full advantage of the possibilities presented by Germany's internal turmoil and international situation. One would expect idiosyncratic factors to be especially important in dictatorships, where one or only a few leaders dominate policymaking, although such factors can be significant in democracies as well. In democracies, idiosyncratic factors are likely to play a larger role in the foreign policy process than in the domestic policy process since leaders generally are given greater leeway in the foreign policy arena. Clearly, for example, President Truman's more suspicious and assertive attitude toward the Soviet Union contrasted with his predecessor's

Adolf Hitler (left) chatting with his air force marshal shortly after becoming the leader (*Der Führer*) of Germany in 1934.

relatively accommodative approach, and rather significantly shaped the development of U.S.-Soviet relations after World War II, although it is possible that President Roosevelt might also have adjusted his view of the Soviets in response to international events in the late forties had he lived into the postwar period. Likewise, without a leader of Nehru's dynamic qualities and neutralist persuasion present at the birth of India in 1947, it is open to question whether India's foreign policy behavior would have taken the turn it did in the postwar period, particularly its active role in the nonaligned movement and its commitment to membership in numerous multilateral international organizations despite scarce resources.

One reason individuals make a difference is that they do not all see their environment the same way. Harold and Margaret Sprout were among the first to draw attention to the distinction between the decision maker's "objective" and "psychological" environments—the difference between reality and an individual's *perception* or **image** of reality.[35] Kenneth Boulding has likewise noted that

> we must recognize that the people whose decisions determine the policies and actions of nations do not respond to the "objective" facts of the situation, whatever that may mean, but to their "image" of the situation. It is what we think the world is like, not what it is really like, that determines our behavior.[36]

Individuals can differ not only in their worldviews but also in *personality* traits such as temperament. The brashness or impulsiveness of leaders, or the extent to which they are tolerant of opposing viewpoints, can have important implications for foreign policy decisions. Some researchers have examined the impact of early childhood experiences on the adult behavior of leaders. For example, it has been argued that Woodrow Wilson's "authoritarian personality," derived from his strict parental upbringing, affected his dealings with other world leaders and members of the U.S. Senate and was at least partly responsible for the failure of the Senate to approve U.S. membership in the League of Nations after World War I.[37]

Personality variables must be treated with caution, however. For example, those who argue that women are inherently less warlike than men might have been confounded by Indira Gandhi's Bangladesh war against Pakistan in 1971, by Golda Meir's 1973 clashes with Syria and Egypt, and by Margaret Thatcher's dispatch of a naval armada to the Falklands in 1982.[38] Each of these leaders built a reputation for strong leadership, exemplified by Thatcher's designation as the "Iron Lady" of British politics. In all three cases there were other factors at work than simply personality. Meir, for instance, did hesitate to strike first against Arab threats in 1973, but seemingly for reasons that any Israeli leader might have been sensitive to; she did not want Israel again condemned by world leaders as an aggressor, as it had been following its preemptive attack on Egypt in 1967.[39] In many cases, the institutional *role* in which policymakers find themselves (e.g., head of state or commander-in-chief) can be more important in affecting their decisions than their individual characteristics.

Far more germane than early childhood experiences or a leader's gender are a leader's recent political experiences. For example, in 1961, while still new to the presidency, John Kennedy met Nikita Khrushchev in Vienna. By most accounts of the Kennedy years, that summit meeting was to affect profoundly the young President's decisions in dealing with the Soviets. Kennedy came away from the meeting feeling that he had failed to impress Khrushchev, that the Russian leader considered him weak and immature. At least one former

U.S. government official has argued that one reason for Kennedy's initial Vietnam commitment in 1961 was a series of early personal setbacks, including his humiliation at Vienna and his failure to respond to the construction of the Berlin Wall, which produced a felt need to demonstrate that he was not spineless.[40] President Kennedy's concern with his image fits a general pattern of leaders worrying that their adversaries in other countries will misperceive reasonableness as weakness and be tempted to take advantage of such weakness.[41]

Idiosyncratic factors can also affect foreign policy when the right person turns out to be in the right place at the right time. While improvement in U.S.-Chinese relations depended mainly on an end to the Vietnam War and growing worries about the Soviet Union, Richard Nixon was perhaps in a better position to take advantage of the situation than any other American politician would have been. The pro-Taiwan "China lobby" in the United States could not accuse Nixon of being soft on Communism when he traveled to Beijing, since his anti-Communist credentials, fashioned during the Mc-Carthy era of the 1950s, were impeccable. Similarly, Israeli Prime Minister Menachem Begin, a staunch hawk and former terrorist leader in Israel's fight for independence, could hardly be criticized by security-minded Israelis for being overly dovish in 1979 when he agreed with Egyptian President Sadat to return the occupied Sinai territory to the Egyptians.

An individual who is all-powerful at one moment might succumb to environmental forces at another moment. What might appear to be a leader's personal charisma and magnetism can actually be skillful manipulation of political factors in the leader's environment. If the environment is no longer amenable to manipulation, the leader's aura of wisdom and invincibility can fade. In perhaps the premier command performance of the postwar period, Charles de Gaulle—hero of the French resistance against the Germans in World War II—was elected in 1958 President of the Fifth French Republic, which he himself designed. Elected partly on the assumption that he would crush the Algerian attempt to gain independence, he proceeded to arrange a plebescite for Algeria that terminated French rule there. Although French colonialists were incensed and felt betrayed by a leader they had relied on to retain French control of Algeria, de Gaulle's carefully cultivated general support in the French army meant that all opponents ultimately had to bend to the President's policy. However, ten years later, during a French worker-student uprising, de Gaulle's charisma no longer sufficed. Although his government finally satisfied the workers and kept the support of the army, voters rejected many of the President's proposals in a final referendum. Even the man who styled himself as the voice of the French nation could not survive all political storms in his environment.[42]

The example of a de Gaulle or a Sadat shows that a country's foreign policy can change in certain circumstances, but one should not lose sight of continuities. Whether due to bureaucratic inertia or other factors, some countries develop a certain tradition in foreign policy, which tends to be maintained even as national leaders come and go. For instance, when the Socialist François Mitterrand replaced a conservative as French President in 1981, his prior opposition to such long-standing French policies as overseas arms sales and military intervention in Africa largely evaporated. Differences among NATO members on concerns ranging from deployment of nuclear weapons in Europe to establishment of better trade relations with the Soviet Union are better explained by long-standing differences in their approaches to military and economic matters—based on disparities in size, geographical location, historical experience, and domestic political forces—than by differences in the nature of individual leaders.

Based on our discussion in this section, it would seem, insofar as idiosyncratic factors are important, that they have a special impact on the *modus operandi* of foreign policy, particularly on the degree of assertiveness and propensity to use force displayed by a country. See the box on page 180 for a summary of some research findings on the role of idiosyncratic factors in foreign policy.

Conclusion

All three sets of factors—systemic, national attribute, and idiosyncratic variables—*intermingle* as a country's foreign policy makers consider how their state should relate to other states.[43] Systemic factors seem especially important in affecting *alignment* behavior. National attribute factors seem especially important in affecting the *scope* dimension of foreign policy. Idiosyncratic factors can be especially important in accounting for some aspects of a country's *modus operandi.*

Although in a given situation one particular set of factors might be the main influence on foreign policy, frequently all three sets of factors operate simultaneously. When Israel bombed Iraq's nuclear research reactor in June of 1981, the action could be attributed to (1) a growing sense of threat in Israel generated by intelligence reports of Iraqi nuclear weapons potential, together with (2) assumptions that a new and evidently less pro-Arab government in Paris would not oppose the destruction of a French-built reactor (i.e., changes in the *international system*); (3) pressures on the Begin government to demonstrate strong leadership in the face of upcoming parliamentary elections, along with (4) general anxiety in Israel over the possibility of a second holocaust against the Jewish people (i.e., *national attributes*); and perhaps (5) Begin's own personal hawkish inclinations bred over a lifetime of anti-Semitic ordeals and forceful Zionist dedication to the creation and maintenance of a Jewish state (i.e., *idiosyncratic* factors).

With all the official speeches and statements pouring out of foreign

ASSUMPTIONS AND RESEARCH FINDINGS ON IDIOSYNCRATIC FACTORS

Some common assumptions about the effects of idiosyncratic factors on foreign policy behavior:

1. Individual leaders will have a greater impact on foreign policy in economically underdeveloped states than in developed states.

2. Individual leaders will have a greater impact on foreign policy in dictatorships than in democracies.

3. Idiosyncratic factors will have a greater impact on decision making the greater the threat, the shorter the time, and the greater the element of surprise in the decision situation.

4. The more detailed the decision that is required, the less likely will idiosyncratic factors affect decisions. The more ambiguous or uncertain the decision-making situation, the greater the impact of idiosyncratic factors is likely to be.

Some research findings related to the above assumptions:*

1. Although leaders who have "authoritarian personalities" (i.e., feel a need to dominate others) are more likely to approve of highly nationalistic, aggressive foreign policy behavior (Scott), the importance of such personality factors on a country's foreign policy depends at least partly on how much control a leader has over policy (M. Hermann).

2. Individuals who favor the use of force in interpersonal relations will tend to favor the use of force in interstate relations (Etheredge), although the institutional role (senator, president, etc.) a leader finds himself in often outweighs personal dispositions (Singer and Ray).

3. The particular images that individual leaders have of the world tend to affect their attitudes toward defense, foreign aid, and other foreign policy concerns (Loomba), although the exact connection between the images of leaders and differences in nation-state behavior is not well established.

4. "Women are decidedly less given to internalizing the pattern of Cold War severity than are men" and "American men are less likely to acknowledge apprehension over the risk of war than women, and are more prone to accept the strategic use of wars" (Rosenberg).

5. Changes in a country's foreign policy are more likely after a change in leadership rather than during the continuation of leadership, particularly in less developed countries (Rosen).

* Full citations for the specific studies noted in parentheses appear at the end of this chapter. Research findings can depend on the measurements used to test relationships. The findings noted here should be treated as suggestive rather than as the last word on the subject.

ministries "clarifying" or "explaining" various countries' actions, it is often difficult to cut through the verbiage to determine which factors are actually driving a given country's foreign policy at a given moment. For foreign policy makers seeking to make sense of the world, it is difficult enough to come to grips fully with their own motives much less those of counterparts in other countries. Yet this is precisely what foreign policy makers must try to do if they are to act wisely.

Information streaming in from the "objective" international environment is interpreted by leaders as it is passed along through government agencies and subjected to a variety of domestic political pressures. Ultimately, the result is some set of judgments about the world, and some set of actions. What is done with the information has an important bearing on the quality of those judgments and the effectiveness of those actions, as we shall see in the next chapter.

SUMMARY

1. Although many people argue that all foreign policy behavior can be traced to national interests, it is necessary to examine a variety of factors found both inside and outside national boundaries in order to understand why countries act as they do. These factors can generally be classified as (1) systemic, (2) national attribute, and (3) idiosyncratic.

2. Systemic factors are those conditions in a country's external environment that can affect its foreign policy. These include geography, international interactions and links, and the international system structure. For example, as the international environment becomes less threatening, two countries allied militarily may feel less need to continue their alliance relationship.

3. National attributes—demographic, economic, military, and governmental factors— also affect foreign policy behavior. For example, the more economic assets a country has, the greater its ability to pursue global interests, to use economic tools of influence, and to participate in international organizations. A country's military preparedness, rate of economic growth, and access to resources can affect its foreign policy assertiveness. The type of political system a country has can also shape its foreign policy behavior, with leaders in a democracy having to be more concerned about public opinion than their counterparts in a dictatorship. However, in democracies and nondemocracies alike, foreign policy is shaped by a combination of external forces and domestic political pressures.

4. Those who rely on "the great man/woman theory of history," or other explanations of foreign policy that focus on the role of individual decision makers, emphasize the importance of idiosyncratic factors. Although objective conditions such as national attributes and systemic factors impose limits on a state's capacity to act no matter who is at the helm, differences in leadership personality, temperament, and other personal characteristics can have important impacts on foreign policy. For example, one cannot fully account for Chinese and French foreign policy after World War II without noting the special imprint of strong leaders like Mao and de Gaulle.

5. Generally speaking, systemic factors seem especially important in affecting alignment behavior, national attribute factors especially affect the scope of foreign policy, and idiosyncratic factors affect the *modus operandi* of a state. However, frequently all three sets of factors operate simultaneously, intermingling as foreign policy makers consider how their state should relate to other states.

SUGGESTIONS FOR FURTHER READING AND STUDY

General works that provide an inventory of theories and research findings on foreign policy determinants include James E. Dougherty and Robert L. Pfaltzgraff, Jr., *Contending Theories of International Relations*, 2nd ed. (New York: Harper & Row, 1981); Susan D. Jones and J. David Singer, *Beyond Conjecture in International Politics: Abstracts of Data-Based Research* (Itasca, Ill.: F. E. Peacock, 1972); Patrick J. McGowan and Howard B. Shapiro, *The Comparative Study of Foreign Policy: A Survey of Scientific Findings* (Beverly Hills: Sage, 1973); Lloyd Jensen, *Explaining Foreign Policy* (Englewood Cliffs, N.J.: Prentice-Hall, 1982); Michael P. Sullivan, *International Relations: Theories and Evidence* (Englewood Cliffs, N.J.: Prentice-Hall, 1976); and Steve Smith, "Comparing the Comparers," *Millennium*, 10 (Autumn 1981), pp. 240–256. Excellent collections of theoretical articles include James N. Rosenau, ed., *Comparing Foreign Policies: Theories, Findings and Methods* (New York: John Wiley, 1974), especially pp. 117–150 and 201–234; Charles W. Kegley *et al.*, *International Events and the Comparative Analysis of Foreign Policy* (Columbia, S.C.: University of South Carolina Press, 1975); Wolfram F. Hanrieder, ed., *Comparative Foreign Policy: Theoretical Essays* (New York: McKay, 1971); and Patrick McGowan and Charles W. Kegley, *Foreign Policy and the Modern World System* (Beverly Hills: Sage, 1983).

The following works were cited in boxes in this chapter: Hayward R. Alker and Bruce M. Russett, *World Politics in the General Assembly* (New Haven, Conn.: Yale University Press, 1965); Steven J. Brams, "Transaction Flows in the International System," *American Political Science Review*, 60 (December 1966), pp. 880–898; Steve Chan, "Mirror, Mirror on the Wall . . . Are the Freer Countries More Pacific?," *Journal of Conflict Resolution*, 28 (December 1984), pp. 617–648; Roger W. Cobb and Charles Elder, *International Community: A Regional and Global Study* (New York: Holt,

Rinehart and Winston, 1970); William D. Coplin and J. Martin Rochester, "The Permanent Court of International Justice, the International Court of Justice, the League of Nations, and the United Nations: A Comparative Empirical Survey," *American Political Science Review*, 66 (June 1972), pp. 529–550; Robert D. Duval and William R. Thompson, "Reconsidering the Aggregate Relationship Between Size, Economic Development, and Some Types of Foreign Policy Behavior," *American Journal of Political Science*, 24 (August 1980), pp. 511–525; Lloyd S. Etheredge, "Personality Effects on American Foreign Policy, 1898–1968: A Test of Interpersonal Generalization Theory," *American Political Science Review*, 72 (June 1978), pp. 435–451; Wayne H. Ferris, *The Power Capability of Nation-States* (Lexington, Mass.: Lexington Books, 1973); Mark J. Gasiorowski, "Economic Interdependence and International Conflict: Some Cross-National Evidence," *International Studies Quarterly*, 30 (March 1986), pp. 23–38; Michael Haas, "Societal Approaches to the Study of War," *Journal of Peace Research*, 2 (1965), pp. 307–323; Margaret G. Hermann, "Leader Personality and Foreign Policy Behavior," in *Comparing Foreign Policies: Theories, Findings, and Methods*, James N. Rosenau, ed. (New York: John Wiley, 1974), pp. 201–234; Ole R. Holsti *et al., Unity and Disintegration in International Alliances* (New York: John Wiley, 1973); Harold K. Jacobson, *Networks of Interdependence* (New York: Knopf, 1979), ch. 3; Evan Luard, *Conflict and Peace in the Modern International System* (Boston: Little, Brown, 1968); George Modelski, "War and the Great Powers," *Peace Research Society Papers*, 18 (1971), pp. 45–60; Frederic S. Pearson, "Foreign Military Interventions and Domestic Disputes," *International Studies Quarterly*, 18 (September 1974), pp. 259–290; Lewis F. Richardson, *Statistics of Deadly Quarrels* (Pittsburgh: Boxwood Press, 1960); David Rosen, "Leadership Change and Foreign Policy," CREON Abstract #6 (Columbus: Ohio State University, 1975); Milton J. Rosenberg, "Attitude Change and Foreign Policy in the Cold War Era," in *Domestic Sources of Foreign Policy*, James N. Rosenau, ed. (New York: Free Press, 1967), pp. 111–159; Rudolph J. Rummel, "A Social Field Theory of Foreign Conflict Behavior," *Peace Research Society Papers*, 4 (1966), pp. 131–150; Rummel, "Dimensions of Conflict Behavior Within and Between Nations," *General Systems Yearbook*, 8 (1963), pp. 1–50; Rummel, "The Relationship Between National Attributes and Foreign Conflict Behavior," in J. David Singer, ed., *Quantitative International Politics* (New York: Free Press, 1968), pp. 187–214.

Also cited in the boxes were Bruce M. Russett, *International Regions and the International System* (Chicago: Rand McNally, 1967); Quincy Wright, *A Study of War*, 2nd ed. (Chicago: University of Chicago Press, 1964); Steven A. Salmore and Charles F. Hermann, "The Effect of Size, Development and Accountability on Foreign Policy," *Peace Research Society Papers*, 14 (1970), pp. 27–28; William Scott, "Psychological and Social Correlates of International Images," in *International Behavior: A Social-Psychological Analysis*, Herbert C. Kelman, ed. (New York: Holt, Rinehart, & Winston, 1965), pp. 71–103; J. David Singer and Paul Ray, "Decision Making in Conflict: From Inter-Personal to Inter-National Relations," *Bulletin of the Menninger Clinic*, 30 (1966), pp. 300–312; J. David Singer, "The Correlates of War Project: Interim Report and Rationale," *World Politics*, 24 (January 1972), pp. 243–270; Melvin Small and J. David Singer, "Patterns in International Warfare, 1816–1965," *Annals*, 391 (1970), pp. 145–155; Raymond Tanter, "Dimensions of Conflict Behavior Within and Between Nations, 1958–1960," *Journal of Conflict Resolution*, 10 (March 1966), pp. 41–64; Jack E. Vincent, "National Attributes as Predictors of Delegate Attitudes at the United Nations," *American Political Science Review*, 62 (September 1968), pp. 916–931, and

"Predicting Voting Patterns in the General Assembly," *American Political Science Review*, 65 (June 1971), pp. 471–498; Frank W. Wayman, "Bipolarity and War: The Role of Capability Concentration and Alliance Patterns Among Major Powers, 1816–1965," *Journal of Peace Research*, 21 (1984), pp. 61–78; Erich Weede, "Conflict Behavior of Nation-States," *Journal of Peace Research*, 7 (1970), pp. 229–235, and "Democracy and War Involvement," *Journal of Conflict Resolution*, 28 (December 1984), pp. 649–664; Jonathan Wilkenfeld, "Domestic and Foreign Conflict Behavior of Nations," *Journal of Peace Research*, 5 (1968), pp. 56–59, and "Some Further Findings Regarding the Domestic and Foreign Conflict Behavior of Nations," *Journal of Peace Research*, 6 (1969), pp. 147–156; and Eugene R. Wittkopf, "The Distribution of Foreign Aid in Comparative Perspective: An Empirical Study of the Flow of Foreign Economic Assistance, 1961–1967," Ph.D. dissertation (Syracuse: Syracuse University, 1971).

The Foreign Policy Process: A View from the Inside

In the previous chapter, we examined several determinants of foreign policy behavior. We noted that although systemic and national attribute factors tend to place constraints on state action, they alone do not dictate foreign policy behavior but operate in conjunction with other, idiosyncratic factors. In other words, national leaders must still make decisions that involve *choices* among foreign policy ends and means, no matter how much it may seem their hands are "tied" by conditions in their environment.

In this chapter, we will look more closely at the foreign policy–making *process* itself, including some of the more subtle factors at work. Clearly, the institutions and procedures involved in foreign policy-making differ from country to country. However, we are not interested here in the legal-formal aspects of the foreign policy process but rather in the various factors—intellectual, psychological, and otherwise—underlying the decision process in all political systems. For example, the kinds of information and time constraints that operate on American policymakers in a crisis situation can operate in a similar manner on Soviet policymakers or the policymakers of India, China, and any other country and produce comparable behavior in like situations, especially if the individuals involved have similar personalities and dispositions in moments of stress.

Much of the discussion in this chapter follows from the discussion of idiosyncratic factors in Chapter 5. We want to look further *inside* the foreign policy process, seeing how those officials responsible for foreign policy produce decisions under varying circumstances. We especially want to examine whether decisions about foreign policy ends and means (such as using nuclear weapons) are made as carefully and *rationally* as the average citizen might assume or hope. As Graham Allison poignantly notes in his study of the Cuban missile crisis, such concerns are not merely of academic interest:

> The Cuban missile crisis is a seminal event. For thirteen days of October 1962, there was a higher probability that more human lives would end suddenly than ever before in history. Had the worst occurred, the death of 100 million Americans, over 100 million Russians, and millions of Europeans as well would make previous natural calamities and inhumanities appear insignificant. Given the probability of disaster—which President Kennedy estimated as "between one out of three and even"—our escape seems awesome. The event symbolizes a central, if only partially thinkable, fact about our existence. That such consequences could follow from the choices and actions of national governments obliges students of government as well as participants in governance to think hard about these problems.[1]

Does Each Country Have a Foreign Policy?

Six months after an American president assumed office, a newspaper ran the following headline: "Reagan Pressed to Spell Out Foreign Policy."[2] This begged the question: Foreign policy with regard to *what*—the world, Latin America, the Soviet Union, foreign aid, arms sales?

Such headlines conjure up visions of foreign policy as being a single, conscious, overarching "plan"—a master blueprint containing an explicit set of goals and strategies for achieving those goals, into which all other smaller decisions are fitted. References are commonly made to the "architects" of U.S. (or Soviet) policy. National leaders themselves like to reassure their citizenry that they have a plan, and they often accuse national leaders in other states of having their own "grand design." However, to what extent does this square with reality?

Among those who have questioned whether states, particularly those with large government bureaucracies, have such blueprints is Henry Kissinger (at least before he was to become U.S. Secretary of State). The quotation below suggests that any American visions of a tiny clique of Soviet leaders hatching a worldwide conspiracy within the Kremlin walls (or Soviet visions of a cabal of American leaders doing likewise within the Oval Office of the White House) may be the figments of someone's imagination:

> The most frequent question that one is asked when abroad, or by people who are concerned with international affairs and have not seen policy made, is "What is American policy?" . . . [People] attempt to give a rationality and consistency to foreign policy which it simply does not have. I have found it next to impossible to convince Frenchmen that there is no such thing as an American foreign policy, and that a series of moves that have produced a certain result may not have been planned to produce that result.
>
> Foreigners looking at American policy have a tendency to assume that anything that happened was intended and that there is a deep, complicated purpose behind our actions. I wish this were true, but I don't believe that it is. In fact, I think that in any large bureaucracy it probably cannot be true, and this is probably the case with the Soviet Union also. We probably ascribe more consistency to Soviet foreign policy than really exists.[3]

Kissinger may have overstated the case a bit. Franklin Roosevelt, for example, had what he considered a "Great Design" for the post–World War II period, whose centerpiece was an active internationalist role for the United States. As we have noted, later American presidents invoked the "containment doctrine," "détente," or "human rights" as guiding principles of their foreign policy. These themes represented at least to some extent an attempt to give an overall rationale and sense of direction to U.S. foreign affairs. Indeed, every U.S. president has felt compelled, either in his inaugural address or first state of the union address, to announce how the nation's foreign policy would be charted over the next four years. Similar pronouncements can be found in the major addresses of leaders in other countries.

It is not that leaders make no attempt to develop a comprehensive framework for action. The thrust of Kissinger's remarks is that no matter how much a leadership tries to carve out a single, overall foreign policy, it inevitably finds itself having to make decisions about more discrete matters—whether, for example, to grant "most favored nation" trade status to Romania, whether to sell the latest fighter plane technology to Saudi Arabia, whether to give territorial asylum to a Chilean dissident poet, whether to use chemical weapons in Vietnam—and numerous other concerns that do not fit neatly into a "grand plan." As Roger Hilsman has noted: "Very often policy is the sum of a congeries of separate or only vaguely related actions."[4]

A famous episode that illustrates Hilsman's point very well was the Iran-Contra affair during the Reagan presidency. President Reagan had built his entire foreign policy around the general theme of restoring American strength and credibility in the world. This included an avowed hard-line policy against negotiating with terrorist groups and those governments that supported terrorism. Despite such a policy, the Reagan administration entered into a secret "arms for hostages deal" with Iran in 1985 and 1986, providing much-needed military equipment to Iran in exchange for Iranian promises to use their influence with certain militant Shiite Muslim groups in Lebanon to gain the release of several Americans held hostage there. The President entrusted the execution of this covert operation to a few aides on his National Security Council staff, hoping to achieve a quick, quiet return of the American prisoners without anyone learning of the "ransom" payments and, hence, without any damage done to the hard-line image the President was trying to project in the world. Although the President authorized the plan, some specific actions seemingly were undertaken by his staff without his full knowledge or approval, including the illegal diversion of funds from the Iran arms sales to anti-Communist guerrilla fighters in Nicaragua known as the Contras. Indeed, many of the normal channels of consultation on major matters within the U.S. foreign policy establishment, such as the Secretary of State, were virtually bypassed. When knowledge of the deal ultimately became public through media reports, and the hostages were not released, the resulting scandal and public uproar threw into disarray not only Washington's anti-terrorism policy but the entire fabric of American foreign policy as well. The episode also raised puzzling questions about the manner in which American foreign policy was made and who was "in charge" of that policy.

Types of Foreign Policy Decisions

Foreign policy should thus be thought of not as a single overall plan but, more realistically, as a series of hundreds of decisions that have to be made, which may hold together in a coherent fashion but which more likely will not. These hundreds of foreign policy decisions confronting a national government can be classified in a variety of ways. One way to categorize foreign policy decisions is according to *issue-area*—national security policy, economic policy, and so forth.[5] Another typology is based more on the *situational* setting in which decisions are made than on the substantive content of the decisions, for instance crisis as opposed to noncrisis decisions.[6] A number of observers have noted that issue-area and situational variables can structure the foreign policy process in important ways. For example, it is frequently argued that in the national security or military-strategic issue-area, and especially in crisis situations, the role of domestic politics tends to be diminished as leaders seek to behave as "statesmen" rather than "politicians." If we focus on situational features, foreign policy decisions tend to fall into three categories: macro-decisions, micro-decisions, and crisis decisions.

MACRO-DECISIONS

Some of the most important foreign policy decisions that a government must make are in regard to such matters as level of defense spending, level and type of foreign aid to be given or sought, arms control policy, and international trade policy. For a country like the United States with diverse global interests, decisions must also be made on Middle East policy, Asian policy, Latin American policy, and so forth. Narrower, but still fairly broad, decisions might have to be made regarding, say, a reevaluation of relations with China or the terms of peaceful nuclear technology transfer to Third World countries. One can label such decisions **macro-decisions** in the sense that they involve relatively large, general concerns and are designed to establish guidelines or "rules of thumb" to be applied later to specific situations (for example, a request by the Indian government for additional uranium from the United States to fuel a nuclear reactor). Some guidelines are formulated in a relatively elaborate and explicit fashion, and others less so. The existence of well-developed general rules can make it easier for decision makers to handle specific problems as they arise. Macro-decisions are the kinds of decisions that conform most closely to what is ordinarily implied by the term "policy."

These decisions normally occur in a setting in which (1) the need to make the decision has been *anticipated* and is not in response to some sudden, surprise occurrence in the environment, (2) there is a relatively *lengthy time frame* in which to reach a decision, and (3) a *large variety of domestic political actors* inside and outside of the government can become involved in the decision process, although the decision is ultimately made by top-level officials. Such decisions may or may not involve serious "high threat" concerns. Macro-decisions allow for foreign policy *planning* by bureaucratic staffs, although it is commonly noted that policymakers tend to be preoccupied with short-term rather than long-term concerns.

MICRO-DECISIONS

An enormous number of foreign policy decisions can be labeled **micro-decisions** (or, as they are sometimes called, "administrative" decisions). These may or may not involve the element of surprise and may or may not allow for lengthy deliberation. In any case, such decisions by definition normally involve concerns that are (1) relatively *narrow in scope*, (2) *low threat* in seriousness, and (3) handled at the *lower levels of the government bureaucracy*. Examples might include the authorization of a visa by Austrian officials allowing a particular person to travel in Austria, the response to a request from an embassy in Malawi for additional office supplies, the determination of seating arrangements for visiting dignitaries at a British reception in Whitehall, and the approval of a $5 million credit extension allowing Bangladesh to purchase needed farm equipment.

The bulk of foreign policy decisions made by a government are micro-decisions. As one U.S. official noted, "The American State Department in any one day receives about 1300 cables from American diplomatic and consular officials abroad providing information, requesting directions, or seeking permission to make certain decisions in the field. But . . . the Secretary of State will read only . . . 2 percent of the total. The State Department also sends out approximately 1000 cables daily; . . . of these, the Secretary of State may see only six, and the President will have only one or two of the most important communications referred to his office."[7]

Micro-decisions are supposed to be based on macro-decisions, i.e., they are made by bureaucrats applying a standard set of guidelines. For example, U.S. officials use the Munitions List and International Traffic in Arms Rules to process 90 percent of the private arms sales license applications they receive. However, administrative decisions are often made independently of, and possibly at variance with, the general policy. While such decisions by themselves are unlikely to have significant consequences (even if a minor diplomatic incident may be created, for example, by an errant choice of dining utensils, which happened when some "made in Taiwan" chopsticks turned up at a Carter White House dinner honoring officials from mainland China), taken together they can add up to major foreign policy developments.

CRISIS DECISIONS

A number of foreign policy decisions fall somewhere between the two types just discussed. Charles Hermann, for example, has identified eight possible decision "situations," each with its own distinct characteristics affecting the dynamics of the decision-making process.[8] One special category of decisions that has attracted the attention of Hermann and many other scholars in recent years involves crisis situations. **Crisis decisions** are made in situations normally characterized by (1) a *high degree of threat* and potential gravity, (2) a *finite time frame* in which to reach a decision, and (3) involvement of the *very* *highest level* of the foreign policy establishment in the decision process (usually in a small group setting). Hermann's initial definition of a crisis situation included the element of surprise, but he has since dropped that requirement from the definition.[9] Although it is possible that decision makers might not be completely surprised, a crisis ordinarily is occasioned by some change or disturbance in a state's environment—a potential turning point in its relationship with other states in the system—that is seen by its policymakers as threatening. Michael Brecher has defined a crisis as a situation entailing perceptions of "threat to basic values, finite time for response, and the likelihood of involvement in military hostilities."[10] Although a crisis is often associated with short response time, some crises can drag on for a long period of time (e.g., the Iranian hostage "crisis" faced by the Carter administration in 1979 and 1980, which lasted 444 days). At a minimum, a crisis entails a sufficiently serious problem to command the intense, sustained attention of the top leadership. One such situation, the Cuban missile crisis of 1962, may well be the most studied single case in history.

Some argue that much of what passes for foreign policy is really "crisis management," i.e., responding to the latest collapse of the Italian government on Tuesday, the outbreak of civil war in Lebanon on Wednesday, the most recent coup d'état in Benin on Thursday, the skyjacking of an American plane on Friday, and other such events. At times multiple crises can occur simultaneously and compete for attention, as in the case of the bombing of the U.S. Marine headquarters in Beirut and the American invasion of Grenada within the same week in 1983. However, it is a mistake to depict the foreign policy process as consisting of one round after another of crisis management. Foreign policymakers do not spend all their time lurching from one crisis to another any more than they do sitting at their desks pondering grand designs and stratagems. When crises occur, though, policymakers are clearly confronted with some of the most crucial decisions they are called upon to make.

In the foreign policy process, the various types of decisions blend together, often imperceptibly. Some decisions, such as the Kennedy administration's commitment of 10,000 American troops to Vietnam as "advisory" counterinsurgency personnel in 1961, can set in motion a myriad of smaller, administrative decisions, can breed more than one crisis, and can even come to dominate a country's foreign policy agenda for a decade—beyond anyone's expectations or intentions.

The Conventional View of Foreign Policy: States as Rational Actors

Those attempting to understand foreign policy—practitioners, scholars, and laymen alike—commonly view foreign policy as the work of a *unitary* actor

A WEEK OF CRISIS IN U.S. FOREIGN POLICY—LEBANON AND GRENADA (OCTOBER 22–28, 1983)

Clockwise from top left

Saturday, Oct. 22, 5:15 am: President Reagan is briefed in his suite at the Augusta, Ga., National Golf Club by National Security Advisor McFarlane (seated in chair) and Secretary of State Shultz regarding a request by five Caribbean nations for a joint invasion of Grenada in response to a violent coup that had just occurred on the island.

11:45 am: After finishing nine holes of golf, the President and Shultz are given an update on the Grenada situation by McFarlane.

12:45 pm: The Secretary of State, using a telephone on the golf course, speaks with State Department officials about plans for an invasion of the island.

Sunday, Oct. 23, 7:30 am: While en route to Washington on Air Force One, the President confers with Shultz and McFarlane after having learned of the killing of 240 U.S. Marines by a terrorist bombing in Beirut, Lebanon.

Clockwise from top left

8:38 am: The President, arriving at the White House with Mrs. Reagan, meets with news reporters and condemns the Beirut bombing.

9:30 am: The President discusses the Beirut developments in the White House Situation Room with his chief advisors (seated clockwise from the President at the head of the table are Secretary of State Shultz, Deputy CIA Director MacMahon, Presidential Special Assistant Baker, National Security Advisor McFarlane, White House Counsel Meese, General Vessey of the Joint Chiefs of Staff, Secretary of Defense Weinberger, and Vice-President Bush).

Tuesday, Oct. 25, 8:15 am: The Secretary of State briefs members of Congress in the Cabinet Room of the White House regarding the invasion of Grenada, which was announced at a press conference one hour later.

(a nation-state or national government). Every day we hear references in conversation and news reports that "the United States" or "Washington" (or "the Soviet Union" or "Moscow") has "decided" something or "done" something in the international arena. These are not just convenient shorthand expressions but a reflection of a natural tendency to reify the nation-state, i.e., to attribute human qualities to a collectivity. According to this conventional states-as-actors perspective, states are treated like "billiard balls," with their interactions constituting international relations.[11] Put another way, states are viewed here as if they were monolithic "black boxes" cranking out foreign policy decisions and behaviors based on national interest calculations, with the observer not having to look beneath the surface at the internal dynamics of the policymaking process.

Much of international relations can be understood in these "black box" terms. In this book we, too, at times have resorted to the shorthand notation in describing foreign policy behavior and have said that states acting through their national government are the lead players in the drama of international relations. Associated with this conventional view is the assumption that nation-states and their governments are *rational* actors. As Thomas Kreuger notes, in the case of the United States, "most American historians view diplomacy as the outcome of decisions made by rational men in pursuit of the national interest."[12] Likewise, Graham Allison has commented that most people tend to explain international events in terms of a "rational actor" model, as the product of deliberate decisions of unified national governments:

> For example, on confronting the problem posed by the Soviet installation of strategic missiles in Cuba [in 1962] . . . [the] analyst frames the puzzle: Why did the Soviet Union decide to install missiles in Cuba? He then fixes the unit of analysis: governmental choice. Next, he focuses attention on . . . goals and objectives of the nation or government. And finally, he invokes certain patterns of inference: if the nation performed an action of this sort, it must have had a goal of this type. The analyst has "explained" this event when he can show how placing missiles in Cuba was a reasonable action, given Soviet strategic objectives. Predictions about what a nation will do or would have done are generated by calculating the rational thing to do in a certain situation, given specified objectives.[13]

THE RATIONAL ACTOR MODEL

Let us examine the assumptions of the **rational actor model** more closely. When faced with a decision-making situation—i.e., with a problem that requires resolution—rational individuals supposedly follow a certain process in which they

1. define the situation that calls for a decision, basing their assessment on an objective consideration of the facts;
2. specify the goal(s) to be achieved in the situation (and, if there is a conflict among several goals, rank-order them as to priorities);

3. consider all possible alternative means of achieving the goal(s);
4. select the final alternative calculated to maximize achievement of the goal(s); and
5. take the necessary action to implement the decision.

One can add a sixth step, evaluation of the consequences of an individual's actions, assuming that a rational actor will want to determine if the goal in question has been achieved and whether similar actions can be expected to achieve similar goals in similar situations in the future.

This all sounds very simple and obvious, even if somewhat abstract. All of us like to think of ourselves as rational creatures. Yet few if any of us actually behave in the above fashion when having to make a decision. The rational actor model is essentially an "ideal type" that cannot be fully conformed to in the real world, whether the decisions involve which brand of beer to buy or more sober matters such as those confronting foreign policy makers. How many people are capable of viewing the world in a totally objective, unbiased manner? How many undertake the effort to spell out goals and to come to grips with the often agonizing choices between equally desired but mutually incompatible benefits? How many have the time to ponder all conceivable options, or possess the complete information with which to arrive at the very best solution? And when others are being relied on to implement a decision, how many people follow through to ensure that the decision is executed as intended? Finally, how many people bother to review systematically the consequences of their decisions so as to draw proper lessons of possible use in the future?

Although the rational actor model is an ideal type, some decision makers come closer than others to fulfilling the requirements. To the extent that a decision maker approximates the model, that individual can be said to act more or less "rationally." As we have noted, in foreign policymaking rational behavior is associated with the pursuit of national interests, so that the criterion for judging whether a foreign policy decision is a rational, high-quality one is generally whether it is calculated to promote national goals at reasonable costs or risks. One would hope that the greatest rationality would prevail in those instances where the most important foreign policy decisions have to be made. However, this may not always be the case, as the following observers note, only semi-facetiously:

> It is tempting to speculate that the more important the decision, the less likely it is that the decision will be based on pure rationality. . . . Notice how little effort is put into acquiring information, considering alternatives, and making choices for the really big life decisions one makes, like choosing a career or a marriage partner. Here people seem to slide into the path of least resistance and to settle for the first available alternative, rather than conducting a thorough search and selecting that alternative which best fulfills one's basic values. More intellectual effort and rational behavior

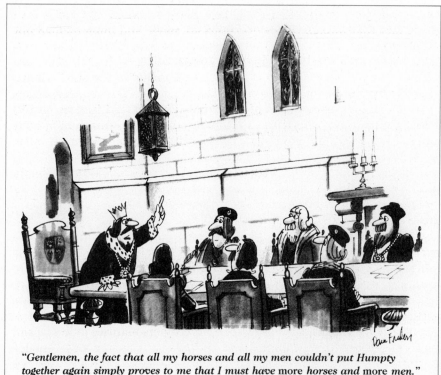

"*Gentlemen, the fact that all my horses and all my men couldn't put Humpty together again simply proves to me that I must have more horses and more men.*"

The rational problem solver at work: Policy evaluation

may typically be put into buying a car or a six-pack of beer, where at least people shop comparatively and gather some information. It is worth asking if the same pattern exists in the realm of foreign policy decisions, where it often appears more time, attention, and energy are given to choosing seating arrangements for a diplomatic reception than to . . . [considering] the effectiveness of the latest weapons system acquired by the Department of Defense.[14]

An Alternative View: States as Collections of Individuals, Groups, and Organizations That May or May Not Act Rationally

As analysis of foreign policy has become more sophisticated in recent years, it has become apparent that many factors can contribute to **nonrational**

behavior on the part of states. This is especially so when one takes into account the fact that foreign policy decisions are made and implemented not by mechanistic actors called "the United States" or "the Soviet Union" but by specific persons who individually or in combination with each other are all capable of human fallibility when acting in the name of the state. Hence an alternative perspective on foreign policy has developed, which incorporates all the various factors discussed in the previous chapter and focuses on the human decision makers themselves as actors responding to stimuli from both their external, international environment and their internal, domestic environment.[15] This alternative view is represented in Figure 6.1.

While the rational actor (state-as-actor) model can provide important insights into nation-state behavior, models that focus on *individuals, groups, and organizations* as actors in the foreign policy process allow us to gain a richer, fuller understanding of such phenomena. In his well-known study of the Cuban missile crisis, Graham Allison argues that the best explanation of the U.S. naval blockade decision can be derived by analyzing the decision from several different "cuts," using not only a rational actor model (interpreting it as the outcome of the leadership's collective deliberations and shared view of what was the best way to protect American national security) but also a "governmental politics" model (interpreting it as the result of intense bargaining and compromise among a group of different personalities who saw the situation from competing viewpoints), and an "organizational process" model (interpreting it as the outcome of various bureaucratic procedures and routines that affected the collection and analysis of intelligence data and other aspects of the decision process).[16]

As we commented in our discussion earlier in this chapter, a country's entire foreign policy establishment does not become mobilized every time there is a decision to be made and implemented. Depending on the nature of the decision—the issue-area or situation—different parts of the foreign policy

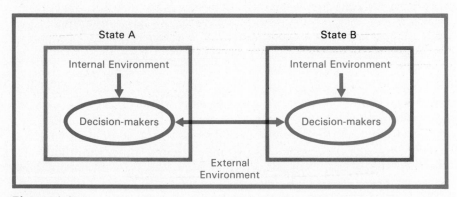

Figure 6.1
AN ALTERNATIVE TO THE "BILLIARD BALL" OR "BLACK BOX" VIEW OF FOREIGN POLICY

apparatus (different individuals, groups, and organizations) will become involved and different factors may come into play that complicate national interest considerations. As in the Iran-Contra case during the Reagan administration, at times the normal workings of a country's foreign policy machinery can become so "short-circuited" that even among the very top leadership the "left hand" may not be aware of what the "right hand" is doing. In the next section we examine the dynamics of foreign policy decision making, noting how nonrational (or at least quasi-rational) factors can intrude throughout the foreign policy process and cause bad decisions.

Nonrational Factors in Foreign Policy

Nonrational (or quasi-rational) factors can operate at various stages in the foreign policy process. This process includes (1) definition of the situation, (2) consideration of goals and means, and (3) the implementation and evaluation stages.

DEFINITION OF THE SITUATION

The need for a foreign policy decision does not exist until somebody identifies a problem "out there" that seems to require a response. We noted in the previous chapter that there can often be a gap between the "objective" environment ("reality") and the "psychological" environment ("image" of reality) of an individual. If the gap is wide, it can seriously distort the character of a problem and cause nonrational decision making from the start, since the definition of the situation—for example, whether some event constitutes a crisis or not—tends to structure the entire decision process, including *who* becomes involved in the decision and the time frame within which officials assume a decision must be reached.

A decision maker's failure to grasp the facts of a situation can have less to do with the quantity or quality of information received ("intelligence failures") than with the manner in which the information is digested ("mental failures"). In order to understand this point, one needs to understand the nature of *images*. All of us have a collection of images of the world, which constitutes a belief system or filter, through which we interpret the myriad events we are exposed to from one day to the next. Images help us construct reality, but they can also blind us to reality or severely bias our assessment of a given occurrence. In particular, there is a common tendency to filter out any stimuli—incoming bits of information—that do not square with our image of the world and, hence, threaten to upset our established mindset. Psychologists speak of *selective attention*, seeing only what we want to see or are habitually inclined to see, as well as *rationalization*, dismissing as unimportant "flukes" any happenings that cannot escape attention but do not conform to our image of things.[17]

Foreign policymakers are as susceptible to distorting reality as are any other decision makers. Robert Jervis has suggested that they have a natural tendency to misperceive their environment to some extent, particularly to view many states as more hostile than they really are and to assume not only that the *other* side is more "ruthless" and "devious" than their own state but also that it is cognizant of this.[18] Associated with such misperception is the tendency of a country's leadership to admonish the other side for what are felt to be aggressive designs and deceitful tactics without realizing that their own behavior may perhaps be a precise mirror image of their opponent's. It has been said that much of the Cold War and especially the nuclear arms race between the United States and the Soviet Union can be explained in terms of mutual distrust based on misperceptions of each other's intentions.[19]

Considerable research has been done in recent years in the area of **threat perception.** In a pioneering article, J. David Singer hypothesized that one nation's perceptions of the degree of threat posed by another nation's actions depends on the former's estimates of the latter's *capability* to do harm and the *intent* to do it.[20] When an adversary suddenly doubles its military spending or mobilizes several divisions of troops, decision makers find themselves of necessity speculating about the underlying intentions behind such behavior, in particular whether it seems to portend an imminent military attack or simply represents a bolstering of national defense. Given the great difficulty in determining an adversary's intentions, a country's foreign policymakers often engage in "worst-case analysis," i.e., assume the *worst* of the adversary and worry not about intentions but only about capabilities (what the latter *can* do). This is a standard tenet emphasized by the military establishment in most countries, based on the assumption that it is easier to estimate an enemy's capabilities than its intentions. However, even capabilities can be grossly misjudged, as in the case of the mythical "missile gap" that was reported to exist between the United States and the Soviet Union in the late fifties based on a top-level U.S. study; there was a gap, but contrary to the study, the United States was in the lead rather than the Soviet Union.

Although it might seem rational to be prepared for any contingency, however improbable, worst-case analysis can produce unwarranted fears that may lead to a conflict neither side wants. It should be added that the lenses through which leaders view the world are not always shaded dark and given to exaggerated perceptions of threat but can at times be rose-tinted and given to "wishful thinking" that can cause leaders to overlook a threat that truly exists. One of the most frequently cited examples of this is the Pearl Harbor attack, when American officials—operating on the assumption that the Japanese would not and could not launch an aerial raid on the U.S. naval base—ignored a stream of information that signaled an impending attack, including the actual radar detection of an approaching squadron of planes.[21]

Since images color reality for foreign policymakers and shape their perceptions of situations, it is important to understand how images themselves are shaped. Some images are based on a nation's *historical experiences*. As such, they may be widely shared among the members of a country's foreign policy establishment and even by its populace as a whole. For example, we noted earlier that the "Munich" experience had a profound impact on an entire generation of Americans after World War II. The problem with historically based images is that they can be misapplied to contemporary circumstances. The failure of the Western democracies to resist aggression in Austria, Ethiopia, Manchuria, and, finally, Czechoslovakia in the 1930s was the first thought that popped into President Truman's mind as he flew from Independence, Missouri, to Washington to handle the fast-breaking events at the start of the Korean War in 1950.[22] Conceivably, the Korean situation could have been interpreted as a civil war or as a confined regional conflict; but Truman, like most of his contemporaries, viewed it in larger terms as part of a global challenge that had to be confronted. A decade later the same Munich analogy was applied again by American leaders to events in Vietnam, a country that was depicted as a "domino"—if it was allowed to fall, the result would be the collapse of all other "dominoes" in Southeast Asia. In the case of both Korea and Vietnam, scholars have argued that a historically based image, wrongly applied, caused a fundamental misreading of the situation and contributed to imprudent U.S. foreign policy decisions. In the words of Ernest May, "history overpowered calculation."[23]

Kenneth Boulding has noted that a nation's image of itself and of others is shaped not only by *specific* historical events such as Munich (which may affect only the generation that lived through them) but even more so by *cumulative* historical experiences as retold in family gatherings or in the civics textbooks to which all children are exposed in school.[24] Some peoples have experienced conflict between each other so often in the past that there develops an ingrained animosity that affects their perceptions of each other. Rivalries that may have been founded on real conflicts of interest, such as border disagreements, can be sustained through the years by less tangible factors. The traditional Franco-German and Russo-Chinese rivalries, for example, have been much discussed.[25] One must be careful not to inflate the importance of such historic rivalries since, as we have noted, there are many instances of rivals at least temporarily "burying the hatchet" when the case for cooperation is compelling (e.g., the Soviet-Chinese security treaty of 1950 and the joint participation of France and West Germany in the European Economic Community after World War II).[26] Clearly, erstwhile enemies can become allies, and vice versa, depending on pragmatic considerations. However, the persistence of Soviet-Chinese, Soviet-German, and Chinese-Vietnamese suspicions, as well as sometimes recurring Franco-German differences, indicate that old negative images die hard.[27] When images based on Francophobia or some other type of **xenophobia** (the fear of foreigners) lead decision makers to act out of hatred or spite, disastrous foreign policy consequences can result.

We have noted that some images are widely shared by the members of a country's foreign policy establishment and by its people, based on a kind of "national memory." However, some images are held much less widely and may be peculiar to only a few individuals, based on their particular past experiences as well as present circumstances. Regarding *personal past experiences*, we have mentioned Kennedy's humiliating meeting with Khrushchev in Vienna, which affected the two leaders' views of each other. The Vienna encounter may have contributed, along with Kennedy's rather restrained policies during the Berlin Wall and Bay of Pigs episodes in 1961, to Khrushchev's expectation that Kennedy would not contest the installation of nuclear missiles in Cuba in October 1962. The Vienna experience also may have contributed in part to Kennedy's perception of Soviet missile deployments as a crisis situation involving a high threat to U.S. security. Some other U.S. officials, like Robert McNamara, defined the situation in much less menacing terms and did not feel it justified going to the brink of war.[28] It has been argued that Kennedy *wanted* to believe that U.S.-Soviet relations could be improved and that Khrushchev would not dare risk a confrontation by deploying missiles ninety miles away from the United States. Given this image of reality, Kennedy initially ignored early intelligence warnings suggesting otherwise—even ordering the cessation of U-2 reconnaissance flights over the western half of Cuba that might have produced conclusive proof of missile deployment earlier than October—and became all the more outraged when later discovery of the missiles ultimately shattered his image.[29]

The *personal present circumstances* of decision makers may also shape their image of the world and, hence, their perception of a situation. It has been pointed out, for example, that where one *sits* in the foreign policy bureaucracy at a given moment may well determine where one *stands* on some issue and, in particular, what "face" of the issue one sees.[30] Even within a country's military bureaucracy, as suggested earlier, disagreements occur between different branches of the armed services: "Every rival group within the American system—the bomber pilots, the fighter jockeys, the missilemen, and the carrier admirals—produces its own interpretation of Soviet behavior to justify its claim for more money."[31] Although this might be an overly cynical view of the American military, there is little question that bureaucratic "blinders" exist, which can subconsciously bias one's definition of a problem.

Although all decision makers approach situations with certain built-in predispositions grounded in their image of reality, some individuals have more *open* images than others, i.e., they are more receptive to information that contradicts their image and are more amenable to revising that image. A classic study of U.S. Secretary of State John Foster Dulles revealed that his image of the world, which was not only based on Munich but reinforced by his strict anti-communist, Presbyterian upbringing, was particularly *closed;* more than most of his contemporaries, Dulles was inflexible in his negative view of the Soviet Union during the 1950s and refused to interpret any Soviet action in a positive light, even when the Soviets planned to reduce their armed forces by 1 million.[32] The degree to which a decision maker is open to new information can depend on the situation itself. Some scholars have hypothesized that in crisis situations, for example, decision makers may feel a need to be as open-minded as possible to get the most accurate picture of reality, but due to conditions of stress and urgency, there may be a tendency to fall back on established, stereotypical images of the enemy.[33]

Until now, we have been speaking primarily in terms of *individual* decision making. It might be argued that the problems we have cited that are associated with individual images are exaggerated, since foreign policy decisions are rarely if ever the product of a single individual but normally result at least indirectly from the input of *groups* and *organizations* involved in the decision process. Can we not assume that "reality testing" will occur and a reasonably accurate definition of a situation will emerge from the competing images likely to be found among many different individuals in either a group or organizational setting?

Although *groups* might be expected to produce better decisions than individuals acting alone, two (or more) heads may not necessarily be better than one. Irving Janis, who has studied small-group dynamics, has noted that under certain circumstances groups can breed their own sort of irrationality and cause individuals to act less rationally than they might if they were alone. In particular, he has described a phenomenon called **groupthink,** whereby pressures for group conformity may lead individual members to suppress any personal doubts they may have about the emerging group consensus regarding the definition of the situation or some other aspect of a foreign policy decision.[34] For example, in the case of the surprise attack on Pearl Harbor, Janis argues that the failure to anticipate the Japanese raid despite several prior intelligence clues was at least partly due to the clubby atmosphere that prevailed among the American admirals in Hawaii, causing any surfacing of individual reservations about the vulnerability of the naval base to be drowned out by a sense of collective invincibility. Janis and others have pointed out that crisis situations, in particular, are dominated by small-group decision making, with the size of the group tending to shrink as the gravity of the situation increases.

One might expect individual or group errors to be minimized by the existence of fairly large *organizations* within the foreign policy bureaucracy of most countries, upon which decision makers rely for information in defining a situation. There are certain "standard operating procedures" whereby problems are brought to the attention of various levels of the foreign policy establishment. Such procedures may appear cut-and-dried. However, when several events break simultaneously and compete for attention, the communications system can become so overloaded that some important problems are placed on the "back burner." In addition, when many different people handle information as it is circulated up and down the bureaucracy and is condensed at various points, the possibility always exists that some key information will be lost or refined beyond recognition along the way.

There is a special problem of subordinates passing along only that information that they think their superiors will want to hear. Patrick McGarvey, a former employee of the U.S. Defense Intelligence Agency (DIA), has written that during the Vietnam War the intelligence reports emanating from DIA field personnel tended to conform to the needs of the Joint Chiefs of Staff; when the generals wanted to show success after the Tet Offensive of 1968, the reports inflated enemy body counts, and later when the generals needed to justify their request for an additional 200,000 men, the reports projected gloomier estimates.[35] One way around this problem is to create multiple sources and channels of information in the hope that "good" information will drive out "bad" information. U.S. leaders, for example, rely not only on the Defense Intelligence Agency but the Central Intelligence Agency (CIA) and a variety of other information-gathering agencies. Still, the dynamics of organizational behavior can further complicate the problems associated with individual and group decision making and contribute to inaccurate definitions of the situation.

CONSIDERATION OF GOALS AND MEANS

Biased views of the world can foster irrationality not only in defining a situation but also in subsequent stages of the decision process, including the consideration of goals and means relevant to the situation. To the extent that decision makers seriously attempt to formulate concrete foreign policy goals, they may at times confuse *national* interests with *personal* interests or goals. The statement by John Kennedy upon discovering the Soviet deployment of missiles in Cuba ("He [Khrushchev] can't do that to *me!*")[36] suggests that it was not only security but prestige at stake in 1962—in particular, Kennedy's own personal prestige and credibility, and not necessarily that of the nation.

Likewise, Lyndon Johnson's escalation of the Vietnam War in a search for "peace with honor" might have been guided more by his own desire to salvage some respect for his presidency after the loss of thousands of American lives than by a need to defend national honor and vindicate the nation's suffering. Admittedly, there can be a fine line between a nation's reputation or credibility being at stake and that of an individual leader, but it is a line that can mean the difference between rationality and nonrationality when it leads to foreign policy decisions based on *machismo*.

We noted earlier that foreign policy makers take into account to some extent the possible domestic political repercussions of their decisions. For leaders in democratic countries, in particular, the goal of reelection may well blur their foreign policy judgments; arms control proposals that might be entirely rational in the context of international politics might represent political suicide in the context of domestic politics, if accepted by a leader in a country where the electorate is clamoring for tougher policies against an adversary. One would expect leaders in crisis situations, more than in other situations, to subordinate domestic political considerations in particular and personal goals in general to the "national interest," although it may be impossible to untangle all these concerns. Even in as explosive a situation as the Cuban missile crisis, there was at least one instance in which domestic political concerns were aired, as one member of ExCom (the Executive Committee of the National Security Council) passed a note to another suggesting "the very real possibility that if we allow Cuba to complete installation . . . of missile bases, the next House of Representatives [after the upcoming November congressional elections] is likely to have a Republican majority."[37] There is no evidence that domestic politics played anything but a marginal role in the blockade decision, but even the possibility that midterm congressional elections could have remotely affected such a momentous decision should give one pause for reflection.

In addition to self-interests, *group* or *organizational* goals can become the overriding preoccupation of officials. Janis's study of groupthink indicates that the maintenance of group cohesion and consensus may become an end in itself and subtly dominate all other considerations. He suggests this was one factor that operated in the deliberations of the "Tuesday lunch group" that advised Lyndon Johnson on bombing and other decisions during the Vietnam War without ever rethinking the basic Vietnam policy.

Many studies, including Graham Allison's, have pointed to the tendency of bureaucrats to articulate foreign policy goals that happen to coincide with the organizational mission of their particular unit. Bureaucratic units at times may feel as threatened by their own possible extinction as by the extinction of the nation, although one is reminded of the remark by a former U.S. Secretary of State that "the nearest thing to immortality on Earth is a government bureau."[38] When President Carter was attempting to reduce the Washington bureaucracy, his acting budget director was quoted as saying: "Only two federal programs have ever been flatly abolished—Uncle Sam no longer makes rum in the Virgin Islands and no longer breeds horses for the U.S. cavalry."[39] Interestingly, the horse cavalry unit within the U.S. Defense Department managed to justify its existence well into the atomic era, with the unit not being disbanded until 1951 and the last army mule retired in 1956. Edward Katzenbach has noted that the U.S. horse cavalry was not alone in its survival instincts and that similar units managed to persist for a long time as part of the armed forces of several European countries as well.[40]

In a bureaucratic society like the Soviet Union as well, decisions that to some outsiders might appear to be carefully aimed at national security concerns may in fact be more a function of the vagaries of **bureaucratic politics.** For example, one writer observed that "new Soviet missiles seem to be born as quadruplets. In the 1960s they deployed the SS–7–8–9–11 missiles; the 1970s generation are the SS–16–17–18 and 19 missiles. In the 1980s they have deployed another generation of four missiles. Why always in fours? U.S. experts say that the organization that designs Soviet missiles has four separate design bureaus, and that each is allowed to design a new generation."[41] Hence, foreign leaders who brood about Soviet strategic intentions thought to underlie such missiles may miss part of the rationale behind them.

We noted earlier that decision makers rarely come close to compiling an exhaustive list of possibilities when searching for alternative means of achieving a given goal. In many instances, particularly in crisis situations, time constraints seriously limit the number of alternatives that can be discussed. In addition, the same images that can distort the definition of the situation can restrict the menu of alternatives considered, foreclosing certain options in the minds of decision makers. Leaders may even feel there is "no choice" but to act in a certain fashion.[42] There is a tendency for one nation's leaders to assume that leaders in other states have a greater range of choices and more decision latitude.[43]

In the final selection of alternatives, the tendency is to engage in "satisficing" rather than "maximizing" behavior, i.e., to choose what seems to be the first satisfactory solution to the problem, which is not necessarily the best alternative.[44] Especially in *organizational* decision making, there is a tendency to make *low-risk* decisions that are calculated to avoid "rocking the boat," the concern being not so much upsetting the ship of state but upsetting existing organizational routines. On the latter point, Joseph de Rivera has hypothesized that "while an individual official might be willing to take great risks, the process of consultation and group decision will produce a more moderate, conservative policy."[45] While a low-risk mentality, based on a concern about "damage limitation," may be a sound approach to foreign policy decision making in general, it may prove harmful if a particular situation or problem calls for more drastic, innovative measures.

Occasionally decision makers engage in the opposite kind of behavior, taking *high-risk* decisions that represent a gigantic "roll of the dice." In contrast to de Rivera, Janis argues that *groups* under certain conditions may be more prone than individuals to act on the basis of passion and emotion rather than reason. He cites the German philosopher Friedrich Nietzsche who observed that "madness is the exception in individuals but the rule in groups."[46] High-risk decisions made without careful consideration of the possible consequences clearly have the potential for more disastrous outcomes than low-risk decisions, although both may contain some element of nonrationality. Scholars have pointed out that crisis situations, almost by definition, involve some degree of heightened commitment to "risk taking" by national leaders.[47]

IMPLEMENTATION AND EVALUATION

Bureaucracies have standard operating procedures not only for channeling information but also for ensuring that decisions taken toward the top will be routinely implemented by those below. Although much implementation occurs routinely, some does not. Especially with "macro" decisions, decision making at the top usually produces only the broad outlines of policy, so that much is left to the discretion of middle-level and low-level bureaucrats involved in the execution of policy. Hence, decisions may be misinterpreted by those responsible for implementation. The implementation of decisions may also be consciously delayed or even totally ignored at times by parts of the bureaucracy that have been ordered to take some action with which they disagree, particularly when it entails a major change in established organizational practices.[48]

The president of the United States has sometimes been referred to as the "single most powerful person in the world," owing to the black code box that always travels with him that can enable him to order a nuclear strike at any moment. However, the president may frequently have great difficulty getting his orders obeyed within his own bureaucracy. The frustrations experienced by Harry Truman were reflected in his much-quoted statement upon handing the presidency over to General Eisenhower in 1952: "He'll sit here and he'll say, 'Do this! Do that!' And nothing will happen. Poor Ike—it won't be a bit like the Army."[49]

Even in a crisis situation, when one would hope that the utmost rationality would prevail throughout the decision process, there may be a gap at the end between the making of a decision and its implementation. The Cuban missile crisis case is rich with examples of presidential decisions that were either ignored or almost ignored. When Khrushchev offered to remove Soviet missiles from Cuba in exchange for the removal of U.S. Jupiter missiles from Turkey, Kennedy became livid as he discovered only at that moment that the obsolete American missiles were still there despite his order for their withdrawal, issued twice in previous months. When an American U-2 plane accidentally strayed into Soviet air space at the height of the crisis, threatening a serious provocation, Kennedy could only remark about the unauthorized act that "there is always some so-and-so who doesn't get the word."[50] Another incident involved Secretary of Defense McNamara, who paid a visit to the office of Admiral Anderson, the Chief of Naval Operations, to ensure personally that the blockade decision reached by ExCom would be implemented by the Navy exactly as the President had intended, i.e., with armed force to be used only as a last resort. McNamara asked Anderson what the Navy would do if a Soviet ship's captain refused to permit an inspection of his cargo, at which point the admiral waved a copy of the *Manual of Naval Regulations* and shouted "It's all in there." McNamara responded: "I don't give a damn what John Paul Jones would have done. I want to know what you are going to do, now." The meeting ended with the admiral admonishing the secretary of defense: "Now, Mr. Secretary, if you and your deputy will go back to your offices, the Navy will run the blockade."[51]

We cite these examples not to suggest that bureaucratic "snafus" are inevitable, only that they can happen and can conceivably have dire, unintended consequences. When a mistake does occur, at whatever point in the decision process, one would hope that corrective actions would be taken to avoid similar mistakes in the future. References are commonly made to the "lessons" of Munich or Vietnam or some other experience, as if foreign policymakers regularly sit down and systematically review the consequences of their decisions.[52] Program evaluation, whereby one assesses the impact of a foreign aid program or some other policy decision, is supposedly an important activity in which bureaucracies engage to determine if goals are being achieved.

However, given the dynamics of individual, group, and organizational decision making, it is questionable how often serious evaluation occurs and how much learning results. Postmortems on the anatomy of decisions may be carefully performed after a catastrophic event such as a major war, but on other occasions evaluation may be a cursory exercise. More thought normally goes into the making of a decision than into the re-examination of one, since foreign policymakers (like most of us) feel too busy to dwell at any length on the past. Careful reflection by statesmen may often have to wait until they write their memoirs, long after their foreign policy decision-making days are over and at a time when their reconstruction of events may be biased by their desire to preserve their place in history in the best possible light.

Even when evaluation does occur, some lessons are misapplied, as in the case of the Munich analogy. Other lessons are never learned, as reflected in the use of strategic bombing of North Vietnamese villages by the United States during the Vietnam War in an effort to lower the enemy's will and ability to resist, despite the findings of U.S. Strategic Bombing Surveys after World War II that showed that similar tactics had failed to have much impact on Nazi Germany.[53] As noted at the outset of this book, many elements of "conventional wisdom" manage to persist among leaders even though history has proved such assumptions to be of dubious validity.

In order to conduct policy evaluation, goals must be sufficiently articulated so that clear-cut criteria can be employed whereby one can determine success or failure. In some cases, however, foreign policy goals can be so sketchy to begin with that it may be impossible to assess performance accurately when it comes time for evaluation. In other cases, where concrete goals have been identified and ample criteria exist to judge the impact of a policy, decision makers are more apt to exaggerate success than admit failure, as with the unwillingness of U.S. officials during the Vietnam War to recognize all the indicators showing that the war was a losing proposition.

We have been discussing evaluation in the context of rationality. However, there is another context in which it can be treated. When one measures success or failure in terms of such criteria as the square miles of territory gained or lost, the number of enemy soldiers or one's own soldiers killed, or the number of friendly dictators one is able or unable to keep in power, one is engaging in the kinds of judgments that move decision making from the realm of rationality into another realm—the realm of *morality*.

Morality and Foreign Policy

It is frequently said, primarily by those harboring realist notions of world politics, that "morality has no place in foreign policymaking." It is not always clear whether such statements mean morality *does not* play any role in foreign policy decisions, or *should not* play any role in foreign policy decisions. Let us briefly examine, then, two distinct issues. One is an empirical question. To what extent, if any, do moral considerations (as opposed to cold, hard calculation of self-interests) influence foreign policy decisions? The second is a normative question: To what extent, if any, should moral considerations be allowed to enter the foreign policy decision calculus?

In addressing the first question, moral principles have regularly been sacrificed to self-interests in the affairs of states, as we stated earlier, notably in the case of the United States, which has consciously cultivated a "do-gooder" image in the world. Still, does this mean morality never affects the foreign policy decisions of the United States or any other country? Only an extreme cynic would answer that morality is totally irrelevant. Indeed, one can cite many examples in the American case and other cases where foreign policymakers freely took action which on balance contributed nothing to national interests and may have even entailed considerable national sacrifice. For example, in 1979, the United States admitted roughly 15,000 Indo-Chinese refugees a month, imposing a substantial economic burden on many local American communities responsible for relocating the "boat people." The skeptic might argue that a large, wealthy country like the United States could afford to absorb a few thousand refugees and that it did so out of a desire to turn world opinion against the Communist regimes of Southeast Asia and out of pangs of conscience for contributing to the refugees' plight, which stemmed from the Vietnam War; the skeptic might also note the tendency of the United States to accept refugees fleeing from left-wing dictatorships more readily than those fleeing from right-wing persecution. However, the fact remains that the rescue of the boat people was in many respects a generous gesture that did not have to be made. If one is prepared to read ulterior motives into every foreign policy action, then admittedly one is not likely to find too many cases of genuine altruism. Earthquake and other international disaster relief efforts undertaken by countries like the United States will be dismissed as world public relations gimmicks; the keeping of commitments and promises will be dismissed as expedients necessary to maintain one's credibility; and so forth.

Although moral pronouncements can often cloak self-serving decisions, there is evidence that even in crisis situations—when one would most expect practical considerations to override all else—ethical concerns may be seriously weighed in the decision-making process. Irving Janis discusses the explicit treatment of moral issues by the members of ExCom during as volatile a situation as the Cuban missile crisis:

> During the Cuban missile crisis, members of the Executive Committee explicitly voiced their concerns about the morality of the policy alternatives they were considering, thus forestalling deceitful, clandestine actions. . . . For example, on the second day of the crisis, George Ball vigorously objected to the air-strike option, arguing that a surprise attack would violate the best traditions of the United States and would harm the moral standing of the nation, whether or not the attack proved to be militarily successful. To the surprise of several members of the group, Robert Kennedy continued the argument, calling attention to the large toll of innocent human lives that would result. Urging a decent regard for humanity, the Attorney General pointed out that a surprise air attack would undermine the United States' position at home and abroad by sacrificing America's humanitarian heritage and ideals. He emphasized this moral stance by stating that he was against acting as the Japanese had in 1941 by resorting to a "Pearl Harbor in reverse."[54]

As the above commentary suggests, there may sometimes be a fine line between morality and self-interest, with the two not necessarily being incompatible. In Robert Kennedy's mind, the thought of launching a surprise attack on Cuba appeared both immoral and against America's long-term interests, with the former concern seemingly weighing at least as heavily as the latter. Some observers have noted also that decision makers generally feel a need to take only those actions which can be publicly justified in some fashion, so that some options will be rejected if they are considered so immoral and indefensible as to defy justification.[55]

Clearly, then, foreign policy decision makers to some extent include moral considerations in their deliberations, although we do not want to exaggerate their role. The question remains, however, whether morality *should* be included in such deliberations. Some students of international politics go so far as to argue that the normal canons of morality observed between individuals—honesty, trustworthiness, and the like—simply do not apply between nations and that any statesman who attempts to behave morally when acting in behalf of the nation is a fool.

It is true that any statesman who seeks to act morally in world affairs faces great difficulties. The first problem involves the issue of "moral relativism." One cannot assume that actions taken on moral grounds will be appreciated by others as such, especially in a system with such sharp ideological and cultural differences as the international system. One of the factors that complicated Jimmy Carter's well-intentioned human rights policy was the fact that the values that Americans seemingly wished to promote ("political rights" such as freedom of speech and press) were not as important to people in some societies as certain other values ("economic rights" such as the right to full employment); in the case of cultures that had no tradition of democratic government or individual liberty, the United States found itself in the position of attempting to impose its value system on other peoples, a posture of questionable morality. While it may be true that there are many competing notions of morality in the world, the moral relativism argument can be carried only so far. There are, after all, at least a few norms that are universally or widely held (e.g., the prohibition against murder).

Another weakness in the Carter human rights policy points to the second problem surrounding moral considerations in international relations: the assumption that one country alone by its example can move others to act morally if they are not so inclined. Carter discovered that trying to save the world by oneself may lead only to martyrdom. When the Carter administration initially withheld nuclear technology and other economic items from certain authoritarian regimes in Latin America and elsewhere, making such benefits contingent upon liberalization of their political systems, those regimes were able to turn to France, West Germany, and other countries for whom the opportunity to do business overrode any moral objections about the customers. Given this example and other similar examples, such as the case of the Carter administration's initial attempt to exercise unilateral restraint in arms sales abroad only to find other countries plugging the gap, it is commonly argued that "if we don't sell it to them, somebody else will, so why should we be the ones to make the sacrifice?"

In other words, this is the familiar "two wrongs make a right" or "everybody does it" problem. Similar arguments have been used to justify the practice of corporate bribery of foreign government officials to obtain lucrative contracts, the logic being that international business is conducted according to a different code of rules than that considered acceptable within national economies. Such arguments are not without cogency, although there is a certain fatalism about them that tends to produce self-fulfilling prophecies.

The third problem is the "ends justify the means" syndrome, i.e., the temptation to excuse the most heinous deeds if they are done in the pursuit of what are thought to be noble causes. Given the ends that may be at stake in international politics, such as national survival, there is a special temptation for statesmen to adopt an "anything goes" attitude. Dropping atomic bombs, supporting ruthless dictators, and assassinating foreign agents have all been done in the name of such things as national defense and the preservation of liberty. Whereas Robert Kennedy felt that a surprise air strike against Cuba in 1962 would have been morally repugnant, Dean Acheson and some other members of ExCom considered it absolutely essential for U.S. security. The atomic bombs that were dropped on Hiroshima and Nagasaki in 1945 were felt to be the only measures capable of convincing the Japanese to surrender unconditionally and, hence, shortening the war and limiting further Allied casualties.[56] Actually, the A-bomb decision did not pose as deep and unprec-

Determining "right" and "wrong" in international relations

edented a moral dilemma for American leaders as sometimes depicted, since decisions made earlier in the war to bomb Dresden and Hamburg as well as Tokyo with conventional weapons had already contributed to more civilian casualties than were to be produced at Hiroshima and Nagasaki.[57] More recently, the Reagan administration invoked national security arguments to justify its secret mining of Nicaraguan harbors aimed at harassing Nicaragua's Marxist government, an action which seemed hardly in character for a country which the President had proclaimed was a "beacon to the world" as an exemplar of civilized and enlightened conduct. Although the ends might often justify the means, relying on this axiom too much may leave a nation physically intact but ethically bankrupt; particularly in a democracy, excessive reliance on secrecy and violence in foreign policy can undermine the very societal values one is presumably seeking to protect. (See the box on pages 212–213 for a discussion of "dirty tricks" played in international relations.)

Related to all these problems is the criticism many realists make that moral considerations may contribute to irrational foreign policy decisions based either on naive sentimentality on the one hand or reckless messianism on the other hand. In this sense, then, morality may be yet another source of nonrationality at times. One can only conclude that the issues associated with morality in international affairs are indeed delicate, although not necessarily so insurmountable that one must dismiss morality as a component of foreign policy decision making.

Conclusion (One Last Thought on Rationality)

It is safe to say that one would generally prefer rational to nonrational behavior on the part of foreign policymakers. However, one cannot assume that a

THE "UNDERSIDE" OF FOREIGN POLICY: THE MORALITY OF CLANDESTINE ACTIVITIES

In 1987, as the construction of a new $190 million U.S. embassy in Moscow neared completion, the Reagan administration announced that it might have to dismantle the building brick by brick and construct another one from scratch, since numerous Soviet electronic eavesdropping devices purportedly had been found embedded within the walls, which were made from prefabricated materials purchased from Soviet suppliers. This followed close on the heels of a sex-spy scandal involving U.S. marines guarding American diplomatic installations in the USSR. The U.S. at the same time threatened to prevent the Soviets from using their new embassy under construction in Washington, D.C., which happened to be located on a hill at one of the highest points in the capital city and hence—with the help of sophisticated antennae and other electronic equipment—would easily be within earshot of not only the gossipy conversations to be picked up at Georgetown dinner parties but also more guarded discussions emanating from the White House and other high-level government offices. In response to American charges of Soviet espionage, Soviet officials themselves revealed "bugging" devices they claimed the Americans had placed in strategic locations in Moscow and in the new Washington embassy.

The kind of chicanery noted above should not have surprised any seasoned observers of U.S.-Soviet relations. Clandestine intelligence-gathering in international affairs—spying—has long been recognized as both necessary and legitimate for national security purposes. Another spy scandal in the late 1980s, the so-called "Pollard Affair," revealed that even the best of international friends (in this case Israel and the U.S.) spy on each other. Intelligence agencies such as the American CIA, the Soviet KGB, and the British MI5 have also been increasingly relying on high-tech electronic and satellite reconnaissance devices ("TECHMINT") as opposed to James Bond–type secret agents ("HUMINT"), although both sources remain important.

The CIA's Technical Services Division has produced a variety of exotic devices over the years, including a radio transmitter in the form of a false tooth, an ordinary pencil that can write invisibly on special paper, an automobile rearview mirror that secretly allows the driver to watch the car's backseat passengers, and a one-person airplane designed to fit into two large suitcases (a project that never went beyond the drawing board).* The CIA is only one of several U.S. agencies responsible for intelligence gathering. The National Security Agency (NSA), whose primary mission is to intercept and decode foreign information and maintain the security of U.S. codes, is so shrouded in secrecy that some say its acronym stands for "No Such Agency." The Defense Department maintains its own Defense Intelligence Agency (DIA), although the CIA Director technically is responsible for overall U.S. intelligence operations.

Far more controversial—and more open to moral question—than the intelligence-gathering function performed by the CIA and KGB is the so-called "covert action" function, i.e., the use of assassination and other "dirty tricks" to intervene actively in the internal affairs of foreign countries. For example, CIA agents reputedly made repeated assassination attempts against Fidel Castro of Cuba in the 1960s; the methods they employed included the use of exploding seashells, a poisoned fountain pen, a diving suit treated with tuberculosis bacteria (to be given to him as a gift), and reliance on Mafia operatives. Intelligence agencies also have engaged in "disinformation" campaigns, planting false stories in the press.

Aside from the moral questions surrounding such activities, one might also question their effectiveness in terms of promoting national security. Generally, assassination attempts can lead to counterattempts and destabilize international relations. Even the practice of spying, if carried to an extreme, may only add to the paranoia and distrust among states rather than enhancing security, although clearly it is more a symptom than a cause of international tensions. Although individuals have been severely punished for spying, as in the famous Rosenberg case of the 1950s involving atomic secrets, it is doubtful that intelligence gathering or covert operations have done much to alter the basic power equation among states.

* These and other devices are described in Victor Marchetti and John D. Marks, *The CIA and the Cult of Intelligence* (New York: Knopf, 1974). Also see John Ranelagh, *The Rise and Decline of the CIA* (New York: Simon and Schuster, 1986).

decision rationally made will necessarily be a "good" one even if a leader follows the rational actor decision process almost perfectly. Passing judgment on the soundness of some foreign policy decision must ultimately await the response of *other* states. As Janis and others have pointed out, although the ExCom decision-making process during the Cuban missile crisis was in many ways the model of rationality, the resultant blockade decision could have easily produced a nuclear holocaust *if the Soviets had decided to react differently than they did.* In Secretary of State Rusk's own words at the time: "We're eyeball to eyeball, and I think the other fellow just blinked."[58]

The simple fact is that the outcome of a given situation depends on the decisions made by *two* sides. It depends on *your* decision as well as *their* decision and the interaction between the two. Hence, we turn in the next chapter to an examination of the dynamics of international *interactions* as we observe the "game" of international politics.

SUMMARY

1. Although the foreign policymaking process differs from country to country, leaders in all countries experience similar psychological pressures and other pressures in their deliberations.

2. Foreign policy is seldom a single overall plan, but rather it is a series of hundreds of decisions that tend to fall into three categories: macro-decisions, micro-decisions, and crisis decisions.

3. Macro-decisions are general decisions that involve such determinations as the level of defense spending or foreign aid. They normally occur in a setting in which the need for a decision has been anticipated, there is a relatively lengthy time frame, and a large variety of actors can be involved in the decision process.

4. Micro-decisions normally involve concerns that are relatively narrow in scope, carry a low threat, and are handled at the lower levels of the bureaucracy. Taken together, however, they can often add up to major foreign policy developments.

5. Crisis decisions are normally characterized by a sense of high threat (including the possibility of military hostilities), a finite time frame, and involvement of officials at the highest levels.

6. Foreign policy is commonly viewed as the work of a unitary, rational actor—"the United States," "the Soviet Union," etc. In this view, foreign policy decision making is assumed to be a rational process in which government officials—responding to stimuli from the international environment—carefully define the situation, specify goals, consider all possible alternative means of achieving these goals, select the final alternative, implement the decision, and evaluate the consequences for the nation.

7. An alternative, and in some respects more realistic, view of foreign policymaking treats the foreign policy establishment as a collection of individuals, groups, and organizations who may or may not act rationally and who respond to domestic stimuli and not only to external stimuli.

8. This latter view recognizes that nonrational factors can operate at all stages of the decision process. For example, the definition of a situation may well be distorted by individual policymakers' images of reality, leading them to misperceive their environment. Such distortion can produce either exaggerated threat perception and paranoia, or wishful thinking—which may cause overreaction or underreaction to an adversary's actions.

9. Some images are held by a nation's people as a whole, based on a nation's historical experiences (e.g., historical Franco-German frictions); other images are developed by specific individuals, based on their personal experiences (e.g., Kennedy's negative view of Khrushchev stemming from their Vienna meeting).

10. The problems associated with individual images are often compounded in group and organizational decision making. Group pressures ("groupthink") can cause individuals to act less rationally than usual. Bureaucratic organizations tend to develop biased images of the world that are consistent with organizational (and not necessarily national) interests.

11. Nonrational factors not only can bias the definition of a situation but also can foreclose certain foreign policy options, lead to excessively low-risk or high-risk decisions, and prevent proper implementation and evaluation of decisions.

12. Although moral principles have regularly been sacrificed to self-interests in international affairs, morality nonetheless frequently enters into foreign policy decisions. There are, however, many difficulties associated with introducing morality into foreign policy. One is the problem of moral relativism, particularly in the presence of sharp ideological and cultural differences among peoples. Another problem is whether one country alone can move others to act morally if they are not so inclined. Still another problem is the temptation to justify questionable means if they are in the pursuit of noble ends. Finally, morality may at times be yet another source of irrationality if it leads to decisions based on naive sentimentality or overly zealous crusading.

SUGGESTIONS FOR FURTHER READING AND STUDY

For a general discussion of the concepts of rationality and nonrationality as applied to the international relations field, see Sidney Verba, "Assumptions of Rationality and Non-Rationality in Models of the International System," in Klaus Knorr and Sidney Verba, eds., *The International System: Theoretical Essays* (Princeton, N.J.: Princeton University Press, 1961), pp. 93–117; and James A. Robinson and Richard C. Snyder, "Decision-Making in International Politics," in Herbert C. Kelman, ed., *International Behavior* (New York: Holt, Rinehart and Winston, 1965), pp. 435–463.

In addition to the writings of Graham Allison cited in the notes for this chapter, many other works have challenged the "rational actor" premises associated with the traditional analysis of foreign policy. Among those scholars who have examined the general role of images and psychological factors as possible sources of nonrationality are Kenneth Boulding, *The Image* (Ann Arbor, Mich.: University of Michigan Press, 1956); Joseph de Rivera, *The Psychological Dimension of Foreign Policy* (Columbus, Ohio: Charles E. Merrill, 1968); and Robert Jervis, *Perception and Misperception in International Politics* (Princeton, N.J.: Princeton University Press, 1976).

There are several volumes that contain a series of brief but insightful case studies of specific foreign policy decisions along with an analytical framework. These include Morton H. Halperin and Arnold Kanter, eds., *Readings in American Foreign Policy: A Bureaucratic Perspective* (Boston: Little, Brown, 1973), focusing primarily on the dynamics of *organizational* decision making; Irving L. Janis, *Groupthink*, 2nd ed. (Boston: Houghton Mifflin, 1982), focusing primarily on the dynamics of *group* decision making; and Lawrence S. Falkowski, *Presidents, Secretaries of State, and Crises in U.S. Foreign Relations: A Model and Predictive Analysis* (Boulder, Colo.: Westview

Press, 1978), ch. 5, focusing on the behavior of *individual* decision makers, particularly in crisis situations. An excellent work that looks at individuals, small groups, and organizations together as three "interrelated subsystems of the policymaking system" and contains numerous examples of "impediments to information processing" in foreign policy is Alexander L. George, *Presidential Decisionmaking in Foreign Policy* (Boulder, Colo.: Westview Press, 1980). For lengthier, in-depth case studies of various foreign policy decisions, see the works cited in the notes, including Allison (on the Cuban missile crisis), Paige (on Korea), and Wohlstetter (on Pearl Harbor). Although all these volumes deal only with U.S. foreign policy, the general conclusions drawn by the authors about the dynamics of foreign policymaking are intended to apply to other countries as well.

Excellent *comparative* studies of the foreign policy process that examine the role of various factors in different countries include Hannes Adomeit and Robert Bordman, *Foreign Policy Making in Communist Countries* (New York: Praeger, 1979); Christopher Clapham, *Foreign Policy Making in Developing States: A Comparative Approach* (Westmead, Eng.: Saxon House, 1977); and William Wallace and W. E. Paterson, eds., *Foreign Policy Making in Western Europe: A Comparative Approach* (New York: Praeger, 1978).

On the role of morality in international relations, see Arnold Wolfers' essay "Statesmanship and Moral Choice" in *Discord and Collaboration* (Baltimore: Johns Hopkins University Press, 1962), pp. 47–65; Stanley Hoffmann, *Duties Beyond Borders: On the Limits and Possibilities of Ethical International Politics* (Syracuse, N.Y.: Syracuse University Press, 1981); Peter L. Berger, "Are Human Rights Universal?" *Commentary* (September 1977), pp. 60–63; and Joseph S. Nye, *Nuclear Ethics* (New York: Free Press, 1986), and Kenneth W. Thompson, *Moralism and Morality in Politics and Diplomacy* (Lanham, Md.: University Press of America, 1985).

7

Playing the Game
of International Relations:
Diplomacy Before Force

International relations can be compared to ballroom dancing. One cannot do it alone. To quote a recent American president, "It takes at least two to tango" in international relations.

While the similarity between ballroom dancing and affairs of state may begin and end with the above observation, a more applicable metaphor can be cited, again with some caution. As suggested in an earlier chapter, international relations has often been depicted as a *game* (or series of games) in which nation-states compete for various stakes. National governments play the game not for the sheer joy of competition but because they hope to achieve certain payoffs from it. How successful a given player is depends essentially on the amount of **influence** that can be exerted on the other player(s) in terms of shaping the latter's behavior in a desired fashion. This chapter examines the way countries *normally* play the game and seek to influence each other.

To many spectators, especially those who rely primarily on front page newspaper headlines as the basis for their observations, the game of international relations seems to involve an inordinate amount of violence. However, while there is usually a war going on somewhere in the world at any given time, the problem of interstate violence is not as common as it might appear if one considers the hundreds of interstate transactions that occur day to day that are largely free of hostilities. Much of international relations is conflictual, but *most* conflict is *nonviolent* in form. Just as resorting to fisticuffs or gunplay is not the norm in poker or chess, resorting to armed force—as a means of influencing the outcome of the game—is not the norm in international politics. One careful estimate is that out of 250 serious confrontations involving major powers since 1815, fewer than 30 (12 percent) have resulted in actual war.[1] In a study focusing on a more recent period and dealing with the entire international system, it was found that "physical conflict" acts accounted for only 7 to 18 percent of all interstate actions observed in the years between 1966 and 1969.[2]

It is especially true in the contemporary nuclear age that national governments, rather than relying on the use of armed force, generally attempt to exercise influence and to achieve desired results through what is commonly called **diplomacy.** The term "diplomacy" has taken on a variety of meanings in the international relations literature. In its traditional sense, diplomacy refers to the formal practices and methods whereby states conduct their foreign relations, including the exchange of ambassadors, the dispatch of messages among official representatives, and participation in face-to-face negotiations; the traditional study of diplomacy focuses on such concerns as the legal status of ambassadors, the functions performed by embassies, and the qualities needed to be a successful negotiator. In recent years the concept of diplomacy has been broadened by scholars to mean the general process whereby states seek to communicate, to influence each other, and to resolve conflicts through *bargaining*—either formal or informal—short of the use of armed force. A few scholars have stretched the concept of diplomacy even further, suggesting that force itself, when applied in a very limited and selective way to make a point, can almost represent a kind of diplomacy (the "diplomacy of violence").

Our treatment of diplomacy in this text conforms only to the first two usages above, and not the third. We will discuss the use of armed force separately in the next chapter; while there admittedly can be a fine line between the use of diplomacy and the use of force as bargaining vehicles, that line constitutes one of the most critical distinctions in all of international relations, since crossing it tends to raise the ante in the game considerably. Leaders generally resort to force only when diplomacy fails or appears likely to fail, although at times force is used before diplomacy has been entirely exhausted.

As practiced by nation-states, diplomacy can be open or secret, bilateral or multilateral, formally or informally conducted. It can take place around green-topped tables with bottles of mineral water and note pads, or across great distances by teletype or "hotlines" installed between government nerve centers. It can occur at the highest official level ("summitry"), or much lower. It can include the making of promises (the "nice guy" or "carrot" approach) as well as threats (the "tough guy" or "stick" approach), designed either to induce or extort concessions from the other side—making opponents an offer they won't, or can't, refuse. It can go on between friends over issues on which they are not far apart, or between enemies whose positions seem intractable. And it can be supported by economic, military, or any other resources employed to influence competitors through means other than outright physical coercion. The various strategies and instruments that can be used to win (or not lose) the game, as well as their relative effectiveness, will be discussed in this chapter.

The Changing Nature of Diplomacy

British diplomat Sir Harold Nicolson, in his classic work *Diplomacy*, cites a conventional definition of diplomacy: "Diplomacy is the management of international relations by negotiation; the method by which these relations are adjusted and managed by ambassadors and envoys. . . ."[3] While much of today's diplomacy still involves the art of negotiation as practiced by ambassadors and envoys, the nature of diplomacy has changed somewhat over the years as conditions in the international system have changed. We will examine a number of ways in which diplomacy in the contemporary era is somewhat different from years past. We will focus on (1) the role of the embassy and the ambassador, (2) the role of public (as opposed to secret) diplomacy, (3) the role of multilateral (as opposed to bilateral) diplomacy, and (4) the role of tacit (as opposed to explicit or formal) diplomacy.

THE ROLE OF THE EMBASSY AND THE AMBASSADOR

Today's **ambassadors** can conceivably trace their roots as far back as prehistoric times, when even the members of primitive societies no doubt occasionally felt the need to deal with mutual concerns through emissaries of some sort. The earliest ambassadors did not come by their roles through any specialized training, although some were more skilled than others. As Nicolson notes in regard to diplomacy during the Middle Ages: "Louis XI sent his barber on a mission to Maria of Burgundy, Florence sent a chemist . . . to Naples, and Dr. de Puebla, who for twenty years represented Spain in London, was so filthy and unkempt that Henry VII expressed the hope that his successor might be a man more fitted for human society."[4] As the nation-state system developed, states gradually established professional, career foreign services from whose ranks ambassadors were normally recruited and who were expected to represent their governments in a more respectable and knowledgeable manner than previously. In some countries, such as the United States, nonprofessionals can still be found in ambassadorial posts—for example, Walter Annenberg, the publisher of *TV Guide*, was appointed by President Nixon as U.S. Ambassador to the Court of St. James's in London, and John Gavin, a movie star of Hispanic heritage, was appointed as U.S. Ambassador to Mexico by President Reagan. However, the emphasis has been increasingly on the development of a professional diplomatic corps to represent states abroad.

Although the practice of dealing with foreign societies through official emissaries is an ancient one, the **embassy** as an institution—i.e., the establishment of *permanent* missions on foreign soil—is of more recent vintage. The concept of a permanent mission to represent a country's interests abroad was first employed by the Italian city-states during the fifteenth century and was later adopted by England and other nation-states that recognized the growing importance of institutionalized diplomacy in managing relations between sovereign entities. In 1815, at the Congress of Vienna following the Napoleonic Wars, the first attempt was made to reach agreement among states on a standard set of rules regarding the appointment of ambassadors and the operation of embassies. This was especially designed to avoid quarrels between states over ambassadorial rank and privileges, such as that which had occurred in London in 1661, when "the coach of the Spanish ambassador tried to push in front of that of the French ambassador, a battle occurred with loss of life among the footmen, . . . diplomatic relations were severed between Paris and Madrid and a very real danger of war arose."[5]

From the start, embassies were found by national governments to be useful institutions for performing a variety of functions, including the continuous collection and transmission of information back to the home country concerning conditions in the host country; the maintenance of a regular line of communication between the home government and the host government; the cultivation of friendly relations with the host government through ongoing social contacts provided by rubbing elbows at embassy balls and other gatherings; the extension of home government protection to one's citizens traveling through host countries; the expansion of commercial interests; and— most notably—expeditious on-the-spot negotiation of issues of concern to home and host governments. Over time, many more routine functions were added, such as processing international travel requests and registering births and deaths of one's citizens living in the host state.

In the nineteenth and early twentieth centuries, embassies tended to be small, sometimes staffed only by an ambassador and a handful of aides. Ambassadors were expected to be generalists, adept at handling a variety of functions. Today, although ambassadors and other diplomatic personnel are still often generalist in aptitude, large embassy staffs include specialists such as information officers (responsible for disseminating "public relations" propaganda), consular officials (responsible for providing legal assistance as well as handling travel requests to and from the host country), commercial attachés (responsible for promoting economic interests in the host country), military attachés or economic development specialists (responsible for dealing with host country military and economic requests), and intelligence officers (sometimes posing as one of the above officials, responsible for monitoring and reporting on local political developments). The increased bureaucratization of embassies has reflected the growing volume and complexity of international transactions in the twentieth century. It should be added, however, that many poorer countries simply lack the money and manpower needed to maintain the kind of modern embassies described above.

It is perhaps ironic today that as the diplomatic service in many countries has become more professionalized, it has also in some respects come to play a lesser role in negotiation, its main historic function. The advanced communications and travel technology of the modern age have made leaders less reliant on their ambassador on the scene as their chief representative in dealing with a foreign government. In the days of carrier pigeons and sailing vessels, a country's ambassador might have had to deal with a host government without benefit of instructions from home for several months. The installation of telephone and teletype lines between home office and embassy has lessened the discretion with which ambassadors abroad can make decisions and the need for them to do so. In an era of supersonic jets and hotlines, many leaders bypass embassy personnel altogether, preferring either to send high-level ministers on "shuttle diplomacy" missions (such as Henry Kissinger's excursions in the Middle East in 1974) or to play the role of diplomat themselves by directly engaging in communications and negotiations with their counterparts in other countries (as in the case of Khrushchev and Kennedy at Vienna in 1961, Nixon and Chou En-lai at Beijing in 1972, and Carter, Begin, and Sadat at Camp David in 1978). This kind of direct, personal contact between heads of state has been labeled **summitry.**

Summit diplomacy is not completely new—even the monarchs of Europe

SIDELIGHT

PORTRAIT OF A NINETEENTH-CENTURY DIPLOMAT

A diplomatic career is seldom as glamorous as it was for Daniel E. Sickles, whose experiences as U.S. Minister to Spain in the 1870s are described below. Yet his case illustrates the occasional impact of politically influential personalities shuttling into and out of diplomatic service. Former New York Governor W. Averill Harriman, for example, played a more significant if less flamboyant role as troubleshooter for six different American presidents in a career that spanned forty years during and after World War II.

The appointment of Daniel E. Sickles as Minister to Spain in 1869 was the culmination of a flamboyant public career. As Secretary of the Legation in London (1853–55), Sickles had helped to arrange the conference of ministers that produced the Ostend Manifesto. He also had his mistress presented to Queen Victoria. As a Democratic Congressman from New York, Sickles gained notoriety for shooting his wife's lover in Lafayette Square, being acquitted of murder, and then forgiving his wife.

At the outbreak of the Civil War, Sickles raised a brigade of volunteers in New York City and maintained them at his own expense until they were taken into the army. He led the "Excelsior Brigade" into battle and rose to the rank of major general and to the command of the Third Corps of the Army of the Potomac. At Gettysburg, he moved his corps to an exposed position and lost most of his troops and his right leg. (The bones of his leg are on display in the Army Medical Museum.) In the spring of 1865, Sickles conducted a diplomatic mission to Colombia to arrange the passage of American troops through Panama.

Sickles was appointed Minister to Spain as a reward for his early support of Grant's campaign for the presidency. He was instructed to offer help to Cuba in purchasing independence from Spain, opening the way to eventual annexation. Spanish opinion was outraged, and General Prim, the Spanish Prime Minister, was assassinated before he could reconsider. After King Amadeo I declined the offer of purchase, Sickles plotted with Spanish republicans in the vain hope that they would be more willing to sell after they came to power.

Sickles lived lavishly in Madrid, renting a box at the opera and having

during the classical era would occasionally meet to exchange pleasantries and discuss mutual concerns. However, summitry has become much more common in the contemporary era. As a form of diplomatic activity, summitry has been both applauded and criticized. On the one hand, meetings of heads of state can help leaders develop greater understanding of each other and can expedite

his secretary, Alvey A. Adee, order fine wines and luxury goods for him from London and Paris. Sickles frequently traveled to Paris, where he had an affair with Isabella II, formerly the Queen of Spain. Isabella herself was notorious for her affairs, and there had been much speculation about the paternity of her children. Parisian society promptly dubbed Sickles "the Yankee king of Spain." Sickles also married Caroline de Creagh, lady-in-waiting to the former Queen.

On October 21, 1873, the Spanish warships captured the steamer *Virginius*, as it carried arms to insurgents in Cuba. After Spanish authorities executed the captain and most of the crew, many of whom were American citizens, the United States demanded the release of the ship and the remaining prisoners. Sickles was instructed to close the legation and return home if the Spanish government did not accept these demands within twelve days. Sickles, however, was ready to close the legation after five days. The crisis was averted when the Spanish government offered to negotiate in Washington rather than Madrid, and Sickles then resigned.

Source: A Short History of the U.S. Department of State, 1781–1981 (Washington, D.C.: U.S. Department of State, 1981), p. 17.

the negotiation process insofar as chief executives are in a position to make foreign policy decisions without requiring clearance from any authorities above them (although democracies often require later ratification of executive decisions by legislative bodies). On the other hand, as U.S. diplomat George Ball commented, such meetings are rarely capable of producing the kind of major diplomatic results that one is led to expect from all the hoopla normally accompanying them:

> What really happens at even the most serious . . . summit conference where there are significant issues to be discussed? Though little serious conversation takes place at the banquet table, the time consumed in eating and drinking is appalling. In the Far East it is not polite to discuss business over food, and in many countries in the Middle East no conversation at all takes place during meals. Wherever the meeting occurs, toasts are normally set speeches. When Communists are present, toasts may be useful for making diplomatic hints—particularly if the toasts are afterward handed out to the press—but by and large the time consumed in communal feeding is time wasted. Nor is anything serious likely to be said over the brandy, for, in spite of the diplomatic mystique with which tradition has surrounded this postprandial ritual, the heads of state are usually too tired to make sensible conversation, which they would probably not be able to remember with precision the next day anyway. . . .
>
> Thus, in trying to measure the period permitted for a substantive exchange of views during ten hours of top-level propinquity, one should deduct at least four hours for eating and drinking, another hour or two for small talk . . . then divide the remainder by two and one half for the translation. What is left is about two or three hours in which positions are stated and ideas exchanged.[6]

Moreover, chief executives are seldom experts in international affairs, often lacking the kind of familiarity with diplomatic procedures and foreign cultures that trained diplomats are able to bring to the negotiating process. Although elaborate pre-summit briefing can help prepare heads of state to some extent, Ball and others have nonetheless lamented the trend toward the theatrics of summitry as a substitute for quiet, behind-the-scenes discussions.

PUBLIC VERSUS SECRET DIPLOMACY

The increase in summitry, with all its "media event" characteristics, reflects another trend in diplomacy, namely the increased role of *public* as opposed to *secret* diplomacy. Although much diplomacy is still conducted secretly, democracies especially have been under increased pressures to open the process and widely publicize the resulting decisions.

It is not clear whether open diplomatic practices produce better international agreements. At least since the time of Woodrow Wilson, many people have argued that "open covenants openly arrived at" would remove much of the suspicion and paranoia that pervade international relations. In other words, many argue that secrecy in the negotiating process is necessarily bad, in terms of not only frustrating the public's "right to know" but also adding to the sense of insecurity and distrust experienced by all nations in the international system. However, many students of diplomacy argue just the opposite, that conducting diplomacy "in a fishbowl" under the glare of television cameras tends to promote "atmospherics"—either empty gestures of friendship or outbursts of rhetoric and the adoption of rigid positions for political gain either at home or abroad—rather than the kind of serious discussion of issues and compromises so essential to effective negotiations. Particularly in the case of highly sensitive and delicate negotiations, even if the final outcome ought ultimately to be publicized, there might be legitimate reasons for keeping the diplomatic process itself insulated from public scrutiny while it is going on.

MULTILATERAL VERSUS BILATERAL DIPLOMACY

The time-honored practice of pairs of countries exchanging ambassadors and maintaining permanent diplomatic missions on each other's soil reflects the traditional emphasis that states have placed on **bilateral** (two country) **diplomacy.** It was not until the late nineteenth century that **multilateral diplomacy** (the meeting together of several countries) became a common mode of diplomacy; prior to that time, multilateral diplomacy was mostly limited to either special meetings called at moments of crisis when war threatened or peace conferences following major wars, such as the Congress of Vienna in 1815, in which winners and losers gathered to determine the division of the spoils and to settle other matters. Even at the turn of the twentieth century, multilateral diplomacy had still not become a highly developed phenomenon.

However, multilateral diplomacy has become increasingly prevalent in the twentieth century, owing to a number of factors: (1) the existence of many problems (not only arms control but economic and environmental concerns and other matters related to the growth of interdependence) that spill over several national boundaries and do not lend themselves to purely bilateral solutions; (2) the proliferation of intergovernmental organizations at the global and regional levels, such as the United Nations and the European Community, which provide ongoing institutional settings for the conduct of multilateral diplomacy; and (3) as noted earlier, the existence of many less developed countries that have come to rely on the UN and other multilateral forums for the bulk of their official diplomatic contacts. While traditional bilateral relations continue to play an extremely prominent role in contemporary diplomacy, several studies have found that "international organizations are by far the most common method of diplomatic contact for most nations— much more so than traditional bilateral exchanges."[7]

Multilateral diplomacy occurs not only through institutions like the UN but also through *ad hoc* conferences convened among states sharing mutual concerns, such as the series of global conferences held during the 1970s and 1980s on problems involving food, population, and the environment. Summit meetings themselves can be both bilateral and multilateral in form, such as the gathering of over a dozen heads of state from developed and underdeveloped countries at the North-South Conference in Cancún, Mexico, in 1981 (which also included over 2000 journalists). Multilateral institutions and conferences are viewed by many observers as playing a constructive role in international relations by involving many relevant participants at once; but others argue that such large open forums—with so many diverse parties represented and with an emphasis on speech-making, parliamentary maneuvering, and voting procedures—complicate problem solving and serious negotiation. In later chapters, we will examine the extent to which multilateral machinery has contributed to the resolution of international conflict and has facilitated cooperation in international problem solving.

TACIT VERSUS FORMAL DIPLOMACY

Although in popular usage "diplomacy" and "negotiation" are often considered synonymous terms, one should keep in mind that **negotiation**—i.e., *formal*, direct communication through face-to-face meetings, cables, or third-party intermediaries—is only one mode of diplomacy. In addition to negotiation, governments often engage in **tacit diplomacy**, i.e., *informal*, indirect communication through words (e.g., press conference statements) and actions (e.g., placing troops on alert) designed to signal intentions or the importance one attaches to some issue. Of course, in practice states tend to combine the two forms, using tacit diplomacy for "posturing" purposes either prior to or during a formal negotiating session in order to reinforce the messages they wish to convey. Apart from being utilized in conjunction with formal negotiations, tacit diplomacy is often employed by itself simply to influence another government's future behavior, particularly when seeking to dissuade the other side from taking some undesired action. For example, when President Johnson ordered "Operation Big Lift" to ferry thousands of U.S. troops to Western Europe in a training exercise during the mid-1960s, he was seeking to communicate to "friend and foe alike" that defense of Europe on short notice was feasible and that any attempted aggression would not succeed.

Tacit diplomacy is not a modern invention. It has always been a part of statecraft along with more formal diplomacy. However, the speed of modern communications technology has enabled leaders to exploit the signaling possibilities of tacit diplomacy much more effectively than in the past. Tacit diplomacy allows communication between governments that for ideological or other reasons do not have official diplomatic relations or whose relations are so strained that they do not wish to be seen formally talking to each other. Such diplomacy, then, can be a useful surrogate for formal diplomacy in managing conflicts.

One problem with tacit diplomacy, however, is that while actions such as troop mobilizations might speak louder than words at a negotiation table, they can also be more easily misinterpreted. The aforementioned Operation Big Lift was meant as a signal of solidarity directed at U.S. allies in Western

Europe, and of capability directed at the Soviet Union; it may even have signaled the Johnson administration's efficiency to the American public. Since such signals are frequently designed for multiple audiences, they can lose impact and clarity. A government can seldom be certain that signaling at long range conveys the desired message unambiguously to the desired target, especially given the large amount of "noise"—random, unrelated events—that can drown out signals in the international arena.

The Concept of Bargaining

Regardless of whether diplomacy is conducted openly or secretly, multilaterally or bilaterally, tacitly or formally, by ambassadors or by heads of state, the essence of diplomacy remains **bargaining**. Bargaining can be thought of as a means of settling differences over priorities between contestants through an exchange of proposals for mutually acceptable solutions. There must be conflict over priorities in order for bargaining to take place, for if there were total agreement there would be nothing to bargain about. Nevertheless, a given conflict can be mild as well as severe. In some cases the differences among disputants might be virtually incompatible and irreconcilable, while in other cases it might be possible for all sides to benefit in some way from the bargaining process.

Bargaining should be a familiar concept, since the same basic process is at work when nations bargain as when friends decide what movie to see on a Saturday night, or when mortal enemies decide where to hold a grudge fight. Even people who are not quite sure how they feel about each other bargain to resolve disputes, which can range from child custody battles in a divorce case to arguments between two drivers over a parking space. Strangers, lovers, statesmen, and assorted other people bargain for the benefits they seek. The elements of both rational and nonrational decision making which were introduced in the last chapter can enter the bargaining process.

A simple example close to home will illustrate the main aspects of bargaining. Suppose a woman is in an automobile showroom seeking to purchase a new car. She has her eye especially on the little red sports car in the corner. The prospective buyer can communicate to the salesperson directly or indirectly what she is willing to settle for in terms of price. That is, she can either *say* that she will not pay more than x dollars for the car, or she can get up and *head for the door* when the dealer quotes what she feels is too high a price. In both cases, the buyer is trying to communicate something about her own terms and about the unacceptability of the dealer's offer. The "game" might boil down to a contest over how many steps toward the door the buyer takes before the dealer gives in. More communications might follow from the dealer, also a presumably rational player—"a free undercoat," "a set of radial tires," "2.9% financing"—whereupon the buyer might counter, "How about the deluxe stereo system?"

Good bargainers, either in an automobile showroom or in the international arena, have a clear idea of their priorities. Participants in the bargaining process presumably have certain minimum and maximum limits regarding how far they are willing to go to reach agreement. The bargaining game consists of each side trying to strike a final agreement as *far* from their own *minimum* and as *close* to their *maximum* demands as possible. The auto dealer tries to pad the price, and the buyer tries to shave the cost; both might settle for less than the maximum, but both will have limits beyond which they cannot afford further concessions. The struggle in any bargaining situation is to push toward your opponent's minimum and your own maximum, along a kind of "bargaining line" as indicated in Figure 7.1.

In Figure 7.1, party A and party B contend along the curved bargaining line of desirable or acceptable outcomes, ranging from A's maximum demand to B's maximum. Lines A and B indicate the values (or "utilities") A and B place on different outcomes, including likes (positive values) and dislikes (negative values). With both bargainers pushing hard for their priorities, the outcome will depend upon a variety of factors, including how accurately each side

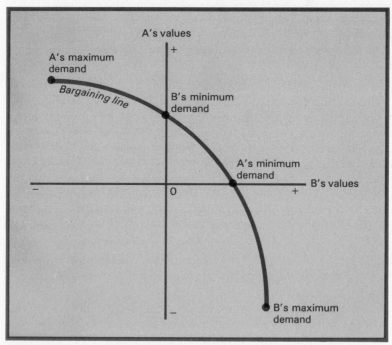

Figure 7.1
THE BARGAINING LINE: MAXIMUM AND MINIMUM DEMANDS

gauges the other's position (for example, whether the auto dealer knows how badly the buyer wants the little red sports car), what tools of influence are available to each side (such as the offer of a free undercoat or the opportunity to walk across the street to another dealer), as well as the skill with which each party bargains. The effectiveness of any bargaining strategy depends in large measure on basic bargaining positions. If you are weaker than your opponent, if you are not wanted or needed in an agreement, or if you time your moves poorly, your bargaining effectiveness is likely to be reduced. Miscalculations, of course, can occur as a result of misperception, emotional involvement, and other problems. Having briefly discussed the general nature of bargaining, let us now examine the various tactics that governments employ in the international bargaining process.

The Dynamics of International Bargaining

THE MANIPULATION OF CARROTS AND STICKS

As the auto showroom example suggests, parties involved in bargaining can attempt to influence each other's behavior through the conscious manipulation of "carrots" and "sticks." In international relations in particular, states make considerable use of both carrot and stick approaches when they rely on four types of bargaining tactics: threats, punishments, promises, and rewards. Two of these tactics (**threats** and **punishments**) represent the stick approach, the former involving some hypothetical action and the latter a real action. The other two tactics (**promises** and **rewards**), which represent the carrot approach, also involve hypothetical and real action. While those who view international politics as being violent and anarchical tend to place greater faith in the stick approach than in the carrot approach, there is no clear evidence that one approach is inherently more effective than the other as a general bargaining strategy. Both can be effective, depending on the context in which they are used.

For example, in 1962, President Kennedy *threatened* Premier Khrushchev with war if the missiles in Cuba were not removed, but at the same time *promised* not to invade Cuba in the future if the Soviets would give in on the missiles. As this example illustrates, states often use threats and promises together, especially when one side wants to provide the other side a face-saving way out of a confrontation.

As states bargain, they often discover that it is more difficult to *compel* than to *deter* certain behavior on the part of another state. In the case of **compellence,** one seeks to persuade the other side to do something it does not wish to do, either to undertake or continue some desired behavior, or to stop some undesired behavior (e.g., the United States attempting to influence South

Africa to grant independence to its colony Namibia, or South-West Africa); in the case of **deterrence,** one seeks to discourage the other side from doing something it might wish to do (e.g., the United States attempting to discourage the Soviets from launching a nuclear strike against intercontinental missiles based in the United States). In other words, with compellence the successful exercise of influence requires one to make something happen; with deterrence, success consists of nothing happening.[8]

In trying to compel or deter a state, the timing of carrot and stick approaches is often crucial. One would ordinarily expect states to exploit the possibilities of promises and threats before employing rewards and punishments. Promises and threats tend to be more efficient tools of influence than rewards and punishments, which entail some actual use and consumption of resources in the bargaining process while promises and threats involve only a hypothetical commitment of resources (even though one might have to make good on them later). It would seem logical to provide rewards only *after* some *desired* behavior has taken place, either to fulfill an earlier promise or (even if no promise was made) to reinforce a continuation of that behavior; likewise, punishments would seem appropriate only *after* some *undesired* behavior persists. However, states do not always follow the logic of delaying rewards and punishments until promises and threats have been given a chance to work. Sometimes punishment is meted out early in the bargaining process, when it is felt that mere threats will be of no avail. Sometimes rewards are bestowed early also, as bribes to induce hoped-for cooperation, but such bribes can backfire, as the example of U.S. policy in relation to South Africa and Namibia suggests. Giving rewards (in the form of promoting continued American private investment in the South African economy as part of the "constructive engagement" policy pursued by the Reagan administration) while the undesirable behavior (South African occupation of Namibia) persists may only reinforce the behavior one is seeking to change.

THE INGREDIENTS OF SUCCESSFUL BARGAINING

It is not enough simply to make timely promises or threats. In order for promises or threats to work, they must also be sufficiently (1) *credible* and (2) *potent*, as perceived by the *other* side. Regarding the element of **credibility,** state A can intend fully to honor a promise or to carry out a threat; however, both are meaningless and unlikely to influence state B's behavior unless B believes that A has the capability and willingness to follow through with its promise or threat. By the same token, a state can be bluffing in its promises or threats; but all that counts is whether the target state is convinced. As Henry Kissinger noted, "A bluff taken seriously is more useful than a serious threat [or promise] interpreted as a bluff."[9] Of course, a state might ultimately be called upon to carry out a threat or promise, and it must be prepared to do so if it values its future credibility.

Regarding the element of **potency,** in order for state A to influence state B to adjust its behavior in a desired direction, a promise or threat by A must not only be believable but it must also be sufficiently weighty in the eyes of the leaders of B—either too attractive to pass up (in the case of a promise) or too potentially harmful to absorb (in the case of a threat). In other words, the carrot must be juicy enough for the target state to want to bite, while the stick must be menacing enough for the target state not to want to test it; the target state might well believe that the other state will execute a given promise or threat, but it might not *care* about the consequences, at least not enough to warrant rethinking its behavior.

Promises and threats that are credible but lack potency are likely to fail in the bargaining process. For example, if we recall Henry Kissinger's flirtations with Moscow in the early seventies, Soviet leaders were quite convinced of Kissinger's willingness to provide agricultural and technological benefits to the Soviet Union in exchange for their cooperation in keeping regional conflicts in Africa and elsewhere under control, especially since he demonstrated his sincerity by rewarding them in advance before any changes in Soviet behavior had even occurred. The failure to influence Soviet behavior as fully as Kissinger had hoped was not due to lack of U.S. credibility but rather at least partially to the fact that the incentives that the United States was offering were not of sufficient weight to induce the Soviets to give up their geopolitical goals. Food and technology might have been important to the Soviets, but they were not so desperate for U.S. exports that they were willing to pass up opportunities to enhance their own influence in Africa and Asia in return. Perhaps if the Soviet Union had been more dependent on U.S. trade, American threats to withhold exports, or promises to expand them, would have been more potent. Indeed, one possible justification for Kissinger's giving the Soviets some benefits without strings attached was precisely the desire to build up Soviet dependencies on the United States and thereby enhance the future potency of American promises and threats in dealing with the Soviet Union. As Kissinger argued, one reason to maintain contact with states even if one disapproves of their form of government is to be in a better position to influence them.[10] However, as we will see later in the chapter when we focus on the use of economic instruments, one should be careful not to overestimate the leverage provided by such ties.

Promises and threats that might be potent but lack credibility are just as likely to fail as those that are credible but lack potency. The need to communicate in a credible fashion is especially important in an era in which misperception and miscalculation can lead to nuclear holocaust. A great deal has been written about how governments can enhance the credibility of their threats as well as their promises, but there are pitfalls in overemphasizing credibility; some critics have noted that the U.S. government became obsessed with the credibility of its pledges to defend allies, and intervened in places like Vietnam to reinforce such credibility (even though Vietnam was never formally an ally). For states wishing to increase credibility, one frequently stated guideline is that "the more specific a promise or threat is, and the more authoritative its source, the greater the credibility of the intentions it expresses."[11] Thus, leaders desiring a particular concession from a foreign state stand a better chance of achieving it if it is spelled out clearly along with the specific consequences that will follow compliance or noncompliance.

Thomas Schelling, who has written many important works dealing with the dynamics of international bargaining, has suggested a number of other ways in which states can increase the credibility of their threats and promises.[12] To Schelling, the "art of commitment" is central to success in the bargaining process. He stresses the importance of reinforcing declarations of intent with the kinds of tacit bargaining actions noted earlier, such as using budgetary allocations, troop mobilizations, and demonstrations of sealift capabilities to buttress threats, or sending a noted diplomat abroad to lend seriousness and authority to one's promises.

One strategy that Schelling suggests can be particularly effective in making threats believable is the "burn all your bridges behind you" approach, i.e., creating a situation in which you convince the other side that if they take a particular action that you wish to deter, you will have *no choice* but to carry out the threat you have posed. A commonly cited example of this type of strategy is the so-called "tripwire" function performed by the 300,000 American troops stationed in Western Europe as part of the NATO defense forces. It is said that the main purpose of having U.S. troops in Europe is to make it more believable to the Soviets that any military aggression on their part in Western Europe would automatically trigger U.S. involvement and force it to honor its commitment to the defense of Western Europe, since it is likely that American soldiers would have been killed as a result of the Soviet action and an American president would have to respond. Of course, the trick—in the nuclear age especially—is somehow to keep your options open, retaining at least one other "bridge," while convincing the other side that all avenues of retreat from your threat have been closed off. Again, in international bargaining, appearance is often more important than reality.

As noted in the previous chapter, a country's foreign policy behavior can produce images in the minds of others, intended or unintended. In an effort to enhance its credibility, a government can try to cultivate a certain image or reputation. A reputation for being "reliable" can be especially helpful in making one's promises believable, while a reputation for being "erratic" or "reckless," which some would argue Libya's Muammar Qaddafi has cultivated, can be helpful in making one's threats believable. A reputation for recklessness can backfire, however, as Qaddafi discovered when foreign leaders began shying away from agreements with him, for example when Tunisian officials quietly ignored an agreement to unify with Libya in the early 1980s.

We have seen that Premier Khrushchev's reckless emplacement of missiles in Cuba in 1962 ultimately helped cost him his job. Previously, in 1958,

Khrushchev had attempted to settle the unresolved status of Berlin and the two Germanys, still lingering issues from World War II, by carrot and stick diplomacy with a tinge of recklessness. As an inducement to the West he offered a general peace treaty recognizing the two Germanys, but providing for removal of Western troops from Berlin, which would have become a "free city" open to East and West. However, if the West refused to sign such an agreement and thereby legitimize East Germany (the German Democratic Republic, or GDR), he threatened to sign a separate peace with East Germany giving the latter effective control over access to Berlin (located well inside GDR territory). Since the Western powers (the United States, Britain, and France) were guaranteed access to Berlin by the Soviets under the Four Power Agreement after World War II, they resisted this ultimatum and let Khrushchev's six-month time limit run out. The ultimate, informal bargain that was struck in 1961, allowing the building of the Berlin Wall dividing the city in half, depended on *changed* bargaining positions after three years of confrontation, and especially on increased acceptance of a divided Berlin. This solution allowed the Soviets to back down from their ultimatum, the East Germans to stem the tide of skilled personnel escaping to West Berlin, and the West to restabilize the situation with continued access to the city.[13]

The Berlin case shows that the international bargaining process often produces an outcome that does not represent a clear victory or defeat for either side. While the construction of an ugly wall through a city cannot be termed an optimal solution, the Berlin case also illustrates how agreements can be based on "prominent solutions." **Prominent solutions** are alternatives that are so self-evidently better than others, even if not optimal, that all parties would tend to settle on them even without clear signals to that effect. As an example, if a group of ten students were deposited one morning in different parts of Manhattan in New York City and were told to find each other before the end of the day, it is likely that, without communicating, they would each show up at a place and time they calculated would have the greatest probability of attracting the others. Surveys have shown that one such prominent solution would be Grand Central Station at noon.[14] Some people argue that a Palestinian state in the West Bank and Gaza areas now occupied by Israel constitutes a prominent solution to the persistent Middle East conflict.

GAME THEORY

A large body of **game theory** literature exists that provides some useful insights into the nature of international bargaining and the way in which cooperation can occur amidst conflict.[15] Two basic types of games are common to discussions of international bargaining: the "zero-sum" game and the "variable-sum" (mixed-motive) game. The **zero-sum game** is structured so that what one party wins, the other party automatically loses; conflict, in other words, is total. An international example would be a territorial dispute in which two states claim the same parcel of land but obviously cannot exercise sovereignty over it at once. However, through creative diplomacy it might be possible to turn such a zero-sum game into a **variable-sum game** in which both parties can simultaneously win something, even though one might benefit more than the other. If the disputants determined that they could share the land, the game would feature a "win-win" outcome.

Most situations in international relations resemble variable-sum (mixed motive) games rather than zero-sum games. Figures 7.2 and 7.3 illustrate two mixed motive games frequently cited as especially relevant to the study of international relations. Such games often have prominent solutions based on the gains or losses expected (with a general rule of thumb being to maximize gains and minimize losses—the so-called "minimax" rule). The first example is the game of "chicken," in which opponents drive toward each other on a single-lane highway, with the first one to swerve considered the loser, or chicken. Each player is faced with essentially two options (swerve or don't swerve), with neither player knowing which option the other will choose and neither one alone able to control the outcome of the game. The hypothetical values (payoffs) gained or lost by each player as a result of swerving or not swerving are represented by the numbers appearing in each cell of the matrix in Figure 7.2. It should be evident that on the basis of projected gains and losses, each party would be better off "cooperating," i.e., swerving to avoid the risk of total and mutual destruction in a collision. This game often is

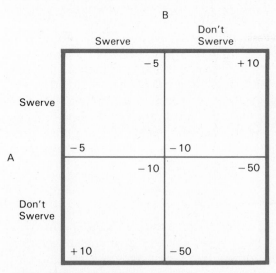

Figure 7.2
THE GAME OF CHICKEN
Payoffs to player A are shown in the lower left-hand corner of each cell, while payoffs to player B are shown in the upper right-hand corner of each cell.

used to illustrate problems of threat and counterthreat, or deterrence in international conflict, particularly relating to the danger of nuclear war (as with the sailing of Soviet ships toward the U.S. naval blockade of Cuba during the 1962 missile crisis).

Figure 7.3 illustrates another simple but somewhat different two-person game, the "prisoners' dilemma." Here it is assumed that two suspects found together are arrested for a crime and are interrogated separately. Each prisoner is told that he will receive the maximum sentence if he remains silent while the other prisoner confesses. On the other hand, he will get probation or go free if he confesses and implicates his partner while the partner remains silent. If both parties confess, they will each receive intermediate sentences; if both remain silent they will receive the minimum sentence. Given the hypothetical payoff values listed in Figure 7.3, the two prisoners—assuming they are both rational players adopting a "minimax" strategy—would probably confess jointly, each thereby receiving moderately long prison terms (e.g., five years). Yet each could get off with much less time in prison if they would jointly cooperate by not confessing. The problem, or "dilemma," is that neither can trust the other to keep quiet, since there is much to gain by pinning the crime on the partner. Each prisoner is worried about the possible maximum (e.g., ten years) prison sentence. The element of trust or enforced compliance is missing, so that neither prisoner can be sure the other will not implicate him if he keeps silent. Thus, the structure of the game tends to produce an unsatisfactory outcome for both players. This situation has been compared to

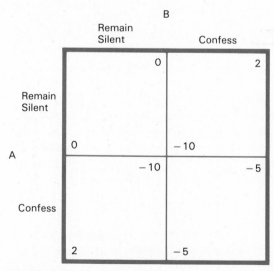

Figure 7.3
THE PRISONERS' DILEMMA GAME
Payoffs to player A are shown in the lower left-hand corner of each cell, while payoffs to player B are shown in the upper right-hand corner of each cell.

international arms races, in which both sides would be better off with reduced defense expenditures and an arms control agreement, but neither trusts that the other will refrain from taking significant advantage of such an agreement.

Although governments often seem to be locked into conflict, as in the case of arms control negotiations, it is possible to develop cooperative strategies over time through trial and error so that the parties can share in winnings rather than losses. Fortunately, in international relations games are seldom one-shot affairs. Often they consist of moves and countermoves, offers and probes. States may back down on some issues but stand firm on others, and in the sequence of events it may be possible to reach a mutually agreeable outcome. The Berlin crisis of 1958–62 can be viewed as such a sequence. There were confrontational elements typical of chicken games, with the United States and the Soviet Union facing possible humiliation in a back-down, and also facing possible mutual destruction in a war over Berlin and its access routes. There were also elements of common interest and distrust typical of the prisoners' dilemma. One complication in many such crises is misperception about what game the opponent is playing. U.S. leaders thought the Soviets were playing chicken with a Berlin ultimatum. Soviet leaders assumed that there was plenty of room for compromise and joint face-saving formulas. The West stood firm on the initial Soviet ultimatum, but ultimately yielded on the building of the wall. The Soviets backed away from their separate peace treaty threat. Gradually the Americans made clear their minimum demands: self-determination and economic survival for West Berliners; continued presence of Western troops in Berlin; freedom of access to Berlin. While Washington signaled intentions to fight for these demands, other related issues were treated as lower priorities, leaving room for a settlement.[16]

Hence, if players can communicate to each other their intention to reward cooperative play, to resist or penalize conflictual play, and to seek mutual benefits, then solutions for difficult disputes can be engineered. It has even been argued that there are "best" ways to play chicken or the prisoners' dilemma which help avert collisions or mutual losses. Frequently such strategies involve signals that cooperation will be rewarded with cooperation while conflictual play will be met with equally conflictual responses. Generally the object is to prevent miscalculations by opponents, minimize ambiguity and maximize predictability of behavior, prevent escalation of hostilities to higher levels, and remove emotional or ideological factors as much as possible from the bargaining process.[17]

The Good Diplomat and Good Diplomacy: Rules to Follow in Negotiations

A number of writers have recommended various "rules" that statesmen ought to follow in order to be good diplomats and to conduct successful diplomacy, particularly in regard to formal negotiations (as opposed to tacit bargaining). Many of these rules are related to the ingredients of successful bargaining discussed earlier. We will first look at the personal characteristics thought to be essential to serving as a model diplomat, and then at what is required for model diplomacy.

RULES FOR GOOD DIPLOMATS

For those who feel the key to diplomatic negotiations is deception, then the chief "virtue" a good diplomat presumably should have is the ability to lie with a straight face. Indeed, diplomacy has often been defined as "the ability to say and do the nastiest thing in the nicest way"; another famous definition describes a diplomat as "an honest man sent abroad to lie for his country."[18] This rather seedy view of diplomats was captured in a statement by a Polish representative assigned to Moscow during the 1940s, who commented on a Soviet diplomat by the name of Vyshinsky: "In a way, Vyshinsky was the perfect diplomat. He was capable of telling an obvious untruth to your face; you knew it was a lie and he knew that you knew it was a lie, but he stubbornly adhered to it. No other diplomat was able to do this with such nonchalance."[19]

Given the importance of the credibility factor that we noted earlier, however, deceitfulness is hardly very useful as a diplomatic quality. While any good bargainer might well wish to conceal certain information, and there can be some occasions when duplicity is necessary, there usually is good reason for a diplomat, on balance, to be honest and truthful when conducting negotiations—if only to retain future credibility and effectiveness. Of the five qualities that Harold Nicolson lists as essential to being an ideal diplomat, the first is truthfulness. The others include precision, in terms of clarity of expression; calmness; modesty, since vanity makes a diplomat more likely to alienate the other side with arrogant behavior or to succumb to its flattery; and loyalty to one's own government, a quality that can sometimes be lost, especially in cases where a diplomat has spent so much time abroad in a particular post that he or she unconsciously develops an affinity for the local culture and people which can affect one's judgment concerning the interests one is representing.[20]

It is sometimes claimed that certain countries, based on ideological or cultural traits, exhibit particular diplomatic "styles" that characterize their negotiating teams in general rather than any individual diplomatic representative.[21] For example, the Soviets are often said to be deliberately brusque and offensive in manner at the negotiating table, while the Japanese are often self-effacing. Much has been made of the fact that many U.S. secretaries of state and other high-level officials in the American diplomatic establishment have been lawyers and have tended to adopt a legalistic approach in diplomatic negotiations. However, too much can be made of these kinds of national negotiating stereotypes. The Soviets have shown themselves to be capable of exercising tact and civility in moments when sound diplomacy called for it, while American negotiators frequently have been quite pragmatic and willing to overlook legal niceties in pursuit of diplomatic goals. The personal factor—the qualities a specific negotiator brings to the bargaining table—should never be completely overlooked, even in an age when emissaries are often mere messengers of their governments.

RULES FOR GOOD DIPLOMACY

Among the rules that diplomats ought to observe in the negotiating process, according to Roger Fisher and many others who have written on bargaining, are the following:[22]

1. *Determine whether the other side is serious about negotiating*. Just because a particular country shows up at the negotiating table does not necessarily mean it is earnestly interested in reaching an agreement through diplomacy. It might merely be using the negotiations as a vehicle for gaining publicity for its cause and promoting propaganda, or for

Drawing by Ziegler; © 1981 The New Yorker Magazine, Inc.

The diplomat: Precision without tact

gathering further information about its opponent's intentions and capabilities. The success of bargaining often depends not so much on the skills of negotiators as on the parties' political interests in a settlement. However, even an "exchange of views" without real negotiation can be helpful in itself if it contributes to greater understanding.

2. *Do not dismiss what might appear to be purely cosmetic or symbolic procedural concerns expressed by the other side*. Sometimes the sticking point in negotiations can occur at the very start, based on such procedural concerns as the shape of the table or the identity of the parties who will be permitted to sit at the table. The United States haggled with the North Vietnamese for several months in Paris over the shape of the negotiating table and who should represent Vietnam, and attempts to organize a Geneva conference on the Middle East involving the Arabs and Israelis have always foundered on the question of whether the Palestine Liberation Organization would be allowed to participate and in what capacity. While the raising of procedural issues often reflects a desire to obstruct negotiations, it can also point up the real crux of the problem in a dispute between countries. Imaginative seating arrangements can often be the start of constructive negotiations.

3. Related to points 1 and 2, *show some empathy and understanding toward the other side's position.* As the nineteenth-century French diplomat Talleyrand is reported to have remarked, "For every hour you negotiate, put yourself in your opponent's position for ten minutes." This does not mean caving in to their demands, only understanding what they can reasonably be expected to accept in negotiations. There is a tendency to be self-righteous in defense of one's position and to admonish the other side for "aggressive" behavior or some other misdeed, on the assumption that feelings of guilt can be inflicted on an opponent. However, chances are the other side feels equally self-righteous, so that by exchanging accusations and insults the two sides will likely be merely talking past each other. As Fisher notes, "How they [other parties] feel about the choice we will be asking them to make is just as important to us as how we feel about it."[23]

4. *Offer proposals that are concrete enough for the other side to think about and respond to.* As we noted earlier, the specificity of promises (and threats) can increase their credibility and effectiveness in the negotiating process. In Fisher's words, give the other side a "yesable proposition."

5. *If a comprehensive settlement of all aspects of a dispute is not possible, slice up the problem into narrower, more manageable issues to be negotiated separately.* When Henry Kissinger did not feel a comprehensive settlement of Arab-Israeli differences was possible at a Geneva conference involving all participants, he resorted to "salami tactics" in approaching Egypt and other Arab countries separately to see if more

modest agreements that excluded the volatile Palestinian issue could be reached between them and Israel. Kissinger's approach eventually bore fruit with the Egyptian-Israeli Camp David accords achieved by the Carter administration, although the fragility of these agreements also showed the problems associated with partial settlements.[24]

6. *Do not humiliate the other side.* Make it as easy as possible for the other side to accept your terms. As long as you get what you want, you might as well let the other side *look* good by providing face-saving concessions. You should not gloat over diplomatic triumphs but instead make them appear to be equitable compromises. Even if one side is practically in a position to dictate the terms, a humiliating outcome is likely to leave feelings of bitterness and pressures for revenge in the future, as the punitive Versailles Peace Treaty did after World War I, contributing heavily to German revanchism in the interwar period.

The Instruments of International Bargaining: Military Resources

Until now, we have discussed the dynamics of international bargaining in general. Let us now focus on specific instruments of bargaining, looking first at military resources and then at economic resources.

Military resources enable a state to bargain through both explicit and implicit threats and promises as well as punishments and rewards. Regarding the use of military instruments as *carrots*, both the United States and the Soviet Union have wooed Third World states with offers of sophisticated military equipment, hoping to win friends by catering to their security needs or to their desire for weapons as status symbols. This tactic can make the recipient state dependent on the donor for spare parts and other military supplies. However, some Third World states also have had carrots available for bargaining purposes, particularly if their location is strategically attractive to a major military power seeking to establish a base in a given area.[25]

Regarding the use of military instruments as *sticks*, many would argue that successful diplomacy depends mainly on the number of guns backing it up. However, as we have already suggested, the relationship between military power and diplomatic effectiveness is far more complicated than this. For one thing, in disputes between some countries (e.g., the United States and Canada) the threat of armed force is largely irrelevant to the bargaining process, due to the implausibility of one side actually employing such weapons against the other no matter what the substance of the dispute. Even in disputes between enemies, where military threats are more plausible, their relevance and ultimate usefulness will depend on a variety of factors and not only on which side has overall military superiority.

Successful bargaining depends not only on relative military capabilities but also on the tenacity with which the parties hold on to their goals, i.e., whether concessions are possible or appealing in light of costs and benefits. Occasionally, clearly weaker parties have refused to bargain, as when Arab states demanded unconditional return of territories occupied by Israel in 1948 and 1967. If the issues at stake involve core political goals, such as territory deemed essential to a country's security and well-being, a country is likely to make fewer concessions and will be more difficult to deal with than if values involve merely prestige or less pressing concerns.

Furthermore, the images and perceptions discussed in Chapter 6 can make bargaining more difficult, especially if mass populations on both sides have grown to hate or fear each other. It was easier for Israelis to bargain with Egypt in 1978 than it would have been for them to bargain with the Palestinians. Egypt and Israel, for all their war-making in the desert, never attacked each other's civilian populations and never claimed the same territory as a major goal. On the other hand, Israeli and Palestinian raiders have killed many civilians on both sides and do not trust the other party to settle for "half a loaf." In mirror image terms, each thinks the other does not recognize the legitimacy of their nationalism and would destroy them as a people. An agreement halfway up the bargaining line under such hostile circumstances is very difficult, despite the advantages peace could bring to both peoples.

MILITARY DETERRENCE

The topic of *deterrence* will be examined more fully in a later chapter on arms races and arms control, particularly in the context of nuclear weapons and averting nuclear war. The deterrence concept also applies to diplomacy and bargaining through the manipulation of military threats in general, a subject we focus on in this section. Although deterrence refers to any attempt by one party to prevent another party from taking some undesired action, the term is most commonly and importantly associated with preventing the other side from taking aggressive *military* action by making the potential costs of such action exceed the potential benefits in the eyes of the would-be aggressor. Billions of dollars are spent yearly in the name of such deterrence, and billions of lives rest on deterrence calculations. Yet it is very difficult to know when a state has been deterred. That depends on whether the state had intended to attack in the first place and on whether it decided not to for fear of retaliation or because of other reasons, such as snafus in its own military operations or the vagaries of weather conditions. If deterrence fails—if the opponent strikes— the game changes from diplomacy to war, from deterrence to defense.

Theoretically, deterrent threats are more likely to work against weaker states than against opponents that are equally powerful or superior in military capabilities. Hence, the logic of the well-worn axiom invoked by leaders to justify increased military spending: to maintain the peace (i.e., to prevent aggression), prepare for war. However, several empirical studies have shown that arming to the teeth provides no assurance that one can deter an attack on oneself or on one's allies, and that other factors can be more crucial to successful deterrence than simply superior military strength. In fact, the saber rattling often associated with arming to the teeth can make the other side increasingly paranoid and provoke the very act one wishes to deter by causing the other side to engage in a preemptive strike. Throughout history, and particularly in the twentieth century, militarily superior states have often failed to deter attacks from weaker states.[26] The most dramatic recent example remains the American experience in Vietnam, when U.S. tank power and air power were insufficient to prevent North Vietnam from pursuing war against South Vietnam.

Recalling a point made earlier, military power—like other forms of power—is issue-specific or situation-specific. In the case of Vietnam, raw military capability was less important than the particular military capability that was *appropriate* to the situation. Also important was the fact that the North Vietnamese placed such a high value on their goal of unifying all of Vietnam under Hanoi's control and had enough political backing in South Vietnam that they were willing to absorb almost any amount of punishment the United States threatened to inflict on them; in other words, the cost-benefit calculus favored North Vietnam. The fact is that even severe threats might not dissuade opponents determined to achieve goals. An attacker might press on unless convinced that a prospective defender will actually stand firm against the attack and that the costs of attacking will be greater than the value of the goals at stake. And the defender must be convinced that the gains from standing firm will be greater than the costs of retreating.[27]

It is generally easier to deter an adversary from attacking one's *own* homeland than to deter it from attacking *another* state, if only because the commitment to retaliate in the first case is invariably stronger. However, certain steps can be taken to deter attacks on allies or other countries, such as the "burn all your bridges behind you" ploy used by the United States to enhance the credibility of its deterrent doctrine in Western Europe. Strong, visible economic and military ties to a threatened state are evidently one of the best ways to extend deterrence. In a study of seventeen cases of deterrence involving protection of a third party ("pawn"), the attacker held back most frequently when there was both economic interdependence and military cooperation between the prospective defender and the threatened state. Formal pronouncements of defense commitments (alliances) were not nearly as effective in deterring aggression.[28]

Another study of deterrence has shown that wishful thinking frequently makes attackers go ahead despite deterrent threats. Leaders who are pressed toward aggressive foreign policies by severe domestic or international problems often redefine reality to suit their needs and miscalculate risks as low and benefits of attack as high. This has been true throughout the twentieth century in crises from Fashoda (in North Africa) to Korea. "To the extent that leaders perceive the need to act, they become insensitive to the interests and commitments of others that stand in the way of success of their policy."[29]

The Instruments of International Bargaining: Economic Resources

As military bargaining has become more problematic and dangerous in the nuclear age, there has been increased attention paid to economic levers of influence.[30] Embargoes, boycotts, multinational investment, frozen assets in banks, and strings attached to foreign aid packages all capture the headlines these days, and all can be used in formal or tacit bargaining. Crowds take to the streets to protest foreign economic exploitation or competition; multinational corporation executives are kidnapped; and OPEC ministers meet under heavy guard—all of these being symbols of the emotional issues at stake in economic bargaining.

Under certain conditions, economic levers can be quite effective, especially with states highly dependent on the influencer in an unequal relationship. In colonial days, a foreign power's economic penetration of another society generally was accompanied by its formal incorporation into that power's empire. Today, economic penetration can produce similar domination in more subtle form (sometimes referred to as **neocolonialism**), although penetrated states frequently can counter with leverage of their own. Among the economic *carrots* that states attempt to use to induce cooperative behavior from other states are foreign aid grants and credits as well as foreign investment funds and "most favored nation" trading status; economic *sticks* include the withdrawal of the latter benefits as well as **embargoes** (refusing to export needed goods to another state), **boycotts** (refusing to import goods from another state), and expropriation or freezing of a foreign state's assets. Economic resources also can enable a state to purchase what political or military pressure will not provide, as when the United States subsidized South Korean and Thai participation in the Vietnam and Laos wars during the 1960s. Economic means have been used both to strengthen friendly governments (by pumping money into their national economies to relieve domestic political pressures) and to weaken unfriendly ones (by damaging their economies or underwriting subversive activities).[31]

It has been argued that while preponderant military power remains concentrated in American and Soviet hands, the ability to influence events around the world has expanded to a variety of relative military weaklings which possess economic prowess, such as Japan, Saudi Arabia, and West Germany (notwithstanding the fact the West Germans have the largest army in Western Europe).[32] However, it bears repeating that diplomatic influence depends on having appropriate resources for the situation at hand. In the case of economic threats, their effectiveness depends upon whether they are relevant to the issue in dispute and whether the country threatened has a sufficient degree of vulnerability to economic penalties.

Klaus Knorr has noted that in order for country A to have "coercive" economic power over country B, the following conditions must exist:

> (1) A must have a high degree of control over the supply of something B values. . . . (2) B's need for this supply must be intensive, and (3) . . . B's cost of compliance must be less than the costs of doing without the supply.[33]

In other words, country B must be not only **sensitive** to the threat posed by country A (i.e., it must have reason to be concerned about the potential damage that might be caused by A's actions) but also **vulnerable** (i.e., it must be unable to make policy adjustments to overcome the damage without suffering prohibitive costs in the process).[34] A fourth requirement seems in order as well, namely that the cost to country A of carrying out the economic sanctions must be lower than the potential benefits, or else country A is not likely to carry them through.

Those who have advocated the use of U.S. agricultural exports as "weapons"—to counter OPEC oil, for example—must reckon with several hard facts of life that do not fit the above requirements. First, other grain exporters, such as Canada and Argentina, are available; even if the United States were somehow able to coordinate with other major suppliers a grain embargo against OPEC countries, it might be difficult to enforce, since grain could reach OPEC countries through nonembargoed countries. In addition, U.S. farmers constitute a powerful interest group opposed to government interference and in favor of exports, since agricultural exports account for roughly one quarter of total annual cash receipts of American farmers. In other words, in an embargo situation the United States might find itself more export dependent than the OPEC countries would be import dependent.[35]

Arab and OPEC states themselves confronted similar facts in 1973,[36] even as they termed their petroleum resources a "weapon ": Western oil companies still controlled most of the refining and distribution of oil; countries could ration and limit oil consumption; oil was available from a variety of sources and remained as difficult to monitor as the international flow of food; the very countries that were the targets of such weapons provided the technology and consumer goods so desired by oil-producing states and also were the markets for investment of surplus petrodollars. OPEC states managed to achieve a measure of success in 1973, but not as much as some expected and not without considerable obstacles.[37] The politics of economic warfare or bargaining, then, are not as simple as they might at first appear.

A study of eighteen attempts at economic sanctions between 1933 and 1967 found that only three could be viewed as even partial successes.[38] Another study has shown that of twenty-two cases of trade sanctions by one state against another, trade restrictions succeeded in achieving foreign policy goals in only four cases, with three more resulting in compromise settlements.[39] The availability of alternate trade sources proved to be a major reason for the fifteen outright failures in the latter study. When the United States tried to punish Cuba during the sixties by boycotting its sugar and embargoing its oil shipments from Western companies, the Cubans were able to turn to the Soviet Union as a market for its sugar and as a source of oil. The ability to engineer ways around the slow-acting effects of economic sanctions also allows countries to resist economic pressure.

The example of South Africa illustrates the many complications surrounding the use of economic sanctions. For years South Africa has weathered relatively half-hearted attempts at international restrictions on its exports and imports, aimed at pressuring the white regime in Pretoria both to relinquish colonial

"If we start using food as a weapon, this could give our side the edge . . . It's Sgt. O'Houlihan's recipe for creamed beef on toast."

Grin and Bear It by Lichty & Wagner. © 1981 Field Enterprises, Inc. Courtesy of Field Newspaper Syndicate

Food as a weapon

rule over Namibia and to end its system of racial discrimination against South African blacks known as apartheid. While the United Nations General Assembly has called for strict sanctions, many countries retain continued interests in the trade of gold, diamonds, platinum, and other goods that South Africa produces or consumes. Western powers also have expressed concern that sanctions directed at South Africa will harm the economies of black African states that depend on ties to South Africa. The South African government has become adept at transshipping goods from one country to another and buying through intermediary agents. The country thus has continued to trade while retaining control over Namibia and maintaining the apartheid system. However, there are many who argue that if the major international trading countries jointly became serious about enforcing sanctions on Pretoria, that government would be hard pressed to continue its policies.

The type and timing of international economic sanctions have much to do with their effectiveness. Where trade embargoes do not work, it is possible that quieter sanctions such as reducing capital flows—either foreign private investment and loans or foreign aid—can succeed. For instance, in 1986, the international banking community's threat to withhold further loans to South Africa because of societal disruptions there (which endangered that state's economy and repayment capabilities) alarmed South African business leaders, shook the country's currency, and spurred the government to announce at least modest "reforms" of apartheid. However, as with trade, the effectiveness of cutting off capital to a country depends on the availability of other states to fill the breach as aid donors or investors. Regarding foreign aid, the United States, the Soviet Union, and other donor countries have discovered in recent years that foreign economic assistance often fails to win friends or buy influence, even though several studies have found that major recipients of Soviet or American aid tend (with some notable exceptions) to vote in agreement with the major donor in the UN General Assembly.[40] Other studies also have shown that sizable foreign investments by corporations do not necessarily give their home (headquarters) country increased control of the country receiving the investments.[41]

Economic threats or punishments involving foreign aid or investment tend to be most effective when the government under pressure is highly dependent on the country applying the pressure and lacks strong domestic support, as in the case of the Manley government in Jamaica during the 1970s. Prime Minister Manley had moved to nationalize American corporate properties in Jamaica. Loans by U.S.-dominated international financial institutions then were denied the Jamaican government, resulting in a decline in Jamaica's foreign currency holdings and driving up the cost of goods to the point where the Manley government was defeated by a pro-U.S. faction in a 1980 election. Similar economic pressures have contributed to the downfall of regimes in Chile and elsewhere in Latin America.[42]

As we will see in later chapters, it is increasingly necessary for countries to forge agreements to coordinate the world's economic transactions. Economic confrontation and coercion not only are often ineffective as a form of international bargaining but also tend to undermine the international economic order by producing disruptive effects on employment, prices, and human welfare in general.

Conclusion

Although this chapter has dealt with diplomacy as something in which national *governments* engage, a variety of actors can become involved in the international bargaining game. Indeed, the game board seems to be expanding today, with "terrorist" or "national liberation" groups (depending on one's perspective) frequently seizing hostages and negotiating with foreign governments, as well as other types of *nonstate* actors getting into the act. Still, students of international relations remain most interested in the game as it is played by nation-states.

Miles Copeland, a former CIA agent, has tried to detail the "game of nations" by focusing on the cat-and-mouse maneuvers of the U.S. and Egyptian governments in the 1950s and 1960s. As Secretary of State Dulles and President Nasser attempted to make use of each other, they employed a variety of tactics—carrots and sticks—some of which involved official diplomatic channels and others more seamy "cloak and dagger" operations. The two sides were trying to convince each other to cooperate in pursuing important goals, or at least not to impede the pursuit of such goals. A feel for the game can be derived by examining the chapter subtitles in Copeland's book, which is essentially as relevant today as it was when it was written; the following fragments call to mind especially the experiences of OPEC members and nonaligned states in general:

> The first prerequisite for winning a game is to know that you're in one.
>
> If you can't change the board, change the players . . . but settle for a true player, not a pawn.
>
> That is to say, the new player you bring into the game will have his *own* objectives and policies . . . and his first objective will be to stay in the game—any way he can.
>
> His second objective will be to strengthen his position by *constructive* means.
>
> The strategy of the weak player is to play off the strong players against one another . . .
>
> . . . and if a single weak player can do this to good effect, a "union" of weak players can do it to better effect.

If you're going to have a union, you've got to make life intolerable for the scabs . . .

. . . and run the risk of pushing their powerful opponents too far . . .

. . . and push upward, beyond what you can afford, the costs of maintaining the facade required of an international power . . .

. . . and the gameboard may change on you, making your role irrelevant . . .

. . . and you are likely to come to a Sad End.[43]

In some ways the game analogy applied to world politics is a very useful one, but in some ways it is also unfortunate. The stakes of international politics are all too real and much weightier than World Series and Super Bowls. Human lives, and in fact the fate of the entire planet, are at stake. The language of American sports pastimes has come to reflect international politics lingo; however, throwing "long bombs" and mounting "blitzes" on Monday Night Football should not be confused with the horrors, broken bodies, and bereaved families caused by such tactics in the real world. Armies, too, play war games, complete with mock battles and fictitious deaths. Hopefully, military officers and civilian leaders can also distinguish between games and the real thing.

The difference between the "game of nations" and other sorts of games is nicely pointed out in a passage in the Copeland book, where the author quotes Egyptian Vice-President Zakaria Mohieddin speaking before the Egyptian War College in 1962; the following remarks provide a fitting transition to the next chapter:

> The Game of Nations . . . differs from other games—poker, . . . commerce—in several important respects. First, each player has his own aims, different from those of the others, which constitute "winning"; second, every player is forced by his own domestic circumstances to make moves in the Game which have nothing to do with winning and which, indeed, might impair chances of winning; third, in the Game of Nations there are no winners, only losers. The objective of each player is not so much to win as to avoid loss.
>
> The common objective of players in the Game of Nations is merely to keep the Game going. The alternative to the Game is war.[44]

SUMMARY

1. In the game of international relations, national governments attempt to exercise influence through diplomacy—the general process whereby states seek to communicate, to influence each other, and to resolve conflicts through bargaining, without the use of force.

2. The nature of diplomacy has changed somewhat over the years. In an era of advanced communications and travel technology that has facilitated direct contact between heads of state, the role of the ambassador as a country's representative abroad has diminished somewhat today. Also, there has been a trend toward greater public diplomacy and multilateral diplomacy, even though much diplomacy remains secret and bilateral in nature. Finally, in addition to formal negotiation, countries increasingly make use of more informal, tacit forms of diplomacy.

3. The essence of diplomacy is bargaining, a process by which each side tries to strike a final agreement as far from their own minimum demands and as close to their maximum demands as possible. Bargaining parties rely heavily on four types of tactics: threats and punishments (the stick approach) and promises and rewards (the carrot approach). The timing of all these approaches is crucial, as is their credibility and their potency.

4. International bargaining can be described and analyzed in terms of two types of games: zero-sum games, in which one party wins and one party loses; and variable-sum, or mixed-motive, games, in which both parties can simultaneously win something. Most situations in international relations resemble mixed-motive games of some sort.

5. Rules that diplomats ought to observe in the negotiating process include the following: (1) Determine whether the other side is serious about negotiating. (2) Do not dismiss apparently cosmetic or symbolic procedural concerns expressed by the other side. (3) Show some empathy and understanding toward the other side's position. (4) Offer proposals concrete enough for the other side to think about and respond to. (5) If a comprehensive settlement is not possible, slice up the problem into narrow, more manageable issues to be negotiated separately. (6) Do not humiliate the other side.

6. States use both military and economic resources as instruments of international bargaining, either to compel or deter certain behavior on the part of other states. Military resources enable a state to bargain through both threats and promises as well as punishments and rewards. However, the relationship between military power and diplomatic effectiveness is complicated by many factors, including the tenacity with which either side holds on to its goals as well as images and perceptions held by both sides. For example, there is no assurance that arming to the teeth will deter an adversary's attack; throughout history, militarily superior states have often failed to deter attacks from weaker states.

7. As problems with the use of military instruments have increased, more attention has been paid to economic tactics in bargaining. Economic means such as embargoes or foreign aid can be used to strengthen friendly governments and weaken unfriendly ones, but the effectiveness of economic carrots or sticks depends on their timing, their relevance to the issue in dispute, and the degree of a country's vulnerability to various forms of economic pressure.

SUGGESTIONS FOR FURTHER READING AND STUDY

For additional pointers on the game of international relations, especially the delicate art of negotiation, see Arthur Lall, *Modern International Negotiation* (New York: Columbia University Press, 1966); Fred C. Iklé, *How Nations Negotiate* (New York:

Harper & Row, 1964); Roger Fisher, *Dear Israelis, Dear Arabs* (New York: Harper & Row, 1972); William Macomber, *The Angels Game: A Handbook of Modern Diplomacy* (New York: Stein and Day, 1975); Edwin H. Fedder, "Negotiating Among Nations: A Review Article," *Background*, 9 (February 1966), pp. 339–350; I. William Zartman, ed., *The 50% Solution* (Garden City, N.Y.: Doubleday, 1976); Zartman, "The Political Analysis of Negotiation: How Who Gets What and When," *World Politics*, 26 (April 1974), pp. 385–399; and William R. Brown, *The Last Crusade: A Negotiator's Middle East Handbook* (Chicago: Nelson-Hall, 1980). For firsthand accounts of personal diplomatic experiences, see Dean G. Acheson, *Present at the Creation* (New York: W. W. Norton, 1969); Nikita S. Khrushchev, *Khrushchev Remembers*, S. Talbot, ed. and trans. (Boston: Little, Brown, 1970); and Henry A. Kissinger, *The White House Years* (Boston: Little, Brown, 1979).

For insights into the dynamics of bargaining in various international situations, see Glenn H. Snyder, "Crisis Bargaining," in *International Crises: Insights from Behavioral Research*, Charles F. Hermann, ed. (New York: Free Press, 1972); Charles Lockhart, *Bargaining in International Conflicts* (New York: Columbia University Press, 1979); and Michael Nicholson, *Conflict Analysis* (New York: Barnes and Noble, 1970). On deterrence, see Alexander L. George and Richard Smoke, *Deterrence in American Foreign Policy* (New York: Columbia University Press, 1974); and Patrick M. Morgan, *Deterrence: A Conceptual Analysis* (Beverly Hills: Sage, 1977). On the use of economic sanctions, see Miroslav Nincic and Peter Wallensteen, *Dilemmas of Economic Coercion: Sanctions in World Politics* (New York: Praeger, 1983); James Mayall, "The Sanctions Problem in International Economic Relations: Reflections in Light of Recent Experience," *International Affairs*, 60 (1984), pp. 631–642; and Gary C. Hufbauer and Jeffrey J. Schott, *Economic Sanctions Reconsidered: History and Current Policy* (Washington, D.C.: Institute for International Economics, 1985).

General theories of bargaining from the perspective of various disciplines are presented in Ian Morley and Geoffrey Stephenson, *The Social Psychology of Bargaining* (London: George Allen and Unwin, 1977); Jeffrey Z. Rubin and Bert R. Brown, *The Social Psychology of Bargaining and Negotiation* (New York: Academic Press, 1975); and John G. Cross, *The Economics of Bargaining* (New York: Basic Books, 1969). Multidisciplinary discussions of bargaining, and particularly game theory, can also be found in issues of the *Journal of Conflict Resolution*. An especially good discussion of taut diplomacy and "the art of diplomatic signalling" can be found in Raymond Cohen, *Theatre of Power* (New York: Longman, 1987).

8

Breakdown in the Game: The Resort to Armed Force

Whem diplomacy breaks down or seems to promise little, governments today as in the past frequently resort to the use of armed force in international relations. Indeed, violence occurs often enough that many observers consider it to be not a breakdown or an aberration but rather a normal part of world politics. For example, one observer notes that "between 3600 B.C. and the present day, there have been only 292 years of peace,"[1] while another remarks that during the 1945–1978 period, "there were not more than twenty-six days . . . in which there was no war [of some kind] somewhere in the world."[2] On an "average" day, about twelve wars were being fought.[3] However, as noted in the previous chapter, violent conflict constitutes only a relatively small fraction of the totality of international interactions. In this chapter, we discuss the reasons leaders cross the line between diplomacy and force, the ways in which force is utilized, and the costs and benefits associated with the resort to arms.

As a starting point, let us consider the following quotations, which illustrate two different, though not necessarily mutually exclusive, ways of viewing the use of force in international affairs:

> War is an instrument of policy. . . . The conduct of war . . . is policy itself which takes up the sword in place of the pen. . . . [4]

> The quest for international security involves the unconditional surrender by every nation, in a certain measure, of its liberty of action. . . . The ill-success . . . of all the efforts . . . to reach this goal leaves us no room to doubt that strong psychological factors are at work, which paralyze these efforts.[5]

According to the first statement, which is by Karl von Clausewitz, a famous nineteenth-century Prussian strategist, war is merely the "continuation of policy by other means." When the diplomacy of the conference table fails to achieve desired goals, force can be used to seize objectives or to apply sufficient pressure to kindle an adversary's interest in negotiation. Bargaining, then, does not necessarily cease when the pen is traded for the sword (or cannon or grenade); leaders still try to convince other leaders to make concessions and adopt acceptable terms of settlement. For example, Iran maintained its embassy and diplomatic relations with Iraq through much of the Gulf war in the 1980s.

Those adopting Clausewitz's view of war assume that cost-benefit, or "rational" calculations, similar to those discussed in Chapter 7, underlie war-making decisions and that war is a *deliberate*, conscious policy designed to achieve political goals. One influential version of this argument posits that individual leaders calculate the "expected utility" of making war before undertaking military action. Such expected utilities consist of the values or priorities the leadership attaches to outcomes that might stem from a war, as well as the leadership's willingness to take risks, and its estimates of various key probabilities—such as the probability of winning an armed struggle against one or more opponents and the probability of receiving help or encountering opposition from other states in the system. The greater the expected utility of going to war as opposed to remaining at peace, the greater the chance that marching orders will be given.

The chief proponent of this view that war is usually a calculated decision is American professor Bruce Bueno de Mesquita, who offers as evidence the fact that of fifty-eight interstate wars he identified between 1815 and 1974, the attacking nation won forty-two, considerably more than one would expect by chance alone. Looked at a bit differently, "only about 10 percent of the wars fought since the defeat of Napoleon at Waterloo have been quickly and decisively lost by the nation that attacked first."[6] Logically, however, the fact that an attacker wins does not necessarily mean that its attack was carefully planned and timed. Indeed, Bueno de Mesquita might well have divided his study into phases, since it appears that while initiators won most wars between 1815 and 1910, they lost three fifths of those fought between 1910 and 1965.[7] Thus, war does not necessarily pay, particularly in the twentieth century.

The goals leaders pursue through warfare can be relatively simple, such as the acquisition of a slice of territory, or complex, as in trying to remake an enemy country's entire political system or to alter fundamentally the world balance of power. It can be argued that wars based on simple or limited objectives and confined to geographically narrow limits are easier to resolve or "win" than wars involving complex goals, many regions, or many participants.[8] Bueno de Mesquita cautions us not to evaluate the "rationality" of war decisions by the saneness or soundness of leaders' goals, or to expect that emotions will play no part in decision making. Rather, rationality depends on leaders clearly ordering priorities, whether or not those priorities make sense to others, and deliberately weighing costs and benefits in pursuing those priorities. Adolf Hitler carried out a systematic plan to conquer Western Europe, and therefore technically was rational, although his ultimate goals—world domination and selective genocide—were diabolical and demented.

Many would argue, however, that emotional instabilities and misperceptions, such as those displayed by Hitler, materially distort leaders' estimates of success or failure probabilities, and hence lead to failure in warfare. Hitler, after all, overextended his forces in attacking the Soviet Union and declaring war on the United States in 1941, hardly rational policy for one intent on building a "1000 Year Reich" (the so-called Third Reich or German Empire). Although Bueno de Mesquita makes a strong case that war usually is a planned strategy for political objectives, he does not specify precisely why wars are fought, especially when decisions to do so appear irrational. For instance, why do *losers* in warfare consent to fight in the first place, rather than make other forms of concessions when confronted by superior forces? Do they misperceive the relative strengths of their own and their enemies' armies, or misperceive the levels of hostility or friendship directed at them in the international system?[9] Are they risk takers who conclude that armed struggle is worth the gamble for perhaps limited gains (as when the Japanese attacked the U.S. in 1941 knowing the high probability that they would lose a long war)? Or does what some have termed "the darker side of human nature" come into play?

Such factors that complicate the rational use of force as a bargaining vehicle are suggested by the second quotation above, from a letter by Albert Einstein in a famous exchange in the 1930s with Sigmund Freud. When emotions become involved in international violence, as Freud argued they inevitably do, reasoned calculations can give way to unlimited and unreasonable applications of force. Freud attributed war to largely unconscious processes of the human mind and speculated that humans have both a life and death wish or instinct, the latter leading them toward world destruction, and the former allowing some hope that culture might be shaped to control destructive impulses.[10]

Those adopting the second viewpoint, then, assume war to be mainly the result of unplanned responses to the environment based on either (1) a human instinct for violence[11] or (2) complex emotions of fear, frustration, and anger of the type discussed in Chapter 6.[12] Whole nations are sometimes categorized, perhaps inaccurately, as frustrated, vengeful, or warlike in mood by those proposing psychologically rooted causes for international violence.[13] Leaders at times might seek to generate, play upon, or respond to such moods. Even small-scale conflict over relatively limited territorial goals can therefore escalate beyond expectations as emotions creep in and produce hardened hatreds. Termination of violence under such circumstances becomes extremely difficult.

No *single* perspective, neither that of Clausewitz nor that of Einstein and Freud, can fully account for the occurrence of international violence. Just as those who see war as a rational bargaining exercise must contend with the often irrational nature of violence, those who see it as the product of deep psychological or biological drives must contend with the fact that not all people fight all of the time; some nations may be warlike at one moment in history and peaceful at other times, while others may be entirely peaceful.[14] Therefore certain conditions must set the stage for, and ultimately trigger, the decision—both calculated and emotional—to go to war. War has been compared to a disease process that, like cancer, seems to occur in multiple forms and have multiple causes.[15] Only by understanding these can we hope to offer possible antidotes to international violence.

Trends in the Use of Armed Force

Traditionally, those who have studied the use of armed force in world politics have been primarily interested in **war.** However, war is only one form of hostilities between nation-states. Other forms include border skirmishes, raids, interventions, and other armed clashes that represent "force without war."[16] In contrast to the latter type of violence, which consists of isolated or intermittent acts often committed by a single party, war in international relations is generally thought of as *sustained* armed combat between the organized military forces of at least two nation-states.

Distinctions between war and other forms of international violence used to be clearer, as wars in the past were definable in *legal* terms and had fairly neat beginnings and endings. A war was usually said to begin when one state issued a formal declaration of war against another state (as in World War II); it normally ended with a formal treaty of peace between the warring parties. Today, however, states tend not to issue formal declarations of war when they begin fighting, perhaps partly because armed aggression is illegal under the United Nations Charter. One reads of "police actions," or "anti-insurgency" or "anti-terrorist" activity, or just plain "self-defense." The result is that war has become less distinguishable from other modes of international violence.

In the midst of confusing labels, it is best to identify different categories of international violence according to the type and extent of fighting that goes on rather than according to what leaders say they are doing. Although the sustained nature of war tends to make for greater loss of life, all forms of international violence can potentially produce large numbers of casualties. Below we examine trends in the use of armed force in three areas: (1) international war, (2) force without war, and (3) civil war.

INTERNATIONAL WAR

Let us first look at the statistics on *war* in the international system, defining war as the onset of sustained military hostilities between at least two states culminating in at least 1000 battle deaths. Using this definition, there have been approximately 118 international wars between 1815 and 1980.[17] The incidence of international war generally has declined over time, although the trend is a modest one. However, even as the number of international wars has diminished, the severity of these wars, as measured by casualties, has mounted with the introduction of new weapons throughout the twentieth century. Although some wars in prior centuries killed proportionately large numbers of people, twice as many soldiers have died in twentieth-century wars (approximately 22.1 million) as in *all* the wars from 1500 to 1899 combined (an estimated 11.2 million).[18]

If one takes into account the enormous proliferation of nation-states since the end of World War II, which has tripled the number of potential candidates for war participation in the international system, then a more impressive case can be made (see Figure 8.1) that the post–World War II period up to recent years has been relatively free of international wars compared to previous eras of world politics. In contemporary times we find many wars dragging on inconclusively for up to a decade or more, but generally there seem to be

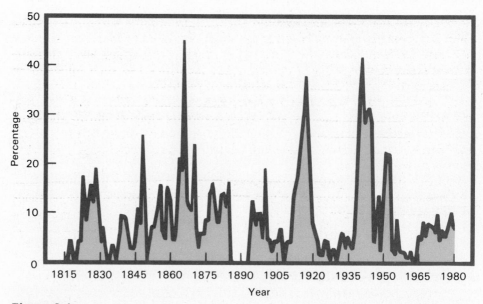

Figure 8.1
PERCENTAGE OF SOVEREIGN STATES ENGAGED IN INTERNATIONAL WARS, 1815–1980

fewer of the very long wars (lasting thirty years and more) that marked prior centuries. Periods of relative peace may be getting longer as periods of warfare become more condensed.[19]

What is perhaps most striking about the war phenomenon since 1945 is the paucity of war involvement by countries considered to be *major* powers and, in particular, the absence of war involvement *between major powers themselves* (unless one counts the Korean conflict, in which the United States and China fought against each other). Although there have been many crises and confrontations between the United States and the Soviet Union since 1945, they have never fought each other directly in war. While in any given year since 1965 roughly 10 percent of the states in the world have been involved in international wars, most of these wars have been waged by lesser powers.[20] Most wars now take place on the territory of and involve the armies of Third World states. However, war-making by the Third World has been facilitated by the increasingly sophisticated weapons supplied primarily by the United States and the Soviet Union.[21]

FORCE WITHOUT WAR

Although the frequency of international war has declined in recent times, notably between major powers, the distinction between war and peace becomes blurred when one takes into account the amount of **force without war** since 1945. For example, one study examines over 200 different incidents between 1945 and 1975 in which the United States has used armed force in some fashion short of war, while a related study identifies 190 such incidents in the case of the Soviet Union.[22] In addition to twenty-eight wars and interventions, another study has tallied twenty-eight border conflicts and rivalries, and twelve blockades, clashes, and crises involving violence during the same period in various regions of the globe.[23] Thus, abundant cases of "force without war" can be found, although the trend in the 1970s seemed to drop somewhat from high levels in the 1960s.

In many instances, force has been used more as a political instrument than as a raw military instrument. When force is used to inflict pain to persuade an adversary to cease or refrain from some undesired behavior, it represents in a certain sense a kind of diplomacy, albeit "coercive diplomacy" or "diplomacy of violence."[24] For example, the Israeli strategy of harsh reprisals against Arab states hosting Palestinian raiders has been aimed not so much at physically injuring those countries or destroying their military capabilities as psychologically convincing them of the intolerable costs of continuing to harbor the Palestinians. In the Israeli case, the coercive use of force has not been notably successful in preventing further raids, although it might have played a role in King Hussein's 1970 decision to oust Palestinian commandos from Jordan.[25] It often happens that people in pain can become more angry and determined to retaliate and fight on; for example, Palestinian acts of violence increased markedly after Jordan's expulsion of the Palestine Liberation Organization (PLO).

In addition to using force to *influence* an adversary, countries can also use force to *seize* what they want from an adversary. For example, when Israel sent fighter planes to destroy Iraq's nuclear reactor in 1981, Israel was not seeking to influence Iraqi decisions about nuclear weapons production but rather to eliminate altogether Iraq's nuclear weapons capability for the near future. Similarly, Israel's 1976 raid against Arab hijackers holding Israeli passengers captive at an airport in Entebbe, Uganda, while partly designed for political purposes to demonstrate Israel's unwillingness to submit to terrorist demands, was primarily a military operation intended not to influence but to obtain forcibly the release of the hostages.

The Israelis have pointed out that their spectacular Entebbe success depended on suitable circumstances, including the fact that Israel had built the Entebbe airport years earlier for the Ugandans and hence was familiar with its layout. In contrast to this operation, Israel's 1982 Lebanese invasion involved far more complicated political and territorial goals. Israel attempted to destroy and expel the entire PLO from Lebanon, and bolster a friendly Christian Lebanese president, achieving only partial and short-lived success at relatively high cost. In using force to achieve goals, it is important not to confuse destroying an opponent with influencing an opponent; depending on what one is trying to accomplish, the latter can be the more effective strategy.

It has been argued by some that along with demonstrative threats to use force (such as troop mobilizations), "acts of minor violence" (such as the dogfight incident between U.S. and Libyan jet fighters over the Mediterranean in 1981) have to some extent become *surrogates for war* in the nuclear age.[26] If the fear of escalation into nuclear holocaust has made many countries—particularly the United States and the Soviet Union—shy away from the large-scale armed combat associated with war, it has not inhibited the use of force short of war. Strategists today speak of the "controlled" use of military force in **limited** (or "low intensity") **conflict** situations. The question remains, however, whether such conflicts can remain under control and be kept from exploding into larger conflagrations.

CIVIL WAR

One cannot meaningfully discuss violence in contemporary world politics without discussing **civil wars.** Civil (internal) wars are clearly not a new or recent phenomenon; as long as there have been nation-states, there have been conflicts *within* states that have led to civil wars, some of which have produced

"I'm warning you—don't provoke me into a total war!"

"Limited war"

a greater death toll than conflicts *between* states (e.g., the T'ai P'ing rebellion in China between 1850 and 1864, which is estimated to have cost as many as 30 million lives).[27] Although civil wars are not a new phenomenon, they have been an especially visible feature of world affairs since 1945, as decolonialization has produced new states often having highly unstable political systems. Civil wars also have taken place in long established states, in Latin America and elsewhere, where such factors as ethnic conflict and economic dissatisfaction have produced political violence within the population. There is evidence that civil wars have increased around the world since 1945, occurring not only with greater regularity but also with greater severity, although civil violence diminished somewhat during the 1970s, especially as certain African and Asian rebellions ended.[28]

Of special consequence for *international* politics has been the increasing tendency over time for civil wars to become *internationalized* (to involve foreign military forces), especially in the period since 1945. According to one study, the "percent of civil wars internationalized" rose from 18 percent in the 1919–1939 period to 27 percent in the 1946–1965 period to 36 percent in the 1966–1977 period.[29] According to another study, out of sixty-seven "internal anti-regime" wars identified between 1945 and 1970, fifty-two (77 percent) involved some degree of outside military intervention.[30] The list of countries that have experienced civil war in conjunction with external military intervention since 1945 is a lengthy one, and would include Lebanon, Yemen, Kampuchea, Laos, Cyprus, Zaire, Ethiopia, Chad, El Salvador, Afghanistan, Angola, and the Dominican Republic. One trend of the 1980s is that more of these disputes have involved conservative "rightist" insurgents fighting against "leftist" governments (as in Afghanistan), largely the reverse of the civil struggles of the 1960s and 1970s.

"Wars of national liberation" constitute a special category of conflict and are exemplified by the efforts of the Algerians to overthrow French colonial rule in the 1950s and of the blacks in Zimbabwe to eliminate British and white minority rule in the 1970s. In these and other cases, **guerrilla warfare** "hit and run" tactics have been found especially useful by revolutionary groups confronting relatively stronger conventional military forces on familiar terrain and in the midst of supportive civilian populations. In reaction to such successes, **counterinsurgency** warfare tactics have been developed, stressing combat in rugged terrain, intelligence operations to identify and destroy guerrilla sanctuaries, and inducements to civilians to report guerrillas to government authorities. Counterinsurgency measures have proved effective in a number of places, such as Bolivia and Malaysia, where the terrain or population has not been conducive to sustained guerrilla operations.

It has become difficult at times to label a conflict an *interstate* or an *intrastate* struggle, since wars today are often hybrid affairs. The terms chosen often depend on the eyes of the beholder. For example, while the United States branded the Soviet movement of troops into Afghanistan in 1979 as an "invasion" and "act of aggression" by one state against another, the Soviets contended it was merely "external assistance" provided to the Afghan government to put down a rebellion that had been instigated by outside groups; similar charges and countercharges have been traded between the United States and the Soviet Union in cases where U.S. forces have become involved in "internal affairs," such as Vietnam. Scholars generally consider conflicts such as Afghanistan and Vietnam to be *interstate* in nature, even though they might essentially be fought on only *one* state's soil and might stem largely from *internal* strife. Based on an extensive data collection, one writer concludes that the latter type of conflict has become the main class of warfare in world politics, noting that "the predominant type of war in our days is the internal war fought within the boundaries of one country . . . with foreign participation" (as opposed to the more traditional wars fought between countries across national frontiers).[31]

HAS THE WORLD BECOME MORE PEACEFUL OR MORE WARLIKE?

If one puts together all the above trends in the use of armed force in world politics, there is reason to be both somewhat hopeful and also concerned about the future level of violence on this planet. On the one hand, there has been no war of global magnitude for well over a generation and international wars in general have declined somewhat in recent times. As seen in Figure 8.2, international disputes involving either the threat, display, or actual use of force, including wars and force without war, generally are no higher on average now than they were in the nineteenth century, allowing for the greater number of independent states today. The countries that could do the most damage to life on the planet have, in particular, been relatively cautious in the "controlled" use of force.

However, the human propensity for political violence remains very much in evidence. Approximately forty major and minor armed conflicts, civil and/or international, were ongoing in the mid-1980s, involving forty-five of the world's approximately 160 states; these conflicts were relatively evenly distributed among the Middle East, Asia, Africa, and Latin America. The combatants had a combined population of 3.3 billion people, with 19 million soldiers under arms, over 4 million soldiers engaged in combat, and an estimated 1 to 5 million killed.[32] As noted above, today's typical violent conflict involves a combination of civil and international strife. The persistence of such violence keeps open the prospect of wider wars, involving major powers in the future.

Moreover, whether in the name of deterrence or defense, countries are *preparing* for ever more sophisticated and exotic forms of warfare, including thermonuclear, chemical, and biological war, as well as wars in space. This, of course, does not even take into account the other, *nonstate* sources of violence in the international system, such as international terrorism. We will

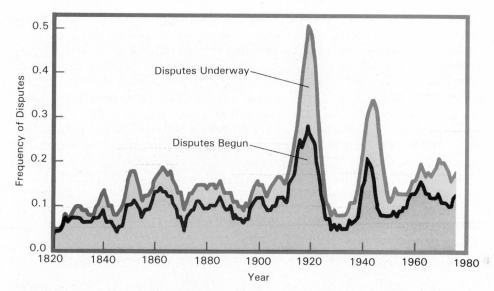

Figure 8.2
FREQUENCY OF MILITARIZED INTERNATIONAL DISPUTES, 1816–1976
These are five-year moving averages of disputes begun and already underway in
any given year in the international system, normalized by the number of independent states in the system. Included are threats to use force, troop alerts, mobilizations, shows of force, blockades, invasions, clashes, and wars.

discuss later in the book what steps the international community is taking
to regulate international violence. But first it is important to understand better
the causes of international violence, and war in particular.

The Causes of War: Theories and Evidence

A POTPOURRI OF THEORIES

The search for causes of war and peace has gone on for centuries and has
included historical, philosophical, and scientific approaches.[33] Among the
more interesting perspectives are those found in anthropological studies of
human warfare over the past two million years. It seems that human history
has been replete with organized violence, although the exact patterns have
varied in different periods and regions. "Primitive" or tribal warfare tended to
be ritualized, with blood revenge, religious duty, individual prestige, and the
capture of possessions—including women and children—impelling the warriors. While relatively few deaths seemed to result, massacres were not
unknown, and the effect of war often was to relieve population pressure on

food and resources.[34] Some of these same motivations and effects also may be present in "modern" warfare. As societies became agriculturally based and settled in fixed locations by the fourth century B.C., large-scale territorial conquest and empire-building became feasible as well; the scale of modern warfare and the preparations for it expanded considerably.

As with the determinants of foreign policy behavior in general, outlined in Chapter 5, it is helpful to focus on *individual, nation-state,* and *international system* levels of analysis in examining theories about the causes of war.[35] When we speak of *individual*-level causes, we are referring to a host of psychological and social-psychological factors related to the use of force. We already have mentioned that aggressive instincts common to all humans have been proposed as a cause of war, but aside from the widespread occurrence of human fighting, there is little empirical evidence to support the instinct theory.[36] Some scholars argue that certain "personality types" (as opposed to human beings in general) are especially prone to violence and that when such

Warfare—a human instinct? "Primitive warfare" rituals among the Yanomamo of South America.

individuals are found in leadership positions in nation-states, the possibilities for their states becoming involved in war increase.[37] Other scholars contend that inherent personality traits of individual leaders are less important than the nature of the decision-making and communication processes that often result in widespread misperceptions of policies and signals.[38] Still others argue that war is often the product of anger, frustration, and other feelings noted earlier, emotions that might have some basis in reality and are not necessarily a matter of misperception or misunderstanding.

Of central concern at the individual level of analysis are the factors in human nature that make the use of force acceptable or desirable. Acts that in other circumstances would be classified as murder become legal when carried out in the name of and at the behest of the state. There are factors at work in the roles individuals play as citizens or government officials that seem to allow this transference from unacceptable to acceptable violence. National leaders act in the name of those they represent, as if they were administering someone's estate as specified in a will. Based on such fiduciary relationships, leaders who feel responsible for the security of their citizens often decide to protect them by force; citizens, in turn, often routinely accept war-making decisions taken from above.

Just as national attributes at the *nation-state* level can affect foreign policy behavior in general, they can influence the resort to violence in particular. For example, a number of scholars have verified that there is a correlation between national strength and hostile tendencies, with countries having sizable military and economic establishments being historically somewhat more inclined to engage in violent conflict than other states, although clearly states of all shapes and sizes have been known to participate in war (especially in recent times).[39] As we noted in Chapter 5, while certain national attributes such as presence or absence of raw materials can affect a state's proclivity toward aggressive behavior, many national characteristics commonly thought to be associated with war-proneness have been found by researchers to be unrelated or only marginally related. Most notably, there is little evidence that type of political system or type of economic system is a key factor associated with war. All types of states—democracies as well as dictatorships, capitalist countries as well as communist countries—seem to have a roughly equal propensity to end up in war at some time, so that "making the world safe for democracy" (or capitalism) would not necessarily produce peace.[40] Likewise, the notion that internal political instability prompts leaders to identify foreign scapegoats and adopt belligerent foreign policies has not been supported by many studies, although such instabilities may tempt foreign leaders to attack or intervene to take advantage of internal problems.[41] Cultural explanations, too (for example, that Germans are militaristic in character), generally have failed to be substantiated by researchers.[42] Some scholars have suggested that war cycles may exist and correspond to "national moods," i.e., there may be initial enthusiasm for war, followed by exhaustion and then disillusionment, followed perhaps in a twenty-year interval by renewed enthusiasm (coinciding with the rise to power of a new generation of leaders untouched by the memory of war).[43] However, most research on such cycles has revealed them to be highly irregular and unpredictable.

At the level of the *international system*, many theorists focus on power relationships as a cause of war, with a favorite explanation being that a balance of power (military parity) between states tends to deter aggression, whereas a breakdown in the military balance tends to invite aggression.[44] However, others argue just the opposite, that war is more likely between equals than unequals, since between unequals "the weaker *dare* not fight and the stronger *need* not."[45] The empirical evidence is inconclusive; as we noted, wars can occur between equals as well as unequals, although the grosser the inequality the less likely it is that war will occur or will be of long duration.[46] It is sometimes suggested that wars result from *changes* in power relationships, and that war is more likely in a period of "power transition," when one state is gaining on another and seeks to be accorded enhanced status. While such changes appear to affect prospects of major power warfare, they are less related to warfare among smaller regional actors.[47]

Some scholars have looked for causes of war in larger aspects of the international system, such as the number and type of alliances, the number of major powers, the number of unresolved disputes, and the flexibility of power centers (degree of polarity) in the system. Some scholars have hypothesized that a multipolar world of flexible alignments tends to be more peaceful than a bipolar world of rigid alliances, while others have argued the contrary.[48] Again, the evidence is mixed and inconclusive, with alliance formation tending to precede the outbreak of war in the twentieth century but not in the nineteenth century.[49] Many systems-level theorists lately have come to explain large-scale wars as struggles for dominance, or "hegemony," in the system, i.e., for control of economic resources, territory, and the power to make rules.[50] Finally, certain action-reaction patterns have tendencies to escalate the level of conflict between states, especially sequences involved in arms races.[51]

The causes of war are difficult to pinpoint because the phenomenon defies single-factor explanation. Some causes might apply to large global wars, and others to more limited, regional wars. Individual, nation-state, and system-level causes also can interact or offset each other, as when individual leaders react to the economic growth or decline of their own or of rival states by seeking dominance in the international system.[52] One way to obtain a better grip on causation is to distinguish long-range or underlying causes of war (*background conditions*) from the more immediate causes (*triggers*).[53] Background causes can be likened to the combustible conditions that make a fire possible, while immediate causes correspond to the spark that sets off the flames. In order to understand the occurrence of any single war, both background and immediate causes must be explored. We focus attention on a few such factors below.

BACKGROUND CONDITIONS

Among the background conditions that tend to set the stage for wars are (1) leaders and citizens who are highly obedient to political authority, (2) military-industrial complexes, and (3) arms races. We have chosen to discuss these partly because they are subject to change and human control and, therefore, offer hope of controlling warfare. Also, these three factors each operate at different levels of analysis: obedience to authority is an individual characteristic; military-industrial complexes are nation-state characteristics; and arms races occur in the international system.

Examining *obedience to authority*, Dr. Stanley Milgram conducted a series of dramatic experiments in the 1960s at Yale University using a sample of American male adults aged twenty to fifty who represented diverse occupations. The experiments showed that the subjects were willing to administer painful and potentially fatal electric shocks to selected victims at the command of individuals posing as authority figures. The victims pretended to receive shocks when unsuspecting subjects were asked by the authority to turn a dial on a control panel to higher voltage levels. Milgram noted that:

> War too moves forward on the triad of an authority which commands a person to destroy the enemy, and perhaps all organized hostility may be viewed as a theme and variation on the three elements of authority, executant, and victim.[54]

Milgram went on to investigate the limits of obedience as he tried to make the victims increasingly human and real to those called upon to administer shocks to them:

> What is the limit of such obedience? At many points we attempted to establish a boundary. Cries from the victim were inserted: not good enough. The victim claimed heart trouble; subjects still shocked him on command. The victim pleaded to be let free, and his answers no longer registered on the signal box; subjects continued to shock him. . . . The final effort . . . was the Touch-Proximity condition. But the very first subject in this condition subdued the victim on command, and proceeded to the highest shock level.[55]

As the subjects became less remote from the victims they were shocking, the average shock they were willing to administer declined; yet 25 percent of the subjects still administered the maximum shock (450 volts), even to victims they had touched. There may be cause for some optimism in the fact that 70 percent of the subjects were willing to defy the authority when they were put in touch contact with the victim, i.e., ordered to force the victim's hand onto the shockplate; yet 30 percent went ahead with shocks even then. Analogously, it has been argued that soldiers find it easier to bomb anonymous victims from the air than to engage people in face-to-face combat.

The Milgram experiments do not indicate that sadism is rampant in New Haven, Connecticut, but rather that modern society seems to have produced authority-obedience relations in which people lose their sense of independent judgment. This loss may or may not transfer to the battlefield; studies of American infantry in World War II have shown that only an average of 15 to 25 percent of soldiers actually fired their weapons at the enemy during the war.[56] Apparently, commanders' orders to fire are not always obeyed. The Vietnam years, in particular, seemed to erode the general willingness of Americans to follow blindly the dictates of their government. Nevertheless, government orders continue to carry considerable authority in all countries, and government interpretations of threats to the nation carry considerable weight. The willingness of a people to go to war and to kill others for their country depends in part on that authority. Obedience to authority, sometimes even unquestioning obedience, would seem to be necessary for wars to begin and continue for long periods, and therefore qualifies as a background condition of war-making.

Citizen obedience to national authorities, especially in long-established states, stems largely from a strong national identity. Such identity is based on socialization processes in each society channeled through educational and cultural institutions. As we have noted, nationalism has been a powerful force in human affairs. It has been called humanity's most fanatical religion and has caused some to define a nation as "the largest group for which one would be willing to die." While identifying as a nation, the group also identifies outsiders as "foreign," in a "we-they" dichotomy. Nationalism was a factor in both world wars—in the First World War as large empires broke up, and in the Second World War as German leaders indulged in hatred and subjugation of foreigners and racial or ethnic minorities, while Soviet, British, and American leaders called on citizens to defend their homelands after suffering attacks.

Although some would contend that **military-industrial complexes** are also a necessary condition for war, the evidence is less conclusive. At the very least, such complexes would seem to be background factors contributing to war-making *potential* and to high armament levels that might not necessarily be warranted by security needs.

When President Eisenhower left office in 1961, the former general commented about the growth of a permanent arms industry and vastly increased peacetime military force in the United States:

> This conjunction of an immense military establishment and a large arms industry is new in the American experience. The total influence—economic, political, even spiritual—is felt in every city, every statehouse, every office of the federal government. We recognize the imperative need for this development. Yet we must not fail to comprehend its grave implications. Our toil, resources, and livelihood are all involved; so is the very structure of our society.

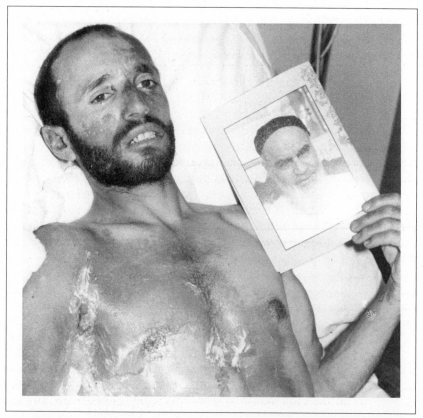

Individual motivation in war—an Iranian soldier, being treated in London for the effects of Iraqi chemical (gas) warfare, displays a photo of the Ayatollah Khomeini, one source of his combat inspiration in 1985.

> In the councils of government, we must guard against the acquisition of unwarranted influence, whether sought or unsought, by the military-industrial complex. The potential for the disastrous rise of misplaced power exists and will persist.[57]

President Eisenhower was primarily troubled by the effects that a powerful alliance between arms manufacturers and defense bureaucrats might have on American democracy. Others have argued that an equally serious concern is the impetus for war-making that such a complex provides when captains of industry and defense collaborate in the pursuit of bigger munitions profits and defense budgets. Leftist thinkers, in the tradition of Marx and Lenin, contend that capitalist societies like the United States naturally come to develop a military-industrial complex geared toward war since supposedly, in addition

THE DEBATE ABOUT THE U.S. MILITARY-INDUSTRIAL COMPLEX

Pros

The military-industrial complex exists and it is dangerous for peace:

1. There is a revolving door through which an elite group rotates between positions in the Department of Defense (DOD) and in corporate board rooms, with generals and admirals retiring to work for munitions companies and corporate executives taking leaves of absence to serve as Pentagon managers. Over 3,000 retired military officers of high rank went on to work for major U.S. defense contracting corporations in the 1980s.

2. The American armed services tailor their weapons orders at least partially to the needs of favored contractors; orders are frequently placed to keep important production lines operating. Close to 70 percent of every federal dollar allotted to research and development goes to military R and D.

3. The main sectors of the U.S. economy have come to depend upon the built-in obsolescence and costly technology typical of military production. Classes of workers and managers now owe their jobs and careers to defense spending. The U.S. Defense Department annually receives the largest single allotment of discretionary funds in the entire federal government budget, and in the 1980s federal defense spending increased markedly. Each day U.S. government military agencies sign 52,000 contracts with manufacturers.

4. The largest industrial firms of the American economy tend to be defense contractors with overseas interests. Over 30,000 U.S. companies are engaged in military production. Such corporations have interests in arms sales to other countries, which can lead to war; local wars might even enhance the markets available to such firms.

5. American states with numerous defense industries and military installations have disproportionate representation on the House and Senate Armed Services Committees in the U.S. Congress. Since these industries and installations are vital to the economies of many local communities, there is a tendency for the local citizenry and their representatives to develop hawkish attitudes on national defense in order to justify and legitimize the continuation of government funding to support these activities. Out of

3,041 U.S. counties, only nine received less than $1000 in Defense Department funds in 1984.

Cons

The military-industrial complex is not a monolith and it does not endanger peace:

1. Most large American corporations derive only a small percentage of their business and profits from defense production. Even major defense contractors tend to have diversified interests. Former military officers can serve important watchdog functions in defense plants to increase efficiency.

2. American military expenditures have not consistently increased over time, especially as a percentage of federal spending and the U.S. gross national product.

3. Other interest group complexes, such as agriculture and medicine, compete with the military complex for government influence.

4. Wars disrupt business operations and can contribute to inflation. During the Vietnam War, the stock market in the United States went up, not down, in response to reports of peace initiatives. It has been U.S. multinational corporations, seeking expanded trade and investment opportunities in the Soviet Union and elsewhere, which have in many cases led the way in attempting to build peaceful East-West bridges.

5. Although individual representatives and senators might be affected by defense interests in their constituencies, their votes on defense issues in Congress have not closely correlated to the number or impact of military facilities in congressional districts.

Source: Most of these and other arguments are presented cogently in Steven Rosen, ed., *Testing the Theory of the Military-Industrial Complex* (Lexington, Mass.: Lexington Books, 1973), especially pp. 23–25. See also Seymour Melman, *Pentagon Capitalism: The Political Economy of War* (New York: McGraw-Hill, 1970); Bruce Russett, *What Price Vigilance?* (New Haven: Yale University Press, 1970); "Militarism in America," *The Defense Monitor*, 15 (Washington, D.C.: Center for Defense Information, 1986); and Bob Adams, "Revolving Door: Contractors Hire Away Watchdogs," *St. Louis Post-Dispatch* (December 17, 1985), pp. 1–7.

to the imperialistic impulses of such societies, it is only through maintaining large armies and arms industries that capitalist systems can continue high levels of employment and prosperity. The point is often made, for example, that it was World War II that brought the United States out of the Great Depression of the 1930s and fueled the post-1945 prosperity.

[handwritten margin note: diversion of resources from more productive/rewarding industries NO!]

However, many scholars have questioned this line of analysis, arguing that even though a military-industrial complex might exist in the United States and dominate decisions about defense spending, it does not necessarily have power over foreign policy in general; moreover, it is questioned whether most elements of the American business community are necessarily hawkish in their foreign policy attitudes and whether they actually tend to benefit from war. The lively debate about the extent and effects of the military-industrial complex in the United States is illustrated in the box on pages 268–269.

It should be added that it is not only the United States and other capitalist societies that would seem susceptible to the development of a military-industrial complex. In various degrees, all modern societies, including the Soviet Union, have well-developed linkages between their industrial and defense establishments. To the extent that there is a connection between such complexes and war, it is generally a case not of individuals directly conspiring to create a hostile international climate but rather of institutionalized societal pressures for arms spending that *indirectly* move a nation toward a war footing. The elevation of military priorities in a society, part of the process of *militarization*, can move that society toward accepting the necessity of war and toward support of increased arms production.

The kind of complexes about which Eisenhower warned therefore have some relation to the excessive obedience problem noted by Milgram. They also relate to **arms races,** which at the system level represent a third important harbinger of war. Arms races are at least partly an action-reaction process between countries and seem to depend on governments' mutual threat perceptions as well as their capacity and desire to pay the costs of armament. Each country increases its armaments in response to the opponent's arms; the race might escalate slowly, become frozen at a point of mutual security, or escalate rapidly. Many scholars have hypothesized that especially when an arms race gets out of control, there is a tendency for it to culminate in war as a result of increasing tension and insecurity.[58]

Not all wars are preceded by arms races. In one study of eighty-four wars ending between 1820 and 1928, only ten were preceded by arms races thought to have been a cause, although several of the other seventy-four were preceded by races of one sort or another.[59] However, several studies have shown the background importance of arms races in creating an atmosphere for war in certain instances. International disputes since 1816 that were accompanied by arms races were much more likely to result in war than those without such races.[60] Lewis Richardson investigated the arms races before World War I and World War II and found evidence of extremely rapid growth in arms competition from 1908 to 1914 between the Allied and Central Powers—an unstable, uncontrolled arms race that culminated in a devastating war between the two opposing alliances. In the World War II case, although Richardson found much arms competition prior to 1939 (such as that between Germany and the Soviet Union), the results for ten nations were not as close to his predictions as the 1914 results.[61]

Another study of thirteen arms races since 1840 concluded that wars resulted in five of the cases.[62] In attempting to explain these findings, Samuel Huntington pointed to (1) the duration of the race, with shorter ones leading to war; and (2) the nature of the race, with competition over numbers of weapons rather than technology evidently more likely to end in war. Of course, causation is difficult to demonstrate in such circumstances, since the contestants could have seen war coming first and then armed themselves; the same factors producing a war could also produce an arms race, so that the latter might merely be a symptom rather than a cause of tension. While military preparation sometimes can lead to war, failure to arm quickly enough, as in the case of the European allies opposing Hitler, also can hasten war's onset. One implication of this is that states supplying weapons to parties in conflict, as in the Middle East, cannot be sure whether supplies will result in stabilizing the region, or instead in opening it to further bloodshed.

Many different background conditions are likely to operate in any given war. Briefly taking World War I as an example, one could identify colonial competition between England and Germany and other states, nationalism, arms races, geographical peculiarities, and the formation of two hostile alliances as important background causes when August 1914 dawned. Germany was surrounded by Russia on the east and France on the west, with Russia and France in a close alliance. Austria, Germany's ally, meanwhile felt threatened by Russian support of Slavic nationalism in Serbia and other parts of the Austro-Hungarian Empire. The delicate house of cards was precariously balanced, waiting for an ill wind to blow it down.

IMMEDIATE CAUSES

In speaking of immediate causes of war, we refer to the triggers, the ill winds, that directly set off the fighting. Often these triggers relate to sudden crises and overburdened diplomacy. For example, the assassination of the Austrian archduke in July 1914 created a crisis situation that set off a chain reaction of troop mobilizations leading to World War I. The sequence of mobilizations is depicted in Table 8.1 Austrian leaders blamed the act on Serbian-trained Slavic nationalists seeking to destroy the Austrian empire; to seize the opportunity and crush such nationalism, Austria issued an ultimatum to Serbia. Germany gave a blank check of support to the Austrian ultimatum, failing to push strongly for diplomatic restraint on the part of its ally. Russia backed Serbia, and the great European powers began to square off. Leaders tended to react to the tense situation by employing existing inflexible military plans. Germany, worried about Russian mobilization and a two-front war, prepared to attack and eliminate France. Russia, limited by a ponderous

Table 8.1
CHAIN REACTION: MOBILIZATION OF ARMIES IN 1914

	Great Britain	France	Russia	Serbia	Monte-negro	Belgium	Austria-Hungary	Germany	Turkey
25 July				180,000			200,000		
26 July									
27 July									
28 July					40,000				
29 July			800,000						
30 July			4,100,000						
31 July						186,000	538,000		
1 August		1,091,000						4,000,000	
2 August									300,000
3 August									
4 August	420,000	50,000							

Source: Ole R. Holsti, *Crisis, Escalation, War* (Montreal: McGill-Queens University Press, 1972), p. 29. Reprinted by permission.

mobilization system, reacted on both the Austrian and German borders. France, worried by German preparations, mobilized and attempted to involve England. The failure to negotiate the disputes sent Europe and the rest of the world headlong over the brink.[63]

Obviously, then, the effectiveness of crisis decision making and diplomacy on the eve of war has much to do with whether or not war actually materializes out of unstable background conditions. As noted in Chapter 6, crises are high-threat situations in which decision makers tend to be under severe stress and are highly susceptible to misperception. Misperception of diplomatic messages and signals, and an exaggerated sense of time pressure, greatly accelerated the slide toward war in 1914. Leaders under stress can react violently to sudden changes in either their domestic environment or their external, international environment. Sudden deterioration of national or international conditions (real or imagined) can therefore trigger war-making decisions.[64] In particular, if a government fears imminent attack by a neighboring state, it is more likely to launch a preemptive attack, as Israel did in 1967, when it struck first after witnessing a major Egyptian troop buildup on its border.

Changes in the environment not only can increase threat perception but also can produce a sense of deprivation and frustration if decision makers are blocked from realizing crucial needs, a factor that has been linked to human aggression in a number of studies.[65] In Chapter 5 we mentioned the "lateral pressures" that operated on Japanese leaders in 1941 when a U.S.-inspired economic embargo had left Japan with only a few months' supply of oil and rubber. When a country with a large and growing population seeks to expand (as Japan had in Southeast Asia during the 1930s) and is confronted by resistance (from the United States, Britain, and the Netherlands East Indies), war can explode.[66]

Crises seem especially likely to result in the use of armed force when a state is faced with sudden loss of control over a region where it is accustomed to exercising influence, witness the dispatch of Soviet troops to Afghanistan in 1979 and of U.S. troops to Lebanon in 1958.[67] Similarly, a people who have had a historical attachment to a certain territory, when suddenly evicted, tend to develop a sense of frustration that can be relieved only through violence. Hence, when Jordan seized the opportunity to occupy part of Jerusalem and the West Bank of the Jordan River during the 1948 Arab-Israeli War, thereby claiming lands that had traditionally been part of Palestine, the Palestinians developed a resentment toward King Hussein's family that remains to this day. The Palestinians' use of violence today is largely based on frustration at the loss of this territory, first to Jordan and later, in 1967, to Israel.

Although frustrations can produce aggressive behavior, they do not invariably do so.[68] The historical evidence is mixed. Countries that at a given moment in time have been growing industrially but remain behind world leaders in standard of living, access to resources, and international influence or status have frequently resorted to war in their push for an increased share of these benefits.[69] Yet such triggers of war often have been defused through diplomacy. We will discuss the causes of *peace* at the end of this chapter.

The Consequences of War

The need to understand the causes of war becomes clearer if one more fully recognizes the *consequences* of war.

HISTORICAL CONSEQUENCES OF WAR

Wars can have profound effects on the international power structure, but not necessarily the effects envisioned by the initiators. In fact it appears that initiators generally expect great and quick success in warfare, yet are often disillusioned.[70] In World War II, Germany and Japan entered the war as major world powers and came out as also-rans, with the emergence of the United States and the Soviet Union as superpowers after 1945. Yet there are those who argue that the effects of war on national power and influence are overrated. Since Germany and Japan have gradually regained international influence and have emerged as the third and fourth leading industrial producers in the world, it is argued that power, like water, finds its own level; if a country has the population and technological skills and resources, it will eventually bounce back from war approximately to the point where it was heading before the war.[71] Still, it would seem that Germany and Japan have not fully recovered the status they enjoyed in 1939, especially in military as opposed to economic terms. It is well to remember, too, that four massive empires crumbled in World War I, and two more in World War II (not to mention two victorious empires crumbling shortly thereafter).

Regardless of whether one wins or loses, war can involve enormous human, political, and economic costs for the participants. As weapons have become more powerful, making it more difficult to discriminate between military and civilian targets, we have seen that war has produced increased carnage in the twentieth century. For example, counting military and civilian casualties, approximately 60 million people died in World War II; altogether, the death toll represented 3 percent of the world's population at that time. Most European countries from Germany eastward lost approximately 10 percent of their populations.[72]

Political leaders are often among the casualties of war, since states participating in wars frequently experience changes in government after the conflict has ended. Ninety-one percent of the losers in World War I and World War II had nonconstitutional changes of government within three years after the war, while 20 percent of the winners underwent such changes. Aggregate data for wars between 1815 and 1965 reveal that 36 percent of the losers and 18 percent of the winners experienced such changes.[73] This means that war is a high-risk proposition for governments; there is nearly a 40 percent probability that they will not be around long if they lose, and a 20 percent risk even if they win. Monumental revolutions throughout history, including those in America and France in the eighteenth century and Russia and China in the twentieth century, developed during or after international wars. War can so weaken governments and embitter populations that old regimes are thrown out. Even Winston Churchill and Charles de Gaulle were quickly voted out of office after World War II, although both made subsequent comebacks.

Other domestic consequences of war—the ones often associated with the ouster of wartime governments—can include changed social values and the disruption of entire economies. The First World War generally is regarded as the origin of the "lost generation" and the "roaring twenties" in which Victorian mores finally were thrown off in a "live for now" era.[74] Although World War II coincided with the end of the Great Depression, it does not appear that war generally is good for economies, at least as judged by the American experience. Although war has often served as a short-term stimulant in reducing unemployment, it has also tended to be accompanied by high inflation in the cost of goods (indicated in Figure 8.3) as well as higher taxes.[75] As President Johnson found during the Vietnam War, it is difficult to wage a "war on poverty" at home at the same time that one is expending billions of dollars to fight a war abroad. For economically less developed countries, with far fewer resources to spread around, such a generalization seems to be especially relevant.

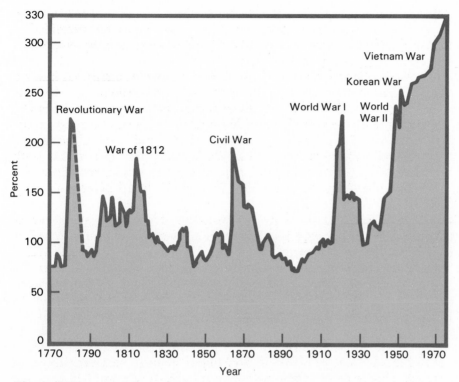

Figure 8.3
WAR AND THE RISE AND FALL OF U.S. WHOLESALE PRICES, 1770–1972

POTENTIAL CONSEQUENCES OF WAR TODAY

As costly as war has been in the past, it has clearly reached new, unprecedented levels of potential destructiveness today. Not only have the new weapons of the twentieth century greatly increased the damage potential of war, they have also shortened the time span needed to reach that potential. In the past, leaders at least had time to reevaluate their decisions to use force, even if they did not always take advantage of the opportunity. Now there are likely to be no second chances to disengage from poor decisions. President Kennedy seemed acutely aware of these dangers when he sought to control escalation during the Cuban missile crisis and referred to the mistakes of World War I and World War II in doing so. A sign outside the U.S. State Department room where ExCom made its decisions during the crisis reminded the participants that "in the nuclear age, superpowers make war like porcupines make love—carefully."[76]

It is tempting to attribute the fact that major powers have not fought each other directly since 1945 to the fear of the horrid destruction of nuclear war.

Survivors of the atomic bomb at Hiroshima, 1945.

If this is so, these weapons have made an important, if ironic, contribution to world peace. Yet the suspicion persists that many military and civilian leaders see nuclear weapons as irrelevant to war-making and assume that conventional wars involving nuclear powers can be fought with little regard to nuclear escalation. We cannot know for sure whether such conventional war could be contained below nuclear thresholds. There is ample reason, however, to think not, especially if one side clearly began to lose.[77]

The question then becomes whether a nuclear war itself, once initiated, could be kept limited. Recent discussions of nuclear doctrine in the United States and the Soviet Union suggest increased thinking among elite circles that "limited nuclear war" is a viable concept, that nuclear weapons could be used in relatively small doses, and that such a war is "fightable" and "winnable." Such discussions assume the possibility of either using tactical or short-range nuclear weapons of the type now deployed in Western Europe, or engaging in larger nuclear strikes with intercontinental or medium-range ballistic missiles aimed at military targets rather than major population centers. However, critics argue that this thinking ignores the fact that current "small-scale" tactical nuclear weapons have several times the explosive power of the 20 kiloton bombs (each equivalent to approximately 20,000 tons of

TNT) that leveled the Japanese cities of Hiroshima and Nagasaki in 1945. It also tends to understate the loss of life and property that would likely occur in the event of even a single hit by an ICBM equipped with a one megaton warhead (having seventy times the destructive power of the Hiroshima bomb). Even if it were targeted only at missile silos in, say, Missouri and the Dakotas, the nearby cities of St. Louis, Kansas City, and Omaha likely would suffer crippling damage, while—depending on the wind—the entire continental United States might become blanketed with deadly radiation. The debris from several such blasts also could blot out sunlight for long periods, bringing on "nuclear winter." The full destructive power of nuclear weapons is evidenced in Figure 8.4. As has been commonly said, "The survivors might envy the dead."

The Causes of Peace: Approaches to World Order

Wartime experiences can affect the probability of another war occurring. A war can foment a desire for revenge or breed a distaste for further hostilities. At least in the immediate aftermath of most major wars, leaders and the citizens they represent seem especially disillusioned and gun-shy. Occasionally this can be a problem (for example, when a state fails to resist a new aggressor), but restraint and war-weariness can also cause serious consideration of peaceful diplomatic options. Although the concept of appeasement was seemingly forever besmirched by British Prime Minister Neville Chamberlain's accession to Hitler's demands at Munich on the eve of World War II, there was a poignancy and a certain logic to Chamberlain's recollections of World War I that might apply to other situations and other times:

> When I think of four terrible years and I think of the 7,000,000 young men who were cut off in their prime, the 13,000,000 who were maimed and mutilated, the misery and the suffering of the mothers and fathers, the sons and daughters, and the relatives and friends of those who were killed and wounded, then I am bound to say again what I have said before, and what I say now not only to you but to all the world—in war, whichever side may call itself victor, there are no winners, but all are losers. It is these thoughts which have made me feel that it was my prime duty to strain every nerve to avoid repetition of the Great War in Europe.[78]

Given the causes of war that we have discussed in this chapter, the following question remains: What can be done to address such causes and to increase the prospects of avoiding war? Just as a plethora of contending theories have been advanced regarding the causes of war, so also has there been a long-

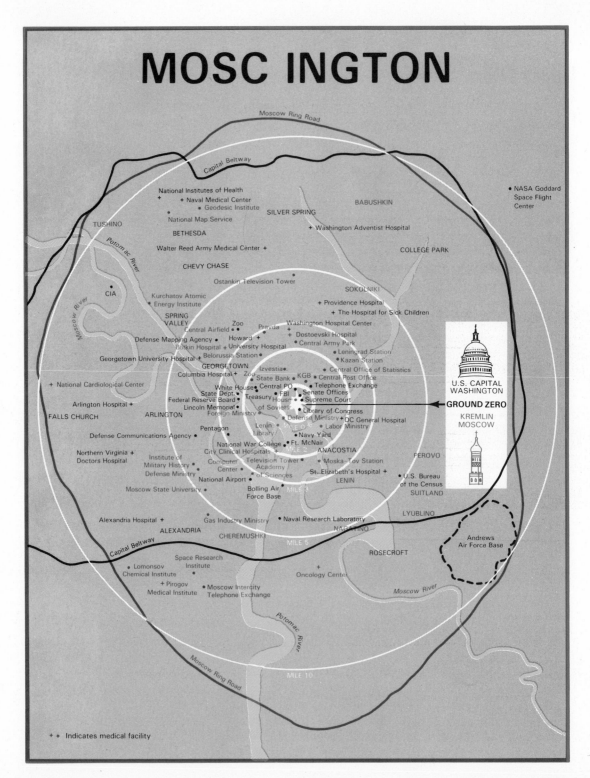

MOSC INGTON

Moscow Ring Road

Capital Beltway

National Institutes of Health
+ Naval Medical Center
• Geodesic Institute

BABUSHKIN

• NASA Goddard
Space Flight
Center

TUSHINO

SILVER SPRING

National Map Service

BETHESDA

+ Washington Adventist Hospital

Walter Reed Army Medical Center +

COLLEGE PARK

CHEVY CHASE

Ostankin Television Tower

SOKOLNIKI

CIA

Kurchatov Atomic
• Energy Institute

• Providence Hospital

• The Hospital for Sick Children

SPRING
VALLEY

Zoo

Pravda

Washington Hospital Center

Central Airfield •
Defense Mapping Agency •
Howard +

• Dostoevski Hospital
• Central Army Park

Botkin Hospital + University Hospital
Georgetown University Hospital + Belorussia Station •

• Leningrad Station
• Kazan Station

GEORGETOWN

Izvestia •

• Central Office of Statistics

Columbia Hospital + Zoo
State Bank •

KGB

• Central Post Office

+ National Cardiological Center

White House •
State Dept. •
Federal Reserve Board •

Central PO •
FBI
Treasury

• Telephone Exchange
Senate Offices

Arlington Hospital +

Lincoln Memorial •

House •

• Supreme Court

FALLS CHURCH

ARLINGTON

Foreign Ministry
of Soviets
Defense Ministry •

• Library of Congress

• DC General Hospital

Defense Communications Agency •

Pentagon

Lenin •
Library

• Labor Ministry

• Navy Yard

ANACOSTIA

National War College •
City Clinical Hospitals +

• Ft. McNair

PEROVO

Northern Virginia +
Doctors Hospital

Institute of
Military History
Defense Ministry

Computer
Center

Television Tower
Academy
of Sciences

• St. Elizabeth's Hospital +

LENIN

National Airport •

Moscow State University •

Bolling Air
Force Base

MILE 3

• U.S. Bureau
of the Census

SUITLAND

LYUBLINO

Alexandria Hospital +

Gas Industry Ministry

• Naval Research Laboratory

NAGATINO

ROSECROFT

ALEXANDRIA

CHEREMUSHKI

MILE 5

Andrews
Air Force Base

Capital Beltway

Space Research
Institute

• Lomonsov
Chemical Institute

+ Pirogov
Medical Institute

• Moscow Intercity
Telephone Exchange

+
Oncology Center

Moscow River

Potomac River

Moscow Ring Road

MILE 10

Potomac River

Moscow River

| U.S. CAPITAL WASHINGTON |
| GROUND ZERO |
| KREMLIN MOSCOW |

+ + Indicates medical facility

278

Effects of a One–Megaton Nuclear Bomb on Each Capital City

Circles of Death*			MOSCOW	WASHINGTON
Circle 1	Epicenter	At ground zero, the surface–burst nuclear weapon (70 times the power of the Hiroshima bomb) creates a crater 300 feet deep and 1,200 feet in diameter. All life and structures are pulverized.	Kremlin	US Capitol
Circle 2	0–.6 mile	People, vehicles, buildings, and thousands of tons of earth are swept into a luminous fireball, with temperatures hotter than the sun. The fireball, rising to a height of more than 6 miles and 1 mile wide, incinerates all life below in less than 10 seconds.	Council of Ministers, Central Committee, House of Soviets, Defense Ministry, Gosplan, Lenin Library, Central Archives.	Senate offices, House of Representatives offices, Supreme Court, Library of Congress, Central Post Office, Union Station, VOA.
Circle 3	.6–2 miles	The flash and heat from the explosion sweep outward from the epicenter at the speed of light. A shock wave of compressed air creates overpressures of 100 pounds per square inch at .6 mile to 9 psi at 2 miles. Structures as well as people are crushed. Lethal radiation covers the area. Virtually everyone dies immediately.	KGB, Supreme Court, Foreign Ministry, State Bank, Central Office of Statistics, Izvestia, Telephone Exchange, Academy of Medicine, Zoo, Moscow Tramways Power Station, Labor Ministry, Health Ministry.	White House, FBI, Executive Offices, National War College, Ft. McNair, Navy Yard, National Archives, Treasury, Federal Reserve Board, Central Telephone Exchange, D.C. General Hospital, Civil Defense.
Circle 4	2–3 miles	Trees, clothes, combustible materials ignite spontaneously. Winds exceed hundreds of miles an hour. Overpressures blow out walls of even the largest buildings. 50 percent of the people die immediately; the rest die more slowly from radioactive poisoning, burns, broken bodies, deeply imbedded fragments of glass.	Central Post Office, Central Army Park, Trotski Barracks, Pravda, Television Tower, Leningrad Station, Belorussia Station Planetarium, Ministry of Commerce, City Clinical Hospital #1, Dostoevski Hospital.	Pentagon, State Department, Bolling Air Force Base, D.C. Armory, National Academy of Science, Washington Monument, Lincoln Memorial, Columbia Hospital, Howard University Hospital, Anacostia.
Circle 5	3–5 miles	Frame buildings are blown out or levelled. Fuel storage tanks explode. Intense heat causes third–degree burns to all exposed skin. A firestorm is highly probable; if it occurs, it sucks oxygen out of underground stations, asphyxiating the occupants. Shelters become ovens. 50 percent of the people die immediately; if there is a firestorm, no one survives the day.	Defense Ministry, Central Airfield, Institute of Military History, Ostankino Television Tower, Computer Center, Academy of Sciences, Moscow State University, Botkin Hospital, Lenin Suburb.	National Airport, Naval Research Laboratory, Defense Communications Agency, Zoo, St. Elizabeth's Hospital, Washington Hospital Center, Providence Hospital, The Hospital for Sick Children, Georgetown, Arlington.
Circle 6	5–10 miles	The shock wave, traveling 1 mile in 5 seconds, reaches the Capital Beltway and Moscow Ring Road 40 seconds after the blast. People in exposed locations suffer second–degree burns. The scorched area covers 200 square miles. Radioactive fallout creates an immediately lethal zone of 400 square miles, causing death through massive damage to the central nervous system and the bone marrow.	Moscow Intercity Telephone Exchange, Space Research Institute, Pirogov Medical Institute, Kurchatov Atomic Energy Institute, Oncology Center National Cardiological Center, Geodesic Institute, National Map Service, Gas Industry Ministry, Moscow Ring Road.	CIA, Andrews Air Force Base, Defense Mapping Agency, Defense Nuclear Agency, NASA Goddard Space Flight Center, Walter Reed Army Medical Center, National Institutes of Health, Naval Medical Center, Bethesda, College Park, Falls Church, Capital Beltway.

Moving downward in a huge plume, fallout also contaminates 20,000 square miles, bringing radon sickness, as well as delayed radiation injuries to the living and to future generations.

*a term born out of the ashes of Hiroshima

Figure 8.4
THE IMPACT OF A ONE-MEGATON NUCLEAR BOMB ON MOSCOW AND WASHINGTON

standing debate over the "causes of peace." In the discussion below, we identify some of the main *approaches to world order* proposed by scholars and policymakers.

BALANCE OF POWER, CONCERT OF POWERS, AND HEGEMONY

We have noted that from the very beginnings of the nation-state system, emerging out of the Peace of Westphalia in the seventeenth century, statesmen have viewed the *balance of power* at the system level as at least a crude mechanism for maintaining order and stability in a world lacking central regulation of the use of force. That is, there has been a widely held assumption that as long as states individually or in alliance with other states do not allow adversaries to gain military superiority, peace will be maintained.

We also have noted, however, that the balance of power often has failed to deter aggression and that states equal in power or even weaker than their adversaries have initiated war at times. Because of the failure of "balance of power politics" to prevent war in the Napoleonic era, the major European powers tried to adopt a somewhat different approach to world order at the **Congress of Vienna** in 1815, following the Napoleonic Wars. They established the **Concert of Europe,** a system of "great power" consultation whereby the great powers would take responsibility together for keeping the peace by convening multilateral conferences to resolve problems any time a dispute threatened to erupt into war.[79] The Concert met over thirty times in the nineteenth century, although with decreasing effectiveness as the consensus against French revolutionary ideas deteriorated. The Concert finally collapsed with the formation of rival alliances on the eve of World War I. The concert of powers approach to world order was to be revived in modified form later by the founders of the League of Nations and the United Nations, both of which were premised in part upon the willingness of the major powers to recognize their mutual interests in resolving their disputes nonviolently and in enforcing the peace against any would-be aggressors.

While many observers have credited the Concert of Europe with making the nineteenth century a relatively peaceful era in world politics (at least in terms of the absence of system-wide war despite numerous lesser wars), others have argued that it was not the great powers in concert who were responsible for enforcing the peace but rather *one* power (the "first among equals")—Great Britain—which through its military and economic dominance was able to maintain whatever international order there was (the so-called "Pax Britannica"). According to the **theory of hegemonic stability,** throughout history large-scale wars involving major powers have tended to produce among the victors one dominant power (a *hegemon,* or leader) capable of maintaining a degree of order over the international system as a whole; just as some point to the Pax Britannica following the Napoleonic wars, it has been suggested that World War II was followed by a period of American leadership over the international political and economic order known as the "Pax Americana," which some have argued ended with the U.S. defeat in Vietnam.[80] The theory posits that a hegemon is able to maintain stability through a combination of coercion (i.e., threatening to use armed force against any state violating the norms or rules of the system established by the hegemon) and positive inducements (i.e., conferring economic and other benefits on states which cooperate in preserving order). Hegemony as a source of order, however, tends to break down eventually as the hegemonic power inevitably declines due to the draining costs of maintaining large armed forces and extensive economic

see
P. Kennedy

commitments; other powers arise to challenge the hegemon, leading ultimately to a new cycle of warfare and postwar reconstruction of world order.

Although this theory may offer useful insights into historical patterns of war and peace and how important changes occur in international relations, it would seem of questionable relevance to the problem of world order in the nuclear age. After all, assuming that any large-scale global war in the future would necessarily involve nuclear weapons, it is highly unlikely that any "victor" would emerge from such a conflict with enough resources intact to play a hegemonic role. Put another way, it is somewhat ludicrous to suggest that such a cataclysmic event could be a source of future world order.[81] If world order is to be maintained in the contemporary age, it may well depend not so much on one state holding a preponderance of power, or on a balance of power or concert of powers, but rather on more positive efforts at international cooperation such as those mentioned below.

ARMS CONTROL AND DISARMAMENT

We have noted that arms races can often lead to war, with adversaries at times driven to match or exceed each other in armaments in order to protect their respective national security, thereby creating spiraling tensions and insecurity (the so-called "security dilemma"). *Arms control* is seen as one way to break the action-reaction sequences that characterize arms races and that lead to conflict escalation. Arms control is commonly thought of as meaning a mutual reduction in armaments, but it can also include agreements freezing armaments at present levels or allowing increases up to a certain ceiling, as well as placing certain limits on weapons testing and deployment. We will discuss various arms control efforts at some length in Chapter 11.

The logic of arms control as an approach to world order is that it can reduce the danger of war not only by removing some of the instruments of war, but more importantly, by opening up lines of communication, developing confidence-building attitudes, and reducing mutual insecurity through the very process of forging and verifying arms agreements. One example often cited in support of this logic is the Rush-Bagot Agreement of 1817, the oldest and perhaps the most successful arms control pact in history, by which the United States and Britain agreed to demilitarize the American-Canadian border and the Great Lakes, thereby paving the way for long-term peaceful relations among these countries.

Curbs on arms races also require controlling or retooling those parts of the military-industrial complexes that generate new arms in various countries. Conversion from weapons to commercial production would be initially costly in most cases, but studies have shown long-run benefits, including employment benefits, outweighing the costs.[82] The example of the Japanese, who have experienced enormous postwar economic prosperity with minimal funds allocated to defense, might cause one to question whether heavy military spending is economically necessary, or for that matter, even conducive to national prosperity.

One must remember, of course, that weapons are more symptoms than causes of international conflict. For the most part, in Hans Morgenthau's words: "Men do not fight because they have arms. They have arms because they deem it necessary to fight."[83] As in the Great Lakes example of U.S.-British arms control, it is necessary to settle the *political* disputes underlying arms races and to promote accurate rather than exaggerated threat perceptions. If somehow the security dilemma that states regularly experience were to be resolved, it might be possible to go beyond arms control to *disarmament*, i.e., the complete elimination of weapons from national arsenals. However, disarmament remains a distant prospect given the nature of the nation-state system.[84]

INTERNATIONAL ORGANIZATION, PEACEFUL SETTLEMENT, AND COLLECTIVE SECURITY

Some have argued that the only way to overcome the security dilemma and to lessen the need for individual national armies in a system of sovereign states is to develop *international organization* machinery that includes both an elaborate set of *peaceful settlement* procedures as well as *collective security* mechanisms. The emphasis is thereby put on states' *common* interests, especially in finding ways out of "chicken" confrontations or "prisoners' dilemmas" (see Chapter 7). Peaceful settlement refers to the formal techniques used to resolve conflicts short of armed force, including diplomatic procedures such as impartial third-party mediation and conciliation (of the type used in labor-management disputes) as well as legal procedures such as arbitration and adjudication. Adjudication, whereby the parties to a dispute agree to submit it to an international tribunal and to accept that body's decision based on international law as binding, is clearly among the most ambitious forms of peaceful settlement. Collective security refers to the agreement by states to use force collectively, through a single international organization, to discipline an aggressor if peaceful settlement procedures fail and certain parties resort to violence. Even proponents of disarmament recognize that there must still be some armed force available in the hands of a central "policeman" in order to deter states from committing aggression and to punish them when they do.

Inis Claude has said that the growth of international organization, particularly in the twentieth century, is "fundamentally, even though not exclusively, a reaction to the problem of war."[85] The League of Nations created after World War I and the United Nations established after World War II both represent attempts to go beyond the balance of power and other power politics approaches to world order and to conduct international affairs on a higher, more civilized plane. Founders of the League and UN, while relying to some extent on the "concert of great powers" notion, sought to introduce a new level of institutionalization into world politics and to make the concepts of peaceful settlement and collective security the institutional cornerstones. We will discuss the extent to which these approaches to world order have had any success in Chapters 9 and 10.

International organizations such as the UN, along with others that exist at the regional level, hold some promise as vehicles for dealing with such causes of war as frustration or lateral pressures—not only because they provide ready machinery for engaging states in peaceful bargaining processes that can resolve specific grievances and defuse crisis situations, but also because they provide multilateral forums for addressing a much broader range of economic and social concerns that often underlie the resort to violence. It is impossible to eliminate all national frustrations and expansive pressures; countries experiencing these cannot and should not be granted everything they want. Nonetheless, through creative bilateral or multilateral diplomacy, it might be possible to discover "prominent solutions" to problems that can satisfy conflicting parties and obviate the resort to armed force.[86]

If war cannot be avoided and violence erupts, the problem shifts from war prevention to war termination. Many of the same techniques and mechanisms available to forestall a war can also be used to terminate one without further bloodshed. If Clausewitz's dictum about war and politics is recalled, and if the awful consequences of war are recognized, it seems imperative that leaders subordinate military goals to political goals, and that no more force be employed than is absolutely necessary. As in all bargaining, agreement on ending wars is possible if the parties achieve at least some of their major aims, if they change or deemphasize certain aims, or if they conclude that achievement of their aims would be too costly.[87] Constructive approaches to war termination can include such possibilities as demilitarized zones, neutralization of disputed territory, and population exchanges.

In time, perhaps national leaders and publics will come to change their perceptions of other states as enemies and of war as a legitimate means of pursuing goals through organized killing. Increasing the accuracy and breadth of news coverage available to citizens throughout the world—a feat technically if not politically feasible in the age of the satellite dish—and making foreigners seem more human might also help restrain unconditional obedience to authority and, thereby, warfare.

Conclusion

War is a type of conflictual social relationship. Earlier in the book, we noted that such conflicts often resemble a social system in which the parties take turns in mimicking each other's behavior—reacting in kind to each other's arms buildups, for example—and engage in strange dances of violence that can last for years. In this sense, war is more than a conscious political decision; it can also be based on unthinking emotional responses. Yet cycles of war and recurrent violence frequently have been broken, and long and stable periods of peace have developed among adversaries. Researchers even speak of **security communities,** groups of states among which war is no longer a serious option for pursuing goals or resolving differences.[88] The United States and Great Britain as well as the United States and Canada, for example, despite considerable tension on a variety of issues, can be labeled security communities today.

The transition from a warlike social system, such as that existing between the United States and both Great Britain and Canada in the early nineteenth century, to a system of "stable peace" is a key mystery for human survival. Social scientists have argued that the successful transition has basically to do with reducing stresses and strains on international relationships, and building trust.[89] If habits of cooperation in solving such gnawing concerns as economic problems can be learned by states, it is conceivable that a much wider, perhaps even global security community could develop among them. The search for community evidenced by the creation of the United Nations and other international organizations would seem to offer some hope in this regard. Indeed, the ultimate solution to the problem of war and related human woes may lie in the further development and strengthening of such institutions, a subject to which we now turn in Part III.

SUMMARY

1. When diplomacy in international relations breaks down, governments frequently resort to the use of armed force. War is sometimes viewed as simply another form of diplomacy—a deliberate, conscious policy designed to achieve political goals. At other times war is seen as the result of unplanned responses to the environment based either on a human instinct for violence or on complex emotions of fear, frustration, and anger. No single perspective provides a complete understanding of war, however; wars occur in multiple forms and have multiple causes.

2. Violence in world politics can be divided into three categories based on the type and the extent of the fighting: international war, force without war, and civil war.

3. International war—sustained military hostilities between at least two states—has become less frequent but more deadly over time. Since 1945, there has been no war between the major powers; most wars now involve Third World states.

4. There have been many cases of force without war. To some extent, the controlled use of military force has become a surrogate for war in the nuclear age.

5. Civil wars have become more frequent and severe since 1945, as well as more internationalized. Wars of national liberation, characterized by guerrilla warfare

and counterinsurgency tactics, constitute a special class of conflict. The persistent occurrence of force without war and of civil war raises the prospect of wider wars developing in the future.

6. The causes of war can be found at the individual, nation-state, and international system levels.

7. It is necessary to distinguish between the background conditions leading to war and the more immediate causes. Among the former are leaders and citizens who are highly obedient to political authority, military-industrial complexes, and arms races.

8. The immediate causes of war, or triggers, often relate to sudden crises and overburdened diplomacy. Crises—high-threat situations in which decision makers tend to be under severe stress and are highly susceptible to misperception—seem especially to result in armed force when a state is faced with sudden loss of control over a region where it is accustomed to exercising influence.

9. War involves enormous human, political, and economic costs for both winners and losers. Today it has reached new, unprecedented levels of potential destructiveness. It is questionable whether conventional war between states armed with nuclear weapons could be contained below nuclear thresholds, and whether nuclear war itself, once initiated, could be kept limited.

10. A number of approaches to reducing war have been proposed. In addition to theories of balance of power, concert of powers, and hegemonic stability (which all emphasize traditional power politics), theories have been developed around the concepts of arms control and disarmament, peaceful settlement, and collective security (which emphasize states' collective interests).

SUGGESTIONS FOR FURTHER READING AND STUDY

A good general work on both the "causes of war" and the "causes of peace" is Seyom Brown's *The Causes and Prevention of War* (New York: St. Martin's Press, 1987). We have shown that war can be analyzed from a variety of perspectives. These can be explored in the following selections, in addition to those cited in the notes to this chapter.

Scientific approaches: Quincy Wright, *A Study of War*, 2 vols., rev. ed. (Chicago: University of Chicago Press, 1965); Dean G. Pruitt and Richard C. Snyder, eds., *Theory and Research on the Causes of War* (Englewood Cliffs, N.J.: Prentice-Hall, 1969); J. David Singer *et al.*, *Explaining War: Selected Papers from the Correlates of War Project* (Beverly Hills: Sage, 1979); Freeman Dyson, *Weapons and Hope* (New York: Harper & Row, 1984); Jack Levy, *War in the Modern Great Power System 1945–1975* (Lexington, Ky.: University of Kentucky Press, 1983).

Political approaches: Robert J. Art and Kenneth N. Waltz, eds., *The Use of Force* (Boston: Little, Brown, 1971); Robert E. Osgood and Robert W. Tucker, *Force, Order, and Justice* (Baltimore: Johns Hopkins University Press, 1967); Richard Smoke, *War: Controlling Escalation* (Cambridge, Mass.: Harvard University Press, 1977); Karel Kara,

"On the Marxist Theory of War and Peace," *Journal of Peace Research*, 6 (1968), pp. 1–27.

Economic approaches: Seymour Melman, *The Permanent War Economy* (New York: Simon and Schuster, 1974); Rodger Owen and Robert Sutcliffe, *Studies in the Theory of Imperialism* (London: Longman, 1972); Richard J. Barnet, *Roots of War* (Baltimore: Penguin, 1972).

Other social science approaches: Leon Bramson and George W. Goethals, eds., *War: Contributions from Psychology, Sociology, and Anthropology* (New York: Basic Books, 1968); Richard A. Falk and Samuel S. Kim, eds., *The War System: An Interdisciplinary Approach* (Boulder, Colo.: Westview, 1980); Dale Givens and Martin A. Nettleship, eds., *Discussions on War and Human Aggression* (The Hague: Mouton, 1976); and a special symposium on "Human Evolution and War," in *International Studies Quarterly*, 31 (March 1987).

Historical approaches: Theodore Ropp, *War in the Modern World* (New York: Collier, 1962); Alfred Vagts, *A History of Militarism* (New York: Free Press, 1967); Michael Howard, *War in European History* (Oxford: Oxford University Press, 1976). See also diplomatic histories of particular wars, such as Barbara Tuchman's *The Guns of August.*

Literary approaches (novels): Stephen Crane, *The Red Badge of Courage*; Ernest Hemingway, *A Farewell to Arms*; Arnold Zweig, *Education at Verdun*; Erich Maria Remarque, *All Quiet on the Western Front*; Norman Mailer, *The Naked and the Dead*; James Jones, *From Here to Eternity*; Kurt Vonnegut, *Slaughterhouse Five*; Günter Grass, *Cat and Mouse*; Joseph Heller, *Catch-22*; Leo Tolstoy, *War and Peace*; Margaret Mitchell, *Gone with the Wind.*

Literary approaches (poetry): E. and E. Humberman, eds., *War: An Anthology*; Victor Selwyn, ed., *Poems of the Second World War*; Alfred Tennyson, "Charge of the Light Brigade"; Rudyard Kipling, *Barrack Room Ballads.*

Philosophical approaches: Glenn Gray, *The Warriors: Reflecting on Men in Battle* (New York: Harper & Row, 1973); John U. Nef, *War and Human Progress* (New York: W.W. Norton, 1963); Douglas P. Lackey, *Moral Principles and Nuclear War* (London: Rowman and Allenheld, 1984); Robert L. Phillips, *War and Justice* (Norman: University of Oklahoma Press, 1984).

Peace research approaches: Robert Pickus and Robert Woito, *To End War*, rev. ed. (New York: Harper & Row, 1970); Israel W. Charney, ed., *Strategies Against Violence: Design for Non-Violent Change* (Boulder, Colo.: Westview, 1978); Morton Deutsch, *The Resolution of Conflict: Constructive and Destructive Processes* (New Haven: Yale University Press, 1973); Richard A. Falk, Samuel S. Kim, and Saul H. Mendlovitz, eds., *Studies on a Just World Order* (Boulder, Colo.: Westview, 1982); Grant Burns, *The Atomic Papers: A Citizen's Guide to Selected Books and Articles on the Bomb, the Arms Race, Nuclear Power, the Peace Movement and Related Issues* (Metuchen, N.J.: Scarecrow, 1984); and *Peace Research Abstracts* (published by the Canadian Peace Research Institute).

PART
III

International Institutions

In relations between nations, the progress of civilization may be seen as movement from force to diplomacy, from diplomacy to law.
LEWIS HENKIN, *How Nations Behave*

No one can observe the international political system without being aware of the fact that order does exist and that this order is related in important ways to . . . a body of law and to a process of law-government.
MORTON A. KAPLAN AND NICHOLAS DEB. KATZENBACH, *The Strategy of World Order: International Law*

We should recognize the United Nations for what it is—an admittedly imperfect but indispensable instrument of nations in working for a peaceful evolution towards a more just and secure world order. The dynamic forces at work in this stage of human history have made world organization necessary.
DAG HAMMARSKJOLD, UN SECRETARY-GENERAL, IN HIS *Annual Report,* August 22, 1957

287

Amidst the din of conflict that surrounds international relations, there does exist some degree of order. In fact, many kinds of transactions across national boundaries, such as mail and travel flows, tend to occur in such a routine, cooperative fashion that they generally go unnoticed by the average citizen. The orderly nature of many international interactions is largely a function of the mutual interests that states share in having at least some modicum of stability in their day-to-day affairs. To this end, states have created a body of international law designed to help regulate relations between countries, as well as a network of intergovernmental organizations designed to facilitate conflict management along with collaboration in economic and social problem solving at the regional and global level. The development of these institutions, "primitive" as they might be, is a manifestation of humanity's continual quest for order in a fragmented system of sovereign nation-states lacking any central authority.

Institutional links among national governments have been increasing in today's interdependent world, with the growth of the United Nations system being the most visible symbol of the international organization phenomenon. Just as governments have been developing greater organized ties across national boundaries, so have private individuals and groups such as multinational corporations, whose contacts and interests transcend national frontiers. In fact, there are many more nongovernmental international organizations than intergovernmental ones. There is some question whether the existing body of international legal rules and intergovernmental organizations are adequate to cope with the burgeoning volume of transnational activities and the new agenda of international issues—energy, the environment, food and population, and other concerns—noted in our earlier discussion of the general setting of contemporary international relations.

Opinions about the effectiveness of international law and organization in a decentralized political system have traditionally ranged from extremely harsh cynicism to extremely naive idealism, and observers today still tend to view international institutions in these terms. Where cynics see international law and international organizations as simply additional instruments that dominant powers in world politics seek to use to maintain the status quo, idealists see these as representing noble experiments in world order possibly leading eventually to world government. In Part III we will examine the role that *international institutions* play in contemporary world politics, focusing on international law (Chapter 9) and a variety of international organizations (Chapter 10). We will attempt to refrain from the excesses of both pessimism and optimism that have characterized so much discussion on this subject over the years.

International Law: Myth or Reality?

On November 4, 1979, fifty-two Americans in the U.S. Embassy in Tehran were seized by a group of Iranian militants. The hostages were to be used to extract certain concessions from the U.S. government, an endeavor that had the blessing of the new regime in Iran headed by Ayatollah Khomeini. It was not until January 20, 1981, after 444 days in captivity, that the American diplomatic personnel were finally released by the Iranian government. Though a somewhat distant memory now, this event preoccupied the nation for over a year and raised some interesting questions about the role of international law in international affairs.

To many, the Iranian hostage episode seemed a vivid illustration of the lawless character of international relations. However, rather than reflecting the nonexistence or impotence of international law, the episode in some respects illustrated its general reliability. In particular, what made the incident

The return of U.S. embassy personnel after 444 days in captivity in Iran, 1981.

such a *cause célèbre* was precisely the fact that it involved a virtually unprecedented violation of one of the most sacred rules of international conduct, namely the immunity of diplomats from host government seizure and punishment. The actions of the Iranian government represented such a departure from the routinely honored canons of state practice that observers at the time feverishly searched through history books to discover the last time such a violation had occurred. There was a certain irony involved, too, since it was in Persia—in the land that is today called Iran—that the principle of **diplomatic immunity** first evolved a thousand years ago.[1]

Still, long after the hostages were returned, questions remained as to what kind of legal system would allow such a violation to go unpunished. There was renewed debate over whether international law has any relevance to the major issues of international politics, or whether it could even be said to exist at all. The believer in international law might ask a number of questions: Why, if international law were irrelevant, would the U.S. State Department Legal Advisor's Office maintain a staff of more than sixty international lawyers, and why would multinational corporations employ hundreds more? Why would a Canadian secretary of state remark that "in my office and in my department, we are, first of all, students of international law"?[2] The skeptic might respond that much of international law is a charade in which states pick and choose to obey those rules that happen to coincide with their interests at a given moment; even if international law is grudgingly acknowledged to exist, it is considered to be feeble in those situations "that really matter." Cynics might note, for example, that the United States, which was so quick to invoke international law in the Iranian hostage case, chose to ignore it in 1986, when Washington refused to acknowledge that its mining of Nicaraguan harbors violated the rule against aggression despite widespread condemnation by international legal experts.

In this chapter we will examine the case for and against international law, investigating the manner in which international law operates and the degree to which it has an impact on international affairs. In our introduction to Part III, we quoted Louis Henkin's eloquent statement that "in relations between nations, the progress of civilization may be seen as movement from force to diplomacy, from diplomacy, to law." We leave it to the reader to judge how much progress has been made.

Is International Law Really Law?

A basic question that arises here is whether or not **international law**, as a body of rules governing relations between states, is really "law." In order to answer this question, we first need to define what law is. Law can be defined as a set of rules or expectations that govern the relations between the members.

of a society, that have an obligational basis, and whose violation is punishable through the application of sanctions by society.[3] It is the obligational character of law that distinguishes it from morality, religion, social mores, or mere protocol. The definition implies that three fundamental conditions must be present if law can be said to exist in a society: (1) a process for developing an identifiable, legally binding set of rules that prescribe certain patterns of behavior among societal members (i.e., a lawmaking process); (2) a process for punishing illegal behavior when it occurs (i.e., a law-enforcement process); and (3) a process for determining whether a particular rule has been violated in a particular instance (i.e., a law-adjudication process).

The reader will recognize these three conditions as the basic characteristics normally associated with domestic law within national societies. Certainly, such conditions exist in the United States or the Soviet Union or any other nation-state. Although some national legal systems might be considerably more effective than others—for example, in achieving compliance with the law—all have the basic elements noted above, as manifested by legislatures, police agencies, and courts.

What about *international* law? How does it compare with law in *national* political systems (commonly called **municipal law**)? The most obvious difference is that the central governmental institutions that are associated with law within nation-states simply do not exist, or operate only very weakly, in relations between nation-states. There is no world government, no supreme lawgiver, no squad of traffic cops riding herd over international affairs, and no court with compulsory jurisdiction. However, if one is willing to overlook the lack of strong central authoritative institutions in the international system—in other words, to abandon the stereotype of law as "a centralized constraint system backed by threat of coercive sanctions"[4]—then it would leave open the possibility of accepting international law as law. At least international law could conceivably fit our definition of law cited above, if not a stricter or more traditional definition. One must be prepared to demonstrate, however, how law can operate in a decentralized political system such as the international system. Let us examine each aspect of the international legal system separately, looking at how international law is made, enforced, and adjudicated, in the absence of a global government.

The Making of International Law: Where Does the Law Come From?

If one is a legal advisor in the foreign ministry of a country involved in an international dispute over maritime boundaries, or a judge on a country's highest court hearing a case involving some international dimension, there is no single body of world statutes that can be consulted to discover what the relevant law is. However, there is an identifiable set of rules accepted by states as legally binding, derived from the *sources* of international law specified in Article 38 of the International Court of Justice Statute that is attached to the United Nations Charter. The officially recognized sources of international law include (1) custom, (2) treaties or conventions, (3) general principles of law recognized by civilized nations, (4) judicial decisions of national and international tribunals, and (5) the writings of legal scholars. Since custom and treaties are by far the most important sources of international law, we will confine our discussion here to them.

CUSTOMARY LAW

Customary rules of international law are those practices that have been widely accepted as binding by states over a period of time as evidenced by repeated usage. In the early life of the international system, custom was an especially important source of international law. Hugo Grotius, a seventeenth-century Dutch writer often cited as the "father of international law" for his classic treatise *On the Law of War and Peace*, noted even in his day the development of certain common practices whose routine observance by governments led to their acceptance as required behavior in relations among states. One such custom was the practice of diplomatic immunity granted by a host government to a foreign government's ambassadors. Another was the designation of a three-mile limit within which coastal states were assumed to exercise sovereignty over territorial waters adjacent to their land; the three-mile limit was based on the effective range of cannon fired from shoreline fortifications. Numerous other rules developed.

Nowhere were any of these rules specifically written down, but they were nonetheless understood to constitute rules of prescribed conduct. Given the decentralized nature of the international system, a customary rule technically became binding only on those states which, through their compliance over time, indicated their willingness to be bound by the rule in question. For example, the Scandinavian countries long insisted on maintaining a four-mile territorial sea while practically all other states observed the three-mile limit. However, once a state demonstrated its acceptance of a customary rule by repeated observance, it was expected to continue to be bound by it; customary law was not something that could be arbitrarily adopted and rejected from one moment to the next.[5]

Today, many customary rules continue to form part of the body of international law. Customary rules of law are to be distinguished from rules of etiquette, known as *comity*; in the case of customary rules, an established pattern of conduct (e.g., diplomatic immunity) is based on a sense of legal obligation (*opinio iuris*) and invites legal penalties if breached, while in the case of comity, it is merely a matter of courtesy (e.g., two ships saluting each other's flag while passing at sea). Admittedly, when states engage in certain standard practices toward each other, it is not always clear whether they do so out of a sense of legal obligation or simply out of politeness. Moreover, given the unwritten nature of customary law, there is great potential for ambiguity and misinterpretation of the rules. For these reasons, there has been an increasing trend in recent years to *codify* customary law, i.e., to embody customary rules in more precise, written *treaty* form to which states can explicitly give or withhold consent.

TREATIES

Treaties or **conventions** are formal written agreements between states, which create legal obligations for the governments that are parties to them. As with customary law, treaties are binding only on those states that consent to be bound by them. A state normally indicates its consent by a two-step process in which its authorized representative *signs* the treaty and its legislature or other constitutionally empowered body *ratifies* the agreement. For example, President Carter in 1979 signed a Strategic Arms Limitation Agreement (SALT II) along with President Brezhnev of the Soviet Union, but failed to win the approval of the U.S. Senate, so that the treaty was not ratified and did not go into effect. Once a state becomes a party to a treaty, it is expected that its government will honor the fundamental principle associated with treaties—*pacta sunt servanda*, which specifies that treaties are to be obeyed.

Many treaties are simply bilateral in nature—agreements between two states seeking, for example, to establish trade relations or an alliance, or regarding the use of each other's air space or the extradition of criminals from each other's territory. Other treaties are multilateral and can involve such subjects as international commerce, patent and copyright regulations, regulation of mail and other communications, use of the oceans for fishing and exploration, treatment of prisoners of war, and development and deployment of various kinds of weapons. Multilateral agreements are the ones of greatest relevance to international law, especially those multilateral treaties that deal with issues of broad importance and seek to involve as many members of the international community as possible, such as the UN Charter.

As we have noted, there have been increased efforts to use treaties to codify traditional, customary rules of international law. For example, the Vienna Convention on Diplomatic Relations of 1961, ratified by almost every country, reiterated the rule of law requiring that the immunity and inviolability of embassies and diplomats be respected. Among the provisions of the treaty are the following: diplomatic agents and members of their families cannot be arrested and prosecuted by the host government for any crimes committed, even a blatant act of murder or a hit-and-run accident; diplomatic agents are immune not only from host state criminal jurisdiction but also from civil jurisdiction, which means that they cannot be prosecuted for damaging someone's property or passing bad checks. In New York City alone, where diplomats abound at UN headquarters, it is estimated that 250,000 parking tickets worth $5 million have gone unpaid as diplomats continue to triple park, block major thoroughfares, and generally go about their business blissfully free from the restrictions that apply to most motorists. However, what might seem to be a grossly unfair system of rules to the New York City cab driver or the person on the street is necessitated by the desire of national governments to ensure that their diplomats are not harassed in any fashion by the host country to which they happen to be assigned. If a diplomat were to abuse such diplomatic immunity, by becoming a mass murderer or a notorious hotrodder and check bouncer, the remedy would be for the host state to request a waiver of immunity from the diplomat's government or to declare the diplomat *persona non grata* and expel him from the country.

Although some treaties simply transcribe customary law into written form, keeping the traditional rules intact, other treaties are designed to revise the customary law. For example, the Law of the Sea Conference, a forum of over 150 states that has met periodically since 1958, has produced several conventions and drafts of others that have incorporated some elements of the traditional law of the sea—such as the right of "innocent passage" enjoyed by all ships in the territorial waters of coastal states, the right of "hot pursuit" by coastal state vessels against foreign ships violating the laws of the coastal state, and absolute freedom of navigation of all ships on the high seas outside any state's boundaries. This forum has also attempted to modify some existing rules, such as extending the width of the territorial seas from three to twelve miles.

In some instances, treaties have been used to develop rules in new areas of concern for which no law has existed or been necessary before. For example, the Outer Space Treaty of 1967, ratified by almost 100 states, requires the signatories to refrain from deploying weapons of mass destruction in outer space and to consider the moon and other celestial bodies *terra nullius*— territory belonging to no one—and beyond any state's sovereign control. As a party to the treaty, had the United States attempted to declare the moon its sovereign territory when it was the first to land there in 1969, the government would have been acting illegally in violation of the 1967 agreement.

It is evident that even in the absence of a world legislature, machinery exists to create written rules that are considered legally binding, with bilateral treaties drafted by the foreign ministries of individual countries and multilateral treaties drafted by the UN International Law Commission or bodies such as the Law of the Sea Conference. There are literally thousands of treaties in effect around the world, and the number is growing as the increased volume and complexity of international interactions lead governments to seek more formalized arrangements in regulating intercourse between states. The proliferation of treaties in modern times is reflected in the fact that in 1892 the official compendium of treaties entered into by the United Kingdom numbered only 190 pages, whereas by 1960 it exceeded 2500 pages.[6]

There is even a treaty on treaties—the Vienna Convention on the Law of Treaties of 1969—which codifies the customary rule of *pacta sunt servanda*. This convention also stipulates the circumstances whereby a state unilaterally can *legally terminate* its involvement in some treaty. A state can back out of a treaty commitment, for example, if the agreement has an "escape hatch" provision (say, a requirement to provide at least six months' advance notification of intent to withdraw). This was the case with the U.S. decision to terminate its mutual defense agreement with Taiwan in 1979 in an effort to cultivate better relations with the Beijing government on the Chinese mainland. A state can also legally terminate its treaty obligations if it can demonstrate that it had been coerced into signing the treaty originally, that the treaty was founded on fraudulent grounds or signed by an unauthorized national representative, or that present conditions are so radically different from those existing at the outset of the treaty as to render it impossible for that party to continue honoring the terms of the pact (the last condition is known as **rebus sic stantibus**). Despite the availability of these loopholes, states tend to use them only sparingly.

Admittedly, the making of international law occurs in a quite different fashion from lawmaking in national political systems. One criticism of international law is that the formulation of rules occurs in such a disjointed manner without any centralized machinery that there remains considerable disagreement over exactly what the rules are at a given moment. However, legal ambiguities—in terms of vaguely worded statutes, unclear judicial precedents, and conflicting interpretations of the law—are not unknown in municipal systems. Indeed, one frequently finds in the United States that legislators are uncertain of the meaning of the U.S. Constitution, bureaucrats are uncertain about the intent of Congressional acts they must implement, and Supreme Court justices reach 5–4 split opinions on the prevailing requirements of the law. The problems associated with discovering the content of the law in the international system are not of a completely different character than those found in municipal systems, only somewhat more pronounced and more serious.

A further criticism of international law has to do with its essentially voluntary nature. Individuals in the United States and other municipal legal systems do not have the prerogative of deciding whether or not to agree to be bound by some rule of law, or whether to terminate their acceptance of some rule. The consent basis of law is generally unheard of in such systems, including democracies; once a rule of law is promulgated, everyone in the society is expected to abide by it regardless of whether everyone approves of it. However, the effectiveness of a legal system may consist not so much in how many members of the society have an obligation to obey the law as how many actually *do* obey the law. We next examine the extent to which international law is obeyed and enforced.

The Breaking of International Law:
How Is the Law Enforced?

The most common indictment of international law is not the absence or ambiguity of the rules but the lack of enforcement—the complaint that international law is broken regularly with impunity due to the lack of a central policing agency. United Nations peacekeeping forces are perhaps the closest thing to an international police body, but they are organized sporadically as temporary responses to certain crisis situations and are designed to maintain peace, not necessarily to enforce law. At least once in its history, the United Nations organized a military force to punish aggression, in the case of North Korea in 1950, but that was exceptional.

Sanctions against violators of international law exist, but they are primarily based on the principle of *self-help*; if one state harms another state (e.g., seizes its financial assets) it is usually left to the aggrieved state to take action to punish the offender through **reprisals** or retaliation of some kind (e.g., reciprocal seizure of the offender's assets held by the aggrieved state's banks). While self-help also operates to some extent in municipal legal systems—for example, defending oneself against assault or reclaiming stolen property or making a citizen's arrest—it tends not to be the norm in those systems.

However, what is most striking about the international legal system is not how often the law is broken but how often it is *obeyed*, despite the lack of "traffic cops" to provide a central coercive threat of punishment against would-be offenders. To be sure, there are frequent violations of international law, most notably those serious breaches that are reported on front pages of newspapers, such as the seizure of the U.S. Embassy in Iran and various acts of violent aggression. While people tend to notice these conspicuous failures of international law, they neglect to notice the ordinary workings of international law in the everyday life of the international system. The fact is that, if one takes into account the myriad treaties and customary rules of international law that exist today, it can be said that most states obey most of the rules most of the time.[7] In other words, international law gets "enforced" in its own way.

To understand why this is so, we need to consider the basic reasons why people obey laws in any society. The first is the already mentioned threat of punishment for illegal behavior (the *coercive* motive). A second is the mutual interests that individuals have in seeing that laws are obeyed (the *utilitarian* motive). A third is the internalization of the rules by the members of the society, i.e., habits of compliance; people obey the law because that is what they have come to accept as the right thing to do (the *identitive* motive). All of these elements can operate to produce obedience to the law. Think for a moment why most people bother to obey a stop sign at an intersection. One reason is the coercive element—the possibility that a police officer might stop you if you do not stop yourself. Another is the utilitarian motive—the possibility that another car might accidentally hit your vehicle if you pass through the intersection without stopping. As powerful as these motives are, the main driving force behind the inclination to stop at a stop sign is probably the simple habitual nature of the act and the fact that it has been inculcated as part of the "code of the road." (Even if one were driving through the middle of Death Valley in California, where no police cars or other vehicles were in evidence for miles, there would be a tendency to stop if somehow one were to encounter a red stop sign sticking out of the desert sand!)

The point here is that law and order can function to some extent even in the absence of police; indeed, any society that relies primarily on coercive threats as the basis for order is one that is terribly fragile. While habits of compliance—the most solid basis for law—are not very well-developed in the international legal system, the mutual interests of states in having a set of rules that prescribe as well as proscribe patterns of behavior provide a foundation for the international legal order. States are willing to tolerate certain constraints on their own behavior because it is widely recognized that international commerce, travel, and other forms of international activity would be exceedingly precarious otherwise.

It is curious that critics argue that international law is virtually nonexistent because it is frequently broken. If one were to apply the same test of effectiveness to municipal law that is generally demanded of international law—i.e., 100 percent conformity to and enforcement of the law, or close to it—then one would have to conclude that there is no law anywhere in the world, not only between nation-states but also within them. One writer comments on the degree to which laws are broken and offenders go unpunished in the American legal system:

> In one study of criminal behavior by adults, people were asked which of forty-nine offenses other than traffic violations they had committed without being caught. Ninety-nine percent of the people admitted they had committed one or more offenses for which they might have received jail or prison sentences had they been caught. Among the males, 26 percent admitted auto theft, 17 percent burglary, and 13 percent grand larceny. Some 64 percent of the males and 29 percent of the females admitted to committing at least one felony for which they they had not been caught.
>
> The fact is that only about a third of all serious crimes (murder, forcible rape, robbery, aggravated assault, burglary, larceny over $50, and auto theft) are ever even reported to the police by the victims. Of all serious crimes reported, in only 19 percent of cases is a suspect ever arrested, although the figure can go as high as 78 percent for murder. Only about half of all suspects arrested are ever convicted. And only a quarter of those convicted actually ever "do time" for their crime.[8]

"You see a car come by here traveling within the speed limit?"

Grin and Bear It by Lichty and Wagner © 1981 Field Enterprises, Inc. Courtesy of Field Newspaper Syndicate.

Law enforcement in municipal law

If one adds the number of people who exceed the speed limit on America's highways, then the effectiveness of law enforcement in the United States becomes much more dubious. (It is true that one can find total obedience to speeding regulations in parts of Europe, such as on the West German Autobahn—but only because there are *no* limits to how fast cars can go on some highways!) More seriously, many national legal systems experience not only methodical violations of speeding laws but also civil violence against the state itself. The international order is not alone, then, in experiencing lawlessness. We do not mean to minimize the problem of law enforcement in international law, only to suggest that unfair and unrealistic standards are sometimes applied in evaluating the effectiveness of international law.

The Adjudicating of International Law: Who Are the Judges?

In municipal legal systems, courts are utilized to determine whether a particular law has been violated in a particular instance when one party accuses another party of an infraction. In the international system, judicial institutions also exist, such as the **International Court of Justice** (commonly referred to as the **World Court**), which can be utilized when one state accuses another of violating the law. However, such international institutions are extremely weak insofar as disputants tend to judge for themselves whether an infraction has occurred, or at least tend to reserve for themselves the decision of whether or not to go to court. Whereas in municipal systems one disputant can normally compel the other party to appear in court, international tribunals like the World Court generally lack any compulsory jurisdiction. As in the *United States Diplomatic and Consular Staff in Tehran* case which the United States brought before the World Court in 1979, one party—in this instance, Iran— can simply refuse to acknowledge the jurisdiction of the Court and to participate in the judicial proceedings. The United States itself refused to accept the jurisdiction of the Court in the 1986 case in which Nicaragua filed suit criticizing the United States for mining Nicaraguan harbors and carrying on illegal intervention.

The World Court consists of fifteen judges whose term of office is nine years. Elected by the UN membership, the judges are generally drawn from every major legal system in the world, with certain countries like the United States and the Soviet Union each assured of one seat at all times; if the Court happens to be hearing a case involving a state that does not have a seat on the Court, that state may appoint one of its own nationals as an *ad hoc* judge for that particular case—despite the fact that judges on the Court are supposed to be impartial international jurists and not representatives of their national governments. Only states are eligible to appear as litigants before the Court, based on the traditional view that only states are "international legal persons" having rights and obligations under international law. If private individuals have a grievance against their own government, they are expected to resolve the matter in their own state's courts; if they have a grievance against a foreign government, they must ordinarily use that country's courts or persuade their own government to take the case before the World Court.

The World Court sits in The Hague, in the Netherlands. Some wags might note that all the Court seems to do for the most part is, indeed, sit. Despite the fact that more than 150 states are parties to the ICJ Statute that established the Court, the Court has heard fewer than sixty contentious cases since its creation in 1946; in roughly one third of these, it has not even been able to render a judgment. In fact, the caseload of the Court has been declining over time, with twenty-nine cases submitted during the 1950s, only six during the

1960s, seven during the 1970s, and three in the 1980s.[9] Again, the lack of business is largely due to the lack of compulsory jurisdiction. Over forty-five states have signed the so-called **Optional Clause** of the ICJ Statute, agreeing to give the Court compulsory jurisdiction in certain kinds of disputes. However, even these states have attached so many reservations to their acceptance of the Court's jurisdiction as to render the clause meaningless; the United States, for example, in the Connally Amendment, agreed to give the Court compulsory jurisdiction except for those "disputes . . . which are essentially within the domestic jurisdiction of the United States *as determined by the United States of America.*"[10]

Where the Court has made a judgment in a case, that judgment has been deemed binding on both the winner and loser. The fundamental problem is that, in disputes involving vital interests, states have been unwilling to entrust a third party with ultimate decision-making competence; and in disputes over more trivial matters, states have not felt the need to use the Court since it is far simpler and cheaper to settle "out of court." In fairness to the Court, it might be said that the great bulk of disputes that arise in domestic law are also settled out of court through a process of bargaining not unlike that found in the international system. Still, even the most charitable apologist for the Court would have to conclude that it has been an extremely ineffective, largely ignored international institution despite its representing the "highest legal aspiration of civilized man."[11]

Fortunately for the international legal system, the World Court is not the only adjudication vehicle. A variety of other courts exist, including several at the regional level, such as the European Court of Justice. More importantly, *national* courts play a key role in the application of international law in those instances in which international issues arise in domestic suits. The constitutions or basic laws of most countries stipulate that treaties and other elements of international law are considered to be the supreme law of the land, at least coequal with the highest national law, and are to be given due respect in the deliberations of national courts; in this sense, national judges are not only agents of municipal law but also international law. It is true that if a conflict exists between some rule of municipal law (say, an act of Parliament in the British system) and a rule of international law (say, a treaty entered into by the United Kingdom), national judges are inclined to favor municipal law. However, these problems do not arise as often as one might think and are not always resolved in favor of the national law. In the United States, for instance, when there is a conflict between an act of Congress and a treaty entered into by the United States, the one that was enacted later in time takes precedence; treaties take precedence over any state or local statutes in the United States, regardless of the timing element.

It is sometimes difficult to separate international law from municipal law. An often overlooked function that international law performs is the *allocation of legal competences*. International law provides the members of the international community with guidelines that help define their rights and obligations vis-à-vis each other, in particular who has what *jurisdiction* to deal with a legal matter in a given situation somewhere in the world.[12] For example, if a Frenchman kills a Pole on a cruise ship owned by a Canadian flying the Panamanian flag in U.S. territorial waters, whose courts have jurisdiction to try the crime? Any state involved in the incident? No state? The flag state? The state on whose territory the incident occurred? The shipowner's state, the victim's state, or the defendant's state? The answers to these questions are found in the box on pages 304–305, where we discuss how jurisdictional problems are sorted out in the international system. Although most situations in international relations involve a much less tangled set of jurisdictional possibilities than the case mentioned here, numerous incidents occur daily that require some determination of jurisdiction. The international system has been able to handle such jurisdictional concerns relatively smoothly, although the problems become more acute as transnational activities increase.

Adjudication, then, like lawmaking and law enforcement, tends to occur in a more convoluted fashion in the international system than in national systems. In many ways, although international law is most criticized for the ineffectiveness of its law-enforcement and lawmaking institutions, it is the adjudication area that is probably the weakest link in the international legal system. Still, an adjudication process does exist, as we have suggested.

Special Problems in Contemporary International Law

In the international system, as in national societies, law is essentially based on politics. That is, the legal rules developed by a society—although they might have some utilitarian value for all members—tend to reflect especially the interests of those members of society who have the most resources with which to influence the rule-making process. Although the law in some societies might be based on a wider, more just set of values and interests than in other societies, underlying political realities nonetheless invariably shape the law.[13] Much of the current body of international law, for example, evolved from the international politics of the nineteenth and early twentieth centuries, when Western capitalist states dominated the international system. The traditional rules that were created to promote freedom of the seas, protection of foreign investment, and many other international activities tended to reflect the needs and interests of these powers.

However, when political realities change along with technological conditions and other factors, pressures mount to *alter* the law so that it better reflects the new environment. The contemporary international system can be

thought of as a society in ferment, with nuclear weapons, economic interdependence and the growth of multinational corporations, and revolutionary
advances in travel and other kinds of technology threatening to render many
of the existing rules obsolete. An even more important impetus for change in
the legal order is provided by the shifting power equation in world politics,
as traditional powers are finding it increasingly difficult to impose their will
on a Third World coalition of states clamoring for a rewriting of the rules
more compatible with the latter's interests. In some problem areas, such as
international terrorism and environmental pollution, a body of international
law is only beginning to evolve.

Hence, many efforts are now underway to expand and revise international
law. These efforts are complicated by wide differences of opinion between the
developed countries of the West, the less developed countries of the Third
World, and Communist countries like the Soviet Union.[14] Even within each
of these groups there are various conflicts of interest. We will discuss the
politics of global problem solving and "regime formation" in Part IV. Before
finishing our discussion of international law, we want to call attention briefly
to three specific problems in contemporary international law: (1) the laws of
war, (2) the treatment of aliens, and (3) human rights.

LAWS OF WAR

Although the bulk of international law consists of the "laws of peace," there
also exist the "laws of war." Some of these laws pertain to the *conduct* of
war, i.e., the kinds of behavior that are legally permissible by governments
once a war is underway, regardless of how it started. Other rules pertain to
the *commencement* of war, i.e., the circumstances under which it is legal for
a state to resort to the use of armed force against another state. If the latter
rules were totally effective, there would be little need for the former.

There is a long history of states attempting to regulate the conduct of war
through agreed-upon rules regarding the rights and obligations of *neutrals*
(e.g., exempting ships of neutral countries from seizure unless they carried
contraband goods destined for one of the warring countries) as well as the
belligerents themselves (e.g., according humane treatment to captured soldiers).
Some of the attempts to inject a dose of civility into warfare have seemed
paradoxical and almost comical, such as the prohibition (embodied in the
Hague Conventions of 1907) against the use of "dum-dum" expanding bullets
and the use of "deceit" in the form of misrepresenting a flag of truce or
wearing Red Cross uniforms as a disguise—especially at a time when poisonous
gas and other atrocities were legally permissible. However absurd as they
might appear and as erratic as their observance has been, the laws governing
the conduct of war have at least succeeded in limiting the savage nature of
war to some extent, notably through such instruments as the 1929 and 1949
Geneva Conventions on the treatment of prisoners of war (POWs).

DETERMINING JURISDICTION IN THE WORLD

What happens if a Frenchman kills a Pole on a ship owned by a Canadian flying the Panamanian flag in U.S. territorial waters?

"Jurisdiction" refers to the competence of a state to prosecute certain acts of individuals in its courts. The subject of jurisdiction is sufficiently complicated to fill hundreds of pages in most international law casebooks. We will try here to summarize briefly the basic aspects of the problem.

One must first understand that any given country is composed of a multitude of individual persons, most of whom are citizens, or *nationals*, of that state. However, also traveling or residing within each state are *aliens*, persons who are nationals of another state or may even be stateless (if their citizenship has been lost for some reason). In general, a "national" refers to a person owing permanent allegiance to a particular state, and it is a status acquired either through birth or through naturalization. Regarding birth, some countries, such as the continental European states, stress the *jus sanguinis* principle, whereby a child automatically acquires the nationality of the parents regardless of where the child is born. Other states, such as the United States, utilize not only the *jus sanguinis* principle but also the *jus soli* principle, whereby any child (with a few minor exceptions) who is born on their soil is eligible for citizenship regardless of the nationality of the parents. Hence, a child born to Belgian parents in the United States would be eligible for both American and Belgian citizenship. The conflicts inherent in dual, and sometimes multiple, citizenship are usually resolved through residency requirements imposed by most states. Nationality can also be gained through naturalization, the process whereby a foreigner attains citizenship after complying with the application procedures stipulated by the state.

Jurisdiction can be claimed by states on five possible grounds:

1. The *territorial* principle, whereby a state may exercise jurisdiction over the acts of anyone—nationals or aliens (except for certain classes of aliens such as foreign diplomats)—committed within its territorial borders (e.g., U.S. courts trying an Englishman for a theft committed in New York City);

2. The *nationality* principle, whereby a state may exercise jurisdiction over any acts perpetrated by its own nationals, no matter where they are committed in the world (e.g., U.S. courts trying an American for a murder committed in Egypt);

3. The *protective* principle, whereby a state may exercise jurisdiction over the acts of any persons—nationals or aliens (with a few exceptions)—committed anywhere in the world, if such acts threaten a state's national security (e.g., U.S. courts trying a Hungarian for counterfeiting U.S. currency in Mexico);

4. The *universality* principle, whereby a state may exercise jurisdiction over the acts of any persons—nationals or aliens (with a few exceptions)—committed anywhere in the world, if such acts constitute crimes against the community of nations (e.g., U.S. courts trying a Belgian for engaging in an act of piracy on the high seas by seizing a French fishing vessel, or trying a Palestinian for skyjacking a Jordanian jetliner);

5. The *passive personality* principle, whereby a state may exercise jurisdiction over any person who has injured one of its nationals, no matter where in the world the act was committed (e.g., U.S. courts trying a Syrian for killing an American in Lebanon).

The first two principles are the most commonly invoked and accepted bases of jurisdiction, with the territorial principle being most adhered to by states in the Anglo-Saxon legal tradition and the nationality principle most recognized by states in the continental European tradition. The other three principles, only occasionally invoked, are exceptions to the general notion that states should not seek to prosecute in their national courts those acts committed by aliens abroad. It is clearly possible for more than one state to have legitimate grounds on which to claim jurisdiction over some act, as in the case of a person shooting across a national frontier and killing a person on the other side. As a practical matter, one state—namely the one that has the offender in custody—is usually in a position to determine whether to exercise jurisdiction itself or to *extradite* that person to another state seeking jurisdiction.

In the hypothetical case cited at the beginning of this box, it is conceivable that France could invoke the nationality principle, Poland the passive personality principle, and the United States or Panama the territorial principle. As a general rule, if the "good order" of the port of the coastal state (here, the United States) were not disturbed by the incident—if a wild shooting spree did not ensue—then the coastal state ordinarily would be willing to defer to the authority of the flag state (Panama), which in turn could decide to hand over the perpetrator to his government (France) for trial. In any event, it is not likely that the Frenchman would go scot-free.

There have also been attempts throughout history to regulate the very outbreak of war, although in the eighteenth and nineteenth centuries legal efforts were devoted more to making war a more civilized affair than actually banning or restricting its occurrence. Not until the twentieth century, with the **League of Nations Covenant** and the **Kellogg-Briand Pact** drawn after the ravages of World War I, were efforts made explicitly to *outlaw* war. The latter treaty, ratified by almost every nation, provided that "the settlement of all disputes . . . of whatever nature . . . shall never be sought except by pacific means."[15] World War II, of course, demonstrated the hollowness of such pious denunciations of violence. In the **United Nations Charter** of 1945, an attempt was made to specify more clearly the proscription against the use of armed force in international relations and to provide stronger enforcement machinery. Under the UN Charter, all members are obligated to "refrain . . . from the threat or use of force against the territorial integrity or political independence of any state." This language has been generally interpreted to mean that not only war but *any first use of armed force* by one state against another state— no matter how limited—is *illegal* today. Force may be legally used only under three conditions: (1) in self-defense by an individual state or alliance of states against the armed attack of another state, (2) in the service of the UN as part of a "collective security" operation, or (3) in the service of a regional peacekeeping organization. In short, armed *aggression* is illegal today, which might be why states no longer have "war departments" but "defense departments."

"Aggression" and "self-defense" naturally are often in the eyes of the beholder, with some states (such as Israel in 1967) at times going so far as to claim the legal right of initiating the use of force in *anticipatory* or *preemptive* self-defense.[16] (It is like the little boy who in attempting to explain to his father whether he or his brother started a fight claims that "it all began when he hit me back!")[17] While we noted in the previous chapter that the resort to armed force continues to be a feature of contemporary international relations, at least one respected observer contends that "the norm against the unilateral national use of force has survived. Indeed, . . . the norm has been largely observed . . . and the kinds of international wars which it sought to prevent [wars between states] have been infrequent."[18] The rub here, however, is that the norm has been much less effective in cases involving what we earlier called force without war.

Moreover, the rules governing the outbreak of hostilities have been especially inadequate to deal with the most common form of international violence today—internal wars involving outside intervention—since in these cases it is not clearly one state engaged in armed attack on another state but rather a government seeking foreign military support to quell a rebellion or a rebel group seeking foreign support to overthrow a government. There is no question that a foreign army's inviting itself into a domestic conflict constitutes aggression and would be a violation of the UN Charter, but what if it is invited in by a government on the brink of collapse? A government has a legal right to invite foreign military assistance only if it can rightly claim to exercise effective control and authority (i.e., sovereignty) over its own population, a condition which is often disputable during a civil war.

Internal wars and military interventionism pose special problems today for the implementation of POW conventions and other rules governing the conduct of warfare because those rules have generally been developed over the years to apply to conventional armed struggle between states.[19] In guerrilla warfare, armies do not normally confront each other across well-defined fronts, and soldiers do not even always wear uniforms. Customary distinctions between civilians and combatants are blurred, as are distinctions between neutrals and belligerents. A national government experiencing rebellion is understandably reluctant to extend to rebels the same status normally reserved for enemy soldiers, preferring to dismiss them as "rioters" or "gangsters" rather than legitimizing them as "freedom fighters." The result is that the rights and obligations traditionally associated with the conduct of warfare have become muddled and often ignored.[20] During the Vietnam War, for example, there was disagreement over whether Communist Viet Cong troops captured by U.S. and South Vietnamese forces ought to have been treated as prisoners of war entitled to protection under the 1949 Geneva Conventions, or as common criminals to be prosecuted for murder, insurrection, and treason against the South Vietnamese government.

Even in those armed conflicts that are purely interstate in nature, the absence of formal declarations of war today can make it difficult to determine whether the rules governing the conduct of war are in effect or not at a given moment. Then, too, the technology of modern warfare—strategic bombing, submarine-launched missiles, napalm, herbicides and defoliants, and the like—has tended to make many of the classic rules practically inoperable, such as the standard proscription against indiscriminate attacks on civilians on land and sea, although governments can still design military strategies to minimize civilian casualties if they are so inclined. Efforts have been made to adapt the laws of war to these new realities, such as the two Geneva Protocols of 1977; but the evolution of international law in this area remains problematical.[21]

TREATMENT OF ALIENS

The distinction between **nationals** and **aliens** was discussed earlier in the context of jurisdiction (see the box on pages 304–305). With the increased volume of transnational business-related and tourist travel in the world, countries are generally finding more aliens visiting or residing within their borders. The basic maxim that has always applied to foreigners is "when in Rome, do as the Romans do." That is, foreigners are expected to obey host country laws and (with the exception of foreign diplomatic personnel) can be prosecuted by the latter's courts for committing crimes of murder or theft, or engaging in any other activities proscribed by the state. However, international law has traditionally stipulated that, in certain respects, aliens are entitled to special treatment different from the manner in which the host government deals with its own nationals. In particular, just because a host government might be a dictatorship that denies its citizens any semblance of due process of law and the right to a fair trial, this does not mean that an alien accused of committing a crime in that country must necessarily settle for the same level of justice reserved for nationals of that state. Governments can invoke a legal right to have their citizens accorded a *minimum international standard of justice* by any host state in which their citizens happen to be present while abroad, no matter what the standard of justice is in the host country. If the minimum standard is not observed, injured parties can request their own government to seek redress from the host state.

These are not mere academic issues and they can critically affect individual lives—for example, if you are an American accused and convicted of theft in Saudi Arabia, where the penalty meted out to Saudis in such cases can be the amputation of an arm; or, as two Australians found out in a celebrated 1986 case, if you are caught possessing a cache of hard drugs in Malaysia, where the automatic penalty is death by hanging. Many governments, notably in the Third World, have increasingly voiced opposition to the customary notion of a minimum *international* standard, viewing it as an artifact of the old colonial era when the United States and other Western states tended to dictate legal norms. Instead, several Third World states today claim their only obligation to foreigners is to ensure that the latter obtain equal treatment with their own citizens in accordance with the established *national* standard. Even for those states that accept the idea of an international standard, differences obviously arise as to what constitutes a "minimum"' degree of justice. Hence, this is another area in which international law is in flux.

Controversy over the treatment of aliens has been especially heated on the subject of **expropriation**, i.e., government seizure of foreign-owned property or assets. It is not surprising that this should be a controversial issue today, at a time when private overseas investment has reached enormous levels; the foreign facilities of American-based companies alone are currently valued at well over $150 billion.[22] The customary rule of international law is that any state has the right to expropriate alien-owned property, but only "for public purposes, if no discrimination is made between aliens and nationals, and if prompt, adequate and effective payment" is provided by the government as compensation.[23] Here, too, many Third World countries have challenged the established rule as an infringement on their sovereignty left over from the colonial era, and they have argued their only obligation is to give "appropriate" compensation based on their national standards. Other Third World countries still acknowledge the customary rule but often disagree with Western states over what constitutes "adequate and effective" compensation, as in the case of several Middle East states that have nationalized foreign oil company facilities in recent years. Attempts at replacing the customary law with multilateral treaties that embody more widely accepted codes of conduct have encountered great difficulty, causing states like the United States to resort instead to a series of bilateral conventions with individual countries.[24]

HUMAN RIGHTS

Since World War II, an ongoing effort has been made to require national governments to observe the minimum international standard of justice not only with regard to aliens within their borders but also with regard to their very own *citizens.* In other words, there has been a movement to extend **human rights** protection under international law to *all* individuals on the globe, regardless of whether they are aliens or nationals. At the **Nuremberg Trials,** following World War II, for example, leaders of Nazi Germany were charged with having committed, along with other crimes, crimes against humanity. In particular, German officials were accused and then convicted of having violated the rights of the indigenous Jewish population in Germany by engaging in genocide against them; several German leaders were sentenced to life imprisonment or execution as a result. The Nuremberg precedent suggested, therefore, that *individuals* have rights (and, indeed, obligations) under international law.

Critics of the Nuremberg Trials have argued that they did not reflect the evolution of international law but simply amounted to "victors' justice," i.e., the winners of a war arbitrarily asserting the existence of certain rules that were used as a pretext to punish the political and military leaders of a vanquished state. These critics point out that the United States, which supported such strong penalties against German leaders at Nuremberg, resisted any calls for international tribunals to hold American officials accountable for atrocities allegedly committed during World War II (and later in Vietnam). Although the United States was not guilty of atrocities on the scale of the Germans, Washington was perhaps guilty of a certain amount of hypocrisy in refusing to permit any scrutiny of its own behavior by an international body.

Still, granted the uneven application of Nuremberg principles, the significance of Nuremberg nonetheless was that it clearly challenged the traditional notion that only *states*—not individuals—were subjects of international law. Nuremberg was followed by the Universal Declaration of Human Rights, a resolution adopted virtually unanimously by the UN General Assembly in 1948. The Declaration, which was a moral pronouncement rather than a legally binding document, urged national governments to promote a variety of human rights, both civil and political (e.g., the right to a fair trial) as well as economic and social (e.g., the right to an adequate standard of living). Since that time, a number of treaties have been drafted that attempt to articulate human rights more clearly and that are binding on those states choosing to ratify them. Included among these are four conventions dealing with genocide, racial discrimination, political and civil rights, and economic and social rights. To date, less than half of the states of the world have ratified these conventions. Part of the problem is getting countries with diverse ideological and cultural backgrounds to agree on a definition of human rights. The more fundamental problem, however, is that national governments tend to resist accepting international legal obligations in this area, since the entire concept of "human rights" is viewed as undermining their sovereign authority within their borders. The Soviet Union and other Communist countries, in particular, have insisted that any attempt to impose international legal obligations on governments vis-à-vis their own citizens constitutes unwarranted interference in the internal affairs of the state and that a state is entitled to treat its own citizens in any manner it pleases. Even the United States, generally an outspoken supporter of human rights over the years, did not ratify the Convention on Genocide until 1986, and has yet to ratify the other three conventions noted above, since certain provisions in these treaties are felt to run counter to current U.S. domestic policy and municipal law in several respects; for example, it is argued by members of the U.S. Senate that the conventions go too far in abolishing capital punishment and guaranteeing paid leave for women before and after childbirth. Despite the drive for "universal" agreement on human rights protection, the greatest progress in this area has occurred at the *regional* level, in Western Europe, where the West Europeans have created institutions such as the European Court of Human Rights, in which individual citizens can bring grievances against their own government before a supranational tribunal.

Respect for even basic human rights, such as free speech, is still very weak in many countries.[25] Nonetheless, the human rights movement persists in the quest for enhanced individual dignity and is part of a larger movement today to bring other kinds of *nonstate* actors directly under the purview of international law.[26] Not only human beings but also international organizations and corporations, as they proliferate, are grudgingly being accorded some degree of status as "international legal persons" alongside nation-states. (In fact, as the Sidelight in this section indicates, even animals are now being recognized as deserving of protection under international law!) Hence, in this area, too, international law is evolving in new directions in response to the changing international environment.

Conclusion

We have noted that international law is a product of international politics. But we have also noted how international politics, in turn, is partly affected

SIDELIGHT

THE DRIVE FOR NONHUMAN RIGHTS

The following news item appeared some time ago under the headline "UN Espouses Animals' Lib," alerting the public that a new dimension had been added to the crusade for a more humane world. Nonhuman rights seemingly were being taken more seriously by some than human rights, although it remained to be seen how they would be enforced.

Man's feathered and four-legged friends have won a Universal Declaration of the Rights of Animals, and they have got the United Nations on their side.

Adopted Sunday at a ceremonial meeting of the UN Educational, Scientific, and Cultural Organization, the Animal Charter opens with the words: "All animals are born with an equal claim on life and the same rights to existence."

The ceremony, attended by statesmen, artists and Nobel prizewinners, included a display of 2.1 million signatures collected around the world in defense of animal rights.

The charter . . . spells out what animal lovers are pushing governments the world over to embody in legislation. Basically, it says that it is wrong to abandon one's dog in the street when one goes on vacation; it is unfeeling to gas stray cats; it is hideous to keep pigs or cattle locked inside container trucks, sweating or freezing, while customs officials settle disputes; it is cruel to raise chickens or rabbits in shoebox-sized cages, drop live lobsters in boiling water or force-feed geese to fatten their livers for foie gras.

Singled out for special condemnation are scientists, the entertainment world and hunters on the grand scale.

"Animal experimentation involving physical or psychological suffering is incompatible with the rights of animals," the charter says. "No animal shall be exploited for the amusement of man. Exhibitions and spectacles involving animals are incompatible with their dignity.

"Scenes of violence involving animals shall be banned from cinema and television, except for humane education.

"Any act involving mass killing of wild animals is genocide, that is, a crime against the species."

Signing of the charter by the 142 member states of UNESCO does not mean that blue-capped UN troops will now be rushed to the defense of persecuted pooches. The organizers hope that it will help animal lovers pressing for animal rights legislation.

Source: "UN Espouses Animals' Lib," *St. Louis Post-Dispatch* (October 16, 1978), p. 10A. Used by permission of the Associated Press.

by international law, in the sense that international law helps to shape the behavior of states and other actors in regard to diplomatic protection, commercial transactions, and other matters. Even in the Iranian hostage crisis, international law—if nothing else—served as the primary medium of communication and bargaining between the United States and Iran, since the conflict was largely played out through the exchange of legal broadsides. The importance of international law can be seen in the debates that are taking place today in the assembly halls of various world bodies, mostly over the question of what rules are going to govern the conduct of international relations; the importance attached to international law can also be seen, less visibly perhaps, in the haggling over the fine print of legal parchments that occurs in the backroom corridors. In the next chapter, we examine the forums in which many future discussions of international law are likely to be held, as we focus on the role of international organizations as actors in world politics.

SUMMARY

1. Three fundamental conditions must be present for law to exist in a society: a lawmaking process, a law-enforcement process, and a law-adjudication process. Despite the lack of a world legislature, a world police force, or other strong central authoritative institutions, international law meets these criteria—although it functions differently from law found in national societies.

2. The officially recognized sources of international law include custom, treaties, general principles of law recognized by civilized nations, judicial decisions of national and international tribunals, and the writings of legal scholars, with the first two being by far the most important.

3. Customary rules and treaties are binding only on those states that consent to them. Given the ambiguity often surrounding customary rules, there has been an increasing trend in recent years to codify them in written treaty form. Treaties are formal written agreements creating legal obligations for the governments that sign and ratify them, and may be bilateral or multilateral. Of special importance are the many multilateral treaties that have been concluded that regulate international interactions in broad areas of concern, such as the law of the sea.

4. The most common criticism of international law is the apparent lack of enforcement, i.e., that rules are violated regularly with no "traffic cop" available to punish offenders. However, the fact is that most states obey most of the rules most of the time, primarily because of their mutual interests in having some degree of order in international relations and their fear of sanctions that individual states might apply in retaliation against lawbreakers.

5. Institutions for adjudicating international law exist but are extremely weak, since disputants cannot ordinarily be compelled to appear in court. The World Court has been an ineffective, largely ignored institution, with little or no compulsory

jurisdiction over states. However, national and regional courts have been more successful in applying international law.

6. When political realities change, along with technological conditions and other factors, pressures mount to alter the law so that it better reflects the new environment. Much of the current body of international law evolved from the nineteenth century, when Western capitalist states dominated the international system and created rules designed to promote freedom of the seas, protection of foreign investment, and other interests. Today, many traditional rules are being rendered obsolete by technological change or are being challenged by Third World and Communist countries as artifacts of the colonial era. Hence, contemporary international law is under great strain.

7. There are three problem areas that exemplify how international law is in flux: the laws of war, the treatment of aliens, and human rights.

8. States have long tried to regulate the conduct of war and have even made some attempts explicitly to outlaw war altogether. Today, armed aggression is illegal. However, rules governing conventional warfare are inadequate in dealing with more common forms of international violence, such as force without war, internal wars, and military interventionism.

9. Traditionally, a host state has been obligated under international law to accord foreigners within its borders a "minimum international standard of justice," even if it treats its own citizens according to different standards. However, many Third World states question whether foreigners are entitled to special treatment. An especially controversial subject is the expropriation of foreign-owned property.

10. Since World War II there has been an ongoing effort to extend human rights protection to all individuals, forcing states to observe a minimum international standard of justice with regard not only to aliens within their borders but also to their own citizens. National governments tend to resist accepting international legal obligations in this area, however, since the entire concept of human rights is viewed as undermining their sovereign authority within their borders.

SUGGESTIONS FOR FURTHER READING AND STUDY

Excellent introductory texts presenting an overview of the rules of international law include a very concise treatment by Michael Akehurst in *A Modern Introduction to International Law*, 5th ed. (London: George Allen and Unwin, 1984), and a more in-depth, lengthier treatment by Gerhard von Glahn in *Law Among Nations*, 5th ed. (New York: Macmillan, 1986). A good reader that explores various contemporary problems in international law is *International Law: A Contemporary Perspective* (Boulder, Colo.: Westview Press, 1985), ed. by Richard Falk *et al*. Also see Robert Bledsoe and Boleslaw Boczek, *The International Law Dictionary* (Santa Barbara: ABC-CLIO, 1987).

A good examination of Western, Communist, and Third World views of international law can be found in A. Sheikh, *International Law and National Behavior* (New York: John Wiley, 1974), especially ch. 11. For specific studies of Soviet attitudes, see Jan F.

Triska and R. M. Slussar, *The Theory, Law, and Policy of Soviet Treaties* (Stanford, Calif.: Stanford University Press, 1962); John Hazard, "Renewed Emphasis upon a Socialist International Law," *American Journal of International Law*, 65 (1971), p. 142; and Isaak Ismail Dore, *International Law and the Superpowers* (New Brunswick, N.J.: Rutgers University Press, 1984). For specific works on Chinese attitudes, see James C. Hsiung, *Law and Policy in China's Foreign Relations* (New York: Columbia University Press, 1972); Jerome A. Cohen, *The People's Republic of China and International Law* (Princeton, N.J.: Princeton University Press, 1970); and Samuel S. Kim, *China, the United Nations, and World Order* (Princeton, N.J.: Princeton University Press, 1979), ch. 8. On the attitudes of Third World states, see R. P. Anand, *New States and International Law* (Delhi, Kans.: University of Kansas Publishing House, 1972); and Adda B. Bozeman, *The Future of Law in a Multicultural World* (Princeton, N.J.: Princeton University Press, 1971).

Among the works that deal generally with the relationship between international law and international politics, see William D. Coplin, "International Law and Assumptions about the State System," *World Politics*, 17 (July 1965), pp. 615–634; Louis Henkin, *How Nations Behave*, 2nd ed. (New York: Columbia University Press, 1971); Karl W. Deutsch and Stanley Hoffmann, eds., *The Relevance of International Law* (Garden City, N.Y.: Doubleday, 1971), especially pp. 177–202; and Hedley Bull, *The Anarchical Society: A Study of Order in World Politics* (New York: Columbia University Press, 1977).

Several case studies exploring the operation of international law in various historical situations are available, including Abram Chayes, *The Cuban Missile Crisis* (New York: Oxford University Press, 1974); Lawrence Scheinman and David Wilkinson, eds., *International Law and Political Crisis* (Boston: Little, Brown, 1968); and Richard B. Finnegan *et al.*, *Law and Politics in the International System: Case Studies in Conflict Resolution* (Washington, D.C.: University Press of America, 1979). Discussions of specific international legal cases and issues can also be found in numerous articles appearing in the *American Journal of International Law*.

International Organizations: Links Between Governments and Between Peoples

Item: Of the top hundred economic units in the world, almost half are corporations, not countries.[1]

Item: It is projected that by the year 2000, there will be 855 IGOs and 9600 NGOs in the world, compared to some 200 nation-states.[2]

Item: The European Economic Community maintains diplomatic missions in several countries, and more than ninety diplomatic missions have been established by nonmember countries in Brussels, the Community's headquarters.[3]

The increased status that lawyers and statesmen have recently accorded nonstate actors in the international *legal* system has coincided with the increased attention that scholars have given those actors as distinctive elements in the international *political* system. Echoing some general observations we offered in Part I, one writer notes that "the state-centered view of world affairs, the interstate model which still enjoys so much popularity in the study of international relations, has now become too simplistic," mainly because "nation-states are not the only actors on the world scene. [In addition to subnational and other actors] some NGOs probably have more power and influence in their respective fields than some of the smaller nation-states. The same applies to several IGOs and undoubtedly to many multinational business enterprises which have more employees and a larger production output than most countries."[4] In this chapter, we will look at "IGOs" and "NGOs"—in common parlance, *international organizations*—and attempt to show how they fit into the overall equation of world politics.

Clearly, international organizations have proliferated greatly in recent times, as was documented in our historical treatment of the development of the international system. There is also no questioning the fact that several international organizations have made valuable contributions to global problem solving. For example, it is an international organization that has been responsible for virtually eradicating smallpox, once one of humanity's most prevalent scourges; another international organization has made it possible for airplanes to fly readily from one country to another despite the potential language barriers between airport control tower personnel and pilots seeking landing permission; and still another international organization permits over 7 billion pieces of mail to flow across national boundaries each year with a minimum of disruption.

However, the significance of international organizations as actors in world politics is still much debated, particularly whether they can be considered as having a life of their own rather than merely being collections of nation-state delegations. As with international law, viewpoints range from the realist perspective that treats international organizations as mere extensions of nation-states or as peripheral to the major power struggles of world politics, to the idealist perspective that envisions international organizations as largely autonomous agents—the possible precursors of a *supranational* government presiding over a world without borders. While the growth of international organizations may be seen as an *integrative* force in human affairs, pulling against the somewhat anarchic, *disintegrative* tendencies of the centuries-old "Westphalian state system," it is open to question how effective such institutions have been in forging world order and whether they can ever expect to displace national sovereignty and national loyalties. Harold Jacobson frames the question nicely when he notes that the idealist perspective

> is vividly, if simplistically, portrayed in the tapestries hung in the *Palais des Nations* in Geneva [the headquarters of the League of Nations in the period between the two world wars, and the frequent site of international conferences today]. They picture international organizations as a stage in the process of humanity combining into ever larger and more stable units for the purpose of governance—first the family, then the tribe, then the city-state, and then the nation—a process which presumably would eventually culminate in the entire world being combined in one political unit. Few if any serious observers would be willing to accept this view so baldly stated as a comprehensive explanation and forecast except in the broadest historical sense and for the most remote future. . . . [However, if] international organizations are not way stations on the route toward the creation of ever larger territorial sovereignties, what then are they?[5]

In order to understand the role of international organizations in contemporary world affairs, and to evaluate the varying claims, we first need to identify the many different types of international organizations that exist today and to describe their major distinguishing characteristics. Not all international organizations look alike, and not all have equal impacts on world politics.

A Typology of International Organizations: IGOs and NGOs

Although the term **international organization** is often equated with the United Nations, it refers to a much larger phenomenon. The United Nations is only one among hundreds of international organizations that come in many different shapes and sizes. In fact, if one defines international organization in the broadest possible sense—i.e., as any group of individuals from at least two different countries that has a formal institutional apparatus that facilitates regular interactions between members across national boundaries—there are literally thousands of such entities in the world. We can classify international organizations according to at least three basic criteria: (1) membership, (2) geographical scope, and (3) functional scope. We will see how the role of international organizations in world politics varies with organizational characteristics.

MEMBERSHIP

The most fundamental basis for categorizing international organizations is in terms of their *membership* characteristics. Some international organizations, labeled **intergovernmental organizations (IGOs),** have *national governments* as members and are created through treaties between states. Other international organizations, labeled **nongovernmental organizations (NGOs),** are generally composed of *private* individuals or groups. Included in the IGO category are such bodies as the United Nations, the World Bank, and the North Atlantic Treaty Organization. Altogether, over 300 IGOs currently exist in the world. Included in the NGO category are such organizations as the International Red Cross, the Baptist World Alliance, the International Confederation of Midwives, and the International Planned Parenthood Association. The *Yearbook of*

Table 10.1

INTERNATIONAL INTERGOVERNMENTAL ORGANIZATIONS: A SAMPLER

Organization	Headquarters
African Groundnut Council	Lagos, Nigeria
Arab Postal Union	Cairo, Egypt
Association of Southeast Asian Nations	Djakarta, Indonesia
Council for Mutual Economic Assistance	Moscow, USSR
European Economic Community	Brussels, Belgium
Food and Agriculture Organization	Rome, Italy
Inter-American Tropical Tuna Commission	La Jolla, Calif.
International Bank for Reconstruction and Development (World Bank)	Washington, D.C.
International Labor Organization	Geneva, Switzerland
International Red Locust Control Organization for Central and Southern Africa	Mbala, Zambia
International Telecommunications Satellite Organization	Washington, D.C.
Latin American Free Trade Association	Montevideo, Uruguay
North Atlantic Treaty Organization	Brussels, Belgium
Organization of African Unity	Addis Ababa, Ethiopia
Organization of American States	Washington, D.C.
Organization of Petroleum Exporting Countries	Vienna, Austria
Union of Banana Exporting Countries	Panama City, Panama
UN Educational, Scientific, and Cultural Organization	Paris, France
United Nations	New York, N.Y.
Warsaw Treaty Organization	Moscow, USSR
World Health Organization	Geneva, Switzerland

Source: Yearbook of International Organizations, 19th ed. (Brussels: Union of International Associations, 1981).

International Organizations, the most comprehensive and authoritative source of information on international organizations, counts over 3,000 NGOs in the world, ten times the number of IGOs. Not included in the *Yearbook* are multinational corporations and transnational revolutionary groups, which are special variants of nongovernmental organizations.[6] See Tables 10.1 and 10.2 for listings of just a few of the IGOs and NGOs in the world.

Several organizations do not fall neatly into the intergovernmental or nongovernmental categories. For example, the International Labor Organization (ILO), an IGO, is composed predominantly of governments but also provides for labor union and employer group representation as well; similarly, the International Telecommunications Satellite Organization (INTELSAT), through which over half of the world's transoceanic telecommunication services are furnished, is an IGO in which business enterprises are members along with governments. On the other hand, the International Criminal Police Organization (INTERPOL), an association of official police agencies from more than 100 countries organized to facilitate worldwide cooperation in fighting

Table 10.2
INTERNATIONAL NONGOVERNMENTAL ORGANIZATIONS: A SAMPLER

Organization	Headquarters
Afro-Asian Peoples' Solidarity Organization	Cairo, Egypt
Amnesty International	London, England
Arab Lawyers Union	Cairo, Egypt
European Broadcasting Union	Geneva, Switzerland
International Air Transport Association	Geneva, Switzerland
International Alliance of Women	London, England
International Chamber of Commerce	Paris, France
International Committee of the Red Cross	Geneva, Switzerland
International Confederation of Accordionists	Surrey, England
International Confederation of Free Trade Unions	Brussels, Belgium
International Council of Scientific Unions	Paris, France
International Criminal Police Organization	Paris, France
International Federation of Air Line Pilots Associations	London, England
International Olympic Committee	Lausanne, Switzerland
International Political Science Association	Brussels, Belgium
International Union Against the Venereal Diseases and the Treponematoses	London, England
Nordic Association of Advertising Agencies	Oslo, Norway
Salvation Army	London, England
World Council of Churches	New York, N.Y.
World Federation of Master Tailors	Paris, France
World Federation of United Nations Associations	New York, N.Y.

Source: Yearbook of International Organizations, 19th ed. (Brussels: Union of International Associations, 1981).

crime, is technically considered an NGO even though its members are governmental bodies. Distinctions can be further complicated by the fact that in many countries today, communist and noncommunist alike, the line between the "public" or "governmental" sector and the "private" or "nongovernmental" sector can be quite blurred. The European Broadcasting Union and the International Air Transport Association are considered NGOs even though most of the members are state-owned radio and television companies in the first case and state-owned airlines in the second case. While the League of Red Cross Societies is an NGO, the USSR chapter—the Soviet Red Cross Alliance—is essentially an arm of the Soviet government; and even the American Red Cross is a quasi-public agency chartered by the U.S. Congress. As we will see, some NGOs and their constituent units are less subject to governmental control than others. Given the difficulty at times in ascertaining the governmental or nongovernmental character of an organization's membership, the ultimate criterion relied on is whether or not it came into being through a formal intergovernmental agreement; if it was created by a treaty, it is an IGO.

GEOGRAPHICAL SCOPE

As Tables 10.1 and 10.2 suggest, another important dimension on which international organizations differ is *geographical scope*. Although there is a common tendency to think of IGOs in *global* terms, along the lines of the United Nations, only roughly one third of all IGOs can be considered truly global, drawing their members from every region in the world. The vast majority of IGOs are primarily *regional* in scope, and in some cases subregional or even bilateral. Regionalism, then, has been a more powerful force than globalism in the development of intergovernmental organizations,[7] which is perhaps not surprising given the tendency for states to have more intense ties at the regional level than the global level, as well as the generally greater ease and lesser expense of regional organizational participation. Such intergovernmental organizations as military alliances and customs unions in particular are found at the regional rather than the global level.

Not all regions are equally represented in the IGO network. Africa, Asia, and Latin America tend to be underrepresented. As noted earlier (in Table 4.2), sixteen of the twenty states that belong to the greatest number of IGOs are found in either Western Europe or North America (along with Australia and Japan); the Europeans, in particular, occupy the top ten spots, led by Denmark.[8] The Western European nations' dominance in IGO membership is owed not only to their heavy participation in global IGOs but, more importantly, to the proliferation of regional IGOs in that part of the world in the 1950s and 1960s related to the formation of the European Community. Although less developed countries may belong to several IGOs and rely on them for diplomatic contacts, the countries with the smallest number of IGO memberships overall tend to be found in Africa and Asia, this being a function primarily of their relatively young age and financial limitations.

A similar pattern can be seen in the NGO network. Only about one fourth of the web of 3,000 NGOs are global. Nearly one fourth of all NGOs are confined to the European region alone, again a factor related to the development of the European Community.[9] Even more than the IGO network, the NGO network draws its members overwhelmingly from Western, developed countries. Fuller participation in the NGO network by Third World countries is inhibited by economic factors, while greater participation by the developed Communist countries is inhibited by political factors (namely, governmental restrictions, the continued East-West rivalry, and the ideological problems entailed by the involvement of such countries in "private" associations). Still, both Second World and Third World countries are gradually being drawn into the web of NGO relationships. Although the Soviets do not belong to the International Chamber of Commerce, Soviet citizens are members of some 200 NGOs.[10]

As with the IGO–NGO distinction, the global-regional distinction is not always clear-cut. Many international organizations, although not global in scope, do draw their members from more than one region. For example, the Organization of Petroleum Exporting Countries (OPEC) includes members from almost every region of the world, excluding only North America and Europe (even though its operational headquarters are in Vienna); the North Atlantic Treaty Organization (NATO) stretches from Canada and the United States to Turkey; the Council on Mutual Economic Assistance (COMECON), while largely an Eastern European and Soviet institution, includes Cuba, Vietnam, and Mongolia as members. As the OPEC example illustrates, membership in many international organizations may be limited not so much by geographical criteria as by political or economic criteria. The main point here, however, is that many international organizations are conceived as "limited membership" institutions, while others are open to any and all countries; only the latter truly approximate "universal" organizations.

FUNCTIONAL SCOPE

Referring again to Tables 10.1 and 10.2, one can discern that international organizations are established to serve a great variety of purposes, some of which seem rather trivial and others more significant. In terms of *functional scope*, some international organizations are general, *multipurpose* organizations, while others are characterized by specific, *limited purposes*. In the case of both IGOs and NGOs, however, limited purpose organizations far outnumber multipurpose ones.

Among IGOs, a few institutions such as the United Nations, the Organization of American States (OAS), and the Organization of African Unity (OAU) have mandates to deal with a broad range of political, economic, and social concerns of members. Most IGOs have more narrow, specialized functions, either military (e.g., NATO), economic (e.g., the European Economic Community), social and cultural (e.g., the United Nations Educational, Scientific, and Cultural Organization), or technical (e.g., the World Health Organization). Economic organizations constitute the largest single category, accounting for more than half of all IGOs.[11] NGOs tend by nature to be single-purpose organizations even more than IGOs, given the fact that nongovernmental organizations ordinarily serve a clientele that shares specialized interests, either economic, religious, social, cultural, educational, or professional. The largest numbers of NGOs are found in the areas of commerce and industry as well as health and medicine.[12]

Trying to classify international organizations according to function can also be complicated. For example, NATO has increasingly become involved in a host of economic, scientific, and technological activities even though it was conceived solely as a military alliance and retains that role as its overriding mission. The European Economic Community (EEC) has become involved in so many aspects of Western European life that calling it a limited-purpose economic organization hardly does it justice. As with the other key dimensions of international organizations, fitting particular institutions into particular pigeonholes on the functional dimension is less important than knowing what the various pigeonholes look like. Figure 10.1 visually summarizes the classification scheme we have presented and includes examples in each category.

The Causes and Effects of International Organization

International organizations require expenditures of money and effort to create and maintain. They exist not for their own sake but presumably because they serve certain purposes, as noted in our discussion of functional scope. Although IGOs and NGOs each have a distinct logic, the common thread running through both types of organizations is the presence of a set of concerns that transcend national frontiers. If IGOs are a bridge between governments, NGOs are a bridge between peoples. Generally speaking, IGOs are considered more important actors on the world stage than NGOs, since IGOs tend to be of more direct interest to national governments. Admittedly, NGOs like the International Confederation of Accordionists and the World Federation of Master Tailors are not likely to alter the course of world affairs. However, certain nongovernmental organizations, such as the Roman Catholic Church, multinational corporations like Exxon or General Motors, and revolutionary groups like the Palestine Liberation Organization, can have significant impact

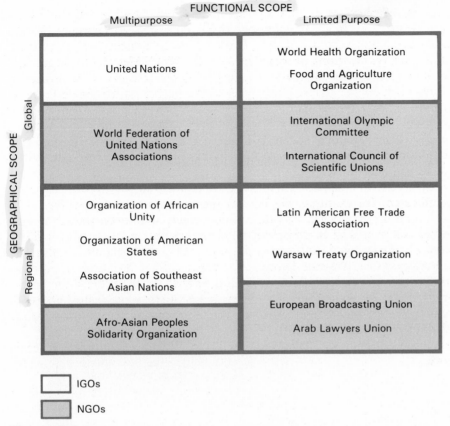

Figure 10.1
THE BASIC TYPES OF INTERNATIONAL ORGANIZATIONS (IGOs and NGOs)

insofar as they are often in a position to act independently of national governments in shaping major events in the international arena.

THE LOGIC OF NGOs

Transnational relations, interactions between private individuals and groups across national boundaries, have existed since the very beginnings of the nation-state system; consider the early wanderings of explorers, missionaries, spice merchants, and slave traders to distant corners of the earth. Nevertheless, it was not until the improved communications and transportation technology that accompanied industrialization in the nineteenth century that large numbers of people were able to interact more readily across national boundaries. Industrialization also created specialized economic and commercial groups for whom national frontiers were somewhat artificial and irrelevant barriers;

not only business executives but also labor union activists, scientists, artists, members of fraternal societies, and professionals of various stripes were added to the ranks of transnational actors. James Field describes the emergence of the "new tribe" of transnational actors:

> Among the humanitarians there developed an international peace movement and international campaigns for the abolition of . . . slavery, for women's rights, and for temperance. Working class groups supported the international labor movement, international socialism. . . . From the managers there came a network of private [agreements] . . . trusts, cartels, and the like—designed to regulate competition abroad as well as at home.
>
> In much of this activity, of course, private and public sectors found themselves intertwined; governments would intermeddle, and private groups would seek governmental aid. Among the actors, governments were . . . the most visible, and the easiest to watch and describe. But while the apparatus of the state continued to grow throughout the period, and particularly from the latter part of the nineteenth century, its role . . . was less one of initiating policy than of responding to conditions produced by nongovernmental factors whose influence increasingly transcended national boundaries.[13]

As transnational interactions—travel, mail exchanges, and other flows—expanded during the nineteenth and twentieth centuries, these ties increasingly became *institutionalized* in the form of nongovernmental organizations designed to provide more durable bonds between transnational actors. The number of NGOs grew from only five in 1850 to 330 by 1914, 730 by 1939, 2,300 by 1970, to the present level of over 3,000.[14] As one would expect, NGO growth has been minimal during major wars and has tended to spurt dramatically after wars, notably after World War II. In many cases, governments themselves have encouraged the creation of NGOs, especially those involving cultural exchanges. The same forces that have contributed to NGO growth in the past—technological developments, industrialization, and urbanization—are likely to continue to operate in the future, even though national governments may well respond by placing increasing restrictions on the transnational activity of their citizenry if threatened by loss of control of some aspect of national policy.

If the reasons that nongovernmental organizations exist are fairly simple and obvious to analyze, assessing the effects of such institutions is more difficult. NGOs are hypothesized to have a number of impacts on world politics. Perhaps the most indirect and subtle impact—and potentially the deepest—has been suggested by Robert Angell in a major empirical study of "transnational participation."[15] Examining hundreds of transnational interactions, Angell concluded that sustained exposure to other peoples and cultures through NGO involvement tends to produce a more cosmopolitan, less nationalistic outlook in participants. If the latter are business executives or other elites having access to high-level foreign policymakers at home, they can promote more accommodative foreign policies and greater understanding among governments themselves; in other words, "international socialization" experienced by private individuals is gradually transferrable to national governments.

However, many scholars consider the connection between NGO participation and foreign policy behavior a weak one, arguing that the flow of influence in the foreign policy process is more complicated than the paragraph above might suggest and that persons who become *too* cosmopolitan in their world view may well lose access to and political effectiveness with their governmental leaders. There is some question, also, about the extent to which business executives and other types of transnational actors are capable of truly shedding their national identity and thinking in larger terms; the fact is that several NGOs are dominated by the citizens, if not the government, of one country. Related to this point, even Angell acknowledges that certain kinds of transnational organizations (e.g., multinational corporations or religious movements) can foster resentment and tension rather than empathy and harmony among different peoples. Familiarity, in other words, can breed contempt, although on balance Angell finds that transnational relations represent "peace on the march."

A second NGO impact is based on the special consultative status that many NGOs have been granted in regional and global IGOs, enabling them to have input into the latter's decision making. Hundreds of NGOs are permitted direct involvement in the activities of several UN agencies, sharing information and advancing proposals as part of a web of governmental, intergovernmental, and nongovernmental efforts aimed at global problem solving. For example, the International Council of Scientific Unions (ICSU), an NGO whose members include the main scientific academies and national research councils in the physical sciences in sixty countries, was responsible for involving the UN in the International Geophysical Year and the International Year of the Quiet Sun; as one writer notes, "Its committees on oceanic research, antarctic research, space research, water research, and science and technology in developing countries all deal with politically significant and sensitive subject areas."[16] The consultative status of NGOs usually allows them to exercise only limited influence over the actual decisions reached by IGOs, although their lobbying efforts can be extremely effective in certain cases. Most notable in this regard are the many transnational agricultural, labor, and manufacturing interest groups that have been organized to promote the concerns of their members in dealing with government officials in the European Community.

A third impact that NGOs have on world politics is more direct and sizable and has nothing to do with informal socialization or formal consultation processes. This impact, alluded to earlier, is the role of some NGOs as distinct, autonomous actors that compete with and threaten the sovereignty of national governments in areas of great international significance. In some cases, the part played by NGOs in the international political system can be quite visible—for example, the role of the Palestine Liberation Organization in affecting tensions between Israel and other Middle Eastern states, of the multinational oil companies in influencing world energy politics, and of the International Olympic Committee in sidestepping the U.S.-Soviet confrontation over Afghanistan and the 1980 Moscow Olympic Games. In other instances, NGOs might have a lower profile but nonetheless significant implications for world politics—for example, the role of the International Federation of Airline Pilots Associations in pressuring governments to adopt stronger air safety and anti-skyjacking measures, or the role played by a handful of agribusiness corporations in determining the world distribution of food and possibly the success or failure of government-imposed grain embargoes. Although, more often than not, governments might "win confrontations" with transnational actors—governments could nationalize foreign corporate assets, the Arab states could conceivably ignore or crush the PLO if they so desired, and so forth—"more relevant than 'who wins' direct confrontations are the new kinds of bargains, coalitions, and alliances being formed between transnational actors and between these actors and segments of governments and [intergovernmental] organizations."[17] As in the case of the PLO, some bargains and coalitions consist of an NGO playing one government off against another in order to advance its particular goals.

The multinational corporation, in particular, is seen by some observers as an alternative form of human organization to the nation-state, pursuing its own objectives apart from those of any national government and—for better or for worse—undermining (or at least confusing) traditional notions of national interest, citizenship, and patriotism. (Note, for example, the curious role of Toyota, the Japanese car manufacturer, as the leading corporate financial sponsor of the 1980 U.S. Olympic Team's training.) We will reserve judgment on the implications of the multinational corporation until Chapter 13, when we focus on its role in the international economy. Multinational corporations, like other NGOs, can have both positive and negative impacts in terms of world order.

THE LOGIC OF IGOs

IGO growth has always lagged behind NGO growth, no doubt due to the simple fact that people have outnumbered governments as potential candidates for forming international organizations and, also, that IGOs have tended to entail a somewhat greater investment of resources. As with NGOs, IGO growth historically has been least pronounced during major wars and most pronounced after major wars, when states normally seek to resurrect some semblance of world order. The network of IGOs has expanded from less than ten in 1870 to almost 50 by 1914, to some 100 by 1945, to more than 200 by 1970, to over 300 today.[18] The substantial growth of IGOs after World War II reflects the impetus of the UN in spawning several other global organizations as part of the UN system, although IGO growth has had even more momentum at the regional level.

States today form intergovernmental organizations for the same practical reasons that have always provided the rationale behind IGOs, i.e., problems exist that either cannot be handled unilaterally within the capabilities of a single state or can be dealt with more efficiently through collaboration with others. Some problems may involve only two states and, hence, may call for merely a two-member IGO (e.g., the St. Lawrence Seaway Authority established by the United States and Canada), while other problems may be defined as requiring regional or global approaches. In a given problem area, the first impulse of governments is not to create an organization but to try to deal with the situation simply through treaties or informal *ad hoc* arrangements, which are less costly. However, if a problem is viewed as an ongoing one, more elaborate collaborative machinery may be found necessary and an intergovernmental organization may be born.

It should be stressed that although IGOs are generally conceived to be instruments of *cooperation*, they also inevitably involve *conflict* and, indeed, can be thought of as forums for managing interstate disagreements as well as mutual problem solving. In fact, member states vie for control of IGOs as they attempt to use international organizations partly as tools for legitimizing various national policies.

The problems that give rise to IGOs can be of the **high politics** or **low politics** variety. "High politics" refers to those issues involving the most crucial and the most controversial interests of states (especially military-security issues); "low politics" refers to those issues that are relatively narrow, technical, and noncontroversial (for example, setting international mail rates, sharing weather forecasting data or cancer research findings, or managing river basins). Although the distinction between "high politics" and "low politics" is a useful one, several issue-areas fall somewhere in between (e.g., regulation of international news information and satellite broadcasting services, reduction of tariff barriers, or dissemination of peaceful nuclear technology). Moreover, even in seemingly low politics areas, issues can become highly politicized, such as the furor raised by the United States over what it felt was growing Marxist influence in the International Labor Organization's activities in the field of worker-management relations, leading to a two-year American withdrawal from the ILO in 1977. The United States, along with Britain, also withdrew from the UN Educational, Scientific, and Cultural Organization (UNESCO) in the 1980s, complaining about not only excessive Marxist influence in the organization's top leadership but also financial mismanagement. In the contemporary era in particular, as military-security, economic, and other issues are becoming more and more intertwined, the high politics-low politics distinction is becoming increasingly blurred.

The typical IGO has at least a plenary assembly or conference in which all member governments discuss and vote on policies, along with a secretariat or bureau that is responsible for implementing decisions and running the organization's administrative apparatus. However, IGOs differ considerably in the amount of decision-making power that states vest in the organization. A few IGOs approach a **supranational** decision-making model, i.e., the organization is empowered to make decisions that are binding on the entire membership, requiring all member states to abide by the collective will no matter whether they are on the winning or losing side of a roll call vote. Far more IGOs, though, are at the opposite extreme, empowered by member states merely to offer recommendations or resolutions of an advisory nature that each individual national government is free to accept or disregard as it sees fit. Other IGOs fall somewhere in between, respecting the sovereignty of individual members in most organizational matters but evidencing a degree of supranationalism in certain areas.

States have generally been more willing to cooperate and entrust decision-making competence in organizations having narrow, well-defined goals rather than in organizations having broader, more open-ended missions. The first IGOs—the Central Commission for the Navigation of the Rhine created in 1815, the European Commission for the Control of the Danube created in 1856, and the International Telegraph Union and Universal Postal Union created a few years later—all were designed to deal with rather specific, technical matters. The ITU and UPU exist to this day as part of the UN system, along with many other limited purpose organizations, which together comprise the Specialized Agencies of the United Nations. These organizations collect and disseminate information, administer programs, and help to develop rules governing relations between states. Several specific purpose organizations do approximate the supranational model in some respects. In the case of UPU and some other organizations, governments have even allowed officials in IGO bureaucracies ("technocrats") to exercise considerable discretion in making and implementing policies on behalf of the entire membership.[19] These IGOs can be said to have a direct impact in several fields of international activity, including health, transportation, education, social welfare, and communications.

The twentieth century has also witnessed the development of multipurpose IGOs designed to deal with a broad range of political concerns, including the "big" questions of war and peace. In addition to the United Nations at the global level, such institutions as the Organization of American States, the Organization of African Unity, the Arab League, and the Association of Southeast Asian Nations have been conceived as "regional security organizations" designed to facilitate general cooperation and peaceful settlement of disputes among their members (and in some cases, even eventual political unification). Although these general purpose IGOs potentially could have far greater impact than the specific purpose IGOs, governments have been much less willing to entrust these organizations with any degree of supranational decision-making competence, given the more volatile nature of the issues that can arise in such forums. Nevertheless, these regional organizations have often played a useful role in preventing or resolving violent conflict between states, as in the case of the "football war" between El Salvador and Honduras in 1969, when the OAS instituted a cease-fire to stop hostilities related to a football match riot and reports of Honduran atrocities against Salvadorans.[20] One scholar, examining nineteen cases of OAS, OAU, and Arab League involvement in regional conflicts, found that these organizations, overall, "helped to abate conflicts among members in more than half of the cases" and "helped to provide a permanent settlement in a third of the cases."[21] We will discuss the UN role in the peacekeeping field later in the chapter.

Many of the same observers who argue that NGOs have an "international socialization" effect on *private* citizens also argue that IGOs have a similar effect on *public* officials who participate in international organizations; one study found, for example, that members of the U.S. Congress who served on the American delegation to the United Nations tended to become more attentive to and supportive of the United Nations in their subsequent congressional speeches and voting behavior.[22] The **functionalist school** of international relations scholars hypothesizes that as states collaborate and surrender some measure of sovereignty to IGOs in low politics issue-areas, their governments will learn *habits* of cooperation that will slowly induce further collaboration and surrender of sovereignty in high politics areas, all leading ultimately to a possible supranational community (i.e., a regional or world government.)[23] In other words, willingness to entrust IGOs with power to make decisions regarding, say, locust control may be the beginning of a process that could eventually "spill over" into the realm of arms control. Some functionalist theorists (called **neofunctionalists**) emphasize that certain sectors of intergovernmental cooperation are more likely candidates for **spillover** than others because they create not only a desire but a need for ever more ambitious cooperation across issue-areas. (An example might be a group of countries discovering that the benefits they have derived from sharing a common fishing ground cannot be sustained without additional collaboration in environmental policymaking pertaining to ocean pollution.)[24]

A number of scholars have criticized functionalist theory, however, noting that some collaborative experiences can be painful and counterproductive, that politics can never be completely removed from even the most seemingly apolitical, technical set of issues, and—most importantly—that there are obvious limits to the extent to which national governments can be expected to relinquish political power to a higher authority in areas that bear on their very survival. Although intergovernmental cooperation in one field might well breed cooperation in other fields, the available evidence indicates that the "spill-over" process does not lead inexorably to supranationalism.[25] Still, even if there is little evidence to support functionalist expectations about supranationalism, there is evidence to support the more modest functionalist view that "entanglement in a web of IGOs would tend to make states less bellicose"; the latter proposition is at least somewhat supported by a recent study which found that the growth of IGOs, particularly since World War II, has coincided with a relative decline in the number of interstate wars.[26]

In general, IGOs thus play a role both as *arenas* for interstate conflict and cooperation and as *actors* in their own right that affect state behavior and outcomes in world politics. In the remainder of this chapter, we will focus on two specific IGOs, the United Nations at the global level and the European Community at the regional level. These institutions are clearly among the most important intergovernmental organizations in the world today, and have a variety of impacts on world affairs.

Global Intergovernmental Organizations: The United Nations and the UN System

After each of the two catastrophic wars in this century, the participants came together at a peace conference, vowed "never again," and proceeded to create a global organization whose primary mission was to preserve the peace. As one would expect, the *winners* were the chief architects of these organizations, the **League of Nations** after World War I and the **United Nations** after World War II. The League set the precedent of a large assembly of nations, which was reincarnated in the UN General Assembly. In creating a peace organization, the winners were also creating an organization designed to promote their own interests in maintaining the postwar status quo as much as possible. The UN, like the League, was founded upon the twentieth-century concept of **collective security,** which envisioned the weight of the entire international community—through the mobilization of the military forces of all the members of a global organization—being thrown against any state intent on committing aggression and upsetting the existing order. Like the founders of the League, the founders of the UN expected that collective security would be implemented primarily through the leadership of a handful of important states. This concept thus resembled in some ways the "concert of great powers" approach to world order borrowed from the nineteenth-century Concert of Europe.

In the case of the United Nations, the "Big Five"—the United States, the Soviet Union, the United Kingdom, France, and China—assigned themselves a special role in 1945 as the "world's policemen" under the new UN Charter. The initial hope was that great-power unity would enable the United Nations to function more successfully than its predecessor, which had been hampered by the absence of several major countries from its membership roster. Although most of the major powers in 1945 were represented in the United Nations, assumptions about great-power cooperation quickly faded as the Cold War between the U.S.-led Western bloc and the Soviet-led Eastern bloc began before the ink had dried on the UN Charter. From the start, the United Nations became a microcosm of world politics, with developments within the institution tending to mirror battles and other happenings occurring outside its walls. We briefly trace the evolution of the United Nations below, in terms of both its structure and activities.

STRUCTURE AND ACTIVITIES

Figure 10.2 is an organization chart of the United Nations and its affiliated agencies that together comprise the "UN system." As the chart indicates, there is a bewildering array of councils, commissions, committees, and assorted other bodies, which can be confusing not only for the casual observer but also for policymakers seeking to understand the workings of the United Nations. As the chart shows, also, the UN is involved in a host of concerns in addition to war and peace.

Under the UN Charter, the **Security Council** was given primary responsibility in the area of peace and security. Chapter VII of the Charter provided that, should **peaceful settlement** procedures (such as mediation and adjudication) under Chapter VI fail, the Council would be empowered to adopt military and economic sanctions on behalf of the UN membership against any nations engaging in actions that constituted a "threat to the peace." Such sanctions were to be the basis for the collective security role of the United Nations, a role that at least on paper was buttressed by far more elaborate machinery than had ever been considered by the League. The powers granted the Security Council in this area were far greater than the powers given any other UN organ, since the Council could theoretically take decisions under Chapter VII that would be *binding* on *all* UN members. However, only once— during the Korean conflict in 1950—have the collective security provisions of Chapter VII actually been used to organize a UN military force against an aggressor. A standing UN army, with contingents drawn from the armed forces of member states and ready to be deployed quickly as needed, was originally provided for in Chapter VII but has never materialized, due mostly to U.S.-Soviet disagreement.

Since 1945, the Security Council has been expanded from eleven members to its present membership of fifteen. This includes the aforementioned Big Five, who were accorded permanent seats under the UN Charter, along with ten other states serving two-year terms on a rotating basis. (The Chinese seat held by Taiwan was assumed by the People's Republic of China in 1971.) Although many objections have been raised recently about the composition of the Security Council—for example, whether countries like Japan or West Germany are not at least as deserving of permanent seats as the United Kingdom and France, or whether any states should even be accorded special status as permanent members—the present arrangements are likely to continue

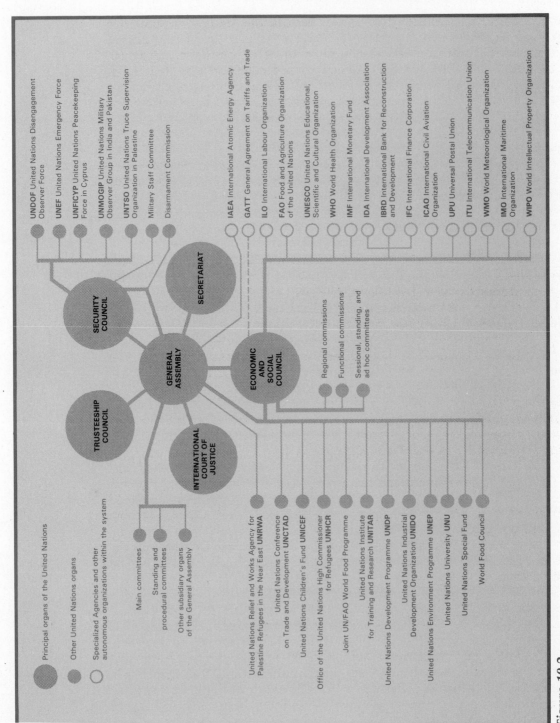

Figure 10.2
THE UNITED NATIONS SYSTEM

for one simple reason: the Charter gives each of the Big Five the power to *veto* any decision taken in regard to collective security operations, Charter amendments, or other substantive matters requiring Security Council approval.

In other words, the Security Council cannot take decisions, binding or otherwise, unless the permanent members are in unanimous agreement (along with at least four other votes needed for passage of a Council resolution). Hence, the veto power gives each permanent member the ability to block a move to oust it from the Security Council. More importantly, the veto enables any permanent member to paralyze Council efforts to enforce the collective security provisions of Chapter VII or to take any other actions that might be objectionable to one of the Big Five. Although the veto rule has been widely criticized, it was inserted in the UN Charter not only to protect the interests of the major powers but also to preserve the organization, ensuring that no key national actor would feel threatened by the organization and be impelled to walk out.

Perhaps no single feature of the UN decision-making apparatus has been more conspicuous than the veto privilege enjoyed by the permanent members of the Security Council. For a long time, the Soviet Union was accused of being particularly obstructionist in its frequent use of the veto to thwart UN action. The Soviet Union cast more than 100 vetoes between 1945 and 1970, while the United States did not use the veto at all until 1970 (when it vetoed a resolution by the Security Council to impose economic sanctions on Rhodesia and South Africa for their white minority government policies against blacks). However, since 1970, the United States has cast more than fifty vetoes (against resolutions dealing with southern Africa, the Middle East, and the admission of Vietnam and Angola into the UN), compared with fewer than twenty vetoes by the Soviet Union.[27] The main explanation for this shift is that the United States found it superfluous in the early postwar period to use its veto power since the composition of the Security Council then was predominantly pro-Western and the Soviets had trouble mustering the necessary majority of votes to pass any resolutions; as the postwar period progressed, however, the temporary seats on the Security Council became increasingly occupied by nonaligned Third World states, thus undermining U.S. control of the Council and forcing the United States to behave as the Soviets had behaved when confronted with objectionable action by the organization.

The gradual loss of American control in the Security Council has been symptomatic of a more general decline of American influence in the United Nations as a whole, which has occurred as the decolonialization process has brought more and more Third World states into the United Nations. Nowhere has the decline of U.S. influence been more in evidence than in the **General Assembly,** the main deliberative body in which the entire UN membership is represented and which is authorized by the Charter to deal with a broad range of political, economic, and social issues. Resolutions passed by the General

Assembly are *nonbinding* on the members; they are only *recommendations* carrying no legal or other obligations. The General Assembly's main power is therefore merely the power to discuss. However, Assembly resolutions, whether pertaining to a redistribution of the world's wealth from North to South or some other issue, at the very least have symbolic significance and create additional pressures for changes in the international system.

The General Assembly has become the primary forum in which Third World states can articulate and promote their positions on a wide variety of concerns. The Assembly originally had only fifty-one members in 1945, with an overwhelming majority being pro-Western; with the exception of the Latin American states, which were heavily influenced by the United States, the only less developed countries in the world body initially were a handful of countries from North Africa and South Asia. By 1980, there were more than 150 members in the General Assembly, with more than 100 of these being less developed countries—often at loggerheads with the United States. Citing evidence of the erosion of U.S. influence in the General Assembly, one scholar notes that the United States found itself on the winning side of General Assembly roll call votes 74 percent of the time between 1946 and 1950, a figure that steadily declined to 35 percent by the mid-1970s.[28] Although the Soviet Union has fared better than the United States recently in the General Assembly, being on the winning side far more often, both countries have grown increasingly wary of Third World interests and votes dominating the General Assembly through the "tyranny of the majority." When the United States was in a position to dominate the General Assembly with its allies in the early postwar period, few Americans spoke of a "tyranny of the majority." Clearly, such criticism from the United States today is hypocritical, although it is understandable given the fact that the United States is the single biggest financial supporter of the United Nations, paying 25 percent of the annual UN budget (compared with only 12 percent for the Soviet Union and less than 1 percent for most member states).

The ranks of the Third World in the United Nations have been swelled in recent years by the addition of such mini-states as Vanuatu, Belize, and Antigua and Barbuda (each having a population of under 100,000 upon their admission in 1981). The admission of so many new members, especially of the mini-state variety, has caused renewed controversy about General Assembly voting procedures. As the UN Charter stipulates, voting in the General Assembly is based on majority rule (a two thirds majority required for "important" questions), with *each state having one vote*. Hence, a country like Seychelles with 75,000 people possesses the same voting power in the General Assembly as the People's Republic of China with 1 billion people. The "one state–one vote" principle is based on the sacred notion of sovereign *equality* among nations. Critics have argued, however, that the voting formula reflects neither power realities nor democratic principles of representation ("one person–one vote") nor fairness in terms of who pays the organization's

The United Nations General Assembly in session, 1982.

bills. The absurdity lies in the fact that a two thirds majority coalition can be formed in the General Assembly by 107 states representing only 8 percent of the world's total population and an even smaller percentage of UN budget contributions. Although various weighted voting schemes based on population or other criteria have been proposed, they are politically controversial and unlikely to replace the current formula in the near future. However, led by the United States, pressures have been increasing to force the General Assembly to be more responsive to the concerns of the major financial supporters, who have threatened to withhold funds if the UN does not change certain practices and programs.

The **Economic and Social Council (ECOSOC)** is a 54-member UN organ charged with offering recommendations, issuing reports, organizing conferences, and coordinating the activities of various UN agencies in the economic and social field. In performing these tasks, ECOSOC works closely with the General Assembly. Much of its work is carried out through five regional economic commissions (for Europe, the Pacific, Latin America, Africa, and

Western Asia) and six functional commissions (including, for example, commissions on population, the status of women, and narcotic drugs).

The **Trusteeship Council,** presently consisting of the five permanent members of the Security Council, has decreased in importance over the years, largely being a victim of its own success in fulfilling the Charter's intention that it preside over the dismantling of colonial empires. Almost all colonial possessions administered as "trust territories" by the British, French, Dutch, and others after 1945 have achieved independence, so that there is little work left for the Council to do. Although less than 1 percent of humanity still lives under colonial rule today, colonialism remains a live issue for those still experiencing it. A few significant colonial conflicts remain, notably the dispute over Namibia (formerly South-West Africa), where South Africa continues to exercise control over a "trust" territory despite a war for independence being fought by the black majority supported by other African states.

The **Secretariat** is the administrative arm of the United Nations. It is headed by a **Secretary-General** whom the Charter designates as "the chief administrative officer of the Organization." The United Nations has had five Secretaries-General to date: Trygve Lie of Norway (1946–1952), Dag Hammarskjold of Sweden (1953–1961), U Thant of Burma (1961–1971), Kurt Waldheim of Austria (1972–1982), and Javier Pérez de Cuéllar of Peru, appointed in 1982. Before his death in an airplane crash while on a UN mission to the Congo, Hammarskjold had elevated the Secretary-General post to one of considerable importance, going beyond mere administrative duties and using Article 99 of the UN Charter as justification for taking political initiatives involving the United Nations in peacekeeping operations. (Article 99 states that "the Secretary-General may bring to the attention of the Security Council any matter which in his opinion may threaten the maintenance of peace and security.") However, Hammarskjold's successors have adopted a much lower profile and have largely confined themselves to a caretaker role of running the day-to-day administrative apparatus of the organization, except for occasionally engaging in "good offices" and other forms of third-party mediation of disputes.

For any candidate aspiring to be Secretary-General or for an incumbent seeking to retain the job, there are considerable pressures to avoid controversy, owing to the selection process. The Secretary-General is selected through nomination by the Security Council, and then election by a majority of the General Assembly for a five-year term subject to possible renewal. Hence, the candidate must be someone who is innocuous enough to be acceptable to all five permanent Council members as well as the bulk of the Assembly membership. It was Hammarskjold's penchant for controversy that angered the Soviets and caused them ultimately to demand his replacement with a "troika" arrangement (three-person executive body), a proposal that was withdrawn after his death.

The "international civil service" that the Secretary-General heads consists of some 18,000 staff members—economists, agronomists, planners, and various managerial personnel—drawn from practically every country, with approximately 6000 members working at UN headquarters in New York City and the remainder scattered among UN offices in Geneva, Nairobi, and elsewhere around the world. While the UN Charter stresses that staff appointments are to be made on the basis of "efficiency, competence, and integrity," it also adds that "due regard shall be paid to the importance of recruiting the staff on as wide a geographical basis as possible." While these two criteria are not incompatible, they reflect a built-in contradiction that characterizes the UN Secretariat—it is expected to be an independent body of technocrats whose primary responsibility is to serve impartially the interests and needs of the *UN* organization as a whole, yet who remain citizens of particular countries subject to potential pressures from their *national* governments. Pressures are particularly felt by those UN civil servants, roughly one third of the entire Secretariat, who are on "fixed term" appointments with the United Nations, i.e., are on temporary loan from their government for one- or two-year periods and must then return to their home government; such temporary appointments have been favored by Communist countries for political reasons (in order to retain as much control as possible over their nationals in the UN bureaucracy) and by less developed countries because of a critical shortage of trained specialists at home. However, even countries that allow their citizens to become career civil servants in the United Nations usually screen applicants to ensure that persons recruited to the Secretariat are loyal to the home country. Hence, in performing UN bookkeeping and other services, in staffing the hundreds of field operations mounted by the United Nations, and in facilitating the 5000 meetings held annually under UN sponsorship, the Secretariat acts as an international civil service yet is not completely free of the nationalism found in other UN organs.[29]

One cannot discuss the United Nations, especially its technical activities, without also noting the global **Specialized Agencies** that are affiliated with the organization. There are over a dozen Specialized Agencies, each essentially a separate IGO having its own membership, budget, secretariat, and decision-making machinery apart from the United Nations but also intimately linked to ECOSOC and other UN organs. For example, the aforementioned Universal Postal Union is headquartered in Berne, Switzerland, and includes as members several states that are not members of the United Nations, such as the Vatican, North and South Korea, and Switzerland itself. We will describe these agencies very briefly here, discussing many of them more fully in subsequent chapters.

The **International Labor Organization** (**ILO**), a holdover from the League of Nations, was created to monitor working conditions worldwide and to promote cooperation in improving the general standard of living of the world's workers through the drafting of an international labor code and other activities. The

PROFILE OF A UN SPECIALIZED AGENCY: THE INTERNATIONAL TELECOMMUNICATION UNION

The International Telecommunication Union (ITU) is in a sense the oldest intergovernmental organization to become a part of the UN system, with its roots going back to 1865, when twenty states created the International Telegraph Union and established a headquarters bureau in Berne, Switzerland, which was to operate through World War II. At the same time, the ITU is an organization that finds itself today involved in the most modernistic of concerns, regulating not only international telephone and telegraph traffic but also space satellite broadcasting and transborder flows of computerized data.

The ITU has more than 150 members and is headquartered in Geneva, Switzerland, where it has a General Secretariat run by its own Secretary-General. The supreme body of the ITU is the Plenipotentiary Conference, which meets every five to seven years to set general policy and draft possible revisions in the International Telecommunication Convention. Each state has one vote in the decision-making process, with efforts made to arrive at decisions through consensus as much as possible. Administrative conferences are convened periodically in two telecommunications areas, one dealing with telephone and telegraph communications and the other with radio and other forms of wireless transmission. A smaller Administrative Council consisting of thirty-six members meets more frequently, at least once a year, to oversee implementation of decisions reached by the larger bodies. In addition, there is an International Frequency Registration Board (IFRB) responsible for maintaining a record of all radio frequencies or wavelengths that have been allocated to countries for various uses.

One must realize that commercial radio stations, coast guard shortwave operators, ham radio enthusiasts, space satellite transmitters, microwave oven cooks, and a host of other users share the same seemingly endless but actually limited range of radio frequencies. ITU reserves specific segments of the "radio frequency spectrum" for specific categories of users and requires member states to notify the IFRB of any new frequency assignments made to individual stations. With the proliferation of space satellites put into orbit by developed countries and broadcasting stations established by less developed countries, the spectrum is becoming overcrowded and interference is increasing among users. Less developed countries are concerned that by the time they develop their own space satellites, there will not be any "slots" left for them in the geostationary orbit, a band roughly 23,000 miles above the equator—a preferred band for economic and other reasons—where satellites are fixed relative to the earth's surface.

It is in ITU conferences where bargaining over the allocation of frequency bands among countries occurs.

The highly technical nature of telecommunications can lead one to overlook the high political stakes potentially involved in ITU deliberations. Space satellite technology has become so advanced that there is the possibility one country's broadcasting stations will be able to beam television programs (not only "Sesame Street" but more propagandistic material) directly into the home receiving sets of people in other countries, further increasing the permeability of national boundaries and threatening the sovereignty of national governments. Through "remote sensing" technology, it is already possible for satellites belonging to the United States and other nations to gather detailed information about any country's soil conditions and food production capabilities, the location of raw materials, and other features of the landscape. Although such data can be extremely helpful to less developed countries in anticipating crop shortages and discovering natural resources, those countries are concerned that developed states may not fully share the information and that the eyes in the sky may represent an unwarranted "invasion of privacy." The less developed states are having to rely already on four Western news agencies—AP, UPI, Reuters, and Agence France-Presse—for the bulk of international news stories, transmitted to Third World press rooms via satellite. The ITU, then, has been a central forum in which the battle over the so-called "New World Information Order" is being waged.

Food and Agriculture Organization (FAO) has engaged in research, technical assistance, and financial support aimed at improving agricultural production and addressing the food needs of less developed countries; among its accomplishments, FAO has played a leading role in bringing the "green revolution" to countries in South Asia and elsewhere, alleviating food shortages through the dissemination of "miracle" high-yield varieties of rice, wheat, and corn. The **World Health Organization (WHO)** has made substantial progress in controlling communicable diseases, including the virtual elimination of smallpox and a dramatic reduction in malaria, in addition to promoting health education and public health services in less developed countries.

The **Universal Postal Union (UPU)**, in accordance with its constitutional mandate to treat the world as "a single postal territory," facilitates the flow of mail across national boundaries through fixing weight limits and maximum postage rates and developing procedures to expedite mail delivery. The **International Telecommunication Union (ITU)** similarly helps to manage the flow of telegraph, telephone, radio, and television communications across the globe; indeed, ITU (profiled in the box on pages 338–339) even deals with communications *above* the globe. The **United Nations Educational, Scientific, and Cultural Organization (UNESCO)** has undertaken a variety of activities designed to improve literacy rates in less developed countries, promote scientific and cultural exchanges, and facilitate the dissemination of information by drafting universal copyright conventions and related rules. UNESCO has also been involved recently in drafting a set of controversial guidelines governing regulation of the mass media, attempting to forge an agreement between the industrialized democracies, the Communist countries, and the Third World regarding the degree of government control over press freedom and the international flow of news information.

The **International Civil Aviation Organization (ICAO)** has been responsible for drafting a number of conventions establishing uniform practices and standards with regard to pilot licensing, aircraft specifications, air traffic control, and anti-skyjacking measures, all of which have contributed immeasurably to international air safety. The **International Maritime Organization (IMO)** has performed a similar function in regard to the oceans, helping to manage international traffic on the two-thirds of the earth's surface that is covered with water. The **World Meteorological Organization (WMO)** engages in the collection and exchange of global weather forecasting data through its World Weather Watch program and monitors conditions relating to the global environment and climatic change.

Among the most important of the Specialized Agencies are several economic institutions. The **International Monetary Fund (IMF)** plays an important role in promoting international monetary cooperation, including stabilizing exchange rates of dollars and other national currencies and providing foreign exchange funds for needy states so that the maximum amount of world trade can occur. The **International Bank for Reconstruction and Development (IBRD)**, commonly called the **World Bank,** annually provides billions of dollars in loans to the governments of less developed countries to finance the building of bridges, dams and roads, and other developmental needs. The World Bank group also includes the International Development Association (IDA), often referred to as the "soft loan window" since it channels capital specifically to governments of the very poorest countries at much lower interest rates, along with the International Finance Corporation (IFC), which provides loans to individuals and companies in the *private* sector of less developed countries. The IMF and World Bank were created after World War II as key elements in the postwar international economic order (often referred to as the "Bretton Woods system," named after the site of the 1944 conference at which UN economic institutions were first planned).

There are many other parts to the UN system, but space does not allow us to even mention them. The system is a maze-like network of organizations with overlapping concerns and complicated linkages. In the case of both the United Nations and its Specialized Agencies, the organizations ultimately work only as effectively as the member governments will permit. Sometimes the level of effectiveness can be quite high, as with those Specialized Agencies whose officials are given considerable discretion to act within their limited sphere of responsibility. Other times, talking far exceeds acting (although as Winston Churchill once said, "jaw-jaw" is better than "war-war").[30] In order to put the United Nations into proper perspective, let us do a quick "cost-benefit" analysis.

AN APPRAISAL: THE UN BALANCE SHEET

It is common to base one's judgment of the United Nations solely on its record in the area of war and peace. Although there have been some successes, the failures and disappointments have undoubtedly been far greater in number. On the only occasion in which the Security Council has taken collective security action under Chapter VII, during the Korean War, a UN military expedition against North Korea was made possible only because the Soviet Union happened to be boycotting the Council (in protest against the occupation of the Chinese seat by Taiwan rather than the People's Republic of China).

However, there have been other occasions when, faced with the paralysis of the Security Council due to the veto, the General Assembly or the Secretary-General has taken action in the peace and security area. At times, such involvement has merely taken the form of mediation and other peaceful settlement efforts under Chapter VI of the Charter, such as U Thant's intervention in the 1962 West Irian conflict between the Netherlands and Indonesia. In other instances, stronger and more visible action has been taken, such as the sending of a peacekeeping force of 6,000 soldiers (UNEF) to the Middle East during the Suez crisis of 1956, and the force of 20,000 (ONUC) dispatched to the Belgian Congo in 1960. In the Suez case, the General Assembly acted on the basis of the "Uniting for Peace Resolution," which

The United Nations as a forum for talking (and listening)

authorizes Assembly involvement in war and peace questions if the Security Council is paralyzed, while in the Belgian Congo case it was essentially Secretary-General Hammarskjold who took the initiative. Strictly speaking, both incidents were *peacekeeping* operations, neither of the "peaceful settlement" variety intended in Chapter VI nor of the "collective security" variety envisioned in Chapter VII; often labeled "Chapter VI and 1/2" actions, they went far beyond a mediating role yet fell short of collective security, since they were sent to provide a neutral military presence rather than punish an aggressor and could be ordered out at any time the host countries desired (as happened when Egypt ordered UNEF's withdrawal in 1967).

The Security Council itself has authorized similar peacekeeping forces over the years, including UNFICYP (in existence since 1964) to help quiet the civil war between Turkish and Greek Cypriots on Cyprus, UNEF–II sent to police the Egyptian-Israeli border following their 1973 war, and UNIFIL sent to help manage the Lebanon civil war in 1978 (approved by the Security Council after only a few minutes of debate).[31] Indeed, since it is the Big Five that have normally been relied on to finance the bulk of UN peacekeeping operations, the formation of such forces without Security Council approval always runs the risk of a financial crisis.[32] Generally speaking, the Security Council has shown itself most likely to take constructive action in those situations, such as the Middle East war of 1973, where the Big Five, particularly the United States and the Soviet Union, share a mutual desire to see a de-escalation of a conflict in which they are not directly involved but which they could be drawn into.

Although one should not exaggerate the UN's successes in the war and peace area—given its conspicuous absence from Vietnam, Central America, and other trouble spots—one should not minimize them either. The United Nations has contributed significantly to peace, especially through the practice of **preventive diplomacy,** helping to keep local conflicts from escalating into larger conflagrations directly involving major powers. One study, examining the 1945–1975 period, found that the UN became involved in over half of all "international crises" in that period (95 out of 160 incidents) and was deemed to have been "effective" in terms of "crisis abatement" in one third of those cases; more impressively, the researchers found that UN involvement and effectiveness tended to increase the more serious and violent the crisis situation.[33] Unfortunately, the UN's record in conflict management has not been as successful in the 1980s.[34]

The United Nations has additionally played a more subtle peacekeeping role as a forum in which countries can vent hostilities verbally rather than physically; unfortunately, there is no way of knowing how many outbreaks of violence the United Nations has averted in this fashion. It is difficult to assess, also, how much the United Nations has contributed to war prevention through its efforts at addressing various economic and social ills that often underlie the resort to violence. While the United Nations is usually judged according to its record in the war-peace area, its work in other fields is no less important. Indeed, the United Nations spends 80 percent of its budget and an even greater share of its energies on economic and social problem solving rather than peacekeeping *per se*.

If the *benefits* produced by the United Nations are modest, the *costs* associated with it are even more modest. Its regular annual operating budget is less than $1 billion (smaller than the annual budget of the New York City Police Department). Considering the fact that the world's governments today spend more than $800 billion a year on weapons of war, the amount spent on the United Nations should seem a bargain. Even if one adds another $2 billion in voluntary contributions to organizations like the United Nations International Children's Emergency Fund (UNICEF) and in assessments to the Specialized Agencies, it would seem that, on balance, the United Nations earns its keep. Although many Americans complain about the financial burden the United States has assumed as the chief benefactor of the United Nations, especially in light of the verbal abuse and setbacks the United States has suffered recently in the General Assembly, it is estimated that it costs the American taxpayer an average of only $2.25 a year (roughly the price of a second-run movie). For the other 5 billion constituents of the United Nations, what has been called "the best hope for mankind" comes even more cheaply.

Regional Intergovernmental Organizations:
The European Community

For those who consider the growth of international organization to be a key to world order, international institution-building efforts at the regional level are sometimes seen as at least modest stepping-stones toward the development of a larger, global community. Nowhere has regional institution-building been more fully attempted than in Western Europe, where a regional entity has been established complete with its own flag and anthem. What is today called the **European Community** is really three IGOs in one: the European Coal and Steel Community (ECSC), the European Economic Community (EEC or Common Market), and the European Atomic Energy Community (EURATOM). This "community" today consists of twelve member states—France, West Germany, the United Kingdom, Italy, the Netherlands, Belgium, Luxembourg, Denmark, Ireland, Greece, Spain, and Portugal—which together constitute the third largest demographic unit in the world, its population of over 320 million exceeded only by China and India. The key question surrounding the European Community, however, is the extent to which it can be considered a *single* unit or actor. As we note below, in some respects it comes close to being a unified, supranational entity, while in many other respects it seems little more than a fragile collection of sovereign states.

The dream of a "United States of Europe" can be found as far back as Dante in the fourteenth century. In the more recent past, Charles de Gaulle and Winston Churchill mused about the possibilities of union between France and Britain when the latter proposed a merger prior to the Nazi occupation of France during World War II.[35] However, it was not until the 1950s that the idea of a European Community was seriously pursued. At first, only six states on the continent (the "inner six," which included France, West Germany, Italy, and the Benelux countries) joined together to form the ECSC in 1952, designed to promote cooperation in coal and steel production and commerce. The same six states signed the Treaty of Rome in 1957, establishing the Common Market and EURATOM, thereby pledging cooperation in all economic sectors as well as atomic energy research and development. The Community expanded to nine in 1973, with the addition of the United Kingdom, Denmark, and Ireland, then to ten with the admission of Greece in 1981, and to twelve with the entrance of Portugal and Spain in 1986 (with Spanish television trumpeting the event with the words "Good evening, citizens of Europe"). Several other Western European states have been invited to apply for membership but have not yet entered for various political and economic reasons. Some states in Western Europe, as well as outside Europe, have been accorded "associate member" status.

Although the two men considered to be the "fathers" of the European Community—Jean Monnet and Robert Schuman, both of France—envisioned eventual *political* unification among the members, most national leaders in the Community have from the start viewed the undertaking in more narrow terms, as a vehicle for joint problem solving mainly in the *economic* sphere. A primary rationale behind the Community was the desire to follow the economic model of the United States, where the absence of trade and related barriers between the constituent units made for a single, large economic market that facilitated economies of scale and generally promoted economic efficiency and prosperity; the hope was that goods and services, labor, and capital would flow as freely between, say, Belgium and France as they did between New York and New Jersey. Although economic integration was not as ambitious a goal as political unification, it nonetheless represented an impressive effort at cooperation that was virtually unprecedented on a continent whose members had fought two major wars in the twentieth century.

The plan was to proceed in several stages: (1) a **free trade area**, in which all tariff barriers were to be eliminated between the member states themselves (so that, for example, French agricultural products could be exported to Belgium without French farmers having to pay an entry duty or tax); (2) a **customs union**, whereby all member states would impose a common external tariff on goods exported to the Community from nonmember states (so that, for example, the French and Belgians would charge the same duty on Japanese automobiles entering their countries); (3) a **common market**, in which not only goods and services but also workers and investment funds would be able to move freely across national boundaries (so that, for example, an Italian construction worker could seek employment in West Germany without worrying about a work permit or other obstacles); and (4) an **economic and monetary union,** in which all member states would harmonize their total economic policies and introduce a single European currency (in place of French francs, German marks, and so forth).

In order to facilitate this process, several institutions were created, with the ECSC, EEC, and EURATOM initially each having its own separate decision-making apparatus. By the 1970s, a single set of institutions had been established to serve the Community as a whole. The European Council, consisting of the heads of state of the twelve member countries, meets three times a year to set broad policy. Brussels, the "capital" of the European Community, is where the Council of Ministers and the European Commission meet. The Council of Ministers, composed of members of the national cabinet from each state (usually the foreign ministers but sometimes agriculture or transportation ministers or other cabinet officials, depending on the issues to be discussed at monthly meetings), is the most powerful decision-making body in the Community other than the European Council. On paper, the Council of Ministers seems to operate in an almost supranational fashion, with the Treaty of Rome assigning states weighted votes based on population (so that France, West Germany, Italy, and the United Kingdom have more voting strength than any of the other states) and with most decisions determined by majority rule rather than unanimity. In practice, however, decisions are normally reached only through general agreement based on consensus among the entire membership. In other words, while a coalition of states could technically impose binding decisions on the other members, there is the practical recognition that engaging in such domineering behavior could jeopardize the continued existence of the whole collective enterprise.

The Council of Ministers, on instructions from their home governments, decides the major economic and related policies of the Community. It is the European Commission that is expected to implement these policies. While the individuals who sit on the Council of Ministers explicitly represent the interests of their particular governments, the sixteen individuals who serve on the Commission theoretically represent the interests of the Community as a whole. Though nominated by their governments for renewable four-year terms (two from each of the "Big Four" and one from each of the other states), these "Eurocrats" along with their 5,000-member staff have tended to display considerable independence of judgment over the years and have generally sought to expand the powers of the Community institutions as much as possible. One of the Commission's main roles is not only to implement Council decisions but to take the initiative in identifying Community problems and proposing policies for consideration by the member states.

The Community political process involves not only interaction between the Council of Ministers and the Commission but also consultation with a variety of other bodies, including the European Parliament and the Economic and Social Committee. The Parliament, situated in Strasbourg, France, is essentially a "watchdog" designed to oversee the functioning of the Commission and other Community institutions and has little legislative power as such. The members of the Parliament were appointed from the individual legislatures of each country until 1979, when citizens were allowed to vote directly for their representatives in the European Parliament (with seats allocated to countries according to population). An interesting feature of the European Parliament is that the political parties are organized across national lines, with Communists from Italy sitting with Communists from France and other states, with Socialists sitting together, with Christian Democrats sitting together, and so forth. While direct election and transnational party organization give the appearance of supranationalism, it must be emphasized that the Parliament is only a consultative body. So, also, is the Economic and Social Committee, composed of representatives from various groups involving agricultural, manufacturing, transportation, and business interests, with both worker and employer groups organized transnationally to lobby in support of or in opposition to various Community proposals that affect them.[36]

The Community political process, then, is a complicated one that involves governmental, intergovernmental, and nongovernmental actors. In addition to the political institutions we have mentioned, there is also a European Court of Justice that sits in Luxembourg and adjudicates disputes related to the Treaty of Rome. The Court has handled hundreds of cases, ranging from hiring and firing grievances filed by Community civil servants to governmental requests for judicial interpretations of Treaty provisions pertaining to social security for migrant workers. Unlike most international tribunals, the Court allows individual citizens to bring suit against their own government, as happened in a 1976 case brought by a Sabena airlines stewardess in which the Court ruled that the state-owned Belgian airline had violated the Treaty of Rome provisions regarding sex discrimination in pay practices.

Despite an impressive institutional infrastructure, the European Community has only partially fulfilled its initial goal of economic integration and remains as far away as ever from the larger aspiration of political unification harbored by some of its founders. While the Community has progressed to the point where it is essentially a single free trade area and customs union, problems still abound in trying to realize a true common market and to coordinate economic policies. On the one hand, the Community has succeeded in forging a common agricultural policy (CAP) with respect to government involvement in the agricultural sector, has facilitated the free movement of people by instituting accident insurance coverage for all motorists throughout the Community and by eliminating work permit requirements along national lines, and has developed a uniform set of safety standards for autos and many other products sold in the Community. On the other hand, economic barriers still persist: French brewers were, until 1987, prevented from selling beer in the German market because their product did not meet "beer purity" standards specified by the Germans; French wine-growers, in turn, have conducted "wine wars" against the cheaper Italian wines that have threatened to flood the French market; the tobacco industry in France and Italy, which is a government-owned monopoly, makes it difficult for tobacco interests in other Community countries to sell their products competitively in those two countries; and doctors, lawyers, and other members of the professional labor force wanting to relocate across national boundaries are inhibited by language and educational training differences that prevent professionals from meeting national licensing requirements. Among the more difficult problems is the need to reconcile the demands of the newer, less advanced member states (Greece, Portugal, and Spain) with the concerns of the more advanced economies in the Community.

The Community's problems are not merely a function of linguistic, cultural, and economic differences but relate to larger political issues. The Franco-German national rivalry continues; indeed, it has been argued that this rivalry was partly responsible for the formation of the Community to begin with, so that the French could "keep an eye on Germany," in addition to gaining access to German iron ore. The British, initially reluctant to join the Community because the customs union concept threatened their traditional Commonwealth ties and posed various trade concerns, continue to be ambivalent about the advantages of Community membership; in particular, despite winning some recent concessions related to the Community's budget, the British see the distribution of costs and benefits as stacked against them and favoring primarily the French farmers, whose products are given privileged access to the British market even though they are more expensive than the butter and other farm goods that used to enter freely from Commonwealth countries. Ideological differences also exist between socialist-oriented governments in Portugal and Greece and more middle-of-the-road or conservative governments in other member states.

It is important to keep in mind that the decision-making competence of Community institutions continues to extend only to economically related matters, although this is a considerable sphere of activity. The Community has no authority to deal with defense issues. The diverse group of twelve national governments has experienced great difficulty in forging a common set of foreign policies. Efforts to coordinate foreign policy through Community institutions have at times produced some degree of unity, as happened during the 1973 war in the Middle East, but more often than not have resulted in disarray, as in the case of the 1980 Moscow Olympic boycott. Rather than presiding over a single community and deciding the great issues of European security and political affairs as envisioned by Monnet, Community officials mostly find themselves sitting in "mirrored halls on centuries-old chairs to argue . . . over the price of a leg of lamb."[37] The range of minutiae ("low politics" issues) dealt with by the Community from month to month can be seen in the Sidelight in this section, which also suggests how the Community manages to shape European life in nontrivial ways.

SIDELIGHT

A MONTH IN THE LIFE OF THE EUROPEAN ECONOMIC COMMUNITY

The following excerpts, which appeared in *The Economist*, describe what might be called a "typical" month in the EEC.

Internal politics

The council of ministers decided to take the European parliament to the court of justice for exceeding its powers to raise spending. But it decided to accept the 1982 budget as amended by Euro-MPs.

Greenland voted to withdraw from the EEC. The Irish voted to elect their EEC commissioner, Mr. Michael O'Kennedy, as an MP instead. Euro-Tories chose a new leader, Sir Henry Plumb (a farmers' man).

Foreign policy

Ministers at last agreed to impose (gentle) sanctions against Russia over Poland. Half of Soviet exports of luxury and manufactured goods to the EEC will be blocked by import quotas. The EEC will also propose . . . that Russia should pay higher interest rates on export credits.

Mr. Wilfried Martens, Belgium's prime minister and EEC president, went to tell President Reagan to change his economic policy. The policy has not changed. EEC ministers also threatened for the umpteenth time to get nasty with Japan unless the Japanese government liberalised its import policy.

Farms and fish

The commission's proposals to raise farm prices by 9 percent got short shrift from farm ministers. Too much, said Britain and Germany; too little, said most of the others.

The question remains whether the substantial progress made thus far toward economic integration will lead to political integration, and whether that progress is even sustainable without further development of the Community's political institutions. The likely prospect is that, rather than moving forward or backward, the Community will continue muddling along in what has become a kind of halfway-house between a collection of sovereign states and a supranational entity.[38] Certainly, the initial euphoric predictions of a United States of Europe that accompanied the Treaty of Rome in the 1950s now seem to have been extremely naive and premature and have given way to more sober analyses of future possibilities. A whole literature sprouted in the 1950s and 1960s dealing with **integration theory** and examining the conditions under which political units tend to merge together and transfer loyalty to a larger community. At that time, when Western Europe seemed on the brink of political integration, theorists pondered whether the European experience

The commission asked member states to stop catching herring only a year after allowing it again, and it took France to the court of justice for its obstruction of Italian wine imports.

Industry and trade

Mr. Christopher Tugendhat decided to push ahead with the third stage of tobacco-tax harmonization. This should help British and American tobacco giants to sell more in France and Italy. But they are not happy, fearing that they will lose out in Britain and Germany; so they persuaded Euro-MPs to oppose the plan.

The commission ripped up a newsprint cartel between two Swedish paper-makers and Feldmuhle of Germany; and stopped the world's biggest sulphur exporter, Cansulex, of Canada, from restricting competition in the EEC.

Court of Justice

Companies can retire men and women at different ages despite the 1976 equal-pay directive, the court ruled in a case concerning British Rail.

Directives and regulations

Ministers approved directives to harmonize laws on electrical equipment used in mines; and to oblige companies quoted on EEC stock exchanges to publish standard accounts every six months.

The commission struck a blow for prettier women. It proposed a change to EEC regulation 76/768 on cosmetics, to authorize the use of some products of barium, strontium, and zirconium, to restrict the use of silver nitrate, and to tighten up the rules on "sell-by" dates.

Source: From "February in the EEC," *The Economist,* March 6, 1982. Copyright by *The Economist* Newspaper, London.

could serve as a model for regional integration in other parts of the world such as Latin America and Africa, where a Latin American Free Trade Association, Central American Common Market, and Arab Common Market were in the process of being born. Today, the European experiment itself is at a crossroads, with most Western Europeans still wedded to the general idea of a European Community but retaining primary loyalty to their individual nation-states.[39]

Conclusion

Despite the justifiable attention that world politics scholars have given subnational, transnational, and supranational phenomena recently, the experiences of the European Community and the United Nations offer a lesson in the staying power of *nationalism* in the contemporary world. In Part IV we will delineate further the relationship between nation-states and nonstate actors, as we examine the congeries of forces involved in the politics of global problem solving in specific issue-areas (arms control, management of the international economy, and other areas). One type of nonstate actor (NGO) we will take a closer look at is the multinational corporation. Although multinational corporations (MNCs) have not erased the boundary lines that separate countries, they have managed to transcend those lines in a manner that is reshaping relations between people across the world in significant ways. More than most institutions, the MNC reflects the tension that exists today between the impulses of nationalism and the impulses of internationalism. In the international economy, as in other parts of the international system, humanity's search for order through global institution-building continues against centrifugal pressures pulling in the opposite direction. We will see where all this is leading in Part IV, as we discuss efforts to create *regimes* in areas where chaos threatens to reign.

SUMMARY

1. International organizations can be classified according to three criteria: membership, geographical scope, and functional scope. Those that have national governments as members and are created through treaties between states are called intergovernmental organizations; those that are composed generally of private individuals or groups are called nongovernmental organizations. There are over 300 IGOs in the world today, compared with more than 3,000 NGOs—which indicates that the bridges between peoples far outnumber the bridges between governments.

2. Although there is a common tendency to think of international organizations as global organizations (like the United Nations), the vast majority are regional or subregional in scope. Western developed countries belong to the most IGOs and NGOs.

3. Some international organizations are general, multipurpose organizations, though far more have specific, limited purposes. More than half of all IGOs are economic; most NGOs are in commerce and industry or health and medicine.

4. As transnational relations expanded during the nineteenth and twentieth centuries, and merchants, scientists, and other groups found that they shared interests that transcended national boundaries, these ties became institutionalized in the form of NGOs. The effects of NGOs are disputed. Their members tend to develop a more cosmopolitan outlook, but the impact of this on relations between governments is uncertain. NGOs sometimes have considerable consultative input into IGO decision making. They can also have a significant impact in their role as autonomous actors who compete with national governments in the international arena.

5. As has been the case with NGOs, IGO growth has been dramatic since World War II. IGOs are instruments for managing interstate disagreements and problems. Problems may involve the most crucial and controversial interstate issues (high politics) or more narrow and technical matters (low politics), with states more willing to cooperate and give decision-making power to IGOs in low politics than high politics issue-areas. Functionalists hypothesize that cooperation in low politics areas will spill over into high politics areas and eventually lead to development of supranational institutions, although little if any supranationalism yet exists.

6. The United Nations is a global IGO created in 1945 as the successor of the League of Nations. The major UN organs are the Security Council (including the "Big Five" who have a veto power); the General Assembly (the plenary body, now dominated by a Third World majority); the Economic and Social Council; the Secretariat (headed by the Secretary-General); and the Specialized Agencies (more than a dozen IGOs affiliated with the United Nations).

7. The United Nations is usually judged on its performance in the war-peace area, but 80 percent of its budget is spent on economic and social problem solving. Although the United Nations has often been ineffective in the war-peace area, it has organized several peacekeeping forces, has mediated disputes, and has served as a surrogate for violence by providing a forum in which states can vent hostilities verbally.

8. The European Community is a regional IGO that consists of twelve Western European states participating in the Common Market, the European Coal and Steel Community, and the European Atomic Energy Community. Started in the 1950s, the Community was designed to create among member countries a single economic market (like that in the United States) that would promote economic efficiency and prosperity. Decision making in the Community occurs through an elaborate set of institutions that make policies binding on all members. Although the Community has made considerable progress toward economic integration— moving from a free trade area to a common market—it has made little progress toward the political integration envisioned by some of its founders.

SUGGESTIONS FOR FURTHER READING AND STUDY

A good general introduction to the concept of international organization, including realist, idealist, Marxist, and other views of the phenomenon, is offered by Clive Archer in *International Organizations* (London: George Allen and Unwin, 1983).

An excellent overview of the NGO phenomenon is provided by Kjell Skjelsbaek in "The Growth of International Nongovernmental Organization in the Twentieth Century," in Robert O. Keohane and Joseph S. Nye, Jr., eds., *Transnational Relations and World Politics* (Cambridge, Mass.: Harvard University Press, 1971), pp. 70–92. The same source also contains several case studies focusing on the role of NGOs and transnational actors in a variety of issue-areas in world politics. Studies examining particular transnational organizations include David Forsythe, *Humanitarian Politics* (Baltimore: Johns Hopkins University Press, 1977), on the International Red Cross;

and Robert Graham, *Vatican Diplomacy: A Study of Church and State on the International Plane* (Princeton, N.J.: Princeton University Press, 1959), on the Roman Catholic Church. Also, see Werner J. Feld, *Nongovernmental Forces in World Politics* (New York: Praeger, 1972).

A good, concise overview of the IGO phenomenon is furnished by Charles Pentland's "International Organizations," in James N. Rosenau *et al.*, eds., *World Politics: An Introduction* (New York: Free Press, 1976), pp. 624–659; a book-length study is Lynn H. Miller, *Organizing Mankind* (Boston: Holbrook Press, 1972). For a discussion of regional IGOs, see Richard A. Falk and Saul H. Mendlovitz, eds., *Regional Politics and World Order* (San Francisco: W. H. Freeman, 1973); and Louis J. Cantori and Steven L. Spiegel, eds., *The International Politics of Regions* (Englewood Cliffs, N.J.: Prentice-Hall, 1970), especially the article by Lynn H. Miller on "Regional Organizations and Subordinate Systems," pp. 357–378. On the European Community, see Anne Daltrop, *Politics and the European Community* (London: Longman, 1982). For a discussion of global IGOs, a basic text is A. LeRoy Bennett, *International Organizations*, 4th ed. (Englewood Cliffs, N.J.: Prentice-Hall, 1988).

A somewhat dated but nonetheless classic work treating the history, problems, and prospects of the United Nations is Inis Claude's *Swords into Plowshares*, 4th ed. (New York: Random House, 1971). Also, see Robert Riggs and Jack Plano, *The United Nations and International Politics* (Greenwood, Ill.: Dorsey, 1987). A good anthology examining the main organs of the United Nations is James Barros, *The United Nations: Past, Present, and Future* (New York: Free Press, 1972). Works focusing on the politics of the United Nations include John G. Stoessinger, *The United Nations and the Superpowers: China, Russia and America*, 4th ed. (New York: Random House, 1977); and Leon Gordenker, ed., *The United Nations in International Politics* (Princeton, N.J.: Princeton University Press, 1971). For more in-depth analysis of decision making, especially in the Specialized Agencies, see Harold K. Jacobson, *Networks of Interdependence*, 2nd ed. (New York: Knopf, 1984); and Robert W. Cox *et al.*, *The Anatomy of Influence: Decision Making in International Organization* (New Haven, Conn.: Yale University Press, 1973). Among the more rigorous studies of the role of the UN in conflict resolution are Mark W. Zacher and J. A. Finlayson, *The United Nations and Collective Security: Retrospect and Prospect* (New York: United Nations Association of America, 1980); Mark W. Zacher, *International Conflicts and Collective Security* (New York: Praeger, 1979); and Ernst B. Haas, Robert L. Butterworth, and Joseph S. Nye, *Conflict Management by International Organizations* (Morristown, N.J.: General Learning Press, 1972). The *UN Chronicle* and the *Yearbook of the United Nations*, published by the UN Office of Public Information, provide summary descriptions of UN activities and developments, as does *Everyone's United Nations*, 10th ed. (1986).

International Organization is an important journal that contains scholarly articles dealing with a wide range of international organizations and transnational activities at the regional and global level, with an emphasis on analyzing their role in world politics. Included are many studies on integration. "Regional Integration: Theory and Research," a special volume that appeared in Autumn 1970, is still a valuable resource.

PART
IV

The Global Condition: The Politics of Global Problem Solving

The traditional agenda of international affairs—the balance among major powers, the security of nations—no longer defines our perils or our possibilities.
HENRY A. KISSINGER, U.S. SECRETARY OF STATE, IN A 1975 SPEECH

We have been more or less brought up to believe that the bonds of community, responsibility, and obligation run only to the [national] frontiers. Should we extend our vision to include all the people of our planet?
BARBARA WARD, *The Lopsided World*

Usually we speak of violence only when it has reached an extreme. But it is also violence when children are dying of malnutrition, when there is no freedom of unions, when there is not enough housing, not enough health care.
ADOLFO PÉREZ ESQUIVÉL, ARGENTINA, 1984

All the preceding quotations have one common thread: the recognition that the contemporary world is beset with numerous problems that are global in scope and require global responses. Human problem solving can occur at several levels—local, national, and international. At the international level, while bilateral and regional approaches might be sufficient to deal with some problems, they necessarily can offer only partial solutions to others, such as nuclear weapons proliferation and climatic disturbances. The existence of problems that are truly global in scale poses unparalleled dangers of international conflict but, perhaps also, unparalleled opportunities for international cooperation.

The notion that all problems must be solvable is in some sense a Western and even a particularly American bias. Nevertheless, governments representing various world cultures, including for example India and China, have campaigned for solutions to such pressing concerns as international violence, poverty, overpopulation, and resource scarcity. Many of the efforts being undertaken today to deal with the new agenda of global issues take the form of *regime-making.* Regimes can be thought of as "recognized patterns of practices around which expectations converge," which "may or may not be accompanied by explicit organizational arrangements."[1] In other words, regimes constitute widely accepted rules, procedures and institutions, or "governing arrangements,"[2] which allow the international community to function and cope with some set of concerns in the absence of a world government. The drafting of treaties and international agreements, the cultivation of shared norms and values, and the creation of international organizational machinery all are part of regime-building. Regimes represent an alternative to each country pursuing strictly its own unilateral foreign policies. In considering global efforts at regime-building, one should bear in mind our initial definition of international politics—the process of deciding who gets what, when, and how in the world. As in national politics, some actors are in a better position than others to shape regimes and, in the process, either to facilitate or frustrate problem solving.

In Part IV, we examine the politics of global problem solving, focusing on three sets of issues: the *control of violence,* particularly nuclear and conventional arms races and terrorism (Chapters 11 and 12); the *promotion of economic well-being,* including both coordination of the global economy and the economic development of impoverished societies (Chapters 13 and 14); and the *management of renewable and nonrenewable resources,* including energy and environmental concerns (Chapter 15). In each chapter, we will (1) define the *nature and magnitude* of the problem; (2) identify the congeries of state and nonstate *actors* whose interests and demands are relevant to the *politics* surrounding the problem; and (3) describe the recent *outcomes* of the political process, including any *regimes* which might have been produced by the international community in response to the problem.

CHAPTER

11

The Control of Violence: Arms Races and Arms Control in the Nuclear Age

Political leaders frequently observe that the need for disarmament is more pressing than ever. These same leaders then frequently turn to their defense budgets and place orders for ever more sophisticated weapons. This paradox was seen at the UN World Disarmament Conference of 1982, which was attended by peaceloving participants ranging from the president of the United States and the foreign minister of the Soviet Union, whose governments were in the process of expanding their multibillion-dollar military budgets to all-time highs, to the UN ambassador from Malta, a country that has an army of 800. Such conferences proceed on the assumption that if the tools of violence can somehow be controlled, the violence itself might be controlled. The argument is, in fact, similar to the gun-control debate in the United States, and it is just as controversial, except that in this case the skeptics conceivably might argue that "bazookas don't kill people. People kill people."

Although violence is obviously not a new phenomenon, we saw in Chapter 8 that humanity's capacity to do violence has reached new heights in the atomic age. Through the use of nuclear explosives, antiship Exocet missiles, TV- or radar-guided "smart bombs," napalm, antitank missile batteries with "night vision" scopes, and assorted other weapons, it has become possible to kill people far more efficiently and in far greater numbers than ever before in history. The development of the "electronic battlefield," with sophisticated weapon control and guidance systems, also has linked the capacity for violence ever more closely with technological capacity. While only a few states appear able to afford the most sophisticated weapons, it is now possible to do greater violence with fewer personnel. Controlling global violence, then, relates to the way states define both their *security* and *technological* needs. This will be seen in this chapter as we focus on international arms races and arms control, one of the most critical dimensions of the larger problem of controlling global violence in the late twentieth century.

The Nature and Magnitude of the Problem

By **arms races,** we generally mean competitive armament by two or more states seeking security and protection against each other. However, as noted in Chapter 8, one country's rate of armament is not always related to another's, or to specific threats by other states. Governments seem to have many additional reasons for arming: to preserve defense industries and jobs; to become dominant regional powers; to gain prestige; to suppress domestic opponents and unrest. Therefore one country can race along with its own armaments quite apart from actions taken by enemy states. Countries engaged in competitive races also confront a "security dilemma," in that the more they arm in the quest for security, the more their adversaries are likely to arm and the *less* secure each side may feel.

States can obtain arms either by manufacturing weapons themselves or by acquiring weapons from another country through gift or purchase. Both methods have the same result: weapons *proliferation*, the spread of weapons among more and more states. Countries manufacture arms by using either the designs of their own engineers or, through licenses, the designs of engineers in other countries. As such weapons as jet fighter planes become more sophisticated and expensive, the weapons business becomes more complex as well. Few countries can design and build an entire aircraft, for example, including airframe, engines, and advanced electronics. Sometimes a small country, such as Israel, can design or manufacture part or most of the weapon system, but must rely on imported components (say, jet engines) to complete the job. Even larger countries, like those in Western Europe, have found it necessary to collaborate in the production of expensive weapon systems.[1]

It is difficult to keep track of the distribution of weapons in the world, partly because governments generally like to keep exact armament levels secret and partly because it is hard to define a weapon. Some states have tried to distinguish between offensive and defensive weapons, the former used to attack targets and the latter to defend against incoming weapons. Other states have called for bans on "inhumane" weapons—presumably those that kill or maim less discriminately than "humane" weapons. But such distinctions break down, especially when "multirole" weapons, such as jet fighter-bombers, are considered. Offense or defense depends on political missions for which weapons are used. The Soviets claimed that the missiles they transferred to Cuban bases in 1962 were defensive (to prevent a U.S. invasion), while Washington countered that they were offensive (aimed at North and South American cities or military bases). A pick-up truck hardly looks like a weapon at all, except in the hands of an angry or drunk driver, but can be easily converted to carry mobile antiaircraft missiles (a Palestine Liberation Organization specialty in recent years). Such uncertainties plague efforts to control arms proliferation.

Both **nuclear** and **conventional weapons** proliferation are causes for concern today. The current world stockpile of nuclear weapons is estimated to contain over 1 million times the explosive power of the atomic bomb that leveled Hiroshima, and to be sufficient to kill an estimated 58 billion people, i.e., twelve times the current world population.[2] If one adds the growing conventional arsenals available to states, the totals become even more mind-boggling. One aspect of arms races gaining particular attention in American and Soviet circles is the prospect for developing space weapons and engaging in space warfare. Some of these weapons are classified as conventional, as in antisatellite (ASAT) missiles for deployment on high-flying jet fighters. Others, the Buck Rogers–type laser and particle beam weapons of the future, are highly unorthodox and difficult to perfect; yet research and development for space wars is proceeding in both Washington and Moscow, and in other states interested in "high tech" capabilities. Such research has been labeled part of the Strategic Defense Initiative (SDI) in the United States, and touted as a potential shield against nuclear attack.

ECONOMIC ASPECTS OF THE PROBLEM

As noted in Chapter 8, arms races may or may not result in war. However, the potential physical destruction that expanding arsenals can cause is only one cost associated with arms races. Even if those weapons were never to be used, the enormous amount of economic resources being devoted to weapons production and acquisition reduces considerably the level of funds available for other, more constructive social purposes. While some argue that military production increases jobs (e.g., 80,000 to 140,000 jobs in Great Britain and Northern Ireland are estimated to depend on British arms exports), it also drains money from other sectors.

Allowing for inflation, world military spending as measured by defense budgets (which include everything from soldiers' socks to nuclear weapons) has increased more than 400 percent since 1948. At constant prices, an estimated $800 billion a year (or $1.5 million per minute) is presently being spent worldwide on arms and military forces. Of this total, the most economically developed states spend approximately 75 percent. From 1981 to 1984, military spending by the United States increased at an annual average of 9.2 percent, by the rest of NATO at 2.5 percent, and by the Warsaw Pact at 2.2 percent. Without these increases, the total global defense budget would probably have declined somewhat due to mounting Third World debts. Still, the total annual military expenditure by all countries in recent years roughly has equaled the entire annual income and the total debt level of the poorest half of the human race. Total development aid given to less developed countries by wealthy, industrialized countries amounts to merely 5 percent of world military spending. Funding of worldwide medical research amounts to less than 25 percent of the support given to military research and development, and the governments of the world spend altogether 57 times more per soldier than per student in the schools and 2500 times more for military activities than for international peacekeeping.[3]

Obviously then, the world's priorities are open to serious question when so many resources are allocated to implements of destruction. The box on page 359 shows how the savings achieved by just a 4 percent reduction in the annual global defense bill could be productively utilized for vital social services in the Third World. Yet poorer countries are not the only ones that stand to benefit from reordered priorities. As the box on page 360 suggests, developed countries like the United States could also address major domestic problems with military budget savings. For example, the United States and the Soviet

---

WHAT 4 PERCENT OF THE GLOBAL MILITARY BUDGET WOULD BUY IN LESS DEVELOPED COUNTRIES

Potable drinking water for all within a decade	$ 7 billion
Direct food aid for 450 million people suffering from hunger or malnutrition	$ 4 billion
Primary schools and teacher training aimed at 130 million children unable to attend elementary school	$ 5 billion
Vaccination protection for the 90 percent of the children born yearly in the Third World who are not immunized	$ 1 billion
Assistance to small farm holdings, to increase food productivity and rural employment	$ 6 billion
Job training programs for unemployed youth	$ 5 billion
	$28 billion

Source: Information from Ruth L. Sivard, *World Military and Social Expenditures, 1981* (Leesburg, Va.: World Priorities, 1981), p. 23; and *World Military and Social Expenditures, 1985* (Washington, D.C.: World Priorities, 1985), p. 33. Identified amounts are *illustrative* only; they are estimates and do not represent stated program needs by development agencies.

Union, which lead the world by far in total military spending (in absolute dollar amounts), rank only *fourteenth* and *fifty-first* respectively among 142 countries in infant mortality.[4] However, there is no guarantee that defense budget savings would be translated automatically into higher social budgetary spending; governments might simply decide to reduce spending in general.

Although arms production and purchases divert resources from economic development projects, poorer countries have clamored as loudly as the rich for new weapons. In addition to the United States and the Soviet Union, their European allies, Japan, the Middle Eastern oil powers, and Israel, poorer states such as China and India rank among the world's top defense spenders. Some one dozen impoverished states (with low per capita GNP) are estimated to spend over 10 percent of their overall GNP on defense. These include Laos, Vietnam, Kampuchea, Cape Verde, Angola, Yemen, Zambia, Nicaragua, Jordan, and Syria. As a whole, the Third World share of military spending increased from 16 percent in 1969 to 23 percent a decade later. Many Third World armies were reequipped in the process, and defense spending decreased slightly after 1982 in many Third World states because they could not absorb much more high-priced equipment.

THE SOCIAL COSTS OF MILITARY SPENDING IN THE UNITED STATES (Circa 1985)

One 155-mm (conventional) high explosive shell ($439)	= 460 meals for [urban homeless]
1986 budget for the M-1 Abrams [main battle] tank ($2.3 billion)	= Proposed 1986 budget cuts in guaranteed student loans and . . . campus-based financial aid [to] students
Two B-1 bombers ($400 million)	= The [approximate] cost of rebuilding Cleveland's water-supply system
The Navy's Trident II submarine and F-18 jet fighter programs ($100 billion)	= Estimated cost of cleaning up 10,000 toxic waste dumps [across the nation]
The Army's Patriot ground-to-air missile system ($12.2 billion)	= 1982–85 cuts in Federal income and nutrition programs . . .
1986 planned research and development for the Strategic Defense Initiative . . . program ($3.7 billion)	= Federal funds [for Connecticut to rebuild bridges and roads]
The Army's single-channel ground and airborne radio system ($5.3 billion)	= . . . A one-third increase in . . . Federal school lunch . . . , food-stamp . . . and Women, Infants and Children (WIC) program(s)

Source: Adapted from Seymour Melman, "The Butter That's Traded Off for Guns," *The New York Times*, April 22, 1985, p. 23, and "Looting the Means of Production," *The New York Times*, July 26, 1981, p. 21.

On a per capita basis, and as a percentage of GNP, the Middle East has led the world in military spending during the 1980s.[5] Israel, Iraq, Oman, Libya, and Saudi Arabia all spent over 30 percent of GNP on the military. By way of comparison, the United States annually spent between 5 and 9 percent of its GNP, and the USSR an estimated 10 percent, in the first half of the decade.[6] The fastest regional military spending growth was in South Asia (Afghanistan, India, Pakistan), Western Europe, and Latin America. Spending reductions occurred mainly in East Asia and Africa (after a period of arms buildup in the 1970s led by South Africa and Nigeria), and even the Middle East began to decline somewhat by mid-decade.

ARMS TRANSFERS

In order to avoid reliance on major-power arms supplies, and to build their technological capabilities, several developing countries, such as Brazil, Argentina, and India, have developed their own arms industries and have been able to supply portions of the military hardware needed by their own armed forces and even to export arms. However, most lack indigenous munitions industries and have had to rely heavily on imports or **arms transfers** from abroad. The Third World imported more than three fourths of all arms traded internationally in the late 1970s and early 1980s, and (as seen in Figure 11.1) about 65 percent of the major arms (excluding small arms such as rifles). The United States and the Soviet Union have continued to be the primary weapons suppliers, providing over two thirds of all arms transfers, trailed by a group of European and Third World suppliers. The combined size of European arms exports has exceeded U.S. totals in some recent years.[7]

Today, the term "arms transfer" refers to both *sales* and *gifts* (military aid grants) of weapons systems, support services such as base construction and

"I look forward to the day when we're civilized and we don't have to spend half our budget on defense . . ."

© 1981 Jim Borgman, *The Cincinnati Enquirer*. Distributed by King Features Syndicate, Inc.

Progress and the arms race

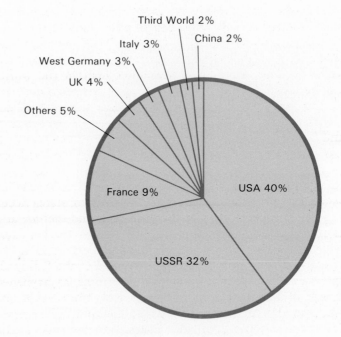

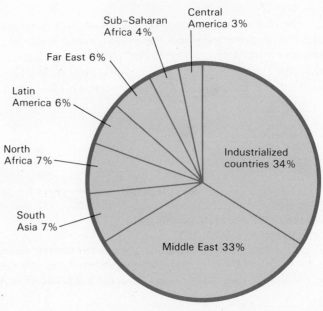

troop training, spare parts, and designs. In recent years the emphasis has shifted from arms transfers in the form of military aid to transfers in the form of military sales, often financed by generous credit arrangements. In contrast to the 1950s, when a large volume of outmoded weaponry was donated to less developed countries, the 1960s saw more advanced weapons offered for purchase in international trade. With the oil price hikes of the 1970s, the sale of sophisticated weaponry to Middle Eastern OPEC members in particular reached staggering proportions; at one point Iran had a larger tank arsenal than Britain as well as the biggest helicopter fleet in the world, and was allowed to obtain any U.S. conventional weapon the Shah desired (evidently in return for the Shah's promise not to "go nuclear"). A "trickle down" effect also began, as the wealthier Third World and industrialized states bought new weapons and handed down their older models to poorer states, creating an international used weapons network, often in the hands of private arms dealers.[8]

One of the problems associated with the arms trade is the "end use" to which weapons are put. Although most arms-supplying states license exports, review the political acceptability of the customer, and include at least some restrictions on end use, enforcement is nearly impossible. For example, arms originally supplied by Britain to foreign customers ended up in the hands of Argentine troops battling British forces for control of the Falkland Islands in 1982. Weapons can be captured by victorious armies (as happened with the vast storehouse of Soviet equipment Israel took from Egypt and Syria in various wars, and the American equipment that North Vietnam acquired), reexported from one country to another, supplied to guerrilla groups, or copied by unauthorized users.[9]

In the 1980s, the trade in conventional arms has been characterized as a "buyers' market," with more suppliers competing in the midst of less overall demand. Most arms suppliers registered real declines in the value of arms agreements with the Third World in 1985, for example. Only the Middle East and nearby South Asia increased arms imports between 1982 and 1985, as the

---

Figure 11.1 (facing page)
WORLD ARMS TRADE, 1980–1984 (MAJOR WEAPONS)
Arms exporters, 1980–1984 *(Above)*
The U.S. and the Soviet Union together account for over 70 percent of world sales of major weapons. But Third World countries like Brazil have now become significant weapon producers and exporters in their own right. The U.S. supplied some 79 countries, and the USSR about 40 countries.
Main arms-importing regions, 1980–1984 *(Below)*
Nearly a third of all exports of major weapons goes to the poorest nations of the world. Another third goes to the conflict-torn Middle East. *Note:* The Far East excludes Japan and China. They are included amongst the group of industrialized countries.

Middle East came to account for over 75 percent of all Third World arms transfer agreements.[10]

NUCLEAR ARMS RACES

Nowhere is concern about arms races greater than in the area of **nuclear proliferation.** American and Soviet strategic nuclear arsenals are compared in Table 11.1. On balance, the Soviet Union has more delivery vehicles, particularly intercontinental ballistic missiles (ICBMs) and submarine-launched ballistic missiles (SLBMs), while the United States has a greater number of warheads (bombs) that can be mounted on bombers or missiles. The U.S. edge in warheads is due mainly to the fact that more of its ICBMs and SLBMs are "MIRVed," i.e., they contain not one but several explosive devices known as "multiple independently targetable reentry vehicles." Although the United States leads in number of warheads and in electronic control sophistication, the Soviets have been closing the gap, and Soviet warheads generally are larger in firepower, giving the Soviet Union an advantage in overall "megatonnage." The Soviet Union relies heavily on land-based missiles, though their submarine fleet is also formidable; the United States relies on the "triad" of land missiles, submarines, and manned bombers (including cruise missile launchers). Protection and defense of the land-based missiles, however, has become progressively more difficult, which has led to various U.S. and Soviet plans to make them mobile (i.e., harder to hit), to "harden" them in more blast-resistant

Table 11.1
U.S. AND SOVIET STRATEGIC NUCLEAR FORCES

Capabilities	U.S.	Soviet
Total Weapons		
On ICBMs	2,170	6,250
On SLBMs	5,632	2,664
On Long-Range Bombers	4,130[a]	832[b]
	11,932	9,746
Total Launchers		
ICBMs	1,000	1,398
Strategic Submarines	36	64
Long-Range Bombers	339	136[c]
	1,375	1,598

[a] Includes self-guided air-launched cruise missiles (ALCMs) launched from bombers.
[b] Includes self-guided air-launched cruise missiles (ALCMs) launched from bombers. Excludes weapons on 145 Soviet Backfire bombers.
[c] Excludes 145 Soviet Backfire bombers which could make one-way flight to U.S.
Source: Force Level Calculator (Washington, D.C.: Center for Defense Information, 1987). Used by permission.

silos, or to protect them through exotic antimissile shields such as SDI. One can see that, depending upon what numbers are used, whether technological developments are included, and what positions their leaders wish to articulate, both sides can claim to be ahead, behind, or even in the nuclear arms race.

Nuclear arms races would be terrifying enough if the United States and the Soviet Union were the only entrants. However, by the 1980s, four other states had joined the "nuclear club"—Britain, France, China, and India (the latter only exploding a nuclear device)—with more than a dozen other states on the brink of joining.[11] Among the leading candidates to join the nuclear club are Israel (assumed to have up to 100 bombs, though none have been formally tested), Iraq, Argentina, Brazil, South Africa, Taiwan, and Pakistan. The ominous threat of regional nuclear arms races is evident in the following description:

> At a closed door seminar at the Institute of Defense Studies in New Delhi, it was the naval officer's turn to speak. With a diffident air, he proposed a crash investment of five billion dollars that would give India a small but effective force of submarine-launched ballistic missiles. . . .
>
> Eight hundred miles away in Bombay, where the Arabian sea laps against the boundary fence of the Bhabha atomic research centre, a scientist also reacts to Pakistan's growing nuclear capability. "We need funds to develop small nuclear warheads to take out major targets in Pakistan without also harming India," he said. "Imagine dropping a three megaton bomb on Lahore. The blast and radioactivity would wash right back on us.[12]

Third World countries lack sophisticated delivery vehicles for nuclear weapons, and the nuclear capabilities of prospective new members of the nuclear club pale by comparison with the United States and the Soviet Union. Nevertheless, nuclear weapons capability of *any* size represents tremendous damage potential. France's *force de frappe* was developed in the 1950s on the assumption that even a token nuclear force would be a good deterrent against possible aggression aimed at France. (The French military establishment was also attracted to nuclear weapons after suffering defeat in Indochina.) In some cases, the mere *reputation* of possibly possessing nuclear weapons can be valuable to a state, with its leaders preferring to let speculation run wild rather than formally announce a successful weapons test. Although nuclear weapons might deter aggression by one state against another, the laws of probability suggest that the more fingers on nuclear triggers, the more likelihood a bomb will go off. Once that happens, it is not known whether a nuclear war could be kept from spreading and involving the United States and the Soviet Union with their vast arsenals, especially given their existing ties with other countries. (For example, as noted in Chapter 4, India has been a military client of the Soviet Union in recent years, while Pakistan has been closely embraced by Washington.)

One complicating factor in nuclear proliferation is the problem of distinguishing "peaceful" from "nonpeaceful" nuclear technology. Peaceful nuclear technology includes such devices as PNEs (peaceful nuclear explosives), which can be used to level mountains or dig holes more efficiently in construction or mining operations, along with nuclear power reactors, which can provide an alternate energy source. More and more countries, both developed and underdeveloped, are seeking such technology. India's explosion of a militarily useful nuclear device in 1974, ostensibly for "mining" purposes, used "peaceful" materials supplied by the United States and a reactor supplied by Canada. In addition to the six members of the nuclear club, sixteen other states had by 1980 built or purchased nuclear reactors capable of producing weapons-grade fuels.[13] In 1981, Israel staged a "preventive strike" against the "research reactor" provided by France to Iraq.

CHEMICAL AND BIOLOGICAL ARMS RACES

Although nuclear proliferation gets the lion's share of the world's scare headlines, the development of **chemical** and **biological weapons** is potentially just as deadly. Chemical gas agents and germ warfare have been around since the early twentieth century. Gas was used with devastating effect in World War I; the British, Americans, and Germans lugged gas cannisters around the battle sites of World War II but never used them for fear of opening the door to retaliation. Biological weapons capable of producing anthrax or cholera epidemics were also available in smaller quantities. Mustard gas was used again recently by Iraq in its Gulf war with Iran. By 1984 an estimated thirty countries and possibly two NGOs—the PLO and the Namibia liberation front (SWAPO)—possessed chemical arms.[14] Such weapons have been increasingly refined over the years. Paralysis, respiratory failure, and death can be caused within a few minutes or hours by not more than .4 milligram of certain nerve gases.

Today's research in nerve and toxic gases and microorganisms is related to civilian chemical and biological programs, and therefore is very difficult to police. Poisonous gases such as hydrogen cyanide and phosgene are useful in manufacturing dyestuffs and other consumer chemicals. Nerve gases are closely related chemically to certain pesticides. It is relatively simple to convert from civilian to military production. Because germ agents are difficult to control, bacteriological warfare research now concentrates on isolating the lethal agents in bacteria as well as in some plants and fungi—so-called "toxins" and "mycotoxins." American government officials accused the Soviets and Vietnamese of using mycotoxins in Laos and Kampuchea in the 1980s, but no proof could be found.[15]

With the widespread use of nuclear fuels as well as chemical and biological products, concern is growing that weapons produced from such substances will be obtained not only by governments but also by private individuals and terrorist organizations. Bomb-making materials produced as by-products of industrial nuclear power generation, such as plutonium 239, are becoming more plentiful. Instructions for making nuclear weapons are also now widely available. A few years ago, a Princeton University undergraduate named John Phillips designed a crude atomic bomb for about $2000. Nuclear wastes generally are packaged in sizes too large to be picked up and carried off by thieves, but theoretically they could be obtained by well-organized criminal or terrorist groups that might be able to hold whole populations at ransom. These dangers make the control of international violence, particularly arms races, an ever more pressing concern.

The Politics of Arms Control

If one wishes to understand why the control of international violence has proved exceedingly difficult, one must consider the variety of actors whose interests and demands affect global problem solving in this area. In this section we discuss the politics of controlling arms races, examining the negotiating positions taken by different states as well as the role of nonstate actors in shaping outcomes.

ACTORS AND ISSUES

Those wishing to stop arms races have advocated *arms control* and/or *disarmament*, two separate but related approaches to peace mentioned in Chapter 8. **Disarmament**, entailing the actual elimination of weapons, is generally a more ambitious undertaking than **arms control**, which can include not only reducing armaments but also more modest measures—"freezing" arsenals at existing levels or placing "ceilings" on future weapons stockpiles, as well as limiting the development, deployment, or use of certain weapons. The failure of the Geneva talks, conducted by the Committee on Disarmament since the 1950s, to achieve substantial disarmament agreements testifies to the difficulties in accomplishing disarmament. There was some progress in arms control in the 1970s, but efforts have been stalled in the 1980s. Although such agreements often have been criticized for allowing parties to forge ahead with favored weapons programs, they nonetheless represent potential solutions, albeit partial ones, to arms race concerns.

Arms control talks have occurred in several settings, including multilateral forums like the Geneva-based Committee on Disarmament (currently composed of forty member states) and special sessions of the UN General Assembly, as well as bilateral forums like the Strategic Arms Limitation Talks (SALT) between the United States and the Soviet Union during the 1970s and the Strategic Arms Reduction Talks (START) of the 1980s. Governments' views on conventional or nuclear arms control depend substantially on their definitions of national interests. For example, Third World states are prone to criticize the United States and the Soviet Union for carrying on unrestrained arms races. But, as noted previously, these critics also insist on their own right to receive or manufacture arms; therefore, they resist any efforts by Washington or Moscow to impose limits or conditions on military sales or on the spread of advanced weapons technology. They argue that until progress is made on disarmament worldwide or in key regions, minor powers cannot risk their security and allow major powers to monopolize sophisticated weapons. Nevertheless, certain less developed countries, such as Costa Rica and Gambia, deliberately have limited the size and budgets of their armed forces and have renounced the acquisition and use of certain types of weapons. In fact, most Third World countries have explicitly agreed not to pursue any nuclear weapons programs. However, their willingness to accept such restraints has been contingent upon promises by the United States and other nuclear states to supply them with the benefits of "peaceful" nuclear technology and to pursue meaningful arms control negotiations. Some developed states, like Japan, have also forsworn nuclear weapons, but might also feel compelled to rethink their positions in the future.

The dilemma for states seeking to maximize their security but to avert arms races is well expressed in the following passage on nuclear proliferation:

> To arrest the spread of nuclear weapons would be to perpetuate an international status quo in which some societies are denied political and strategic assets that other societies, certainly no more deserving, are entitled to have. Yet to condone nuclear proliferation in the interest of reducing the inegalitarian nature of the international system would be to abdicate responsibility for minimizing the risk of nuclear conflict.[16]

The politics of limiting conventional or nuclear weapons proliferation is fraught with cross-pressures. During the Carter administration, for example, the American government initiated a series of talks with the Soviets on limiting the spread of conventional arms (so-called CAT, or Conventional Arms Transfers, talks). During the course of the ultimately unsuccessful negotiations it became clear that the United States and the Soviet Union had basically reversed policies they had advocated during the 1960s, when Washington had proposed limits on arms transfers to the Middle East, only to find Moscow, which was pouring arms into Egypt in those days, unwilling. By 1977, however, America had become the major Middle Eastern and Egyptian arms supplier, and Washington thus proposed that CAT deal mainly with limiting arms supplies to Latin America and Africa, not the Middle East. Moscow, however, countered by proposing limits on Middle Eastern and Chinese arms supplies. The talks broke off, with each side proposing negotiating positions that would hamper the opponent's policies while leaving themselves relatively free to pursue business as usual.[17]

The weapons trade continues because both major and minor powers have deep political and economic interests in it. Major powers distribute weapons to favored clients and allies in order to gain political influence over recipients (such as U.S. arms payoffs to Egypt and Israel for signing the Camp David accords), to balance off hostile forces in key regions, to keep friendly regimes in power, to buy goodwill and concessions such as the right to use military bases in foreign countries, to lessen foreign states' desires for nuclear weapons, and to obtain trade and balance of payments benefits. Minor powers seek weapons for security, access to technology, economic tradeoffs, prestige, and influence.

Proliferation continues even though there is no evidence that the benefits listed above are reliably obtained through arms transfers. For example, arms sales to the Shah of Iran did not prevent his downfall and the disastrous loss of U.S. influence in Tehran; sales to Pakistan evidently have not slowed that country's nuclear weapons program; rather than stabilizing a region by balancing power, U.S. arms frequently have been used by both sides in a regional war; trade benefits are marginal when arms make up only 3 to 5 percent of the total exports of major Western arms producers such as the United States, the United Kingdom, and France; and the security dilemma of weapons acquisition, mentioned earlier, calls into question the security rationale.[18] Rather than questioning the benefits of arms transfers, governments normally operate on the assumption that they offer at least some leverage over foreign states, and some payoff for influential interest groups at home.

One cannot understand the international politics of arms control without also taking into account the domestic political forces that have an impact on the arms spending decisions of states. Earlier in the book, we mentioned the existence of military-industrial complexes in the United States and elsewhere. Among the actors who comprise such complexes are scientists working on weapons research, politicians seeking military contracts and other income-generating defense activities for their local constituencies, military and civilian officials in defense department bureaucracies that draw up arms shopping lists, and munitions manufacturers themselves. Many of these actors within the United States, in conjunction with counterparts in West Germany, Britain, Japan, Israel, and other states, have indicated special interest of late in joining in work on SDI because of the technological advantages to be gained as well as potential profits in subsidized research and development. Although such actors often have conflicting views among themselves,[19] all tend to have a stake in maintaining large defense expenditures and, at least indirectly, maintaining international arms races.

Although national governments have been the primary buyers and sellers of arms (with over 80 percent of U.S. arms sales to other countries being based on government-to-government agreements), much of the equipment is manufactured and marketed by private arms industries that sell to governments, either in their own country or abroad. In certain countries, the government

An "Apache Indian" heralds the rollout of the first production AH-64A Apache Attack Helicopter for the U.S. Army in 1983.

itself directly owns and operates weapons research, development, and production facilities. In the Soviet Union, for example, the government operates all arms production plants, though rival government-sponsored design teams are sometimes employed. In Western capitalist states, private defense contractors sometimes compete, especially where the home and export market is large enough to support multiple manufacturers. Otherwise, governments subsidize or encourage the consolidation of defense manufacturers so that they can compete with those of other countries. International arms "co-production" by combinations of industries from different countries has increased, particularly in Europe, whose companies are hard pressed to compete with larger American and Soviet arms manufacturers. Governments frequently balance purchases from each defense contractor in their country, in order to keep valued production lines in operation and design teams employed in case they are needed in wartime. Some states, including the United States, place rather strict and politically motivated limits on the amount of defense goods they will import, even if foreign prices are lower, in order to maximize the independence of their armed forces and the business of their defense contractors. In short, high-technology weapons are designed, produced, and merchandised with close company-government cooperation.

Weapons are promoted and marketed today much as cars or toys are, with giant exhibitions complete with attractive models trying to convince buyers of the merits of their wares. The "Madison Avenue" approach to arms peddling is vividly captured in the Sidelight in this section, which contains Anthony Sampson's account of a helicopter sales convention in Washington. In the weapons business, shadowy middlemen often are hired to ease the way for sales to certain countries where they have government connections. These agents normally take a 20 percent commission on the sale price and frequently have been accused of bribery. Agents' commissions, manufacturers' cost-overruns, and government agencies' overhead charges all add to the weapons export price inflation of recent years. Intermediaries can also help conceal the identity of arms buyers and sellers, thereby avoiding political embarrassment or "end use" violation charges. Israeli, American, and Russian arms turned

SIDELIGHT

THE ARMS BAZAAR

The whole basement looked like a giant toyshop or fairground, and at the stalls of each of the chief manufacturers—Boeing, Hughes, Sikorsky, or Bell—salesmen stood by tables of drinks and canapes to welcome the visitors. At the Air Force Association stall a man in a bright red jacket with a permanent smile invited guests to win a prize by guiding beans through a maze. As the evening developed the cocktail parties filled up with guests. . . . There were men from the Army, Navy and Air Force, with their wives; there were Congressmen diligently escorted by lobbyists; and there were solitary and earnest-looking officers and attachés from abroad. . . .

The names of the helicopters—the Sea Knight, the Chinook, the Sea Stallion—emphasized their playfulness. . . . The "Incredible Lifting Machine" could lower girders onto bridges, the "Big Mother" could rescue troops from impossible places, and one film showed two giant helicopters dancing round each other backwards and forward, to ballet music. . . .

On the television screens the peaceful antics of the helicopters were abruptly interrupted by outbreaks of killing. One moment the creatures were cavorting comically in the air, the next moment shooting off a quick burst of missiles, exploding in orange fire.

Source: From *The Arms Bazaar* by Anthony Sampson. Copyright © 1977 by Anthony Sampson. Reprinted by permission of Viking Penguin Inc; and Sterling Lord Literistic.

up in the Lebanese civil war, in the Iran-Iraq war, and in other conflicts during the late 1970s and early 1980s, distributed through a network of covert and third-party connections. This complicated traffic flow is one reason why arms embargoes, such as that imposed by the UN Security Council against South Africa, are so difficult to enforce. For clients wishing to purchase relatively portable weapons, such as rifles, private traders offer vast storehouses of equipment. One such firm, Interarms Ltd. of Manchester, England, with offices in North and South America, has generated up to $100 million a year in such sales.[20]

With so many elements contributing to arms races, it is a wonder that any arms control occurs at all. However, many actors furnish support for arms control efforts—including domestic interest groups such as antinuclear protesters in Europe, Japan, the South Pacific, and North America that apply public pressure on their governments; officials in the United Nations and other IGOs that facilitate arms control talks; and certain national government agencies that are specifically charged with responsibility for arms control (such as the U.S. Arms Control and Disarmament Agency). In recent years, in the wake of growing concern over nuclear weapons, even city councils and boards of aldermen in the United States have passed resolutions calling for a U.S.-Soviet nuclear weapons freeze. In 1983, the American Catholic bishops issued a pastoral letter criticizing many aspects of prevailing nuclear strategy as immoral; this may have been one of the factors leading both to changed views and changed rhetoric in Washington concerning nuclear weapons. The Reagan administration began to speak of doing away with such arms through defensive shields. In countries like the United States and the Soviet Union, defense department officials and others who are inclined toward heavy arms spending often themselves recognize the need for some degree of arms control, if only to preserve some current military advantage or to prevent the spread of highly sensitive and dangerous weapons technology to potential enemies.

NUCLEAR DETERRENCE AND ARMS CONTROL

One complication in nuclear arms control negotiations is the need to preserve "stability" in the nuclear arms race, i.e., to maintain the so-called "balance of terror" which in theory at least *deters* the use of nuclear weapons. **Nuclear deterrence** is a specific form of military dissuasion, of the type discussed in Chapter 7, and a separate logic and language have grown up around it (see the box on page 373). In the case of nuclear deterrence, the government of a nuclear-armed nation threatens to use nuclear weapons if an adversary initiates a nuclear or perhaps even a conventional strike against it or its allies. As applied to allies, this is a variation of deterrence called *extended* deterrence. For example, during the 1950s, Secretary of State Dulles threatened "massive retaliation" with America's largest nuclear weapons if the Soviet Union committed even the smallest conventional aggression in Western Europe or

THE LANGUAGE OF NUCLEAR DETERRENCE

In connection with the Strategic Arms Limitation Talks (SALT) between the United States and the Soviet Union during the 1970s, the U.S. Arms Control and Disarmament Agency compiled a short dictionary—the "SALT Lexicon"—to make the terms of nuclear deterrence understandable, if not "strangelovable." Here is a sample:

ICBM: Intercontinental ballistic missile.

Counterforce strike: A threatened attack aimed at an adversary's military capability, especially strategic military capability.

Countervalue strike: A threatened attack aimed at an opponent's cities.

MIRV: Multiple independently targetable reentry vehicle.

Bus: The part of a MIRVed missile's payload that carries the reentry vehicles.

Cold launch: The technique of ejecting a missile from a silo before full ignition of the main engine, sometimes called "pop-up."

Collateral damage: The damage to surrounding human and nonhuman resources, either military or nonmilitary, as the result of action or strikes directed . . . against enemy forces or military facilities.

Launch-on-warning: A doctrine calling for the launch of ballistic missiles when a missile attack against them is detected and before the attacking warheads reach their targets.

Megaton: A measure of the yield of a nuclear weapon equivalent to one million tons of TNT.

Penetration aids: Devices carried toward offensive delivery vehicles to neutralize the effect of defensive systems.

Throw-weight: The maximum useful weight which has been flight tested on the boost stages of the missile.

TRIAD: The term describing the basic structure of the U.S. strategic deterrent force . . . comprised of land-based ICBMs, the strategic bomber force, and the . . . submarine fleet.

Unacceptable damage: Degrees of destruction anticipated from an enemy second strike, which is sufficient to deter a nuclear power from launching a first strike.

Source: SALT Lexicon, rev. ed. (Washington, D.C.: U.S. Arms Control and Disarmament Agency, 1975).

elsewhere. Even after the Soviets developed **intercontinental ballistic missiles (ICBMs)** capable of hitting the continental United States in the 1960s, thereby eliminating any credibility the massive retaliation doctrine might have had, the United States continued to hold out the possibility of responding with nuclear weapons if Warsaw Pact countries, generally ahead of the West in quantities of conventional weapons such as tanks, launched any kind of attack on NATO countries. Indeed, the apparent imbalance of conventional forces, and the sense that nuclear threats enhance extended deterrence, are the main reasons why the United States has not accepted Soviet offers of a "no first use of nuclear weapons" pledge.

Since 1945, no state has employed atomic or nuclear weapons against another state, leading many observers to argue that such weapons are "usable" today only for *deterrent* purposes, to discourage aggression rather than to defend against it. It is also argued that such weapons allow "nuclear blackmail" by enabling nuclear powers to coerce submissiveness from other states through intimidation; Americans frequently have expressed concern that modern Soviet nuclear arsenals aimed at Western Europe are designed not so much to be used on Western Europe as to cause NATO allies to soften their opposition to Soviet foreign policy (thus bringing about the so-called "Finlandization" of Western Europe).

Although nuclear weapons are in a sense designed precisely *not* to be used— i.e., to be so frightening that opponents will refrain from war—the fact remains that weapons are always designed not only for deterrence purposes but for the combat needs of military services as well; therefore, they also are ultimately intended for possible use. This paradox complicates deterrence. For example, the Soviets have vowed not to be the first to use nuclear weapons but have warned that if their forces are attacked with such weapons (for instance in Central Europe in an escalating military confrontation with NATO), they would be prepared to widen the war by targeting the mainland of the United States with nuclear missiles. Their intention is to make sure American leaders are not deluded into thinking the United States could ride out another major war with damage confined only to Europe.[21] Many Western Europeans themselves, even those supporting strong nuclear forces stationed on their soil as a deterrent to Soviet aggression, have expressed concern over the possibility that those arsenals might actually be used in a future "limited nuclear war." In such a case, they feel, the "defense" of Europe would probably result in its destruction.

There is disagreement about whether nuclear war could be limited if it broke out, whether *tactical* (battlefield) or *intermediate-range* weapons could be used without ultimate escalation to **strategic weapons** (of global range capable of hitting the territory of the superpowers). For the United States and the Soviet Union, nuclear deterrence has meant, above all, convincing each other that a first nuclear strike by one side on the other's homeland would be suicidal—causing the state that suffered the first blow to retaliate with a devastating second strike on the aggressor. In order for such deterrent threats to be effective, the would-be aggressor must be convinced that the other side (1) would still have a second-strike capability left after absorbing the first blow, (2) would be willing to unleash the second strike, and (3) would be able to inflict "unacceptable damage" on the aggressor. Former U.S. Defense Secretary Robert McNamara maintained persuasively that *both* the United States and the Soviet Union should possess **mutually assured destruction (MAD)** capability, and that both should place their missiles in impenetrable silos (to be augmented by undetectable submarines) so that no first strike could disable them and prevent retaliation. The result, presumably, would be stable deterrence and peace.

Since the 1960s, American strategic posture has been that any disruption to such stable deterrence should be avoided. Even such policies as building fallout shelters in U.S. cities have been discouraged (even though smaller countries located near potential war zones, such as Finland and Sweden, have extensive public shelter programs). It is argued that shelters or **anti-ballistic missile (ABM)** defenses might signal to the opponent that the United States had the intention and capability of surviving a nuclear war, and therefore might be tempted to start one. This in turn might make Soviet leaders more trigger-happy and might cause them to contemplate a preemptive strike themselves against American ICBMs.

The advance of technology, however, has called some of the assumptions and premises of MAD into question. In particular, the increased number of nuclear warheads since MIRVs (multiple independently targeted reentry vehicles) were introduced to overwhelm possible ABM defenses in the 1970s, and the increased accuracy of delivery systems, have meant that nuclear explosions could conceivably knock out even hardened missile silos, thereby endangering retaliatory capability. Therefore, worried American or Soviet commanders might have a tendency to "launch on warning," i.e., not to wait for verification of an enemy attack, but to launch missiles at the first computer or radar warnings in order to avoid having these missiles destroyed on the ground. This lowers the threshold of nuclear war.

Furthermore, technological advances in radars, lasers, particle beam generators, and other electronic systems tempt leaders to devise defenses against missile attacks, such as the Strategic Defense Initiative. (See Figure 11.2 on page 376.) However, in addition to technical difficulties in mounting and protecting defenses against nuclear weapons, such systems also raise the same problems for strategic stability as the older ABM proposals: namely, they signal that one intends to survive a nuclear exchange. The entire future of land-based ICBMs remains in question, with advocates of SDI arguing that defenses either could make them obsolete or protect them on the ground, others noting that technological improvements in defensive systems are likely to encourage development of new ICBMs and offensive technologies to overwhelm the radars, and disarmament advocates calling for abolition of the vulnerable ICBMs by agreement. If anti-submarine weapons improve significantly in the next few years, the same arguments will be heard about the future of **submarine-launched ballistic missiles (SLBMs)**.

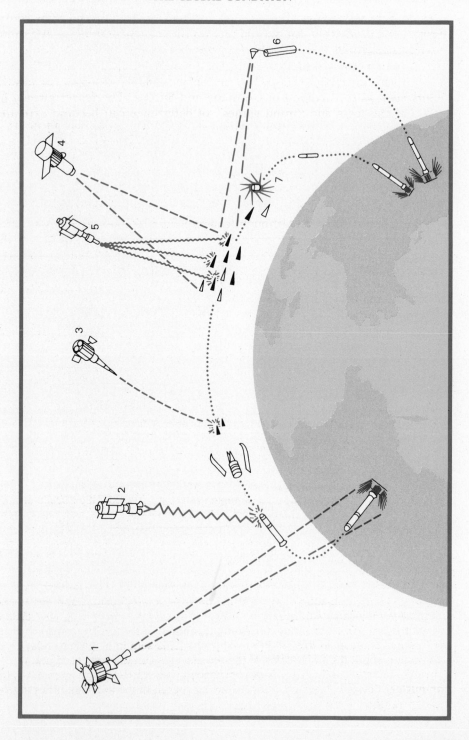

Aside from technology, the problem for nuclear strategy and arms control negotiations is whether one should rely on the logic of deterrence and should move to strengthen MAD capabilities, or whether one should abandon MAD and move to a different form of security. It is still not clear whether the peace among major powers since 1945 is due to the balance of terror, or to other factors such as the division of Germany and Europe. The reader already has seen that the logic and "mind games" of deterrence can become extremely convoluted and complex: "What do we think the opponent would think we think we could get away with if we took this action?" Recent articles have called into question the credibility of deterrent threats and warnings.[22] It has been clear since China attacked American forces in Korea in 1950, thereby facing possible retaliation by the world's preeminent nuclear power, that if a political goal is important enough to a government, it might even risk nuclear devastation to achieve it. Although leaders would be likely to hesitate before bringing on the incineration of their own societies, no one knows to what extent or for how long they would hesitate. This probable hesitation upholds deterrence and makes us safer; yet it also undermines the credibility of retaliatory threats, and might make us more vulnerable if a nuclear risk-taker launches a war expecting to get away unscathed.

Responses to Arms Race Problems: Arms Control Regimes

As noted in Chapters 9 and 10, the UN Charter essentially outlaws the use of armed force by states (except in self-defense), provides alternative mecha-

---

Figure 11.2 (facing page)
STAR WARS: LAYERED DEFENSE AGAINST BALLISTIC MISSILE ATTACK
The diagram shows how a layered defense system against ballistic missile attack might work. For simplicity, the diagram only shows single missiles. In reality there might be thousands involved. Similarly, there would be many more SDI platforms. The four layers of the defense might be as follows. An early-warning satellite (1) picks up the rocket launch. The first layer is a laser (2) which attacks rockets as they are climbing out of the earth's atmosphere. In the second layer, the "bus" which dispenses the warheads and decoys is attacked by an electro-magnetic railgun (3). In the mid-course phase of the defense, a target-acquisition and tracking satellite (4) locates and passes on information about the surviving warheads so that they can be attacked by, for example, another laser (5). The fourth layer is the terminal defense. In this, an infra-red probe (6) is sent into space to relay information about the trajectories of the remaining incoming warheads and to discriminate between live warheads and decoys. The warheads are intercepted by non-nuclear devices (7) which, after launch by rocket, home in using infra-red heat-seeking sensors.

FORMAL ARMS CONTROL AGREEMENTS (STATUS AS OF 1985)

Protocol for the Prohibition of the Use in War of Asphyxiating, Poisonous or Other Gases, and Bacteriological Methods of Warfare (Geneva Protocol) Declares that the parties agree to be bound by the above prohibition. Reservations by a number of states have limited the applicability of the Protocol to nations party to it and to first use only. Also, no prohibition of the manufacture of such weapons. Signed and entered into force: 1925; number of parties: 118.

Antarctic Treaty Declares the Antarctic an area to be used exclusively for peaceful purposes. Prohibits military bases, fortifications, maneuvers, and weapons testing there, as well as nuclear explosions and waste material storage, subject to possible future agreement. The question of territorial sovereignty in Antarctica has not definitely been resolved, although the contracting parties meet together periodically to discuss outstanding issues. Signed: 1959; entered into force: 1961; number of parties: 30.

Partial Test Ban Treaty Prohibits nuclear weapons tests or any nuclear explosions in the atmosphere, outer space, and under water. It has helped curb radioactive pollution caused by nuclear fallout. But testing underground has continued, making it possible for parties to the treaty to develop new generations of nuclear warheads. Signed and entered into force: 1963; number of parties: 111.

Outer Space Treaty Prohibits the emplacement in orbit around the earth of any objects carrying nuclear weapons or any other kinds of weapons of mass destruction, the installation of such weapons on celestial bodies, or the stationing of them in outer space in any other manner. The establishment of military bases, installations, and fortifications, the testing of any type of weapons, and the conduct of military maneuvers on celestial bodies are also forbidden. Outer space has remained open, however, for the passage of ballistic missiles carrying nuclear weapons, and for the deployment of weapons not capable of mass destruction. Signed and entered into force: 1967; number of parties: 81.

Treaty of Tlatelolco Prohibits nuclear weapons in Latin America, and provides for agreements to be concluded with the International Atomic Energy Agency (IAEA) for safeguards. It thus established the first internationally recognized nuclear-weapon-free zone in a populated region of the world. Also, non–Latin American states are obliged to keep their territories which lie within the zone free of nuclear weapons, while the nuclear powers undertake not to use or threaten to use nuclear weapons against the zonal states. However, neither Argentina nor Brazil, the two potential nuclear powers in the region, are full parties to the treaty. Signed: 1967; entered into force: 1968; number of parties: 25.

Treaty on the Non-Proliferation of Nuclear Weapons (NPT) Prohibits the transfer of nuclear weapons by nuclear states and the acquisition of such weapons by non–nuclear weapon states. The latter are subject to IAEA safeguards to prevent diversion of nuclear energy from peaceful uses to nuclear explosive devices. The parties undertake to make the benefits of peaceful nuclear technology available to non–nuclear weapon states adhering to the treaty. Signed: 1968; entered into force: 1970; number of parties: 129.

Sea-Bed Treaty Prohibits emplacement on the sea-bed and the ocean floor and in the subsoil thereof beyond a twelve-mile zone of any nuclear weapon or other weapon of mass destruction, as well as structures or facilities for storing, testing, or using such weapons. However, the treaty presents no obstacle to a nuclear arms race in the whole of the marine environment. Signed: 1971; entered into force: 1972; number of parties: 74.

Accidents Measures Agreement Pledges the United States and the Soviet Union to improve safeguards against accidental or unintended use of nuclear weapons. (An executive agreement rather than a treaty.) Signed and entered into force: 1971; number of parties: 2.

Biological Weapons Convention Prohibits biological means of warfare, including development, production, and stockpiling of bacteriologic and toxin weapons, and calls for their destruction not later than nine months after the entry into force of the Convention. However, chemical weapons, which are more controllable and predictable than most biological arms, are still the subject of disarmament negotiations, particularly on the subject of verification of compliance. Signed: 1972; entered into force: 1975; number of parties: 99.

Anti-Ballistic Missile Treaty (ABM Treaty) Imposes limitations on U.S. and Soviet anti-ballistic missile defenses, confining such defenses to one site in each country (as of 1974), and prohibiting development and deployment of new systems, though not research on such systems. Signed and entered into force: 1972; number of parties: 2.

Prevention of Nuclear War Agreement Requires consultation between the United States and the Soviet Union if there is danger of nuclear war. (An executive agreement rather than a treaty.) Signed and entered into force: 1972; number of parties: 2.

Helsinki Declaration Contains confidence-building measures included in the Final Act of the Conference on Security and Cooperation in Europe. Provides for notification of major (at least 25,000 troops) military maneuvers in Europe at least twenty-one days in advance or as soon as possible for short-notice maneuvers. States may invite observers to attend the maneuvers. Signed and entered into force: 1975; number of parties: 35.

Environmental Modification Convention Bans military or other hostile use of techniques to produce "widespread," "long-lasting," or "severe" changes in weather patterns, ocean currents, the ozone layer, or ecological balance. Signed: 1977; entered into force: 1978; number of parties: 45.

Protocols additional to the 1949 Geneva Conventions Provide for the protection of victims of international and non-international armed conflicts. Reiterate the rule of international law that it is prohibited to use weapons and methods of war that cause unnecessary suffering, and expands prohibitions on indiscriminate attacks to cover bombardment of cities or other areas containing similar concentrations of civilians. Dams, dikes, and nuclear electric power generators are placed under special protection, and guerrilla fighters are accorded rights as prisoners of war. These provisions constitute a step forward in the development of humane laws of war, but do not specifically define notions such as "unnecessary" or "excessive" suffering or ban specific weapons producing such effects. U.S. military interpretations are that only "undefended" cities and towns constitute protected civilian targets. Signed: 1977; entered into force: 1978; number of parties: 48 (protocol on international armed conflict) and 41 (protocol on non-international armed conflict).

Inhumane Weapons Convention Bans the use of fragmentation bombs in the human body; bans the use against civilians of mines, booby traps, and incendiaries. Signed and entered into force: 1981; number of parties: 26.

South Pacific Nuclear Free Zone Treaty Bars the possession, testing, and use of nuclear weapons or dumping of nuclear waste in the South Pacific. Spurred by continued French nuclear testing in the region. Signed and entered into force: 1986; number of parties: 8.

Sources: SIPRI, *Armament or Disarmament? The Crucial Choice* (Stockholm: 1982), pp. 26–30; John Turner and SIPRI, *Arms in the '80s* (London: Taylor and Francis, 1985), pp. 102–110; Ruth Leger Sivard, *World Military and Social Expenditures, 1985* (Washington, D.C.: World Priorities, 1985), p. 30; and "Australia OKs Treaty on Nuclear-Free Zone," *Christian Science Monitor* (December 9, 1986), p. 2.

nisms whereby states can resolve their differences peaceably (through the World Court and other vehicles), and establishes enforcement procedures for applying sanctions against states should aggression occur (through the Security Council).[23]

The UN Charter, along with the machinery established by it, is a central component of a global regime for controlling violence. Related to this regime are a number of treaties and institutions dealing specifically with arms control that have been created in recent years. As with the UN Charter, the arms control regime is imperfect. Not all states have ratified relevant agreements; even among those states that have, compliance can be erratic as governments hedge on fulfilling certain conditions; verification of whether agreements are being honored is often difficult; many issues are not covered by agreements; and treaties expire and must be renewed. Nevertheless, global cooperation is emerging to lessen the worst effects of arms races.

One observer has noted that "it seems that the agreements already concluded . . . are designed not to halt or reverse the arms race but rather to institutionalize it and regulate it."[24] Although there is much truth to this statement, particularly as regards the U.S.-Soviet arms competition, it somewhat understates the degree of arms control that has occurred since World War II. The box on pages 378–380 lists major bilateral and multilateral arms control agreements in effect in recent years. Negotiations also are continuing on such issues as "mutual and balanced force reductions" (MBFR) in Europe, strategic and theater nuclear arms limitations, arms in outer space, further nuclear test bans, and a chemical weapons ban. In the area of unilateral restraints on nuclear weapons, the Soviet Union suspended nuclear tests for an extended period in 1985, suspended tests on anti-satellite weapons in 1982, had a freeze on the deployment of medium-range missiles in Europe in 1985, and offered a "no first use" pledge in 1982. Previously the United States unilaterally halted production of biological weapons in 1969, leading later to a multilateral ban on biological weapons, and suspended work on the "neutron bomb" (designed to kill enemy troops with less collateral damage to surrounding buildings) during the Carter years only to resume development under the Reagan administration. As one can see, numerous restrictions have been imposed on the testing, production, stockpiling, transfer, deployment, and use of various kinds of weapons. As one also can see, however, there remain several weaknesses in existing treaties as well as several areas in which negotiations have thus far failed to produce agreement.

In particular, agreements have been reached mainly on projects and activities that were not of very high priority (e.g., militarizing the sea bed or the moon) or that were especially frightening or destabilizing (e.g., nuclear proliferation and ABM development; the latter was also thought to be impractical at the time of the ABM treaty, before the emergence of new radar and particle beam technologies which brought SDI plans into conflict with that treaty). On the issue of nuclear testing, for example, efforts to broaden the 1963 above-ground test ban agreement to prohibit underground testing as well have been stalled by American desires to perfect new nuclear devices, in part for the SDI program. Since 1963, the United States has conducted approximately 450 underground nuclear tests and the Soviet Union approximately 400; France and China, which tested in the atmosphere until 1974 and 1980 respectively (since they were not parties to the 1963 agreement), have conducted along with Britain at least another 178 tests.[25]

The arms control regime can be divided into those agreements dealing with nuclear (or "strategic") weapons and those concerning conventional weapons. The nuclear category includes bans on the testing of nuclear weapons anywhere except beneath the ground; bans on the placement of nuclear weapons in orbit around the earth, on the moon, on the ocean floor; prohibitions on the transfer of nuclear weapons from nuclear to nonnuclear states; and limitations on the size and nature of the nuclear arsenals of the major powers. Interestingly, there is no rule that explicitly forbids a state from *using* nuclear weapons first (in the event it is attacked and is engaged in a war).

The biggest controversy surrounding nuclear arms control has centered on the bilateral **Strategic Arms Limitation (SALT) agreements** between the United States and the Soviet Union. The SALT I Treaty and Interim Agreement of 1972 set ceilings on the number of offensive nuclear launch vehicles (missiles and bombers) as well as antiballistic missile emplacements that the two sides could possess. The SALT II agreement, necessitated by the expiration of the SALT I Interim Agreement in 1977, was designed to lower the ceilings and limit the number of MIRVs. However, it was not approved by the U.S. Senate. Although the failure to ratify was ostensibly due to the Soviet intervention in Afghanistan, strong opposition to the treaty had surfaced in the Senate, especially among those who argued that it would allow the Soviet Union to gain or maintain a strategic weapons lead.

The Reagan administration took office in 1981 vowing to renegotiate a treaty remedying SALT's deficiencies. Washington's new Strategic Arms Reduction (START) proposals concentrated on reducing the number of warheads on land-based missiles available to the two sides, in the process striking at Russia's main nuclear strength. The negotiations were broken down into three interconnected parts: strategic (long-range) forces, intermediate-range European and Asian theater nuclear forces (INF), and space weapons. The Soviets were concerned about American SDI initiatives, and came to offer deep cuts in ballistic missiles and a comprehensive nuclear test ban in return for long delays in the development and deployment of SDI. Terms were left somewhat vague, and *verification* of agreements remained open to question. While both sides had adhered informally to most SALT II provisions, the U.S. exceeded the SALT II nuclear limits by deploying additional strategic weapons in 1986. In the public debate that followed, the prospect of a restructuring of nuclear deterrence, possibly including elimination of superpower nuclear arms in Europe, frightened some Western leaders who feared that reduced nuclear deterrence might increase the risk of conventional war. The "prominent solution" in the U.S.-Soviet START negotiations appeared to be in the vicinity of a 50 percent cut in strategic weapons, major reductions in theater (European and Asian based) weapons, including missiles, bombers, and warheads, together with an approximately ten-year reaffirmation of the ABM treaty, which would include elaboration of what would happen if either or both sides perfected SDI-type defenses.[26] At some point, British and French weapons might also be brought into the European theater agreements. Despite the rhetoric in Washington and Moscow about eliminating nuclear weapons, it appears that the nuclear genie will remain out of the bottle for many years to come and will represent a continuing challenge for arms controllers.

Another basic ingredient of the arms control regime is the **Nuclear Non-Proliferation Treaty (NPT) of 1970,** which the United States and the Soviet Union both actively promoted. The NPT was partly responsible for the advent of SALT negotiations, since both countries had promised to undertake serious bilateral nuclear arms talks in return for the nuclear restraint shown by the rest of the international community. Nuclear states that are parties to the NPT agreement are pledged not to transfer nuclear weapons to nuclear have-nots, while the latter are pledged not to attempt to acquire nuclear weapons. Although more than 100 countries have ratified the treaty, several nuclear powers (France, China, India) as well as potential developers of nuclear weapons (such as Israel, Pakistan, and Brazil) have refused to do so. While France and China have not provided nuclear weapons to other states, they have objected to NPT on the grounds that it is inherently biased in favor of preserving American-Soviet nuclear dominance over the rest of the world.

Control of nuclear weapons is incomplete without limits on potential warfare in outer space. The **Outer Space Treaty of 1967,** banning the placement of "mass destruction" weapons in orbit around the earth or on celestial bodies, leaves obvious gaps into which hunter-killer satellites, particle beam lasers, and partial orbit weapons can sail. Satellites have become vitally important as communications and intelligence links in warfare; however, there are currently no prohibitions against weapons that can destroy satellites in efforts to blind the enemy. The United States and the Soviet Union held discussions in Helsinki in the late seventies about limiting the arms race in space, but these broke off with the defeat of the Carter administration. When, in 1981 at the United Nations, the Soviet Union offered a treaty banning antisatellite weapons, there was no favorable U.S. response. The U.S. Congress later placed restrictions on the testing of such weapons, however.

Since World War II, conventional arms control has been given somewhat lower priority than nuclear arms control but has proceeded along at least two main avenues: (1) agreements designed to promote basic trust and cooperation and (2) agreements designed to limit or reduce armament levels.[27] In the first category are the "confidence building measures" of the Helsinki accords produced by the 1975 Conference on Security and Cooperation in Europe, whereby NATO and Warsaw Pact countries agreed to notify each other in advance of troop movements and war games. Efforts to achieve agreement on mutual balanced force reduction in Europe, which made some progress in the 1980s, fall in the second category, along with agreements controlling the use of "inhumane" weapons such as plastic explosives, claymore mines, booby traps, and biological and chemical weapons.

The **Geneva Protocol of 1925** prohibits the first use of lethal biological and chemical weapons by the signatories against each other. Now ratified by more than 100 states, the Protocol has been widely honored, although some violations have been reported and disputes have arisen about whether nontoxic herbicides and tear gases are covered by the agreement. The **Biological Weapons Convention of 1972,** also signed by most states, goes further than the Geneva Protocol in outlawing germ warfare, insofar as it forbids not only the use of biological weapons but even their production and stockpiling. Hence, countries that are party to the agreement, such as the United States and the Soviet Union, have been obliged to destroy any biological arsenals in their possession (although possession of chemical weapons is still permissible). In this sense, the 1972 Convention is a measure not only of arms control but of actual disarmament.

Certain agreements in the arms control regime are less verifiable than others. The Biological Weapons Convention, for example, has no inspection machinery; the United States and the Soviet Union have *ingredients* for biological weapons and carry on "defensive" research to combat each other's research programs. On the chemical warfare side, the Soviets offered to allow inspection of their chemical weapons facilities in the mid-1980s, but not of herbicide and other factories which could conceivably produce such substances. By contrast, information on compliance is easy to obtain in the case of Antarctic demilitarization agreements, since all expeditions to the area must be reported and can be photographed. Notification of activities in outer space is also generally sent to the UN Secretary-General, though the exact nature of satellite missions is often withheld. The SALT I agreement became feasible after the perfection of satellite photography in the 1960s, which made verification of compliance easier.

The **International Atomic Energy Agency (IAEA)** is responsible for safeguards on the use of nuclear fuels and disposal of wastes associated with the NPT agreement and the Treaty of Tlatelolco, which established a nuclear-weapons-free zone in Latin America. NPT signatories receiving nuclear fuels from other governments for power generation or research must return weapons-grade wastes (such as plutonium) to the donor country for disposal and must not use such fuels to manufacture weapons. The IAEA can inspect the civilian nuclear plants and warehouses of NPT signatories to detect any attempted diversion of fuels to weapons, and has placed photographic, TV, and other monitors in such plants for continuous surveillance. While no on-site inspections are required of the major nuclear powers, both the Americans and Soviets have agreed to on-site observations of peaceful explosions to verify that they do not violate the Partial Test Ban Treaty.

Immediately after World War II, the United States proposed the Baruch Plan whereby all atomic weapons would be placed under UN ownership and control. The Soviets—behind in atomic technology—refused, and so the nuclear arms regime came to include not UN ownership but instead the more modest IAEA "night-watchman" role of trying to detect arms control violations. In 1980 alone, IAEA conducted more than 1,100 inspections of more than 500 nuclear facilities around the world. In 1981, 80 tons of plutonium, 12 tons of highly enriched uranium, 5,000 tons of low enriched uranium, and 18,000 tons of natural uranium were accounted for under IAEA supervision.[28]

Nevertheless, the inspection procedures of the IAEA have frequently been criticized as inadequate to the task of preventing nuclear proliferation. However, the system was never designed to be foolproof. The NPT agreement sets no limit on how close countries can come to assembling nuclear weapons without actually doing so.[29] The 1980 attack by Israel (a nonsignatory of NPT) on the nuclear reactor in Iraq (a signatory) showed the Israelis' lack of confidence in IAEA safeguards. Although nuclear fuels have been largely accounted for by the IAEA, small amounts of weapons-grade materials have disappeared over the years; and some states, such as Israel itself, have acquired nuclear supplies through unknown channels. Although the night watchman can "blow the whistle" on an apparent nuclear violation or discrepancy in nuclear supply totals, it has little or no enforcement power. It can only refer the matter to the UN Security Council, call for the return of material and technical assistance already supplied, or suspend the offending state from IAEA membership.

Rapidly improving weapons technologies make verification of arms control, especially by "national technical means" such as spy satellites, increasingly difficult:

> Easy-to-detect systems—large, fixed, land-based ballistic missiles, and lumbering bombers—are becoming rare species in the nuclear arms competition. New generations of smaller, multi-mission weapons, such as cruise missiles, have been developed for use in the next decade. Farther away are aerodynamic and electromagnetic innovations, represented by the so-called "Stealth" technologies, which will enable airborne platforms to evade radar detection.... Large scale deployments of binary chemical weapons will compound already severe difficulties in monitoring CW stockpiles. With binaries, the nerve-gas precursors can be stored and transported separately and under less stringent safety conditions.[30]

It is easy to despair of the chances for arms control under such circumstances. How can one count the number of country X's planes or missiles when, through "Stealth," they cannot even be seen on radar? How can one tell whether country Y possesses nerve gases if such substances can be decomposed into separate parts and reassembled later? Yet important violations in the past were often detected not so much by super-sophisticated techniques but by old-fashioned spies, inadvertent leaks of information in publications or even in bars (information on Cuban missiles was gleaned this way in 1962), by aerial photography, and by careful analysis of technical data on the capabilities of the weapons of other states. It is important to bear in mind, as well, the political importance countries frequently attach to making agreements work. Neither the United States nor the Soviet Union wants nuclear weapons to be distributed widely around the world; the Soviets and Americans have informed each other of potential violations of the NPT and other agreements, including the discovery of a nuclear testing site in South Africa in 1979 (since dismantled) and a suspected nuclear explosion off the coast of South Africa in 1981 (which remains unexplained).

With all its flaws, the arms control regime has produced some major benefits for the world's population. For example, the **Partial Test Ban Treaty of 1963**

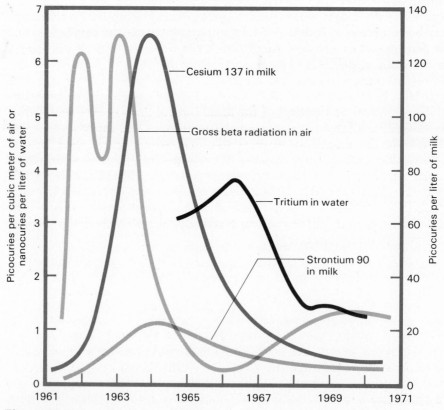

Figure 11.3
EFFECTIVENESS OF THE 1963 PARTIAL TEST BAN TREATY: RADIOACTIVE FALLOUT, 1961–1971

clearly has improved the environment by reducing atmospheric radiation and contamination of the food chain, as Figure 11.3 demonstrates. By going on record as unwilling to acquire nuclear weapons, more than 100 nonnuclear nations adhering to the NPT have made it politically embarrassing for themselves to test and build such weapons. Most of them, even if capable of developing nuclear arms, refrain from doing so because they simply do not need, want, or expect to afford such weapons, and because of political conflicts with neighbors they would face if they "went nuclear." They can repudiate, opt out of, or perhaps even evade the NPT agreement; but it will be impossible to hide their plans and far more costly politically to manufacture nuclear weapons than if there were no NPT. SALT allowed the United States and the Soviet Union to go on building new nuclear weapons, but at least set some ceilings on the numbers produced. As evidence of the importance of limits, both Washington and Moscow have been reluctant to abandon those set in the now expired SALT I and even in the unratified SALT II treaties. Removing all limits and embarking on an open-ended arms race would force the superpowers into burdensome spending programs for weapons that had previously been limited. It would also fundamentally change the psychology and threat perceptions involved in American-Soviet relations, and could thereby make the world a much less safe place in which to live.

The arms control regime, in summary, evidences conflict as well as cooperation. It is speculated that one reason the Reagan administration, basically suspicious and critical of the arms control process, was tempted by Soviet offers to cut large numbers of ballistic missiles was the advantage this would give to the defense in projects like SDI, which would then have to knock down far fewer enemy weapons. By the same token the Soviets insisted that their offers were contingent upon American concessions in limiting SDI development. Each side seeks advantages at the bargaining table, but the *joint* advantage in reducing the arms race is also an ever-present factor. The superpowers cooperate quite openly and actively on their joint desire to limit nuclear proliferation, for example.

Conclusion

Peaceful solutions to the world's pressing conflicts are necessary if arms races are to be contained. Although the 1982 UN World Disarmament Conference that was mentioned at the beginning of this chapter produced little of substance, it did symbolize humanity's continued quest to fulfill the biblical prophecy that nations "shall beat their swords into plowshares, and their spears into pruning hooks . . . and neither shall they learn war anymore."[31] If nothing else, the General Assembly *unanimously* expressed "its profound preoccupation over the danger of war, in particular nuclear war, the prevention of which remains the most acute and urgent task of the present day."

Unfortunately, despite the arms control regime, weapons are likely to remain plentifully available in the coming years. One particularly nightmarish concern is that lethal weapons of mass destruction could end up in the possession of nonstate actors such as terrorist organizations. Arms control and anti-terrorism regimes, then, seem intricately linked. As one nuclear strategist has put it, referring to the danger of nuclear terrorism, "The best way to keep weapons and weapons-material out of the hands of nongovernmental entities is to keep them out of the hands of national governments."[32] In the next chapter we look at another dimension of the problem of controlling global violence as we consider the morally and politically complicated issues related to international terrorism.

SUMMARY

1. Improved technologies have vastly increased the ability of humans to do violence to each other in the international arena. Both security and technological interests are involved in arms races.

2. The proliferation of both nuclear and conventional arms, as countries engage in competitive arms races, is a source of major concern. Even if such weapons are never used, their enormous cost diverts funds from more constructive social purposes. Poor countries are as eager as rich countries for new weapons and must rely heavily on arms transfers from abroad—from the United States, the Soviet Union, and European and Third World suppliers.

3. Six states now are members of the "nuclear club," with more than a dozen others on the verge of developing nuclear weapons capabilities. Although American and Soviet arsenals—which are roughly equal—dwarf those of all other states, nuclear capability of any size represents tremendous damage potential.

4. Chemical and biological weapons are potentially as deadly as nuclear weapons and are extremely difficult to police.

5. Nuclear arms control is complicated by concerns about nuclear deterrence. A debate has emerged recently about the benefits of relying on a balance of terror to keep the peace, as opposed to greater technological and political efforts to do away with nuclear weapons.

6. Given the mutual distrust among nation-states, arms control—i.e., reductions or restrictions in armaments—is a more realistic solution to arms race problems than is outright disarmament. However, even arms control is difficult, given the state and nonstate actors who see benefits in weapons procurement. Nonetheless, much progress has been made since World War II in developing an arms control regime that includes such agreements as the Nuclear Non-Proliferation Treaty, the Biological Weapons Convention, and the ABM agreements.

7. States seek both individual and joint benefits in the arms control regime, but agreements generally extend mainly to areas where the superpowers can agree or to issues of less than the highest priorities to the parties.

SUGGESTIONS FOR FURTHER READING AND STUDY

There are three major research groups that attempt to keep track of international arms levels. They utilize different definitions and measurements, however, and their estimates must be used carefully: (1) the Stockholm International Peace Research Institute (SIPRI), which publishes *Yearbooks on World Armaments and Disarmament;* (2) the International Institute for Strategic Studies (London), which annually publishes *World Military Balance;* and (3) the U.S. Arms Control and Disarmament Agency (ACDA), which issues annual reports in *World Military Expenditures and Arms Transfers* (covering ten-year periods). See also Michael Brzoska, "Arms Transfer Data Sources," *Journal of Conflict Resolution,* 26 (March 1982), pp. 39–75. For studies of global armament, see Hugh G. Mosley, *The Arms Race: Economic and Social Consequences* (Lexington, Mass.: Heath, 1985); and Peter Wallensteen, Johan Galtung, and Carlos Portales, *Global Militarization* (Boulder, Colo.: Westview Press, 1985).

On the dangers of nuclear arms races, see Michael D. Wallace, Brian L. Crissey, and Linn I. Sinnott, "Accidental Nuclear War: A Risk Assessment," *Journal of Peace Research,* 23 (1986), pp. 9–27; Robert McNamara, *Blundering into Disaster: Surviving the First Century of the Nuclear Age* (New York: Pantheon, 1986); Theresa C. Smith and Indu B. Singh, eds. *Security vs. Survival: The Nuclear Arms Race* (Boulder, Colo.: Rienner, 1985); and Jonathan Schell, *The Fate of the Earth* (New York: Knopf, 1982).

Among the best discussions of nuclear arms proliferation and control are William Epstein, *The Last Chance: Nuclear Proliferation and Arms Control* (New York: Free Press, 1976); Leonard S. Spector, *Nuclear Proliferation Today* (New York: Vintage, 1984); Ralph M. Goldman, *Arms Control and Peacekeeping: Feeling Safe in This World* (New York: Random House, 1982); William G. Hyland *et al., Nuclear Weapons in Europe* (New York: Council on Foreign Relations, 1984); *Progress in Arms Control? Readings from Scientific American* (San Francisco: W. H. Freeman, 1979); Bhupendra Jasani and Christopher Lee, *Countdown to Space War* (London: Taylor and Francis, for SIPRI, 1984); Richard Falk, "Toward a Legal Regime for Nuclear Weapons," in Falk *et al.,* eds., *International Law: A Contemporary Perspective* (Boulder, Colo.: Westview Press, 1985); and Alva Myrdal, *The Game of Disarmament: How the United States and Russia Run the Arms Race* (New York: Pantheon, 1976). Publications under the auspices of the Arms Control Association in Washington and the Council for Arms Control in London are also quite timely, as is the journal *Arms Control,* published by the University of Lancaster (England), Centre for the Study of Arms Control and International Security.

Conventional arms proliferation and control are discussed in Uri Ra'anan *et al., Arms Transfers to the Third World* (Boulder, Colo.: Westview Press, 1978); Cindy Cannizzo, ed., *The Gun Merchants* (New York: Pergamon, 1980); Stephanie G. Neuman and Robert E. Harkavy, eds., *Arms Transfers in the Modern World* (New York: Praeger,

1980); Michael T. Klare, *American Arms Supermarket* (Austin: University of Texas Press, 1984); Philip J. Farley *et al., Arms Across the Sea* (Washington, D.C.: Brookings Institution, 1978); "Soviet Weapons Exports: Russian Roulette in the Third World," *The Defense Monitor*, 8 (January 1979); and John Stanley and Maurice Pearton, *The International Trade in Arms* (London: Chatto and Windus, 1972). The characteristics of weapons and weapons-related programs and sales are often described in the magazines *Aviation Week and Space Technology; Defense and Diplomacy;* and *Jane's Defense Weekly.*

The Control of Violence:
Combatting International
Terrorism

In October of 1985, four armed Palestinians boarded an Italian cruise ship, the *Achille Lauro*, apparently planning to disembark at the Israeli port city of Ashdod where they intended to attack Israeli targets and pressure authorities to release several comrades held in Israeli jails. When the plot was discovered, the Palestinians seized the ship and took more than 400 passengers hostage. They proceeded to shoot an elderly, disabled American Jew named Leon Klinghoffer, pushing him together with his wheelchair overboard into the Mediterranean Sea. The episode ended with the hijackers fleeing from the ship and eventually being apprehended and tried in an Italian court.

The *Achille Lauro* incident was only one of some 800 cases of international "terrorism" that were reported in 1985,[1] although it was perhaps the most grisly. Other such incidents that year included the storming of the Palace of Justice building in Bogota, Colombia, by M-19 guerrillas, resulting in the deaths of more than 100 people, including over half the members of the Colombian Supreme Court; the mysterious explosion of an Air India jumbo jet, killing over 500 passengers; the skyjacking of a TWA airliner to Lebanon and the killing of an American navy diver on board; the skyjacking of an Egyptair Boeing airliner to Malta leading to 59 fatalities; and assorted other acts as violent if not as bloody.

As front-page headlines frequently remind us, terrorism is a growing international concern, although one that is complicated by the fact that there is considerable disagreement over what constitutes terrorism and over what are the proper responses for combatting the problem. In this chapter we seek to go beyond the headlines and explore the phenomenon in greater depth.

The Nature and Magnitude of the Problem

DEFINITIONAL QUESTIONS

There is no general agreement among scholars or lawyers on a clear definition of **terrorism.** Not everyone would concur that all the incidents noted above necessarily were the acts of terrorists. It has been said that one person's "terrorist" is another person's "freedom fighter." According to this logic, George Washington and the American revolutionaries could have been considered terrorists, at least in the eyes of the British authorities they were trying to overthrow. Likewise, Yassir Arafat and his followers in the Palestine Liberation Organization (PLO), fighting against Israeli occupation of what they consider their homeland, contend it was hypocritical for Menachem Begin, as Israeli Prime Minister in the 1970s, to denounce the PLO as "murdering terrorists." Begin himself had engaged in similar sorts of actions as a leader of the main Israeli underground movement (the Irgun) that struggled against

By permission of Johnny Hart and Field Enterprises, Inc.

One person's terrorist is another person's national liberation hero

the British in the late 1940s; the Irgun was responsible for blowing up the King David Hotel, killing many British soldiers as well as bystanders, and committing other acts of violence in the name of liberating "the Jewish homeland" from British rule and creating the state of Israel.[2]

However, the problem with this logic is that, if one accepts the view that "one person's terrorist is another's national liberation hero" and that the distinction is completely arbitrary and dependent upon which side of the fence one sits on, then any act of violence can be excused and legitimized so long as someone invents a justification. Aside from being a recipe for chaos and anarchy, this type of logic ignores the principle that not all acts of violence are equally acceptable and condonable. At a minimum, certain acts (such as the aforementioned murder of Leon Klinghoffer) seem so barbaric and insensitive to nearly universal standards of civilized behavior that one can reasonably label such acts "terrorist" in nature.[3] There are additional characteristics as well that would seem to distinguish terrorism from other acts of violence. Despite the conceptual problems we have mentioned, and the absence of any universal agreement on a clear definition, we can identify certain elements that tend to be associated with terrorism.

According to one authoritative definition, terrorism is "the use of violence for purposes of political extortion, coercion, and publicity for a political cause."[4] This definition suggests that terrorism entails a combination of at least three elements. First, terrorism ordinarily involves the threatened or actual use of *unconventional* violence—violence that is spectacular, violates accepted social mores, and is designed to *shock* so as to gain publicity and instill fear. Even in the most deadly interstate warfare—during World War II, for example—certain rules have been observed widely by the combatants (e.g., those rules governing treatment of POWs). Terrorists, however, generally observe no "rules" of conduct whatsoever; there are virtually no limits to the degree or type of violence they are prepared to utilize.[5] The tactics they resort to can include hijackings (of anything from a jumbo jet to an elevator);

kidnappings; letter, car, and other bombings; assassinations; and injections of
deadly substances. (In 1978, a Bulgarian journalist was stabbed in a London
subway with an umbrella treated with a deadly toxin derivative of castor
beans.) Such acts need not even be costly: would-be terrorists need only the
price of a phone call, since they can *threaten* any of the above acts and, if
believed, achieve the desired effect.

Terrorism is characterized, secondly, not only by unconventional violence
but also by violence that is politically motivated. The political context of
terrorism distinguishes it from mere criminal behavior such as Bonny-and-
Clyde type armed robbery or gangland slayings, which may be every bit as
bizarre or spectacular but which are driven ordinarily by nonpolitical (private
rather than public) motives. One would not call the Mafia, for example, a
terrorist organization—even though it is heavily involved in international
drug trafficking and other criminal activities, at times in league with terrorist
groups—precisely because its existence and activities are not motivated by
any recognizable political goals.[6] In contrast, incidents like the *Achille Lauro*
affair and others noted at the outset of this chapter are clearly motivated by
political goals, ranging from the creation of a national homeland to the
elimination of foreign cultural influence in a region to the total political and
economic transformation of society. One can debate whether these goals are
legitimate or not, and whether "political" offenses committed in pursuit of
these goals should be punished in the same manner as "criminal" offenses,
but in any case the inherently political nature of terrorism must be understood.

A third key distinguishing characteristic of terrorism, following from the
first two, is the almost *incidental* nature of the *targets* against whom violence
is committed. That is, the immediate targets of terrorism—whether persons
or property, civilian or military—usually bear only an indirect relation to the
larger aims impelling the terrorist. Sometimes the targets are carefully chosen
individuals—well-known businessmen, government leaders, or diplomats,
such as the oil ministers at a 1975 OPEC meeting in Vienna who were held
hostage by the notorious international terrorist named "Carlos"; at other
times the targets are faceless, nondescript masses—ordinary men, women and
children, as in the random slaughter that has occurred in airports, department
stores, and other public places. In any case, the victims are merely pawns
used in violence that is staged with the intent of reaching a much wider
audience.

One might add a fourth ingredient of terrorism, having to do with the
nature of the *perpetrators* of such violence. It can be argued, with some
qualifications, that organized terrorism is an activity engaged in essentially
by *nonstate* actors; i.e., it is mainly the tactic of "outgroups" denied legitimate
status and of the politically weak and frustrated (e.g., the PLO, the Irish
Republican Army in Northern Ireland, the Red Brigades in Italy), who see
terror as the best tool for contesting the vast armies and police forces possessed
by the governments of nation-states.[7] A distinction perhaps can be made

between, on the one hand, those groups that operate relatively openly as armed revolutionary or guerrilla forces (limiting their attacks primarily to military targets) and, on the other hand, those groups that operate in a highly "clandestine and sporadic" fashion with random targets; the latter are clearly terrorists, although in practice the distinction can often be blurred.[8]

It is true, of course, that governments frequently use violence and armed force, either internally as part of the "police" function or externally as part of the "defense" or "security" function. While certain excessive forms of violence used by authorities are sometimes referred to as "state terrorism"— in particular, the systematic torture and repression a government inflicts on dissidents within its own society, or assassinations and "dirty tricks" committed by secret state agencies against foreigners—the terrorism label normally does not apply to actions taken by official governmental bodies.[9] For example, however repugnant one might find the Soviet Air Force's shooting down of the KAL 007 Korean airliner that strayed into Soviet airspace in 1983 (resulting in the deaths of all 269 passengers), few if any observers would characterize it as an act of terrorism. Similarly, although some have called the dropping of the atomic bomb on Hiroshima in 1945 an act of terrorism—because it represents to them seemingly indiscriminate violence against innocent civilians—this would seem to confuse terrorism with interstate warfare. It should be added that many governments do at least indirectly support and sponsor terrorist groups (e.g., the relationship between the Iranian government and the Shiite Muslim movement known as Islamic Jihad in the 1980s).[10] We will elaborate on this point in our later discussion of the politics of combatting terrorism.

TRENDS IN INTERNATIONAL TERRORISM

Terrorism is not a new problem. The term itself can be traced to the Reign of Terror during the French Revolution in the eighteenth century. It was a terrorist's bullet that set off World War I with the assassination of Austria's Archduke Franz-Ferdinand. A classic historical example of prolonged terrorism is the struggle of the Irish Republican Army (IRA) to pressure Britain to grant Ireland independence, beginning with the Easter rebellion of 1916, continuing through the establishment of the Irish Republic (Eire), and extending into contemporary times in Northern Ireland.

Although terrorism is not new, it is a more serious concern today in several respects. Modern industrial society seems especially vulnerable to spectacular displays of violence, given such inviting targets as jumbo jets and nuclear power stations. The existence of modern communications technology enables terrorists to receive instant publicity through the world's mass media and can contribute to an epidemic effect worldwide. This same technology permits terrorists to operate on a global scale. Where terrorism in the past was primarily a domestic concern, frequently associated with civil wars, today's hijackers and other terrorists tend to have strong international ties that often enable them to coordinate their efforts throughout the world.

Statistical surveys confirm the common impression that international terrorism has been on the rise. According to the U.S. State Department, there were more than 5,000 international terrorist incidents worldwide between 1975 and 1985, averaging approximately 500 incidents annually, with 1985 witnessing an upsurge to over 800 incidents reported.[11] Over the past decade an estimated 4,000 people were killed and 8,000 wounded in such attacks, although most terrorist incidents (75 percent of all attacks) have not resulted in casualties. There is evidence that terrorism is becoming more deadly; where in the 1970s terrorists tended to concentrate their attacks on property, the 1980s have witnessed increased attacks on people. Bombings have tended to be the main instrument used, accounting for roughly half of all incidents in recent years. Armed attacks and kidnapping also have been prevalent techniques. The flashier tactics of hostage-taking and hijackings have constituted only 2 percent of all terrorist incidents.

Western Europe has been the primary scene of international terrorist activity in recent years, providing the geographical locale for some 40 percent of all international terrorist incidents between 1975 and 1985; the Middle East has been the locale of 30 percent, Latin America 20 percent, and other regions the rest.[12] American citizens and property abroad have been primary targets, with Americans targeted in over one-third of all incidents reported in 1985. Among the other "most victimized nationalities" in recent years have been the British, French, Israelis, Iraqis, and Libyans. If Western European soil has been the most prominent site of international terrorism, the Middle East has been the most fertile source, with Middle East terrorists responsible for almost half of all incidents reported worldwide in 1985; the most lethal terrorist violence has been inflicted by Arabs against fellow Arabs in various parts of the world.

One reason that terrorism has become such a popular pursuit is that it often produces precisely those results that terrorists seek, at least in terms of attracting vast international attention to themselves and their causes. The hijackings, kidnappings, and killings carried out by various Palestinian nationalist groups (such as the slaying of Israeli athletes at the 1972 Olympic Games in Munich), while technically not always successful in achieving political objectives, clearly helped make "Palestinian" a household word throughout the world. In the early 1970s Golda Meir, the Israeli Premier, wondered "Who are the Palestinians?" and maintained that no such recognizable group existed. By the 1980s, no leader could make such a claim, even for propaganda purposes.

In addition to attracting attention, terrorism has frequently paid off in concrete terms. Terrorists generally have been remarkably successful in achieving their immediate goals relative to the costs they have incurred. One study of sixty-three major kidnappings and barricade operations between 1968 and 1974 produced the following statistics: terrorists had an 87 percent success rate in seizing hostages; there was a 79 percent probability of all members of the terrorist team involved in an operation escaping punishment or death, a 40 percent chance that at least some of their demands would be met, a 29 percent chance of full compliance with their demands, and an almost 100 percent probability of obtaining major publicity. Another study revealed that terrorists suffer casualties in only 14 percent of all incidents.[13]

On the other hand, many of these statistics reflect only short-term success for terrorists. Larger causes and ultimate political goals are rarely realized through terrorist methods. As one student of terrorism has put it: "Terrorism has indeed resulted in political change, but it has had a lasting effect only in fairly rare circumstances when political mass movements used terrorist tactics in the framework of a wider strategy. There is no known case in modern history of a small terrorist group seizing political power; society usually tolerates terrorism only so long as it is no more than a nuisance."[14]

The Politics of Combatting Terrorism

Terrorism has become something more than a "nuisance." While one can take some consolation in the fact that terrorism seems to be a futile pursuit, in terms of rarely achieving any major long-term goals sought by its practitioners, the phenomenon nonetheless poses a serious threat to society because of the disruptive violence and fear it generates within and across national boundaries. Efforts to combat the problem have come up against a variety of competing interests represented by nonstate as well as nation-state actors. In this section, we look further into the actors involved in terrorism, their motivations and demands, and the politics surrounding the attempt to forge a global counterterrorist consensus.

THE DILEMMAS OF COMBATTING TERRORISM

On May 9, 1978, Italian police found the crumpled, bullet-ridden body of former Italian Prime Minister Aldo Moro in the trunk of a car, after weeks of desperate searching for his kidnappers, who had identified themselves as the Red Brigades, a group intent on overhauling all of Italy's societal institutions. The Italian government, composed of some of Moro's closest friends and former colleagues, had refused to deal with the terrorists or consider their demands and had ignored Moro's poignant letters pleading for assistance. Aldo Moro, one of the most noted of history's terrorist victims, was "tried and convicted" by a "People's Court" and executed by its order. (Moro's kidnappers were themselves sentenced to life imprisonment by an Italian court in 1983.)[15]

The Moro case illustrates the perplexing dilemmas that can be experienced in the attempt to control terrorism. The Italian government was roundly

The body of Aldo Moro, former Italian Premier kidnapped in 1978, is found in a car on a Roman road.

criticized by some for inflexibly refusing to negotiate for the life of a statesman. Yet the leaders reasoned that any negotiations under such duress would encourage future kidnappings and put national leaders as well as ordinary citizens at further risk. The horrifying impact of the Moro murder hardened the Italian authorities, so that when the same Red Brigades group four years later expanded their operations into the international arena and kidnapped American NATO General James Dozier, the Italian government's refusal to negotiate along with a well-coordinated manhunt resulted in the release of the hostage and the deaths of the terrorists. It also resulted in the decline of the Red Brigades, as most of the leaders either were imprisoned or fled the country; an organization that had numbered in the hundreds had been reduced to a mere handful.

While the success of the Italian government in combatting the Red Brigades suggests the virtues of adopting a hard-line strategy toward terrorists, the problem has not been eliminated. Many Red Brigades members are thought to be hiding out in France where, despite Italian efforts to have them extradited back to Italy to stand trial, they are protected by the traditional French attachment to the right to political asylum. Some members still operate in

Italy and carry out occasional terrorist attacks. Moreover, other terrorist groups both indigenous to Italy and of external origin have filled whatever void was left by the demise of the Red Brigades.[16] It is not clear, then, that hard-line strategies necessarily deter terrorism, since terrorists are generally dedicated, even fanatical, in the pursuit of their goals. It is also not clear that negotiations generally encourage terrorists to be any bolder than they otherwise would be, though repeated refusals to bargain or make concessions could discourage terrorism against specific states.[17]

Terrorism is difficult to combat as a political tactic for a variety of reasons. Open, democratic political systems cannot patrol all public places, search all citizens and foreign travelers, and monitor everyone's political connections. And whatever the type of political system they operate within, many terrorist groups are tightly organized by cells, so that members do not know the identity of members in other cells or those in command, and therefore cannot expose them under interrogation or torture.[18] Elaborate routines are developed to separate advance teams of planners from those actually entrusted with the execution of terrorist actions, with only the top leadership knowing the various elements of the organization.

Many countries prepare specially trained counterterrorist squads, such as West Germany's G-9 Group, to combat terrorists. Private security firms also are employed to train business executives and public officials in methods to avoid terrorist attack. (Many of the directions given to potential victims—such as varying their schedules and routes to and from work—can become as complex as the plans used by terrorist cells.) These efforts seem worthwhile, yet if the fight against terrorism is carried beyond certain limits, basic human and civil rights can be abridged and endangered. Governments must balance the costs of terrorism against the costs of the political repression necessary to stop it. Does the population want constant searches in public places and private homes, with troops lining the streets? Can a democracy survive using such means? At some point the remedies can become politically intolerable, though judging by examples from Israel and Northern Ireland, civilian populations will accept stiff, prolonged police measures in the interest of safe streets. As the following discussion will show, the internal politics of combatting terrorism is in many respects not nearly as troublesome as the international politics.

A "FREEMASONRY"[19] OF TERRORISTS: ACTORS AND LINKAGES

Who are the most important actors involved in terrorism, and what links exist among them internationally? We have noted that organized terrorism is mainly the tactic of "outgroups," such as the Red Brigades, seeking to upset the established order in some fashion. Distinctions between terrorist groups can be made according to their goals, which include (1) creation of new states (e.g., Croatians in Yugoslavia, Basques in Spain, Kurds in Iraq and Iran, and

the Front de Libération de Québec in Canada); (2) destruction of existing states
(e.g., the Popular Front for the Liberation of Palestine); (3) liberation of territory
from the control of others (e.g., Armed Forces for National Liberation of Puerto
Rico, Irish Republican Army, and the Palestine Liberation Organization [PLO]);
(4) subversion of regimes (e.g., Tupamaro guerrillas in Uruguay, M-19 guerrillas
in Colombia, and Shining Path in Peru); (5) elimination of foreign cultural
influence from a region (e.g., Islamic Jihad); and (6) complete transformation
of the world political and economic order (e.g., Red Brigades in Italy, Red
Army Faction in West Germany, United Red Army in Japan, and Direct Action
in France).[20] Some terrorist groups have fairly well-developed and clear political
demands; others lack clear manifestos and seem to indulge mainly in symbolic
violence against the establishment. Some groups, such as the IRA, have long
lives, while others have short lives and are then replaced by another group,
as the old Baader-Meinhof gang was succeeded by the Red Army Faction in
West Germany in the 1980s.

Terrorist organizations often experience internal dissension among their
membership over goals and strategies, so that splinter factions can develop
and produce a further proliferation of terrorist groups. For example, the
Palestine Liberation Organization is not so much a distinct organization as it
is an umbrella movement that encompasses several autonomous Palestinian
factions—including Fatah led by Yassir Arafat, the Palestine Liberation Front,
and the Arab Liberation Front—united only by their common animosity
toward Israel. In addition, other more extremist Palestinian groups have split
off from the PLO, such as the Democratic Front for the Liberation of Palestine
and the Popular Front for the Liberation of Palestine, oriented more toward
Marxist ideology as well as more violent tactics in pursuit of a Palestinian
homeland.[21] It is often hard to know which groups are responsible for which
specific acts of violence.

Despite the rivalries that exist among various terrorist groups, there is
much cooperation. Indeed, there is much evidence that transnational ties
among terrorist groups are increasing. Some Palestinian elements, for example,
have reputedly helped to train members of the Red Army Faction of West
Germany, M-19 guerrillas in Latin America, and members of the Irish
Republican Army as well as the Japanese Red Army. Palestinians have also
had strong ties with the Red Brigades, evidenced by the joint communiqués
issued by the latter and a Lebanese extremist group in 1984, taking responsibility for the murder of Leamon Hunt, an American diplomat in charge of a
multinational team supervising an Egyptian-Israeli truce agreement.

Until now, the discussion has focused on terrorism as a practice engaged
in by *nonstate* actors. However, governments also can and do participate in
terrorism, even if not as openly. Some governments funnel financial support
to foreign terrorists engaged in skyjacking, kneecapping (the practice of shooting
a victim's legs, a particular favorite of the Red Brigades), and bombing activities.
Others are more directly involved in assassinations and other acts of political
violence through clandestine agencies.[22] The complex ties that connect

nonstate and state actors can be seen in the box on page 402, which describes the web of terrorism in the Middle East existing in the mid-1980s. Clearly, the politics of controlling international terrorism is complicated by the fact that the world's governments are not universally opposed to terrorism (or at least do not all define it the same way).

In UN General Assembly sessions and in other forums where controls on international terrorism have been discussed, states have often taken conflicting positions. In the early 1970s the United States introduced a draft convention on terrorism requiring the extradition or prompt trial of hijackers and kidnappers, especially in cases where hostages were government officials. Generally, the United States and other industrialized states favored the principle that terrorists are criminals and that the world community shares a responsibility to apprehend them and bring them to trial. In contrast, Third World states, while deploring the deaths of innocent victims, argued that terrorism is often the only available weapon of the oppressed, and that before it can be outlawed, measures should be adopted to rectify the political and economic injustices perpetrated particularly by industrialized states and their allies. The latter argument, for example, was invoked to condone PLO violence against Israel and to justify Third World support for rebel groups in southern Africa. Latin American countries and other Third World states were also concerned about the traditional right of states to offer asylum to "political prisoners" or sanctuary to those fighting in "national liberation" movements.

The ultimate fate of the American draft convention and of similar antiterrorism measures is discussed below in our examination of international responses to global violence. It has often taken nonstate actors to move the international community toward some acceptance of controls on terrorism. One cannot fully describe the politics of controlling skyjacking, for example, without noting the role of an IGO like the International Civil Aviation Organization (ICAO) in helping to draft anti-skyjacking conventions, as well as the role of an NGO like the International Federation of Air Line Pilots Associations (IFALPA) in pressuring governments to adopt stronger air safety measures and to refuse asylum to skyjackers. It was IFALPA—in essence, a transnational labor union—that threatened not to fly into countries harboring skyjackers, following a particularly brutal murder of a Lufthansa Airlines pilot during a 1977 skyjacking. The IFALPA action, combined with pressure from the United States and other governments, resulted in a token but nonetheless unprecedented UN General Assembly resolution condemning aerial hijacking.

Responses to Terrorism Problems: Antiterrorism Regimes

It is possible for countries individually to develop improved capabilities for combatting terrorism. Counterterrorist techniques might include: launching

THE WEB OF TERRORISM IN THE MIDDLE EAST

Basic, uncluttered political causes drive Middle Eastern terrorists, who [according to congressional testimony given by Robert Oakley, the head of the U.S. State Department's Office of Counter-Terrorism] ... fall mainly into two groups—"fanatical Palestinians who have split off from the main-line Palestine Liberation Organization led by Arafat and often have the direct support of Libya, Syria, and/or Iran; and Shia [Shiite] zealots from various Arab countries, especially Lebanon, who are inspired and trained, often armed and financed, and, to varying degrees, guided by Iran." Diplomats and intelligence people are split on the degree to which Iran, Libya, and Syria actually direct and support the groups. Not a great deal is known for certain, but the consensus runs like this: Syria uses terrorism against Americans wherever its interests collide with those of the United States, as in Lebanon, but Syria apparently isn't involved with the hit teams sent to Europe to kill Americans. Libya's Qaddafi blusters and threatens, but the larger part of the terrorism he exports is directed against Libyan dissidents, whom he calls terrorists. Among governments, Iran's is the most committed in a doctrinal, or ideological, sense to terrorism, and it does control some of the Lebanese Shiite groups operating in the Bekaa Valley, even though the area lies within Syria's zone of influence. There are several Lebanese groups, but two main ones—Amal (*amal* is the Arabic word for "hope") and the Lebanese Armed Revolutionary Faction. Amal, which isn't controlled by Iran, is supposedly somewhat more conservative than LARF. Intelligence people work hard at distinguishing the two groups and trying to identify their members. A member of Amal, it seems, can move freely into LARF, but there is no movement in the other direction, because LARF is Marxist, and Amal won't accept Marxists. LARF, according to the consensus, is responsible for most of the murders and attempted murders of American diplomats in Europe (and certainly takes credit for them). This assumption troubles some experts, one of whom—an American—says, "You can't say this action was committed by LARF and that one by Amal and another by Islamic Jihad"—the group that has claimed credit for the attacks on the American Embassy in Beirut. "These are all people selected to perform bold missions. They are a continuum of cellular units. There may be a brain—a clever brain—behind it, but the whole is animated by religious passion."

Source: John Newhouse, "A Freemasonry of Terrorism," *The New Yorker,* July 8, 1985, p. 51. Reprinted by permission; © 1985 John Newhouse.

preemptive strikes against terrorist bases before terrorists can act; launching retaliatory strikes against terrorist bases following terrorist incidents, both for punishment and deterrent purposes; improving intelligence-gathering methods so as to penetrate and subvert terrorist groups; strengthening the protection of likely terrorist targets such as embassies and airports; and creating elite rescue and counterterrorist units (SWAT teams) capable of intervening in hostage-taking and other crisis situations (e.g., the U.S. Army's Delta Force and the Navy's SEAL teams). The success of such measures depends very much on circumstances; terrorist bases seldom can be isolated from the surrounding countryside, and attacking them in foreign countries can have grave political consequences.

Because of the international character of much contemporary terrorism, unilateral efforts by governments to combat the problem are not as likely to succeed as concerted efforts taken by governments acting together. As with the arms control regime, steps to control international terrorism have involved mainly the drafting of treaties. National and international judicial institutions have also come into play since terrorism cannot be stopped without the arrest, trial, extradition, or jailing of terrorists. Under international law, a state traditionally has been free to choose whether to return fugitives sought by other states, to prosecute those individuals in its own courts, or to set them free. Only if a state has an extradition treaty with another state does it incur obligations to surrender fugitives, although even these treaties normally do not require the return of those accused of "political" crimes. However, the concept of global responsibility for preventing certain wanton acts of terrorist violence and for apprehending terrorists has slowly been gaining acceptance in recent years. Even bitter rivals like the United States and Cuba have sometimes agreed on the need to control hijackings and assassinations, to protect diplomats, and to extradite or refuse asylum to terrorists.

Increased global concern about terrorism was particularly evident following the slaughter of Israeli Olympic athletes by Palestinian commandos at Munich in 1972. This led to efforts to prevent both kidnappings and assassinations, especially of so-called "internationally protected persons" (diplomats and other national representatives). The UN General Assembly passed a resolution on the status of such persons in 1973, and a UN Convention on the Prevention and Punishment of Crimes Against Internationally Protected Persons Including Diplomatic Agents was opened for ratification in the same year. A UN Committee on International Terrorism also was established. Eventually, after many years of debate—particularly on terrorism's role in national liberation struggles—an International Convention Against the Taking of Hostages was drafted in 1979; during the 1980s, more than forty countries, including the United States, signed it. The convention provides that states shall prosecute or extradite all hostage-takers, though rights of national liberation movements are recognized.[23]

Three other conventions, developed by the International Civil Aviation

Controlling terrorism?

Organization, specifically address crimes relating to air travel. The **Tokyo Convention of 1963** obligates signatory states to effect the safe release of hijacked aircraft, passengers, and crew entering their borders. The **Hague Convention of 1970** goes further in requiring states to extradite or prosecute hijackers in their custody. The **Montreal Convention of 1971** broadens the Hague provisions to include not only skyjackers but anyone committing any acts of sabotage against airports or aircraft on the ground, with the ICAO empowered to suspend air travel to states that fail to comply. These conventions have been only "the first stage in the development of an international regime for the control of aircraft hijacking."[24] Loopholes in their coverage, and the fact that many states have not yet ratified them, allow the harboring of skyjackers to continue, but skyjacking is more difficult than it was when no consensus on the need for travel safety and airport security existed.

Certain regional IGOs have gone even further to outlaw certain types of terror tactics. For example, in 1976 the Council of Europe (composed of most Western European states) decided that political causes would be no excuse for leniency in punishing or extraditing terrorists committing offenses involving various lethal devices, although again several European states did not ratify the agreement and some that did stated reservations qualifying the extent of their obligations.[25]

In addition, states have shared technological innovations aimed at countering terrorism. Electronic search devices have been installed in airports and other public buildings. Air hijackings have been greatly reduced in states with increased airport security. The movements of terrorists are tracked through international police agencies such as INTERPOL, and information from national computer data banks is exchanged between states.[26] Yet none of these measures guarantee success against terrorism; Italian police ignored Turkish warnings about the terrorist who eventually shot Pope John Paul II in 1981, and other warnings were ignored in a little-known but shattering 1977 incident described as follows:

> So complex is our modern world and so close the margins for error that terrorist disruptions can produce unforeseen tragedies. The explosion of a time bomb in the airport flower shop on Gran Canaria in March 1977 by a little-known terrorist group seeking independence for the Canary Islands from Spain was responsible for the diversion of air traffic to the airport at Santa Cruz de Tenerife. Two jumbo jetliners that had been redirected to Tenerife collided, producing the worst civil aviation disaster in history.[27]

One modest but hopeful sign of growing global recognition of the terrorism problem appeared two months after the brutal slaying of Leon Klinghoffer in the *Achille Lauro* affair. On December 9, 1985, the UN General Assembly for the first time, by unanimous approval, passed a resolution containing a blanket condemnation of all terrorism. The resolution "unequivocally [condemned] all acts . . . of terrorism whenever and by whomever committed" and "deeply [deplored] the loss of human lives which results from such acts of terrorism." It also called upon all states to "refrain from organizing, instigating, assisting, or participating in terrorist acts." The resolution even managed to embody a single if vague agreement on the definition of terrorism, as acts "that endanger or take innocent human lives, jeopardize fundamental freedoms, and seriously impair the dignity of human beings." The problem has remained one of getting universal agreement in the application of these general principles to specific cases.

Conclusion

A variety of approaches can be utilized to combat terrorism, ranging from unilateral national policies to global regime-building, highly visible displays of force to more quiet behind-the-scenes intelligence work, and actions directed at government sponsors of terrorism to actions directed at terrorist groups themselves. Counterterrorist tactics in many cases, however, fail to come to grips with the root causes of the problem and therefore provide only momentary relief.

We have noted that terrorist groups are driven by a variety of motivations.

While some groups are almost wholly nihilistic, calling for sweeping changes that amount to the total destruction of society, others are animated at least somewhat by more persuasive concerns, even if their methods are extremely questionable. If humanity hopes to achieve the goal of maintaining *peace* and reducing "physical" violence in the world—whether it takes the form of terrorism or more traditional warfare—it is unlikely this can be done without also addressing concerns about *justice* and what has been called "structural" violence, i.e., hunger, poor health care, and other forms of economic deprivation that can kill and maim no less effectively than guns and that so often underlie the resort to violence. Hence, in the next two chapters we turn to international economic concerns, focusing first on the functioning of the global economy as a whole and then on the economic development of the Third World.

SUMMARY

1. There is considerable disagreement over which groups and which actions can be considered "terrorist" in nature, with the argument frequently made that "one person's terrorist is another's national liberation hero."

2. However, terrorism conceptually tends to be characterized by at least three common ingredients: (1) it involves the threatened or actual use of unconventional violence designed to shock so as to gain publicity and instill fear; (2) it is politically motivated; and (3) the immediate targets or victims, whether persons or property, usually bear only an indirect relation to the larger aims impelling such violence.

3. One might add a fourth characteristic: the tendency for the perpetrators to be nonstate actors, i.e., "outgroups" denied legitimate status and seeking to upset the established order in some fashion, although some states and their governments do participate at least indirectly in terrorism either through clandestine agencies or by funneling arms and other forms of support to terrorist groups.

4. Although terrorism is not a new phenomenon, it has become a more serious concern in the contemporary era due to the increased vulnerability of modern industrial civilization, the existence of communications and travel technologies that permit terrorists to operate on a global scale, and the expanded ties among terrorist groups across national boundaries.

5. Between 1975 and 1985, there were an average of 500 international terrorist incidents reported annually, with the most recent trend data showing an upsurge of such activity. Although only one-quarter of all such incidents have resulted in casualties, the trend is toward increased bloodshed. Western Europe has been the most frequent locale of terrorist attacks, with American property and citizens being the primary target along with Western Europeans and Arabs. The Middle East has been the main source of terrorism, particularly various Palestinian groups and Islamic fundamentalists, although terrorist groups can be found in every region of the world.

6. Terrorists generally have been highly successful in achieving their immediate goals relative to the costs incurred, even if their larger aspirations—which can range from creation of an independent homeland, to the elimination of foreign cultural influence

from a region, to the transformation of the world political and economic order—
are rarely fulfilled.

7. Efforts to combat terrorism are complicated by the fact that governments often
have conflicting definitions of terrorism, with some, particularly in the Third World,
arguing that it is a legitimate weapon of the oppressed. However, the concept of
global responsibility for combatting terrorism has slowly been gaining acceptance,
manifested by the Hague, Montreal, and Tokyo anti-skyjacking conventions

---

SUGGESTIONS FOR FURTHER READING AND STUDY

Several research groups carefully monitor trends in international terrorism. Two in
particular which prepare often-cited annual reports are the U.S. State Department's
Office of Counter-Terrorism (in its *Patterns of Global Terrorism* series) and the Rand
Corporation's Program on Political Violence headed by Brian Jenkins (in its *Chronologies
of International Terrorism* and *Trends in International Terrorism* series).

Good conceptual treatments of terrorism can be found in the following works:
Grant Wardlaw, *Political Terrorism* (New York: Cambridge University Press, 1983);
Yonah Alexander, ed., *International Terrorism: National, Regional and Global Per-
spectives* (New York: Praeger, 1976); J. Bowyer Bell, *Transnational Terror* (Washington,
D.C.: American Enterprise Institute, 1975); John Dugard, "International Terrorism:
Problems of Definition," *International Affairs*, 50 (January 1974), pp. 67–81; Martha
Crenshaw Hutchinson, "The Concept of Revolutionary Terrorism," *Journal of Conflict
Resolution*, 16 (September 1972), pp. 383–396; Walter Laqueur, *Terrorism* (Boston:
Little, Brown, 1977); and Paul Wilkinson, *Political Terrorism* (New York: John Wiley,
1975).

On the threat posed by terrorism in the nuclear age, see Robert K. Muller, "Mass
Destruction and Terrorism," *Journal of International Affairs*, 32 (Spring/Summer 1978),
pp. 63–89; and Brian M. Jenkins, "Will Terrorists Go Nuclear?" *Orbis*, 29 (Fall 1985),
pp. 507–515. The dilemmas of dealing with terrorism are examined in Richard
Clutterbuck, *Living with Terrorism* (London: Faber and Faber, 1975); Edward F.
Mickolus, "Negotiating for Hostages: A Policy Dilemma," *Orbis*, 19 (Winter 1976),
pp. 1309–1325; and William P. Lineberry, *The Struggle Against Terrorism* (New York:
H. W. Wilson, 1977).

There are many case studies of specific groups, such as Helena Cobban, *The
Palestinian Liberation Organization: People, Power and Politics* (New York: Cambridge
University Press, 1984); Robert P. Clark, *The Basque Insurgents* (Madison: University
of Wisconsin Press, 1984); and J. Bowyer Bell, *The Secret Army: A History of the IRA,
1916–1970* (Cambridge, Mass.: MIT Press, 1974). A study in "state terrorism," as
practiced by Argentina, is provided by Jacobo Timerman, *Prisoner Without a Name,
Cell Without a Number* (New York: Knopf, 1981). For an excellent review of the
literature on terrorism, together with references to terrorism bibliographies, see
Augustus Richard Norton, "Review Essay: International Terrorism," *Armed Forces
and Society*, 7 (Summer 1981), pp. 597–627.

The Promotion of Prosperity: Keeping the World Economy Running

All countries today find themselves part of a larger global economy that has become sufficiently interdependent to move some observers to speak of the world as a "global shopping center" or "marketplace."[1] Along these lines, the U.S. State Department in recent years has supplemented U.S. Commerce Department reports on Gross National Product with its own periodic reports on the "Planetary Product"—the sum of the GNPs of all nation-states—which had reached $10 trillion by 1980.

The existence of a *world* economy is manifested in many different ways. We have already commented on the intricate international ties that characterize the global arms trade. More visibly, Americans traveling abroad will find McDonald's hamburgers sold in Kuwait, Kent cigarettes in Romania, Pepsi in the Soviet Union, and Coca-Cola in China (the latter product is reputedly served 180,000 times a minute worldwide).[2] Japanese travelers will find Toyotas peddled in West Germany, Nikon cameras in Brazil, and Minolta copiers in the United States. French tourists will find Michelin tires, French designer clothes, cosmetics, and wines sold not only throughout the European Community but throughout the world. Other nationalities can likewise find their "native" products advertised on billboards in various corners of the globe, although the financing, production, and distribution of goods and services around the world are becoming so internationalized that it is difficult to determine the national identity of many products. We noted at the beginning of this book the creation of the "world car," the Ford Escort, with shock absorbers made in Spain, steering gears in Britain, rear brakes in Brazil, door lifts in Mexico, wiring in Taiwan, and assorted other parts from other countries, all assembled in the United States and sold in showrooms in America and abroad.

Escorts are not the only "American" products that are in reality manufactured largely *outside* the United States for import into the United States and other markets. Most Singer sewing machines, Kodak cameras, and even the baseballs used in the "all-American" game of major league baseball are produced overseas. Moreover, many items that are "made in U.S.A." and are commonly assumed to be "as American as apple pie"—such as Alka-Seltzer, Nestlé-chocolate bars, Foster Grant sunglasses, Pepsodent toothpaste, and Girl Scout cookies—are produced by companies owned by foreign interests. (An especially poignant example of this phenomenon is the jeep, made famous by the U.S. Army during World War II, which is manufactured by American Motors, a company whose name belies the fact that in the 1980s it was taken over for several years by Renault, a car company owned and operated by the French government.)

Clearly, the international economy is characterized by a complicated web of relationships that cut across national boundaries and touch every part of the globe. However, recalling our earlier discussion of interdependence, it is important to keep in mind that the flow of international trade and other economic activities is uneven. Some countries, such as those in Western

Europe, have especially strong regional ties while others have intense bilateral ties. Not all countries are equally involved in the international economy and not all share equally in the planetary product. Some countries deliberately choose not to become more involved, while others seek to expand their participation but are prevented from doing so by various barriers that inhibit free economic transactions among states. Attempts to eliminate these impediments and to integrate the international economy through global institutions in the UN system have met with only partial success. Hence, in thinking of an interdependent world economy, one should not lose sight of the fact that national borders continue to pose major economic barriers and that central regulative institutions remain weak.

In this chapter we want to convey a sense of the overall structure and dynamics of the international economy. We will examine the problems associated with the coordination of the international economy, the politics of economic problem solving, and the various regime-building efforts that have been undertaken. Comparing regime-building in the economic sphere with that in the peace and security (control of violence) area, one observer comments: "Conflict and cooperation are, of course, commingled in both [economic and security] issues, but . . . economic issues are characterized far more by elaborate networks of rules, norms, and institutions."[3] Still, people disagree not only over how much coordination of the international economy is necessary, but also what purposes coordination should serve—for example, greater overall economic growth and efficiency, or also economic justice (a more equitable distribution of wealth). There is also disagreement over what role international institutions should play in the process. Before examining the problems, politics, and regimes found in specific sectors of the international economy, we first should review a number of widely different, conflicting perspectives on the nature of international economic relations as a whole.

The Nature and Magnitude of the Problem: Alternative Views

It is commonly observed that the first three decades after World War II generally were characterized by steady economic growth and rising employment worldwide. These trends began to be reversed in the early seventies, after the OPEC-induced "oil price shocks" and other developments resulted in growing economic problems for developed and less developed countries alike. Whereas in the 1960s Western developed states had grown economically at an average rate of roughly 5 percent a year, this rate of growth declined to 3.2 percent in the 1970s, and fell still lower in the 1980s, to barely 1 percent. By the early 1980s, unemployment in major Western developed states was on average over 8 percent, and in some countries like the United States and Britain had reached double-digit levels. Economic problems spanned the ideological divide, as Communist developed states also experienced economic troubles, reflected in the decline of the Soviet Union's annual growth rate from 5 percent to 2.5 percent in the 1980s. The economic growth rates of the less developed countries, except for OPEC and a few other more advanced developing countries, decreased on average from 4.5 percent in the 1960s to 2 percent by the 1980s, with recession in the West aggravating the already depressed economies of the Third World.

Taken as a whole, a world economy that had expanded robustly at a rate of about 5 percent annually in the 1950s and 1960s contracted to only 2 percent growth during the 1980s. Coincident with this trend was a contraction of world trade; total world exports had grown rapidly since World War II and had reached a volume of $2 trillion by 1980, but then leveled off and even declined subsequently. The picture that emerged in the 1980s, then, was a world economy in trouble. Despite some progress made in some countries on some fronts, such as the Reagan administration's somewhat successful efforts at combatting inflation and unemployment in the U.S., the signs all continue to point to serious structural problems within and between national economies.[4] There are different schools of opinion on what can and should be done by the international community to revive the world economy.

THE CLASSICAL LIBERAL INTERNATIONALIST SCHOOL

This school of thought developed in reaction to the so-called **mercantilist school** of international economics, which predominated in the seventeenth and eighteenth centuries. The main tenets of mercantilism were the following: the pursuit of *national* power and wealth were the primary ends of foreign policy, with power dependent upon wealth and vice-versa; in order to maximize national interests, a state's international economic transactions had to be subject to strict *governmental control,* including restrictions on exports and imports, foreign investment, and other economic activity; and, given the presumed absence of any harmony of interests among states, economic decision making had to be based on *unilateral* policies rather than collective problem solving through consultation and participation in international institutions.[5]

In contrast, the **liberal internationalist school,** first championed by Britain in the nineteenth century and later by the United States after World War II, holds that even though national governments can be expected to pursue foreign economic policies designed primarily to serve the national interests of their own individual societies, there are benefits to be derived from *cooperation* with other states.[6] In the process of interstate competition over the distribution of the world's wealth, states are likely to share certain mutual interests in collaborating to open up trade and investment opportunities for each other so as to maximize the special economic advantages of each country. Some countries have low labor costs, others high technology, still others raw materials, and so forth. Ultimately, consumers in all nations can expect to benefit from an international economy that is based on the most efficient allocation and use of resources among countries. To this end, classic economic liberals argue that governments should reduce tariffs and other barriers to international economic activity, allowing goods and services to flow as freely as possible across national boundaries.

From the perspective of the liberal internationalist school, the role of international institutions such as the International Monetary Fund and the World Bank should be to maintain as much order and stability as possible in economic relations between states while helping to facilitate international economic activity and expand the planetary product. This view of the international economy is one that is widely held in developed capitalist societies today.

THE *DEPENDENCIA* SCHOOL

According to the **dependencia** school, the international economy, rather than consisting of over 150 national economic units competing on roughly equal terms, instead consists of two sets of states pitted against each other in a pattern of interstate competition that clearly favors one group at the expense of the other.[7] In particular, *dependencia* theorists argue that the world economy is divided into an exploitive Northern tier of developed states ("the core") and a dependent Southern tier of less developed states ("the periphery"). This relationship, which can be traced back to the colonial era, is supposedly perpetuated by an international division of labor whereby the North concentrates on producing and exporting more lucrative, high-priced technology and manufactured products while the South concentrates on producing and exporting relatively low-priced raw materials, agricultural commodities, and unfinished goods. The result of this unequal exchange, the *dependencia* school contends, is massive poverty in the South and massive wealth in the North.

From the *dependencia* perspective, the role of international institutions should not be to maintain order and stability in economic relations between states but to *change* those relations in a way that redistributes wealth more evenly between the core and the periphery. *Dependencia* ideas, originally developed in the context of U.S.–Latin American economic relations, have come to be accepted throughout much of the Third World.

THE WORLD SYSTEM SCHOOL

The **world system school** is similar to the *dependencia* school in that it also conceives of the world economy in terms of core and periphery areas.[8] However, rather than viewing international economic relations as interactions between states controlled by national governments, the world system school tends to focus attention on interactions between *nonstate* actors, namely economic elites and non-elites that often transcend national frontiers. This school argues that the international economy is not driven by national interests but by the interests of economic elites in various countries, particularly in developed capitalist societies, who compete with each other in accumulating wealth. National governments are generally assumed to be the instruments of economic elites, although conflicts can arise between political and economic leadership circles. Instead of national political capitals (like Washington, Bonn, and Ottawa) being the key loci of economic decision making in the world, it is the financial capitals (like New York, Frankfurt, and Toronto) that are thought to be the major power centers; in places such as London, Paris and Tokyo, the political and economic capitals happen to be in the same location. These three cities are in fact among a dozen "global cities"—the "command and control centers" of the world economy that are the headquarters sites of the world's largest multinational corporations and banks.[9] Strictly speaking, this network of global cities, and not the North as a whole, is the core of the international economy, although these cities are generally found in the Northern Hemisphere. The surrounding towns, villages, and urban areas of the world constitute the semiperiphery and periphery, with wealth "trickling down" to the masses more and more slowly the farther one lives from the global cities.

The world system school essentially takes a Marxist approach to international economics, i.e., viewing international economic relations not so much as a contest between rich and poor states but as a struggle between rich and poor classes in a world society. According to this analytical perspective, multinational corporations and intergovernmental organizations are simply the latest institutional responses of modern economic elites to a changing world, just as economic elites in an earlier era developed the nation-state as the chief mode of human organization fitted to their needs. The world system perspective shares much in common with *dependencia* thought, but calls for drastic change rather than mere reform of existing economic relationships. It is an approach that has been adopted in various parts of the world, both by some social scientists seeking to obtain a better understanding of the connection between international economics and international politics and by radical thinkers seeking to revolutionize the world.

THE ANALYSIS OF INTERNATIONAL ECONOMIC RELATIONS

It should be clear from the previous comments that there are many different ways one can think about the international economy and analyze current problems. In addition to liberal, *dependencia*, and Marxist perspectives, one might add a fourth viewpoint as well—the "realist" perspective, which holds that these various economic schools of thought neglect the real driving force behind the workings of the international economy; i.e., rather than the management of international economic relations being about the promotion of global prosperity, justice, or efficiency, it is about the pursuit of national self-interest and power that characterizes all international relations.[10] While realists rightly remind us of the mercantilist tendencies of all states, that school cannot account fully for the many cooperative linkages that have developed across national boundaries among governmental and nongovernmental actors enmeshed in economic interdependence. In the discussion that follows, we will draw on insights from all these schools as we focus on specific sectors of the international economy.

One can conceptualize the international economy as consisting of three distinct but interrelated components (the "three c's"):[11] (1) the commerce sector, (2) the currency sector, and (3) the capital sector. Within each of these sectors, we will examine the issues at stake as they relate to three sets of national actors: (1) the developed capitalist states, (2) the developed Communist states, and (3) the countries of the Third World. While considerable diversity exists within each of these groups, they nonetheless represent three fairly distinct sets of actors with particular roles in the international economy. Within each of the three sectors, we will also examine the relevant international institutions that have been established to help manage the global economy. Special attention will be devoted to multinational corporations and how they relate to national governments, both their own "home" government (of the country in which they are headquartered) as well as "host" governments (of countries in which they do business). We will address the question of whether multinational corporations are merely extensions of the nation-state, or autonomous actors that compete with governments in running the world economy.

The Commerce Sector:
Problems, Politics, and Regimes

When most people think about the international economy, they usually think first of international **commerce,** or trade—imports and exports of oil, autos, coffee, oranges, television sets, computers, zinc, and countless other commodities and products that flow across national boundaries. There are many reasons why countries engage in international trade. In many cases, certain goods, such as petroleum or coffee, are simply unavailable at home and are impossible to produce domestically given the climatic or other physical features of the country; even if a state does have indigenous supplies, they might not be sufficient to meet the demands of the population. In the case of such items as computers and nuclear reactors, countries may lack the technological capabilities to produce these goods within their borders. In still other cases, with shoes and textiles for example, countries might well be able to supply all their own needs through domestic sources but choose to obtain these from foreign producers because the latter are more cheaply priced for consumers. Just as countries **import** goods for various reasons, they also **export** them for various reasons, one of which is simply to pay for their imports. Countries also seek to expand exports since foreign markets offer additional opportunities for the growth of their domestic industries, including increased jobs at home. All of these motives for participating in international trade are economic in nature and are in addition to the political motives noted earlier when we discussed the use of economic tools as bargaining instruments, for example, to develop friendlier ties with countries having strategic value.

The classical liberal internationalist school emphasizes the virtues of **free trade,** i.e., encouraging as much international trade as possible by removing "artificial" government-imposed tariff and nontariff barriers between states and instead relying on the "natural" forces of supply and demand. It was Adam Smith, a Scottish economist and author of *The Wealth of Nations*, published in 1776, who became identified as the "father of free trade," arguing that the same capitalist *laissez-faire* economic principles and rules of commerce that were being introduced *within* the emerging industrialized countries of Western Europe should also apply *between* them; a minimum of government regulation in national and international economics, he argued, would enable all countries to make the best use of their resources and to prosper. Another eighteenth-century economist, David Ricardo, buttressed Smith's arguments with his *theory of comparative advantage*, positing that countries should specialize in producing those goods that they can produce most efficiently and trade these for other needed goods from other countries. Both Smith and Ricardo were reacting against the mercantilist policies that governments had traditionally used to control economic activity and that fostered economic nationalism rather than an open international economy.

Although we have noted many good reasons for engaging in international trade, there are also many reasons why countries historically have frequently sought to limit their international commercial involvement. Free trade brings numerous benefits, but also possible costs. If countries are attempting to develop "infant industries" at home that are not yet competitive with more established and more efficient foreign producers, free trade can result in a flood of cheaper imports that outsell the domestic line and prevent the new domestic industries from growing. In many instances, domestic opposition to free trade comes not from infant industries but from workers and managers in older industries that have failed to adapt to changing conditions and have become inefficient compared with their counterparts abroad; at least in the short run, free trade can damage these local industries severely and cause massive plant shutdowns and layoffs. Then, too, in specializing in certain economic areas (say, computers) and relying on foreign industries for other needed goods (say, shipbuilding or auto parts), countries risk becoming excessively dependent on external sources of supplies that might be cut off during wartime or in crisis situations. Pressures for restricting imports can also arise when a country finds itself with a negative **balance of trade**—the value of its imports exceeding the value of its exports—which signals that the nation might be living beyond its means. Even exports, which one would expect governments normally to promote as much as possible, might be curtailed if the effect of selling certain goods (for example, tons of wheat) on the world market is to create shortages of that good along with higher prices at home. For all these reasons, in addition to politically inspired boycotts and embargoes, national governments often opt for restricting trade rather than expanding it.

There are a variety of ways governments attempt to protect domestic producers from foreign competition, all of which have the effect of constraining international trade. The most blatant approach is simply to prohibit certain foreign goods from entering one's territory or to impose a **quota** regarding the maximum volume of allowable imports (tons of steel, numbers of cars, etc.). A more common instrument is a **tariff,** or import tax, which is imposed on foreign products entering a country and which has the effect of raising the selling price of those goods relative to domestically produced goods, thereby making the latter more attractive to consumers. Governments also often rely on more subtle techniques to inhibit imports, such as requiring all products sold in one's market to meet certain safety standards or technical specifications as to labeling or size or some other product feature—regulations designed not so much to protect the domestic public from defective foreign merchandise as to add further obstacles for foreign producers who must spend extra money retooling their production lines to comply with the local standards. While these tariff and nontariff barriers are usually instituted by states acting individually, they can also be instituted by groups of states acting collectively against outsiders through regional customs unions or common markets, such as the European Community.

As appealing as protectionism might seem to a country experiencing domestic economic problems, it is a two-edged sword. Not only does it tend to reward inefficient domestic industries at the expense of consumers who would otherwise benefit from lower-priced foreign imports, but it also invites retaliation from targeted countries and, hence, damages one's own export-oriented sectors. Therefore governments are often faced with difficult choices as to what sectors might have to be sacrificed if the national economy as a whole is to benefit. Most economists agree that the high degree of protectionism that was practiced after World War I, in contrast to the relatively free trade of the nineteenth century, contributed significantly to the contraction of business activity and increased worldwide unemployment leading to the Great

Table 13.1
DESTINATION OF EXPORTS, BY GROUPS OF COUNTRIES, 1980

Note: Data do not include trade among the centrally planned economies of Asia.

From:	DEVELOPED MARKET ECONOMIES ($ BILLIONS)	(%)	DEVELOPING MARKET ECONOMIES (INCLUDING OPEC) ($ BILLIONS)	(%)	CENTRALLY PLANNED ECONOMIES ($ BILLIONS)	(%)	WORLD* ($ BILLIONS)	(%)	EXPORTS AS PERCENTAGE OF TOTAL WORLD EXPORTS
Developed market economies	911.3	70.5	300.7	23.3	64.0	5.0	1,292.5	100.0	64.5
OPEC	217.4	74.0	70.3	23.9	4.5	1.5	293.8	100.0	14.7
Non-OPEC developing market economies	152.8	63.2	70.6	29.2	15.8	6.5	242.0	100.0	12.1
Centrally planned economies	57.1	32.6	32.1	18.3	85.9	49.1	175.1	100.0	8.7
World	1,338.6	66.8	473.6	23.6	170.2	8.5	2,003.4	100.0	100.0

*Includes certain exports that, because their regions of destination could not be determined, are not included elsewhere in this table.

Source: Roger D. Hansen and Contributors for the Overseas Development Council, U.S. Foreign Policy and the Third World: Agenda 1982 (New York: Praeger Publishers for the Overseas Development Council, 1982), pp. 204–205. Used by permission.

Depression in the 1930s. This is precisely why after World War II major efforts were made to lower trade barriers so that the "beggar thy neighbor" mistakes of the interwar period would not be repeated.

World trade did, indeed, increase more than tenfold between 1945 and 1980. However, not all countries have shared equally in this growth. As indicated in Table 13.1, the major traders are Western developed capitalist countries ("market economies"), selling mostly to each other but also conducting substantial trade with less developed countries of the Third World. Not shown in the table, the United States is the single most active trading country in the world, accounting for roughly 10 percent of total world trade; the European Community as a whole, however, accounts for one fourth of world imports and exports.[12] The developed Communist states ("centrally planned economies"), led by the Soviet Union, have participated relatively little in the international commerce sector, trading mostly with each other rather than with the capitalist developed states or Third World states. The minor role played by the Soviet Union and other Eastern bloc states is partly due to the fact that these states over the years have attempted to pursue a policy of **autarky** (economic self-sufficiency) within the "Communist Commonwealth," seeking to insulate themselves from Western trade winds that could upset their planned economies and create unwanted dependencies. In recent years, the Communist developed states have evidenced increased interest in obtaining advanced technology, consumer goods, and farm products from the West, but have had little to offer in return (except raw materials) and, hence, have often lacked the ability to purchase those goods without Western credits. They have also had little to offer less developed countries, although their trade with the Third World as well as with the West has been on the increase.

The marginal role that the Communist developed states play in the international trade sector (and, as we will see, in the international economy as a whole) explains why the West is far more relevant than the East to the North-South *dependencia* debate, and why the capitalist states are more often targeted for criticism than the Communist states. Table 13.1 shows that, although the developed capitalist states trade mostly with each other, they have come to rely on less developed countries as an important source of imports as well as markets for their exports. Over 25 percent of the exports of developed capitalist states have gone to less developed countries in the 1980s. These are mostly industrial products and technology, including tractors and farm equipment, refrigerators, computers, and machine tools that have to be imported by developing countries in order for them to meet their economic modernization needs; some developed countries, such as the United States, also sell developing countries wheat and other agricultural commodities along with weapons. In order to help pay for these costly imports, the less developed countries export various goods to the developed capitalist states. These are mostly primary products, either agricultural commodities such as bananas, sugar, or coffee, or raw materials such as petroleum, copper, or chromium.

However, led by a few "newly industrializing countries" (NICs), such as Taiwan, Brazil, South Korea, and Mexico, and taking advantage of cheap labor, Third World countries have begun to shift the composition of their exports away from primary commodities to labor-intensive consumer goods (shoes, textiles, toys) and semifinished or finished manufactures.[13] Altogether, approximately 75 percent of the exports of less developed countries go to developed countries, with the less developed countries engaging in relatively little commerce between themselves, mainly because (except for the OPEC nations and a few others) they lack sufficient purchasing power to generate a significant trade volume.

As *dependencia* theorists point out, the pattern of trade relations between North and South has tended to favor the former, for a variety of reasons. First, the technologically sophisticated finished products sold by the North tend to carry a higher price tag than the primary and unfinished or processed goods sold by the South, even though many Northern products could not be made without the raw materials and other inputs from the South. Second, many less developed countries are still excessively dependent on certain items, such as bananas or tin, for the bulk of their export earnings and, hence, are extremely vulnerable to world recession and other conditions that can cause price fluctuations and economic uncertainty. Third, even developing countries, such as the NICs, that have diversified their economies have encountered tariff barriers thrown up by developed states seeking to protect domestic producers from a flood of cheap footwear, china dolls, and other manufactures, just as cane sugar growers and other agricultural producers in the South have frequently encountered quotas, excise taxes, and other barriers in the North. Although the Third World as a whole has accounted for a growing percentage of total world exports in the last two decades, the growth in Third World exports has been contributed mostly by just a few countries, the OPEC states along with the NICs.

Despite adverse terms of trade, less developed countries find themselves so reliant on international trade that it is difficult to extricate themselves from the present web of relationships. As a group, less developed countries depend on international trade for 40 percent of their combined gross domestic products (GDPs). Developed countries as a group are somewhat less dependent, with international trade accounting for 30 percent of their combined GDPs.[14] However, some individual developed states, notably in Western Europe, are heavily dependent on international commerce. If a country's **trade dependence** is defined as the sum of its imports and exports as a percentage of its GDP, the following figures may be noted: the United Kingdom, 58 percent; West Germany, 50 percent; and France, 41 percent. In contrast are the figures for Japan, 20 percent, and the United States, 19 percent.[15]

In the U.S. case, even though it is the world's largest single trading nation in terms of the absolute dollar volume of its imports and exports, its domestic economy is so huge that international trade accounts for relatively little of its overall $4 trillion GNP. Still, the dependence of the United States on foreign *imports* of oil and other key raw materials used in industry cannot be minimized; the United States depends on imports to meet over half of its consumption needs in a dozen categories of industrial raw materials, as indicated in Figure 13.1.[16] Less commonly recognized is the growing *export* dependence of the United States, with sales abroad accounting for more than one fourth of all cash receipts in the U.S. agricultural sector as well as one out of every eight jobs in manufacturing. Indeed, trade has become so important to many localities that mayors and governors are becoming U.S. "trade ambassadors" alongside federal officials, as subnational political units increas-

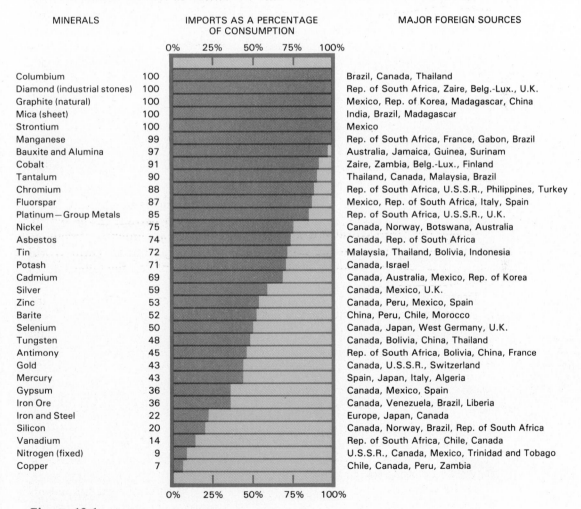

MINERALS	IMPORTS AS A PERCENTAGE OF CONSUMPTION	MAJOR FOREIGN SOURCES
Columbium	100	Brazil, Canada, Thailand
Diamond (industrial stones)	100	Rep. of South Africa, Zaire, Belg.-Lux., U.K.
Graphite (natural)	100	Mexico, Rep. of Korea, Madagascar, China
Mica (sheet)	100	India, Brazil, Madagascar
Strontium	100	Mexico
Manganese	99	Rep. of South Africa, France, Gabon, Brazil
Bauxite and Alumina	97	Australia, Jamaica, Guinea, Surinam
Cobalt	91	Zaire, Zambia, Belg.-Lux., Finland
Tantalum	90	Thailand, Canada, Malaysia, Brazil
Chromium	88	Rep. of South Africa, U.S.S.R., Philippines, Turkey
Fluorspar	87	Mexico, Rep. of South Africa, Italy, Spain
Platinum—Group Metals	85	Rep. of South Africa, U.S.S.R., U.K.
Nickel	75	Canada, Norway, Botswana, Australia
Asbestos	74	Canada, Rep. of South Africa
Tin	72	Malaysia, Thailand, Bolivia, Indonesia
Potash	71	Canada, Israel
Cadmium	69	Canada, Australia, Mexico, Rep. of Korea
Silver	59	Canada, Mexico, U.K.
Zinc	53	Canada, Peru, Mexico, Spain
Barite	52	China, Peru, Chile, Morocco
Selenium	50	Canada, Japan, West Germany, U.K.
Tungsten	48	Canada, Bolivia, China, Thailand
Antimony	45	Rep. of South Africa, Bolivia, China, France
Gold	43	Canada, U.S.S.R., Switzerland
Mercury	43	Spain, Japan, Italy, Algeria
Gypsum	36	Canada, Mexico, Spain
Iron Ore	36	Canada, Venezuela, Brazil, Liberia
Iron and Steel	22	Europe, Japan, Canada
Silicon	20	Canada, Norway, Brazil, Rep. of South Africa
Vanadium	14	Rep. of South Africa, Chile, Canada
Nitrogen (fixed)	9	U.S.S.R., Canada, Mexico, Trinidad and Tobago
Copper	7	Chile, Canada, Peru, Zambia

Figure 13.1
U.S. MINERAL IMPORT RELIANCE, 1982

ingly see themselves as competitors in a world economy. "More than half of our states [the fifty U.S. states] now have trade offices overseas, up from only nineteen states as recently as 1976."[17]

Recognizing the benefits of international trade, governments have attempted to cooperate through various intergovernmental organizations established after World War II to deal with trade problems. Initial attempts to create an International Trade Organization as a United Nations agency alongside the World Bank and International Monetary Fund failed. In its place, the **General Agreement on Tariffs and Trade (GATT)** was created in 1947 to serve as a global forum for multinational negotiations aimed at reducing tariff and nontariff barriers. Although GATT membership is open to all states, many Communist states and less developed states have refused to participate, viewing the organization as an instrument of the capitalist developed countries. Still, GATT remains a major international trade forum, with its more than ninety member states responsible for more than four-fifths of all world trade. In the words of one official: "GATT has provided a rule of law for world trade" and has represented "an attempt to banish into history the jungle of restrictions and bilateral dealings that strangled world trade in the 1930s like jungle weed."[18]

The main principles adopted by GATT have been the following. First, where governments feel a need to protect domestic industries, protection should be accomplished primarily through tariffs rather than quotas. Second, governments should work gradually toward reduction of the general level of tariffs through multilateral negotiations based on the **most favored nation principle**; i.e., whenever one member state lowers tariffs on certain kinds of imports from another member state, all member states are entitled to the same favorable treatment with regard to their goods. Third, any trade disputes that arise among members should be settled through established procedures in GATT. A series of GATT negotiations have been conducted over the years, including the so-called Kennedy Round in the 1960s and the Tokyo Round in the 1970s, which have succeeded in substantial tariff reductions in certain areas. In particular, tariffs on industrial goods have been cut by an average of 35 percent from their 1945 level. Yet much of world trade, especially in agriculture, is still not covered under GATT.

Although much progress has been made in relaxing trade barriers since 1945, further progress has been stalled by a revival of protectionist sentiment in many countries experiencing domestic problems in recent years. As we noted at the outset, compared with the rapid growth of world trade in the first three decades after World War II, the volume of world trade has stagnated and even declined somewhat in the 1980s.[19]

Even the United States, which has been the champion of free trade since World War II, has retrenched somewhat from that role, particularly since 1971, when the United States experienced its first negative trade balance in almost eighty years. The U.S. trade deficit reached $150 billion in 1985. The

U.S. government has come under increasing pressure from American management and labor unions in slumping industries such as textiles, electronics, automobiles, steel, and shoes to impose quotas on imports from Japan and other countries if their governments do not agree to "voluntary" limits. A particular complaint by American producers is that Japanese companies are able to "dump" television sets and other goods on the American market at prices lower than their U.S. competition (and even lower than the same products sell for in Japan) because their production costs are partially offset by subsidies from the Japanese government. Although the U.S. government also has indulged in subsidizing certain exports—a practice that goes against the spirit of free trade—Japan has been notorious for blocking foreign access to the Japanese market through a variety of subtle nontariff barriers, including administrative regulations such as import licenses, technical requirements regarding product size and markings, and assorted taxes and fees that are tacked on to the cost of imported items (and which, for example, can raise the price of an American-made car from $6,000 to $20,000 between the Yokohama dock and the Tokyo showroom). The European Community also remains protectionist in several areas, notably in the agricultural sector, where Community farmers are shielded from American and other foreign competition by government subsidies as well as continued tariff walls. In the industrial sector, Community members engage in trade restrictions of a formal and informal nature; for example, Italy in recent years has explicitly allowed an upper limit of only 5,000 Japanese cars to be imported annually into the country, while Britain and France have had informal "understandings" with Japan that only a fixed percentage of their domestic markets would be open to Japanese auto imports (10 percent in Britain and 3 percent in France).[20] EEC members and other developed states have also become increasingly protectionist toward developing countries, fearful of a flood of cheap imports capturing Northern markets and undercutting Northern producers.

As for less developed countries, they have generally supported lower trade barriers in those areas where they can compete best with foreign producers—in labor-intensive industrial goods and textiles as well as raw materials and agricultural commodities—while insisting on their prerogatives to protect other, more vulnerable domestic industries and service sectors. Rather than relying on GATT for trade negotiations, the less developed countries have preferred using the **United Nations Conference on Trade and Development (UNCTAD)**, a UN General Assembly organ established in 1964, to supplement GATT as a world trade forum. (UNCTAD will be discussed in greater detail in the next chapter when we focus on Third World economic development.)

Such was the backdrop against which a new round of GATT trade talks—the Uruguay Round—began in 1986, with the postwar trade regime under strain and the outlines of a future trade regime uncertain. Clearly, then, even though most states today "talk" free trade, the specter of economic nationalism and trade wars persists. At the same time that trade liberalization is occurring in some areas, "neomercantilism" seems on the rise in other areas. These conflicting tendencies are also at work in sectors of the international economic system other than trade.

The Currency Sector: Problems, Politics, and Regimes

The international economy is generally not a barter economy, in which people exchange one set of goods (say, apples) for another (say, oranges). It is rather an economy in which people exchange goods and services for *money*. Some barter exists, and may even be increasing, as in the recent Chinese efforts to persuade Fiat and Toyota to accept hams and rugs in return for technology and equipment from the two car companies. However, such arrangements are relatively rare.

What complicates transactions in the international economy is that not all countries have the same **currency** to use as a medium of exchange. The United States has as its major monetary unit the dollar, while the Japanese have the yen, the West Germans the mark, the British the pound, the Indians the rupee, the Soviets the ruble, the Brazilians the cruzeiro, and so forth. When a government or any of its citizens buys something from another state (oil, cars, or whatever), the seller ordinarily will accept payment only in the seller's national currency or in a currency whose value is fairly stable relative to other national currencies. Otherwise, the sellers may find they have been paid in money which has become worthless or greatly depreciated in value. Hence, most international economic transactions are based on a few select, widely accepted "international" (or "hard") currencies, such as the dollar or mark, as well as gold. In other words, many countries, particularly in the Third World but also East bloc states including the Soviet Union, find that their national currencies are usable only within their own borders and perhaps in a few other nations. The fact that the hard currencies are those belonging to the developed capitalist states naturally contributes to the pivotal role of these countries in the international economy.

Because each national monetary system has its own logic, national currencies differ in terms of the value attached to each monetary unit. Put simply, one U.S. dollar, for example, does not equal one Italian lira; one U.S. dollar equals roughly 1000 Italian lira, so that one would much rather have a million dollars than a million lira. The rate at which one country's currency can be purchased with another country's currency is called the **exchange rate.** The exchange rate is the mechanism through which different national currencies are reconciled for trading and other purposes. The exchange rate determines what people in a given country must pay for foreign goods. Hence it would take one U.S. dollar to purchase an item that is priced at 1000 lira in Italy. Table 13.2 indicates recent exchange rates of various currencies.

Table 13.2

SELECTED CURRENCIES AND EXCHANGE RATES, MAY 1987

CURRENCY	U.S. DOLLAR EQUIVALENCE
1 U.S. dollar	1.00
1 West German mark	0.57
1 British pound	1.68
1 French franc	0.17
1 Italian lira	0.0008
1 Canadian dollar	0.74
1 Japanese yen	0.007
1 Indian rupee	0.08

Source: Data from *Wall Street Journal,* May 5, 1987.

It needs to be added that the exchange rates can fluctuate from year to year and, indeed, from day to day. For example, a British pound shown in the table to be worth $1.68 in May of 1987 had been down to $1.43 just six months earlier. Exchange rates are determined either by agreement between governments or, more commonly, by market forces of supply and demand. Although the value of such international currencies as the dollar and mark is subject to change, wild fluctuations that could erode confidence in these currencies among traders have generally been prevented through joint action by governments.

Since international currencies like the dollar are readily *convertible* into other currencies and are therefore readily usable in international economic transactions, countries seek to accumulate sizable reserves of these hard currencies for foreign exchange. Some countries are able to accumulate more reserves than others. When states import goods, they ordinarily spend hard currency. When they export, they earn hard currency. If the value of a country's imports exceeds the value of its exports, this negative trade balance can exhaust all of its foreign exchange holdings, so that theoretically it cannot engage in further international economic transactions. However, it is important to understand that international trade is only one type of international economic transaction whereby hard currency can be obtained or lost. Foreign aid and foreign investment, which will be discussed later in this chapter, also involve hard currency transfers, as do international tourism and many other kinds of activities. Hence, a country can try to compensate for an adverse trade balance by accumulating hard currency in other areas.

Because it is difficult to participate in the international economy without adequate reserves of foreign exchange monies, national governments carefully monitor their state's overall record of foreign expenditures and earnings. A state's **balance of payments** is a financial statement of its economic transactions with the rest of the world that takes into account both outflows and inflows of money. If a state is spending more in other countries than it is receiving from other countries, then the state is running a *deficit;* conversely, if it is receiving from other countries more than it is spending abroad, it is running a *surplus.* National governments much prefer surpluses to deficits, just as any household bookkeeper would.

The balance of payments can be thought of as an accounting ledger, with certain types of activities producing an inflow of funds and appearing as entries on the *credit* side, and other kinds of activities producing an outflow of funds and appearing on the *debit* side. Figure 13.2 shows the main ways in which countries accumulate credits and debits in their yearly balance of payments computations.

A country experiencing a balance of payments deficit can unilaterally pursue several possible policies in an effort to lessen the deficit. One strategy is to try to *reduce* the *outflow* of funds, through either raising tariffs and other barriers to imports, cutting back foreign aid (if one is a foreign aid donor), increasing restrictions on the amount of foreign investment abroad by one's citizens, reducing overseas military commitments (if one has bases overseas), or limiting foreign travel by one's citizens. However, each of these strategies involves potential costs. Raising trade barriers invites retaliation from foreign governments; reducing foreign aid donations and overseas military bases could pose political and security problems; restricting foreign investment risks alienating not only one's own corporate and banking community but also other governments dependent on such funds, and additionally might even be counterproductive in the long run in terms of reducing the flow of investment

Credits	Debits
Trade exports from Country X to other countries	Trade imports into Country X from other countries
Foreign investments by other countries in Country X	Foreign investment by Country X in other countries
Profits returned (repatriated) to Country X from its investments in other countries	Profits returned (repatriated) to other countries from their investments in Country X
Foreign aid received by Country X from other countries	Foreign aid sent by Country X to other countries
Military expenditures by other countries to support overseas bases in Country X	Military expenditures by Country X to support its overseas bases in other countries
Money spent by foreign tourists visiting Country X	Money spent by Country X visiting other countries

Figure 13.2
THE BALANCE OF PAYMENTS LEDGER (FOR COUNTRY X)

income returning as profits to the investing country; restricting foreign travel likewise can alienate tourists and the countries to which they travel.

Another strategy for reducing a deficit is to try to *promote* a greater *inflow* of funds, through government subsidies or improved labor productivity measures that support export expansion, tax benefits and other inducements to attract more foreign investment funds, and development of one's own tourist industry aimed at the international globetrotter. Some of the approaches can also present problems; in particular, the encouragement of foreign investment in one's economy might produce economic benefits but political costs if foreign penetration of the national economy leads to foreign domination.

One special technique available to a government attempting to grapple with a balance of payments deficit is currency **devaluation.** A government deliberately can decide to lower the value of its currency relative to other currencies, thereby increasing the buying power of foreigners seeking to purchase its goods and services while at the same time decreasing the buying power of its own people abroad (without markedly affecting its internal economy). In other words, when a country devalues its currency, this tends to enhance its ability to export goods and to attract foreign tourists while making it more expensive and difficult for its own citizenry to buy imported products and to travel abroad. For example, the aforementioned rise in the value of the British pound from $1.43 in November 1986 to $1.68 in May 1987—largely a result of a conscious strategy by the Reagan administration to allow the value of the dollar to fall in order to rectify a growing U.S. trade deficit problem—tended to make it harder for Americans to purchase British goods and to travel in Britain, and easier for Britons to partake of American goods and travel.

Although devaluation might seem a very useful "quick fix" for a deficit problem, it is usually viewed only as a last resort, since it upsets foreigners who happen to be holding large quantities of the devalued currency and undermines confidence in the currency; in addition to its international repercussions, devaluation can harm the domestic economy, possibly leading to higher prices and inflation if one has no choice but to import certain items such as oil from abroad. There are clearly no easy solutions to a balance of payments problem, although a deficit can be erased through a careful blend of policies.

If many countries are simultaneously experiencing balance of payments problems, a serious global problem can result for two reasons. First, major shortages of hard currency resulting from deficits mean that countries lack the ability to finance their imports and other international economic activities, so that overall world trade is likely to dry up, producing in its wake decreased worldwide production and increased worldwide unemployment. The inadequacy of international currency reserves to keep the international economy going is known as a "liquidity" problem. Second, if several governments attempt to solve their deficit problems by resorting to currency devaluation, this can spur other governments to devalue their own currencies in a counterattack in order to regain a competitive edge in the international economy. The resulting instability in exchange rates can shake the very foundations of the international economic order.

It was precisely in anticipation of these kinds of monetary problems that the United States after World War II took the lead in establishing the so-called "Bretton Woods system" as the basis for global management of international monetary affairs. First discussed in 1944 at a wartime conference in Bretton Woods, New Hampshire, this system—which tied together concerns in the commerce, currency, and capital sectors—featured the creation of the International Monetary Fund (IMF) as a key Specialized Agency of the United Nations designed to (1) provide a central fund of hard currency reserves that could be made available to countries with periodic deficits in order to ease liquidity problems, and (2) provide a central forum for negotiating adjustments in currency values in order to prevent disruptive fluctuations in exchange rates.

Between 1945 and 1971, the system operated essentially on the basis of "fixed" foreign exchange rates, with most currencies valued in relation to the U.S. dollar as well as to gold. The central role of the American dollar was owed simply to the economic primacy of the United States after World War II. The value of the dollar itself was fixed at $35 per ounce of gold, which meant that any foreigners holding dollars could redeem them for a set guaranteed amount of gold if they wished. This "gold and dollar standard," founded on the assumption that "the dollar was as good as gold," worked fairly well as long as the United States had sufficient gold reserves in Fort Knox to make good on any claims made by foreigners seeking to exchange their dollar holdings for gold. However, when foreign dollar holdings had reached the point where they exceeded U.S. gold reserves in 1960, after chronic American balance of payments deficits arising from extensive overseas commitments, confidence in the dollar began to wane. U.S. deficits continued throughout the 1960s, fueled largely by the huge American expenditures in Vietnam. The U.S. balance of payments deficit had soared to a record $9.5 billion by 1971, aggravated by the first *trade* deficit the United States had experienced since 1893. With foreigners concerned that the United States might be forced to devalue the dollar in order to cope with its rising balance of payments deficit, pressures mounted to turn dollars in for gold and other "harder" currencies such as the German mark. Finally, the Nixon administration took the drastic step of terminating the sale of gold at $35 an ounce and allowing the price of gold to be determined by market forces, which were eventually to raise the price drastically, at one point to over $800 an ounce. With this decision, the Bretton Woods monetary regime crumbled.

Since 1971, the international monetary system has operated on the basis of "floating" exchange rates, with the relationships between different currencies determined mostly by what values they have on the open market. Some degree of intergovernmental coordination remains, however, with implicit agreement among IMF members to keep currency fluctuations within reasonable limits. Although the IMF has over 140 members, the capitalist developed states as a group dominate decision making in the organization, having two thirds of the votes due to a system of weighted voting based on each state's financial contributions to the central fund of currency reserves.

The majority of less developed countries belong to the IMF. In the case of some of them, such as the former French colonies in Africa that comprise the "franc zone," the value of their national currency is directly tied to the value of the "mother country's" currency. Rumania, Hungary, and Poland are the only East bloc countries that are IMF members, with the Soviet Union and other developed Communist states refusing to join an organization dominated by capitalist countries. Given their absence from the IMF and the nonconvertibility of their currencies, the Soviet Union and the Eastern European countries play a virtually nonexistent role in the international currency sector—one even more marginal than their role in the international commerce sector.

Just as the developed capitalist states dominate IMF decision making with regard to exchange rate concerns, they likewise dominate IMF efforts to deal with liquidity problems. The way IMF has attempted to deal with liquidity problems is for member governments to deposit assigned shares of gold and currency in a central fund, which then entitles them to borrow from the fund at times when they are short on foreign exchange holdings. In recent years, the IMF has multiplied its reserves through the creation of Special Drawing Rights (SDRs), or "paper gold," a new international currency that represents a combination of several hard currencies that adds to the assets available to the international community. Since less developed countries, in particular, regularly experience shortages of hard cash, they often have to prevail upon the IMF to make its currency reserves available. As we note later, the less developed countries are making demands for changes not only in the trade sector but also in the currency sector of the international economy.

In the international currency sector, as in the international commerce sector, one can see a tension between pressures for unilateral policymaking on the one hand and the felt need for multilateral cooperation on the other hand. There are obvious limits to the willingness of states to integrate the international economy in this area, for example to create a single common currency worldwide in place of individual national currencies (although the creation of SDRs, in a sense, represents a modest start in this direction). Yet amidst great diversity and divisiveness, there does exist some degree of central management in the international monetary system.[21]

The Capital Sector:
Problems, Politics, and Regimes

The **capital** sector of the international economy refers to the flow of resources across national boundaries that are invested in a country's economy and contribute to economic development and growth. Capital is to an economy what blood is to the human body. Virtually all countries partially rely on external infusion of capital to nurture their economy rather than relying solely on their own capital formation, although some countries are more dependent than others on outside stimulants. Two general types of capital flows warrant discussion here: (1) foreign aid and (2) foreign investment.

Foreign aid is a transfer of resources between governments, either bilaterally (from one government to another) or multilaterally (from an IGO to a government), on generous "concessionary" terms. It can take several forms: grants, in the form of money or food or other resources that are donated as gifts (e.g., disaster relief provided to countries experiencing earthquakes or other catastrophes); loans, which must be repaid but carry little or no interest charges (ordinarily used by the recipient country to finance the building of dams, roads, and other economic infrastructure); export credits, which enable the recipient to purchase the donor country's exports; technical assistance, which helps meet the needs of a country in agriculture, engineering, or other fields where skilled personnel might be in short supply (e.g., U.S. Peace Corps volunteers or the United Nations Development Program); and military assistance, either giving a country weapons or selling it weapons at below market value, as well as providing military training.

Foreign investment can likewise take a variety of forms: an investor can buy foreign stocks and bonds; banks in one country can make loans to businesses or to the government of another country; corporations can build manufacturing or sales facilities abroad, and contract with foreign governments to develop and manage various concerns, such as mining operations. Much foreign investment is of a *portfolio* nature, where investors merely seek a return on their financial contribution but do not seek to exercise any controlling interest in the overseas operations that utilize the capital. Somewhat less prevalent, but far more controversial, is *direct* foreign investment, where finance capital is used by a firm (say, Ford Motors) to create new overseas enterprises or to buy up existing overseas enterprises as subsidiaries of the parent company, which exercises control over pricing, production levels, and other economic decisions of the foreign operations.

Before discussing foreign investment, we first will examine the flow of foreign aid in the contemporary international economy. The *donor* countries, giving aid directly or channeling it through multilateral institutions, are mostly developed capitalist states; while the *recipient* countries tend to be less developed states (although the Marshall Plan, the first large-scale aid program in the postwar era, was targeted at the developed states of war-ravaged Western Europe). The developed capitalist states as a group account for over 75 percent of all foreign aid given in the world, although their total aid still amounts only to .35 percent of their combined GNPs.[22] The United States, which has never been a recipient of foreign aid in the postwar period, has been the single biggest national donor, contributing roughly $10 billion annually in recent years but ranking near the bottom of aid donors in terms of relative ability to pay (.25 percent of its GNP). The bloc of developed Communist states, led by the Soviet Union, has played a much smaller role as foreign aid donors, accounting for only 8 percent of all aid given annually (representing only .17 percent of their combined GNPs).[23] Although Third World countries generally have not been in a position to serve as aid donors, a few have managed to contribute foreign aid in recent years. In particular, the OPEC countries as a whole have accounted for 15 percent of all aid given in recent years, with the aid performance of some OPEC members being especially impressive as a percentage of their GNP (for example, Kuwait's aid constituting 2 percent of its GNP and Saudi Arabia's amounting to 4.7 percent in the 1980s, despite declining oil revenues).[24]

As we have noted, the recipients of foreign aid today are not surprisingly almost exclusively less developed countries. The bulk of foreign aid is dispensed to these countries through bilateral means, such as the U.S. Agency for International Development (AID), allowing the donor government to exercise total discretion as to which governments should receive the assistance and under what terms. As one would expect, the political aims of the donor state play at least as much a role in determining aid relationships as the economic needs of the recipients. Although foreign aid is commonly viewed as a form of charity, one should keep in mind that most aid is in the form of loans rather than outright gifts and hence must be paid back, usually with interest. In addition, much aid is "tied," i.e., the donor attaches strings that require the recipient to use the aid funds to purchase donor products even if those goods can be obtained from other countries more cheaply. Moreover, a large quantity of aid is military in nature, given to countries of strategic value to the donor and not usable for economic development purposes.

The developed capitalist states, the developed Communist states, and the OPEC states have all been selective in their allocation of foreign aid. The French, for example, have channeled most of their aid to their former colonies in Africa, with whom they retain special trade ties. The United States has given much more aid to pro-Western countries like Israel and Egypt than to neutralist countries like India. (Indeed, in the Reagan administration's foreign aid program request submitted to Congress in 1987, almost half of all U.S. bilateral assistance was targeted at just Israel and Egypt.) The Soviets funnel aid primarily to their East European allies and to client states with left-wing regimes in various parts of the world, such as Cuba and South Yemen. The OPEC members (more precisely, the Arab group) have given aid almost entirely to fellow Arab or Muslim states.

Although most aid is given bilaterally, multilateral institutions at the regional and global level also play a significant role. Even though individual foreign aid donors lose some degree of control over the purse strings when channeling aid through multilateral institutions, certain countries are still able to dominate foreign aid decisions in many of these institutions. In the case of the World Bank, the chief global institution in the capital sector of the international economy, the developed capitalist states generally and the United States in particular have tended to dominate. Headquartered in Washington, D.C., the World Bank consists of more than 140 members, including almost all the developed capitalist and Third World states but few of the developed Communist states. The Soviets have found it difficult to join an organization whose recent presidents have included Robert McNamara, former head of the Ford Motor Company and U.S. Secretary of Defense in the 1960s, and A. W. Clausen, former head of the Bank of America.

Decision making in the World Bank is based on weighted voting. Member governments are assigned voting power according to the size of their capital contribution to the Bank, with the United States being the largest single contributor. The Bank obtains its funds mainly through soliciting government subscriptions and issuing interest-bearing bonds and notes that are purchased by governments as well as investors in the private sector. These funds are then supposed to be loaned to needy governments on relatively generous terms, particularly by the International Development Association, the "soft loan window" of the Bank, which is capable of offering fifty-year repayment periods at low interest rates. However, the major recipients of World Bank loans generally have been countries like Mexico and Brazil, which are among the more advanced Third World states and among those judged most friendly by the United States. While the World Bank has played an indispensable role in providing capital to less developed countries, many problems have arisen, not the least of which is the servicing of the more than $1 trillion debt that the Third World has accumulated over the years (half of which is owed to private banks in the West). We will discuss these problems in the next chapter when we examine international economic development.

Because foreign aid frequently has failed to produce the political and economic results intended by the donor, many donor countries have suffered "donor fatigue" recently and have scaled down their foreign assistance programs.[25] Given the limited supply of foreign aid, many less developed countries have increasingly turned to foreign private investors as an additional source of capital, particularly to promote industrial capabilities. As with foreign aid, the major *providers* of investment capital are the developed capitalist states, led by the United States. However, unlike foreign aid, the developed capitalist states are also the main *targets* of foreign investment, especially direct investment, since they tend to offer a more favorable investment climate than politically unstable developing states. During the 1970s, roughly 70 percent of the direct foreign investment by developed capitalist countries was in other developed capitalist countries, mostly in the manufacturing and sales areas.[26] This pattern has continued in the 1980s; for example, only one fourth of U.S. overseas direct investment in recent years has been in developing countries.[27] Even the few less developed countries with the means to engage in overseas investment, such as the OPEC countries, have channeled most of their investment funds into developed capitalist states rather than into fellow Third World states. As for the developed Communist countries, their government-run economies have not been very suited for foreign investment activity, although their state companies have entered into "joint ventures" with Fiat, Pepsi, and other Western companies, and private Western banks have financed certain operations in Poland and elsewhere.[28]

Although the bulk of finance capital flows from developed states to other developed states, substantial foreign investments have occurred in certain sectors of developing country economies. Traditionally, the primary or extractive sector of less developed countries—mineral mining, oil drilling, and agriculture—has attracted major direct investment from the likes of Alcoa (in the Caribbean), Exxon (in the Middle East), and United Fruit Company (in Central and South America). More recently, the lure of cheap labor has attracted increased direct investment in manufacturing by companies such as Ford and General Electric in a number of Third World countries, particularly in Asia. For less developed countries, such direct investment poses a serious dilemma, bringing in much needed capital but adding to the foreign penetration of economies that are already heavily dependent on outsiders. The growing involvement of foreign interests in national economies has also been a source of concern for developed capitalist states, many of which are themselves highly penetrated. In order to understand these concerns, it is necessary to examine the nature of the *multinational corporation* and its relationship to the nation-state.

THE MULTINATIONAL CORPORATION

The **multinational corporation (MNC)** has become a key agent for the globalization of the international economy, with its tentacles connecting national economies in every corner of the planet. One finds many different definitions as to what makes a company "multinational." One study defines a multinational corporation as any company that appears on the *"Fortune 500"* list of top industrial firms and has manufacturing subsidiaries in six or more foreign countries.[29] However, this is a very narrow definition insofar as it includes only the largest MNCs and only those engaged in industrial activity. Another, far broader definition considers MNCs to be "corporations which have their home in one country but operate and live under the laws and customs of other countries as well."[30] Still another definition of MNC is a "cluster of corporations of diverse nationality joined together by ties of common ownership and responsive to a common management strategy."[31] Whatever definition one uses, the key feature of an MNC is that it has branch operations abroad that are connected with and subordinate to a headquarters office in another country.[32]

MNCs are not exactly new actors on the world scene. The British East India Company and other trading companies chartered by the British, Dutch,

SIDELIGHT

PROFILE OF A MULTINATIONAL CORPORATION: THE CHAMPION SPARK PLUG COMPANY

The Champion Spark Plug Company is a U.S. corporation that is headquartered in Toledo, Ohio, and does business in 160 countries around the world. In 1920, when Americans owned 10 million of the 12 million cars then found in the world, Champion's operations were largely confined to the United States. However, by 1980, when almost 60 percent of the world's cars were on roads outside the United States, Champion had become a far-flung multinational.

In 1981, Champion's sales of spark plugs, windshield wipers and assorted other automotive and motorcycle products totaled $818 million. Half of all the spark plugs it produces are now sold outside the United States, helped by 325 sales representatives in its various foreign markets, all of whom are nationals of those countries. Champion not only maintains sales facilities abroad but also has spark plug manufacturing plants in thirteen countries (including Belgium, where the spark plug was invented) as well as five other foreign plants making wiper products. Over 40 percent of its annual gross income in recent years has come from its *foreign* operations.

Despite its cosmopolitan features, Champion remains very much an American company, with its ownership and top management at its corporate headquarters consisting almost entirely of Americans. Like most MNCs, multinationalism only goes so far. In the case of the Champion Spark Plug Company, all roads still lead to its world headquarters in Toledo.

Source: Based on remarks by Donald A. Ramsdell, Vice-President, Champion Spark Plug Company, at the Annual Meeting of the International Studies Association, Cincinnati, Ohio, March 25, 1982.

and other governments in the seventeenth century were the ancestors of present-day MNCs, and the big oil companies were already beginning to stake out claims to the Middle East oil fields in the nineteenth century. International Nickel and other mining companies had established extractive operations overseas by the turn of the century; Singer Sewing Machines already had an overseas factory in Scotland in 1878; Ford Motors had an assembly plant in Europe in 1911; and Woolworth, General Electric, and Otis Elevator were among other U.S. companies establishing foreign subsidiaries prior to World War I. Indeed, as early as 1902, F. A. MacKensie's *The American Invaders* was warning Europeans about increasing U.S. penetration of European economies, much as J. J. Servan-Schreiber's *The American Challenge* was to do sixty years later.[33]

Although the beginnings of multinational operations can be traced far back, the MNC phenomenon did not really take off until after World War II, when a number of factors spurred spectacular growth in direct foreign investment. First, rather than trying to break through tariff and other trade barriers to export their goods to foreign markets, many companies found it easier to gain access simply by building separate production facilities inside those countries, especially if they could save transportation and other costs that would make their goods more competitive. Second, many countries offered cheap labor, special tax treatment, lax pollution laws and other advantages to foreign firms willing to invest in their economies, prompting many firms to build overseas plants from which they could serve not only their foreign markets but their home market as well. Third, the new technology, including advances in the speed of communications and travel, the containerization of cargo, and the development of computers capable of storing large amounts of data, all made it possible for MNCs to expand their operations. Fourth, the economic primacy of the United States and the special status of the dollar after World War II enabled U.S.-based corporations, in particular, to expand their overseas investment rapidly, with direct foreign investment by American companies alone increasing tenfold between 1950 and 1970. The "bottom line" explanation for the growth of MNCs is that, purely and simply, foreign investment has been found increasingly profitable by corporations; in 1980, for example, nearly half of the "Fortune 500" corporations depended on their international operations for over 40 percent of their profits.[34]

Today, there are over 5,000 MNCs in the world.[35] The United States continues to be headquarters for a majority of MNCs, being the base of operations for roughly half of the 500 largest corporations. However, MNCs headquartered in Western Europe and Japan have been proliferating, challenging American MNCs in various areas.[36] MNCs have grown to the point where their resources now exceed those of many nation-states. As indicated in Table 13.3, if the annual product of nation-states and MNCs are compared, almost half of the top 100 economic units in the world are corporations. General Motors is "bigger" than Nigeria and Norway, not to mention Vanuatu.[37] It is estimated that the 350 biggest MNCs, with over 25,000 subsidiaries, account for well over one quarter of the non-Communist world's total production of goods and services,[38] in addition to controlling most of the world's capital, technology and managerial skills. On other measures of comparison between states and MNCs, Exxon has three times as many employees stationed overseas as the U.S. State Department; and IBM has a bigger research and development budget than most national governments in the world.

As impressive as the MNC appears in statistical comparisons with nation-states, the statistics only hint at the potential power and impact of MNCs in the world. As two writers note, "In the process of developing a new world, the managers of firms like GM, IBM, . . . Volkswagen . . . and a few hundred others are making daily business decisions which have more impact than those of most sovereign governments on where people live; what work, if any, they will do; what they will eat, drink, and wear; what sorts of knowledge

Table 13.3

RANKING OF COUNTRIES AND CORPORATIONS ACCORDING TO SIZE OF ANNUAL PRODUCT, 1980

Countries are ranked according to gross national product. Corporations (headquarters in parentheses) are ranked according to total sales. While not exactly comparable, they are sufficiently close to illustrate size relationships.

RANK	ECONOMIC ENTITY	U.S. DOLLARS (BILLIONS)	RANK	ECONOMIC ENTITY	U.S. DOLLARS (BILLIONS)
1	United States	2,377.10	28	**Mobil** (US)	59.51
2	Soviet Union	1,082.30	29	Turkey	58.76
3	Japan	1,019.48	30	**General Motors**	
4	West Germany	717.66		(US)	57.73
5	France	531.33	31	South Korea	55.93
6	People's Republic of		32	Nigeria	55.31
	China	475.00	33	Yugoslavia	53.79
7	United Kingdom	353.63	34	Indonesia	52.20
8	Italy	298.20	35	**Texaco** (US)	51.20
9	Canada	228.44	36	South Africa	48.99
10	Brazil	207.27	37	**British Petroleum**	
11	Spain	162.33		(UK)	48.04
12	Netherlands	143.24	38	Venezuela	45.15
13	Poland	135.45	39	Norway	43.52
14	Australia	130.67	40	Rumania	41.83
15	India	125.99	41	Hungary	41.27
16	Mexico	107.62	42	**Standard Oil of**	
17	East Germany	107.61		**Calif.** (US)	40.48
18	Belgium	107.32	43	Finland	39.43
19	**Exxon** (US)	103.14	44	**Ford Motor** (US)	37.09
20	Sweden	98.58	45	Greece	36.71
21	Switzerland	89.89	46	Bulgaria	32.73
22	Czechoslovakia	80.53	47	Iraq	30.43
23	**Royal Dutch/Shell**		48	Algeria	28.94
	(Neth./UK)	77.11	49	Philippines	28.11
24	Austria	64.64	50	**ENI** (Italy)	27.19
25	Saudi Arabia	62.64	51	Thailand	26.92
26	Argentina	60.98	52	**Gulf Oil** (US)	26.48
27	Denmark	60.83	53	Colombia	26.39

schools and universities will encourage, and what kind of society their children will inherit.[39] MNCs have been labeled "invisible empires"[40] and "the new sovereigns,"[41] referring to the desire and ability of MNCs to escape the constraints of national boundaries. One scholar has characterized the emerging relationship between MNCs and national governments as "sovereignty at bay," meaning that the power and authority of national governments is being at least challenged, if not overtaken, by MNCs.[42] MNCs are seen as having

Table 13.3 (Continued)

RANK	ECONOMIC ENTITY	U.S. DOLLARS (BILLIONS)	RANK	ECONOMIC ENTITY	U.S. DOLLARS (BILLIONS)
54	IBM (US)	26.21	78	Siemens (W. Germany)	17.95
55	Standard Oil of Indiana (US)	26.13	79	Daimler-Benz (W. Germany)	17.11
56	Fiat (Italy)	25.16	80	Peugeot (France)	16.85
57	General Electric (US)	24.96	81	Hoechst (W. Germany)	16.48
58	Française des Pétroles (France)	23.94	82	Bayer (W. Germany)	15.89
59	Atlantic Richfield (US)	23.74	83	Israel	15.71
60	Unilever (UK/Neth.)	23.60	84	Thyssen (W. Germany)	15.24
61	Libya	23.40	85	BASF (W. Germany)	15.23
62	Kuwait	21.87	86	Petrobras (Brazil)	14.84
63	Portugal	21.30	87	Pemex (Mexico)	14.81
64	Pakistan	20.99	88	Nestlé (Switzerland)	14.62
65	Shell Oil (US)	19.83	89	Morocco	14.46
66	North Korea	19.72	90	Toyota Motor (Japan)	14.23
67	New Zealand	19.19	91	Cuba	13.92
68	Renault (France)	18.98	92	Nissan Motor (Japan)	13.85
69	Petroleos de Venezuela (Ven.)	18.82	93	Ireland	13.79
70	Egypt	18.60	94	E. I. Du Pont de Nemours (US)	13.65
71	ITT (US)	18.53	95	Phillips Petroleum (US)	13.38
72	Chile	18.44	96	Imperial Chemical (UK)	13.29
73	Elf Aquitaine (France)	18.43	97	Tenneco (US)	13.23
74	Philips Gloeilampen-fabrieken (Netherlands)	18.40	98	Nippon Steel (Japan)	13.10
75	Volkswagenwerk (W. Germany)	18.34	99	United Arab Emirates	12.99
76	Conoco (US)	18.33	100	Sun (US)	12.95
77	Malaysia	17.96			

Source: GNP data are from World Bank Atlas (Washington, D.C., 1980), pp. 12–21; sales data are from Fortune, August 10, 1981, p. 205.

implications not only for government-business relations but government-labor relations, as the transnational enterprise phenomenon is providing added impetus to the formation of transnational labor unions among MNC employees in different countries.

The latter observations all tend to buttress the arguments of those who view the international economy from a world system perspective, which emphasizes the role of nonstate actors in shaping the international economy.

However, there are many others who argue that the major decisions affecting international relations, economic or otherwise, continue to be made in official governmental circles rather than in corporate board rooms, and that MNCs have only limited autonomy vis-à-vis governments.[43] In assessing the impact of the MNC, two kinds of relationships need to be examined: (1) MNC–host government relations and (2) MNC–home government relations.

MNC–Host Government Relations. By **host government,** we are referring to the government of a country in which a foreign-based MNC operates subsidiaries. For various reasons, foreign MNCs and host governments tend to have a "love-hate" relationship. On the one hand, in less developed countries especially, MNCs are often credited with creating jobs, introducing modern technology, and generally helping the host country's balance of payments by bringing in fresh capital and helping to develop export industries through their subsidiaries. On the other hand, Third World critics of MNCs argue that they ultimately take more out of a country than they contribute, using a variety of devices to evade host government taxes, squeezing out smaller local firms, drawing away the most talented indigenous human resources (creating a "brain drain"), engaging in advertising that creates local demand for expensive Western consumer goods, and reaping enormous profits that are repatriated to the home country rather than reinvested in the host country.

In the view of *dependencia* theorists, in particular, MNCs are not only exploitive of less developed countries but are often so enmeshed in the economy of a host country that they are able to dominate its political life as well. Although the "one-company country" (e.g., Liberia under the half-century control of Firestone Rubber) is rarely if ever found today, many foreign MNCs control huge sectors of host country economies in the Third World. For example, one writer notes that "in 1980, foreign investors controlled 25 percent of all assets and 40 percent of all sales of Brazilian industry." The assets they controlled included "88 percent of the office equipment industry, 75 percent of electrical products, 54 percent of domestic appliances, 78 percent of tractors, 78 percent of drugs, and 100 percent of automobiles."[44]

Given their pervasive presence in Third World economies, foreign MNCs have often been in a position to exert considerable influence over host government domestic and foreign policy. However, as Third World countries have become increasingly sensitive about foreign penetration, they have become more assertive in their dealings with MNCs, using the threat of expropriation and other sanctions to bring MNCs under greater control.[45] The most obvious case of host governments exercising power against MNCs has been the successful efforts by OPEC countries to gain ownership of (i.e., at least 51 percent controlling interest in) the oil production facilities operated by oil companies within their borders. Although many Third World countries have tried to follow the OPEC example, few have had the degree of leverage enjoyed by the oil producers, so that "get tough" policies against MNCs have frequently resulted in their closing up shop in the host country and transferring their movable assets elsewhere to a more hospitable business environment, even if they have had to absorb some losses in the process.

Sensitivity to foreign economic penetration is not confined to less developed economies. As suggested in Servan-Schreiber's *The American Challenge*, many developed countries in Western Europe and elsewhere have expressed concern over growing foreign MNC involvement in their economies. Although the governments of these countries have usually been in a position to exercise greater control over MNC activity than their counterparts in the Third World, they have often found MNC subsidiaries within their borders resistant to their authority (e.g., the West German government has had difficulty in getting subsidiaries of U.S. firms to abide by the German national policy of facilitating worker representation on corporate boards of directors).

Perhaps nowhere is there a better example of foreign penetration of a developed economy than in Canada, where U.S. companies alone in recent years have owned or controlled over 90 percent of Canada's theaters, 55 percent of its manufacturing sector,[46] and 70 percent of its oil and gas industry,[47] figures which help account for the fact that Canada remains America's single biggest trade partner, both as a market for U.S. exports and as a source of U.S. imports. The Canadian government has been under increasing domestic political pressure to lessen foreign control, particularly in the energy sector, where a policy of "nationalization" of foreign-owned facilities has been undertaken over the objections of both U.S. companies and the U.S. government.

Even in the United States, where the domestic economy is so large that foreign penetration accounts for only a small fraction of total economic activity, there has been growing concern over increased direct investment by foreign interests engaged in "the buying of America"[48]—the slices of "Americana" include Beverly Hills estates and hotels (by Arab interests), Saks Fifth Avenue and Sinclair (by the British), Houston's One Shell Plaza and Pennzoil Place (by the Germans). In fact, by the mid-1980s, the U.S.—long the predominant home (headquarters) country of MNCs—had become the predominant host country as well, attracting more direct foreign investment than any other single state (over one quarter of the world's direct investment). The trillion dollars in total American investments held abroad (including both portfolio and direct investments) is matched by roughly the same amount of foreign ownership of assets in the U.S. today.[49]

In some cases, foreign investment in the United States has been perceived by Americans as economically healthy and has been encouraged (e.g., the offer of a $40 million loan by the state of Pennsylvania to Volkswagen, which would allow the German automaker to build a new plant in the state that would employ thousands of workers). In other cases, foreign investment has been viewed as potentially risky in terms of national security and has been severely restricted (e.g., the U.S. government's restriction on foreign investment

in the communications and air transport sectors of the American economy).
Special concerns have been raised about the growth of Japanese banks in the
U.S. and the increasing financial power exercised by the Japanese in the
American economy. In the agricultural sector, although foreigners own less
than 1 percent of the 1 billion acres of private farmland in the United States,
compared with much more sizable holdings by United Brands and other U.S.-
based agribusiness MNCs in Latin America and elsewhere, many states in the
American farm belt have become so alarmed at the prospect of foreign takeovers
that they have passed legislation that bans or severely restricts foreign
ownership of farmland.

   In the case of both less developed and developed countries, one can see that
host governments are extremely ambivalent about foreign MNCs within their
borders. While foreign firms can provide important benefits to host countries,
they also can produce invidious effects, such as the 1984 disaster in Bhopal,
India, where a chemical leak from a Union Carbide plant caused the deaths
of over 2,000 people and injuries to 50,000 others. Such incidents have renewed
calls in the United Nations and elsewhere for the establishment of a uniform
code of conduct that would spell out MNC responsibilities and obligations
toward host states in which they operate, as part of a general MNC regime.
There is a special concern that subsidiaries controlled from abroad will become
"Trojan horses," serving the interests of the home country in which the parent
country is headquartered rather than the host country.[50] This leads us to
consider the nature of MNC–home government relations.

MNC–Home Government Relations. If MNCs often pose problems for host
governments, what about MNC relations with their **home government?** It is
curious that although MNCs are commonly portrayed by *dependencia* theorists
and other observers as agents of home government "imperialism" and "neocolonialism," the evidence is mixed as to whether MNCs fully act in the
interest and under the control of their home state. As they do with host
governments, MNCs tend to have a "love-hate" relationship with home
governments as well.

   On the one hand, it is true that MNCs typically have special bonds with
the nation-state in which they are headquartered, insofar as their ownership
and top management tend to consist predominantly if not exclusively of
nationals of the home country. In a few cases such as Unilever, the giant
British-Dutch conglomerate that makes Pepsodent and Close-Up toothpaste
and numerous other products, there is joint control by two countries. However,
such internationalization of ownership and management is rare. The typical
case is Nestlé, the Swiss-based MNC, which has almost 100,000 stockholders
drawn from many different countries but which is required to have 51 percent
of the voting stock held by Swiss citizens. Ties between Japanese MNCs and
the Japanese government are so close that Japan is often referred to as "Japan,
Inc." In terms of ownership and top management, then, MNCs are closely
associated with their home country.

It is also true that MNCs have often been used as instruments of home state foreign policy. Attempts by the U.S. government to use foreign subsidiaries of American MNCs to serve U.S. foreign policy ends are well documented. For example, the U.S. government used its control over IBM to prevent IBM's French subsidiary from selling computers to the French government for France's nuclear program during the 1960s, and also from exporting high technology from France to the Soviet Union and other East bloc countries. In banning such exports to the East bloc, the United States was attempting to extend U.S. law—the Trading with the Enemy Act—to operate within French borders and to shape French foreign economic policy. In 1979, in an effort to pressure the Iranian government to release American diplomatic personnel held hostage, the Carter administration ordered the overseas branches of Chase Manhattan and other U.S. banks to cooperate in freezing any Iranian assets they held. In the early 1970s, the U.S. Central Intelligence Agency and International Telephone and Telegraph followed a parallel course in helping to create economic chaos in Chile designed to undermine the Allende government, although it was not clear whether ITT was serving as an instrument of the U.S. government or whether the U.S. government was simply responding to the threat posed to ITT and other American MNCs in Chile.[51] The sense of partnership between the U.S. government and U.S. MNCs over the years is captured in Raymond Vernon's observation that in support of American business abroad, Washington "has landed Marines in half a dozen Caribbean countries, threatened to cut off aid to several dozen others from Peru to Sri Lanka, and at some point put other forms of pressure on almost every [other government]."[52]

However, tensions can arise between MNCs and their home government, in the U.S. case as well as other cases, with MNCs at times engaging in activities that are seemingly at odds with home state interests and beyond home government control. Home government attempts to adopt "tight money" policies to dampen high domestic inflation in the price of goods are often frustrated by the ability of MNCs to borrow money readily through their overseas channels. Home government problems in reducing domestic unemployment are often aggravated by "runaway shops," whereby MNCs relocate their factories from the home country (where the average hourly compensation for manufacturing workers might be $12.00) to, say, South Korea (where the prevailing rate might be $1.50). Even in regard to foreign policy concerns, MNC and home government policies are not always "in synch." By the early 1980s, Pittsburgh-based Gulf Oil had invested over $500 million in Angolan facilities and maintained a cordial working relationship with the Marxist Angolan government, at a time when 15,000 Cuban troops were helping that government ward off a pro-Western faction seeking power with the support of the Reagan administration. A Philippine subsidiary of Exxon refused to sell oil to the U.S. Navy at Subic Bay during the Arab oil embargo of 1973. At the beginning of World War II, the U.S. State Department had difficulty getting U.S. oil and chemical companies to terminate their close ties with German companies operating in Latin America. And in the 1970s, U.S.-based Lockheed Corporation made under-the-table payments to Japanese Prime Minister Tanaka to influence Japanese government purchases of Lockheed aircraft, violating U.S. laws prohibiting bribery of and political donations to foreign officials, and in the process creating embarrassment in U.S.-Japanese relations.[53]

Acknowledging the ambivalent nature of MNC–home government relations, Raymond Vernon has added that as these relations evolve, the identity of MNCs "is likely to become more and more ambiguous in national terms. Commingling human and material resources of many nations, formulating problems and solutions on lines uninhibited by national boundaries, multi-national enterprises may not be easy to classify in terms of national associa-tion."[54] Charles Kindleberger has suggested that the divorce is already final: "The international corporation has no country to which it owes more loyalty than any other, nor any country where it feels completely at home."[55] One of the strongest expressions of MNC detachment from its national roots, at least in terms of aspirations, came from the chairman of a major MNC, the Dow Chemical Company:

> I have long dreamed of buying an island owned by no nation, and of establishing the World Headquarters of the Dow company on the truly neutral ground of such an island, beholden to no nation or society. If we were located on such truly neutral ground we could then really operate in the United States as U.S. citizens, in Japan as Japanese citizens and in Brazil as Brazilians rather than being governed in prime by the laws of the United States.[56]

The detachment of the MNC from the nation-state is still just that—a dream. Most MNCs are still firmly anchored to the home country. As for those MNCs that forget their national roots, home governments still have the authority ultimately to restore control over them, given the vast regulative role that modern societies have assigned to government. In fact, pressured by domestic labor unions damaged by runaway shops, the U.S. government and the governments of other developed countries have considered imposing further restrictions on the level and type of foreign investment their MNCs can engage in overseas. Then, too—to paraphrase Stalin's famous remark about the limits of *power* possessed by the Pope—General Motors and other MNCs have no (army) divisions. In short, national governments would still appear to be in charge of "the global shopping center."

Conclusion

Although governments are still running the world economy, that economy sputtered through much of the 1980s as many countries experienced recession and serious economic problems. Nowhere are the problems greater than in the Third World, where the "debt bomb" and other troubles are threatening to produce not only disaster in less developed countries but a worldwide financial crisis as well. As we have noted, the liberal international economic order that was created under American leadership after World War II, commonly referred to as "the Bretton Woods system," can be credited with expanding the planetary product and providing a degree of management over trade, monetary, and aid relations through institutions such as GATT, the IMF, and the World Bank. However, as we have also noted, this system and the regimes associated with it have come under increasing strain and are now threatened with collapse. While many in the developed capitalist states believe the system can be saved, others in the Third World have called for a "New International Economic Order," a subject to be taken up in the next chapter.

SUMMARY

1. There are three predominant schools of thought on the international economy. The classical liberal internationalist school, which developed in reaction to mercantilist thought that predominated in the seventeenth and eighteenth centuries and which is popular in developed capitalist countries today, argues that goods and services should flow as freely as possible across national boundaries. In this way, consumers in all nations can benefit from the cheapest prices based on the most efficient allocation of resources among countries. The role of international institutions is to maintain stability in international economic affairs and to help expand the planetary product.

2. The *dependencia* school argues that the world is divided into two sets of states— the developed, exploitive Northern states and the less developed, dependent Southern states—and that international institutions should act to redistribute wealth more evenly between the two sides.

3. The world system school also posits an exploitive relationship but focuses on the role of nonstate actors, namely economic elites found inside and across national boundaries. Adopting a Marxist approach, this school views international economic relations as a struggle between the rich and poor classes in a world society.

4. The international economy has three interrelated components: the commerce sector, the currency sector, and the capital sector. The international economy can also be examined in terms of three sets of actors: the developed capitalist states, the developed Communist states, and the countries of the Third World.

5. In the commerce sector, free trade carries both benefits and costs. It increases the availability of goods, often at favorable prices, as well as opportunities for growth of certain local industries. However, it can also damage a country's "infant" industries or older, inefficient industries unable to compete with foreign producers, and thus lead to higher unemployment at home and excessive dependence on external sources of supply. To constrain international trade, countries can use quotas and tariffs as well as more subtle protectionist measures.

6. The major participants in world trade have been the developed capitalist countries, with the Communist countries trading mostly with each other. The developed countries rely on the less developed countries as sources of raw material imports as well as markets for their exports of technology and manufactured goods, with the terms of trade tending to favor the developed states. Despite postwar efforts at relaxing trade barriers through organizations such as GATT, there has been a recent revival of protectionist sentiment (neomercantilism).

7. Most international economic transactions are based on a few "hard" currencies belonging to developed capitalist states. Because of the importance of maintaining adequate supplies of hard currencies, countries carefully monitor their balance of payments, attempt to correct deficits by adjusting the outflow or inflow of funds (in such areas as tourism, foreign investment, and trade). If many countries experience balance of payments problems at once, a serious global problem can result if there is not enough "liquidity" to finance international economic activity and if countries resort to currency devaluation as a solution.

8. The international monetary system now operates on the basis of floating exchange rates. Intergovernmental coordination occurs primarily through the IMF, which provides a central fund of hard currency reserves as well as a forum for controlling disruptive currency fluctuations. The Soviet Union and most Communist states generally do not participate in the IMF and are insignificant actors in the currency sector of the international economy.

9. The capital sector consists of foreign aid and investment. Foreign aid, either bilateral or multilateral, can be in the form of grants, loans, export credits, technical assistance, or military assistance. Donor countries are mostly the developed capitalist states, although the Soviet Union and other developed Communist states have also provided foreign aid. The chief multilateral source of aid, the World Bank, is dominated by the developed capitalist states, primarily the United States.

10. Unlike foreign aid, foreign investment has been targeted at both developed and less developed countries. An important vehicle for foreign investment has been the multinational corporation. The enormous assets controlled by MNCs make them influential both in their home states where they are headquartered and in the host countries in which they operate subsidiaries.

11. Although MNCs bring capital, jobs, and technology to developing countries, critics argue that they take even more out than they contribute; they also exert considerable influence over host government domestic and foreign policy. Third World as well as developed countries have become increasingly sensitive about foreign penetration of their economies.

12. Tension can also arise between MNCs and their home government, with MNCs at times acting seemingly at odds with home state interests. Nevertheless, MNCs tend to be closely associated with their home countries and have often been used as instruments of foreign policy by their home governments.

13. The international economic order that was created after World War II, commonly referred to as the "Bretton Woods system," has been able to achieve some success in managing trade, monetary, and aid relations through institutions such as GATT, the IMF, and the World Bank. However, these regimes have been viewed as ignoring

the needs of less developed states; and even among developed capitalist states they have become increasingly fragile and given to collapse in recent years as countries have experienced domestic economic problems.

SUGGESTIONS FOR FURTHER READING AND STUDY

For an excellent introductory overview of the international economy, especially the relationship between international economics and international politics, see David H. Blake and Robert S. Walters, *The Politics of Global Economic Relations*, 3rd ed. (Englewood Cliffs, N.J.: Prentice-Hall, 1987); and Joan E. Spero, *The Politics of International Economic Relations*, 3rd ed. (New York: St. Martin's Press, 1985). A good reader on "international political economy" is Jeffrey A. Frieden and David A. Lake, eds., *International Political Economy* (New York: St. Martin's Press, 1987).

Writings that focus on the international trade sector, particularly relations between developed capitalist states, include Miriam Camps and William Diebold, Jr., *The New Multilateralism: Can the World Trading System Be Saved?* (New York: Council on Foreign Relations, 1983); William R. Cline, *Trade Policy in the 1980s* (Washington, D.C.: Institute for International Economics, 1983); Robert B. Reich, "Beyond Free Trade," *Foreign Affairs*, 61 (Spring 1983), pp. 773–804; and Gary Hufbauer and Jeffrey J. Schott, *Trading for Growth: The Next Round of Trade Negotiations* (Washington, D.C.: Institute for International Economics, 1985). On North-South trade relations, see Roger D. Hansen, *Beyond the North-South Stalemate* (New York: McGraw-Hill, 1979); David Yoffie, *Power and Protectionism: Strategies of the Newly Industrializing Countries* (New York: Columbia University Press, 1983); and Robert L. Rothstein, *Global Bargaining: UNCTAD and the Quest for a New International Economic Order* (Princeton: N.J.: Princeton University Press, 1979). On East-West trade, see the Atlantic Council's *East-West Trade: Managing Encounter and Accommodation* (Boulder, Colo.: Westview Press, 1977); and Alec Nove, *East-West Trade: Problems, Prospects, Issues* (Beverly Hills: Sage, 1978).

Works that focus on the international currency sector include Benjamin J. Cohen, *Organizing the World's Money* (New York: Basic Books, 1977); Frank A. Southard, Jr., and William McChesney Martin, *The International Monetary System in Transition* (Washington, D.C.: The Atlantic Council, 1980); Sidney E. Rolfe and James Burtle, *The Great Wheel: The World Monetary System* (New York: Quadrangle, 1973); Henry C. Wallich *et al.*, *World Money and National Policies* (New York: Group of Thirty, 1983); and Anthony Sampson, *The Money Lenders* (New York: Penguin, 1981).

On foreign aid, see Jagdish Bhagwati and Richard S. Eckans, eds., *Foreign Aid* (Harmondsworth, England: Penguin, 1970); Edward S. Mason and Robert E. Asher, *The World Bank Since Bretton Woods* (Washington, D.C.: Brookings Institution, 1973); and David Wall, *The Charity of Nations: The Political Economy of Foreign Aid* (New York: Basic Books, 1973). For a variety of viewpoints on MNCs and foreign investment, see Robert Gilpin, *U.S. Power and the Multinational Corporation: The Political Economy of Direct Foreign Investment* (New York: Basic Books, 1975); Anthony Sampson, *The Sovereign State of ITT* (New York: Stein and Day, 1973); John Robinson, *Multinationals and Political Control* (New York: St. Martin's Press, 1983); Isaiah

Frank, *Foreign Enterprise in Developing Countries* (Baltimore: Johns Hopkins University Press, 1980); and Sanjaya Lall and Paul Streeter, *Foreign Investment, Transnationals and Developing Countries* (London: Macmillan, 1977). See also Barnet and Muller and other works cited in the notes for this chapter.

For data on international economic activity, the following sources are especially helpful: *Direction of Trade,* published by the International Monetary Fund; *World Bank Atlas,* published by the World Bank; *Handbook of International Trade and Development Statistics,* published by UNCTAD; *Survey of Current Business,* U.S. Department of Commerce; and *Fortune* magazine.

A good historical perspective on the development of the Bretton Woods system of regimes in the postwar era is furnished by William Diebold, Jr., in "The United States in the World Economy: A Fifty Year Perspective," *Foreign Affairs,* 62 (Fall 1983), pp. 81–104. On whether the "world economy" is now disintegrating with the collapse of postwar regimes, see Albert Bressand, "Mastering the World Economy," *Foreign Affairs,* 61 (Spring 1983), pp. 745–772. An interesting discussion of "liberal," "socialist," and "realist" views of "global economic problems and solutions"—related to our discussion of the various economic schools of thought—is provided by R. D. McKinlay and R. Little, *Global Problems and World Order* (Madison: University of Wisconsin Press, 1986), Part III.

Economic Development:
The Call for a New
International Economic Order

They came to the balmy shores of the Mexican island resort of Cancún in October of 1981. They came, the leaders of twenty-two nations representing two thirds of the world's population, to discuss relations between the world's rich and poor states—to continue the so-called North-South dialogue. They came to hotel suites equipped with Jacuzzi hot-tubs, with a Mexican hairdresser on call daily for British Prime Minister Margaret Thatcher, and a planeload of furniture flown in from Manila for then Philippine President Ferdinand Marcos.[1] They came at a time when world economic recession saw the United States drop to eighth place in per capita income, behind Kuwait, Switzerland, Sweden, Denmark, West Germany, Belgium, and Norway—all with per capita incomes of over $10,000. This was to be compared with Bhutan, Bangladesh, Chad, Ethiopia, Nepal, Mali, Burma, Afghanistan, Burundi, Upper Volta, and India at the bottom of the list, with per capita GNPs of approximately $200 per year. They came as Robert McNamara was retiring as president of the World Bank and predicted that the gap between the world's rich and poor would continue to increase; between 1950 and 1980, the average per capita income of industrial countries had more than doubled (to $10,600), while that of low-income countries rose by less than 50 percent (to $250).[2] They came to see if, in the relaxed seaside atmosphere, anything could be done to close the ever-widening gulf between the "have" and "have-not" nations.

Four years later, during the summer of 1985, 72,000 people thronged to London's Wembley Stadium while 90,000 filled Philadelphia's John F. Kennedy Stadium to hear simultaneously some of the world's best-known rock musicians in the "Live Aid" concert to benefit African famine relief. This first global rock concert and telethon (Bangladesh famine relief had inspired a U.S. rock concert in 1971) was beamed by satellite to an estimated 1.9 billion viewers in 152 countries, raising an estimated $70 million ($30 million in the U.S.).[3] Irish musician Bob Geldof, the concert coordinator, stressed direct aid to victims on the spot in Ethiopia and other drought-ridden African countries; he flew off to supervise truck convoys that would deliver the goods, and spoke of promoting self-help among African populations to stave off future food crises. The compelling issue of global poverty and starvation had struck a chord in the prosperous countries; to quote the successful benefit album by Michael Jackson (who was unable to attend "Live Aid") and other major American stars, "We Are the World!"

Cancún and Live Aid constitute a spectrum of global concern about questions of economic development and poverty, ranging from governmental to private citizen initiatives. Indeed, we will see in this chapter that the Cancún meeting itself produced much disagreement about the proper role of governmental and private enterprise approaches to development. It remains unclear, however, whether—as the star-studded glitter wears off and African rains relieve the acute famine—people will still identify intensely with global economic suffering to the point of singing "We Are the World." In this chapter, we

The "Live Aid" concert at Wembley Stadium in July 1985.

review the developing world's food, population, and economic dilemmas and the politics of problem solving.

The Nature and Magnitude of the Problem

Before examining efforts to address the global problem of poverty and under-development, it would be well to consider the exact nature of the world's rich-poor gap. The meeting at Cancún was occasioned in part by the report of an independent study commission on world economic problems, chaired by former West German Chancellor Willy Brandt, in cooperation with the United Nations. The so-called Brandt Commission Report, published in 1980, followed years of controversy over Third World demands for a **New International Economic Order (NIEO)** which, based on preferential trade and aid arrangements, would supposedly produce a more even redistribution of wealth from the generally well-to-do North to the generally impoverished South.[4] The Brandt Report, now translated into over twenty languages, was not the first documentation of world poverty (the Pearson Commission had reported a decade earlier); but it made a considerable stir as it described the razor-thin edge of economic survival experienced by a majority of the world's people.

The stark reality of the "rich-poor gap" in human terms is expressed in the first chapter of the Brandt Report:

> The North including Eastern Europe has a quarter of the world's population and four fifths of its income; the South including China has...three quarters of the world's population but living on one fifth of the world's income. In the North, the average person can expect to live for more than seventy years; he or she will rarely be hungry, and will be educated at least up to secondary level. In the countries of the South the great majority of people have a life expectancy of closer to fifty years; in the poorest countries one out of every four children dies before the age of five; one-fifth or more of all the people in the South suffer from hunger and malnutrition; fifty per cent have no chance to become literate.[5]

Although the North-South debate is ordinarily couched in terms of the rich-poor gap *between* states, there is also a large rich-poor gap *within* states, which is another dimension of the problem of world poverty. Within both developed and less developed states, one finds huge differences in wealth among the citizenry. However, disparities tend to be particularly pronounced in less developed countries, where the richest 20 percent often receive 60 to 70 percent of the total national income (compared, for example, with only 40 percent in the United States). As McNamara pointed out, it is not enough for less developed countries (LDCs) to experience economic growth; for poverty to be conquered, the fruits of economic growth must be more equally distributed between elites and masses in these countries, so that the poorest of the poor can benefit as well as the wealthy few living on palatial estates.

The World Bank has developed two scenarios about the world's economic future—the "good news" view, and the "bad news" projection. Optimistically, "the number of people living in absolute poverty would decline between 1980 and 1990 to 630 million from 750 million; average per capita GNP for the poorest nations would grow to $260 from $220; average per capita GNP for the noncommunist industrial nations would rise to $14,520 from $10,660."[6] Corresponding figures under the pessimistic view would be 850 million in poverty, and per capita incomes of $230 in the South and $13,380 in the North. The difference between good and bad news in this case seems very slight.

Living conditions in much of the South are likely to improve, at least in absolute terms if not as related to the North. Oil revenues and government programs have brought electricity and improved sanitation to remote Mexican villages, for example. However, the fall of oil revenues in the 1980s and the resultant cutoff of government programs could generate frustration and anger in those same villages. Substantial economic improvement relative to the North will depend upon several factors associated with **economic development,** to be discussed below. In the past, development has been equated with industrialization on the Northern model, i.e., economic growth based on the application of sophisticated technologies (including automation), as well as urbanization (the movement of masses of people to the cities to work in manufacturing). However, the Brandt Report notes that development primarily has to do with "improvements in income distribution and employment" as well as "greater human dignity and justice," and that there are several routes a country can take toward these goals (for example, better use of labor-intensive technologies of production rather than resorting to automation).[7] Development can be taken to mean improving techniques of production and distribution of goods and services, with less waste of resources or human energy. In this sense, all countries are still developing, but some have much further to go than others.

Development, then, entails the establishment of conditions that enable the average man or woman, on the street or on the farm, to engage in productive work and attain a decent standard of living. Yet jobs that allow such productivity are difficult to create in the Third World. For example, the International Labor Organization issued a report prior to the Cancún Conference showing that $76 billion worth of MNC investments in the Third World had produced only 4 million jobs, or 0.5 percent of the total Southern work force. The ILO also has estimated that 1 billion jobs will have to be added in the South by the end of the century.[8] As difficult as it is to generate new or conserve old jobs even in the prosperous North, consider the problem of a country like India, which by some estimates must create 8 million new jobs each year until the year 2000 just to keep up with population growth and employment needs. "With 600 million people, India has a GNP two fifths the size of that of the United Kingdom, which has 55 million people,"[9] so the money to invest in new jobs is indeed scarce. In the developing countries as a whole, an estimated 500 million people have been unemployed or employed in only marginal jobs in recent years.[10]

As noted previously, economic conditions vary considerably among regions and countries of the South, so that one can speak of a South-South gap as well as a North-South gap. Table 14.1 illustrates some differences among LDCs. In the 1970s, during the period of high global inflation rates and high oil prices, certain LDCs did better than others. Oil exporters generally prospered; however, countries dependent on oil imports, for example to run irrigation pumps as part of agricultural development projects, suffered massive inflation. Inflation, which also hit the industrialized world, caused crippling increases in the cost of manufactured items LDCs needed to import. Markets for LDC exports, frequently basic commodities such as tin or rubber, tended to dry up as manufacturing output declined in the industrialized states. Economic growth rates of the lowest income countries fell far more than those of "middle income" and "newly industrializing" LDCs (the latter having invested heavily in manufacturing and taken advantage of relatively low wage rates to expand their exports).[11] Newly industrializing countries (NICs), such as Brazil, Argentina, and Mexico, also borrowed heavily on international financial markets to

Table 14.1

A PROFILE OF THE THIRD WORLD: AVERAGE ANNUAL PER CAPITA GNP IN SELECTED COUNTRIES, 1984

OIL-EXPORTING DEVELOPING COUNTRIES[a]

Indonesia	$ 540	Ecuador	$1,220	Saudi Arabia	$10,740
Nigeria	770	Algeria	2,380	Kuwait	15,410

"ADVANCED" OR "NEWLY INDUSTRIALIZING" COUNTRIES[b]

Brazil	$1,710	S. Korea	$2,090	Taiwan	$ 2,670
Mexico	2,060	Argentina	2,230	Singapore	7,260

"MIDDLE-INCOME" DEVELOPING COUNTRIES[c]

Bolivia	$ 410	El Salvador	$ 710	Jordan	$ 1,710
Morocco	670	Cameroon	810	Panama	2,100

"LOW-INCOME" DEVELOPING COUNTRIES[d]

Chad	$ 80	India	$ 260	Haiti	$ 320
Ethiopia	110	China	300	Pakistan	380

[a] The countries listed here are among 13 countries that are members of OPEC.
[b] The countries listed here are among a dozen countries considered to be NICs.
[c] The countries listed here are among some 50 countries with per capita incomes between $400 and $5,000 that are not OPEC or advanced developing countries.
[d] The countries listed here are among 35 countries with per capita incomes less than $400.

Source: Adapted from *World Bank Atlas, 1986* (Washington, D.C.: World Bank, 1986).

finance their rapid expansion, relying on continued prosperity to pay back the loans. However, this strategy also came "unstuck" in the 1980s as oil prices collapsed, interest rates soared, and a global recession took hold. NICs and their creditors, usually Western banks and international lending agencies, were left holding an extremely heavy debt load.

Generally, Latin American and Middle Eastern countries were better off economically than African and most Asian states throughout the 1970s and 1980s, not only in terms of per capita income but on most other indicators of development as well, such as literacy and infant mortality rates. However, some East Asian developing states, such as South Korea, Taiwan, and Singapore, made great economic strides during these decades. These Asian NICs put great stress on development of export-oriented products and hence maintained better balances of payments and lower foreign debts than many Latin American states, which saw much of their investment capital leave the country.[12] However, even relatively prosperous Asian states remained economically dependent on U.S. and Japanese markets, so that their economies slumped when Washington and Tokyo experienced economic downturns. Among prosperous LDCs, some have distributed wealth more evenly within their societies and have put funds to more socially beneficial uses than others. Among the oil-rich, for example, Iraq and Kuwait did more to raise national standards of hygiene and medical care, at least prior to the dislocations of the Iran-Iraq war, than did Iran or Saudi Arabia.[13]

The problem of economic development is really several problems in one, all of which are *interrelated*. It is difficult for the North and the South to agree on the causes of world poverty, let alone the cures. The trick will be somehow to feed, clothe, shelter, and employ between 6 and 15 billion people in the twenty-first century on a planet of limited resources administered by governments that cannot now manage acceptable living standards for over 3 billion of its inhabitants. Population control, health care, education, social welfare, agricultural management, land distribution, energy research, transportation, labor productivity, capital formation, and technology transfer are the key development policy issues for the future.

We focus on three specific dimensions of the economic development problem in this chapter: *food, population,* and *the transfer of capital and technology.* Keep in mind as we review these concerns that they strongly affect each other. Capital is needed to improve a country's food production and distribution network; food supply has to meet population demands; poorly fed people get sick more often and become less productive; lack of production contributes to poverty; poor people cannot afford food, and so on.

FOOD

Most Northerners have seen photos of starving African and Asian children with distended bellies and listless stares. Televised starvation in distant lands seems almost unreal at times. Yet starvation is very real, as the African famine of the early 1980s drove home with the deaths of an estimated 5 million children in 1984 alone.[14] In addition to millions who die from hunger and related health problems, current estimates are that at least 500 million of the world's people suffer from malnutrition. The global hunger problem is difficult to comprehend, partly because it comes and goes and affects some regions more severely than others. One year Bangladesh will have ruinous weather and famine, and the next it will have relatively abundant harvests. Wars and their accompanying refugee problems can suddenly tilt delicate food balances— as they did in Ethiopia, Somalia, and Chad—adding to the problems of drought. It is difficult to know where famine will strike next, and what type of food assistance to provide—whether to aim for immediate famine relief or for long-term food self-sufficiency.

Optimists can point to some improvements in the food picture in recent years and hopeful possibilities for the future. World food production surged ahead during the third quarter of this century, and outstripped population growth rates. Although these food production rates have slowed during the last decade, grain production has continued to exceed population growth. Some formerly famine-ridden countries, such as China and India, have succeeded in providing their populations with more than adequate nutrition.[15]

(India, the world's largest food aid recipient in the 1960s and early 1970s, by 1986 was no longer a "food deficit" country and was running an annual agricultural trade surplus of over $1 billion.) There still remain some vast tracts of land in Brazil's Amazon jungle, in Argentina, in Central Africa, and in Southeast Asia that could be made arable, depending on land use decisions and the ability to deal with such problems as erosion or flooding. Ocean farming could be developed as another source of food production. Existing agricultural acreage might be made more productive with more efficient farming methods and new hybrid seeds such as those which have helped push the cornbelt further north.

Yet the trends are not altogether encouraging. Deaths related to hunger and malnutrition have been averaging 50,000 a day in the 1980s. "As recently as 1970, Africa was essentially self-sufficient in food. In 1984, however, some 140 million Africans—out of a total of 531 million—were fed with grain from abroad."[16] Africa is the one region where food production per person has *consistently* declined since 1970. Given the expected growth in world population, there is clearly a long-term problem of food supply in other regions as well, especially if one considers difficulties in opening up new farmland or trying to make more productive use of existing acreage. Only 15 percent of the land area on the globe is suitable for agriculture; half of it is already under cultivation. The remaining half consists of land that would be the most difficult and costly to cultivate. The world's oceans have also suffered from overfishing in recent years, with the world catch of tuna and other fish in decline after dramatic growth between 1950 and 1970.

Despite concerns about food scarcity, there are currently sufficient food stocks to feed the world's hungry. Indeed, there is agricultural overproduction in some countries such as the U.S., where grain storage silos have been overflowing in recent years as American farmers have been unable to sell in the world marketplace all that they produce. A major part of the world food problem is distribution, i.e., the lack of purchasing power by many people in Africa and elsewhere means that food often never gets to those places where it is most needed. In a survey of the world food situation in 1986, one study noted that "food held in the silos and cold stores of America, Europe, and Japan could meet the food needs of Africa five times over," with American storage facilities alone having "enough surplus . . . to produce 27 loaves of bread for everyone in the world."[17]

Distribution problems are also complicated by land-holding patterns. In Latin America, the poorest 70 percent of the people own less than 3 percent of the land.[18] Much of the land is owned by foreign interests, concerned more about producing farm products for export than meeting local food needs. For example, although beef production doubled in the last twenty years in Guatemala and Costa Rica, per capita beef consumption in those countries declined as more than half of the beef products were exported, primarily to the United States for fast-food chains.[19] Even among native farmers, land is sometimes used to grow cash crops, such as cotton, coffee, or even opium, to support farmers' debts rather than for production of food grains.

A long-term solution to the global food problem could lie in making as many Southern states as possible more self-sufficient in food production. Self-reliance in some instances requires introduction of new farming methods and high-yielding seeds developed since World War II. This so-called **green revolution** is based on the heavy application of petroleum-based chemical fertilizers and on extensive irrigation.[20] These in turn depend on expensive foreign imports. While OPEC states have assisted a few hard-hit Southern countries, the majority of LDCs have had little assistance in footing the hefty import bills. The "green revolution" also tends mainly to help richer farmers able to afford and make use of the new technology on large plots of land, leaving the bulk of the rural poor in many countries to remain in poverty or to join the ranks of urban slum dwellers searching in vain for employment. Complicating matters further have been shortages and poor distribution of seeds, especially in famine zones where the population has been forced to eat the seed supply. There is a need, then, to supplement the "green revolution" with more egalitarian land reform along with better use of the rural labor supply and traditional farming techniques. Yet overall food production might suffer, at least in the short run, if radical land reform measures were to take land away from many technologically advanced farmers.

POPULATION

At least since the time of Thomas Malthus, an eighteenth-century English economist who became famous for his prediction that the world's population would inevitably outstrip its food supply and cause massive famine, the problems of food and population have been intimately linked. However, man

By permission of Johnny Hart and Field Enterprises, Inc.

A matter of priorities: Crops for food, or cash?

does not live by bread alone. The growth in the world's population today poses many concerns that go far beyond food problems.

Not only is world population growing, but the growth over the centuries has been accelerating at an alarming pace. It took roughly two million years—until 1830—for the human population of the earth to reach 1 billion; it took only 100 years for the total to grow by another billion, and just 50 years for that number to double again. Today, the equivalent of a city the size of Dayton, Ohio (which has a population of 200,000) is added to the planet every 24 hours!

Population growth has been most dramatic in the South, where the introduction of advanced medical care since World War II has lowered death rates somewhat while birth rates have remained relatively high. Whereas many developed states of the North have become virtually "ZPG" (zero population growth) countries, many less developed states are experiencing population growth rates of more than 2 or 3 percent annually. This situation is particularly acute in Africa, the only region to have experienced *consistently* increasing rates of population growth since 1960 (see Figure 14.1).

Population problems are aggravated by the fact that the age distribution in less developed countries is increasingly weighted toward the young. These young people, in addition to being of prime childbearing age, are restless for job opportunities and are moving from the countryside to cities in search of a better life. Hence, a "population bomb" is ticking away:

> [In the next century] Nigeria and Bangladesh are projected to have as many people as the United States and USSR do today, and India will have at least 1.2 billion inhabitants. The cities of the Third World are growing even faster than the total populations, and the biggest of them are likely to exceed 30 million by the end of this century.[21]

By the year 2010, it is projected that more than half the human race will live in urban areas, with one-fifth crowded into seventy-eight cities, mainly in the Third World, having populations of at least 4 million. Twenty "mega-cities" are expected to have populations exceeding 10 million.[22] (See the growth of such cities in Table 14.2.) Mexico City seems the prime candidate to be the world's largest city in the twenty-first century, with an expected population larger than Canada's.

Aside from causing overcrowding, such population growth places tremendous strains on a nation's economy. Even with Mexico's remarkable 6 percent average annual economic growth rate between 1940 and 1980 and its emerging oil industry, roughly 20 percent of the total Mexican work force has been driven to seek employment, often illegally, in the United States in recent years. Many of the economic gains made in the Third World have been eroded by burgeoning populations demanding more and more housing, education, and

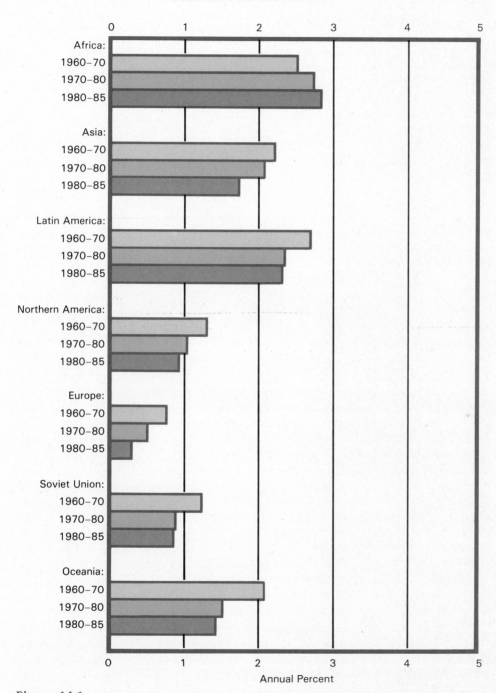

Figure 14.1
WORLD POPULATION—ANNUAL GROWTH RATE, BY CONTINENT: 1960 TO 1985

Table 14.2

HOW THE WORLD'S 12 LARGEST CITIES ARE GROWING (all figures in millions of people)

1975	POP. IN MILLIONS	1990	POP. IN MILLIONS	2000	POP. IN MILLIONS
Greater New York	19.8	Tokyo-Yokohama	23.4	Mexico City	31.0
Tokyo-Yokohama	17.7	Mexico City	22.9	Sao Paulo	25.8
Mexico City	11.9	Greater New York	21.8	Tokyo-Yokohama	24.2
Shanghai	11.6	Sao Paulo	19.9	Greater New York	22.8
Los Angeles-Long Beach	10.8	Shanghai	17.7	Shanghai	22.7
Sao Paulo	10.7	Beijing	15.3	Beijing	19.9
London	10.4	Rio de Janeiro	14.7	Rio de Janeiro	19.0
Buenos Aires	9.3	Los Angeles-Long Beach	13.3	Bombay	17.1
Rhein-Ruhr	9.3	Bombay	12.0	Calcutta	16.7
Paris	9.2	Calcutta	11.9	Jakarta	16.6
Rio de Janeiro	8.9	Buenos Aires	11.4	Seoul	14.2
Peking	8.7	Seoul	11.3	Los Angeles-Long Beach	14.2

Source: David K. Willis, "The Supercities," *Christian Science Monitor,* August 7, 1984, pp. 18–19. Reprinted by permission. © 1984. The Christian Science Publishing Society. All rights reserved.

other social services.[23] Education is a particularly serious problem in a world in which one-third of the total adult population is estimated to be illiterate and, hence, lacking in essential skills to participate in a modern economy.

Despite the problems that seem to be associated with population growth, people and governments do not fully agree on its implications or remedies. The North in the past has urged the South simply to control its numbers; the South in turn has argued that its mass of humanity would not be such a problem if more wealth were available to distribute among its people. Social scientists have indeed found evidence, as seen in Soviet and European growth rates in Figure 14.1, that the population growth rate almost invariably declines when people in a society improve their income. Large families are no longer necessary when parents have sufficient income, since fewer children are needed to work, to provide old-age security, and to serve as status symbols. The problem, of course, is that of the chicken and the egg—how to produce improved economic conditions when such progress is hampered by the very population growth it could curb.

Some less developed countries, forced by intense population pressure, have tried to solve the population paradox through implementation of national birth control policies. For years, China officially encouraged late marriages, and more recently it has imposed heavy financial penalties on couples having more than two children and has adopted a goal of one-child families. Experiments with mandatory sterilization have been tried in India, along with mass birth control education programs. Some of these are dire remedies, meant to solve dire problems. Population control efforts have begun to produce results in several Third World countries. Birth rates have declined in some countries (in China, faster than the death rate). In fact, a hopeful sign is that the world population *growth rate* has declined from 1.9 percent per year in the 1970s to 1.7 percent in the 1980s (even though 79 million people were added annually in the eighties compared to 70 million in the seventies).[24] Projections that just a few years ago had humanity doubling to 8 billion by the year 2000 now have been modified to show "only" a 50 percent increase to 6 billion.

We have noted that death rates have been lowered throughout much of the South through medical advances, notably in eliminating smallpox and reducing the incidence of cholera and malaria. However, serious problems remain as growing populations put added burdens on already inadequate health care systems. In the United States there was one doctor for every 549 persons in 1980, while in Mozambique there was one for every 23,883; there were 171 people per hospital bed in the United States, and 3,470 in Afghanistan.[25] Doctors in the Third World as well as the United States tend to be concentrated in cities. Sixty percent of Thailand's physicians reside in Bangkok, which contains only 8 percent of the population; in Guatemala, with six times more doctors in urban areas than in rural areas, the average Guatemalan visits a hospital or clinic only once every five years. It is little wonder, then, that six relatively easily preventable diseases—polio, measles, diphtheria, tetanus, whooping cough, and tuberculosis—kill one-third of the 15 million children dying each year in the Third World, or that something as mundane as diarrhea is the biggest single killer—accounting for another third of the childhood deaths.[26]

Therefore health care delivery is a key development concern. The United Nations has estimated that to reach its suggested minimum global standard of one doctor per 10,000 people, an additional 3.5 million doctors would have to be trained at a cost of $100 million. Yet only about 12,000 new African doctors graduate yearly. Research needs over the next twenty years are likely to be very costly as well, especially given the devastating effects of relatively difficult diseases such as acquired immune deficiency syndrome (AIDS) in tropical Africa and Haiti. Looking at the situation a bit differently, however, it has been estimated that every newborn child could be vaccinated against the six major childhood killer diseases for $5.00 per child. Oral rehydration is a relatively easy and effective antidote to diarrhea, using readily available ingredients.

The health problem in LDCs, then, is more complicated than merely the scarcity of medical personnel. Even with vaccinations against disease, infant mortality still often increases in LDCs because of socioeconomic problems, such as lack of money for nutrition, poor community water and sanitation systems, belief in traditional or folk medicine (some of which can be beneficial and some not), and time pressures on women (especially in Africa, where in some locations they do 70 to 80 percent of the agricultural work).[27]

As many as 1 billion people in the South are thought to lack potable water, and an estimated 80 percent of Third World infections are water-borne. The Brandt Commission estimates that the condition known as river blindness affects 20 million Africans along the fertile rivers of West Africa, while sleeping sickness claims 35 million victims and parasitic schistosomiasis, or bilharzia (spread by river snails), another 180 to 200 million. It is encouraging that 15 million more rural people in the developing world were served by adequate water supplies in 1983 than in 1980, but such improvements remain among the most expensive preventive health care programs.[28]

THE TRANSFER OF CAPITAL AND TECHNOLOGY

In reviewing development problems, it is clear that societies must have funds at their disposal to invest in job-creating industries, food production, population control programs, health care, and social services in general. Yet capital tends to be scarce in Southern countries, especially when people cannot afford to pass savings along to banks or to the government (through taxes) for reinvestment in the economy. Foreign aid and foreign investment as well as funds earned from exports can provide an alternative source of capital for countries lacking sufficient domestic resources, but problems of corruption often sap those funds.

As noted in our earlier discussion of the international economy, the Third World claims existing international economic relationships benefit the North more than the South. In the trade sector, many Southern countries continue to depend excessively on money earned from the export of a few commodities, which makes them vulnerable to the vagaries of global supply and demand for these products. In fact, some fifty LDCs are still "one-commodity countries," i.e., dependent on a single commodity to provide more than half of their export earnings.[29] Therefore, not enough hard foreign currency comes in to pay for increasingly expensive imports. In the words of the Brandt Commission, "Without adequate finance, imports cannot be paid for; without essential imports, production and exports decline; and without adequate exports, countries are not sufficiently creditworthy to borrow and cannot service their debts."[30]

An example of the mushrooming effects of trade problems comes from the depressed world cocoa market in 1981, which had so reduced revenues from Ghana's chief cash crop that crucial imports could not be bought. The price of a loaf of bread equaled two days' wages, and the country owed neighboring Nigeria—the sole source of Ghana's petroleum—$90 million for past purchases. With strict rationing in force, there was only a few weeks' reserve of oil supplies.[31] A military coup soon followed in Ghana, produced by the same kind of economic hardships that have caused political instability in many Third World countries.

We have already commented on the tendency of NICs and other LDCs to accumulate heavy international debt burdens—a problem traceable to their own mismanagement, to worsening global economic conditions, and to questionable bank lending practices. The "debt crisis" became acute when it appeared in the early 1980s that the largest debtor nations might default on their loan principal and interest ("debt servicing") payments, hence threatening the solvency of the international banking system (with Western commercial banks holding about 60 percent of the global debt). As a U.S. Treasury official reportedly put it, the crisis began in 1982 when the Mexican Finance Minister "showed up on our doorstep and turned his pockets inside out."[32] Indeed, the situation had reached the point by 1983 where the net flow of investment capital, which is theoretically supposed to go from Northern advanced economies to Southern LDCs for development to occur, had actually reversed, with more money going from South to North in order to pay off international debts. LDCs were forced to mortgage their exports (one-third of all Latin American exports in the mid-1980s went to debt servicing) in order to pay their creditors; little if any hard currency was left to finance development projects. Fewer new loans were made available to debt-ridden LDCs, further cutting available investment capital. International commercial lending dipped by 50 percent between 1982 and 1983.[33] Some governments, such as Nigeria and Peru, announced unilateral slowdowns on debt repayment, but most began negotiations on "rescheduling" (lengthening the time for loan repayment) or "restructuring" (lowering loan interest rates) of their debts. By the late 1980s the acute crisis for banks had eased somewhat with internationally coordinated approaches to debt repayment. However, a chronic shortage of investment funds in the developing world remained.

In addition to trade and commercial lending, foreign aid is a major source of capital for development. As we have noted, aid can be given bilaterally or multilaterally and can include grants as well as concessionary (low interest) loans. Bilateral economic (as distinct from military) assistance by donors such as the United States has been reduced since the 1970s by budgetary constraints and political considerations; most such assistance goes to middle income LDCs. At a UN conference in Paris in 1981, the industrialized countries agreed either to double their official development assistance by 1985 to the neediest thirty-six countries in the world (mostly in Africa and South Asia), or to achieve an aid level of .15 percent of their own GNPs. However, they fell well short of the targets. Development assistance has provided nearly 90 percent of low income LDCs' external revenues, but only Denmark, the Netherlands, Norway, Sweden, and Belgium reached the .15 percent goal in the 1980s. Overall, the percentage of GNP given in aid to low income countries has fallen rather than risen since 1980. More aid was distributed through multilateral agencies, though not enough to offset the decline in bilateral programs.[34]

Foreign private investment by multinational corporations also has presented opportunities for Third World capital formation but often has resulted instead in net losses of capital, as MNC profits are repatriated to the home country rather than reinvested in the host country. Foreign investment also has been restrained by mutual suspicions—MNCs fear disruptions in operating conditions, taxation, renegotiation of contracts, and political risks in LDCs; host countries fear "exploitation," unfair contracts, concealed information, restrictive business practices, distortion of pay scales, and political interference by the MNCs.[35]

MNCs are viewed by Third World countries not only as a key potential source of capital but also as a major source of modern technology, although technology transfers from North to South have occurred almost as slowly and unevenly as capital transfers. While certain high-technology labor-saving devices are probably inappropriate to the needs of many less developed countries, at least some technological advancement is needed if Third World countries are to progress economically and to become less dependent on the North.

The communications and information sector is one area in which the North-South technology gap is especially troublesome for the Third World. Figure 14.2, which shows the worldwide distribution of telephones, suggests the heavy advantage this wonder of communication affords the Northern Hemisphere; for example, if you want to make a telephone call between Egypt

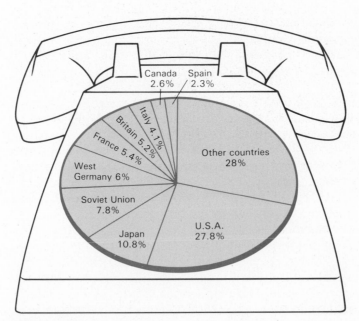

Figure 14.2
WHERE THE TELEPHONES ARE
72 percent of the world's 424 million access lines are concentrated in nine countries.

and South Africa today, it is still easier to place the call through London. The "communications gap" goes well beyond telephones. While computers have become more evident in Third World countries ranging from Kenya to Peru, and while much computer assembly and manufacturing take place in the South, computer design technologies and software are mainly Northern owned. Over 80 percent of the world's computers used for high-speed information processing were found in only six Northern states in 1980.[36] Many Third World states also lack modern news gathering and dissemination capabilities, which means that, for example, people in Ghana learn about events less than 400 miles away in Nigeria through reports from the Reuters News Agency thousands of miles away in London.[37] As telephone, television, and other forms of communication come to depend increasingly on satellites, controlled mainly by advanced industrialized countries, the LDCs' access to vital information (even about such topics as their own natural resources and arable land) may depend even more on the North.

The technology gap can be closed only if the North is willing to facilitate greater technology transfer. However, international technology transfer occurs primarily through the buying and selling of patents and licenses, with most of these held by MNCs. The flow of technology has run mainly among Northern states themselves rather than between North and South; an advanced country like Japan has obtained far more new technology from abroad than have less developed states.[38] Some Third World countries, such as India, have developed indigenous corps of technicians, engineers, and scientists; but when the most talented Southern minds are sent abroad to study in Northern universities, many fail to return to their home country, contributing to the **brain drain** of recent years.

All of these concerns have been closely tied to the larger debate over the New International Economic Order (often referred to as NIEO) that occurred in the 1970s and similar debates that have occurred since. Having conveyed some sense of the nature and magnitude of Third World development problems, we now turn to an examination of the global political process and the formation of regimes related to those problems.

The Politics of
Economic Development and NIEO

A variety of actors with interests in the politics of economic development and NIEO can be identified. These include nation-states and their governments, interest groups within nations, and both IGOs and NGOs. In the 1970s the debate centered on a set of Southern demands constituting the NIEO. With the 1981 Cancún meeting and criticism by many economists, NIEO as a package of proposals was largely rejected by the North; but elements of it are still on the bargaining agenda, as will be seen in the remainder of this chapter.

Among nation-states, two main bargaining groups have participated in the North-South debate. One is the so-called **Group of 77** countries representing the South or Third World (which numbers more than 100 countries). Although the sheer size of this group along with the aforementioned South-South gap has made it difficult at times to forge a single Southern negotiating position on economic issues, the Group of 77 has displayed a generally high level of solidarity in emphasizing the need for a new set of international economic relationships. The second bargaining group is the **Organization for Economic Cooperation and Development (OECD)** representing the North. Consisting of the developed states of North America and Western Europe and Japan, OECD was an outgrowth of efforts by the United States to help rebuild Western European economies after World War II and to promote economic cooperation among the industrialized democracies. Although many differences exist within this group also, OECD members have consulted with each other closely and have largely agreed on basic economic principles.

Of course, there are subgroupings on both sides, with such organizations as OPEC or the "Group of 24" in the IMF representing some Southern states in certain forums, and organizations such as the EEC or the Club of Paris (on questions of debt) sometimes speaking for segments of the North. (As noted earlier, the Soviet Union and other developed Communist states of the North have generally been peripheral to the NIEO dialogue, professing to champion the Southern cause but not being very relevant to Southern needs.)

One can see that IGOs serve partly as vehicles for articulating the interests of different sets of *states*. IGOs, through their secretariats, also seek to articulate and promote *organizational* interests of their own, such as bigger budgets and expanded powers. In addition to the World Bank and the IMF, many other IGOs in the UN system are involved in economic development concerns and have a stake in NIEO politics. A partial listing would include the Food and Agriculture Organization (FAO), World Health Organization (WHO), Education, Scientific and Cultural Organization (UNESCO), and International Labor Organization (ILO). The UN General Assembly itself has been the central forum for much of the NIEO debate. Within the United Nations, the Economic and Social Council (ECOSOC) and its regional economic commissions, the UN Conference on Trade and Development (UNCTAD), the UN Industrial Development Organization (UNIDO), the UN Development Program (UNDP), and the UN Children's Fund (UNICEF) are among the many agencies active in the economic development area. To this list of global IGOs can be added regional development banks and other regional organizations. Finally, among nonstate actors, one cannot overlook the role played by private banks, multinational corporations, and other nongovernmental entities in affecting economic relations between North and South.

The Group of 77 has prepared an extensive "shopping list" of demands over the years as part of their call for a New International Economic Order, campaigning for greater access to Northern capital and technology as well as more favorable trade terms. They have focused attention especially on the need to reshape global economic institutions so that the latter might be more responsive to Third World concerns. The Group of 77 has argued that the major UN agencies concerned with economic development are underfunded, overly restrictive in their rules, and generally controlled by developed states.

Some Southern leaders have proposed a more comprehensive World Development Authority, to be run by a board elected by the Third World–dominated UN General Assembly and empowered to regulate short- and long-term credit, expand trade opportunities, and supervise global efforts to address development problems involving population, food, and other issues. Included in such an Authority would be an International Central Bank, a Development Fund, a World Trade Organization, and a World Food Authority.[39] Some Northern states also have concluded that the economic machinery established shortly after World War II needs reform, but there is no consensus that the Southern proposal is practical. (Given the fact that the twelve European states of the EEC have so far been unable to form a unified central bank at the regional level, the idea that a world central bank could be formed in the next fifty years seems quite fanciful.)

North-South discussions have occurred in several different places, ranging from UNCTAD conferences, convened every four years, to smaller select meetings like Cancún. Periodic special sessions of the UN General Assembly have also been organized, such as those in 1974 and 1975, which produced a Declaration on the Establishment of a New International Economic Order and a Program of Action. North and South have each tried to exercise a certain leverage. The North has feared increased Southern control over supplies and raw materials. A new issue in the trade debate concerns increased Southern exports of manufactured products at relatively low prices. Such "cheap labor" production has threatened traditional Northern industries such as textiles, shoes, and steel.[40] Some Northern political and economic leaders argue that the North should abandon such production to the South and concentrate instead on "hi-tech" items and services; others argue for a concerted Northern effort to win back the "basic industries." On the other hand, Southern dependence on the North as an export market and a source of hard currency and technology has limited the South's freedom to maneuver. With momentum shifting back and forth, the Group of 77 and OECD remain essentially locked in a political stalemate.[41]

Three political factions have emerged during the course of the NIEO debate: (1) the radicals (including such Southern states as Cuba, Algeria, and Benin), who have called for a complete overhauling of the international economic system; (2) the moderates (including some of the richer Southern states such as South Korea, Singapore, and the Ivory Coast, as well as several Northern states such as Canada, Australia, and especially the Netherlands and the Scandinavian countries), who have been supportive of NIEO proposals but lean more toward making practical reforms within the existing institutions rather than necessarily seeking drastic changes; and (3) the conservatives (including some of the major economic powers, such as the United States, West Germany, and Japan), who, while amenable to certain limited reforms, have been generally suspicious of and resistant to NIEO proposals.

The tactics of the conservative group have included "delay, ambiguous verbal concessions, and minimal concessions that might split some of the developing countries away from others."[42] Some of these tactics were evident in the relatively conservative political stance taken by the United States at Cancún. President Reagan generally opposed the idea of global negotiations between North and South aimed at broad changes in international economic relations. Instead, the Americans stressed the notions of self-help and free enterprise, placing the onus on Third World countries to undertake *internal* political and economic reforms within their society as the key to development. President Reagan, Prime Minister Thatcher, and other conservatives argued that weak Third World economies could be attributed largely to ineffective governments.

Southerners took a different view, however. While agreeing that corrupt and bloated governments existed, they doubted that free enterprise alone would solve the South's problems. An exclusively free enterprise approach might merely add to urban slums and neglect of the rural population as wealth became even more concentrated in the hands of a few. Moreover, it was argued that a series of natural disasters and devastating international economic forces, previously alluded to, were more responsible for recent Southern economic woes than bad governments.

The North-South confrontation has been compared to the confrontation between management and labor during negotiations for a new contract. Southern governments have mostly operated within the general framework of the existing rules and institutions while working for change. There have been relatively few "strikes" on the part of the South (i.e., boycotts of the industrialized North, repudiation of debt obligations, or refusals to honor patent rights and pay royalties), although on occasion Southern governments have taken actions against the established order (e.g., expropriation of MNC property without compensation). Although the entire fabric of rules governing international economic relations has been on the brink of unraveling in recent years, Northern and Southern governments alike have at least continued both bilateral and multilateral negotiations to prevent regime collapse; national central banks are in constant touch with each other trying to shore up shaky currencies, for example, while the Board of the IMF debates overall regime rules, such as the amount of reserve currencies IMF will hold and the terms by which members will have access to them.[43]

With this backdrop, let us focus in greater detail on the politics and regimes found in the specific issue-areas of food, population, and capital and technology transfer. In so doing, we should note that it has been easiest to develop widely accepted norms and rules in those instances where both North and South have stood to benefit jointly. It has been easier, for example, to generate consensus behind the rescheduling of Southern debt repayment than behind the creation of a new international aid agency. The former benefits both Northern and Southern economic interests, preventing debt default. In contrast, a new international aid agency might lessen Northern control of development funds.[44] The task for regime formation, here as elsewhere, is one of discovering mutual interests.

Food: Politics and Regimes

In global food politics the debate centers on the fact that world food supplies are unevenly distributed, with certain Northern countries accounting for the bulk of production, consuming disproportionate amounts and controlling distribution. Southerners point out that more grain is consumed by livestock in the United States and the Soviet Union than by the human inhabitants of less developed countries.[45]

The 1974 UN-sponsored **World Food Conference** in Rome made a series of recommendations for improving the world food situation that were endorsed by the UN General Assembly in 1975, at a time of high grain prices and dangerously low reserve food supplies. The recommendations included (1) increased agricultural development funds; (2) a global early-warning system to share information about projected weather patterns, harvests, and other factors that would make it possible to anticipate and deal with imminent food shortages; (3) an internationally coordinated system of nationally held grain reserves; (4) an annual world food aid target of 10 million tons; and (5) more international institutions, such as a World Food Council, devoted to food problems.[46]

As the world's largest food exporting country, the United States has played a pivotal role in the international politics of food. Secretary of State Kissinger's call in 1974 for an end to global malnutrition was seen as an important commitment. However, questions remained after the World Food Conference as to who would pay for the elaborate institutional network and for the stockpiling of emergency food stocks, and what impact such measures might have on agricultural markets and prices in the United States and elsewhere. Some recommendations of the 1974 Conference have been implemented. In particular, a number of proposed agencies were established, adding to an already elaborate network of UN institutions associated with the global food regime. The World Food Council, created in 1975 and consisting of representatives from thirty-six countries along with a secretariat staff, reports to ECOSOC and is charged with monitoring and coordinating all aspects of the UN food security system. An International Fund for Agricultural Development

(IFAD) was started in 1977 as a vehicle to help the poorest of the rural poor in developing countries to improve food production. IFAD is directed jointly by developed and developing states and supplements the funding provided by the World Bank and UN Development Program (UNDP). A Global Information and Early Warning System also has been established to collect and disseminate data on weather patterns and other conditions that might allow the international community to anticipate possible food shortages.

The above agencies work closely with the Food and Agriculture Organization (FAO), as does the World Food Program, established by the UN in the 1960s to provide emergency assistance (for example, sending 1,500 tons of food per month to one region of Uganda alone in early 1981).[47] While the World Food Council holds extensive discussions of food problems at its annual meetings, the main action in promoting food production is carried on by FAO, with its staff of 8,000, offices in Rome and throughout the world, and half-billion-dollar annual budget. Assorted other UN agencies (e.g., UNICEF, the UN Children's Fund) help deal with technical assistance needs, nutrition problems, and other food-related concerns.

Despite all this impressive machinery, implementation of the food regime objectives has still fallen short in many respects. Although some major food-producing nations have accumulated reserve stocks, there is no effective mechanism for committing these supplies quickly to needy areas of the world. "Grain mountains" have rotted in storage and in LDC ports for lack of effective distribution and insufficient consumer purchasing power. Heaping food aid on a stricken country also can undercut the market for that country's own farm products. The FAO, therefore, has tried to promote greater food exchanges between neighboring LDCs, some of which produce too much and some too little food. The problem of malnutrition is likely to be alleviated only by greater food self-sufficiency and, more importantly, through a greater transfer of purchasing power to the masses of the South.

Northerners have demanded that Southern governments undertake, in conjunction with agricultural development funds provided through IGOs, agricultural reforms within their own societies. In particular, the North has urged an end to Southern governments' subsidization of food prices, which keeps food costs artificially low so that they are within reach of the urban poor. It is argued that such subsidies discourage Southern farmers from producing more and making needed investments, drain government treasuries, and ultimately lead to higher prices. Yet Southern governments risk urban riots and possible overthrow if food prices are allowed to skyrocket overnight.

Southerners, in turn, have demanded that the seed banks, currently supported by the FAO and World Bank, which conserve precious plant seed stocks, be administered by a Third World–controlled agency. In 1986, the U.S. government threatened to withhold its FAO contributions if such an agency were created along with rules to override patents on new seed varieties usually developed in Northern countries. As plant and animal genetic engineering progresses and becomes commercially rewarding, such battles over "genetic imperialism" are likely to intensify.

Private interests, ranging from domestic farm groups to transnational grain marketeers and food-processing companies, also can find themselves embroiled in global food politics in many different ways. For example, multinational food companies such as Swiss-based Nestlé have, ironically, been blamed for contributing to malnutrition by marketing nutritious baby formula in the Third World. It seems that mothers, initially given the formula free at maternity centers, stopped breast-feeding their babies and then began diluting the formula (often with polluted water) to cut costs when they discovered they could not afford to buy it. In 1982 the World Health Organization passed a voluntary code of conduct for companies selling such items in the South, with the United States being the only country to vote against the code (based on the argument that the code represented overregulation of the private sector). Nestlé, seeking to end a consumer boycott of its products, promised to comply.

Of more widespread impact on world food concerns are the large grain dealers that speculate on the commodity markets and control vast stocks of food. Some of these companies, together with lax oversight by the U.S. government, were responsible for massive grain sales at bargain prices to the Soviet Union in 1972 and 1975, at a time when Soviet harvests were very poor and world food demand potentially very high. The shock wave of these massive sales sent world grain prices spiraling upward and led to global hoarding in those years. Activities of the "Big Five" grain dealers are described in the Sidelight on pages 470–471. They clearly have a major role to play in any global food regime.

Population: Politics and Regimes

At the 1974 **World Population Conference** in Bucharest, also sponsored by the United Nations, Southern governments generally argued that attempts to limit population growth were unfairly aimed at the South, where growth rates were highest. They labeled the Northern call for the South to control its numbers a subtle form of racism, noting that high per capita consumption in affluent developed countries was putting at least as much pressure on global resources as growing populations in the Third World. Hence, Southerners demanded that population issues be dealt with in the context of NIEO and that a redistribution of wealth between North and South be effected as part of the solution to the world population problem.

A decade later, however, as 149 countries met at the UN International Conference on Population in Mexico City, many of these same LDC leaders

SIDELIGHT

GRAIN TRADE AND THE BIG FIVE

In the 1970s, much was heard about cartels of Third World raw materials suppliers such as OPEC. Less attention has been paid to the century-old grain cartel among five companies owned by seven American and European families: Cargill, Continental, Bunge, Louis Dreyfus, and André. Their exploits are vividly revealed by Dan Morgan in *The Merchants of Grain*:

In Joseph Heller's *Catch-22*, Milo Minderbinder keeps the Air Force messes supplied with fresh eggs. Milo buys the eggs in Malta for 7 cents, sells them to the mess halls for 5—and still makes a profit. Everybody has a share, and it isn't as hard as it sounds. Milo first buys the eggs in Sicily for only a penny "at the hen." He transfers them secretly to Malta, sells them for 4½ cents, buys them back for 7, and resells them to the Air Force for 5. When his friend Yossarian expresses puzzlement, he explains, "I'm the people I buy them from." . . . [M]odern grain companies operate in a very similar fashion. . . . [T]he resource by which they live is grown by millions of farmers all over the world.

The Big Five are at the center of the global system by which grain is distributed and processed. The grain companies invest in shipping, grain elevators, communications, and processing plants—grain "refineries" which make wheat into flour, soybeans into cooking oil or animal meal, and corn into animal-feeding compounds or liquid sweeteners for soft drinks and ice

were openly advocating population control. In the words of Niger's President Kountche:

It is established . . . that our rate of demographic growth is not at all in step with our economic growth rate. . . . How [can we] reconcile demographic growth and economic growth taking into account, of course, the sacrosanct regulations of Islam and the traditional values which we have inherited? . . . Is it normal to impose on a woman successive pregnancies which impair the life of the mother and that of the child? Is it normal to inflict on our sisters in the towns and particularly in the country, the almost inevitable obligations to become old before their time, crushed under the weight of daily work and ravaged by almost constant nursing? . . . "[48]

The persistent cross-pressures experienced by LDCs on such questions were reflected in a statement by Malaysian Prime Minister Hahathir bin Mohammed: "We must have a sufficiently large domestic base if we are going to industrialize. . . . A big population is not harmful if the people are productive."[49]

cream. They also operate the grain "pipeline"—all the way from farmer to foreign consumer. Together, Cargill and Continental handle half of all the grain exported from the United States—and the United States exports half of all the grain in world trade (in some years, Cargill has even been the leading exporter of wheat from France, the world's third or fourth largest wheat trader). The Big Five dominate the grain trade of the Common Market; the Canadian barley trade; the South African maize trade; the Argentine wheat trade. In the 1960s, these same companies expanded into trading in sugar, meat, and tapioca. And the directorates of these firms channeled money into facilities "upstream," closer to farms. Cargill runs 50- to 100-car freight trains full of grain from the interior of the United States to the ports. And the dollars circulating through the companies come in very large figures.

While the structure of the international grain trade remains quite "oligopolistic" (i.e., dominated by a few distributors), agricultural *exports* as a percentage of total world agricultural production have been declining recently (down 16 percent in the 1980s) as many countries have managed greater food self-sufficiency. Even a country like Sudan in North Africa has experienced "grain gluts" and has entered the export market along with China, Europe, and Brazil. Thus the U.S. share of the market has diminished somewhat.

Source: Excerpted material is from *The Merchants of Grain* by Dan Morgan. Copyright © 1979 by Dan Morgan. Reprinted by permission of Viking Penguin Inc. On grain markets in the 1980s, see Wendy L. Wall, "World's Grain Output Surges as Nations Seek Food Self-Sufficiency," *Wall Street Journal* (April 6, 1987), pp. 1 and 12; and Jean Marie Brow, "US Wheat Has Little Appeal for Soviets," *Wall Street Journal* (March 20, 1987), p. 13.

Ironically, while many Southerners were by 1984 coming to see the need for population planning, combined with health, education, and employment programs, some in the North were reconsidering their traditional support for population control programs, and particularly those involving abortion. In 1985 the U.S. Congress and the Reagan administration cut off American contributions to the UN Fund for Population Activities (UNFPA), a program begun in the late 1960s under U.S. auspices to head off the threat that overpopulation would lead to political instability and Third World revolutions. UNFPA had established links with 134 nations. American policy reverted mainly to bilateral programs and voluntary agencies stressing child health care and private enterprise–oriented economic development, thus depleting the UNFPA budget by about $25 million.[50]

Although the politics of global population has tended to pit the North against the South, the picture is actually more complex. A great variety of actors have attempted to shape policies on population growth—either pro-birth (pro-natalist) or pro-control (anti-natalist). In fact, in addition to the more than 130 national governments represented at the 1974 World Population Conference, there were observers from more than 100 IGOs and NGOs.

In recognition of the seriousness of the problem, government-sponsored birth control campaigns have been mounted not only in China and India but in more than half of all Third World countries. UNFPA, financed by voluntary contributions, has been more active in promoting birth control and family planning than the UN General Assembly itself, which represents a wider variety of national viewpoints. Among NGOs, the International Planned Parenthood Federation and the World Council of Churches have promoted birth control programs and family planning, helping to account for the proliferation of such programs in the Third World; most less developed countries now have family planning associations.[51]

On the "pro-birth" side, the Catholic Church and the governments of certain largely Catholic nation-states have campaigned to emphasize economic development rather than population control. Ironically, certain Marxist states have taken similar positions in the past, creating an "unholy alliance" of sorts between Roman Catholicism and atheistic communism, although even some Catholic thinkers and Marxist ideologues have begun to recognize the population problem. Latin America's lowest birth rate is in Cuba, which has sponsored family planning efforts and alternate employment opportunities for women. Throughout Latin America, which is 90 percent Catholic, individual governments in at least twenty out of thirty-three countries permit population control programs.[52] The Islamic League also has opposed family planning; certain Islamic states have been slow to promote family planning, partly because they are not under heavy population pressure.

The 1974 World Population Conference adopted a compromise plan of action, setting targets for controlling world population growth and extending life expectancy. The plan reaffirmed the "right of all couples and individuals to decide freely and responsibly the number and spacing of their children" (as enunciated in the Universal Declaration of Human Rights) and added their "right to have information, education, and means to do so."[53] In acknowledging government's increased role in facilitating birth control, the Conference also recognized the dangers of eroding individual rights (for example, if governments imposed one- or two-child limits on families). Because of the reference to "means" of control, the Vatican later dissociated itself from the plan. Both the 1974 and 1984 global population conferences reiterated the principle that even though international action on the population problem is essential, each state retains the sovereign right to determine its own national population policies in light of its social traditions and needs.

One often overlooked aspect of the population problem (and the food problem as well) is the imbalance caused by the migration of *refugees.* Worldwide refugee problems, present at least since World War I, have worsened recently with an outpouring of desperate people fleeing their homelands because of war, famine, or political repression. Estimates have put the refugee population at 10 to 15 million and growing. Among the actors dealing with refugees is the UN High Commission for Refugees (UNHCR), which won the Nobel Peace Prize in 1981 for the second time. Through persistent efforts, the High Commissioner, former Danish Prime Minister Poul Hartling, succeeded in raising $400 million in general and emergency assistance funds in 1985, with 30 percent of the total coming from the United States. Yet this was hardly sufficient to deal with the steady flow of humanity from such places as Afghanistan, Haiti, Ethiopia, Vietnam, El Salvador, and Kampuchea.

Refugees, left homeless and stateless, represent difficult burdens for the countries hosting them. The UN High Commissioner has campaigned for better living conditions as well as an easing of repression and an end to wars so that repatriation might be possible. Although most recent refugees have come from states aligned with the Soviet Union, that country has yet to contribute a single ruble to the UNHCR's budget. States whose citizens become refugees traditionally have been embarrassed and reluctant to admit the problem exists. Other governments have argued that UN refugee relief programs—as in the case of Palestinian or African (Ethiopian-Somalian) refugees—merely perpetuate political conflicts by subsidizing refugee camps and the governments that host them.[54] Therefore the UNHCR must carry on delicate negotiations with national governments, of the type that finally helped ease Vietnamese refugees out of death boats and into an orderly 1000-per-month release program.[55]

Although there have been calls for international legal conventions on the status of refugees, the issue has been too politically volatile for agreement. One possibility for alleviating refugee problems is for international agencies to arrange the migration of people from overpopulated countries to countries needing population. For example, after thousands of Haitian refugees entered the United States in 1980 to escape economic and political conditions in Haiti, the Geneva-based International Committee for Migration managed to resettle some Haitians in newly independent Belize, which had approximately the same land area as Haiti but six million fewer inhabitants.[56]

Numerous actors also are involved in health concerns related to population, including NGOs such as the International Red Cross and IGOs such as the ten-nation International Agency for Research on Cancer. The major global institution in the health care field, the World Health Organization (WHO), has become increasingly involved in servicing the health needs of the Third World. The North-South battle lines have not been as clearly drawn in WHO as in some other international institutions, partly because it is recognized that diseases do not respect national or regional boundaries. The WHO/UNICEF International Conference on Primary Health Care, held at Alma-Ata in the Soviet Union in 1978, identified a number of health needs and objectives, including provision for primary health care in national rural and urban development plans, stress on education and prevention, community-oriented medical programs, improved training and incentives for work in field operations, and international assistance for needy countries. UNICEF, in its annual report on "The State of the World's Children 1987," cited new regional agreements in Central America and South Asia for mutual assistance in saving children. Government troops and guerrillas ceased firing for one day a month in El Salvador so that children could be immunized; Honduras provided

In Cameroon, DDT being used to eradicate malaria. Unfortunately, while the WHO chemical war on mosquito-carried diseases continues, mosquitoes have developed resistance to the main insecticides in use. Regular spraying of homes and villages also is socially disruptive, and causes people to resist the programs.

Guatemala and El Salvador with oral rehydration salts, while Guatemala assisted with immunizations in El Salvador and Nicaragua.[57]

However, global problem solving in the area of health care has not been as politically uncontroversial as one might hope. Although WHO has succeeded in campaigns against major killer diseases such as smallpox, and has launched new worldwide efforts against AIDS, it has come up against a variety of political forces that have frustrated attempts to deal with other health concerns. For instance, there are many governments unwilling to notify WHO of outbreaks of cholera and other communicable diseases, lest official announcements of local epidemics damage port traffic and tourism. In its efforts to regulate the global marketing of products that it deems dangerous or needlessly expensive, WHO has had to combat MNCs that market such products as pharmaceuticals in the Third World. In working with the UN Commission on Narcotic Drugs to counter drug abuse problems, WHO must deal with cash-hungry governments and NGOs reliant on drug sales. Burmese rebels and other guerrilla groups in the "Golden Triangle" of Southeast Asia have financed their activities partly through dealings with an international ring of drug traffickers. WHO officials even find themselves involved in bureaucratic politics with officials in other IGOs, such as UN environmentalists who oppose the use of DDT and other insecticides that contribute to ocean pollution and other ecological problems at the same time that they kill malaria-carrying mosquitoes. Swamp draining efforts to combat malaria also have caused conflicts with environmentalists.[58]

Health care is one area in which regime formation has included the drafting of explicit rules (in the form of conventions and regulatory codes) designed to raise global standards. Central to this effort has been the World Health Assembly, the plenary body of WHO that meets annually to determine the broad policies of the organization, with each of the more than 140 member states having one vote. Among the rules that have been widely accepted are a series of International Sanitary Conventions, covering such matters as what can and cannot be done on ships and aircraft to prevent the spread of diseases. The World Health Assembly also has the power to adopt technical regulations that promote uniform classification of diseases and pharmaceuticals (so that morbidity statistics can be compared and treatment standardized across national boundaries), a uniform code of standards regarding the safety, labeling, and advertising of health products sold internationally, and uniform procedures for reporting and responding to epidemics. Assembly regulations, administered by the WHO secretariat in Geneva, are binding on all member governments except those that within a specified time limit expressly reject the rule in question.[59] Hence, when purchasing drugs from the neighborhood pharmacy, one is receiving products that have probably been subject not only to local, state, and national regulation, but also to international regulation.

As with population matters in general, the international community has been careful to respect national sovereignty in the health field. WHO mainly has served as a facilitator of improvements in national health care programs rather than acting as a supranational agency. Major WHO programs in developing countries have dealt with immunization, research and training in tropical diseases, onchocerciasis (river blindness) control, and sanitation. Other UN agencies have cooperated with WHO. For example, FAO, UNDP, and the World Bank have helped to reopen fertile land along the Volta River area of Africa by supporting the use of insecticides against the blackfly that transmits river blindness. The UN Conference on Human Settlements and the UN Water Conference in the late 1970s set various sanitation priorities. The latter conference designated the 1980s as the International Drinking Water Supply and Sanitation Decade and endorsed the goal of adequate drinking water for all people by 1990, although it was left to national governments to figure out how to carry out conference recommendations.[60]

In a sense, the world is involved in a population race toward stability. In the long run—if economic development problems can be overcome—improvements in personal income, education, and employment opportunities for women will tend to reduce birth rates, as improved health care extends life expectancies throughout the world. With global population growth already slowing somewhat, projections are for a "steady-state" global population of approximately 11 billion around the year 2090. The problem, though, is that 11 billion may be too many, depending upon resources available at that time. If birth rates can be made to decline faster, the steady-state population, when reached, would be smaller and easier to support (8 billion, for example, if a one percent net reproduction rate were reached in 2000 instead of 2020 as expected). World population efforts continue to be hampered, however, by the inability of the world's leaders and citizens to agree on an "optimal" population level and on the means of achieving it.

Transfer of Capital and Technology: Politics and Regimes

Since the NIEO debate of the seventies, LDC demands have been most pointed in regard to the transfer of capital and technology, and have involved congeries of actors—nation-states, MNCs, global IGOs, and private banks. Specifically, the South has sought reform in the rules governing international trade, aid and investment, monetary matters, and the dissemination of information and technology. The International Development Strategy for the Third "Development Decade" (1981–1990), adopted by the UN General Assembly, set targets of an annual 7 percent increase in gross domestic products in the Third World, 8 percent annual growth in trade, and 1 percent of the combined GNPs of developed states to be allocated to development aid. None of these targets are likely to be met.

High on the South's list for trade improvements, articulated primarily through UNCTAD, have been (1) **commodity agreements,** like those already in effect for coffee and rubber, to raise and stabilize agricultural and raw material prices and to create "buffer stocks" that could be released in controlled ways on the market; (2) a common fund to back these commodity arrangements financially and to aid against the competition of synthetic products; (3) reductions in Northern tariff and nontariff barriers against Southern products, such as textiles, without Northern insistence on reciprocal reductions in Southern trade barriers; (4) other trade preferences for Southern products in Northern markets, including more equitable shipping and insurance rates; and (5) Northern domestic economic policies to phase out production of goods that the South can produce more cheaply. It has been estimated that without any additional foreign aid, if the North dismantled existing trade barriers against Southern goods, billions of dollars yearly would be added to the South's export earnings.

Southern priorities in the area of foreign aid have included (1) greater efforts by developed states to meet the aid target established by the UN; (2) increased Northern financial commitments to the various emergency funds set up to deal with problems stemming from food and other price increases; (3) greater Northern willingness to cancel debts of Southern states in serious balance of payments difficulties, or to renegotiate longer repayment schedules; and (4) loans at cheaper interest rates with fewer strings attached. Particularly gnawing to Third World governments is the tendency of the World Bank, IMF, and other lending institutions to require loan recipients to adopt austerity measures in their economy (higher taxes, reductions in government social services, and so forth). What the IMF sees as sound fiscal management might be a recipe for political suicide to Third World governments.

In the area of international monetary reform, in addition to a greater voice in IMF decision making, the South would also like to see higher levels of international currency reserves and Special Drawing Rights set aside for developing countries. Southern states, especially the poorest and least strategically important ones, object to the hit-or-miss nature of international economic assistance, and want guaranteed funds administered by international agencies backed by mandatory rather than voluntary government contributions. Finally, they also want resumption of North-South dialogues like the Cancún conference, to deal with international monetary and financial problems blocking development.[61]

In the area of foreign investment, Southern states have pushed for greater access to investment funds contributed by MNCs. They want greater control over foreign operations within their borders, and they have attempted to establish codes of conduct for MNCs that would limit the profits MNCs could repatriate to their home country, prohibit MNC interference in host country domestic politics, impose stricter obligations on MNCs to obey local laws, strengthen host government authority to tax and expropriate foreign property, and promote greater participation by host country nationals in the ownership and management of foreign subsidiaries.

In the area of technology transfer, the South has campaigned for changes in patent and licensing procedures that tend to penalize less developed countries, as well as increased funding of Southern scientific and research institutions. Regulations to slow or prevent the "brain drain" from South to North have also been requested. In an effort to counter what is perceived as "information imperialism," the South has sought Northern assistance in developing its news-gathering, data-processing, and other information-related capabilities as well as protection from possible Northern "invasion of privacy" by satellite reconnaissance. This controversial "New World Information Order" has been discussed at UNESCO and International Telecommunications Union conferences focusing on specific technological questions and at more general conferences such as the 1978 UN Conference on Science and Technology for Development.

Naturally, creating a set of negotiating demands is one thing, but having them accepted is quite another. Although some Northerners feel a moral or practical obligation to assist less developed countries, many Northern criticisms of Southern demands have surfaced at Cancún, at UN General Assembly meetings, and in other forums. Northerners have noted that price stabilization of raw materials and other commodities is contrary to the laws of supply and demand and is likely to result in higher prices for Northern consumers, while also adversely affecting the poorest countries that must import such items. On foreign aid, it is argued that the South is unrealistic in expecting major increases in aid when many Northern economies are suffering increased economic problems themselves, and that too much aid goes to prop up repressive regimes. It is felt that moratoriums on debt repayment might simply further harm the credit rating of Southern states wishing to borrow in private commercial markets and would lessen pressures on such states to become self-reliant. MNC executives have objected to increased attempts by Third World governments to regulate them, contending that such policies are likely to discourage foreign investment and add to capital shortages for many countries. On the technology front, the North generally has found Southern proposals one-sided in seeking to tap technological advances costing Northern states millions of dollars in research funds without offering concessions in return (such as allowing greater freedom of the press in the South).

However, there have been some positive international responses to the problems of capital shortages and technology gaps, even though most of the South's demands for a new economic order remain unfulfilled. Southern states have used their voting power in the UN General Assembly to pass NIEO-related resolutions that they contend have the status of international law, although Northern states have refused to recognize General Assembly resolutions as conferring any binding obligations on them. Although General Assembly resolutions remain merely advisory in nature, they do contribute to regime formation insofar as they express evolving norms in the international system. As one example of efforts to translate principles into practice, note the **Charter of Economic Rights and Duties of States,** passed by the UN General Assembly in 1974, which contains as a central tenet the following provision:

> Every state has and shall freely exercise full permanent sovereignty, including possession, use, and disposal, over all its wealth, natural resources, and economic activities. [This includes competence] to nationalize, expropriate, or transfer ownership of foreign property.

The UN Centre for Transnational Corporations, formed to deal with foreign investment issues, has thus far failed to produce a uniform code of conduct that more clearly spells out MNC–host government relations. However, OECD members have formulated a set of guidelines that reflect increased sensitivity to Third World concerns about MNC business practices.

The militant positions taken by Third World states during the NIEO debate of the 1970s (reflected in the 1974 Charter) lessened somewhat in the 1980s, as the growing debt crisis caused LDCs to scramble to attract foreign MNC investment and other sources of capital. Foreign investment has been seen not so much as a form of imperialism as an alternative to expensive loans. As private investment in the developing world shrank by about 50 percent in the early 1980s, the World Bank formed a billion-dollar insurance agency, the Multilateral Investment Guarantee Agency, to promote renewed MNC interest in LDCs.[62]

Considerable progress has been made over the years in forging commodity agreements aimed at stabilizing the prices of Third World exports. However, there has been a tendency for states to ignore provisions or withdraw from agreements when differences have risen. One such cooperative venture, the International Tin Council, composed of twenty-two leading tin producing and consuming countries (including the U.S. until its withdrawal in 1982), collapsed in 1985. The ITC ran out of money to purchase tin for buffer stocks, and tin trading on the London Metal Exchange had to shut down completely. When large tin producing states, such as Indonesia, Malaysia, Bolivia, and Thailand, failed to contribute the necessary extra funds to keep the ITC going, the price of tin fell by more than 25 percent. Some of these states, such as Malaysia, did not depend heavily on tin for exports; others like Bolivia did. With lower cost competition from Brazil and other tin producers not belonging to the ITC, with a general world recession, and with Northern sentiment running against government-subsidized commodity prices, ITC solidarity diminished. Similarly, the International Cocoa Agreement (also without U.S. participation) lost momentum and suspended cocoa price supports in 1982.[63] However, there has been continued success on the part of the International Coffee Organization (with U.S. participation) in regulating, through a system of export quotas, the coffee market and generally keeping export prices within a range of $1.20 to $1.40 per pound in the 1980s.[64]

Both regional and global approaches to commodity trade problems have been pursued. On a regional level, the EEC committed itself in the 1975 Lomé Convention to assist former dependencies in the Third World with compensation for marketing problems through a system called STABEX. However, coverage under this scheme has been limited to relatively few products (40 percent of proceeds in the first five years went to countries producing groundnut products), with disagreements about when a price crisis could be said to exist. In global negotiations over commodity agreements conducted through UNCTAD, ten primary products accounting for the bulk of Third World export earnings have been designated for stockpiling and price stabilization. A Common Fund for Commodities was established in the 1980s, with over twenty states participating, including major industrial nations. However, Southern producers, especially of food commodities, remain in a difficult bargaining position. The North generally needs industrial raw materials more than it needs or can absorb additional bananas.[65]

In regard to foreign aid, assistance patterns of the 1970s generally have persisted in the 1980s. Northern bilateral assistance increasingly has been tied to specific purchase agreements, especially in sales of armaments on long-term moderate- or low-interest credit. Nonmilitary development needs have not generally been given such generous credit, except in high-technology fields in which Northern firms are trying hard to peddle their wares. For example, Canada, anxious to market its CANDU heavy-water nuclear power stations amidst heavy competition from American and French firms, promised Mexico generous financing and export credits in a $30 billion deal in 1982. Interestingly, Canada and Mexico, two countries dealing in atomic energy and oil and trying to avoid U.S. economic domination, were the co-chairs of the Cancún conference.[66]

The World Bank and the IMF, with their commercial banking principles and weighted voting schemes based on contributions, remain the chief multilateral aid vehicles. Although a UN Capital Development Fund with equal voting provisions exists, Northern states have been reluctant to contribute to an aid institution dominated by the Southern majority. The United States, in particular, has reduced its funding of the International Development Association, the World Bank's "low interest" window, while placing greater emphasis on the private enterprise–oriented but much smaller International Finance Corporation branch of the World Bank system.[67]

By and large, the international debt problem has been handled on a case-by-case basis through negotiations among the World Bank, IMF, regional development banks, consortia of private banks, and lender and debtor governments. In emergencies, such as Mexico's near-default in 1982, the coordinated response among these actors can be swift.[68] Long-term and sustained debt relief is more difficult, however. Some debtors, such as Zaire, have conformed readily to international demands for domestic economic reforms in return for renewed lines of credit, only to find that their somewhat improved budgetary positions have not attracted the expected foreign investment, trade, and aid to spur development. The possible economic bankruptcy of its major Latin American trading partners brought the United States to propose the Baker Plan for debt relief in 1985. The American Treasury Secretary, James W. Baker, called on commercial banks and international development banks to participate in a three-year $20 billion program of lending to promote economic growth among the fifteen major debtor states. In return, borrowers would be expected to emphasize private enterprise and market-oriented approaches to development. With skepticism about debt repayments running high, however, it proved difficult to obtain the needed bank commitments to launch the Baker initiative. Third World critics of the proposal, especially those in the Cartagena Group of eleven Latin American debtor states, noted that it did not go far enough and begged the question of relief for existing debts. The Cartagena Group sought a series of further measures, including greatly reduced interest rates and improved repayment terms, increased IMF funding to make up for falling commodity prices, and extension of the Baker Plan to cover smaller Third World states.[69] Thus, it remains unclear whether Third World economies can both grow domestically and pay large percentages of their export earnings to Northern creditors.[70] (See the box on pages 482–483 for a focused look at the international debt problem and some proposed remedies.)

One must keep in mind that the policies of the World Bank and the IMF are ultimately the policies of the national governments that run these institutions, since the boards of governors in both cases consist of the finance or treasury ministers of member states. As with regimes in other issue-areas, then, the future effectiveness of international institutions in solving problems of capital and technology transfer will depend on the willingness of Northern and Southern governments to cooperate with each other.

Conclusion

Although a New International Economic Order has not dawned, the Third World at the very least has been able to give economic development concerns much greater visibility on the global agenda. We have said very little, however, about another set of issues that is crowding the global agenda and creating complications for economic development problem solving: the management of energy and nonrenewable resources, and protection of the natural environment.

Many Northerners in the 1970s were warning of threats posed to human existence by resource scarcities and environmental pollution. While Northerners spoke of the "limits to growth" in the world economy, arguing the

POSSIBLE REMEDIES FOR INTERNATIONAL DEBT

The "international debt crisis" mounted in the 1980s, with Third World debt reaching $1 trillion by 1987. A number of possible remedies have been offered, in addition to the Baker Plan which we have discussed. Some officials, such as New Jersey Senator Bill Bradley, proposed that creditor nations and commercial banks forgive a certain percentage of the debt, say three percentage points of interest and principal over three years, while debtor states would reduce trade barriers and spur economic growth. Others objected that such forgiveness would merely encourage increased borrowing and resistance to repayment. Alternate proposals include lowering interest rates and stretching out repayments, along with government loan guarantees, and a British-French proposal to ease the debt burden of the poorest states, particularly in Africa.

A recent innovation has been the so-called "debt-equity swap." Pioneered elsewhere in Latin America, it has been picked up by the Mexican government. As shown in the illustration below, it works as follows:

> An American company planning, for example, a cassette-tape plant in Mexico, purchases $1 million worth of Mexican debt from an American bank that loaned the money to Mexico. The bank sells the $1 million IOU for just $600,000, happy to wipe the shaky loan from its books rather than wait years in hope of repayment. The company then presents the $1 million IOU to the Mexican government, which, after applying a 10 percent discount, "buys" the note for $900,000 worth of pesos to be spent on the new plant.

need for altering high-consumption habits represented by gas-guzzling automobiles and all-electric kitchens, Southerners contended that they had yet to enjoy these benefits fully and would continue to seek them. Nevertheless, economic hardship has also forced Southerners to recycle and conserve. In Brazil, for example, citizens of Recife are noted for turning old bottles, cans, tires, and electric lightbulbs into salable figurines, lamps, sandals, bed-webbing, and ashtrays. Elsewhere in Brazil, of course, people avidly sign up on multiyear waiting lists for Volkswagen automobiles, roads are being carved through once remote Amazon jungles, and the country's timber is being cut at alarming rates and the land is being subjected to ravaging erosion.

Many of the North's achievements as well as its problems are being transferred to the South, and many of the South's responses are both creative and destructive. Even international lending agencies have been asking ques-

While the Mexican government would be subsidizing a foreign investor, and at the same time repaying a loan, it would also use local currency and keep scarce capital within the country rather than seeing it go abroad. New jobs could be created in the process. It does little, however, to relieve the Mexicans' overall dependence on foreign investment and ownership. And since the Mexican government would be printing pesos to cover the cost of the swap, the plan could aggravate inflation.

MEXICO'S DEBT-EQUITY SWAP PROGRAM

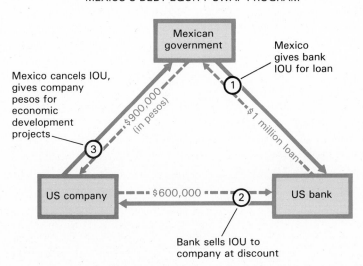

Source: Howard La Franchi, "U.S. Firms Help Lighten Mexico's Debt," *Christian Science Monitor* (April 13, 1987), p. 3; and John Yemma, "FYI: International Debt Crisis," *Christian Science Monitor* (March 19, 1987), pp. 18–19.

tions about the environmental impact of proposed development projects such as dam and road construction in the Third World. We turn next to an examination of how modern industrial civilization is putting pressure on the "carrying capacity" of the earth's oceans, air, and land, and how the global political system is attempting to cope with the threat to the global ecosystem.

SUMMARY

1. A rich-poor gap exists both between states (the North versus the South) and within states (particularly in less developed countries). Substantial improvement in the lot of the poor depends on economic development, which in turn is associated with three interrelated problems: food supply, population growth, and the transfer of capital and technology.

2. Although world food production has been growing, efforts to relieve global hunger are hampered by lack of effective food distribution networks along with inadequate water and energy supplies and agricultural research. The "green revolution" has made a partial dent in the problem of Third World food self-sufficiency, although the impact has been uneven and particularly weak in Africa.

3. Food problems are intimately linked with population problems. Population growth has accelerated at an alarming rate since World War II, particularly in the South, though the growth rate has begun to decline recently except in Africa. The North has urged the South to control its numbers; the South has responded with extensive birth control programs, but also notes that lower birth rates would occur if the standard of living in Southern countries were raised.

4. Although medical advances have lowered death rates in the South, serious problems remain, particularly in the areas of health care delivery, nutrition, and sanitation.

5. Although foreign aid and foreign investment as well as funds earned from exports provide important sources of capital for the Third World, these countries feel that existing international economic relationships help the rich more than the poor. The flow of advanced technology, for example, tends to be North-North rather than North-South. Capital also has tended to flow to the North in loan repayments and investments.

6. All these problems are closely associated with the politics of the "New International Economic Order," a system being demanded by Third World countries as a way of redistributing wealth more equally between North and South. The South has sought reform in the rules governing international trade, aid and investment, monetary matters, and the dissemination of technology. But Southern demands have met with criticism from Northern states, which have tended to blame corrupt and inefficient Third World governments for at least part of the South's poverty problem.

7. The two main bargaining groups in the NIEO debate have been the Group of 77 (representing the South) and OECD (representing the North). Nonstate actors involved in North-South politics have included agribusiness corporations, private banks, and a variety of IGOs and NGOs.

8. An international development regime is emerging that partially incorporates Southern demands, particularly in areas benefiting both North and South.

9. Although some recommendations of the 1974 World Food Conference have been implemented, global food reserves are still inadequate and distribution methods ineffective. Malnutrition in the Third World can probably be alleviated only through greater food self-sufficiency and purchasing power in those countries.

10. The 1974 and 1984 World Population Conferences somewhat reconciled the Southern and Northern views on the relation between economic development and population control, but provided little machinery for enforcing recommendations.

11. In the area of health care, conventions and regulatory codes have been established through the World Health Organization and have helped to raise global standards.

12. Although there have been some positive international responses to the problems of capital shortages and technology gaps, certain aspects of the international

development regime have broken down (e.g., commodity agreements) or are still in transition between case-by-case and comprehensive approaches (e.g., debt relief). Most NIEO demands remain unrealized.

SUGGESTIONS FOR FURTHER READING AND STUDY

General works dealing with the problems surrounding economic development include Charles K. Wilbur, ed., *The Political Economy of Development and Underdevelopment* (New York: Random House, 1973); Denis Goulet, *The Cruel Choice* (New York: Atheneum, 1971); James H. Weaver and Kenneth P. Jameson, *Economic Development: Competing Paradigms—Competing Parables* (Washington, D.C.: Agency for International Development, 1978), Development Studies Program, Occasional Paper 3; Hans Singer and Javed Ansari, *Rich and Poor Countries*, 3rd ed. (London: Allen and Unwin, 1982); and Altaf Gauhar, *The Rich and the Poor: Development, Negotiations and Cooperation* (London: Third World Foundation, 1983).

In addition to the works cited in Note 4, other general discussions of NIEO and international political economy can be found in Mahbub ul Haq, *The Poverty Curtain* (New York: Columbia University Press, 1976); H. Chenery *et al.*, *Redistribution with Growth* (Oxford: Oxford University Press, 1977); Jan Tinbergen, *Reshaping the International Order* (New York: Dutton, 1976); Paul Alpert, *Partnership or Confrontation? Poor Lands and Rich* (New York: Free Press, 1973); Robert W. Tucker, *The Inequality of Nations* (New York: Basic Books, 1977); and Robert A. Mortimer, *The Third World Coalition in International Politics* (Boulder, Colo.: Westview Press, 1984).

Works that focus on the food problem are Neal Spivack and Ann Florini, *Food on the Table* (New York: United Nations Association, 1986); and George R. Lucas, Jr., and Thomas W. Ogletree, eds., *Lifeboat Ethics: The Moral Dilemmas of World Hunger* (New York: Harper and Row, 1976). On population, see Lester R. Brown, *In the Human Interest* (New York: W. W. Norton, 1974); and Richard L. Rubenstein, *The Age of Triage: Fear and Hope in an Overcrowded World* (Boston: Beacon, 1983). On technology, see Frances Steward, *Technology and Underdevelopment* (Boulder, Colo.: Westview Press, 1977); Anthony Smith, *The Geopolitics of Information* (New York: Oxford University Press, 1980); and John V. Granger, *Technology and International Relations* (San Francisco: W. H. Freeman, 1979).

On global debt, trade, and capital flows, see John H. Makin, *The Global Debt Crisis: America's Growing Involvement* (New York: Basic Books, 1984); and John W. Sewell *et al.*, eds., *U.S. Foreign Policy and the Third World: Agenda 1985–86* (Washington, D.C.: Overseas Development Council, 1985).

Additional information can be found in the official publications of such UN agencies as the World Bank and IMF; in such magazines and newspapers as *The Wall Street Journal*, *The Economist*, *World Development*, and *South: The Third World Magazine*; in reports and publications of the Overseas Development Council (Washington, D.C.); and in the *State of the World* series, edited by the staff of the Worldwatch Institute and Lester R. Brown.

The Management of Resources: Negotiating the World's Troubled Waters, Land, and Air

On December 17, 1970, the United Nations General Assembly passed Resolution 2749 by a vote of 108 yeas, 0 nays, and 14 abstentions. The resolution contained the following statement:

> The sea-bed and the ocean floor, and the subsoil thereof beyond the limits of a national jurisdiction, as well as the resources of the area, are the common heritage of mankind. The area shall not be subject to appropriation by any means by States or persons ... and no State shall claim or exercise ... sovereign rights over any part thereof.

The term "common heritage of mankind" included in this resolution potentially has profound implications. The resolution refers specifically to the oceans, which altogether cover 70 percent of the earth's surface. But, in a sense, it might just as well apply to the entire ecosystem upon which life on the planet depends: minerals, energy sources, oxygen, plant and animal species, and other natural resources. When one views photos of the earth taken from outer space, one can appreciate the extent to which human beings all coexist on a lovely and delicate orb and possess a common heritage.

However, as compelling as "Spaceship Earth" imagery is, the view from the ground up looks quite different. Instead of a common heritage, the dominant reality "down here" is that different actors compete to control and exploit the world's natural resources, including outer space itself. Questions about ownership of the world's resources can be treated in the context of what social scientists call *collective goods* and *private goods*. **Collective goods** are those resources that can be used by one party without diminishing the supply available to other parties, i.e., they are *jointly available,* like public parks and clean air. Such goods are *indivisible;* they cannot be parcelled out for the benefit of some individuals while being denied to others. In contrast, **private goods** are resources that can be possessed by individuals and can be divided up.

The tension between collective goods and private goods in international relations can be seen in the law of the sea debate. The traditional notion of "freedom of the seas," a fixture of international law over the centuries, implied that the vast stretches of the oceans—unlike land masses and the waters immediately adjacent to them—were to be considered a collective good, a commons subject to no state's ownership or jurisdiction. As the seventeenth-century legal scholar Grotius stated, "The sea, since it is incapable of being seized as the air, cannot be attached to the possessions of any particular nation."[1] The 1970 UN resolution noted above was essentially a reaffirmation of this basic principle.

However, the virtually unanimous vote in support of the resolution disguised some major disagreements. These disagreements surfaced at the UN **Conference on the Law of the Sea** held during the 1970s, which was attended by almost every country in the world, coastal and landlocked states alike. At the conference, the common heritage concept was challenged as many participants proposed to treat the oceans as a private good, i.e., a commodity to be carved up and claimed by individual countries for their own exclusive use—whether in the form of national economic zones (for exploiting offshore oil and gas), fishing zones (for controlling access to nearby fish stocks threatened with depletion), or restricted areas of various other sorts. The law of the sea debate continued during the 1980s.

Similar conflicts have occurred recently over whether air space and outer space are to be considered the "common heritage of mankind" or are to be subject to extended national claims. In this chapter, we discuss the continuing tension between those who advocate sharing the common heritage widely, those who seek to use the lion's share for their own individual purposes, and those who would inhibit use as much as possible in order to conserve natural resources and protect the environment. Clearly, the key resources of the "common heritage" can be divided up and treated as private goods. The questions are to what extent will they be divided and between whom, and what will be the impact on global ecology?

The Nature and Magnitude of the Problem

Scientists have distinguished between **primary, secondary,** and **tertiary resources** (see Figure 15.1). In a sense, all resources on earth stem from primary solar power; sunlight is the driving force of life for plants and animals. This primary solar energy has been trapped in fossil fuels (coal, oil, etc.) that we use today. The brew of primary resources many millennia ago produced the secondary resources—minerals, vegetables, and animals. These have been processed by humans into various tertiary resources, which have then been used to produce other items. In the discussion of the global management, or mismanagement, of resources that follows, we will concentrate on primary and secondary resources. In particular, we will review the political struggles over the *atmosphere, outer space, land,* and *oceans,* and over commercially exploitable secondary resources in the form of *animals,* vegetable-based and fossil *fuels,* and *minerals.* In line with the theme of the last chapter, it is clear that human health and prosperity and the quality of the earth's environment are interdependent.

Another way of classifying the world's resources is in terms of **nonrenewable** and **renewable resources.** The former include raw materials like copper, zinc, and nickel, as well as such energy sources as oil and natural gas, all of which are in finite supply and are capable of being exhausted. Resources that are renewable, such as air and water, are threatened not so much by exhaustion as by pollution and spoilage. Modern industrial civilization—characterized by

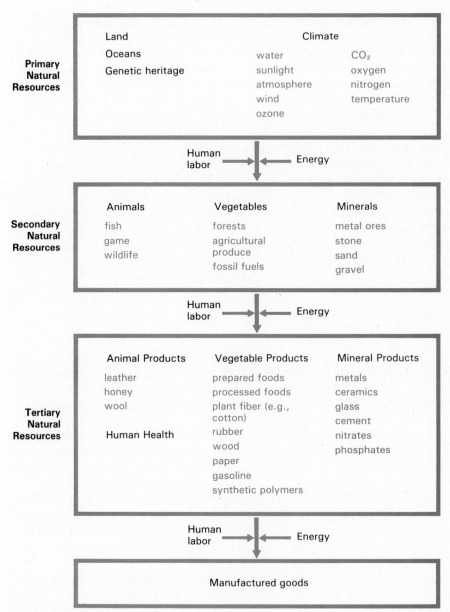

Figure 15.1
CLASSIFICATION OF NATURAL RESOURCES

high technology, energy-intensive means of production, and mass consumption—puts an increased burden on both kinds of resources.

Scientists do not agree on exactly how serious the threat to global resources is. In the early 1970s, doomsday predictions about imminent resource scarcities and environmental decay mounted and produced a movement to limit growth in world population and consumption. Especially provocative was a 1972 study by the Club of Rome entitled *The Limits to Growth,* which concluded that economic growth would have to be halted in the late twentieth century if civilization was to survive.[2] Alarms were sounded at the 1972 UN Conference on the Human Environment that the world would soon be out of fuel and raw materials, if it did not first suffocate from pollution. It now appears that some of the predictions of the **limits to growth school** were erroneous and based on faulty computer models that included exaggerated rates of consumption, population growth, industrialization, and pollution. Such models may have underrated such factors as human innovation, economic slowdowns, and the abundance of raw materials available at higher market prices.[3] Nevertheless, warnings about the finiteness of key resources and the fragility of ecological balances are still valid.

PRIMARY RESOURCES

The Atmosphere. The atmosphere performs a number of important functions for life on the planet: filtering out harmful solar radiation; providing oxygen and carbon dioxide for animal and plant respiration; holding moisture and heat; conducting sound waves; and soaking up industrial wastes. Hence, the atmosphere can be treated to some extent as a collective good.

However, with the continuing effects of industrial pollution, some would argue it is becoming a "collective bad." Wind-borne pollutants know no national boundaries as they circle the globe. The world in recent years has seen "killer smogs in London and Los Angeles and the widespread use of gas masks in Tokyo."[4] While natural pollutants (e.g., forest fires and volcanoes) have been around since before human memory, the largest contributors to today's air pollution are the burning of fossil fuels and the chemical processing of hydrocarbons by human beings.

Air pollution impairs plant growth, alters climatic conditions, and threatens animal and human life. Even the great cultural monuments of Rome and Venice have been ravaged by industrial chemicals, hydrocarbon fallout, and "acid rain" (evidently caused by sulfuric acid accumulation in the atmosphere). The accumulation of carbon dioxide caused by the burning of coal and other fossil fuels is thought to produce a **greenhouse effect,** trapping heat and raising the earth's temperature. Atmospheric carbon dioxide has been steadily building, and is estimated to have raised global temperatures by 0.25 degree centigrade— enough perhaps to trigger abnormal droughts. If continued, it is feared that such temperature elevations eventually could melt the polar ice caps and therefore flood major coastal cities and farms. Some climatologists have called attention to an opposite problem, noting that the massive accumulation of dust and other particles in the air might conceivably block the sun's rays so much as to lower temperatures and produce another Ice Age. Aerosol spray cans have been banned in some countries, since the buildup of gas propellants (fluorocarbons) has been linked, along with natural causes such as volcanic eruptions, to the depletion of the atmosphere's ozone layer , which shields us from the sun's ultraviolet rays and helps to prevent skin cancer.[5]

In addition to accidental changes in climate caused by pollution, it now seems increasingly feasible to modify the weather deliberately. Human capacity to interfere with nature has reached new heights with the use of cloud seeding to produce rain or to control typhoons, although the technology is still primitive and unpredictable. Climatic changes produced by one country are bound to affect neighbors. If a storm is induced to shed excess rain early in its path, there will be less rainfall later for parched neighboring countries. As with countries along a common river, such "diversion" by "upstream" states is likely to provoke protests from those "downstream."

Land. Land-based resources are being threatened partly by changing atmospheric conditions and partly by other factors. Creeping "desertification"—the spread of deserts to previously arable land (the Sahara has increased by 250,000 square miles in recent years)—has been traced to long-term atmospheric changes as well as to overgrazing, overfarming, and deforestation (especially of tropical forests). Deserts now cover one third of the earth's land area and are encroaching upon another 20 percent; an estimated 25 billion tons of topsoil are eroding and blowing away each year. It has been estimated that 25 to 40 percent of the tropical rainforests that existed prior to the twentieth century now have been eliminated, and that an area the size of Austria is "deforested" each year.

Deforestation is economically devastating, especially in the Third World, where wood remains the major fuel source. A U.S. government study has

By permission of Johnny Hart and Field Enterprises, Inc

Measuring global pollution: An acid test

concluded that deforestation may be the single major factor leading to the extinction of one fifth of the world's plant and animal species: "If present trends continue, increasing numbers of people will be dependent on the genetic strains of perhaps only two dozen plant and animal species."[6] Such species could become highly susceptible to pests and diseases, which could thereby doom tens of millions of humans, making the nineteenth-century Irish potato famine look like small potatoes indeed.

The land, and creatures living upon it, are also threatened by deposits of toxic substances, including heavy metals (like mercury), nuclear wastes, pesticides, and herbicides. In 1962, Rachel Carson's book *The Silent Spring* alerted people to the danger of bird and animal extinction due to ingested pesticides (which weaken eggshells), expanding cities and industries (which destroy animal habitats), and general pollution.

Water. Water is now also a matter of global concern, as evidenced by the convening of a UN Water Conference in 1977. Although water blankets much of the earth, drinkable water is in short supply: "Viewed globally, fresh water is still undeniably abundant. For each human inhabitant there is now an annual renewable supply of 8,300 cubic meters, which is enough to fill a six-meter-square room 38 times. . . . [But this] water is not always available when and where it is most needed."[7] The uneven distribution of global fresh water supplies is illustrated in Figure 15.2.

Ninety-nine percent of the world's water is inaccessibly tied up in salty oceans or frozen polar caps; over half of the remaining one percent is located more than a mile underground, beyond the reach of today's drills. Almost two-thirds of each year's rain and snow runoff flows away in floods. Hence, lakes and rivers, representing only a tiny fraction (less than one percent) of total global water resources, constitute the bulk of available fresh water supplies. The lakes and rivers themselves are being subjected to increased pollution and deterioration of water quality. The "Blue Danube" in Europe, for example, is now commonly referred to as the "Brown Danube." Currently, 80 percent of the world's population have no access to tap water and must rely on often contaminated streams and wells.

With worldwide water demand possibly tripling by the early twenty-first century, fresh water could indeed become "the world's scarcest resource, more valuable than petroleum."[8] Desalinization technology along with the "towing" of icebergs to desert regions could conceivably relieve shortages in such places as the Sahara. However, neither is commercially feasible yet. The use of "fossil water" (left underground from the Ice Age), rainwater catch basins, and plant breeding for brackish water cultivation offer additional hope, but may not eliminate water shortages.[9]

Land-based pollutants—industrial effluents, chemical fertilizers, nuclear wastes, DDT, and raw sewage—which enter rivers and lakes ultimately are fed into the world's oceans. The connection between land and sea is shown

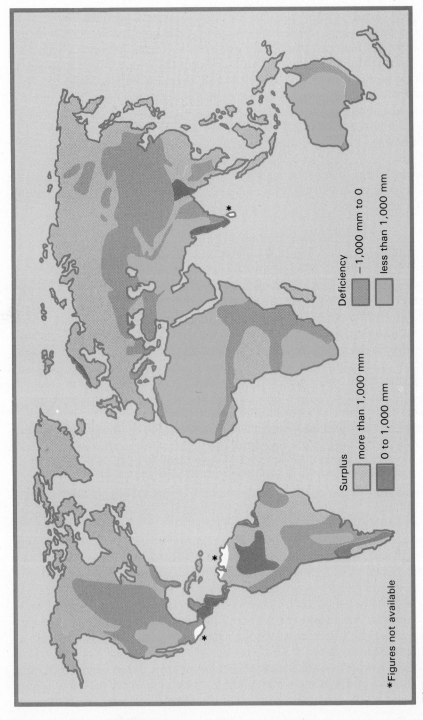

Surplus

☐ more than 1,000 mm

■ 0 to 1,000 mm

Deficiency

▨ –1,000 mm to 0

▥ less than 1,000 mm

*Figures not available

Figure 15.2
WORLD WATER SUPPLIES

in the ecology of the Nile valley. If one travels to Egypt and views the mouth of the Nile, it is disturbingly clear that the Aswan High Dam, meant to solve agricultural problems and control yearly floods, has led to a host of unanticipated environmental problems. The land along the coast is washing away rapidly, along with much of Egypt's rich Nile valley topsoil, due to intensive agriculture the dam made possible and the loss of seasonal floods to replenish the soil. This erosion of the land into the sea symbolizes the interrelated problems of land masses and oceans: "Every pollutant that can be carried by water eventually reaches the ocean, and those that do not decompose accumulate and become more concentrated with time."[10] Additionally, much of the 6 million tons of oil that have spilled annually into the seas from supertankers not only destroys ocean life but also often ends up on land and despoils shorelines.

It is obvious that water pollution, like air pollution, does not respect national boundaries. It is also clear that the revolution in marine technology, designed to exploit the sea for the benefit of humanity, is rendering the oceans increasingly vulnerable to destruction. (See the box on page 496.) The oceans serve many functions at once as the earth's major source of oxygen, commercial laboratories for deep-sea mining, transport lanes for tankers and freighters, food baskets and potential farms, industrial wastebins, and the aquatic home for animals—functions that are not all completely compatible.

The oceans also are a source of mystical beauty providing a unique contentment—both quite scarce resources these days. The fact that deserts in the United States and Middle East were once vast seas, that continents still drift apart (or together), that some of the earth's highest mountain peaks are submerged, all testify to the immense natural forces that dwarf the power of nations.

SECONDARY RESOURCES

The environmental problems plaguing the earth's oceans and other realms are closely related to concerns about food supplies, fossil fuel energy resources, and minerals—all secondary resources obtained from the biosphere.

Food Supplies. As noted earlier, animal life and plant life that serve as *food sources* for humans are threatened on land and in the sea. Yet there are grounds for some optimism. Fish, for example, still represent untapped food potential. Already the annual fish harvest exceeds global beef production, and provides 23 percent of all animal protein consumed commercially. Only about fifteen countries mount major fishing efforts, with Japan and the Soviet Union leading the way; together the fifteen account for 75 percent of the global catch. Most of the catch comes from the Pacific and the Atlantic; the Indian Ocean has been relatively underutilized, though overfished for some species. Many varieties of fish are being rapidly and alarmingly depleted, and mammals such as whales slaughtered; however, other species are underutilized and represent

THE REVOLUTION IN MARINE TECHNOLOGY

Man's industry now extends from the airspace above the water, throughout the water column, down to and beneath the seabed. Oil, natural gas, and a variety of industrially useful minerals and chemicals have joined food as materials that can be extracted from the ocean.

Aircraft and satellite-carried sensors measure sea level, water temperature, and currents; underwater acoustical instruments and cameras contribute to refined geological surveys; today's oil drilling technology permits seabed penetration to 1000 meters in waters 6000 meters deep; and mining of ores rich in copper, nickel, and other valuable metals is projected for depths of 12,000 to 20,000 feet.

Fishing grounds are frequented by long-distance fishermen on giant factory ships equipped with electronic tracking and catching devices, as well as with freezing and processing plants.

Normal intercontinental transportation now takes place above the surface, on the surface, and beneath the surface.

Oil is carried in tankers with capacities of as much as 500,000 tons. . . .

Artificial ports are being constructed tens of miles from shore.

The seabed is increasingly used for storage facilities and for anchorage for a wide variety of . . . installations.

Nuclear reactors on the seabed are being planned, and scientists are progressing toward harnessing the energy in the sea's tides and currents.

Meanwhile, the disposal of man-made wastes in the ocean is increasing exponentially.

Source: Seyom Brown, Nina W. Cornell, Larry L. Fabian, and Edith Brown Weiss, *Regimes for the Ocean, Outer Space, and Weather* (Washington, D.C.: Brookings Institution, 1977), p. 20.

a potentially renewable food source if fishing is properly managed. The Food and Agriculture Organization (FAO) estimates that more than 100 sea-food species are commercially available, but only twenty-two are heavily fished, and just five (herring, cod, jacks, redfish, and mackerel) constitute over half the annual catch.[11]

Energy. In addition to food resources, the oceans harbor vast *energy* supplies. Huge petroleum deposits are found under the continental shelf, and smaller and less accessible amounts of oil and coal also lie on the bed of the deep sea. (The potentially most valuable resources found on the deep seabed are mineral deposits of manganese, nickel, cobalt, copper, and precious metals.) Every cubic kilometer of seawater contains about 30 million metric tons of dissolved chemical elements potentially valued at a billion dollars.[12] However, even with rapidly developing technology, exploitation of ocean resources remains difficult and is complicated by political disputes over ownership of these resources.

Should less developed countries somehow seek to emulate the energy consumption patterns of industrialized Northern states, the pressure on resources could become intolerable. Presently, only fifteen countries, with 65 percent of the world's population, consume about 80 percent of the world's commercial energy (excluding traditional forms of energy such as firewood and animal dung). The United States alone, with only about 6 percent of the world's population, accounts for some 30 percent of annual global energy consumption. The fifteen major energy-consuming nations include most of the large industrial powers, plus such developing states as China, India, and Brazil. Most industrial powers, including the United States, increased energy conservation and (partly because of economic recession) cut consumption rates after energy price increases in the 1970s. Still, while experts disagree, most predict a 125 percent global increase in energy demand by the year 2025.[13]

The earth's primary power source, the sun, is free, and solar energy is never used up—it simply changes from more usable to less usable forms (such as waste heat). Costs accrue only with the need for equipment and technology to harness solar rays or other energy sources. However, it is difficult to tap the sun directly as an energy source since its rays are highly diffuse and large land areas are needed for solar collectors. In addition, since solar energy can be collected at any one place on earth for only part of every twenty-four hours, and then only if cloud cover does not interfere, elaborate solar storage facilities are needed. It is estimated that only about 1 percent of the solar energy that reaches the earth's surface is recoverable, but even that eventually could make a dent in world energy needs. Of course, solar energy is all around us: in renewable forms such as wind and crops that can be converted to gasohol, and in such nonrenewable forms as coal, oil, and gas deposits. Efforts are being made to convert to renewable energy sources, but for the foreseeable future the world will rely on oil, coal, gas, and nuclear power for its commercial energy.

The nuclear industry currently relies on fuels derived from finite, non-renewable supplies of uranium. Using uranium 235, a fission process (which involves the splitting of atoms) creates both usable heat and dangerous radioactive waste products. To compensate for limited supplies of U235, "fast breeder" reactors have been developed to convert more plentiful U238 to plutonium, a highly toxic fuel that is also useful for producing nuclear weapons. In the future, nuclear engineers hope to perfect safer breeder reactors and to solve the waste disposal problem. However, the fact that highly radioactive wastes must be stored safely for 10,000 years in order to do no harm suggests the magnitude of the disposal problem.

Saudi Arabia's "other" resource—the vast photovoltaic solar power plant serving three villages near Riyadh.

Engineers hope ultimately to shift to "fusion" reactors (fusing together atomic particles), using widely available, renewable elements. Waste products of the fusion process would be nontoxic helium gas. This theoretical energy panacea has one major drawback, however: "Controlling a fusion reaction is like trying to confine a hydrogen bomb explosion in a room the size of a small office without allowing the reactants to touch the walls."[14] Despite these difficulties, scientists in the United States, Europe, Japan, and the Soviet Union are proceeding with intensive fusion research.

Although nuclear plants provided 65 percent of France's electricity, 52 percent of Taiwan's, 42 percent of Sweden's, and over a quarter of Japan's during the 1980s, nuclear energy currently accounts for only about 3 percent of commercial energy usage worldwide, with petroleum accounting for 54 percent, coal for 18 percent, natural gas for 18 percent, and hydropower for 7 percent.[15] The explosion of the Soviet Chernobyl nuclear plant in 1986 added to worldwide fears of nuclear power. No new nuclear plant has been built in the United States in the last several years, and Western Europe has curtailed plans for increased nuclear power production as well, with Sweden deciding by popular vote in 1980 to phase out all twelve of its nuclear plants.

Among fossil fuels, coal is the most plentiful and most widely distributed on the globe. Although it is especially abundant in North America and the

Soviet Union, every continent except Africa and Latin America has a generous supply. Serious environmental problems are associated with the expanded use of coal, however, including increased air pollution and increased damage to land areas caused by strip mining. Furthermore, until coal liquefaction or gasification technologies are developed, coal will have limited utility in the transportation sector.

Oil supplies are far more concentrated than coal deposits. The bulk of known oil reserves (60 percent) is concentrated in the Middle East. Four Middle Eastern states (Saudi Arabia, Kuwait, Iran, and Iraq) control over half the proven reserves, though the Soviet Union is the top producer and the United States enjoys significant domestic supplies as well. Natural gas tends to be concentrated near oil fields, with the Soviet Union having one third of all known reserves.

Although oil and gas "scarcities" in the 1970s seemed politically and economically contrived rather than physically real, there is evidence that the world's petroleum and natural gas supplies are being slowly drained. World petroleum reserves were estimated at between 500 and 700 billion barrels in 1976. However, no one knows for sure how much oil will be available in the future, since higher prices and new technologies could make further reserves exploitable. Recent estimates place recoverable petroleum at 2,000 billion barrels. New reserves are being discovered, but at a decreasing rate. Based on projected reserves, there could be a 100-year global supply; however, strains on oil and natural gas supplies are expected by the turn of the century, and energy prices are expected to rise.[16]

The environmental problems of both coal and nuclear energy along with oil and gas supply uncertainties make a *mix* of energy strategies, including greater use of renewable resources, crucial for the future. "Countries situated in the higher latitudes are favored with wind resources; mountainous countries have falling water; tropical countries can produce organic materials for fuel throughout the year, and countries in desert areas have an abundance of sunlight."[17] Such variations leave room for controlled use of nuclear power as well, especially in countries with few energy alternatives. Certain fuels may also be utilized best in certain sectors of the economy; for example, petroleum is being diverted more and more to transportation as opposed to electric power generation.

Nonfuel Minerals. Finally, turning to problems associated with nonfuel minerals, one finds that these reserves are generally more widely distributed than fossil fuel reserves, but that some areas are highly dependent on imported supplies. (See Table 15.1 for the location of major mineral reserves.) The Japanese and Western Europeans are particularly short of key minerals, relying on imports to meet over 90 percent of their needs in several industrial raw material categories. Recalling our earlier discussion of trade dependence in the international economy, the United States also has a heavy "mineral import

Table 15.1

WORLD MINERAL RESERVES

	PERCENTAGE OF WORLD RESERVES		PERCENTAGE OF WORLD RESERVES
Bauxite		Lead	
Australia	26	United States	36
Guinea	26	Canada	12
Brazil	15	Soviet Union	11
Chromite		Australia	11
South Africa	62	Manganese	
Zimbabwe	33	South Africa	45
Cobalt		Soviet Union	38
Zaire	28	Australia	8
Oceania	27	Molybdenum	
Zambia	14	United States	49
Cuba	14	Soviet Union	15
Soviet Union	8	Canada	14
Copper		Chile	14
United States	20	Nickel	
Chile	20	New Caledonia	44
Canada	9	Canada	16
Soviet Union	9	Soviet Union	10
Iron ore		Australia	9
Soviet Union	31	Indonesia	8
Brazil	17	Tin	
Canada	12	China	24
Australia	10	Thailand	15
Zinc		Malaysia	12
Canada	23	Bolivia	10
United States	20	Indonesia	8
Australia	12	Tungsten	
Soviet Union	8	China	54
		Canada	12
		Soviet Union	9

Source: Adapted from Bureau of Mines, *Mineral Facts and Problems,* 1975 ed. (Washington, D.C.: Government Printing Office, 1976); found in Dennis Pirages, *Global Ecopolitics* (North Scituate, Mass.: Duxbury, 1978), p. 154.

reliance" despite being blessed with various raw materials found within its own borders.

In order to judge the potential for mineral supply crises, one must assess many factors: the importance of each mineral in industry; its abundance in various countries; the likelihood that producers could agree politically to restrict supply; the availability and price of substitutes; the power of MNCs to control the market and make up for shortages; the effect of price increases on new exploration; the ease of storage or shipment (for building stockpiles);

and the level of reserves in relation to demand. There is no reason to assume that the energy crisis will necessarily be repeated in a series of minerals crises.

For example, iron, very important in a number of industrial processes and in the military sector, has few substitutes but is abundantly and widely available. Bauxite is similarly widely available for aluminum production; bauxite-producing states that are members of the International Bauxite Association (IBA) are ideologically and economically quite diverse, and have found agreement to control supplies difficult. In addition, new producers such as Brazil have entered the bauxite market and undermined IBA prices.[18] Manganese, once mined largely in the Soviet Union, was found in greater abundance worldwide after World War II. Nickel, used in stainless steel, has likewise been more widely available since the price doubled in the 1970s and discoveries were made on the sea floor. On the other hand, chromium is currently available through only a few sources, some of which are considered unreliable because of political instability or for other reasons: the Soviet Union, Turkey, Zimbabwe, and South Africa. The platinum metals pose similar concerns to Western consumers.[19]

Slowed economic growth and increased conservation since the 1970s, along with new discoveries of mineral reserves, have caused doomsday projections about exhaustion of global raw materials to be modified somewhat. It does not now appear that any major metals will disappear in this century. According to one study, "The threat of widespread physical scarcities should not loom for at least thirty years."[20] New technologies, conservation, diminished consumption, recycling, and development of synthetics might ease such scarcities even then. However, the costs of future raw materials and their distribution patterns cannot easily be predicted.

Although the stimulus of higher prices might increase exploration for and extraction of raw materials, thereby enlarging global supplies, there is a law of diminishing returns that has been compared to squeezing the last drops out of a sponge. It is unlikely that the deepest mineral deposit, or the last drop of oil or gas, will ever be tapped, because its extraction probably will be economically prohibitive even if technologically possible. At the point when the costs and energy required for extraction exceed the value of the resources, the mines and wells will close and industrial civilization—if it is to continue— will need other resource bases.[21]

The Politics of Resource Management

Although all human beings seemingly have a common stake in achieving better management of resources, major conflicts nonetheless exist among various actors involved in the global politics of resource management. These actors include not only *nation-states* (ranging from the resource-rich to the resource-starved, industrial to underdeveloped, and coastal to landlocked) but also *nonstate* actors, such as subnational interest groups (ranging from conservationist and wildlife groups to mining and fishing interests within countries), multinational corporations, NGOs (like Greenpeace, organized to protect whales and other endangered species), and IGOs (like the International Whaling Commission and other bodies affiliated with the United Nations).

As noted in the previous chapter, the South as a whole seldom echoes Northern calls for resource conservation, unless such conservation is accompanied by redistribution of wealth. However, the politics of resource management is not quite this simple. Southerners tend to argue for more internationalized management of resources through IGOs, especially in the case of the oceans. They frequently base their arguments on the "common heritage" concept discussed at the beginning of this chapter, and have criticized industrialized states for seeking unfettered rights to extract and exploit resources through MNCs. Northerners disagree among themselves about rights to stake out ownership of and derive profits from natural resources, as well as about the priorities of conservation, protection of endangered species, pollution control, industrial expansion and economic growth, and energy self-sufficiency.

The importance of environmental protection and resource conservation has gained recognition in both the North and the South, with a growing number and network of environmental organizations around the world. The U.S. State Department lists over fifty ongoing multilateral agreements (with seventy more being negotiated) and more than 275 bilateral agreements, involving over seventy countries, on environmental issues.[22] In the remainder of this chapter we examine the politics surrounding the formation of regimes governing the world's oceans, air and outer space, and land-based resources.

The Oceans: Politics and Regimes

The "freedom of the sea" concept goes back a long way in history. Even the ancient Romans spoke of the free, public use of the oceans by all peoples. It is true that a few states in the fifteenth and sixteenth centuries made extravagant claims of ownership of large ocean areas (for example, Spain claimed possession of the Pacific Ocean). However, these claims had been generally discredited by the time Grotius initiated the notion of *mare liberum* (open seas) in his seventeenth-century international law treatises. The British and the Dutch, great seafaring and trading nations, led the way in pushing for universal acceptance of the freedom of the sea doctrine.

The basic principle that became widely accepted was that no state could exercise sovereignty or control over any part of the oceans except for the waters immediately adjacent to its coast—the so-called **territorial sea,** in which the coastal state could regulate navigation and any other activities in the interest of its security. This area was to be distinguished from the **high seas,** where no regulation was permissible. Practically all coastal states established territorial seas three nautical miles in width, based on the prevailing range of seventeenth-century cannon, although a few states did attempt to assert rights of up to twelve miles. Even within a state's territorial sea, where it had sovereign jurisdiction, it could not deny another state's vessels the legal **right of innocent passage** (the right to pass through a state's coastal waters as long as it is done peaceably).

Hence, for centuries the oceans were relatively calm in terms of rule consensus. However, in the mid-twentieth century the "laissez-faire" approach to managing the oceans came to be challenged for a variety of reasons. First, as land-based resources began to dry up, states intensified their search for ocean-based resources and discovered oil, gas, and mineral deposits in the seabed. Second, with new technologies, such as sonar fishing that could sweep huge expanses of the ocean clean of fish and supertankers that could spill oil over huge stretches of shoreline, humans were faced for the first time in history with the prospect that the oceans could become depleted and even destroyed if not regulated in some fashion; coastal states suddenly had to be concerned about policing commercial activities not only within their territorial seas but in coastal waters beyond a three-mile limit.

Ironically, it was the United States, a major naval power and long-time champion of the freedom of the sea doctrine, that set a key precedent for expanded national claims on the oceans. With Americans pioneering deep-sea drilling, the Truman administration proclaimed in 1945 the exclusive right of the United States to exploit the oil and other resources on its *continental shelf* to a depth of 200 meters (extending well beyond three miles). This action sparked a wave of new claims to assorted segments of the oceans, with many states claiming twelve-mile territorial seas or even 200-mile limits (as in the case of several Latin American countries seeking to compensate for the fact they had no continental shelf to exploit), others claiming 12- to 200-mile exclusive fishing zones, and still others claiming 12- to 200-mile zones in which they had a right to regulate pollution.

Numerous disputes arose over these claims. Major maritime powers, including the United States, became alarmed that 200-mile zones, especially around vast island archipelagos like Indonesia, would endanger the principle of the open sea that allowed maximum freedom of operation for their large far-flung navies, scientific research expeditions, and fishing fleets. Coastal states lacking such maritime prowess felt they benefited more from an "enclosure" policy that limited other countries' access to their offshore waters than from an "open sea" policy that gave free rein to anyone who had the capability to exploit the oceans. Smaller, less developed states, then, tended to advocate increased national control over their coastal waters. They also later sought to restrict certain activities on the high seas as well, urging

international regulation through the United Nations to ensure that technologically advanced states did not exploit the deep seabed for their exclusive
gain. Landlocked states were somewhat wary of all coastal states—big and
small alike—and voiced concerns about how they too might share in the
riches of the sea.

Law of the sea politics occurred at several levels. Subnational groups, such
as hard-pressed U.S. fishermen, waded into the fray and muddied the waters
further, often disagreeing among themselves over what legal positions best
served the "national interest" of their country. For example, American
fishermen on the East Coast, generally operating with small boats in nearby
waters and having to compete with mechanized Soviet floating fish factories,
favored a 200-mile exclusive fishing zone; in contrast, West Coast tuna
fishermen, plying the distant waters off the coasts of Ecuador and Peru,
supported the principle of a more limited twelve-mile zone so that they would
not be excluded entirely from Latin American waters. Various governmental
agencies also often took conflicting positions and engaged in domestic bureaucratic politics to have their particular views accepted as official national
policy. American Defense Department officials—concerned primarily about
the free passage of U.S. warships on the high seas—sought to retain the narrow
three-mile territorial sea, although expressing a willingness to tolerate a
twelve-mile territorial limit as long as the principle of "unimpeded transit"
applied to international straits falling in the extended band; on the other hand,
Interior Department officials—primarily concerned about managing U.S. coastal
resources, including policing would-be polluters and exploiting offshore
wealth—were less supportive of the freedom of the sea doctrine and instead
wanted to expand the national zone of jurisdiction to 200 miles for certain
purposes. Battles between defense and interior ministries were fought not
only in the United States but in other countries as well.

Despite efforts in the 1950s and 1960s to reconcile differing viewpoints
through UN conferences, disagreements persisted. The first UN Conference
on the Law of the Sea (UNCLOS I), held in Geneva in 1958 and attended by
eighty-six states, managed to produce four conventions that codified some
traditional customary rules (e.g., the right of innocent passage in territorial
waters) along with some new ones (e.g., the right of coastal states to exploit
the continental shelf to a depth of 200 meters). However, UNCLOS I as well
as a similar conference held in 1960 (UNCLOS II) failed to reach agreement
on several key issues, particularly the width of the territorial sea. Agreement
became increasingly difficult as more and more independently minded Third
World nations entered the United Nations. The Third World viewed the
oceans—particularly the mineral-rich deep seabed—as a means of facilitating
a global redistribution of wealth; a 1967 UN agenda item introduced by
Malta's UN Ambassador, Arvid Pardo, called for "the use of [seabed] resources
in the interest of mankind," i.e., as a "common heritage."[23]

By 1973, however, unilateral claims to expanded territorial seas and other parts of the oceans had reached such proportions that the 65 percent of the oceans that represented an unclaimed "common heritage" in 1958 had shrunk to 35 percent.[24] Almost all the harvestable fish and readily exploitable oil and gas resources were to be found within these newly claimed coastal areas rather than further out to sea in the commons.

Such was the setting for UNCLOS III, as officials from 149 states along with numerous nongovernmental bodies met in Caracas, Venezuela, in 1973 to forge a new regime. The goal was nothing less than producing a *single comprehensive* agreement on the rules governing well over half the earth's surface; the complete spectrum of issues was to be addressed—territorial seas, economic and fishing zones, continental shelves, high seas, the deep seabed and ocean floor, marine pollution, and the transfer of technology. In the words of one writer, UNCLOS III was "the largest single international legal undertaking since the time of Grotius."[25] The agreement was to be based on consensus as much as possible and otherwise by a two-thirds vote. Little did the participants know that UNCLOS III would last over eight years.

To illustrate the political complications of UNCLOS III, we need look only at the tortuous decision making of the European Economic Community (EEC), just one of the groups of states participating. In 1974, the EEC Commission proposed a common Euro-policy for the UNCLOS proceedings in Caracas, including support for a twelve-mile territorial sea and 200-mile economic zone, an International Authority to exercise jurisdiction beyond 200 miles, and regional cooperation to settle fishing disputes. Yet EEC members were initially unable to agree among themselves on these Commission proposals since various European states had divergent interests. In Britain, for example, although commercial fishing interests provided only 20,000 jobs, they had considerable political clout, with eighteen major fishing ports possessing twenty-two parliamentary seats and with anti-EEC politicians looking for issues to exploit. Thus, in support of its fishermen, who mostly worked the coasts off Ireland and Iceland, London pushed hard for narrow limits on exclusive fishing zones, while at the same time seeking exclusive economic zones to protect North Sea gas and oil fields. West Germany and the Benelux group, with short coasts and few offshore resources, did not entirely share such interests. Most EEC states had extensive commercial shipping enterprises and were suspicious of strong coastal state pollution regulations that could hamper navigation. Some, however, like France, suffered the effects of growing pollution in the English Channel and the North Sea and supported regulation. Differences between European governments had to be ironed out before the Community could bargain with the rest of the world.[26]

Europeans and other UNCLOS delegations began to harmonize their positions when it became clear by 1976 that if a Law of the Sea Treaty could not be produced, other states—including major powers like the United States—

were prepared to enforce 200-mile economic zones off their coasts and to begin ocean mining beyond those zones unilaterally without clear legal authority. Howard Hughes' Summa Mining Corporation and Tenneco Deep Sea Ventures were bringing strong pressures to bear on the U.S. Congress to authorize American companies' deep-sea mining, despite Third World objections that such unregulated action would violate the common heritage doctrine expressed in the 1970 UN resolution. In the interests of self-protection and of not being left out, EEC states ultimately agreed to support a twelve-mile territorial sea and a 200-mile fishing and commercial zone, although special fishing privileges were to be accorded EEC states by fellow Community members.[27]

By the late 1970s, a virtual consensus had been achieved among all states (including the thirty or so landlocked states) behind a twelve-mile territorial sea with unimpeded transit through international straits, a 200-mile exclusive fishing zone for coastal states, a similar zone covering nonliving resources, and an **International Seabed Authority** for regulating deep-sea mining and distributing the resultant revenues between private investors and developing countries. A draft convention was finally readied in 1980.

However, the adoption of the draft treaty was delayed when the incoming Reagan administration decided to renounce the product of eight years' labor primarily because of objections to the International Seabed Authority. Two competing positions had emerged at UNCLOS III about the Authority. Technologically advanced Western states wanted the Authority's powers limited to licensing private, public, or joint venture enterprises. They argued that a free enterprise and open exploitation system would maximize the economic return to the whole world. In contrast, Third World states wanted a strong Authority, composed of all states, to govern the exploration, extraction, and marketing of seabed mineral resources and to determine how the proceeds were to be distributed. Third World states that relied on the sale of minerals for the bulk of their export earnings (for example, the so-called "three Z's"—Zaire, Zambia, and Zimbabwe) were especially concerned that unlimited mining of manganese nodules might produce a world raw materials glut and depress prices. A compromise was finally reached. However, the United States continued to push for modifications in the proposed mining regime to benefit private mining companies. These included priority in the first mining contracts for five Western consortia of companies, four of which were dominated by American corporations; more Western voting power in the Authority, with a U.S. veto over proposed amendments to the convention; and the return of mining sites not exploited by the Authority to private developers.

When the **Law of the Sea Treaty** finally came to a vote in April of 1982, it was adopted by a margin of 130 to 4, with 17 abstentions. Since then, over 150 countries have signed the treaty and are in the process of ratifying it. Only the United States among the major world powers has remained opposed. Washington might eventually accept the treaty, since the United States has much to gain from a widely ratified agreement despite some drawbacks. The decision by American companies to go ahead and mine the oceans without a codified set of rules could invite "claim-jumping" by other states, with little legal recourse for the companies. Moreover, it is estimated that, if the treaty provisions pertaining to expanded territorial areas and economic zones were ratified, the United States—with one of the longest coastlines in the world—would obtain clear legal title to some 3 million square miles, the biggest "territorial acquisition" in U.S. history.[28] The United States has declared its intention to abide by the treaty provisions except for those pertaining to deep seabed mining.

The Law of the Sea Treaty now is so widely accepted that it is already part of customary international law. However, many questions remain regarding the exact scope of coastal state power to regulate navigation, to police polluters, to prevent access to fishing grounds, and to control other activities in various ocean areas. Questions also remain over what powers international bodies have in regulating activities on the high seas and deep-sea floor. The treaty contains language that is vague and open to differing interpretations on several subjects.[29] Hence, the law of the sea is still somewhat in flux, although a fragile consensus seems to be emerging around some traditional and some new elements.

Under the UNCLOS III treaty provisions on seabed mining, for example, common heritage concepts call for states to share in the proceeds, whether or not they do any extraction of minerals. Under the compromise noted earlier, the International Seabed Authority would allow national mining enterprises, including private corporations, to operate on the ocean floor under certain specified conditions. Any firm applying for a mining permit would have to submit two sites to the Authority, which would then decide which site to award to the firm and which to retain for its own exploitation on behalf of the international community as a whole. In this way the Authority would take advantage of private mining expertise. Funds from payments to the Authority and from the sale of minerals under its control would be shared among the needy Third World states, including those exporting land-based minerals that might suffer from sea-based competition. Such a regime is a radical development insofar as a global body for the first time would have its own direct source of revenue rather than being reliant on individual nation-state contributions. Still, financial contributions from national governments are needed initially to establish the Authority; and it may prove difficult to make it operational without the support of the United States, which had been counted on as a major donor.

A less controversial body that has been in existence since 1958 is the major international agency overseeing ocean navigation and pollution control today. The International Maritime Organization (IMO), formerly called the Inter-Governmental Maritime Consultative Organization, is a UN Specialized Agency with well over 100 members. From its inception, IMO has been charged with facilitating international cooperation on maritime issues, specifically promoting maritime safety, efficiency, and fair practices among shipping interests. The Torrey Canyon tanker disaster, which occurred off the British coast in 1967, added oil pollution to IMO's concerns.

IMO helps to formulate rules for preventing collisions at sea, standards for ship construction and safety, and pollution safeguards. It is merely an advisory body, having the power only to recommend. Nonetheless, it has had some success in convincing states to ratify conventions and accept uniform practices regarding ship-to-shore communications, traffic control in congested waters, minimum standards for ship crews, and handling of dangerous cargoes. The task of drafting regulatory conventions and codes is handled mainly by a Council and Maritime Safety Committee, both dominated traditionally by states with significant shipping interests, although recent reforms have permitted broader representation. Critics have charged that IMO seldom proposes regulations strongly opposed by shipping companies, such as ship design specifications.[30]

On the question of pollution at sea, the International Convention for the Prevention of Pollution from Ships is expected to replace an earlier IMO treaty. Areas particularly vulnerable to oil spills are designated in the convention, and all oil discharges in those zones would be prohibited (including the major European and Middle Eastern seas and gulfs). Several other treaties deal with problems of accidental oil spills; they include provisions placing responsibility for damages squarely on ship owners, and requiring both insurance and compensation of pollution victims. In addition, under the UNCLOS III treaty, coastal states are entitled to prosecute polluters entering their harbors regardless of where at sea the offenses took place.[31] In general, under the treaty, all ships (including warships) have a right of unrestricted transit on the high seas and through international straits, such as the busy Straits of Malacca, the shortcut between the Indian and Pacific Oceans. Yet within their territorial waters, coastal states can deny passage to ships carrying military weapons or unsafe cargo, and can restrict scientific expeditions and any other activities they deem potentially harmful.[32]

A special issue that has plagued IMO is the "flag of convenience" problem. The international shipping industry is split between those countries and companies that adhere to strict regulatory practices and those countries offering, and companies seeking, "flags of convenience." Flags of convenience are registrations and licenses issued by such states as Liberia, Panama, Cyprus, and Singapore, which enforce fewer safety and personnel standards and, hence, require less financial investment or ship upkeep. Ratification and enforcement of IMO treaties are often held up as maritime states resist regulations that might put them at a disadvantage against competitors in a shrinking market. In the search for cheap labor, inexperienced crews with no common language often are recruited, leading to safety problems and shipwrecks. Some shippers maintain that flags of convenience have become "flags of necessity" because of high shipping costs and the need to compete; yet reputable shippers, including several multinational oil companies, pay the higher costs and abide by IMO regulations. A UN Conference on Conditions for Registration of Ships has met periodically in the 1980s, aiming for a treaty requiring at least somewhat more correspondence between the flag a ship flies and the nationality of its owners and crew.

There is considerably less international machinery for managing fisheries and wildlife than for regulating shipping and navigation. The establishment of 200-mile fishing zones has gone far toward satisfying the concerns of coastal state fishing interests, although there is still some question over whether foreign fishing interests that have traditionally fished another country's waters are entitled to continue operating there if the coastal state cannot fully utilize the "maximum sustainable yield" itself. Hence, there is a need for further international coordination to regulate fishing zones and, also, to conserve endangered species and regulate high seas fishing. At present, the main international coordination occurs through regional bodies, such as the Inter-American Tuna Commission, the International Pacific Halibut Commission, and the EEC Commission, which tend to have limited powers.[33]

The small boats of the Greenpeace Foundation speeding out to stand between Soviet and Japanese harpoonists and the whales they hunted, in the early 1980s, alerted the world to the politics of the International Whaling Commission (IWC). Traditionally, the IWC had been strongly influenced by states with major whaling interests. Animal conservationists had futilely tried to penetrate IWC annual meetings to push for a complete ban on whaling. IWC membership expanded in the 1970s, however, to include several non-whaling states, adding to the voting strength of the conservationist forces. In 1982, the IWC moved toward a moratorium on all commercial whaling. Given vigorous protests by the Japanese, who consider whaling part of their cultural and economic heritage, as well as foot dragging by the Soviet Union, Norway, Iceland, and South Korea, and lack of IWC enforcement powers, it remained to be seen whether the ban would be effective.

Not only whales but other marine species—such as the Antarctic seal, the North Pacific fur seal, and the polar bear—are in trouble despite the existence of an International Endangered Species Convention, a World Heritage Trust Treaty, and other rules designed to regulate exploitation of marine life. Regimes dealing with fishing and animal hunting must confront states' demands for an "equitable share" and the traditional claims of fishermen and hunters who have been traveling to certain waters for centuries. To resolve these contradictions, some have argued for separating the right of access to fishing and hunting grounds from the right to benefit from those grounds. For example, the North Pacific Fur Seal Commission has set provisions whereby seals are hunted only by countries on whose islands they breed—the Soviet Union and the United States, for instance. States that previously captured seals on the high seas agreed to stop doing so in return for a share of the skins. Therefore, fewer seals are indiscriminately slaughtered and the herd is maintained.

Air and Outer Space: Politics and Regimes

Many of the disputes concerning atmospheric and outer space resources are similar to disputes about the oceans, especially those regarding what constitutes the common heritage and what is up for grabs by individual states. Indeed, ocean controversies have been directly related to air space controversies because national sovereignty over a state's territorial sea has—at least since the advent of the airplane—also included sovereignty over the skies above the territorial sea. These skies, along with those above a country's land mass itself, have been considered **national air space**—a column of air in which a state exercises total jurisdiction and can even deny overflight rights to foreign aircraft. Hence, the U.S. Air Force was as concerned as the U.S. Navy about expanded territorial seas.

There has been no attempt to develop a multilateral "Law of the Air Treaty" akin to the Law of the Sea Treaty. Presently a state has no right to utilize the national air space of another state unless the latter has granted specific permission through a bilateral agreement. The International Civil Aviation Organization (ICAO) helps to develop uniform air safety standards but has little control over air traffic.

Although it is clear that each state has sovereignty over its air space (up to where it meets "outer space"), there remain conflicts over certain airborne activities such as weather modification and atmospheric pollution. Canada has complained in recent years, for example, that half of its acid rain comes from the United States. Lamenting American slowness in developing a bilateral treaty obligating each side to limit sulfur emissions, the Canadian Environment Minister in 1982 commented that acid rain was "the single most important irritant, or issue, in Canadian-American relations."[35] An issue such as acid rain, which affects certain parts of North America and Europe more than others, shows that international environmental politics have become interrelated with domestic environmental politics, and just as heated. American western and midwestern states, especially those with coal mining interests, have seen far less need for costly sulfur dioxide controls than eastern states or Canadian provinces suffering under the wind-blown acid fallout. Anticipation of Congressional action on the matter might have been one factor, along with Canadian pressure, leading the Reagan administration to formulate a general, if somewhat vague, acid rain agreement with Canada in 1986, thus recognizing the need for coordinated ecological responses.

In 1972, the **UN Conference on the Human Environment** in Stockholm articulated the general principle that states "have the responsibility to ensure that activities within their jurisdiction or control do not cause damage to the environment of other States or of areas beyond the limits of national jurisdiction"; states are expected to inform and consult with other states likely to be affected by a pending activity if there is an "appreciable risk of effects on climate." Adopting these principles, the Scandinavian states agreed to a Nordic Environmental Protection Convention in 1974, under which enterprises must obtain permits to carry out potentially harmful activities and must notify all affected states that are parties to the agreement.[36]

Until the Chernobyl nuclear accident in the Soviet Union, which many felt was not reported quickly enough under provisions of the 1974 treaty, little progress had been made in establishing international environmental management. In the wake of the Chernobyl accident, however, there were new mandatory agreements under the International Atomic Energy Agency (IAEA) to share information on potential environmental disasters openly and quickly, and to provide coordinated emergency assistance. The IAEA had been invited to study the Chernobyl site and reported somewhat optimistically on the likely extent of long-term health damage from radiation, as well as on the future of nuclear power. Other experts disputed these findings, and European and American studies predicted roughly 50-50 chances of a major nuclear accident in the next five years.[37]

The major global environmental agency is the **UN Environmental Program (UNEP)**, created after the Stockholm Conference. The UNEP annual budget has remained relatively static since its inception. States generally have been left to their own devices for checking pollution, because many governments are suspicious of any international agency that could impose limits on industrial activity, especially in hard economic times. UNEP's main contribution has been to coordinate the "Earthwatch" network that gathers worldwide data on the environment and monitors any changes in the atmosphere and elsewhere that could pose dangers. In these efforts, UNEP has worked closely with the World Meteorological Organization (WMO), although both agencies remain information-gathering more than rulemaking organizations. Under WMO auspices, for example, international weather and climatological data are shared by countries participating in the World Weather Watch program. Efforts are underway to extend such crucial weather forecasts to drought-stricken African farmers.[38] UNEP has also organized a number of environmental conferences, including a commemorative second UN Conference on the Human Environment in Nairobi, Kenya, in 1982, as well as a landmark 1987 conference in Montreal to deal with the decay of the ozone layer that protects humanity from the sun's rays. The latter conference resulted in the Montreal Protocol signed by twenty-four nations, including the U.S., Canada, and the members of the European Community, each of which pledged itself to reduce production of chlorofluorocarbons and other ozone-depleting chemicals by fifty percent before the end of the century.

Much of the earth's atmosphere—all the air over the high seas—remains *terra nullius*, territory belonging to no one. The moon and celestial bodies and outer space as a whole are also considered *terra nullius*. Northern, technologically advanced states (including the United States and the Soviet Union), while agreeing that outer space cannot be claimed as sovereign territory by any state, interpret *terra nullius* to mean that it is nonetheless open to free use and exploitation on a "first come, first served" basis. Countries lacking space technology, notably Third World countries, have interpreted *terra nullius* to mean that outer space is part of the common heritage, jointly owned by everyone and subject to international regulation (i.e., more properly, "*terra communis*").

The different perspectives could be seen in disagreements between the Soviet Union and Argentina during negotiations over a Moon Treaty in the 1970s. The Soviets refused to accept the common heritage notion, insisting that space belonged to *no one* (not everyone) and hence was available for use by any state. Argentina, on the other hand, pointed out that when Soviet moon probes brought back samples of moon rocks, Moscow in effect was taking ownership of space property. In an argument reminiscent of the deep seabed debate, Argentina urged that rules be developed for sharing space benefits widely and equitably, especially as future technology would likely enable states to build permanent space stations and to exploit gases, metals, and various other space resources.[39]

In addition to nation-states (the roughly twenty countries presently capable of launching satellites as well as the remaining "have-nots"), the group of actors potentially involved in space politics also includes MNCs and other enterprises that build, launch, and rent satellites or contract for services from space (such as utilizing data gained from remote sensing devices); IGOs like the International Telecommunications Satellite Consortium (INTELSAT) and International Telecommunication Union (ITU), whose role in regulating the satellite uses of space and allocation of radio frequencies was discussed in Chapter 10; and even the many individuals all over the world who tune their TV sets to hundreds of satellite TV channels. At future Law of Space conferences, all of these actors will no doubt be contending that "the Force" is with them. (See the Sidelight "Space: The Last Frontier," page 514.)

Although air space and outer space are connected, the regimes governing the two domains are quite different. The Outer Space Treaty of 1967 prohibits sovereignty or ownership over any part of outer space. Up to now, no state has attempted to restrict the movements of space satellites flying over its territory. In other words, unlike airplanes, satellites can fly freely over any country. This is a key difference between the air space and outer space regimes, and is mainly in deference to the laws of physics; i.e., planes can more easily be rerouted around forbidden areas than can satellites in orbit!

However, with the growing network of satellites surveying world crop patterns, connecting transoceanic telephone calls, spying on military installations, and beaming World Cup soccer games to all continents, states have recognized the need for some degree of coordination and regulation. A Unispace Conference, held in 1982, sought to develop rules requiring technologically advanced states to share with Third World states any data on the latter's weather and agricultural conditions derived from remote sensing satellites. In addition to dealing with peaceful uses of space, Unispace also sought to limit military ventures as well, in recognition of the fact that approximately 80 percent of the satellites launched since Sputnik in 1957 have been for military purposes. States launching satellites into outer space must currently register them with the United Nations and are liable for any damages caused by such objects falling to earth (under the Convention on Liability for Damage Caused by Objects Launched into Outer Space). Additionally, there is an Agreement on the Rescue of Astronauts.

With the failure to obtain agreement on the creation of a Space Commission, the main body responsible for developing space law is the UN Committee on the Peaceful Uses of Outer Space (COPUOS). COPUOS prepared the UN Draft Treaty Relating to the Moon, which was opened to ratification in 1979. This treaty, which the U.S. has been reluctant to ratify, culminated ten years of debate triggered by humanity's first steps on the moon in 1969. The treaty augmented the principles of the 1967 Outer Space Treaty and banned the exploitation of moon resources for profit (a blow to private enterprise in space). States would be free to explore the moon and to collect rocks and minerals, however. Stations established on the moon could not interfere with other states' access, and their presence there would not imply permanent ownership. Parties to the agreement also are pledged to establish an international regime to "govern the exploitation of the natural resources of the moon."[40] Although it is difficult to establish such agreements for sharing the common heritage in a world of sovereign states, most states are on record as willing to try.

Land-Based Resources: Politics and Regimes

Controversies over land-based resources mainly pit those who want coordination among countries to push up resource prices or control supplies on one side versus those who want freer access to materials at lower cost on the other side. The former, following the OPEC cartel example, want maximum economic payoffs for raw materials taken from their territory. The latter, consumer states that import heavily, want guarantees of secure and reasonably priced supplies. Often in between are MNCs that dominate global extraction and distribution operations. Dennis Pirages notes the following:

SIDELIGHT

SPACE: "THE LAST FRONTIER"

Perplexing legal problems in outer space are revealed in the following excerpts from a *Wall Street Journal* article that was written shortly before the fatal crash of the Challenger spacecraft in 1986.

During a quiet moment in space two years ago, a fleck of cosmic junk hurtled at 17,500 miles an hour into the windshield of the space shuttle Challenger. Fortunately the high-speed collision only pitted the glass. A larger object might have broken through, killing or injuring the five crew members, disabling the $1 billion spacecraft and damaging its valuable payload.

If a similar kind of disaster occurred at sea—a drilling rig, for instance, tumbled from a barge and sank the towboat alongside, injuring the crew—maritime law, developed over centuries, would apply. Surviving sailors would stand a good chance of collecting damages from the ship builder, the shipowner, the rig owner, the barge operator and even the barge itself. Other parties would probably collect as well.

But no one knows for sure whether the surviving astronauts—or any of the other parties—would have been able to win damages in the space-shuttle case. As the U.S. starts its commercial thrust into outer space, astronauts and space entrepreneurs are moving into a legal wasteland, where liability, national sovereignty, commercial codes, criminal laws and government regulations are veritable black holes. . . .

Already some 350 companies are gearing up for space exploitation, drawn by predictions that the industry will generate 10 million jobs and $65 billion or more in revenue by the year 2010. . . .

Often, nations are characterized as importers or exporters of commodities, and it is assumed that political leaders control the flow of commodities across their borders. In reality, the extent to which the flow of commodities is subject to control by political elites varies among nations. Transnational economic actors (multinational corporations) are responsible for many decisions in both exporting and importing nations, and they can effectively inhibit or aid exporter cartel formation.

Each mineral market is characterized by a greater or lesser dominance of nonnational actors, and each nation is characterized by a different degree of government intervention in trade. This variety results in a complex matrix of semi-independent national actors and semi-independent multinational corporations that criss-crosses the world mineral marketplace. Cartels are most likely to develop in markets where national actors control exports and where the private sector controls most imports.[41]

The U.S. Apollo and Soviet Soyuz rendezvoused in space 10 years ago, but on earth the two nations remain locked in a 15-year debate over space treaties. The Soviets have attempted to outlaw private industry from space; the Americans have threatened to abandon the United Nations' top space committee.

The few U.S. laws that extend into space are equally deficient. It's illegal, for instance, to kill a fellow astronaut in the space shuttle—but not on the moon, in a space station or during a space walk. Any tycoon can avoid paying U.S. taxes on some income earned in a foreign country, but not in space, which the Internal Revenue Service has described as "no place at all.". . .

No international law yet exists to effectively govern space pollution. The North American Air Defense Command, or NORAD, counts 5,330 man-made objects circling the earth, a veritable trash dump of spent boosters, dead satellites and lost space gloves rushing along at 17,500 miles an hour. . . . International law also remains poorly equipped to deal with junk that tumbles back to earth. Much of it burns into dust and gas, but not all. . . .

The most severe space fallout . . . occurred in 1978, when the nuclear powered Cosmos 954 crashed in northern Canada. Canada spent $14 million to clean up radioactive debris, but because nobody was hit and no property was damaged, the Soviet Union argued that it wasn't liable under international treaties. After outcries . . . and years of negotiation, the Soviets paid $3 million. To space powers like the U.S. and Russia, "the concern is the launch pad. For all other nations, it's the end that matters. . . ."

Source: Mark Zieman, "Lack of Law May Slow the Use of Outer Space by Private Enterprise," *Wall Street Journal* (August 20, 1985), pp. 1 and 5. Reprinted by permission. © Dow Jones & Company, Inc. 1985. All rights reserved.

The box on pages 516–517 lists the major actors concerned with the export of selected raw materials. As one can see, with some materials (e.g., tin), there have been attempts to develop organizations that include both exporter and importer interests. With others (e.g., copper), more exclusive organizations have been formed among producer countries only, although the unwillingness of some major producers to participate and disagreements among members themselves have limited the effectiveness of cartel efforts. These efforts have also been weakened by the existence of alternative and ocean-based supplies in some cases.

In the future, supplies of all types of secondary resources will depend as much on economics and politics as on geological conditions. For example, for every barrel of oil refined and sold over the last hundred years or so, an estimated four barrels remain, unrecovered or undiscovered, in the ground.

THE POLITICS OF RAW MATERIALS: MAJOR ACTORS

Resource	Actors
Copper:	Intergovernmental Council of Copper Exporting Countries (CIPEC)—Chile, Peru, Zaire, Indonesia, Zambia (accounting for 65 percent of world exports). Other major producers: United States, Canada, Soviet Union. Major importers: Japan and Western European states. Private dealers, such as those on the London Metal Exchange. Major MNCs, such as Kennecott, Anaconda, and Corro.
Iron ore:	Association of Iron Ore Exporting Countries (AIOEC)—Algeria, Australia, Brazil, Chile, Gabon, India, Liberia, Malaysia, Mauritania, Peru, Venezuela, Sweden. Other major producers: United States, Canada, Soviet Union. Major importers: Japan and Western European states. MNCs, such as U.S. Steel, Bethlehem, Kaiser, and Marcona Mining, as well as ore-buying syndicates of steel companies (especially European).
Sulfur:	SULEXCO, an export cartel of U.S. MNCs. Major producers: Canada (largest exporter), France, Mexico, Poland, Cuba, Iran, Iraq, Kuwait.
Uranium:	Uranium Institute, composed of major exporting and importing states, including Australia, Canada, South Africa, France, and United Kingdom (with limited participation

Oil companies and oil-producing states decide how much oil to search for, to drill, to refine, and to sell; these decisions tend to be based on the economic return and political leverage that can be generated. Therefore, as we approach the year 2000, resource politics will involve efforts by MNCs to manage global supplies so that prices stay high enough to make exploration and extraction financially worthwhile. Governments of producer states and consumer states, often having divergent interests from those of MNCs, might organize their own enterprises to extract raw materials and compete with MNCs in order to keep the latter honest.

by United States, West Germany, and Soviet Union and with China and India not participating).

Mining companies and energy-related MNCs.

Bauxite: International Bauxite Association (IBA)—Australia, Guinea, Guyana, Jamaica, Sierra Leone, Surinam, Yugoslavia, Dominican Republic, Ghana, and Haiti (together producing 65 percent of world supply and accounting for 80 percent of exports); new producers such as Brazil.

Major importers: United States, Japan, Western Europe.

Assocalex, cartel between Alcoa and other aluminum MNCs through which they bargain in unison with host country governments.

Mercury: Producers' association, including Spain (largest producer), Italy, Mexico, Algeria, Yugoslavia, Turkey, and Canada.

Chemical MNCs.

Tin: International Tin Council (ITC), including major exporting states—Australia, Bolivia, Indonesia, Malaysia, Nigeria, Thailand, Zaire—and major importing states—Australia, Belgium, Bulgaria, Canada, Czechoslovakia, Denmark, West Germany, France, Hungary, India, Ireland, Italy, Luxembourg, Japan, Netherlands, Poland, South Korea, Rumania, Spain, Turkey, United Kingdom, Soviet Union, Yugoslavia (with the United States participating partially and China not at all).

Miners, smelters, dealers, investors, creditors, industrial users, new producers such as Brazil.

Source: Data from Zuhayr Mikdashi, *The International Politics of Natural Resources* (Ithaca, N.Y: Cornell University Press, 1976), ch. 3; and Richard J. Barnet, *The Lean Years: Politics in the Age of Scarcity* (New York: Simon and Schuster, 1980), ch. 5.

Few global institutions exist to manage raw materials supplies, although the UN system has become increasingly involved through its role in forging a New International Economic Order. In the field of energy resources, the oil crisis of 1973 led to the establishment of the International Energy Agency (IEA). The United States helped generate support for the organization by promising to make its own oil supplies available to member states in time of energy shortage. The IEA aims include (1) providing security against new oil embargoes through cooperation to build and share oil stocks; (2) sharing equitably among industrialized countries the cost of and responsibility for energy conservation; and (3) stimulating alternative energy source development. The goal is a ninety-day reserve supply of oil and coordinated conservation moves to ease consumption.[42] The IEA, however, is confined basically to industrialized noncommunist states, and as such cannot coordinate global energy resources.

Other international organizations also concern themselves with energy supplies and conservation. The EEC has published numerous energy consumption surveys, and member states have pledged themselves to a series of conservation measures including insulation of buildings and planning for the use of certain fuels in certain segments of the economy. The energy supplies of the Eastern bloc are also coordinated to an extent through the Council on Mutual Economic Assistance, although the Soviet Union tends to dictate the distribution and price of oil and gas supplies, sometimes to the disadvantage of Eastern European states.

One area in which there has been considerable regime development is the management of inland waterways. The Danube River Commission and Rhine River Commission, both going back to the early nineteenth century, have attempted to regulate navigation, pollution, power generation, and other activities among the several European states through which the rivers pass. Recently, a canal project has been engineered to join the Rhine and Danube rivers, thereby linking Western and Eastern Europe with a vast river highway. Although this would fulfill a centuries-old transportation dream, the project has also subjected the Danube and Rhine commissions to political controversies about the extent of Soviet shipping dominance, especially in West European waterways.

While the Danube and Rhine commissions have attempted to deal with environmental concerns, the rivers remain heavily polluted. According to one observer, the Rhine River is not only "the world's busiest waterway, it is also the dirtiest."[43] Canada and the United States have been somewhat more successful in managing their common waterways. The International Joint Commission and the Boundary-Waters Treaty of 1909 has been a model regime in many respects, with more than 100 disputes between the two countries settled through established procedures over the years. This commission has tackled such murky problems as Great Lakes pollution and distribution of benefits from Columbia River development. The United States has also reached understandings with Mexico regarding mutual responsibilities for maintaining the water quality of the Colorado River and other shared waterways, including a 1973 agreement by the United States to desalinate water leaving Texas.[44] On a global scale the International Convention on Trans-boundary Pollution (1979) and the International Tropical Timber Agreement (1985) offer some hope of establishing environmental safeguards.[45] Such agreements and others pledging prior consultation before environmentally hazardous policies are adopted are important precedents for the management of all the world's resources.

Conclusion

Industrial and "high-tech" civilization, based on raw materials exploitation, has spread a uniform culture around much of the world—from the sporting of designer jeans to the smell of auto exhaust fumes, from blips of computers and hospital intensive care monitors to cash registers in fast food chains. Contemporary civilization will be remembered for a variety of good and bad developments, ranging from women's liberation to nuclear explosions. Perhaps in the future, cultural diversity also will be fostered and nations will develop economic and social styles well-suited to their own individual needs.[46] If one travels through Israel and sees thousands of rooftop solar collectors for water heating, irrigation systems turning deserts green, pools of Dead Sea water drying in the scorching sun for the extraction of minerals, fish farms with self-feeding devices and raceways for trout (and if one remembers that even in biblical times roofs had rainwater catch basins), one realizes how far some states have gone and how far others must go in adapting to their natural environments and making the best of them.

In addition to national responses to environmental problems, there will be a continued need for international responses. On the eve of his departure from the White House in 1980, outgoing U.S. President Carter received the results of "The Global 2000 Report to the President," a three-year study he had commissioned. As one news service characterized it, the study was "gloom and doom quantified," since it tended to paint an extremely pessimistic picture of the world resource situation. Although many—especially in the subsequent Reagan administration—felt the report exaggerated the severity of global problems, few could quarrel with the general conclusion of the authors:

> The only solutions. . . are complex and long-term. . . . The needed changes go far beyond the capability and responsibility of this or any other single nation. An era of unprecedented cooperation and commitment is essential.[47]

Whether greater international cooperation in managing global resources will be forthcoming remains to be seen. If resources are going to cost much more, and if the environment is increasingly fouled, economic growth may be seriously slowed even if resources are physically available in sufficient supplies. If the world economy moves toward a slow or no-growth "steady state," the politics determining "who gets what, when, and how" will become even more hotly contested. Labor union members and other workers will vie for higher wages and jobs, and the funds will have to come from somewhere. India, Pakistan, and Brazil will vie for energy resources at affordable prices, and the supplies will have to come from somewhere. Tourists will vie for space on a clean beach, and the pollution controls will have to come from somewhere. Children will vie for survival, and the foresight and vision of parents will have to come from somewhere.

SUMMARY

1. Although the earth's natural resources can be viewed as a common heritage (collective goods), different actors compete to control and exploit them (as private goods).

2. Scientists distinguish between primary, secondary, and tertiary resources, as well as between renewable and nonrenewable resources. Many have questioned the "limits to growth" thesis that continued economic growth will soon exhaust the earth's nonrenewable resources and destroy renewable resources. While doomsday predictions seem premature, warnings about the finiteness of key resources and the fragility of ecological balances are still valid.

3. Our primary resources are affected by a number of environmental problems that transcend national boundaries. The atmosphere is subject to severe pollution from industrial and automobile emissions. Land-based resources are threatened by desertification and deforestation. Oceans, lakes, and rivers are being spoiled by chemical wastes and industrial effluents.

4. These same environmental problems also affect secondary resources such as food and energy supplies. While much of the South still relies on such traditional energy sources as wood and dung, the North relies on fossil fuels, including oil, gas, and coal, in addition to nuclear power. Increased pressures on resources are likely to occur as the South shifts to fossil fuels. The environmental problems of coal and nuclear energy along with oil and gas supply uncertainties make a mix of energy strategies crucial for the future.

5. Reserves of nonfuel minerals are generally more widely distributed than fossil fuel reserves, making a mineral supply crisis unlikely in the near future, although some countries are heavily dependent on just a few suppliers for imports of certain vital raw materials. Political and economic factors are likely to dominate the minerals situation more than physical scarcities will.

6. Major conflicts surround the global politics of resource management, as seen in debates over the law of the sea. Southerners generally argue for more internationalized control of resources and redistribution of the benefits; Northerners disagree among themselves about the priorities of conservation, pollution control, economic growth, and energy self-sufficiency. Among the nonstate actors involved in law of the sea politics are defense departments and interior departments, multinational corporations, IGOs like the United Nations and the International Whaling Commission, and NGOs like Greenpeace.

7. International regimes governing the management of the world's oceans, land masses, and air and outer space differ in scope and effectiveness. Although the success of the Law of the Sea Treaty is uncertain, several customary rules and principles regarding territorial seas and economic zones have become widely accepted.

8. Since the 1972 Stockholm Conference on the Environment and the 1986 Chernobyl nuclear disaster, some progress has been made in global regulation and monitoring of atmospheric pollution; some countries also have reached bilateral and regional agreements.

9. Under existing treaties, states are prohibited from claiming sovereignty over the moon or any part of outer space. However, just as there are debates over ownership of resources beneath the high seas, there is disagreement regarding outer space and whether it is to be considered *terra nullius*—territory belonging to no one and hence free to be exploited—or *terra communis*—territory belonging to everyone and hence subject to international control.

SUGGESTIONS FOR FURTHER READING AND STUDY

Among the classic studies of world environmental problems, focusing on primary resources, are Barbara Ward and René Dubos, *Only One Earth: The Care and Maintenance of a Small Planet* (New York: Penguin, 1972); Barbara Ward, *Progress for a Small Planet* (London: Temple Smith, 1979); and Rachel Carson, *The Silent Spring* (New York: Houghton Mifflin, 1962). In addition, see Gerald O. Barney, ed., *The Global 2000 Report to the President of the United States: Entering the 21st Century*, vol. 1 (New York: Pergamon, 1980); Kenneth E. Maxwell, *Environment of Life*, 4th ed. (Belmont, Calif.: Dickenson, 1985); Alden D. Hinckley, *Renewable Resources in Our Future* (New York: Pergamon, 1980); Stephen H. Schneider, *The Genesis Strategy: Climate and Global Survival* (New York: Plenum, 1976); *World Conservation Strategy* (New York: UNIPUB, 1980); Lynton K. Caldwell, *International Environmental Policy: Emergence and Dimensions* (Durham, N.C.: Duke University Press, 1984); Erik P. Eckholm, *Down to Earth: Environment and Human Needs* (New York: W. W. Norton, 1982); and Kenneth A. Dahlberg *et al., Environment and the Global Arena* (Durham, N.C.: Duke University Press, 1985).

On the management of secondary resources, including energy and nonfuel minerals, see Richard J. Barnet, *The Lean Years: Politics in the Age of Scarcity* (New York: Simon and Schuster, 1980); Gary A. Klee, ed., *World Systems of Traditional Resources Management* (New York: Halstead, 1980); Gunnar Alexandersson and Bjorn-Ivan Klevebring, *World Resources: Energy, Metals, Minerals* (New York: Walter de Gruyter, 1978); Yuan-li Wu, *Raw Materials in a Multipolar World*, 2nd ed. (New York: Crane, Russak, 1979); Denis Hayes, *Rays of Hope: The Transition to a Post-Petroleum World* (New York: W. W. Norton, 1977); Daniel Yergin and Martin Hillenbrand, eds., *Global Insecurity: A Strategy for Energy and Economic Renewal* (New York: Penguin, 1983); and Barry B. Hughes *et al., Energy in the Global Arena* (Durham, N.C.: Duke University Press, 1985). An excellent treatment of the entire "limits to growth" controversy is William Ophuls' *Ecology and the Politics of Scarcity* (San Francisco: W. H. Freeman, 1977).

Works that focus specifically on the oceans are *Restructuring Ocean Regimes*, special issue of *International Organization* (Winter 1977); Barry Buzan, *Seabed Politics* (New York: Praeger, 1976); Robert L. Friedheim, ed., *Managing Ocean Resources: A Primer* (Boulder, Colo.: Westview Press, 1979); and Bernard H. Oxman, David D. Caron, and Charles L. O. Buderi, eds., *Law of the Seas: U.S. Policy Dilemma* (San Francisco: ICS Press, 1983). See also Antony Dolman, *Global Planning and Resource Management: Toward International Decision Making in a Divided World* (New York: Pergamon, 1980). On air and outer space, see Jonathan F. Galloway, *The Politics and Technology of Satellite Communications* (Lexington, Mass.: Lexington Books, 1972); Gerhard von Glahn, *Law Among Nations*, 5th ed. (New York: Macmillan, 1986), ch. 19; and Michael Akehurst, *A Modern Introduction to International Law*, 5th ed. (London: Allen and Unwin, 1984), ch. 19. On resource regimes generally, see Oran R. Young and Stephen Krasner, eds., *Resource Regimes: Natural Resources and Social Institutions* (Berkeley: University of California Press, 1982). Discussion of regimes can also be found in the *American Journal of International Law*.

Useful information on recent developments can also be found by browsing through the following periodicals: *Environment Magazine, Nature, Ecologist Magazine, Science, Scientific American*, and publications produced by Worldwatch Institute and Resources for the Future, Inc.

PART
V

Conclusion

The world is unhappy. It is unhappy because it does not know where it is going and because it senses that if it knew, it would discover that it was heading for disaster.
VALÉRY GISCARD D'ESTAING, PRESIDENT OF FRANCE, IN A 1974 SPEECH

The age of nations is past; the task before us, if we would survive, is to build the earth.
PIERRE TEILHARD DE CHARDIN

523

In Part V we offer some concluding observations about the global condition in the late twentieth century, and where the world seems to be heading. There is room for both pessimism and optimism. We noted near the outset of this book that one can find in international relations over the centuries elements of continuity as well as change. The continuities are such that one well-known writer, reflecting upon the persistent theme of interstate competition and conflict that has characterized human affairs since the days of antiquity, asserts: "In honesty, one must question whether or not twentieth century students of international relations know anything that Thucydides and his fifth century [B.C.] compatriots did not know about the behavior of states."[1] Yet another writer, reflecting upon political life in the nuclear age, sees at least one fundamental change today from the past that might require a rethinking of world politics: "It has historically been one thing to die *for* your country. It is a different thing [today] to die *with* your country."[2]

In our last chapter (Chapter 16), we attempt to provide some further perspective on the past and, even more, the *future,* as we examine a variety of "alternative world order models." We are interested here not only in how the nation-state system can be made more peaceful (as discussed in Chapter 8), but also in the broader question of whether other systems (such as regional or world government) are possible, and whether they would promote a number of human values in addition to peace.

16

Toward the Year 2000 and Beyond

W e have just concluded our discussion of some of the great issues on the global agenda. There are hundreds of other, not-so-great issues that, despite their triviality, can affect the lives of people everywhere in the world. Consider the crusade for a "world plug and socket system,"

SIDELIGHT

GLOBAL PROBLEM SOLVING AND YOU

Travel can be fun. It can also be a nightmare of delays, strikes, lost reservations and an occasional hijacking. But worst of all is the electric plug that won't fit.

Imagine a world in which your electric shaver or hair dryer worked instantly everywhere you went. Well, the idea has been imagined for 74 years now, and the news is bad: It may soon be abandoned.

At a meeting this June, a final attempt will be made to reach agreement on a "world plug and socket system"—familiarly known as "whoops." The meeting, in Rio de Janeiro, is being convened by the International Electrotechnical Commission.

Founded in 1906, the IEC now has 43 member states, including the United States, the Soviet Union, China and India. Members represent 80 percent of the world's population and generate 95 percent of global electric power.

"We dislike puns," says an official at IEC headquarters here, "but it would be fair to say that our members are still poles apart." He adds, "The whole concept of a standard plug and socket may die." In a sense, it already has died: The current (we don't mind puns) proposal by IEC engineers envisions two systems, not one. The proposal, which the IEC likes to describe as a "universal system with two varieties," calls for a 250-volt round-pin plug for most of the world— the plug pictured here—and a 125-volt flat-pin, or rectangular, plug for North America and Japan.

Two varieties would be a great help. There now are hundreds of different plugs and sockets in the world, the IEC says, often as many as 20 different types in one country alone.

Of course, there are adapters on the market, but they can't allow for the hundreds of different sockets around the world, and there are many countries described in the Sidelight below. That a global conference would even be convened to address such a concern shows how far the world has come in terms of the range of problems now being treated at the global level. That no politically acceptable solutions have yet been found for such a seemingly

where adapters simply can't be found—many places in the Third World, for instance. To fit any possible situation anywhere, you would have to lug around a separate suitcase full of adapters.

Governments first began thinking of a universal system in 1908 when national standardization started. But it was only in 1970 that real negotiations were opened within the IEC. At first everyone fully backed the idea of world standardization. When a design was proposed four years later, however, the problems began. Governments promptly said the principle of a global plug and socket was fine *provided* it was based on their own national system.

Mr. Folcker [a Swede, head of IEC] concedes that adoption of a universal system would be extremely expensive. He estimates that it would cost $175 to change all the plugs and outlets in a normal-size home. That would put the total bill at $700 million in Sweden alone.

Voting procedures in the "whoops" committee require approval of draft designs by a four-fifths majority. That has proved impossible.

In 1977, the United States rejected one proposal because it was so unlike the American system that it would have meant rewiring the entire country. A year later the French had everyone applauding when, after years of opposition, they finally accepted the basic concept of one world, one plug. "On condition it is the French system," the delegate from Paris added when people stopped clapping.

Japan in 1979 produced what it called a prototype world plug. Other committee members were pleased by the design.

"Delight quickly faded when the experts took the plug apart and discovered it wasn't a prototype at all," one IEC official discloses. "It turned out to be a real production model and Japan had production lines all ready to go as soon as the so-called prototype was accepted."

As for the IEC engineers' latest proposal, Britain has already made it known that it will reject a round-pin plug. The British want rectangular pins and say that round pins would give some countries an unfair economic advantage. Countries with round pins say a rectangular system would be unfair to them.

Actually, the IEC people say, the existing round-pin "Europlug" does work in Britain. "But you need a matchstick to make it fit and that's dangerous," a frustrated spokesman says.

Source: Excerpted from John Calcott, "A World-Wide Plug Faces Disconnection After 74-Year Effort," *Wall Street Journal* (April 1, 1982), p. 1. Reprinted by permission of Dow Jones & Company, Inc. © 1982. All rights reserved.

mundane, technical matter shows how far the world still has to go to become a true global community with effective problem-solving machinery. This example is offered as a humorous, and also somewhat sad, commentary on the state of the world in the late twentieth century.

In this chapter, we look to the *future* and speculate about how human beings will be organizing themselves to cope with large and small problems as the twenty-first century approaches. We noted in Chapter 2 that the history of humankind could be viewed as the ongoing search for the optimal political unit, with the pendulum swinging between a virtually single universal order (such as the empire of Alexander the Great) and much more fragmented, smaller political communities (such as those that existed in the feudal era). Some observers argue that just as the nation-state came into being as the primary unit of political organization some 300 years ago, the world today is on the threshold of another great transformation—this one of epic proportions. According to this view,

> the world is at a psychological moment comparable to that time, some 5,000 to 15,000 years past, when human society moved from an essentially nomadic-hunting existence to an essentially territorial-agricultural way of life. Just as the breakdown of old myths and values led to the territorial-agricultural unit . . . , so now . . . the breakdown of statist myths and values, hastened by our growing sensitivity to humankind's ecopolitical inter-relatedness, is leading to the long-term emergence of a truly planetary civilization.[1]

Controlling the fate of the earth

Although many other observers reject such Spaceship Earth notions as naive "globaloney," even the realists have acknowledged the strains on the present nation-state system and the pressures for change. The father of the realist school, Hans Morgenthau, lamenting the growing threat to human existence posed by nuclear weapons and other hazards, wrote toward the end of his life that

> the technological revolutions of our age have rendered the Nation-State's principle of political organization as obsolete as the first modern industrial revolution of the steam engine did feudalism. The governments of Nation-States are no longer able to perform the functions for the sake of which civilized governments have been instituted in the first place: to defend and promote the life, liberty, and pursuit of happiness of its citizenry. Unable to perform these functions with regard to their own citizens, these governments are incapable of performing them in their relations with each other.[2]

There is admittedly a tendency for every generation to be temporocentric, i.e., to assume that it is living in an era that is at the crossroads of history and that its actions will be the pivotal ones upon which the entire future of humanity will hinge. However, the current generation may be more justified in its temporocentrism than past generations, if only because it has only been in the nuclear age that "mankind as a whole has had to live with the prospect of its extinction as a *species.*"[3] Whether such awesome responsibility for the fate of the planet requires fundamental changes in the world political order, and whether people are prepared to accept such changes, remains to be seen. One can rightly ask: If not the nation-state, then *what*? How else might, or should, human affairs be organized?

Thinking About the Future

In conjecturing about the world politics of the future, it is helpful to think in terms of **alternative world order models,** ways in which human beings could conceivably organize themselves politically. Scholars who engage in such crystal-ball gazing generally pose two basic questions: (1) What alternative world order models are *possible*? (2) Which are *desirable*? The first is an empirical question, and calls for a judgment about what kind of world one can realistically expect to see in the future. The second is a normative question and calls for a value judgment about what kind of world one would ideally like to see.

Regarding the empirical question, it is almost as difficult today for the average person to envision a world without nation-states as it was for people in an earlier time to envision a world that was round rather than flat. Yet, as we have noted, the nation-state is a human creation that has not always existed and will not necessarily be with us for all time. Indeed, it seems extremely unlikely that the world map in, say, the year 3000 will look even remotely like the world map of today, delineated by nation-state boundaries in dark colors. While the year 3000 is admittedly too far off to ponder, let us take a more manageable time frame and look ahead to the year 2000. Given the trends we have described throughout this book, what might the world look like in the next century, a few short years away?

Regarding the normative question, there is much disagreement over the criteria to be applied in evaluating the merits of alternative world order models. For example, one group of scholars participating in the World Order Models Project has suggested that alternative world order systems be judged in terms of how well they would promote the following four "human" values: peace, individual freedom and dignity, economic justice, and ecological balance.[4] Other people, however, might add such goals as cultural diversity, national unity, or economic efficiency. A world that is conducive to one set of values might well be detrimental to another set of values. What kind of world should we be striving for in the next few years?

Of course, one hopes that the way the world is heading happens to coincide with the direction one wishes to see it take, or that it at least can be moved in that direction. In considering what is possible and desirable, people tend to become either overly cynical and resigned to the present reality or overly optimistic and idealistic about what could be. The former are obsessed with what *is*, and are incapable of opening their minds to new possibilities; the latter are preoccupied with what *ought to be*, to the exclusion of what can practically be attained. The future is difficult to predict, precisely because it partly depends on what we want the future to look like. Within limits, humanity has the ability to shape the future, to continue or to alter the existing course.

We will now examine a number of alternative world order models. In each case, we will attempt to assess the likelihood of the world's resembling that model in the twenty-first century. We will also consider whether the model in question would necessarily represent an improvement on the current international system in terms of various values one might seek to promote.

Alternative World Order Models

THE CONTEMPORARY NATION-STATE SYSTEM

One distinct possibility in the year 2000 and beyond is that the world will look much as it does today. We have spent virtually this entire book describing the contemporary international system. As we have shown, the dominant feature of this system remains the competition between the governments of sovereign nation-states, although IGOs and other nonstate actors are part of an expanding web of human relationships that cut across state lines and complicate world politics. This is a complex system not only in terms of the congeries of actors involved in world politics but also the range of issues that concern them, with economic and other issues vying for attention with traditional military-security ones. Central guidance mechanisms remain weak despite increased interdependence and attempts at coordination.

Although the pace of change today may be so great that the least likely future is one that resembles the present, there seems to be a strong probability that—barring a nuclear holocaust or some other global cataclysm—the contemporary system will last into the next century, at least in its basic characteristics. In other words, one would expect nation-states still to be the key units of political organization in the world even if technological and other developments increasingly threaten to undermine their sovereignty. Several variants of the nation-state system are possible, though. For example, interdependence might increase to the point where efforts at regime-building become more intensified and increased regulatory power is vested in global IGOs like the United Nations or in regional IGOs. Or just the opposite might occur, as national governments seek to reduce interdependence (say, by restricting transnational activities of their citizens) and to return to a more clearly "state-centric" system. In place of the current *bimultipolar* world, one might find neater alignment patterns, possibly even a *concert of great powers* attempting to exercise a global condominium in the absence of a world government. Alternatively, if more and more states were to develop nuclear weapons, there might be a *unit veto* system in which no single state or group of states could dominate but all would be at a standoff.[5]

It is difficult to say which of these directions the nation-state system might take. Interdependence can possibly be reduced, but it cannot be undone in the modern age. It is difficult to envision a concert of great powers imposing their will on the world when some powers today already have what seem to be unparalleled means of influence at their disposal yet are failing to take advantage of it; although countries like the United States and the Soviet Union might have more leverage if they worked together, such "grand coalitions" have a way of falling apart. As for the unit veto system, if it ever did come into being, the number of fingers on the nuclear trigger suggests it would not last very long.

Normatively speaking, a unit veto system would resemble the nineteenth-century American Wild West at High Noon, with each individual living by the gun. Nationalism and cultural diversity would be preserved, but the survival of the human race might be questionable. In fact, as the quotation from Hans Morgenthau on page 529 indicates, some have questioned whether *any* variant of the nation-state system, including the contemporary system, is capable of preventing the destruction of civilization. In the words of Robert North, "One may entertain serious doubts whether the competitive, often violent nation-state system as it now exists is any longer safe for the human race."[6] Perhaps if a concert of great powers that enjoyed unchallenged power and a high degree of cohesiveness could somehow emerge, it might be able to maintain order and minimize violent conflict. However, as Robert Johansen points out, "Because such a system would be hierarchical and inequitable, it would doubtless be exploitative. It probably would not attack worldwide poverty, political repression, or ecological decay."[7] If one wishes to maximize the chances not only for peace but for other values to be realized, then maybe the only road open within the framework of a nation-state system is to continue to "muddle along," trying to strengthen regimes as much as possible through negotiation and compromise among multiple actors.

REGIONALISM

An alternative to the nation-state system is a system of regional units. Instead of more than 160 nation-states, the world's people might be organized in five or six region-states—the United States of Europe, the United States of Africa, and so forth. We noted the euphoria that surrounded the creation of the European Community in the 1950s and the predictions by some that it would not only lead to a United States of Europe but would also serve as a model for similar integration movements in other parts of the world. We noted, too, that these predictions have proved erroneous, with regional integration efforts failing in Africa and elsewhere and with the European experiment itself stalling in recent years. Still, **regionalism** remains a significant phenomenon in international relations, with regional organizations growing far more rapidly than global organizations. It is not inconceivable that sometime in the future, because of mutual security or economic concerns, national units might merge into larger regional political communities. Such regionalization is likely to be an uneven process, as the transfer of loyalty and authority to regional institutions is likely to occur in some geographical areas sooner than in others. As a world order model, regionalism would still be a decentralized system, with sovereignty residing in the individual regional units.

Would this necessarily be a better world than the present one? Since it would be a somewhat more centralized political system in which agreement would have to be reached among only a few actors rather than many, it would probably be a more manageable world in many respects. Such a system would be particularly effective in dealing with problems that are primarily regional rather than global in scope. Some have also suggested that regional units would represent "stepping stones" toward a global community and world government, or at least would be "islands of peace." There is evidence to suggest that the regional arrangements that have developed thus far, modest as they are, have helped "to control certain types of conflicts among their members and prevent them from spreading."[8] Others, however, argue that regional units would simply be nation-states writ large, with the same propensity for conflict and with far more firepower with which to pursue their interests. Conflicts that today might be confined to a relatively localized area on the world map would in a future regional system likely pit very large areas of the globe against each other, especially if leaders of regional units felt they could maintain regional cohesion only by inventing external scapegoats. As difficult as it is for many national leaders today to sustain national unity and patriotism among their people, loyalty to a regional state would be even more diluted and difficult to maintain. It is not clear, either, whether regionalism would promote values of economic justice and individual freedom.

One variation on regionalism could be increased organization among groups of less developed countries, in order to confront the superior economic or military power of industrialized states. While the precedent of OPEC does not clearly indicate that cartels of raw material suppliers can transform the international power structure, the Southern challenge to the existing global distribution of wealth is likely to become more serious as time goes on—as resources are gradually depleted, as world population trends promise an increasing Southern majority, and as more military techniques are acquired by developing countries. The availability of "cheap" Southern labor, the South as a market for Northern goods, assured Northern access to natural resources in the South, and the continued availability of military outposts in the South all will be called into question in the coming century, with the bargaining over such issues becoming more heated as the South calls for greater Northern concessions in return. Just as much in question, though, is whether the South, given its own internal divisions, is capable of becoming a truly cohesive entity with a "regional" (hemispheric) identity. Indeed, to the extent that parts of the Third World, such as the NICs, succeed in modernizing their societies and posing challenges for the North, they are likely to distance themselves from their less fortunate Southern brethren. Rather than presenting a common front against the North, the South may experience decreasing unity over time.

WORLD GOVERNMENT

Another world order model is **world government**—a political system in which one central set of institutions would preside over all human beings and political units on the planet. Several variations of this model have been contemplated. The most ambitious proposal calls for nation-states surrendering total sovereignty to a supreme global authority that would rule directly over all citizens of the world. Almost equally ambitious would be a *federation*, in which nation-states would share power and authority with a central world government; the world government would be delegated specific powers in certain areas (e.g., maintenance and deployment of armed forces) and the nation-states allowed to exercise jurisdiction over other areas (e.g., education, health care). This would resemble the model used by the Founding Fathers of the United States in creating a nation in 1787. Another possibility would be a *confederation*, in which a world government would enjoy some limited degree of power and authority but the bulk would be clearly retained by the constituent nation-state units. Still another approach to world government might be the creation of several separate global authorities in different functional areas, along the lines of the International Seabed Authority proposed at UNCLOS III.

Various model constitutions have been drafted over the years to flesh out what the elements of a world government might look like in terms of executive, legislative, and judicial organs. Among the most widely discussed plans is one by Grenville Clark and Louis Sohn who, in *World Peace Through World Law*, envisioned a permanent world police force with a monopoly on the legitimate use of force.[9] A starting point for world government might be a change in UN General Assembly voting procedures whereby each state's voting strength would be based on population or some criterion other than sovereign equality; no state would have a veto, and resolutions would be binding rather than merely advisory.

Speculating about the prospects for world government admittedly borders on science fiction. By the year 2600—the setting for *Star Trek*—humankind's sense of the universe may indeed have expanded to the point where earthlings will view each other as one people with a common destiny. However, short of a Martian invasion, the vision of a single supranational community under one roof is not likely to materialize by the year 2000.

Even if a world government were possible, though, would it necessarily be a panacea for all our problems? It is true that a centralized system would facilitate a more concerted global effort to deal with environmental problems; it would be less possible, for example, for states to offer themselves to multinational corporations as "pollution havens" where few environmental regulations were enforced (as Brazil and some other countries now do to attract foreign industry). Such a system might also allow for a more equitable distribution of wealth, although probably at the expense of some individuals and states that are now in a privileged position. There is serious question whether such a system would promote freedom and democracy. Who would determine the nature of the political institutions? Where would the "capital" be located? There are complaints today that even in a democracy like the United States the average person has little access to the decision-making centers of power. One would imagine the problem would be greatly magnified with a world government. A world government would be in a better position to enforce the Universal Declaration of Human Rights than the United Nations is today, since national governments that practice repression could not then invoke sovereign privileges against foreign interference in their internal affairs; yet some of the same governments might be the ones controlling the world government and defining the nature of the "rights" enjoyed by Americans and other peoples.

The one value that a world government would most likely maximize, according to conventional wisdom, is peace. However, just as central governments of nation-states today are often incapable of preventing the outbreak of large-scale domestic violence and civil war, there is no reason to assume that a world government could necessarily keep its house in order. In fact, some have suggested that the more "amalgamated" a political community is (in terms of having a common set of governmental institutions), the more prone it can be to instability and disintegration; instead, it might be better to work toward a "pluralistic" community with constituent units sharing common values and interests but not necessarily tied together under one government.[10]

POLIS

Regionalism and world government models are based on increased centralization of the global political system. However, another possibility is increased *decentralization*, with political life on the planet revolving around even smaller and more fragmented units than the present nation-states. It is estimated that there are as many as 1500 distinct nationality or ethnic groups in the world. Potentially, each might form its own state. Or smaller units might be based not on common ethnicity but on the special needs of local populations. The attempts by the "flower children" in the United States during the 1960s to form relatively isolated, self-sufficient communes represented a desire to "drop out" from both a nation and a world that seemed alien to them. Although most observers have commented on the trend toward growing centralization of decision making in the world, some have noticed a countertrend. Jackson Davis has noted that

> in the recent past, local governments in the United States have grown faster than the federal government in terms of budget. . . . A trend toward decentralization is not confined to the United States, nor even to industrial nations; rather, it is global in scope. If continued, trends such as these could culminate eventually in a confederacy of small, relatively autonomous local governments, perhaps coordinated and represented internationally by central governments that are vastly reduced from today's unwieldy bureaucracies.[11]

Although a world order system made up of subnational local entities as the dominant political units is conceivable, it seems at least as unlikely as world government. The world might be organized in communes after a nuclear war, as Jonathan Schell has suggested in *The Fate of the Earth*.[12] Otherwise, it would seem a utopian idea. As a utopian model, one can again ask whether it would necessarily be an improvement on the current system or any of the other alternative world order models that have been mentioned. Those who believe greater decentralization would be a positive development include

"New Left" thinkers who seek greater democracy in the workplace and in other areas, as well as some "limits to growth" thinkers who urge a "small is beautiful" approach to life. The common thread is a concern that the world has become too big and complicated for individuals to relate meaningfully to it, and a resultant desire to return to smaller "human-scale" communities—along the lines of the ancient Greek city-states, which stressed the concept of **polis.**

Although such decentralization might well maximize individual freedom, democracy, and economic justice, some central guidance mechanism would still be needed to address global issues such as ecological problems that are not likely to disappear from the planet. Traditional security concerns would also have to be addressed somehow. The specter of Peoria, Poughkeepsie, and Portland saber rattling with nuclear weapons is hardly any more reassuring than the likes of the United States and the Soviet Union doing it. Given the nature of the problems we have discussed in this book, a "stop the world, I want to get off" approach does not seem appropriate. Some degree of decentralization might be both possible and desirable, but only within limits.

OTHER WORLD ORDER MODELS

All the models we have discussed here tend to assume a *territorial* basis for human organization. Even world government models generally assume that, in addition to a global orientation, people will retain some degree of identity with smaller territorial units, be they regional, national, or subnational. However, other futures are conceivable. Indeed, we noted in Chapter 13 that some observers—world system theorists—already see the world organized around nonterritorial principles, with transnational economic elites and the pursuit of corporate interests overshadowing national governments and the pursuit of national interests. Although world system theorists seem to underestimate the forces of nationalism, it is possible that at some time in the future, if the multinational corporation phenomenon continues to grow, the world political map might consist of units defined more by corporate logos than geographical boundaries. For this to occur, though, present trends of economic nationalism would have to be reversed and the MNC would have to extend its tentacles into communist systems. Howard Perlmutter has sketched what the "emerging global industrial system" might look like, complete with a global central bank and tax and patent authority, world annual reports, global universities, and a global telecommunications system.[13] In this world society, human beings would be primarily employees and managers of MNCs rather than citizens of nation-states. The General Motors auto worker in St. Louis would feel a greater bond of community with his fellow GM worker in Brazil than with his next-door neighbor employed by Ford Motors.

Alternatively, the world might be organized along Marxist lines, with corporations and other vestiges of capitalism removed and replaced by communist institutions. The kind of classless and stateless world society envisioned by Karl Marx, however, seems even more remote from reality than the MNC-centered world pondered by Perlmutter.

In a variety of ways the future world system could be based on "networks" of nongovernmental organizations. Today various groups around the world—not only MNCs and terrorist organizations—already meet and communicate over the heads of or underground from national governments. For example, networks today address the status of women in many different countries. During International Women's Year in 1975, which followed a World Conference of Women held in Mexico City, an International Feminists Network was formed in Brussels to emphasize person-to-person contacts. With the development of instantaneous telecommunications and computer terminal networks, it is becoming increasingly feasible to bring people from remote parts of the globe into direct contact.

The problem with such world society scenarios is that even though *government* of some sort would still be needed, it is not clear how it would function. It is also not clear what the implications of these scenarios would be for various world order values. In an MNC-centered world, for example, although there would seemingly be less international conflict as we know it, there might be intensified transnational class conflict. Although the drive for profit maximization would presumably contribute to economic growth and some economic efficiencies, concerns about economic justice and environmental protection would probably suffer. To paraphrase an old slogan, what is good for General Motors might not necessarily be good for the world.

Toward the Year 2000: Onward and Upward

There is little doubt that space-age technology will be changing our lives in many ways that will go far beyond microwave ovens and home computers, and that along with improvements in the human condition will also come new, unforeseeable problems. Looking ahead to the twenty-first century, in addition to these unforeseeable problems, we can expect older, more familiar problems to remain on the global agenda. In compiling his "agenda for the twenty-first century," Robert McNamara has listed as the top two concerns the "threat of nuclear war" and the "imbalance of population growth rates on the one hand and social and economic rates of advance on the other"; he also lists as major concerns the tensions associated with the East-West conflict, the decay of traditional democratic and moral values, and the need for new global institution-building.[14]

This leads us back to our discussion of alternative world order models. All the alternative world order models we have discussed have potential drawbacks. There are no obvious solutions to the human predicament that are both ideally perfect and realistically attainable. It may be that the *present* system, with some tinkering here and there (centralizing some aspects and decentralizing others), could be the best of all possible worlds. We do not want to engage in false optimism, especially given all the global problems we have noted. However, there is reason to be cautiously hopeful. In a world where several human beings have landed on the moon and—perhaps more amazingly—Soviet and Western astronauts have "broken bread" together and dined on creamed crab in a joint space voyage, we do not want to sell future possibilities short.[15] Just as certain centuries-old human institutions once thought unchangeable have been changed for the better—for example, the virtual eradication of slavery—other deeply embedded human institutions, such as war, might also become relics of the past. The seemingly impossible occasionally does happen.

At the outset of this book, we distinguished between the differing perspectives of policymakers, scholars, and laymen as observers of international relations. Policymakers and laymen will probably continue to be preoccupied with more immediate, less philosophical and theoretical matters than the futuristic issues discussed above, leaving scholars to ponder the long term. Nevertheless, rather than asking "What has posterity ever done for me?"[16] *all* of us could accept some responsibility for the future world we bequeath to tomorrow's children. For policymakers and laymen, no less than scholars, the starting point in working toward a better world is *understanding* how the world works—overcoming the ignorance that blinds people both to the seriousness of recent developments and to the vision of future possibilities.

As the year 2000 approaches, the current generation is faced with entering not only a new century but a new *millennium.* No generation will experience such a moment for another thousand years. As the last years of the twentieth century tick away, then, this would seem as good a time as any to pause and reflect upon the global condition and what might be done to improve it. More than ever, the future is now.

SUGGESTIONS FOR FURTHER READING AND STUDY

An excellent general work on futurism as a field of study is *Political Science and the Study of the Future,* a collection of articles edited by Albert Somit (Hinsdale, Ill.: Dryden Press, 1974). Also worthwhile are Willis W. Harmon, *An Incomplete Guide to the Future* (New York: W. W. Norton, 1979); Daniel Bell, "The Study of the Future," *The Public Interest,* I (Fall 1965), pp. 119–130; and John Platt, "How Men Can Shape Their Futures," *Futures* (March 1971). On the problems of predicting events in international relations, see Nazli Choucri and Thomas Robinson, *Forecasting and*

International Relations: Theory, Methods, Problems, Prospects (San Francisco: W. H. Freeman, 1977).

Among the scholarly works that offer a negative view of the world's future, perhaps the most gloomy is Robert Heilbroner's *An Inquiry into the Human Prospect* (New York: W. W. Norton, 1975); the work that most clearly addresses the issue of human extinction is Jonathan Schell's *The Fate of the Earth* (New York: Knopf, 1982). Also see Gerald Barney, *The Global 2000 Report to the President of the United States: Entering the 21st Century*, vol. 1 (New York: Pergamon, 1980). Guardedly optimistic views of the future that foresee the need for fundamental changes in world order can be found in L. S. Stavrianos, *The Promise of the Coming Dark Age* (San Francisco: W. H. Freeman, 1976); W. Jackson Davis, *The Seventh Year: Industrial Civilization in Transition* (New York: W. W. Norton, 1979); Robert C. North, *The World That Could Be* (New York: W. W. Norton, 1976); Gerald and Patricia Miche, *Toward a Human World Order* (New York: Paulist Press, 1977); and W. Warren Wagar, *Building the City of Man* (San Francisco: W. H. Freeman, 1971).

Among those scholars who have been optimistic about recent trends and foresee little need to alter course are most notably Herman Kahn and Julian Simon. See Kahn et al., *The Next Two Hundred Years* (New York: Morrow, 1976); Kahn, *The Coming Boom* (New York: Simon and Schuster, 1982); Simon, *The Ultimate Resource* (Princeton, N.J.: Princeton University Press, 1982); and Kahn and Simon, eds, *The Resourceful Earth: A Response to Global 2000* (Oxford: Basil Blackwell, 1984). Another work that argues that the nation-state system is here to stay and that we might as well make the best of it is David Fromkin, *The Independence of Nations* (New York: Praeger, 1981).

Special attention to normative concerns from a "globalist" perspective can be found in the World Order Models Project series, in such works as Richard A. Falk, *A Study of Future Worlds* (New York: Free Press, 1975); Rajni Kothari, *Footsteps into the Future* (New York: Free Press, 1974); and Samuel S. Kim, *The Quest for a Just World Order* (Boulder, Colo.: Westview Press, 1983). Robert J. Johansen examines the normative implications of different directions American foreign policy might take in the future, comparing traditional "national interest" concerns with "human interest" concerns, in *The National Interest and Human Interest* (Princeton, N.J.: Princeton University Press, 1980). A critique of the WOMP project is provided by Tom J. Farer in "The Greening of the Globe: A Preliminary Appraisal of the World Order Models Project," *International Organization*, 31 (Winter 1977), pp. 129–147. Also see Barry B. Hughes, *World Futures: A Critical Analysis of Alternatives* (Baltimore: Johns Hopkins University Press, 1985).

Novels that offer fictitious accounts of future societies, either utopias or dystopias, include the following: George Orwell, *1984* (New York: Harcourt, Brace, 1949); Ernest Callenbach, *Ectotopia* (New York: Bantam, 1975); H. G. Wells, *A Modern Utopia* (1905; reprint, Lincoln: University of Nebraska Press, 1967); and Cecilia Holland, *Floating Worlds* (New York: Knopf, 1976). See also *International Relations Through Science Fiction*, Martin Harry Greenberg and Joseph D. Olander, eds. (New York: Franklin Watts, 1978); and Dennis Livingston, "Science Fiction Modes of Future World Order Systems," *International Organization*, 25 (Spring 1971), pp. 254–270. Additional articles on world futures can be found in the journal *Alternative Futures* as well as in publications of the Institute of World Order, 777 United Nations Plaza, New York, NY 10017.

Notes

Chapter 1.   The Study of International Relations, or Getting a Handle on the World

1. Based on CBS Evening News and KMOX-TV newscasts on August 25, 1980.
2. For example, see George F. Brown and Lester R. Silverman, *The Retail Price of Heroin: Estimation and Applications* (Washington, D.C.: Drug Abuse Council, 1973), ch. 4; also, Roger D. Blair and Ronald J. Vogel, "Heroin Addiction and Urban Crime," *Public Finance Quarterly*, 1 (October 1974), pp. 457–466.
3. *The Defense Monitor*, XI (Washington, D.C.: Center for Defense Information, 1982), p. 3. In the 1980s, the Soviet Union competed closely with the United States as the leading arms exporter in the world.
4. Stephen H. Schneider, *The Genesis Strategy* (New York: Plenum Press, 1976), pp. 5–9.
5. Stephen K. Bailey, "Education in the Public Interest," *Public Administration Review*, (November/December 1976), p. 678. The reference to "global village" is from McLuhan's *Understanding Media: The Extension of Man* (New York: McGraw-Hill, 1965), p. 93; the reference to "Spaceship Earth" is from Ward's *The Lopsided World* (New York: W. W. Norton, 1968), p. 26.
6. "Only About Half of Public Knows U.S. Has to Import Oil, Gallup Survey Shows," *New York Times*, June 2, 1977. A 1981 study showed that even in the early 1980s, half of the American people still felt the United States was basically self-sufficient in oil and another 13 percent were not sure. *The Emerging Consensus: Public Attitudes on America's Ability to Compete in the World* (New York: Cambridge Reports, 1981), p. 24.
7. Sheldon Appleton, *United States Foreign Policy* (Boston: Little, Brown, 1968), p. 280.
8. See the 1981 Washington Post–ABC News poll, reported in *Interdependent*, 7 (November 1981), p. 1; also, the 1983 CBS News–New York Times poll cited in *National Journal* (August 8, 1983), p. 1658; and the 1987 Overseas Development Council poll cited in *Interdependent*, 13 (April/May 1987), p. 1.
9. Moreover, even on those occasions when there is widespread interest in an issue—such as the Panama Canal Treaties debate in the seventies—the public still remains largely uninformed. A Gallup Poll during the 1978 debate showed that, even among those who followed the debate, only 25 percent were able to answer correctly some key substantive questions about the Canal. *The Gallup Opinion Index*, Report #153 (April, 1978). For a general discussion of the American public's level of knowledge about international affairs, see Barry B. Hughes, *The Domestic Context of American Foreign Policy* (San Francisco: W. H. Freeman, 1978), chs. 2 and 4; and Charles W. Kegley and Eugene R. Wittkopf, *American Foreign Policy: Pattern and Process*, 2nd ed. (New York: St. Martin's Press, 1982), ch. 8.
10. See Ronald Inglehart and J. R. Rabier, "Europe Elects a Parliament: Cognitive Mobilization," *Government and Opposition*, 14 (Autumn 1979), pp. 478–507; "Information on the European Community," *Euro-Barometre*, July 1978, pp. 17–20; and *Euro-Barometre*, May 1979, pp. 3–6.
11. *Webster's Third New International Dictionary* (Springfield, Mass.: G. and C. Merriam Co., 1968), p. 1181.

12. James N. Rosenau, ed., *International Politics and Foreign Policy*, rev. ed. (New York: Free Press, 1969), p. 1.

13. *Ibid.*, pp. 1–29.

14. The various categories of "nonstate" actors will be discussed in the last section of the book.

15. Harold D. Lasswell, *Politics: Who Gets What, When, How?* (Cleveland: World Publishing, 1958).

16. John Stoessinger, *The Might of Nations*, 7th ed. (New York: Random House, 1982), p. 5. Of course, similar struggles go on *within* nations as well, particularly in many less developed countries in Africa, Asia, and elsewhere, where such conflicts can be every bit as violent as conflicts between nations. The main point here, however, is that within nations central authoritative institutions do exist, however weakly they may actually function in many instances. For a discussion comparing the stability of international and intranational politics, see Fred W. Riggs, "International Relations as a Prismatic System," *World Politics*, 14 (October 1961), pp. 141–181. Also, see Hedley Bull, *The Anarchical Society* (New York: Columbia University Press, 1977).

17. There has been debate in the international relations field over the question of whether or not interdependence has in fact been increasing. A few scholars (such as Kenneth Waltz) argue that it has actually been *decreasing*, while others (such as Edward Morse, Richard Rosecrance, and Arthur Stein) argue that there is at least contradictory evidence to be found and that the phenomenon is more complex than commonly conceived. See Kenneth N. Waltz, "The Myth of National Interdependence," in *The International Corporation: A Symposium*, Charles P. Kindleberger, ed. (Cambridge, Mass.: M.I.T. Press, 1970), pp. 205–223; Edward L. Morse, "Interdependence in World Affairs," in *World Politics*, James N. Rosenau, Kenneth W. Thompson, and Gavin Boyd, eds. (New York: Free Press, 1976), pp. 660–681; and Richard N. Rosecrance and Arthur Stein, "Interdependence: Myth or Reality?" *World Politics*, 26 (October 1973), pp. 1–27. We will discuss the various arguments and evidence in detail in later chapters. Suffice it to say at this point that the weight of the evidence would seem to justify the minimal assertion that "we live in an era of interdependence." Robert O. Keohane and Joseph S. Nye, *Power and Interdependence* (Boston: Little, Brown, 1977), p. 3.

18. Robert C. Angell, *Peace on the March: Transnational Participation* (New York: Van Nostrand Reinhold, 1969).

19. Lester R. Brown, *World Without Borders* (New York: Vintage, 1972).

20. The concept of international "regimes" was introduced by Robert O. Keohane and Joseph S. Nye. They define regimes as "governing arrangements" among nation-states. See Keohane and Nye, *op. cit.*, p. 5.

21. For an elaborate discussion of the meaning of the term, see Thomas S. Kuhn, *The Structure of Scientific Revolution* (Chicago: University of Chicago Press, 1962).

22. See J. Martin Rochester, "The Paradigm Debate in International Relations and Its Implications for Foreign Policy Making," *Western Political Quarterly*, 31 (March 1978), pp. 48–58.

23. Dante Alighieri, *On World Government*, trans. Herbert W. Schneider, 2nd rev. ed. (New York: Liberal Arts Press, 1957).

24. Albert Fried, ed., *A Day of Dedication: The Essential Writings and Speeches of Woodrow Wilson* (New York: Macmillan, 1965).

25. R. S. Baker, *Woodrow Wilson and World Settlement* (Gloucester, Mass.: P. Smith, 1922), p. 93. Wilson's statement also points to a seedier side of idealism, i.e., the sometimes fanatical missionary zeal with which idealists attempt to reform the world, even to the point of producing the very conflict they ostensibly seek to avoid. Wilson's own "messianic liberalism" is discussed in Alexander L. George and Juliette George, *Woodrow Wilson and Colonel House* (New York: John Day, 1956).

26. E. H. Carr, *The Twenty Years' Crisis, 1919–1939* (London: Macmillan, 1939).

27. Hans J. Morgenthau, *Politics Among Nations* (New York: Knopf, 1948). Other "realist" works include George F. Kennan, *American Diplomacy, 1900–1950* (Chicago: University of Chicago Press, 1951); Arnold Wolfers, *Discord and Collaboration* (Baltimore: Johns Hopkins University

Press, 1962); and Henry A. Kissinger, *American Foreign Policy: Three Essays* (New York: W. W. Norton, 1969).

28. See, for example, Robert G. Gilpin, *War and Change in World Politics* (Cambridge: Cambridge University Press, 1981). For a general discussion of neorealism, see Robert O. Keohane, ed., *Neorealism and Its Critics* (New York: Columbia University Press, 1986).

29. See Keohane and Nye, *op. cit.*; Richard W. Mansbach, Yale G. Ferguson, and Donald E. Lampert, *The Web of World Politics: Nonstate Actors in the Global System* (Englewood Cliffs, N.J.: Prentice-Hall, 1976); and Edward L. Morse, *Modernization and the Transformation of International Relations* (New York: Free Press, 1976). A variation of the "globalist" paradigm is the "world society" approach, as represented by John W. Burton, *World Society* (Cambridge: Cambridge University Press, 1972).

30. Robert O. Keohane and Joseph S. Nye, eds., *Transnational Relations and World Politics* (Cambridge, Mass.: Harvard University Press, 1971). Among the precursors of the globalists was John Herz, who in the 1950s already pointed to the increased "permeability" of national boundaries and envisioned the "demise of the territorial state," although he later had second thoughts about the latter prediction. See John Herz, *International Politics in the Atomic Age* (New York: Columbia University Press, 1959).

31. Realists acknowledge the existence of actors other than the nation-state but consider them to be relatively peripheral to international politics. See Wolfers, *op. cit.*, pp. 3–24.

32. For an excellent discussion of methodological issues, see Klaus Knorr and James N. Rosenau, eds., *Contending Approaches to International Politics* (Princeton, N.J.: Princeton University Press, 1969). For a discussion of both methodological and paradigmatic issues, see James E. Dougherty and Robert L. Pfaltzgraff, *Contending Theories of International Relations*, 2nd ed. (New York: Harper and Row, 1981).

33. A few scholars, such as Quincy Wright, used behavioralist approaches well before the 1960s, but it was only in the latter part of that decade that the behavioralist tide swept the discipline. See Quincy Wright, *A Study of War*, vols. 1 and 2 (Chicago: University of Chicago Press, 1942).

34. Some behavioralists like Deutsch urged *both* "quantitative" and "qualitative" analysis, while others like Singer were more unequivocal in their criticism of traditional approaches and in their use of quantitative techniques. See, for example, Karl W. Deutsch, "Toward an Inventory of Basic Trends and Patterns in Comparative and International Politics," *American Political Science Review*, 54 (March 1960), pp. 34–57; J. David Singer, "The Behavioral Science Approach to International Relations: Payoff and Prospect," *SAIS Review*, 10 (Summer 1966), pp. 12–20; and James N. Rosenau, *The Scientific Study of Foreign Policy* (New York: Free Press, 1971).

35. Even though Hans Morgenthau's work has been called "the first 'scientific' treatment of world politics," in the sense that he did attempt to develop an explicit empirical theory, his methods were still essentially traditionalist ones. See Stanley Hoffmann, "An American Social Science: International Relations," *Daedalus*, 106 (Summer 1977), p. 43.

36. The continued hold that realist thought has had since World War II in determining the research topics and agendas of even the most ardent of "scientific" international relations scholars is demonstrated by William D. Coplin *et al.* in "Color It Morgenthau: A Data-Based Assessment of Quantitative International Relations Research," paper presented at the Annual Meeting of the International Studies Association, New York, 1973.

37. Charles A. McClelland, "International Relations: Wisdom or Science?," in James N. Rosenau, ed., *International Politics and Foreign Policy*, rev. ed. (New York: Free Press, 1969), p. 4.

38. See Benjamin Jowett, trans., *The Republic of Plato*, 4th ed. (Fair Lawn, N.J.: Oxford University Press, 1953); Niccolo Machiavelli, *The Prince*, T. G. Bergin, trans. and ed. (New York: Appleton-Century-Crofts, 1947).

39. For a discussion of the relationship between the scholarly community and the policymaking community, see Raymond Tanter and Richard H. Ullman eds., *Theory and Policy in International Relations* (Princeton, N.J.: Princeton University Press, 1972); of particular

interest is the article by Allen S. Whiting entitled "The Scholar and the Policy-Maker," pp. 229–247.

40. Much of this discussion owes a debt to William Coplin. See William D. Coplin and Charles W. Kegley, eds., *A Multi-Method Introduction to International Politics* (Chicago: Markham Publishing, 1971). The discussion also relates to the taxonomy of cognitive skills developed by Benjamin S. Bloom *et al.*, *Taxonomy of Educational Objectives, Handbook I: Cognitive Domain* (New York: McKay, 1956). The latter suggests that there is a certain hierarchy of skills that build on each other, ranging from the most basic skill of factual literacy to more sophisticated skills that include comprehension and ultimately evaluation and application. In our scheme of things in this section, factual literacy is roughly related to description, comprehension to what we call explanation, evaluation to what we call normative analysis, and application to what we call prescription.

41. A country's per capita gross national product equals its gross national product (i.e., the total value of all goods and services produced in the national economy over a given time period) divided by its total population. The distribution of wealth in the world is skewed by the fact that two countries—China and India, with a PGNP of $300 and $260 respectively—together constitute roughly one third of humanity. It should be added that PGNP is only one of several indicators that one might use to measure national wealth. The data were obtained from the *World Bank Atlas, 1986* (Washington, D.C.: World Bank, 1986), pp. 16–17.

Chapter 2.   A Glimpse Into the Past: The Historical Development of the International System

1. Barbara W. Tuchman, "Is This the Summer of 1914?" *Washington Post*, May 11, 1980, p. C–7. It should be noted that Tuchman has often strayed into the *déjà vu* school, most recently in *A Distant Mirror* (New York: Knopf, 1978), where she draws a sweeping parallel between the economic dislocation and political chaos of the fourteenth century and the troubles of the twentieth century.
2. Alvin Toffler, *Future Shock* (New York: Bantam Books, 1970), p. 17
3. Kenneth N. Waltz, *Theory of International Politics* (Reading, Mass.: Addison-Wesley, 1979), pp. 65–66.
4. George Santayana, *Life of Reason,* I (New York: Scribner's, 1954), p. 12. A more extreme version of this *déjà vu* view was offered by the historian Crane Brinton, who once remarked that "while those who do not know history are bound to repeat it, those who know it are bound to repeat it as well." Cited in Jagdish Bhagwati, "Economics and World Order from the 1970s to the 1990s: The Key Issues," in *Economics and World Order*, J. Bhagwati, ed. (London: Macmillan, 1972), p. 4.
5. F. S. Northedge and M. J. Grieve, *A Hundred Years of International Relations* (New York: Praeger, 1971), p. 351. On the general theme of continuity and change in international relations, see George Liska, "Continuity and Change in International Systems," *World Politics*, 16 (October 1963), pp. 118–136.
6. For example, Morton Kaplan suggests the international system has changed only once since the seventeenth century, that being after World War II. William Coplin and K. J. Holsti suggest there have been two major changes, one coming at the beginning of the nineteenth century and the other in 1945 after World War II. Evan Luard likewise notes two major changes but lists the dates as 1789 and 1914. Richard Rosecrance has identified nine different "system-periods" between the mid-eighteenth century and the mid-twentieth century. Geoffrey Barraclough argues that the period between 1890 and 1960 was a key transition period between the "modern" era and the "contemporary" era of world affairs. See Morton A. Kaplan, *System and Process in International Politics*, science ed. (New York: John Wiley, 1964); William D. Coplin, *Introduction to International Politics*, 3rd ed. (Englewood Cliffs, N.J.: Prentice-Hall, 1980), pp. 23–52; K. J. Holsti, *International Politics: A Framework for*

Analysis, 4th ed. (Englewood Cliffs, N.J.: Prentice-Hall, 1983), pp. 57–94; Richard Rosecrance, *Action and Reaction in World Politics* (Boston: Little, Brown, 1963); Geoffrey Barraclough, *An Introduction to Contemporary History* (Baltimore: Penguin Books, 1967), ch. 1; and Evan Luard, *Types of International Society* (New York: Free Press, 1976).

7. Coplin, *op. cit.;* Holsti, *op. cit.* These authors, however, do not cite 1973 as a watershed year.

8. The concept of "interconnectedness" as one aspect of interdependence is discussed by Alex Inkeles in "The Emerging Social Structure of the World," *World Politics,* 27 (July, 1975), pp. 468–495. The concept of "mutual sensitivity and vulnerability" as another aspect of interdependence is discussed by Keohane and Nye, *Power and Interdependence,* pp. 8–22. Other "properties" of the international system can be identified. For a discussion of some of the difficult conceptual problems involved in defining what an "international system" is and in distinguishing between different international systems, see Dina A. Zinnes, "Prerequisites for the Study of System Transformation," in Ole R. Holsti *et al.,* eds., *Change in the International System* (Boulder, Colo.: Westview Press, 1980), pp. 3–21.

9. Trends toward "universalism" and "particularism" are discussed in Mansbach *et al., The Web of World Politics,* ch. 1. For a survey of various historical state systems, including the city-state systems of Ancient Greece and Renaissance Italy, see Martin Wight, *Systems of States* (London: Leicester University Press, 1977).

10. Some monarchs were more assertive of their authority than others, notably Elizabeth I of England, who warned "my dogs shall wear no collars but mine own." Still, all monarchs encountered difficulty in enforcing their will. England actually possessed many attributes of a territorial state as early as 1400.

11. For a discussion of the feudal era and the emergence of nation-states, see C. J. H. Hayes, *The Historical Evolution of Modern Nationalism* (New York: Macmillan, 1948).

12. For a detailed discussion of how the "balance of power" operated in the seventeenth and eighteenth centuries, see John B. Wolf, *Louis XIV* (New York: W. W. Norton, 1968). The "balance of power" notion was not identified solely with the classical era but was to be applied also to international politics in subsequent eras as well.

13. The conceptual problems surrounding the term "balance of power" are discussed by Ernst Haas in "The Balance of Power: Prescription, Concept, or Propaganda?" *World Politics,* 5 (July 1953), pp. 442–477; and by Dina A. Zinnes, "An Analytical Study of the Balance of Power Theories," *Journal of Peace Research,* 4 (1967), pp. 270–288.

14. The term "prismatic" was used originally by Fred Riggs to describe developing *countries* that were passing through an intermediate stage from traditional to modern societies in which old and new cultures collided. See Fred W. Riggs, *Administration in Developing Countries: The Theory of Prismatic Society* (Boston: Houghton Mifflin, 1964).

15. "Universal adult suffrage" (at least among males) was not to be achieved in most European countries until the late nineteenth and early twentieth centuries, while in many other countries voting was rendered meaningless by either the persistence of monarchical rule or the emergence of "one-party" regimes.

16. Lester R. Brown, *The Twenty-Ninth Day* (New York: W. W. Norton, 1978), ch. 8. It should be added that there were a few exceptions to the concentration of poverty in the Southern Hemisphere, notably Australia and South Africa. For a discussion of the historical development of the rich-poor gap, see Patrick J. McGowan, "Imperialism in World-System Perspective," *International Studies Quarterly,* 25 (March 1981), pp. 45–46.

17. Waltz's listing in Table 2.1 conforms roughly to the listings compiled by many other scholars. See J. David Singer, ed., *The Correlates of War I* (New York: Free Press, 1979), p. 241; and Charles F. Doran and Wes Parsons, "War and the Cycle of Relative Power," *American Political Science Review,* 74 (December 1980), p. 953.

18. Barraclough, *op. cit.,* pp. 110–111. See Barraclough, chs. 2–5, for general historical background on political, economic, and social trends affecting international relations during the nineteenth and early twentieth centuries.

19. Many observers had anticipated the emergence of the United States and Russia as "super-

powers" well before 1945. As early as 1835, Alexis de Tocqueville had written that "there are, at the present time, two great nations in the world which seem to tend toward the same end. . . . I allude to the Russians and the Americans . . . each of which seems to be marked out . . . to sway the destinies of half the globe." *Democracy in America*, part I, Henry Reeve, trans. (New York: J. H. G. Langley, 1841), pp. 470–471. Likewise, Sir John Seeley noted in 1883 that the United States and Russia were "enormous political aggregations" that would eventually "completely dwarf such European states as France and Germany and depress them into a second class." Cited in Richard J. Barnet, *The Giants* (New York: Simon and Schuster, 1977), p. 14.

20. Mass democracy in countries such as England and France meant that the public had to be consulted or at least mobilized in support of foreign policy decisions; the new military technology meant that alliances had to be more institutionalized and defense planning among allies more coordinated. Despite the rigidity that these elements tended to introduce, Britain was almost prepared to ally with Germany at "the eleventh hour" in 1914. See Northedge and Grieve, *op. cit.*, ch. 5.

21. For a discussion of the new military technology, see David W. Ziegler, *War, Peace, and International Politics* (Boston: Little, Brown, 1979), pp. 14–16.

22. "[Of 1,300,000 French troops initially put into combat] they suffered in August 1914 alone 600,000 casualties. . . . On one day alone, July 1, 1916, the British attacked with 140,000 troops and suffered 60,000 casualties. On another occasion it cost the French 160,000 casualties to gain 7000 yards. At Passchendaele it cost the British 370,000 casualties for no gain at all." *Ibid.*, p. 21.

23. It is estimated that a total of 30 million combatants and civilians died in World War I, while twice as many died during World War II.

24. As noted by Hornell Hart, "In 1944 [the 'killing area' within which people could be killed from a given base] . . . surpassed the size of the largest governing area ever attained. . . . The development of refueling in the air . . . [has] extended the potential killing radius to globe-encircling dimensions." Hornell Hart, "The Hypothesis of Cultural Lag," in Francis R. Allen *et al.*, *Technology and Social Change* (New York: Appleton-Century-Crofts, 1957), p. 428.

25. Waltz especially stresses the fact that the two major powers in the post–World War II era—the United States and the Soviet Union—had little to do with each other economically, compared with the intricate economic ties that the European powers had in the late nineteenth and early twentieth centuries. See Waltz, *op. cit.*, pp. 138–160.

26. Asa Briggs, "The World Economy: Interdependence and Planning," in C. L. Mowat, ed., *The New Cambridge Modern History*, vol. 12 (Cambridge: Cambridge University Press, 1968); cited in Waltz, *op. cit.*, p. 140.

27. Erich Marcks, *Männer und Zeiten* (Leipzig, 1911); cited in Barraclough, *op. cit.*, p. 53.

28. For trends in world trade, see Simon Kuznets, *Modern Economic Growth* (New Haven, Conn.: Yale University Press, 1966), pp. 306–307. Several analysts have pointed out the misleading nature of using "trade as percentage of GNP" as an indicator of interdependence. See, for example, Edward L. Morse, "Transnational Economic Processes," in *Transnational Relations and World Politics*, Robert O. Keohane and Joseph S. Nye, eds. (Cambridge, Mass.: Harvard University Press, 1970), pp. 23–47.

29. Although the number of people *immigrating* to one country from another never again reached the high pre–World War I levels (due to stricter immigration barriers imposed by governments), the number of people *traveling* across national boundaries increased enormously after World War II (as personal mobility was increased by improved transportation technology). For data on these and other trends related to interdependence, see Morse, *op. cit.*, as well as Rosecrance and Stein, *op. cit.*, and Inkeles, *op. cit.* Inkeles notes that "recent decades reveal a general tendency for many forms of human interconnectedness across national boundaries to be doubling every ten years." *Ibid.*, p. 479.

30. Although it was not until much later, well into the post–World War II era, that Jean-Jacques Servan-Schreiber was to write *The American Challenge*, in which he warned of the challenges

posed by American corporations establishing marketing and manufacturing facilities through-out Western Europe, F. A. MacKenzie had anticipated the scale of the MNC phenomenon as early as 1902 in his *The American Invaders* (London: Oxford, 1902).

31. We will discuss these different types of international organizations in Chapter 10.

32. As Inis Claude suggests, the Hague Conferences of 1899 and 1907, convened to discuss ways of settling disputes peacefully, symbolized the shifting nature of the international system at the turn of the century: "Whereas the first conference was attended by only twenty-six states and was preponderantly European in composition, the second involved representatives of forty-four states, including the bulk of the Latin American republics [as well as Asian states]." Inis L. Claude, *Swords into Plowshares*, 4th ed. (New York: Random House, 1971), p. 29.

33. Barbara Ward, *The Lopsided World* (New York: W. W. Norton, 1968).

34. For a discussion of the impact of nuclear weapons on various aspects of world politics, see Michael Mandelbaum, *The Nuclear Revolution: International Politics Before and After Hiroshima* (New York: Cambridge University Press, 1981). For an unconventional view, which argues that the effects of nuclear weapons on world politics have been exaggerated, see A. F. K. Organski, *World Politics*, 2nd ed. (New York: Knopf, 1968), pp. 313–335.

35. The United States actually enjoyed an atomic monopoly until 1949, when the Soviet Union acquired its first atomic weapons and along with the United States developed massive military superiority in the international system.

36. Charles W. Maynes and Richard H. Ullman, "Ten Years of Foreign Policy," *Foreign Policy*, Fall 1980, p. 5.

37. Much of our discussion of the origins and dynamics of the East-West conflict and the rivalry between the United States and the Soviet Union is left to Chapter 4, where we focus in detail on the foreign policy behavior of these two countries over the years. Also in Chapter 4, we will examine China's foreign policy behavior and note how it gradually gravitated out of the Soviet orbit during the 1960s and 1970s and moved more closely toward the United States. We also examine India's behavior as a leader of the "nonaligned" movement.

38. The United States helped to launch the postwar independence boom by granting the Philippines independence on July 4, 1946. Fifteen new nations, almost entirely in the Middle East and Asia, came into being between 1945 and 1955. The big wave of independence, however, was to occur in the 1960s, when forty-four states (including seventeen in 1960 alone), mostly in sub-Saharan Africa, were created.

39. Soviet territorial annexation ceased with the absorption of Estonia, Lithuania, and Latvia at the very end of World War II. While territorial issues were not important to the superpowers, they were still of concern to other lesser states (e.g., the disputes between Morocco, Mauritania, and Algeria over the Spanish Sahara, between Argentina and Chile over the Beagle Channel and other border areas, and between Israel and various Arab states over lands controlled by Israel following its achieving statehood).

40. The Suez crisis was sparked when Egypt's President Nasser seized the Suez Canal from the British, who had administered the Egyptian waterway since the nineteenth century. The British responded by launching air attacks to recapture the Canal, joined by the French, who were angered by Nasser's assistance to Algeria in the latter's struggle for independence, and by the Israelis, who were concerned about threats posed by Nasser to Israeli shipping and other interests. The United States and Soviet Union joined with Canada and others to organize a United Nations peacekeeping force, which helped to defuse the crisis. On the Suez crisis, see Kennett Love, *The Twice-Fought War* (New York: McGraw-Hill, 1969).

41. The Hungarians were not seeking to overturn the Communist regime in Budapest but rather to adopt a more independent posture vis-à-vis Moscow, along the lines of Communist Yugoslavia. For a discussion of the Hungarian Revolution and its implication for Eastern solidarity, see Ghita Ionescu, *The Break-up of the Soviet Empire in Eastern Europe* (Baltimore: Penguin Books, 1965), pp. 68–86.

42. Ronald Steel, *The End of Alliance: America and the Future of Europe* (New York: Viking Press, 1964). In regard to the Western alliance, in particular, U.S. allies expressed doubts about the reliability of the American guarantee to use nuclear weapons to counter a possible Soviet aggression in Western Europe, given the fact that Soviet ICBMs might then be aimed directly at the U.S homeland.

43. France remained in the North Atlantic Treaty Organization (NATO) alliance, but withdrew from the military command structure in 1966. Rumania remained in the Warsaw Pact, the Eastern European counterpart to NATO, but refused to allow joint military maneuvers on Rumanian soil.

44. The six states that had exploded atomic bombs by the early seventies were the United States, the Soviet Union, the United Kingdom, France, Communist China, and India. The United States and the Soviet Union remained far superior, however, in terms of numbers of weapons and types of delivery systems.

45. The *Pueblo* was an American naval vessel seized by North Korea on the grounds that it was spying in North Korean waters. Despite U.S. denials and demands that the ship be released, the North Koreans kept the eighty-three-man crew for almost a year before setting the group free (which included one deceased crewman) after a formal American apology.

46. The Soviet Union had helped arm and train the Egyptian military personnel against Israel. However, Anwar Sadat, Nasser's successor as president of Egypt, became suspicious of Soviet motives in the Middle East and ordered Soviet advisers out of the country. He was to utilize Soviet help again during the Arab-Israeli war of 1973, only to move closer to the United States later.

Chapter 3.   A Bird's-Eye View of the Present: The Contemporary International System

1. Jordan contributed troops to the Syrian effort but did not get directly involved in the fighting. Regarding the Palestinian question, the Arabs claimed that over 200,000 Palestinians had been expelled from their homeland in 1948 when the state of Israel was created out of what had previously been British-controlled Palestine. The Israelis argued that the refugees were simply casualties of war and that the Arab states had aggravated the refugee problem by encouraging Palestinians to abandon their homes to fight with other Arabs against Israeli independence. By 1973, there were over 700,000 Palestinians living in refugee camps scattered across Egypt, Syria, Lebanon, Jordan, and elsewhere in the Middle East. For general background discussion on the roots and dynamics of the Arab-Israeli conflict, see Fred J. Khouri, *The Arab-Israeli Dilemma*, 2nd ed. (Syracuse, N.Y.: Syracuse University Press, 1976).

2. The lines of conflict in the Middle East were never clearly drawn between East and West, however. As noted in Chapter 2, the United States parted company with France, Britain, and Israel in support of Egypt during the Suez conflict of 1956, while Egyptian suspicions about Soviet motives in the Middle East caused Egypt to expel Soviet advisers in 1972, only to momentarily mend fences with Moscow in 1973. The Americans and Soviets both could find friends as well as enemies in the Arab world.

3. Actually, the oil companies were already on the defensive by 1972, when they failed to extract favorable new agreements from several oil-exporting states and failed to counteract expropriation of oil company assets by the governments of Libya and Iraq. However, the strength of OPEC's bargaining position was not fully realized until 1973. For a general discussion of the economic disputes between oil-producing and oil-consuming countries and the events leading up to the oil embargo, see Leonard Mosley, *Power Play: Oil in the Middle East* (Baltimore: Penguin Books, 1974).

4. The statistics on oil production, consumption, and imports used here and elsewhere in this case study are taken from Joel Darmstadter and Hans H. Landsberg, "The Economic Background," in *The Oil Crisis*, ed. by Raymond Vernon (New York: W. W. Norton, 1976), pp. 15–37. Whereas Western Europe as a whole had relied on petroleum for only 25 percent of its aggregate energy needs in 1955, it was up to 75 percent by 1972; petroleum usage

likewise accounted for 75 percent of aggregate energy consumption in Japan by 1972. It should be added that not all Western European countries were equally dependent on oil imports. The United Kingdom and Norway, in particular, were about to begin exploitation of their own oil reserves discovered in the North Sea. The Netherlands, more so than other countries in Western Europe, made considerable use of natural gas as an energy supplement to oil.

5. For a discussion of the entire embargo episode and its political and economic ramifications, see Vernon, *op. cit.*

6. The Dutch were apparently also targeted because of the crucial position of Rotterdam as the chief port of entry for Middle East oil destined for West Germany, a leading industrialized state the Arabs were indirectly attempting to pressure. See Frederic S. Pearson, "Netherlands Foreign Policy and the 1973–74 Oil Embargo—The Effects of Transnationalism," in Forest L. Grieves, ed., *Transnationalism in World Politics and Business* (New York: Pergamon Press, 1979), pp. 114–138.

7. Between December 1973 and March 1974, the availability of petroleum in Britain was only about 1 percent lower than it had been in the same period a year earlier; France suffered only a 7 percent drop, and the Germans 12 percent. The Italians even managed a 4 percent increase.

8. The decline of OPEC in the 1980s is discussed by Mohammed E. Ahrari in *OPEC: The Failing Giant* (Lexington: University of Kentucky Press, 1986); by Douglas J. Feith in "The Oil Weapon De-Mystified," *Policy Review*, no. 15 (Winter 1981), pp. 19–39; and in "Mideast Oil: A Cartel Crisis," *The Middle East*, 6th ed. (Washington, D.C.: Congressional Quarterly, 1986).

9. Charles W. Maynes and Richard H. Ullmann, "Ten Years of Foreign Policy," *Foreign Policy*, Fall 1980, p. 6.

10. The materials are aluminum, chromium, cobalt, manganese, natural rubber, nickel, tin, tungsten, and zinc. See *International Economic Report of the President, 1977* (Washington, D.C.: U.S. Government Printing Office, 1977), p. 187; and John W. Sewell, *U.S. Foreign Policy and the Third World: Agenda 1985–86* (New Brunswick, N.J.: Transaction Books, 1986), p. 188. One writing that plays down U.S. mineral import dependence but acknowledges the seriousness of mineral import dependencies experienced by American allies is Michael Shafer, "Mineral Myths," *Foreign Policy* (Summer 1982), pp. 154–171. For problems of oil dependency, see David A. Deere and Joseph S. Nye, eds., *Energy and Security* (Cambridge, Mass.: Ballinger, 1980).

11. Soviet import dependence on food varies with the weather and other factors. See Michael R. Dolan, "Export Specialization and Import Dependence in the Soviet Economy, 1970–1977," in *Soviet Economy in a Time of Change* (Washington, D.C.: U.S. Government Printing Office, 1979), p. 353; and Karl-Eugen Wadekin, "Soviet Agriculture's Dependence on the West," *Foreign Affairs* (Spring 1982) pp. 882-903.

12. One of the best statements on the changed role of military power in the nuclear age is found in Klaus Knorr's *On the Uses of Military Power in the Nuclear Age* (Princeton, N.J.: Princeton, University Press, 1966).

13. To be a member of the "nuclear club," a state must conduct a test explosion of a nuclear bomb. For a list of those states that are thought to presently have such a capability or to be on the brink of acquiring a capability, see Thomas C. Schelling, "Who Will Have the Bomb?" *International Security*, 1 (Summer 1976), pp. 77–91; Leonard S. Spector, *Nuclear Proliferation Today* (New York: Random House, 1984); and Spector, "Proliferation: The Silent Spread," *Foreign Policy* (Spring 1985) pp. 53–78.

14. Kenneth N. Waltz, *Theory of International Politics* (Reading, Mass.: Addison-Wesley, 1979), p. 170.

15. Henry A. Kissinger, *American Foreign Policy*, 3rd ed. (New York: W. W. Norton, 1977), p. 416. While Kissinger has often spoken about multiple power centers, many observers have pointed out that during his tenure as U.S. Secretary of State he tended to view the world in terms of an "American-Soviet condominium."

16. Elmer Plischke, *Microstates in World Affairs* (Washington, D.C.: American Enterprise Institute for Public Policy Research, 1977), pp. 2, 19–21.

17. J. David Singer, "Reconstructing the Correlates of War Data Set on Material Capabilities of States, 1816–1985," paper presented to the Annual Meeting of the International Studies Association, Washington, D.C., April 1987; see also Richard L. Merritt and Dina A. Zinnes, "From National Capabilities to National Power: Indicators and Indices," paper presented to the Annual Meeting of the International Studies Association, Washington, D.C., April 1987; and Steven L. Spiegel, *Dominance and Diversity* (Boston: Little, Brown, 1972), pp. 93–96.

18. At least one analyst suggests that "will" can be measured with some degree of precision. See Ray Cline, *World Power Assessment: A Calculus of Strategic Drift* (Washington, D.C.: Georgetown University Center for Strategic and International Studies, 1975).

19. "I still believe he [President Lyndon Johnson] found it viscerally inconceivable that what Walt Rostow [Johnson's chief national security adviser] kept telling him was 'the greatest power in the world' could not dispose of a collection of night-riders in black pajamas." Quoted from Arthur Schlesinger, Jr., "The Quagmire Papers," *New York Review of Books*, December 16, 1971, p. 41.

20. In other words, power is not completely "fungible" in terms of being equally usable and effective for a variety of purposes. While power in international relations has always been "issue-specific" in a sense, it is especially the case today with so many variables being relevant to the power equation. The notion that power is issue-specific and, hence, that identifying a single power hierarchy in a political system is somewhat simplistic has been discussed by several scholars in the context of both domestic politics and international politics. See Robert Dahl, *Who Governs: Democracy and Power in an American City* (New Haven, Conn.: Yale University Press, 1961), in which the notion of "polyarchy" is developed; William D. Coplin and Michael K. O'Leary, *Everyman's Prince* (North Scituate, Mass.: Duxbury Press, 1972); and Robert O. Keohane and Joseph S. Nye, *Power and Interdependence* (Boston: Little, Brown, 1977). The concept of "issue-area" was first developed in the international relations field by James Rosenau. See his article "Pre-Theories and Theories of Foreign Policy," in R. Barry Farrell, ed., *Approaches to Comparative and International Politics* (Evanston, Ill.: Northwestern University Press, 1966), pp. 27–92.

21. See *World Bank Atlas, 1986* (Washington, D.C.: World Bank, 1986).

22. See *ibid.*, p. 20; and *World Development Report, 1984* (Washington, D.C.: World Bank, 1984). Further statistics on the rich-poor gap are cited in Chapter 14.

23. The Overseas Development Council has pioneered this concept. See Morris D. Morris, *Measuring the Condition of the World's Poor: The Physical Quality of Life Index* (Washington, D.C.: Overseas Development Council, 1979).

24. John Stoessinger, *The Might of Nations*, 6th ed. (New York: Random House, 1979), p. 5.

25. The "Group of 77" is a term that began to be used in the 1960s to refer to the 77 less developed countries which formed the United Nations Conference on Trade and Development in 1964 in an early attempt to press economic demands against developed countries. The term is still used to refer to the Third World even though the ranks of the less developed countries had swelled to over 100 by 1980.

26. Richard J. Barnet, *The Giants: Russia and America* (New York: Simon and Schuster, 1977), p. 145.

27. The term was first coined by Richard Rosecrance in 1966 to describe a hypothetical system that he felt might exist in the future but did not yet exist at the time. See Richard N. Rosecrance, "Bipolarity, Multipolarity, and the Future," *Journal of Conflict Resolution*, 10 (September 1966), pp. 314–327. John Spanier has used similar terminology to describe the present system, calling it "bipolycentric." See John Spanier, *Games Nations Play*, 4th ed. (New York: Holt, Rinehart and Winston, 1981), p. 273. Stanley Hoffmann also notes the bipolar character of the international system on one level and the multipolar character on another level. See Stanley Hoffmann, *Gulliver's Troubles, or the Setting of American Foreign Policy* (New York: McGraw-Hill, 1968), pp. 21–46.

28. Patrick M. Morgan, *Theories and Approaches to International Politics: What Are We to Think?* (San Francisco: Consensus Publishers, 1972), pp. 227–228.

29. Stanley Hoffmann, "Choices," *Foreign Policy*, Fall 1973, p. 5.

30. Speech before the Institute of World Affairs of the University of Wisconsin, U.S. Department of State News Release, July 14, 1975.

31. The term is Robert L. Paarlberg's in "Domesticating Global Management," *Foreign Affairs*, 54 (April 1976), pp. 563–576.

32. Harold and Margaret Sprout, *Toward a Politics of the Planet Earth* (New York: Van Nostrand Reinhold, 1971), p. 14. For a similar view of international relations, see Dennis Pirages, *The New Context for International Relations: Global Ecopolitics* (North Scituate, Mass.: Duxbury Press, 1978).

33. Paarlberg, *op. cit.*

34. Studying the period between 1965 and 1974, Knorr found that military expenditures in constant dollars rose by 28 percent, military manpower by 24 percent, and arms imports by 60 percent. See Klaus Knorr, "Is International Coercion Waning or Rising?" *International Security* (Spring 1977), pp. 93–94. By 1985, total world military spending had approached nearly $1 trillion annually. See U.S. Arms Control and Disarmament Agency, *World Military Expenditures and Arms Transfers, 1985* (Washington, D.C.: U.S. ACDA, 1985).

35. Alex Inkeles, "The Emerging Social Structure of the World," *World Politics*, 27 (July 1975), p. 479.

36. John Herz was among the first to call attention to this "permeability," in his *International Politics in the Atomic Age* (New York: Columbia University Press, 1959).

37. Inkeles, *op. cit.*, p. 484.

38. John W. Sewell *et al.*, *The United States and World Development, Agenda 1980* (New York: Praeger, 1980), pp. 196–197. In the mid-1980s, the developed capitalist countries had a 70 percent share of total world exports. See *Direction of Trade Statistics Yearbook, 1986* (Washington, D.C.: International Monetary Fund, 1986), p. 6.

39. Kjell Skjelsbaek, "The Growth of International Nongovernmental Organization in the Twentieth Century," in Robert O. Keohane and Joseph S. Nye, eds., *Transnational Relations and World Politics* (Cambridge, Mass.: Harvard University Press, 1971), p. 82.

40. Harold K. Jacobson, *Networks of Interdependence* (New York: Knopf, 1984), pp. 53–54.

41. The distinction between "sensitivity" and "vulnerability" is discussed in Keohane and Nye, pp. 12–19. We use the terms here to mean that a country may well have reason to be concerned about the potential damage caused by another country's actions, yet it can withstand those actions by making some policy adjustments without suffering major costs in the process. In fact, it has been argued that the Nixon administration was not entirely upset by the oil embargo's impact on the more vulnerable Western European and Japanese economies, since Europe and Japan had become highly competitive economically with the United States.

42. The United States must import 95 percent of the cobalt it consumes.

43. The role of economic dependencies in affecting power relationships between countries is discussed in Chapter 7.

44. K. J. Holsti, "Change in the International System: Interdependence, Integration, and Fragmentation," in Ole R. Holsti *et al.*, eds., *Change in the International System* (Boulder, Colo.: Westview Press, 1980), p. 41.

45. Given the global nature of oil politics, it may be harder to treat the Middle East as an autonomous subsystem today than in the past. For an examination of the Middle East as a distinct subsystem in the past, see Leonard Binder, "The Middle East as a Subordinate International System," *World Politics*, 10 (April 1958), pp. 408–429. For a more recent perspective on this, see Frederic S. Pearson, "The Dynamics of 'Middle Eastern' Conflict," *General Systems Yearbook*, XIX (1974), pp. 103–113.

46. The term "discontinuities" was introduced by Oran R. Young in "Political Discontinuities in the International System," *World Politics*, 20 (April 1968), pp. 369–392. For an examination

of regional subsystems, see Louis J. Cantori and Steven L. Spiegel, *The International Politics of Regions* (Englewood Cliffs, N.J.: Prentice-Hall, 1970).

47. See Keohane and Nye, *op. cit.*; Young W. Kihl, *Conflict Issues and International Civil Aviation Decisions: Three Cases* (Denver: University of Denver Press, 1971); Kenneth A. Dahlberg *et al.*, *Environment and the Global Arena* (Durham, N.C.: Duke University Press, 1985); Barry B. Hughes *et al.*, *Energy in the Global Arena* (Durham, N.C.: Duke University Press, 1985); Jonathan Aronson, "Multiple Actors in the Transformation of the International Monetary System," paper presented at the Annual Meeting of the International Studies Association, Toronto, February 25, 1976; and David P. Forsythe, "The Red Cross as Transnational Movement: Conserving and Changing the Nation-State System," *International Organization*, 30 (Autumn 1976), pp. 608–630. For a systematic empirical analysis that attempts to assess the relative significance of state and nonstate actors, see Richard W. Mansbach *et al.*, *The Web of World Politics* (Englewood Cliffs, N.J.: Prentice-Hall, 1976).

48. Charles Kindleberger, *American Business Abroad* (New Haven, Conn.: Yale University Press, 1969), p. 207.

49. George W. Ball, "The Promise of the Multinational Corporation," *Fortune*, June 1, 1967, p. 80. George Ball was a U.S. Assistant Under Secretary of State during Lyndon Johnson's administration.

50. Zbigniew Brzezinski, *Between Two Ages: America's Role in the Technotronic Era* (New York: Viking, 1970), p. 275. Brzezinski had to change his orientation toward the world somewhat when he found himself in the position of chief U.S. national security adviser to President Carter in the late 1970s.

51. Out of 132 states identified in 1970, only 12 (9 percent) were homogeneous in terms of common ethnic and cultural characteristics within their societies. See Walker Connor, "Nation-Building or Nation-Destroying?" *World Politics*, 24 (April 1972), pp. 320–321. Another source of disintegration is the further break-up of colonial empires; by 1984, there were still 17 territories listed by the United Nations as "Non-Self-Governing." See *Everyone's United Nations* (New York: UN, 1986), pp. 332–335.

52. In a 1978 survey, it was found that only 36 percent of the world's people lived in countries whose political systems could be classified as "free," with 21 percent living in countries that were only "partly free" and 43 percent living in countries that were "not free." Freedom House, *Freedom at Issue*, 44 (February 1978), p. 2. The "free" societies, as defined in the study, tended to be predominantly Western, capitalist, developed societies. A 1985 follow-up study found only 53 countries that could be called "free," compared with 59 that were "partly free" and 55 labeled "not free," and noted that "since the first survey [of freedom] published in . . . 1973, . . . worldwide the percentage of people living in freedom or the percentage of free nations has not changed noticeably." Raymond G. Gastil, *Freedom in the World: Political Rights and Civil Liberties, 1984–1985* (Westport, Conn.: Greenwood Press, 1985), pp. 11 and 25.

PART II.   NATIONAL ACTORS AND INTERNATIONAL INTERACTIONS

1. Hedley Bull, *The Anarchical Society: A Study of Order in World Politics* (New York: Columbia University Press, 1977), p. 8.

2. One attempt to develop a "standardized" list was undertaken by Bruce Russett, J. David Singer, and Melvin Small. See "National Political Units in the Twentieth Century: A Standardized List," *American Political Science Review*, 62 (September 1968), pp. 932–952. For a more current listing of "independent territorial units," see Harold K. Jacobson, *Networks of Interdependence*, 2nd ed. (New York: Knopf, 1984), Appendix C.

Chapter 4. Describing Foreign Policy Behavior: What Is It Nation-States Do?

1. Arnold Wolfers, *Discord and Collaboration* (Baltimore: Johns Hopkins University Press, 1962), pp. 81–102.

2. On alliance concepts and policies, see Edwin H. Fedder, "The Concept of Alliance," *International Studies Quarterly*, 12 (March 1968), reprinted in *The Theory and Practice of International Relations*, David McLellan, William C. Olsen, and Fred Sondermann, eds., 4th ed. (Englewood Cliffs, N.J.: Prentice-Hall, 1974); Fedder, *NATO: The Dynamics of Alliance in the Postwar World* (New York: Dodd, Mead, 1973); Francis A. Beer, *Alliances: Latent War Communities in the Contemporary World* (New York: Holt, Rinehart and Winston, 1970); and George Liska, *Nations in Alliance* (Baltimore: Johns Hopkins University Press, 1962).

3. On neutrality concepts and practice, see Cecil V. Crabb, Jr., *Nations in a Multipolar World* (New York: Harper and Row, 1968), ch. 15, and *The Elephants and the Grass: A Study of Nonalignment* (New York: Praeger, 1965).

4. The Swiss position on neutrality is a complicated one. Over the years the Swiss have joined certain specialized UN agencies such as the Universal Postal Union and World Health Organization, and even Western-oriented economic organizations such as the Organization of Economic Cooperation and Development. In a 1986 national referendum, 75 percent of the Swiss voters voted against Switzerland joining the UN.

5. The Burmese case is a curious one since it was during the height of their isolation that a Burmese citizen, U Thant, happened to be head of the United Nations, serving as Secretary-General of the world organization between 1962 and 1972.

6. Treaty data are from Gerhard von Glahn, *Law Among Nations*, 4th ed. (New York: Macmillan, 1981), p. 54; other data are from Elmer Plischke, *Microstates in World Affairs* (Washington, D.C.: American Enterprise Institute for Public Policy Research, 1977), pp. 134 and 140. Plischke also notes that out of 50 major multilateral treaties identified as of 1977, China had ratified only 5 (compared to 45 for the United States and 44 for Soviet Union) and had attended only 3 out of 45 major multilateral conferences since 1945 (compared to 45 for United States and 36 for Soviet Union).

7. See K. J. Holsti, "National Role Conceptions in the Study of Foreign Policy," *International Studies Quarterly*, 14 (September 1970), pp. 233–309; and Naomi B. Wish, "Foreign Policy Makers: Their National Role Conceptions," *International Studies Quarterly*, 24 (December 1980), pp. 532–554. See also the distinctions between active versus passive, planned versus opportunistic, and uncompromising versus bargaining leadership styles made by Harold and Margaret Sprout in their *Toward a Politics of the Planet Earth* (New York: Van Nostrand Reinhold, 1971), p. 161.

8. On accommodation in history and especially regarding the German threat, see Peter Karsten, "Response to Threat Perception: Accommodation as a Special Case," in *Historical Dimensions of National Security Problems*, Klaus Knorr, ed. (Lawrence: University of Kansas Press, 1976), pp. 120—163. Historians have noted also that the French army and populace might not have resisted the Nazi invasion very effectively in part because of French anti-Communism and anti-Semitism. The moving film *The Sorrow and the Pity* documents the divisions in French society, which in many cases resulted in collaboration with the Germans. In a slightly different vein, Italy accommodated itself to changing wartime circumstances and left the losing side in time to avoid damaging consequences in both world wars.

9. Interventions in colonies are counted. See John R. Van Wingen and Herbert K. Tillema, "British Military Intervention," *Journal of Peace Research*, 17 (1980), pp. 291–303; and Tillema and Van Wingen, "Law and Power in Military Intervention: Major States After World War II," *International Studies Quarterly*, 26 (June 1982), pp. 220–250. Also, see J. H. Wyllie, *The Influence of British Arms: An Analysis of British Military Intervention Since 1956* (London: George Allen and Unwin, 1984).

10. The term "new nation" refers to the fact that the United States was the first major colony to break away from colonial rule and achieve sovereign independence. See Seymour Martin Lipset, *The First New Nation* (New York: W. W. Norton, 1979). For a discussion of U.S. foreign policy in the early years of the nation, see Alexander De Conde, *A History of American Foreign Policy*, vol. 1, 3rd ed. (New York: Scribner's, 1978).

11. For a review of America's continuing fascination with China, see John K. Fairbank, *The United States and China*, 4th ed. (Cambridge, Mass.: Harvard University Press, 1979); Warren Cohen, *America's Response to China: An Interpretative History of Sino-American Relations*, 2nd ed. (New York: John Wiley, 1980); and Harold Isaacs, *Scratches on Our Minds: American Images of China and India* (Westport, Conn.: Greenwood Press, 1973).

12. Some historians see American expansion as planned and imperialistic, while others see it as somewhat reluctant, defensive, or idealistically aimed at uplifting foreign countries. Reality may have been a mixture of both. See William A. Williams, *The Contours of American History* (Chicago: Quadrangle Press, 1966) and *The Tragedy of American Diplomacy* (New York: Dell, 1962); Richard Van Alstyne, *The Rising American Empire* (Oxford: Quadrangle, 1960); Sidney Lens, *The Forging of the American Empire: A History of American Imperialism from the Revolution to Vietnam* (New York: Thomas Y. Crowell, 1974); Foster Rhea Dulles, *America's Rise to World Power, 1898–1954* (New York: Harper Torchbooks, 1963); and Dexter Perkins, *The Evolution of American Foreign Policy*, 2nd ed. (New York: Oxford University Press, 1966).

13. The moralistic-legalistic thread running through much of U.S. foreign policy history is ably discussed by George Kennan in *American Diplomacy 1900–1950* (Chicago: University of Chicago Press, 1951). See also Stanley Hoffmann, *Gulliver's Troubles, or the Setting of American Foreign Policy* (New York: McGraw-Hill, 1969), ch. 5.

14. See Lloyd Gardner, "A Progressive Foreign Policy 1900–1921," in *From Colony to Empire: Essays in the History of American Foreign Relations*, William Appleman Williams, ed. (New York: John Wiley, 1972), pp. 225–251 (see also pp. 481–482); and Martin Sklar, "Woodrow Wilson and the Political Economy of Modern United States Liberalism," *A New History of Leviathan*, Ronald Radosh and Murray N. Rothbard, eds. (New York: Dutton, 1972), pp. 7–64.

15. The United States was faced with increasing Japanese warfare in China throughout the thirties. President Roosevelt had to decide whether to recognize or resist Japanese gains; in holding out for China's "territorial integrity," he finally employed trade sanctions against the Japanese, then as now one of America's leading trade partners. The cutoff of oil supplies to resource-starved Japan led eventually to the desperation attack to oust the United States from the Western Pacific. On Pearl Harbor, see Herbert Feis, *The Road to Pearl Harbor* (Princeton, N.J.: Princeton University Press, 1950); Kennan, *American Diplomacy*, op. cit.; and William Neumann, *America Encounters Japan* (New York: Harper, 1965), chs. 10–13.

16. Stephen Ambrose notes that in 1939, the United States had an army of 185,000 and a defense budget of less than $500 million. With the impetus of World War II, the army was to grow to millions and the budget to hundreds of billions. See Stephen Ambrose, *America's Rise to Globalism: American Foreign Policy Since 1938*, 4th ed. (New York: Penguin, 1985), pp. xiii–xiv. For an overview of American foreign policy in the post–World War II period, through several different administrations, see James E. Dougherty and Robert L. Pfaltzgraff, Jr., *American Foreign Policy: FDR to Reagan* (New York: Harper and Row, 1986).

17. Aside from security needs, there were other reasons the Soviets felt U.S. and British concessions were called for. The Soviet Union had allowed Britain, France, and the United States to enter Berlin and share the occupation of Germany even though allied troops had not arrived in the German capital during the war. The Stalin government in Moscow had already accumulated grievances against the West, including the failure to open a second fighting front in Europe until 1944 (the Normandy invasion). From Stalin's viewpoint, Russia had been bled of nearly twenty million lives before Britain and America ventured onto the European continent. Of course, from the Western viewpoint, it was necessary to be sure Moscow would stay in the

war before risking troops in an offensive against Germany. Stalin also was irritated by American-British cooperation in atomic bomb research and President Truman's use of the bomb to end the Pacific war before Russia could become involved. For one version of atomic diplomacy, see Gar Alperovitz, *Atomic Diplomacy: Hiroshima and Potsdam* (New York: Vintage, 1967).

18. The United States failure to understand local or regional issues was typified by American policy regarding the Greek Civil War in 1947. The Truman administration moved to oppose the Communist-supported side in that war, yet also aided Stalin's main Communist rival, Marshal Tito of Yugoslavia, on the mistaken assumption that Stalin, not Tito, was behind the leftist insurgency in Greece. Thus, America unwittingly aided both sides in the Greek war.

19. In October 1944, near the end of World War II, Churchill himself had sat across a conference table from Stalin passing slips of paper on which were written the names of certain Southern and Eastern European countries together with the proposed percentage of British or Soviet influence over those countries. After checking off approval on each slip, Churchill asked if they should not be burned. Stalin replied, "No, you can keep them." So descended the "Iron Curtain" in the Balkan countries. See Winston Churchill, *Triumph and Tragedy* (Boston: Houghton Mifflin, 1953), pp. 226 ff. On the origins of the Cold War, see Lynn Ethridge Davis, *The Cold War Begins* (Princeton, N.J.: Princeton University Press, 1974); Louis Halle, *The Cold War as History* (New York: Harper and Row, 1974); Walter LaFeber, *America, Russia, and the Cold War, 1945–1967*, 2nd ed. (New York: John Wiley, 1972); Daniel Yergin, *Shattered Peace: Origins of the Cold War and the National Security State* (Boston: Houghton Mifflin, 1978); Adam Ulam, *The Rivals: America and Russia Since World War II* (New York: Penguin, 1976); and John Lewis Gaddis, *The United States and the Origins of the Cold War, 1941–1947* (New York: Columbia University Press, 1972).

20. Kennan argued that if the Soviets were prevented from expanding in Europe or the Mediterranean areas, their top-heavy political system would collapse, a prediction somewhat similar to Lenin's observations about Western imperialist states. In later years, Mr. X argued that he never meant containment to be a worldwide concept, as it was viewed by subsequent U.S. administrations, or, especially, to involve the United States in Asian land wars. But the "logic" of *extended* containment was difficult to avoid once the containment concept itself was accepted.

21. While NATO committed all members to consider an attack on one equivalent to an attack on all, members promised only to consult together and take such action as was "constitutionally appropriate" in response. Originally the European states desired an alliance as much to guard against a resurgent Germany as against the Soviet Union. By 1960, the United States had a network of alliances in addition to NATO, including SEATO (Southeast Asia Treaty Organization, now lapsed), ANZUS (a treaty with Australia and New Zealand), and the OAS (Organization of American States), with the NATO commitment remaining the strongest. The United States had moved firmly from neutrality to alliance in world affairs. See Fedder, *NATO: The Dynamics of Alliance in the Postwar World.*

22. For a discussion of the crises over Berlin and Germany, see John Mander, *Berlin: Hostage for the West* (Baltimore: Penguin, 1962); Paul Y. Hammond, *Cold War and Détente: The American Foreign Policy Process Since 1945* (New York: Harcourt Brace Jovanovich, 1975), pp. 169–170; and Jack Smith, *The Berlin Crisis 1958–1962* (Philadelphia: University of Pennsylvania Press, 1971).

23. Taken from the documentary film, *I. F. Stone's Weekly*, directed by Jerry Bruch.

24. The Cuban missile crisis is discussed briefly in this chapter under the Soviet foreign policy profile.

25. The SALT agreements and other arms control agreements will be discussed in Chapter 11. On Kissinger's designs, see Henry A. Kissinger, *American Foreign Policy*, 2nd and 3rd eds. (New York: W. W. Norton, 1974 and 1977); and *The White House Years* (Boston: Little, Brown, 1979).

26. His pragmatism notwithstanding, Kissinger also could be as anti-Communist as John Foster Dulles. He reportedly asked a meeting of the U.S. National Security Council dealing with the nationalization of American corporate property by the Allende government in Chile, "Why should we stand by and watch a country go Communist merely because of the irresponsibility of its own people?" Cited in James A. Nathan and James K. Oliver, *United States Foreign Policy and World Order* (Boston: Little, Brown, 1976), p. 496.

27. The proposed overhauling of American foreign policy was articulated by Carter in May 1977 in an address at Notre Dame University's commencement exercises. See *U.S. Department of State Bulletin*, 76 (June 13, 1977), p. 622.

28. See Frederic S. Pearson, "U.S. Arms Transfer Policy: The Feasibility of Restraint," *Arms Control*, 2 (May 1981), pp. 25–65.

29. We should note that European allies have also used a "Lone Ranger" approach at times, as when France and Britain tried to obtain special privileges from the Arab oil states in 1973. At times also, U.S. officials have tried to forge joint policies with major allies, as when Kissinger led the way in forming the International Energy Agency in 1974.

30. For an exhaustive discussion of early Soviet foreign policy, see Adam Ulam, *Expansion and Coexistence: A History of Soviet Foreign Policy 1917–1973*, 2nd ed. (New York: Praeger, 1974). On the later years, see Joseph L. Nogee and Robert H. Donaldson, *Soviet Foreign Policy Since World War II* (Oxford: Pergamon, 1981).

31. *Ibid.*, pp. 149–152.

32. See *Derzu Urzawa*, a beautiful Japanese film about the Russo-Chinese border area at the turn of the century.

33. Ulam, *Expansion and Coexistence*, pp. 250–279.

34. In comparison, the United States suffered 405,000 casualties during World War II. See Martha Boyd Hoyle, *A World in Flames* (New York: Atheneum, 1970).

35. On the diplomacy of Allied wartime conferences, see Gaddis, *op. cit.*, pp. 135–173; and Diane Shaver Clemens, *Yalta* (New York: Oxford University Press, 1970).

36. In an effort to preclude that entry, Moscow had offered in 1952 to allow a reunified but neutral Germany. See Richard J. Barnet, *The Giants* (New York: Simon and Schuster, 1977), p. 17.

37. Samuel L. Sharp, "U.S.-USSR: From Détente to Cold Peace," lecture at the University of Missouri–St. Louis, April 17, 1980.

38. Galia Golan, "The Soviet Union and the Israeli Action in Lebanon," *International Affairs*, 59 (Winter 1983), p. 7. On superpower security commitments in the Third World, see Mohammed Ayoob, "Third World Security: The Worm May Be About to Turn," *International Affairs*, 60 (Winter 1984). On Soviet military intervention, see Alex P. Schmid, *Soviet Military Interventions Since 1945* (New Brunswick, N.J.: Transactions Books, 1985).

39. A. Doak Barnett, *China and the Major Powers in East Asia* (Washington, D.C.: Brookings Institution, 1977).

40. Samuel Kim, *China, the United Nations, and World Order* (Princeton, N.J.: Princeton University Press, 1979).

41. *Ibid.*, p. 24.

42. On Soviet-Chinese suspicions and prejudice, see Harrison Salisbury, *War Between Russia and China* (New York: Bantam, 1970).

43. *The Military Balance, 1985–86* (London: International Institute for Strategic Studies, 1986). For a discussion of Chinese foreign policy in the 1980s, see Harry Harding, ed., *China's Foreign Policy in the 1980s* (New Haven, Conn.: Yale University Press, 1984); and Samuel Kim, ed., *China and the World: Chinese Foreign Policy in the Post-Mao Era* (Boulder, Colo.: Westview Press, 1984).

44. See Stanley Wolpert, *A New History of India* (New York: Oxford University Press, 1977).

45. See the foreword by American political scientists Harold D. Lasswell and Quincy Wright in the excellent study of Indian political thought by K. Satchidananda Murty, *Indian Foreign*

Policy (Calcutta: Scientific Book Agency, 1964); see also A. Appadorai, *Essays in Politics and International Relations* (London: Asian Publishing House, 1969), chs. 7–8.

46. See W. Norman Brown, *The United States and India, Pakistan, Bangladesh* (Cambridge, Mass.: Harvard University Press, 1972), ch. 11.

47. Many scientists, however, leave the country to work in the West, or are underutilized at home. On India's recent efforts in the areas of nuclear technology and space technology, see Raju G. C. Thomas, "India's Nuclear and Space Programs: Defense or Development?" *World Politics*, 38 (January 1986), pp. 315–342.

Chapter 5.   Explaining Foreign Policy Behavior:
Why Do Nation-States Do What They Do?

1. Winston Churchill, radio broadcast, London, October 1, 1939.

2. As with Hans Morgenthau's and Arnold Wolfers' use of the term, "national interests" are sometimes referred to as the "core values" held by a national society. Not all analysts agree on the exact identity of these values, but the three mentioned here are the most often cited. See Hans Morgenthau, "Another Great Debate: The National Interest of the United States," *American Political Science Review*, 46 (December 1952), pp. 961–988; and Arnold Wolfers, *Discord and Collaboration* (Baltimore: Johns Hopkins University Press, 1962), pp. 67–80. For a discussion of problems associated with the concept, see Alexander L. George and Robert O. Keohane, "The Concept of National Interests: Uses and Limitations," in George, ed., *Presidential Decisionmaking in Foreign Policy* (Boulder, Colo.: Westview Press, 1980), pp. 217–237.

3. Much work in this area of inquiry owes an intellectual debt to James Rosenau, who developed a "pre-theory" of foreign policy behavior. See James N. Rosenau, "Pre-Theories and Theories of Foreign Policy," in R. Barry Farrell, ed., *Approaches to Comparative and International Politics* (Evanston, Ill.: Northwestern University Press, 1966), pp. 27–92; also, see Rosenau, *The Scientific Study of Foreign Policy*, rev. ed. (London: Frances Pinter, 1980), ch. 6. For a discussion of "levels of analysis" and the relative merits of viewing states from "inside-out" as opposed to "outside-in" perspectives, see J. David Singer, "The Level-of-Analysis Problem in International Relations," in Klaus Knorr and Sidney Verba, eds., *The International System: Theoretical Essays* (Princeton, N.J.: Princeton University Press, 1961), pp. 77–92; and Kenneth N. Waltz, *Theory of International Politics* (Reading, Mass.: Addison-Wesley, 1979), especially ch. 4.

4. Trudy Rubin, "Why Sadat, Begin Plan Summit," *Christian Science Monitor*, May 29, 1981, p. 13.

5. Two influential theorists, one American and one British, have stressed the importance of controlling particular sea-lanes or land masses. Late in the nineteenth century, U.S. Admiral Alfred Thayer Mahan identified control of the seas as the key to world power. World leaders from Teddy Roosevelt to Leonid Brezhnev seem to have been influenced by this notion. However, British geographer Sir Halford J. MacKinder later disputed the importance of naval power, and worried about potential German or Russian domination of the key Eurasian land mass, or the "world island," which included Africa as well. More recently, scholars have argued that technology has greatly diminished the importance of geography. See Raymond F. Hopkins and Richard W. Mansbach, *Structure and Process in International Politics* (New York: Harper and Row, 1973), p. 148.

6. See Frederic S. Pearson, *The Weak State in International Crisis: The Case of the Netherlands in the German Invasion Crisis of 1939–40* (Washington, D.C.: University Press of America, 1981), ch. 3.

7. On the importance of geography in conflictual interactions, see Richardson, *Statistics of Deadly Quarrels* (Pittsburgh: Boxwood Press, 1960), pp. 176–177; Quincy Wright, *A Study* *of War* (Chicago: University of Chicago Press, 1965), p. 1240, ch. 46, appendix 5; Frederic S. Pearson, "Geographic Proximity and Foreign Military Intervention," *Journal of Conflict Resolution*, 18 (September 1974), pp. 432–460; Herman van der Wusten, "The Geography of Conflict Since 1945," in *The Geography of Peace and War*, ed. by David Pepper and Alan Jenkins (Oxford: Basil Blackwell, 1985), pp. 13–28; Harvey Starr and Benjamin Most, "The Substance and Study of Borders in International Relations Research," *International Studies Quarterly*, 20 (December 1976), pp. 581–620; and J. N. H. Douglass, "Conflict Between States," in *Progress in Political Geography*, ed. by Michael Pacione (London: Croom Helm, 1985).

8. On the importance of geography in cooperative interactions, see Richard L. Merritt, "Distance and Interaction Among Political Communities," *General Systems Yearbook*, 9 (1964), pp. 255–263; Steven J. Brams, "Transaction Flows in the International System," *American Political Science Review*, 60 (December 1966), pp. 880–898; Bruce M. Russett, *International Regions and the International System* (Westport, Conn.: Greenwood Press, 1975).

9. See the excellent summary of the work on distances by Deutsch, Organski, Morgenthau, Schuman, Wright, Klingberg, Rummel and others in Rudolph J. Rummel, *The Dimensions of Nations* (Beverly Hills: Sage, 1972), ch. 16, and propositions on pp. 407 and 410.

10. See A. F. K. Organski, *World Politics*, 2nd ed. (New York: Knopf, 1968), pp. 293–295.

11. See Kenneth Waltz, "The Stability of a Bipolar World," *Daedalus*, 93 (Summer 1964), pp. 881–909, and "International Structure, National Force, and the Balance of Power," *Journal of International Affairs*, 21 (1967), pp. 215–231.

12. See Karl W. Deutsch and J. David Singer, "Multipolar Power Systems and International Stability," *World Politics*, 16 (April 1964), pp. 390–406; and Richard N. Rosecrance, "Bipolarity, Multipolarity, and the Future," *Journal of Conflict Resolution*, 10 (September 1966), pp. 314–327.

13. For a synthesis of some studies, see Michael P. Sullivan, *International Relations: Theories and Evidence* (Englewood Cliffs, N.J.: Prentice-Hall, 1976), pp. 169–200. Also see Michael D. Wallace, "Alliance Polarization, Cross-Cutting, and International War, 1815–1964," and Bruce Bueno de Mesquita, "Systemic Polarization and the Occurrence and Duration of War," in *Explaining War: Selected Papers from the Correlates of War Project*, J. David Singer, ed. (Beverly Hills: Sage, 1979), chs. 4 and 5; A. F. K. Organski and Jacek Kugler, *The War Ledger* (Chicago: University of Chicago Press, 1980); Randolph M. Siverson and Michael R. Tennefoss, "Power, Alliance, and the Escalation of International Conflict, 1815–1965," *American Political Science Review*, 78 (December 1984), pp. 1057–1069; and Jeffrey A. Hart, "Polarity, Hegemony, and the Distribution of Power," paper presented to the Annual Meeting of the American Political Science Association, Washington, D.C., 1986.

14. Egyptian President Sadat's historic trip to Jerusalem in 1977 to seek a peace treaty with Prime Minister Begin of Israel was strongly influenced by systemic factors. In Jimmy Carter's early days as president he spoke of a possible joint U.S.-Soviet approach to a Middle East settlement. Fearing a superpower-imposed solution, Sadat and Begin determined that they could regain the initiative and keep the Soviets out by getting together themselves.

15. See Bruce M. Russett, "Pearl Harbor: Deterrence Theory and Decision Theory," *Journal of Peace Research*, no. 2 (1967), pp. 89–106.

16. See Nazli Choucri and Robert C. North, *Nations in Conflict* (San Francisco: W. H. Freeman, 1975); and North, Nobutaka Ike, and Jan F. Triska, *The World of Superpowers*, rev. ed. (Stanford, Calif.: Notrik Press, 1985).

17. In referring to national characteristics we are *not* reviving the traditional and largely discredited notion of "national character." While it is possible that at certain times a country's population has certain clear preferences about, for example, the use of force, there is no evidence that certain nations are inherently more peace-loving or warlike, more practical or romantic, more cowardly or courageous than others. Yet commentators still sometimes refer to the "naive Americans," the "brutal Russians," the "inscrutable Chinese," the "fun-loving Italians," or the "militaristic Germans." Most societies are complex enough that it is possible to find

many individuals with these traits in almost every country. When countries develop behavior patterns like the "m.o.'s" described in Chapter 4, they are usually reacting to historical and cultural experience rather than genetic traits.

18. Governments can become paranoid about dissident ethnic groups, especially in wartime. Thousands of loyal Americans of Japanese descent were interned in camps and lost their property during World War II in the United States because it was assumed that they represented a "fifth column" for Japanese infiltration and because of racist attitudes in certain parts of the country. See Bill Hosokawa, *The Quiet Americans* (New York: Morrow, 1969); and Roger Daniels, *Concentration Camps U.S.A.: Japanese Americans and World War II* (New York: Holt, Rinehart and Winston, 1972).

19. North, Ike, and Triska, *op. cit.*, ch. 1.

20. Harold K. Jacobson, *Networks of Interdependence*, 2nd ed. (New York: Knopf, 1984), p. 50.

21. For a discussion of these claims and counterclaims, see Bernard S. Morris, *Imperialism and Revolution* (Bloomington, Ind.: Indiana University Press, 1973). See also Frederic S. Pearson, "American Military Intervention Abroad: A Test of Economic and Noneconomic Explanations," in *The Politics of Aid, Trade, and Investment*, Satish Raichur and Craige Liske, eds. (New York: John Wiley, 1976), ch. 2.

22. For a fuller discussion of the respective merits of U.S. and Soviet forces, see Lawrence J. Korb, "FY 1980–84 Defense Program: Issues and Trends," *AEI Foreign Policy and Defense Review*, 1, no. 4 (1980); The Boston Study Group, *The Price of Defense* (New York: New York Times Books, 1979); and Barry R. Posen and Stephen W. Van Evera, "Overarming and Underwhelming," *Foreign Policy*, 40 (Fall 1980), pp. 99–118.

23. See Pearson, *The Weak State, op. cit.*, ch. 3.

24. George F. Kennan, *Memoirs, 1925–1950* (Boston: Little, Brown, 1976), p. 53.

25. George F. Kennan, *American Diplomacy, 1900–1950* (Chicago: University of Chicago Press, 1951), p. 59.

26. See William L. Shirer, *The Rise and Fall of the Third Reich* (New York: Simon and Schuster, 1960); and Hopkins and Mansbach, *op. cit.*, pp. 182–184.

27. See Townsend Hoopes, *The Limits of Intervention* (New York: McKay, 1973), ch. 4.

28. See Edward R. F. Sheehan, "How Kissinger Did It: Step by Step in the Middle East," *Foreign Policy*, no. 22 (Spring 1976), p. 53.

29. Henry L. Mason, "War Comes to the Netherlands: September 1939–May 1940," *Political Science Quarterly*, 78 (1963), pp. 548–580.

30. See Morton H. Halperin, *Bureaucratic Politics and Foreign Policy* (Washington, D.C.: The Brookings Institution, 1974).

31. It is not always easy to predict the sides in such bureaucratic battles. On Lebanon, the Pentagon reportedly opposed risky military action favored by the State Department; on the other hand, the Defense Department took a more hawkish view on the SALT II agreement, unconcerned about State Department fears about negative allied reaction to the failure of arms control.

32. It has been argued that President Johnson utilized inaccurate reports of North Vietnamese attacks on U.S. patrol boats in the Tonkin Gulf to gather the Senate votes needed to pass the Tonkin Gulf Resolution in 1964, giving him a "blank check" in using force. In addition, his campaign statement about American boys fighting was artfully phrased to avoid an outright lie; he could argue that he only promised that U.S. soldiers would not do the fighting Asian boys should do, not that they would do no fighting at all. See James A. Nathan and James K. Oliver, *United States Foreign Policy and World Order*, 2nd ed. (Boston: Little, Brown, 1981), pp. 328–330; *The Pentagon Papers*, Gravel Edition, vol. 3 (Boston: Beacon Press, 1971), pp. 180–192; and Harry S. Ashmore and William C. Boggs, *Mission to Hanoi: A Chronicle of Double-Dealing in High Places* (New York: Putnam's-Berkley, 1968).

33. See Nathan and Oliver, *op. cit.*, pp. 335–358; and Hoopes, *op. cit.*, chs. 5 and 6. President Johnson also avoided raising taxes during the Vietnam years, a move that some economists

blame for the origin of American inflation in the late 1960s and 1970s. To move to a stringent wartime financial policy would have aroused even more public controversy about the war.

34. Blaise Pascal, *Lettres Provinçiales, 1656–1956*, no. 162; and Ronald Steel, interview with Robert F. Kennedy, *New York Review of Books*, March 13, 1962, p. 22. For a general discussion of the impact individual decision makers can have on foreign policy behavior, see Margaret G. Hermann, "Effects of Personal Characteristics of Political Leaders on Foreign Policy," in Maurice A. East *et al.*, *Why Nations Act: Theoretical Perspectives for Comparative Foreign Policy Studies* (Beverly Hills: Sage, 1978), pp. 49–68.

35. Harold Sprout and Margaret Sprout, "Man-Milieu Relationship Hypotheses in the Context of International Politics," Center for International Studies, Princeton University, research monograph (Princeton, N.J.: 1956); and "Environmental Factors in the Study of International Politics," *Journal of Conflict Resolution*, 1 (December 1957), pp. 309–328.

36. Kenneth Boulding, "National Images and International Systems," *Journal of Conflict Resolution*, 3 (June 1959), p. 120.

37. Alexander L. George and Juliette George, *Woodrow Wilson and Colonel House* (New York: John Day, 1956). For discussions on the role of personality in shaping foreign policy, see Stephen G. Walker, "The Motivational Foundations of Political Belief Systems: A Reanalysis of the Operational Code Construct," *International Studies Quarterly*, 27 (June 1983), pp. 179–202; Lloyd S. Etheredge, "Personality Effects on American Foreign Policy, 1898–1968: A Test of Interpersonal Generalization Theory," *American Political Science Review*, 72 (June 1978), pp. 435–436; Etheredge, *A World of Men: The Private Sources of American Foreign Policy* (Cambridge, Mass.: MIT Press, 1979); E. Victor Wolfenstein, *Personality and Politics* (Belmont, Calif.: Dickenson, 1969); and Robert A. Isaak, *Individuals and World Politics* (North Scituate, Mass.: Duxbury Press, 1975).

38. Feminists can counter that these examples are not valid since Gandhi, Meir, and Thatcher were women ruling in male-dominated societies. There have been female leaders of smaller countries, such as Norway and Sri Lanka, whose governments have not participated in foreign wars. Yet it is difficult to conceive of a perfect laboratory setting to examine the effects of gender on foreign policy.

39. See Michael Brecher and Benjamin Geist, "Crisis Behavior: Israel, 1973," *The Jerusalem Journal of International Relations*, 3 (Winter-Spring 1978), pp. 197–228.

40. Lecture by Paul M. Kattenburg at the University of Missouri–St. Louis on March 30, 1978; and his book, *The Vietnam Trauma in American Foreign Policy, 1945–75* (New Brunswick, N.J.: Transaction Books, 1980), pp. 113–115. See also Richard E. Neustadt and Graham T. Allison, "Afterword," in Robert F. Kennedy, *Thirteen Days* (New York: W. W. Norton, 1971), p. 123.

41. See William D. Davidson and Joseph V. Montville, "Foreign Policy According to Freud," *Foreign Policy*, 45 (Winter 1981–82), pp. 145–157.

42. See Bernard E. Brown, *Protest in Paris: Anatomy of a Revolt* (Morristown, N.J.: General Learning Press, 1974).

43. A good illustration of how individual, nation-state, and systemic factors interact is provided by Michael Ng-Quinn in his attempt to explain Chinese foreign policy behavior using a framework similar to the one used in this chapter. See "The Analytic Study of Chinese Foreign Policy," *International Studies Quarterly*, 27 (June 1983), pp. 203–224.

Chapter 6. The Foreign Policy Process: A View from the Inside

1. Graham T. Allison, "Conceptual Models and the Cuban Missile Crisis," *American Political Science Review*, 63 (September 1969), p. 689.

2. *St. Louis Post-Dispatch*, June 14, 1981, p. 1.

3. Henry A. Kissinger, "Bureaucracy and Policymaking: The Effects of Insiders and Outsiders on the Policy Process," in Morton H. Halperin and Arnold Kanter, eds., *Readings in American*

Foreign Policy: A Bureaucratic Perspective (Boston: Little, Brown, 1973), p. 85. The essay originally appeared in a 1968 volume shortly before Kissinger became the chief foreign policy adviser to Richard Nixon.

4. Roger Hilsman, *To Move a Nation: The Politics of Foreign Policy in the Administration of John F. Kennedy* (Garden City, N.Y.: Doubleday, 1967), p. 5.

5. One set of authors has developed a four-fold issue-area typology: military-security, economic-developmental, political-diplomatic, and cultural-status. See Michael Brecher *et al.*, "A Framework for Research on Foreign Policy Behavior," *Journal of Conflict Resolution* (March 1969), pp. 75–101. Also, see William Zimmerman, "Issue Area and Foreign Policy Process: A Research Note in Search of a General Theory," *American Political Science Review*, 67 (December 1973), pp. 1204–1212; and William C. Potter, "Issue Area and Foreign Policy Analysis," *International Organization*, 34 (Summer 1980), pp. 405–427.

6. Linda B. Brady, "The Situation and Foreign Policy," in Maurice A. East, Stephen A. Salmore, and Charles F. Hermann, *Why Nations Act: Theoretical Perspectives for Comparative Foreign Policy Studies* (Beverly Hills: Sage, 1978), pp. 173–190.

7. Testimony of Secretary of State Dean Rusk to a Senate subcommittee, reported in *Time*, 83 (January 1964), p. 19, as summarized by K. J. Holsti, *International Politics: A Framework for Analysis*, 3rd ed. (Englewood Cliffs, N.J.: Prentice-Hall, 1977), p. 402. Similar estimates are reported in Lincoln P. Bloomfield, *The Foreign Policy Process: A Modern Primer* (Englewood Cliffs, N.J.: Prentice-Hall, 1982), p. 143.

8. Charles F. Hermann, "International Crisis as a Situational Variable," in James N. Rosenau, ed., *International Politics and Foreign Policy*, rev. ed. (New York: Free Press, 1969), pp. 409–421.

9. See Charles F. Hermann, *International Crisis: Insights from Behavioral Research* (New York: Free Press, 1972).

10. Michael Brecher and Jonathan Wilkenfeld, "Crises in World Politics," *World Politics*, 34 (April 1982), p. 381. For a fuller discussion of crises, see Brecher, *Decisions in Crisis: Israel, 1967 and 1973* (Berkeley: University of California Press, 1980).

11. The term "billiard ball" perspective was coined by Arnold Wolfers. See his chapter "The Actors in International Politics" in *Discord and Collaboration* (Baltimore: Johns Hopkins University Press, 1962), pp. 3–24.

12. Thomas A. Kreuger, "The Social Origins of Recent American Foreign Policy," *Journal of Social History*, 7 (Fall 1973), p. 93.

13. Graham T. Allison, *Essence of Decision* (Boston: Little, Brown, 1971), pp. 4–5.

14. Charles W. Kegley and Eugene R. Wittkopf, *American Foreign Policy: Pattern and Process* (New York: St. Martin's Press, 1979), p. 337.

15. The so-called "decision-making approach" to the study of foreign policy was pioneered by Richard C. Snyder, H. W. Bruck, and Burton M. Sapin in *Foreign Policy Decision Making: An Approach to the Study of International Politics* (New York: Free Press, 1962). Snyder, Bruck, and Sapin were criticized for giving too much attention to idiosyncratic factors to the exclusion of other factors in their study. See Benjamin A. Most and Harvey Starr, "International Relations Theory, Foreign Policy Substitutability, and 'Nice' Laws," *World Politics*, 36 (April 1984), pp. 383–406.

16. Allison, *Essence of Decision, op. cit.* For additional models, see Barbara Kellerman, "Allison Redux: Three More Decision-Making Models," *Polity*, 15 (Spring 1983), pp. 351–367.

17. Selective attention and rationalization are devices for avoiding or resolving "cognitive dissonance," the tension we can experience between our existing view of the world and our exposure to stimuli that are at odds with the latter. See Leon Festinger, *A Theory of Cognitive Dissonance* (Stanford, Calif.: Stanford University Press, 1962).

18. See Robert Jervis, "Hypotheses on Misperception," *World Politics*, 20 (April 1968), pp. 454–479.

19. The "spiral of misconceptions" is discussed in John G. Stoessinger, *Nations in Darkness: China, Russia, and America*, 2nd ed. (New York: Random House, 1975), ch. 11. Empirical

evidence supporting the contention that both the United States and Soviet Union have misperceived each other's behavior since World War II can be found in William A. Gamson and André Modigliani, *Untangling the Cold War* (Boston: Little, Brown, 1971), p. 108.

20. J. David Singer, "Threat Perception and the Armament-Tension Dilemma," *Journal of Conflict Resolution*, 2 (March 1958), pp. 90–105. See also Dean G. Pruitt, "Definition of the Situation as a Determinant of International Action," in Herbert C. Kelman, ed., *International Behavior* (New York: Holt, Rinehart & Winston, 1965), pp. 393–432.

21. U.S. leaders realized the Japanese might attack somewhere, but *not* Pearl Harbor. See Roberta Wohlstetter, *Pearl Harbor: Warning and Decision* (Stanford, Calif.: Stanford University Press, 1962). Another study, on the decisions leading up to World War I, indicates that the flurry of messages exchanged between Berlin, Vienna, St. Petersburg, London and Paris on the eve of World War I was characterized by overestimation of the threat by one side and underestimation by the other side. See Ole R. Holsti *et al.*, "Perception and Action in the 1914 Crisis," in J. David Singer, ed., *Quantitative International Politics* (New York: Free Press, 1968), p. 157. Jack Levy has noted the tendencies to underestimate or overestimate an adversary's hostile intentions and capabilities. See Jack S. Levy, "Misperception and the Causes of War," *World Politics*, 36 (October 1983), pp. 76–99.

22. Joseph de Rivera, *The Psychological Dimension of Foreign Policy* (Columbus, Ohio: Charles E. Merrill, 1968), p. 133. See also Glenn D. Paige, *The Korean Decision* (New York: Free Press, 1968).

23. Ernest R. May, *"Lessons" of the Past: The Use and Misuse of History in American Foreign Policy* (New York: Oxford University Press, 1973), p. 52. On Korea, see *ibid.*, ch. 3, and Marshal D. Shulman, *Stalin's Foreign Policy Reappraised* (New York: Atheneum, 1966), ch. 6. On Vietnam, see May, *op. cit.*, ch. 4, and James C. Thomson, "How Could Vietnam Happen? An Autopsy," in Halperin and Kanter, *op. cit.*, pp. 98–110. American leaders also seemingly forgot some elements of Vietnam history, in particular the disaster suffered by the French at Dienbienphu in 1954, when their forces were routed by Vietnamese nationalists and France was forced to give up colonial rule.

24. Kenneth Boulding, "National Images and International Systems," *Journal of Conflict Resolution*, 3 (June 1959), pp. 120–131.

25. On the Russo-Chinese relationship, see Stoessinger, *op. cit.*, ch. 14. On the Franco-German relationship, see G. P. Gooch, *Franco-German Relations, 1871–1914* (New York: Russell and Russell, 1967). Gooch, writing after World War I, noted: "The story of Franco-German relations since 1871 is the record of France's endeavor to regain her lost territories and of Germany's attempt to retain them. The one [Germany] remembered the aggression of 1870, the other [France] the settlement of 1871; and the writers of schoolbooks took good care that the children should inherit the passions of their elders. There were pauses between the rounds, but the wrestlers never left the arena" (p. 5).

26. One of the founding fathers of the European Community was Robert Schuman, who as French foreign minister in 1950 urged that "the gathering together of European nations requires the elimination of the age-old opposition between France and Germany." Cited in Richard Mayne, *The Community of Europe* (New York: W. W. Norton, 1962), p. 86.

27. The stability and durability of national images is discussed by Karl W. Deutsch and Richard L. Merritt in "Effects of Events on National and International Images," in Kelman, *op. cit.*, pp. 132–187.

28. McNamara contended that the placement of intermediate-range ballistic missiles in Cuba created no new dramatic threat to U.S. security that was not already posed by existing Soviet intercontinental ballistic missiles based in the Soviet Union. McNamara's argument was summed up by his statement that "a missile is a missile." Hilsman, *op. cit.*, p. 195. For the different perceptions of U.S. officials involved in the Cuban missile crisis decision, see *ibid.*, ch. 15, and Allison, "Conceptual Models and the Cuban Missile Crisis," pp. 712–715.

29. There is some disagreement over Kennedy's motive for discontinuing U–2 flights over the western half of the island. Some analysts argue it had as much to do with Kennedy's desire

to avoid a diplomatic incident over a possible shooting down of an American plane as with his subconscious desire to avoid information that might disturb his image. For discussion of this question, see Hilsman, *op. cit.*, ch. 14; Alexander George and Richard Smoke, *Deterrence in American Foreign Policy: Theory and Practice* (New York: Columbia University Press, 1974), pp. 472–491; and Roberta Wohlstetter, "Cuba vs. Pearl Harbor: Hindsight and Foresight," *Foreign Affairs*, 43 (July 1965), pp. 691–707.

30. Allison, *Essence of Decision*, pp. 176–178. Also, see Morton H. Halperin, *Bureaucratic Politics and Foreign Policy* (Washington, D.C.: Brookings Institution, 1974); and Jerel A. Rosati, "Developing a Systematic Decisionmaking Framework: Bureaucratic Politics in Perspective," *World Politics*, 33 (January 1981), pp. 234–252.

31. Les Aspin, "Misreading Intelligence," *Foreign Policy*, Summer 1981, p. 168.

32. Ole R. Holsti, "The Belief System and National Images: A Case Study," *Journal of Conflict Resolution*, 6 (September 1962), pp. 248–249.

33. Ole R. Holsti, "The 1914 Case," *American Political Science Review*, 59 (June 1965), pp. 375–376; Hermann, *International Crisis, op. cit.*; and Frederic S. Pearson, *The Weak State in International Crisis: The Case of the Netherlands in the German Invasion Crisis of 1939–40* (Washington, D.C.: University Press of America, 1981).

34. Irving L. Janis, *Groupthink*, 2nd ed. (Boston: Houghton Mifflin, 1982).

35. Patrick J. McGarvey, "DIA: Intelligence to Please," in Halperin and Kanter, *op. cit.*, p. 325; reprinted from *The Washington Monthly*, July 1970.

36. Cited in Allison, *Essence of Decision*, p. 193.

37. Theodore Sorensen, *Kennedy* (New York: Harper and Row, 1965), p. 675. See Barry B. Hughes, *The Domestic Context of American Foreign Policy* (San Francisco: W. H. Freeman, 1978) for a theoretical and empirical examination of the role of domestic politics in foreign policy, in the U.S. context.

38. The remark has been attributed to James F. Byrnes, Secretary of State under President Truman.

39. Cited in David V. Edwards, *The American Political Experience* (Englewood Cliffs, N.J.: Prentice-Hall, 1979), p. 223.

40. Edward L. Katzenbach, "The Horse Cavalry in the Twentieth Century, " *Public Policy*, 8 (1958), pp. 120–149.

41. Deborah Shapley, "Technological Creep and the Arms Race: ICBM Problem a Sleeper," *Science*, 201 (September 22, 1978), p. 105. For a discussion of the impact of bureaucratic pressures on Soviet perceptions of international reality, see Vernon V. Aspaturian, "The Soviet Military-Industrial Complex: Does It Exist?" in Steven Rosen, ed., *Testing the Theory of the Military-Industrial Complex* (Lexington, Mass.: Lexington Books, 1973), pp. 103–134; and Andrew Cockburn, *The Threat: Inside the Soviet Military Machine* (New York: Random House, 1983). On the reasons behind U.S. and Soviet weapons procurement policies, see James Kurth, "Why We Buy the Weapons We Do," *Foreign Policy*, 11 (Summer 1973), pp. 33–56; and Matthew A. Evangelista, "Why the Soviets Buy the Weapons They Do," *World Politics*, 36 (July 1984), pp. 597–618.

42. Robert Kennedy, for example, commenting on the necessity of a U.S. naval blockade during the Cuban missile crisis, said: "I just don't think there was any choice." Robert F. Kennedy, *Thirteen Days* (New York: W. W. Norton, 1971), p. 45.

43. See L. L. Farrar, "The Limits of Choice: July 1914 Reconsidered," *Journal of Conflict Resolution*, 16 (March 1972), pp. 1–23.

44. James C. March and Herbert A. Simon, *Organizations* (New York: John Wiley, 1958); and Herbert A. Simon, *Administrative Behavior*, 2nd ed. (New York: Free Press, 1957).

45. De Rivera, *op. cit.*, p. 139.

46. Janis, *op. cit.*, p. 3.

47. See Hannes Adomeit, *Soviet Risk-Taking Behavior: A Theoretical and Empirical Analysis* (London: George Allen and Unwin, 1982), pp. 44–49.

48. For a discussion of implementation problems, see Michael Clarke, "Foreign Policy Imple-

mentation: Problems and Approaches," *British Journal of International Studies*, 5 (1979), pp. 112–128; and Halperin, *op. cit.*, chs. 13–15.

49. Richard E. Neustadt, *Presidential Power*, 2nd ed. (New York: John Wiley, 1976), p. 77.

50. Hilsman, *op. cit.*, p. 221.

51. The complete incident is discussed in Allison, *Essence of Decision, op. cit.*, pp. 131–132.

52. An excellent examination of the "lessons" seemingly learned by American leaders from the Vietnam experience, based on a "foreign policy leadership" opinion survey, can be found in Ole R. Holsti and James N. Rosenau, "Cold War Axioms in the Post-Vietnam Era," in Ole R. Holsti *et al.*, eds., *Change in the International System* (Boulder, Colo.: Westview Press, 1980), pp. 263–301.

53. In an extensive discussion of the Strategic Bombing Surveys, Bernard Brodie notes that the aerial bombing of German cities did lower German morale somewhat but did not have much effect on the ability of the German economic and military machine to continue functioning. See Bernard Brodie, *Strategy in the Missile Age* (Princeton, N.J.: Princeton University Press, 1959), pp. 131–138. In a personal account, John Kenneth Galbraith reports similar conclusions and notes that the Air Force attempted to summarize the USSBS in a way that inflated the success of their bombing missions. See *A Life in Our Times: Memoirs* (Boston: Houghton Mifflin, 1982), chs. 13 and 14.

54. Janis, *op. cit.*, p. 157. Robert Kennedy was further quoted as saying "my brother is not going to be the Tojo of the 1960s," referring to the Japanese commander who ordered the Pearl Harbor attacks; cited in Ronald Steel, "The Kennedys and the Missile Crisis," in Halperin and Kanter, *op. cit.*, p. 205. According to Theodore Sorensen, Robert Kennedy had intended to address the general question of morality in international relations in his memoirs, before his life was abruptly ended by assassination in 1968; see Kennedy, *op. cit.*, p. 106.

55. See Paul A. Anderson, "Justification and Precedents as Constraints in Foreign Policy Decision-Making," *American Journal of Political Science*, 25 (November 1981), pp. 738–761.

56. There have been many different interpretations of the A-bomb decision and why U.S. leaders felt it necessary to use such a weapon. For various views on this, see Len Giovannitti and Fred Freed, *The Decision to Drop the Bomb* (New York: Coward-McCann, 1965).

57. In one conventional bombing raid on Tokyo, only a few months before Hiroshima, over 80,000 persons died. This was less than the number of Japanese deaths reported at Hiroshima in 1945. It must be noted, however, that not all Hiroshima casualties have been accounted for. Additional casualties beyond those originally counted are still being uncovered due to the long-term effects of radiation causing cancer and other diseases. The Hiroshima victims would have been even more numerous had the atomic bomb exploded at ground level rather than as an air burst.

58. Quoted by Allison, *Essence of Decision*, p. 131.

Chapter 7.   Playing the Game of International Relations: Diplomacy Before Force

1. J. David Singer, "Accounting for International War: The State of the Discipline," *Annual Review of Sociology*, 6 (1960), p. 353. War is defined and identified according to type of combat, participants, and number of battle-related casualties. Put a bit differently, between 1816 and 1976, states involved in serious international disputes, including at least the threatened use of force, pulled back from the brink of war in nine out of ten cases. See Charles S. Gochman and Zeev Moas, "Militarized Interstate Disputes, 1816–1976," in *International War: An Anthology and Study Guide*, ed. by Melvin Small and J. David Singer (Homewood, Ill.: Dorsey Press, 1985), pp. 27–36. Other researchers have found many more major-power incidents, though not necessarily "serious" ones, and a considerable frequency of wars involving minor powers, especially in the twentieth century. See Barry M. Blechman and Stephen S. Kaplan, *Force Without War* (Washington, D.C.: Brookings Institution, 1978);

Istvan Kende, "Twenty-five Years of Local Wars," *Journal of Peace Research*, 8, no. 1 (1971), pp. 5–22; and Kende, "Wars of Ten Years," *Journal of Peace Research*, 15, no. 3 (1978), pp. 227–241.

2. Gary A. Hill, "The Flow of International Events, July-December, 1970: A General Survey and a Look at the Jordanian Crisis," Interim Technical Report, mimeo (Los Angeles: University of Southern California, 1971). The analysis is based on the coding of events reported in the *New York Times* and *Times* of London (not merely on the front page). If anything, such "events data analysis" tends to overreport acts involving high levels of conflict.

3. Sir Harold Nicolson, *Diplomacy* (1939; reprint, New York: Oxford University Press, 1964), pp. 4–5.

4. Sir Harold Nicolson, *The Evolution of Diplomacy* (London: Constable, 1956), pp. 50–51.

5. *Ibid.*, p. 63.

6. George Ball, *Diplomacy for a Crowded World* (Boston: Little, Brown, 1976), pp. 35–36.

7. Patrick J. McGowan and Howard B. Shapiro, *The Comparative Study of Foreign Policy* (Beverly Hills: Sage, 1973), p. 140. For research studies, see Michael K. O'Leary, "Linkages Between Domestic and International Politics in Underdeveloped Nations," in James N. Rosenau, ed., *Linkage Politics* (New York: Free Press, 1969), pp. 324–326; and Elmer Plishke, *Microstates in World Affairs* (Washington, D.C.: American Enterprise Institute, 1977), ch. 4.

8. The distinction between compellence and deterrence is discussed in Thomas C. Schelling, *Arms and Influence* (New Haven, Conn.: Yale University Press, 1966), pp. 69–78. See also J. David Singer, "Inter-Nation Influence: A Formal Model," in James N. Rosenau, ed., *International Politics and Foreign Policy*, 2nd ed. (New York: Free Press, 1969), pp. 380–391.

9. Henry A. Kissinger, *American Foreign Policy* (New York: W. W. Norton, 1974), p. 61.

10. For a discussion of Kissinger's timing of promises and rewards, see Alexander L. George, "Domestic Constraints on Regime Change in U.S. Foreign Policy: The Need for Policy Legitimacy," in Ole R. Holsti *et al.*, eds., *Change in the International System* (Boulder, Colo.: Westview Press, 1980), pp. 251–258.

11. John P. Lovell, *Foreign Policy in Perspective: Strategy, Adaptation, Decision-Making* (New York: Holt, Rinehart and Winston, 1970), p. 80.

12. See Schelling, *op. cit.*, especially ch. 2 on "The Art of Commitment." Also, see Thomas C. Schelling's *The Strategy of Conflict* (New York: Oxford University Press, 1960).

13. The bargaining that occurred over Berlin is discussed among many other examples and cases in the excellent work by Glen H. Snyder and Paul Diesing, *Conflict Among Nations: Bargaining, Decision Making, and System Structure in International Crisis* (Princeton: Princeton University Press, 1977), p. 69.

14. Schelling, *The Strategy of Conflict*, pp. 55–56.

15. See Anatol Rapoport, *Fights, Games, and Debates* (Ann Arbor, Mich.: The University of Michigan Press, 1960); John Von Neumann and Oscar Morgenstern, *Theory of Games and Economic Behavior* (Princeton, N.J.: Princeton University Press, 1964); and various issues of the *Journal of Conflict Resolution*.

16. See Snyder and Diesing, *op. cit.*, ch. 2.

17. On such constructive solutions, see Robert Axelrod, *The Evolution of Basic Cooperation* (New York: Basic Books, 1985); Anatol Rapoport and Albert Chammah, *The Prisoner's Dilemma* (Ann Arbor, Mich.: University of Michigan Press, 1970); Thomas Schelling and Morton Halperin, *Strategy and Arms Control*, 2nd ed. (New York: Pergamon, 1985); and Charles E. Osgood, *An Alternative to War or Surrender* (Urbana, Ill.: University of Illinois Press, 1962).

18. The definition has been attributed to Sir Henry Wooten, an ambassador of King James I of England in the seventeenth century; cited in Arthur Lall, *Modern International Negotiation* (New York: Columbia University Press, 1966), p. 151.

19. Cited in David J. Dallin, *Soviet Foreign Policy After Stalin* (Philadelphia: J. B. Lippincott, 1961), p. 9.

20. Nicolson, *Diplomacy*, pp. 55–67.

21. For a discussion of "East" and "West" negotiating styles, see Fred C. Iklé, *How Nations Negotiate* (New York: Harper and Row, 1964), ch. 12.

22. Roger Fisher, *International Conflict for Beginners* (New York: Harper and Row, 1969).

23. *Ibid.*, p. 11.

24. In a recent study, T. C. Morgan has argued that the separation of issues on the bargaining agenda and the sequence in which they are addressed materially affect the prospects for settlement of crises. Morgan, "Bargaining Agendas in International Crises," paper presented to the Annual Meeting of the American Political Science Association, Washington, D.C., August 1986.

25. See Klaus Knorr, *The Power of Nations: The Political Economy of International Relations* (New York: Basic Books, 1975), pp. 7–8; and Andrew J. Pierre, *The Global Politics of Arms Sales* (Princeton: Princeton University Press, 1982).

26. See Raoul Naroll, *Military Deterrence in History* (Albany, N.Y.: State University of New York, 1974), p. 328; Wayne Ferris, *The Power Capabilities of Nation-States* (Lexington, Mass.: D. C. Heath, 1973); and Bruce M. Russett, "The Calculus of Deterrence," *Journal of Conflict Resolution*, 7 (June 1963), pp. 97–109.

27. Russett, *op. cit.*, p. 106.

28. *Ibid.*, pp. 106–108. See also Paul Huth and Russett, "What Makes Deterrence Work?" *World Politics*, 36 (July 1984), pp. 496–526; and Clifton Fink, "More Calculations about Deterrence," in Naomi Rosenbaum, ed., *Readings on the International Political System* (Englewood Cliffs, N.J.: Prentice-Hall, 1970), p. 191.

29. Richard Ned Lebow, *Between Peace and War: The Nature of International Crisis* (Baltimore: Johns Hopkins University Press, 1981), pp. 274–275.

30. See David A. Baldwin, *Economic Statecraft* (Princeton: Princeton University Press, 1985).

31. Knorr, *op. cit.*, pp. 134–138; and Knorr, "International Economic Leverage and Its Uses," in *Economic Issues and National Security*, Knorr and Frank N. Trager, eds. (Lawrence, Kansas: Regents Press of Kansas, 1977), ch. 4.

32. See James A. Caporaso and Michael D. Ward, "The United States in an Interdependent World: The Emergence of Economic Power," in *Challenges to America: United States Foreign Policy in the 1980's*, Charles W. Kegley, Jr., and Patrick J. McGowan, eds. (Beverly Hills: Sage, 1979), ch. 6.

33. Knorr, "Economic Leverage," p. 103.

34. This relates to earlier comments in Chapter 3. See Robert O. Keohane and Joseph S. Nye, *Power and Interdependence* (Boston: Little, Brown, 1977), pp. 12–19.

35. For a thorough discussion of the problems associated with using food as a weapon, see Cheryl Christiansen, "Food and National Security," in Knorr and Trager, *op. cit.*, ch. 11; and Peter Wallensteen, "Scarce Goods as Political Weapons: The Case of Food," *Journal of Peace Research*, 13, no. 4 (1976), pp. 277–298.

36. Stephen D. Krasner, "The Great Oil Sheikdown," *Foreign Policy*, no. 13 (Winter 1973–74), pp. 123–138.

37. See Hanns Maull, "Oil and Influence: The Oil Weapon Examined," in Knorr and Trager, *op. cit.*, ch. 10; also, Klaus Knorr, "The Limits of Economic and Military Power," in *The Oil Crisis*, Raymond Vernon, ed. (New York: W. W. Norton, 1976), pp. 229–243.

38. Peter Wallensteen, "Characteristics of Economic Sanctions," *Journal of Peace Research*, 5, no. 3 (1968), pp. 248–267; such findings are further substantiated by Margaret P. Doxey, *Economic Sanctions and International Enforcement*, 2nd ed. (New York: Oxford University Press, 1980), ch. 2; and James T. Bennett and Walter E. Williams, *Strategic Minerals: The Economic Impact of Supplier Disruptions* (Washington, D.C.: The Heritage Foundation, 1981).

39. Knorr, *The Power of Nations*. One study of 103 cases of economic sanctions since 1914 identifies certain "limited circumstances" in which they can work; see Gary Hufbauer and Jeffrey Schott, *Economic Sanctions in Support of Foreign Policy Goals* (Washington, D.C.: Institute for International Economics, 1983). James T. Lindsay has shown that while trade

sanctions usually fail if the goal is compliance, subversion, or deterrence, they retain great appeal as international and domestic political symbols. See Lindsay, "Trade Sanctions as Policy Instruments: A Re-examination," *International Studies Quarterly*, 30 (June 1986), pp. 153–173.

40. The tendency of foreign aid decisions to be made by donor countries based on political rather than economic criteria is discussed in R. D. McKinlay and R. Little, "A Foreign Policy Model of Bilateral Aid Allocation," *World Politics*, 30 (October 1977), pp. 58–86. On the relationship between aid and influence, see Joan M. Nelson, *Aid, Influence, and Foreign Policy* (New York: Macmillan, 1968); and Philip G. Roder, "The Ties that Bind: Aid, Trade, and Political Compliance in Soviet–Third World Relations," *International Studies Quarterly*, 29 (June 1985), pp. 191–216.

41. The lack of home country domination has especially been noted in U.S.-Canadian relations. See Joseph S. Nye, "Transnational Relations and Interstate Conflict: An Empirical Analysis," *International Organization*, 28 (Autumn 1974), pp. 961–998; David Leyton-Brown, "The Multinational Enterprise and Conflict in Canadian-American Relations," *International Organization*, 28 (Autumn 1974), pp. 733–754; and Keohane and Nye, *op. cit.*, ch. 7.

42. Richard S. Olson, "Economic Coercion in World Politics," *World Politics*, 31 (July 1979), pp. 471–494.

43. Miles Copeland, *The Game of Nations: The Amorality of Power Politics* (London: Weidenfeld and Nicolson, 1969).

44. *Ibid.*, p. 9.

Chapter 8. Breakdown in the Game: The Resort to Armed Force

1. The quote, based on the findings of Norman Cousins, is from Francis A. Beer, *Peace Against War: The Ecology of International Violence* (San Francisco: W. H. Freeman, 1981), p. 20.

2. Anthony Sampson, "Want to Start a War?" *Esquire* (March 1978), p. 60.

3. Stockholm International Peace Research Institute (SIPRI), *Yearbook of World Armaments and Disarmament* (Stockholm: Almquist and Wiksell, 1976), p. 48.

4. Karl von Clausewitz, *On War*, Anatol Rapoport, ed. (Baltimore: Penguin, 1968), p. 410.

5. Albert Einstein, correspondence with Sigmund Freud, in *Readings in World Politics*, Robert Goldwin and Tony Pearce, eds. (New York: Oxford University Press, 1970), p. 125.

6. See Bruce Bueno de Mesquita, *The War Trap* (New Haven, Conn.: Yale University Press, 1981).

7. Lloyd Jensen, *Explaining Foreign Policy* (Englewood Cliffs, N.J.: Prentice-Hall, 1982), p. 217.

8. Of course, wars can also end in deadlock or stalemate without being won or lost. On war settlement, see Robert F. Randle, *The Origins of Peace: A Study of Peacemaking and the Structure of Peace Settlements* (New York: Free Press, 1973); and Richard E. Barringer, *War: Patterns of Conflict* (Cambridge, Mass.: MIT Press, 1972); for a fuller classification of more or less complex wars, see also Manus I. Midlarsky, *On War: Political Violence in the International System* (New York: Free Press, 1975), pp. 8–14.

9. Dagobert L. Brito and Michael D. Intrilligator, "Conflict, War, and Redistribution," *American Political Science Review*, 79 (December 1985), p. 945. See also Jack S. Levy, "Misperception and the Causes of War: Theoretical Linkages and Analytical Problems," *World Politics*, 36 (October 1983), pp. 76–99.

10. See Albert Einstein and Sigmund Freud, "Why War?" *International Journal for the Reduction of Group Tensions*, 1 (January-March 1971), pp. 9–25; Freud, *Civilization and Its Discontents*, J. Strachey, ed. and trans. (New York: W. W. Norton, 1962), p. 58; and *The Standard Edition of the Complete Psychological Works of Sigmund Freud*, J. Strachey, ed. (London: Hogarth Press, 1953–1954), vols. 14 and 22, for a comparison with Freud's early, more pessimistic views on controlling or abolishing war.

11. See the work of Konrad Lorenz, *On Aggression* (New York: Bantam, 1967); F. Fornari, *The Psychoanalysis of War*, A. Pfeifer, trans. (Bloomington, Ind.: Indiana University Press, 1974);

and James A. Schellenberg, *The Science of Conflict* (New York: Oxford University Press, 1982).

12. See Ivo K. Feierabend, Rosalind L. Feierabend, and Ted R. Gurr, eds., *Anger, Violence, and Politics* (Englewood Cliffs, N.J.: Prentice-Hall, 1972); and Gurr, ed., *Handbook of Conflict Theory and Research* (New York: Free Press, 1980).

13. See Ted R. Gurr and V. F. Bishop, "Violent Nations and Others," *Journal of Conflict Resolution*, 20 (March 1976), pp. 79–110; and Frank L. Klingberg, "The Historical Alternation of Moods in American Foreign Policy," *World Politics*, 4 (March 1952), pp. 239–273.

14. See D. Fabbro, "Peaceful Societies: An Introduction," *Journal of Peace Research*, 15, no. 1 (1978), pp. 67-83; Ashley Montagu, *The Nature of Human Aggression* (New York: Oxford University Press, 1976); and I. Eibl-Eibesfeldt, *The Biology of Peace and War* (New York: Viking, 1979).

15. The disease analogy is fully developed by Beer, *op. cit.*, ch. 1; and criticized by Urs Luterbacher, "Last Words About War? A Review Article," *Journal of Conflict Resolution*, 28 (March 1984), pp. 165–182.

16. See Philip D. Zelikow, "Force Without War, 1975–82," *The Journal of Strategic Studies*, 7 (March 1984), pp. 29–54. For studies of American and Soviet uses of force short of war since 1945, see Stephen S. Kaplan, *Diplomacy of Power: Soviet Armed Forces as a Political Instrument* (Washington, D.C.: Brookings Institution, 1981); and Barry M. Blechman and Kaplan, *Force Without War: U.S. Armed Forces as a Political Instrument* (Washington, D.C.: Brookings Institution, 1979).

17. This definition and finding are drawn from the Correlates of War project directed by J. David Singer. Included here are "wars of national liberation" and other such conflicts between a colonial power and a colony seeking independence. See Melvin Small and J. David Singer, "Patterns in International Warfare, 1816–1980," in *International War: An Anthology and Study Guide*, ed. by Small and Singer (Homewood, Ill.: Dorsey Press, 1985). Also, see Small and Singer, "Conflict in the International System, 1816–1977: Historical Trends and Policy Futures," in Charles W. Kegley, Jr., and Patrick J. McGowan, eds., *Challenges to America: United States Foreign Policy in the 1980s* (Beverly Hills: Sage, 1979), pp. 89–115. The problems involved in developing an operational definition of war and measuring its occurrence are discussed in Singer and Small, *The Wages of War, 1816–1965: A Statistical Handbook* (New York: John Wiley, 1972), pp. 1–39.

18. Figures are derived from Jack S. Levy and T. Clifton Morgan, "The Frequency and Seriousness of International War: An Inverse Relationship," *Journal of Conflict Resolution*, 28 (December 1984), p. 742. On increased casualties, see also Beer, *op. cit.*, ch. 2; and Gwynn Dyer, *War* (Homewood, Ill.: Dorsey Press, 1985).

19. See Beer, *op. cit.* p. 41. In a study of 118 wars from 1816 to 1980, Melvin Small concludes that "international war appears to be neither on the rise or the decline." Small and Singer, "Patterns in International Warfare, 1816-1980," p. 13.

20. See Harold K. Jacobson, *Networks of Interdependence*, 2nd ed. (New York: Knopf, 1984), p. 192; and Small and Singer, "Conflict in the International System," pp. 97–99, for data on military confrontations involving at least one major power.

21. See Ruth L. Sivard, *World Military and Social Expenditures, 1985* (Washington, D.C.: World Priorities, 1985), p. 14; Istvan Kende, "Wars of Ten Years (1967–1976)," *Journal of Peace Research*, 15, no. 3 (1978), pp. 227–241; and Kende, "Dynamics of Wars, of Arms Trade and of Military Expenditures in the 'Third World,' 1945–1976," *Instant Research on Peace and Violence*, 7, no. 2 (1977), pp. 59–67.

22. Blechman and Kaplan, *op. cit.*, and Kaplan, *op. cit.* Many of these cases, however, involve only physical movements of military forces for intimidation or other political purposes without necessarily producing bloodshed, so that they are closer in nature to some of the phenomena discussed in Chapter 7.

23. William Eckhardt and Edward A. Azar, "Major World Conflicts and Interventions, 1945 to 1975," *International Interactions*, 5 (1978), pp. 78–83.

24. The concept of "diplomacy of violence" is developed by Thomas Schelling in *Arms and Influence* (New Haven, Conn.: Yale University Press, 1966), ch. 1. The concept of "coercive diplomacy" is developed by Alexander L. George, David K. Hall, and William R. Simons in *The Limits of Coercive Diplomacy* (Boston: Little, Brown, 1971).

25. Their potential threat to the Jordanian monarchy could have been another factor behind Hussein's decision to oust the Palestinians.

26. Glenn H. Snyder and Paul Diesing, *Conflict Among Nations: Bargaining, Decision Making, and System Structure in International Crises* (Princeton, N.J.: Princeton University Press, 1977), pp. 453–455.

27. Roy L. Prosterman, *Surviving to 3000* (Belmont, Calif.,: Duxbury Press, 1973), p. 33.

28. See Eckhardt and Azar, *op. cit.*, p. 85. See also Donald Blackburn *et al.*, *Restricted Engagement Options* (Vienna, Va.: BND Corporation, 1973), cited in Charles W. Kegley, Jr., and Eugene R. Wittkopf, *World Politics: Trend and Transformation* (New York: St. Martin's Press, 1981), p. 371; and Small and Singer, "Conflict in the International System," pp. 101–102.

29. Small and Singer, *ibid.*, p. 100.

30. Istvan Kende, "Twenty-five Years of Local Wars," *Journal of Peace Research*, 8, no. 1 (1971), pp. 5–22. A similar point is made by Eckhardt and Azar, *op. cit.*, p. 78, who counted thirty-six civil/international conflicts from 1945 to 1975.

31. Kende, "Twenty-five Years," p. 12. For another quantitative study of foreign military intervention in civil wars, see Richard Little, *Intervention: External Involvement in Civil Wars* (Totowa, N.J.: Rowman and Littlefield, 1975). For a more focused examination of revolutionary and counterrevolutionary struggles in recent times, see Nathan Leites and Charles Wolfe, Jr., *Rebellion and Authority: An Analytic Essay on Insurgent Conflicts* (Chicago: Markham, 1970). The film *The Battle of Algiers* (1966) also provides useful insight on this subject.

32. "A World at War—1983," *The Defense Monitor*, 12 (Washington, D.C.: Center for Defense Information, 1983).

33. For one of the earliest efforts, see Thucydides, *History of the Peloponnesian War*, R. Warner, trans. (Harmondsworth, England: Penguin, 1972). On philosophical approaches, see Keith L. Nelson and Spencer C. Olin, Jr., *Why War? Ideology, Theory and History* (Berkeley, Calif.: University of California Press, 1979); and Kenneth N. Waltz, *Man, the State, and War: A Theoretical Analysis* (New York: Columbia University Press, 1959). An excellent historical analysis is presented by Geoffrey Blainey, *The Causes of War* (New York: Free Press, 1973). The scientific approach is epitomized by the work of J. David Singer, *Correlates of War*, 2 vols. (New York: Free Press, 1979 and 1980).

34. See Ralph M. Goldman, *Arms Control and Peacekeeping: Feeling Safe in This World* (New York: Random House, 1982), pp. 2–8; Morton Fried *et al.*, *War: The Anthropology of Armed Conflict and Aggression* (Garden City, N.Y.: Natural History Press, 1967); and Andrew P. Vayda, *War in Ecological Perspective: Persistence, Change, and Adaptive Processes in Three Oceanic Societies* (New York: Plenum, 1976).

35. See Waltz, *op. cit.*

36. In animals, instincts are identified when individuals raised apart from others of their species nevertheless display behavior typical of that species. See Lorenz, *op. cit.*, and Robert Ardry, *The Territorial Imperative* (New York: Atheneum, 1966). Since such experiments are nearly impossible to conduct on humans, human instincts are extremely difficult to demonstrate. Researchers argue that if a behavior is found in all countries, regardless of culture, it can be assumed to result from instincts. Thus far, the only universal human behavior seems to be the showing of some form of deference (bowing, handshakes, etc.) when meeting strangers and the raising of eyebrows to indicate surprise.

37. An author who has emphatically argued that individual *personalities* have had a major impact on the outbreak of war is John Stoessinger, in *Why Nations Go to War*, 4th ed. (New York: St. Martin's Press, 1985).

38. See Ralph K. White, *Nobody Wanted War* (Garden City, N.Y.: Doubleday, 1968); and Ole R. Holsti, Robert C. North, and Richard A. Brody, "Perception and Action in the 1914 Crisis," in *Quantitative International Politics: Insights and Evidence,* J. David Singer, ed. (New York: Free Press, 1968), pp. 123–158, and Levy, *op. cit.*

39. Stuart A. Bremer, "National Capabilities and War Proneness," in J. David Singer, ed., *Correlates of War II: Testing Some Realpolitik Models* (New York: Free Press, 1980); Nazli Choucri and Robert C. North, *Nations in Conflict* (San Francisco: W. H. Freeman, 1975); and Erich Weede, "Conflict Behavior of Nation-States," *Journal of Peace Research,* 7, no. 3 (1970), pp. 229–235; and Charles F. Doran, "War and Power Dynamics: Economic Underpinnings," *International Studies Quarterly,* 27 (December 1983), pp. 419–441.

40. See Nelson and Olin, *op. cit.,* ch. 3; Quincy Wright, *A Study of War* (Chicago: University of Chicago Press, 1942); Erich Weede, "Democracy and War Involvement," *Journal of Conflict Resolution,* 28 (December 1984), pp. 649–664; and Steve Chan, "Mirror, Mirror on the Wall . . . Are the Free Countries More Pacific?" *Journal of Conflict Resolution,* 28 (December 1984), pp. 617–648.

41. See Joseph M. Scolnick, Jr., "An Appraisal of Studies of the Linkage between Domestic and International Conflict," *Comparative Political Studies,* 6 (January 1974), pp. 485–509; and Arthur Stein, "Conflict and Cohesion: A Review of the Literature," *Journal of Conflict Resolution,* 20 (March 1976), pp. 143–172.

42. Tom Broch and Johan Galtung, "Belligerence among the Primitives," *Journal of Peace Research,* (1966), pp. 33–45; and Wright, *op. cit.*

43. Beer, *op. cit.,* pp. 49–51; Frank Denton and Warren Phillips, "Some Patterns in the History of Violence," *Journal of Conflict Resolution,* 12 (June 1968), p. 193; and Arnold J. Toynbee, *A Study of History,* vol. 9 (London: Oxford University Press, 1954).

44. Inis Claude, *Power and International Relations* (New York: Random House, 1962), p. 56.

45. J. David Singer, "Accounting for International War: The State of the Discipline," *Journal of Peace Research,* 18, no. 1 (1981), p. 10.

46. See Michael P. Sullivan, *International Relations: Theories and Evidence* (Englewood Cliffs, N.J.: Prentice-Hall, 1976), pp. 179–189, for a review of research findings on power relationships; see also Singer, "Accounting for International War," pp. 10—11.

47. See especially A. F. K. Organski, *World Politics,* 2nd ed. (New York: Knopf, 1968), ch. 14; Organski and Jacek Kugler, *The War Ledger* (Chicago: University of Chicago Press, 1980); and Luterbacher, *op. cit.*

48. Karl W. Deutsch and J. David Singer, "Multipolar Power Systems and International Stability," *World Politics,* 16 (April 1964), pp. 390–406; and Kenneth W. Waltz, "The Stability of a Bipolar World," *Daedalus,* 93 (Summer 1964), pp. 881–909. See also Manus Midlarsky, "A Hierarchical Equilibrium Theory of Systemic War," *International Studies Quarterly,* 30 (March 1986), pp. 75–105.

49. For a review of empirical research in this area, see Sullivan, *op. cit.,* pp. 189–199; and Singer, "Accounting for International War," pp. 8–10. See also Randolph M. Siverson and John King, "Attributes of National Alliance Membership and War Participation, 1815–1964," *American Journal of Political Science,* 24 (February 1980), pp. 1–15.

50. See Jack S. Levy, "Theories of General War," *World Politics,* 37 (April 1985), pp. 344–374.

51. See Lewis F. Richardson, *Arms and Insecurity* (Pittsburgh: Boxwood, 1960); Michael Intrilligator and Dagobert L. Brito, "Can Arms Races Lead to the Outbreak of War?" *Journal of Conflict Resolution,* 28 (March 1984), pp. 63–84; George W. Downs, David M. Rockes and Randolph M. Siverson, "Arms Races and Cooperation," *World Politics,* 38 (October 1985), pp. 118–146; and Michael D. Wallace, "Armaments and Escalation: Two Competing Hypotheses," *International Studies Quarterly,* 26 (March 1982), pp. 37–56, and "Arms Races and Escalation: Some New Evidence," *Journal of Conflict Resolution,* 23 (March 1979), pp. 3–16.

52. Doran, *op. cit.,* and Doran and Wes Parsons, "War and the Cycle of Relative Power," *American Political Science Review,* 74 (December 1980), pp. 947–965.

53. Richard Ned Lebow, *Between Peace and War: The Nature of International Crisis* (Baltimore: Johns Hopkins University Press, 1981), preface and ch. 1.

54. Stanley Milgram, "Some Conditions of Obedience and Disobedience to Authority," *Human Relations*, 18 (February 1965), pp. 57–75; reprinted in Prosterman, *op. cit.*, p. 85.

55. *Ibid.*, p. 101.

56. S. L. A. Marshall, *Men Against Fire* (New York: Morrow, 1947).

57. Dwight D. Eisenhower, "Farewell Radio and Television Address to the American People," January 1961, *Public Papers of the President of the United States, Dwight D. Eisenhower, 1960–61* (Washington, D.C.: Government Printing Office, 1961), p. 1037; reprinted in *The Military-Industrial Complex*, Carroll W. Purcell, Jr., ed. (New York: Harper and Row, 1971), p. 206.

58. See Wallace, *op. cit.*; Richardson, *Arms and Insecurity*; and Anatol Rapoport, "Lewis Richardson's Mathematical Theory of War," *Journal of Conflict Resolution*, 1 (September 1957), pp. 249–299.

59. Lewis F. Richardson, *Statistics of Deadly Quarrels* (Pittsburgh: Boxwood, 1960).

60. Wallace, "Arms Races and Escalation."

61. Richardson, *Arms and Insecurity*, chs. 2 and 3. See useful summaries by Anatol Rapoport, *Conflict in Man-Made Environment* (Baltimore: Penguin, 1974), p. 161; and Kenneth E. Boulding, *Conflict and Defense: A General Theory* (New York: Harper and Row, 1962), ch. 2.

62. Samuel Huntington, "Arms Races: Prerequisites and Results," in *Approaches to Measurement in International Relations*, John Mueller, ed. (New York: Appleton-Century-Crofts, 1969), pp. 15–33.

63. For discussions of the beginnings of World War I, see Holsti *et al.*, *op. cit.*; Holsti, *Crisis, Escalation, War* (Montreal, Canada: McGill-Queens University Press, 1972); L. L. Farrar, Jr., "The Limits of Choice: July 1914 Reconsidered," *Journal of Conflict Resolution*, 16 (March 1972), pp. 1–23; and Paul Schroeder, "World War I as Galloping Gertie," *Journal of Modern History*, 44 (September 1972), pp. 319–345.

64. See Lebow, *op. cit.*; and Michael Brecher, ed., *Studies in Crisis Behavior* (Jerusalem: Hebrew University, 1978).

65. Frustration-aggression explanations have been applied to all types of violence, ranging from murder, to urban riots, to terrorism and international warfare. See John Dollard, Leonard W. Doob, *et al.*, *Frustration and Aggression* (New Haven: Conn.: Yale University Press, 1939); and Hugh D. Graham and Ted R. Gurr, eds., *Violence in America: Historical and Comparative Perspectives* (New York: Bantam, 1969).

66. On lateral pressure, see Nazli Choucri and Robert North, "Alternative Dynamics of International Conflict: Population, Resources, Technology, and Some Implications for Policy," in *Theory and Policy in International Relations*, Raymond Tanter and Richard Ullman, eds. (Princeton, N.J.: Princeton University Press, 1972); Choucri, *Population Dynamics and International Violence: Propositions, Insights, and Evidence* (Lexington, Mass.: D. C. Heath, 1974); Choucri and North, *Nations in Conflict*.

67. On this point, see Midlarsky, *On War*, chs. 2 and 3.

68. It is sometimes argued that "relative deprivation"—a gap between one's current situation and one's expectations—is a more important determinant of violence than one's absolute condition. According to "relative deprivation" theories applied to domestic politics, revolutions occur not when the masses are destitute and hopeless or when people are very rich, but rather when people's conditions have begun to improve, raising their expectations without fully satisfying them. See especially Ted R. Gurr, *Why Men Rebel* (Princeton, N.J.: Princeton University Press, 1970), ch. 2.

69. See Johan Galtung, "A Structural Theory of Aggression," *Journal of Peace Research*, 1, no. 2 (1964), pp. 95–119; Midlarsky, *On War*, ch. 5; Michael D. Wallace, "Power, Status, and International War," *Journal of Peace Research*, 8, no. 1 (1971), pp. 23–35; and Maurice East, "Status Discrepancy and Violence in the International System: An Empirical Analysis," in

The Analysis of International Politics, Vincent Davis *et al.,* eds. (New York: Free Press, 1972), pp. 299–319.

70. Blainey, *op. cit.,* ch. 3.

71. See A. F. K. Organski and Jacek Kugler, "The Costs of Major Wars," *American Political Science Review,* 71 (September 1977), pp. 1347–1366; Organski and Kugler, *The War Ledger;* and Organski, *World Politics,* pp. 207–215.

72. David W. Ziegler, *War, Peace, and International Politics* (Boston: Little, Brown, 1977), p. 1; and Dyer, *op. cit.,* photo caption facing p. 101.

73. Randolph M. Siverson, "War and Change in the International System," in Ole R. Holsti *et al.,* eds., *Change in the International System* (Boulder, Colo.: Westview Press, 1980), pp. 216–217.

74. See the works of F. Scott Fitzgerald and of historians such as Frederick Lewis Allen, *Only Yesterday: An Informal History of the 1920s* (New York: Harper and Row, 1964).

75. Although most economic recessions in the United States have historically occurred during periods of peace, so have most economic booms. See J. A. Thornton, "Wars, Peace, and Prosperity," L. L. Farrar, ed., *War: A Historical, Political, and Social Study* (Santa Barbara, Calif.: ABC-CLIO, 1978), p. 195; see also Harvey Starr *et al.,* "The Relationship Between Defense Spending and Inflation," *Journal of Conflict Resolution,* 28 (March 1984), pp. 103–122.

76. Richard E. Neustadt and Graham T. Allison, "Afterword," in *Thirteen Days,* by Robert F. Kennedy (New York: W. W. Norton, 1971), p. 115.

77. For a discussion of the myth that nuclear weapons will deter conventional war, or that nuclear weapons would not be used to repel an overwhelming conventional attack, see Bernard Brodie, *War and Politics* (New York: Macmillan, 1973), pp. 392–404.

78. Duncan Keith Shaw, *Prime Minister Neville Chamberlain* (London: Wells Gardner, updated), pp. 111–112, as quoted by Siverson, *op. cit.,* p. 216.

79. A good comparison of the balance of power and concert of powers approaches to world order is presented by Robert Jervis, "From Balance to Concert: A Study of International Security Cooperation," *World Politics,* 38 (October 1985), pp. 58–79.

80. On the theory of hegemonic stability, see Robert G. Gilpin, *War and Change in World Politics* (Cambridge: Cambridge University Press, 1981); and George Modelski, *Long Cycles in World Politics* (Seattle: University of Washington Press, 1987). A good overview of this literature is provided in Richard Rosecrance, "Long Cycle Theory and International Relations," *International Organization* 41 (Spring 1987), pp. 283–301.

81. See Robert O. Keohane, *After Hegemony: Cooperation and Discord in the World Political Economy* (Princeton: Princeton University Press, 1984).

82. Steven Rosen, ed., *Testing Theories of the Military-Industrial Complex* (Lexington, Mass.: Lexington Books, 1973), pp. 23–24.

83. Hans J. Morgenthau, *Politics Among Nations,* 5th ed. (New York: Knopf, 1973), p. 400.

84. See Kurt Gasteyger, *Searching for World Security: Understanding Global Armament and Disarmament* (London: Frances Pinter, 1985). See also U.S. scholar/diplomat George Kennan's eloquent plea to end the nuclear arms race, in remarks on receiving the Einstein Peace Prize in 1981, reprinted by Lloyd Shearer, "Intelligence Report," *Parade,* July 19, 1981.

85. Inis L. Claude, Jr., *Swords Into Plowshares,* 3rd. ed. (New York: Random House, 1964), p. 197.

86. The general problem of achieving cooperation in an anarchy-prone international system, and the role international institutions can play in conflict resolution, are ably discussed by Robert Axelrod and Robert O. Keohane, "Achieving Cooperation Under Anarchy: Strategies and Institutions," *World Politics,* 38 (October 1985), pp. 226–254.

87. For a variety of approaches to war termination and settlement, see Randle, *op. cit.,* especially chapter 2; and Barringer, *op. cit.* pp. 98–129.

88. Karl W. Deutsch *et al.*, "Political Community and the North Atlantic Area," *International Political Communities: An Anthology* (Garden City, N.Y.: Doubleday, 1966), pp. 1–91.

89. Kenneth E. Boulding, *Stable Peace* (Austin, Tex.: University of Texas Press, 1978), ch. 2.

PART III.   INTERNATIONAL INSTITUTIONS

Chapter 9.   International Law: Myth or Reality?

1. Lincoln P. Bloomfield, *The Foreign Policy Process: A Primer* (Englewood Cliffs, N.J.: Prentice-Hall, 1982), p. 139.

2. Paul Martin, Canadian Secretary of State for External Affairs, cited in *External Affairs*, 16 (1964).

3. This definition is based on a discussion by William D. Coplin in his *The Functions of International Law* (Chicago: Rand McNally, 1966), pp. 1–3.

4. This is the traditional notion of law attributed primarily to John Austin, a British writer in the nineteenth century; cited in Edward Collins, Jr., ed., *International Law in a Changing World* (New York: Random House, 1970), p. 2. For a discussion of how law and order can exist in a decentralized political system such as the international system, see Hedley Bull, *The Anarchical Society: A Study of Order in World Politics* (New York: Columbia University Press, 1977).

5. There is some disagreement over the consensual nature of customary international law, particularly as it applies to states that have just achieved independence and joined the international community. For a discussion of this issue, see Michael Akehurst, *A Modern Introduction to International Law*, 5th ed. (London: George Allen and Unwin, 1984), pp. 31–33.

6. *Ibid.*, p. 25. On trends in codification of international law and other aspects of lawmaking in the international system, see Nicholas G. Onuf, ed., *Law Making in the Global Community* (Durham, N.C.: Carolina Academic Press, 1982).

7. For a discussion of law observance, see Louis Henkin, *How Nations Behave*, 2nd ed. (New York: Columbia University Press, 1979), pp. 46–47; and Bull, *op. cit.*, p. 137.

8. David V. Edwards, *The American Political Experience*, 3rd ed. (Englewood Cliffs, N.J.: Prentice-Hall, 1985), pp. 374–375. Law enforcement is not much better in the British criminal justice system, with 59 percent of the serious crimes known to the police going unsolved. Akehurst, *op. cit.*, p. 2.

9. Data on the caseload of the Court, including a listing of the individual cases, can be found in A. LeRoy Bennett, *International Organizations*, 4th ed. (Englewood Cliffs, N.J.: Prentice-Hall, 1988), pp. 179–182; also, see *UN Chronicle*, 20, no. 11 (1983), pp. 47–53.

10. On the tendency of defendant states to refuse to participate in ICJ proceedings despite court rulings that the court has jurisdiction, see Dana D. Fischer, "Decisions to Use the International Court of Justice," *International Studies Quarterly*, 26 (June 1982), pp. 251–277.

11. These are the words of Benjamin Civiletti, former U.S. Attorney General, in his oral argument presented before the World Court on December 10, 1979, during the proceedings of the *US Diplomatic and Consular Staff in Tehran* case; cited in U.S. Department of State, Bureau of Public Affairs, Current Policy No. 118 (December 1979), p. 1.

12. The term "allocation of legal competences" is borrowed from Coplin, *op. cit.* See chapter 2 of his book for a discussion of the way in which international law performs this function.

13. One of the best statements of the relationship between law and politics in international relations is found in Morton A. Kaplan and Nicholas DeB. Katzenbach, *The Political Foundations of International Law* (New York: John Wiley, 1961).

14. For a discussion of Western, Communist, and Third World views of international law, see Akehurst, *op. cit.*, ch. 2.

15. In the case of the League of Nations Covenant, the only obligation of states to refrain from war was that they at least exhaust all peaceful settlement procedures first. For a discussion of the Covenant and the Kellogg-Briand Pact, see Bennett, *op. cit.*, ch. 2.

16. One of the most widely accepted definitions of "self-defense" was offered by U.S. Secretary of State Daniel Webster in condemning British actions in the Caroline case during the nineteenth century. Webster argued that the use of force in self-defense was permissible "only when the necessity for action is instant, overwhelming and leaving no choice of means, and no moment for deliberation." See Collins, *op. cit.*, pp. 336–337.

17. This remark is owed to Samuel Sharp, made in a presentation at the University of Missouri–St. Louis on April 17, 1980.

18. Henkin, *op. cit.*, p. 146.

19. Article 3 of the 1949 Geneva Convention dealt with treatment of prisoners in civil wars, but only weakly.

20. One scholar has found evidence, however, that in a large proportion of internal conflicts since World War II, the warring parties have honored the obligations contained in the 1949 Geneva Conventions regarding civil war. See David P. Forsythe, "Legal Management of Internal War: The 1977 Protocol on Non-International Armed Conflict," *American Journal of International Law*, 72 (1978), pp. 275–276.

21. For a discussion of these protocols and recent attempts to develop rules in this area, see *ibid.*; William V. O'Brien, *The Conduct of Just and Limited War* (New York: Praeger, 1981); Geoffrey Best, *Humanity in Warfare* (New York: Columbia University Press, 1980); and Michael Bothe *et al.*, eds., *New Rules for Victims of Armed Conflicts* (The Hague: Martinus Nijhoff, 1982).

22. Raymond Vernon, "Multinationals: No Strings Attached," *Foreign Policy*, Winter 1978–79, p. 122.

23. See Collins, *op. cit.*, p. 254.

24. For a discussion of the "minimum international standard" issue in general and the expropriation issue in particular, see Akehurst, *op. cit.*, ch. 7.

25. As noted in an earlier note, a recent survey found that only one-third of the world's people live in countries whose political systems could be classified as "free." Altogether, fifty-three nations were deemed "free," fifty-nine "partly free," and fifty-five "not free." Raymond G. Gastil, *Freedom in the World: Political Rights and Civil Liberties, 1984–85* (Westport, Conn.: Greenwood Press, 1985), pp. 11 and 25.

26. For a discussion of human rights and international law, see Abdul Said, ed., *Human Rights and World Order* (New Brunswick, N.J.: Rutgers University Press, 1978); Richard Falk, *Human Rights and State Sovereignty* (New York: Holmes and Meier, 1982); and David P. Forsythe, *Human Rights and World Politics* (Lincoln: University of Nebraska Press, 1983).

Chapter 10. International Organizations: Links Between Governments and Between Peoples

1. *Fortune* (August 13, 1979), p. 208.

2. *Yearbook of International Organizations*, 15th ed. (Brussels: Union of International Associations, 1974), pp. S33–37.

3. Werner J. Feld, *The European Community in World Affairs* (Sherman Oaks, Calif.: Alfred, 1976), p. 35.

4. Kjell Skjelsbaek, "The Growth of International Nongovernmental Organization in the Twentieth Century," *International Organization*, 25 (Summer 1971), pp. 435–436.

5. Harold K. Jacobson, *Networks of Interdependence*, 2nd ed. (New York: Knopf, 1984), p. 14.

6. Depending on the criteria used, one might find over 600 IGOs and 6000 NGOs in the world; see Jacobson, *op. cit.*, pp. 9–10. For a discussion of membership classification, see Werner J.

Feld and Roger A. Coate, *The Role of International Nongovernmental Organizations in World Politics* (New York: Learning Resources in International Studies, 1976), pp. 1–9.

7. For a comparison of regional and global IGO growth, see Charles W. Kegley, Jr., and J. Martin Rochester, "Assessing the Impact of Trends on the International System: The Growth of Intergovernmental Organizations," in William D. Coplin and Kegley, eds., *A Multi-Method Introduction to International Politics* (Chicago: Markham, 1971), p. 404; Jacobson, *op. cit.*, pp. 47–50; and Jacobson *et al.*, "National Entanglements in International Governmental Organizations," *American Political Science Review*, 80 (March 1986), pp. 145–147.

8. Jacobson *et al.*, "National Entanglements," p. 149.

9. Werner J. Feld, *International Relations: A Transnational Approach* (Sherman Oaks, Calif: Alfred, 1979), p. 259.

10. *Ibid.*

11. Jacobson, *Networks of Interdependence*, p. 49.

12. Feld, *International Relations*, p. 256.

13. James A. Field, Jr., "Transnationalism and the New Tribe," *International Organization*, 25 (Summer 1971), pp. 355–356.

14. Jacobson, *Networks of Interdependence*, p. 10.

15. Robert C. Angell, *Peace on the March: Transnational Participation* (New York: Van Nostrand Reinhold, 1969). Included in his definition of "transnational participation" are activities engaged in by representatives of national governments, such as U.S. Peace Corps volunteers and delegates to IGOs, although most of his study focuses on nongovernmental actors.

16. A. LeRoy Bennett, *International Organizations*, 3rd ed. (Englewood Cliffs, N.J.: Prentice-Hall, 1984), p. 421.

17. Joseph S. Nye, Jr., and Robert O. Keohane, "Transnational Relations and World Politics: A Conclusion," *International Organization*, 25 (Summer 1971), p. 723.

18. Jacobson, *Networks of Interdependence*, pp. 9 and 48.

19. For a discussion of decision making in IGOs, especially the Specialized Agencies, see Robert W. Cox *et al.*, *The Anatomy of Influence: Decision Making in International Organization* (New Haven, Conn.: Yale University Press, 1973).

20. The football match riot was merely the incident that touched off the hostilities. Tensions had been building for some time between Honduras and El Salvador over the latter's complaints about Honduran mistreatment of thousands of Salvadoran workers in Honduras.

21. Joseph S. Nye, *Peace in Parts* (Boston: Little, Brown, 1971), p. 169. The OAS was the most successful, followed by the OAU and Arab League.

22. Robert E. Riggs, "One Small Step for Functionalism: UN Participation and Congressional Attitude Change," *International Organization*, 31 (Summer 1977), pp. 515–539. Similar findings on the effects of IGO participation were reported in an earlier study by Chadwick F. Alger in "United Nations Participation as a Learning Experience," *Public Opinion Quarterly*, 27 (Fall 1963), pp. 411–426.

23. The classic formulation of functionalist theory is David Mitrany, *A Working Peace System: An Argument for the Functional Development of International Organization* (London: Royal Institute of International Affairs, 1943). An analysis of Mitrany is provided by James P. Sewell, *Functionalism and World Politics* (Princeton, N.J.: Princeton University Press, 1966), pp. 28–72.

24. For the "neofunctionalist" viewpoint and discussion of the "spill-over" concept, see Ernst B. Haas, "International Integration: The European and the Universal Process," in *International Political Communities* (New York: Doubleday Anchor, 1966), pp. 93–130; and Leon N. Lindberg and Stuart A. Scheingold, *Europe's Would-Be Polity* (Englewood Cliffs, N.J.: Prentice-Hall, 1970), pp. 117–120 especially.

25. James A. Caporaso, *Functionalism and Regional Integration: A Logical and Empirical Assessment* (Beverly Hills: Sage, 1972). See also Peter Wolf, "International Organization and Attitude Change: A Re-Examination of the Functionalist Approach," *International Organization*, 27 (Summer 1973), pp. 347–371.

26. Jacobson *et al.*, "National Entanglements," p. 152. Jacobson and his co-authors acknowledge that IGO growth is not the only explanation for the drop in interstate wars since World War II, but they argue it has been a contributing factor.

27. See Richard Bernstein, "The UN Versus the U.S.," *The New York Times Magazine*, January 22, 1984, p. 21; and Robert E. Riggs, "The United States and Diffusion of Power in the Security Council," *International Studies Quarterly*, 22 (December 1978), p. 529. The other three permanent members of the Security Council have been less inclined to use the veto than either the United States or the Soviet Union.

28. Riggs, "The United States and Diffusion of Power," p. 525. Also, see Bernstein, *op. cit.*, and M. J. Peterson, *The General Assembly in World Politics* (London: Allen and Unwin, 1986).

29. For a general discussion of the "loyalty" question and other issues related to the UN Secretariat, see Bennett, *op. cit.*, ch. 15; and Theodor Meron, *The United Nations Secretariat* (Lexington, Mass.: D. C. Heath, 1977).

30. Cited in *Chronicle*, published by the Dag Hammarskjold Information Centre on the Study of Violence and Peace, 2 (March 1982), p. 12.

31. For a good discussion of these and other UN peacekeeping activities, see Bennett, *op. cit.*, ch. 7; and John F. Murphy, *The United Nations and the Control of International Violence* (Totowa, N.J.: Allanheld, Osmun, 1983).

32. The so-called "Article 17 crisis" occurred during the 1960s over the financing of the UN peacekeeping force (ONUC) in the Congo. The Soviet Union refused to pay its share, arguing that the Secretary-General had exceeded his authority and the instructions of the Security Council in administering the operation. Article 17 of the Charter stipulates that any member who is negligent in paying its assessed contributions to the United Nations can be suspended. The United States ended up paying for most of the Congo operation, choosing not to pursue the possible suspension or expulsion of the Soviet Union from the United Nations. However, financial problems continue to plague the organization and have worsened in recent years.

33. The authors found that the UN was active in 29 of 32 cases involving "full scale war" and was effective in 13 of these cases. Jonathan Wilkenfeld and Michael Brecher, "International Crises 1945–1975: The UN Dimension," *International Studies Quarterly*, 28 (March 1984), pp. 45–67.

34. One study that questions the effectiveness of the UN and finds the organization becoming increasingly ineffective since 1970 is Ernst B. Haas, "Regime Decay: Conflict Management and International Organizations, 1945–1981," *International Organization*, 37 (Spring 1983), pp. 189–256; also, Haas, *Why We Still Need the UN* (Berkeley: U. of California, 1986).

35. Lindberg and Scheingold, *op. cit.*, p. 2.

36. An excellent discussion of the formal structure as well as the political process of the European Community can be found in Roy Pryce, *The Politics of the European Community* (Totowa, N.J.: Rowman and Littlefield, 1973), especially ch. 3.

37. The quote is attributed to Geoffrey Ripon, a chief negotiator representing Britain when it entered the Community in 1973; cited in *New York Times*, March 21, 1982, p. 6.

38. See Roger Hansen's review essay "European Integration: Forward March, Parade Rest, or Dismissed?" in *International Organization*, 27 (Spring 1973), pp. 225–254. For the view that recent trends point more toward disintegration than integration, see Paul Taylor, "Intergovernmentalism in the European Communities in the 1970s: Patterns and Perspectives," *International Organization*, 26 (Autumn 1982), pp. 741–766.

39. An annual poll taken in the spring of 1981 found that 69 percent of the respondents reacted positively to the general question, "In general, are you for or against efforts being made to unify Western Europe?" Luxembourg, Italy, and the Netherlands were most supportive, with Denmark, the United Kingdom, and Greece being least supportive. There was less overall positive response when more pointed questions were asked about the surrender of national sovereignty. See *Euro-Barometre*, no. 15 (June 1981), pp. 15–45. See also Ronald Inglehart, "The New Europeans: Inward or Outward-Looking?" *International Organization*, 24 (Winter 1970), pp. 129–139.

PART IV.　THE GLOBAL CONDITION: THE POLITICS OF GLOBAL PROBLEM SOLVING

1. Oran R. Young, "International Regimes: Problems of Concept Formation," *World Politics*, 32 (April 1980), pp. 332–333.
2. Robert O. Keohane and Joseph S. Nye, *Power and Interdependence* (Boston: Little, Brown, 1977), p. 5. On the concept of regimes, see Stephen D. Krasner, ed., *International Regimes* (Ithaca, N.Y.: Cornell University Press, 1983); and the review essay by Oran R. Young, "International Regimes: Toward a New Theory of Institutions," in *World Politics*, 39 (October 1986), pp. 104–122.

Chapter 11.　The Control of Violence: Arms Races and Arms Control in the Nuclear Age

1. For descriptions of the "weapons game," see Helena Tuomi and Raimo Vayrynen, *Transnational Corporations, Armaments and Development* (London: Gower, 1982); Russell Warren Howe, *Arms, Money and Diplomacy* (London: Sphere Books, 1981); and J. S. Mehta, ed., *Third World Militarization: A Challenge to Third World Diplomacy* (Austin: L. B. Johnson School of Public Affairs, University of Texas, 1985).
2. See Ruth L. Sivard, *World Military and Social Expenditures, 1981* (Leesburg, Va.: World Priorities, 1981), p. 5, and *World Military and Social Expenditures, 1985* (Washington, D.C.: World Priorities, 1985), p. 5.
3. These figures are taken from Sivard, *op. cit.*, 1981 and 1985; Stockholm International Peace Research Institute (SIPRI), *Arms Uncontrolled*, prepared by Frank Barnaby and Ronald Huisken (Cambridge, Mass.: Harvard University Press, 1975), pp. 1–7; and John Turner and SIPRI, *Arms in the 80s* (London: Taylor and Francis, 1985), pp. 11–13.
4. Sivard, *op. cit.*, 1985, p. 39.
5. *World Military Expenditures and Arms Transfers, 1985* (Washington, D.C.: US Arms Control and Disarmament Agency, 1985), pp. 1–11; see also Turner and SIPRI, *op. cit.*, pp. 59–68.
6. *World Military Expenditures and Arms Transfers, 1985*, p. 6.
7. Richard F. Grimmett, *Trends in Conventional Arms Transfers to the Third World by Major Supplier, 1978–1985* (Washington, D.C.: Congressional Research Service, 1986), p. 1.
8. Trends in arms transfers are discussed by Andrew J. Pierre, *The Global Politics of Arms Sales* (Princeton, N.J.: Princeton University Press, 1982); and by Leslie H. Gelb, "Arms Sales," *Foreign Policy*, no. 25 (Winter 1976–77), pp. 3–23.
9. *Arming the World: An Introduction to the International Arms Trade and Alternatives* (London: Campaign Against Arms Trade, 1980), pp. 15–17.
10. Grimmett, *op. cit.*, pp. 1–2.
11. For a discussion of "candidates for the nuclear club," see Leonard Spector, "Nuclear Proliferation: The Silent Threat," *National Forum*, 66 (Fall 1986), pp. 5–7.
12. Colin Smith and Shyam Bhatia, "Proliferation: Atoms for War," *The Observer* (London), December 16, 1979.
13. SIPRI, *Armament or Disarmament? The Crucial Choice* (Stockholm: SIPRI, 1979), p. 15.
14. Turner and SIPRI, *op. cit.*, pp. 55–56.
15. "Can the Lid Be Kept On?" *The Economist*, July 23, 1982, pp. 78–79.
16. David C. Gompert, "Introduction: Nuclear Proliferation and the 1980s Project," in *Nuclear Proliferation: Motivations, Capabilities, and Strategies for Control*, Ted Greenwood, Harold Feiveson, and Theodore B. Taylor, eds. (New York: McGraw-Hill, 1977), p. 1.
17. On CAT, see Gelb, *op. cit.*
18. Pierre, *Arms Sales, op. cit.*, pp. 14–38.
19. On bureaucratic politics within the U.S. Defense Department, see Asa Clark, "Armies Walk, Air Forces Fly, Navies Sail, . . . and Military Services Compete: Interservice Competition and US Defense Policy," paper delivered at annual meeting of the International Studies Association, Cincinnati, March 1982.

20. Anthony Sampson, *The Arms Bazaar* (London: Hodder and Stoughton, 1977), pp. 23–30; see also, Patrick Brogan and Albert Zarca, *Deadly Business: Sam Cummings, Interarms, and the Arms Trade* (New York: W. W. Norton, 1983).

21. See Freeman Dyson, *Weapons and Hope* (New York: Harper and Row, 1984), pt. 4.

22. See Erich Weede, "Some (Western) Dilemmas in Managing Extended Deterrence," *Journal of Peace Research*, 22, no. 4 (1985), pp. 223–238; R. Ned Lebow, "Deterrence Reconsidered: The Challenges of Recent Research," *Survival*, 27 (January-February 1985), pp. 20–28; and Eckhard Lubkemeier, "Extended Deterrence: Implications for Arms Limitation and Reduction," *Bulletin of Peace Proposals*, 16, no. 3 (1985), pp. 249–254. See also Richard Pipes, "Why the Soviet Union Thinks It Could Fight and Win a Nuclear War," *Commentary*, 64 (July 1977), pp. 21–34.

23. For excellent reviews of peacekeeping dilemmas, see Anthony Verrier, *International Peacekeeping: United Nations Forces in a Troubled World* (New York: Penguin, 1981); and Indar Jit Rikhye, Michael Harbottle, and Bjorn Egge, *The Thin Blue Line: International Peacekeeping and Its Future* (New Haven: Yale University Press, 1974).

24. The statement was made by William Epstein, cited in *Progress in Arms Control?* (San Francisco: W. H. Freeman, 1978), p. 183.

25. Michael R. Gordon, "The Arms Race Shows No Signs of Slowing Down," *New York Times*, March 23, 1986, p. E-3, based on SIPRI data.

26. See "Arms Control: The Gap Narrows," *The Economist*, June 21, 1986, p. 47; Chalmers Hardenbergh, "News of Negotiations," *ADIU Report*, 8 (Brighton, U.K.: Armament and Disarmament Information Unit, Sussex University, March-April, 1986), pp. 19–21; and Elizabeth Pond, "Quiet Talks Continue on Arms Control," *Christian Science Monitor*, November 17, 1986, pp. 1 and 48.

27. Efforts to control conventional weapons, both before and after World War II, are discussed by Frank Gregory, in "Conventional Arms Control: A Survey and Analysis," *ADIU Report*, 3 (May-June 1981), pp. 7–9.

28. Mark F. Imber, "Arms Control Verification: The Special Case of IAEA-NPT Special Inspection," paper presented to Seminar on Arms Control Verification, Lancaster, England, The University of Lancaster, April 1982, p. 7.

29. SIPRI, *Armament or Disarmament?*, p. 16.

30. James A. Schear, "Arms Control and Verification: Learning from Experience," paper presented to the Seminar on Arms Control Verification, Lancaster, England, University of Lancaster, April 1982, pp. 16–17; and William H. Kincaide, "Challenge to Verification: New and Old," Seminar on Arms Control Verification.

31. Isaiah 2:4.

32. Thomas C. Schelling, "Thinking About Nuclear Terrorism," *International Security*, 6 (Spring 1982), p. 76.

Chapter 12. The Control of Violence: Combatting International Terrorism

1. This was roughly the number of incidents counted by the U.S. State Department's Office of Counter-Terrorism; cited in *The Economist*, July 26, 1986, p. 44.

2. See Thurston Clarke, *By Blood and Fire: The Attack on the King David Hotel* (New York: Putnam, 1981).

3. One observer who argues that the line between terrorists and freedom fighters is very clear is James Q. Wilson in "Thinking About Terrorism," *Commentary*, 72 (July 1981), pp. 34–39. For a different view, see Benjamin B. Ferencz, "When One Person's Terrorism Is Another Person's Heroism," *Human Rights*, 9 (Summer 1981), pp. 39–43.

4. Frank H. Perez, Deputy Director, Office for Combatting Terrorism, U.S. State Department, cited in U.S. State Department Bureau of Public Affairs, Current Policy No. 402 (June 10, 1982). Similar definitions are offered in Timothy B. Garrigan and George A. Lopez, *Terrorism: A Problem of Political Violence* (Columbus, Ohio: Consortium for International Studies

Education, 1978), pp. 1–2; Andrew J. Pierre, "The Politics of International Terrorism," *Orbis*, 19 (Winter 1976), pp. 1251–1270; and Alan D. Buckley, "Editor's Foreword," *Journal of International Affairs*, 32 (Spring-Summer 1978).

5. See Walter Laqueur, *Terrorism* (London: Weidenfeld and Nicolson, 1977).

6. On this point, see Ted Robert Gurr, "Some Characteristics of Political Terrorism in the 1960s," in Michael Stohl, ed., *The Politics of Terrorism*, 2nd ed. (New York: Marcel Dekker, 1983), p. 27.

7. On the use of terrorism by groups seeking to seize state power, see Edward Luttwak, *Coup d' Etat: A Practical Handbook* (Cambridge: Harvard University Press, 1979).

8. See Gurr, *op. cit.*, p. 25.

9. For the view that states commit terrorist acts no less than nonstate actors, see Michael Stohl and George A. Lopez, eds., *The State as Terrorist: The Dynamics of Governmental Violence and Repression* (Greenwood, Ill.: Greenwood Press, 1984).

10. On links between state and nonstate actors, especially the role of the Soviet Union, see Claire Sterling, *The Terror Network* (New York: Holt, Rinehart and Winston, 1981).

11. "International Terrorism," *GIST* (Washington, D.C.: U.S. State Department, August 1985) and *Patterns of Global Terrorism: 1985* (Washington, D.C.: U.S. State Department, November 1986). The trend data mentioned in this section of the text are taken from surveys conducted by the U.S. State Department's Office of Counter-Terrorism. These data tend to understate the amount of terrorism since the data include only those acts considered to be "international terrorism," i.e., involving the citizens or territory of more than one country, and exclude completely indigenous acts of terrorism. The data are also somewhat controversial in that they may underreport the degree of political violence occurring in certain regions of the world such as Africa. Data compiled by the Rand Corporation generally are consistent with the U.S. State Department findings, although somewhat different counting procedures are used; see the Rand Corporation Chronologies of International Terrorism, directed by Brian Jenkins.

12. Edward Mickolus makes the point that, while domestic terrorism may occur most often in less developed states, "international forms of political terrorism" occur most often in developed, Western states. For an overview of international terrorism trends between 1968 and 1980, see Mickolus, "International Terrorism," in Michael Stohl, ed., *The Politics of Terrorism*, 2nd ed. (New York: Marcel Dekker, 1983), pp. 221–253. Also, see Brian Jenkins, "International Terrorism: Trends and Potentialities," *Journal of International Affairs*, 32 (Spring-Summer 1978), pp. 122–135.

13. David L. Milbank, "International and Transnational Terrorism: Diagnosis and Prognosis" (Washington, D.C.: U.S. Central Intelligence Agency, April 1976); and Chalmers Johnson, "Perspectives on Terrorism, Summary Report of the Conference on International Terrorism" (Washington, D.C.: U.S. Department of State, 1976). Both are cited in Garrigan and Lopez, *op. cit.*, pp. 5–6.

14. Laqueur, *op. cit.*, p. 221. Also, see Laqueur, "The Futility of Terrorism," *Harper's*, March 1976. Political scientist Ted Gurr examined eighty-seven countries between 1960 and 1976, and found measurable changes made in the political systems traceable to terrorism in only a half-dozen cases; cited in Neil C. Livingstone, "Is Terrorism Effective?" *International Security Review* (Fall 1981), pp. 387–409.

15. See Robert Katz, *Days of Wrath: The Ordeal of Aldo Moro, The Kidnapping, The Execution, The Aftermath* (New York: Doubleday, 1980); and Daniela Salvoni and Anders Stephanson, "Reflections on the Red Brigades," *Orbis*, 29 (Fall 1985), pp. 489–506.

16. John Newhouse, "A Freemasonry of Terrorism," *The New Yorker*, July 8, 1985, pp. 55–58.

17. See Paul Wilkinson, *Terrorism and the Liberal State* (London: Macmillan, 1977), p. 228.

18. See J. D. Zawodny, "Infrastructures of Terrorist Organizations," in Lawrence Z. Freedman and Yonah Alexander, eds., *Perspectives on Terrorism* (Wilmington, Del.: Scholarly Resources, Inc., 1983), pp. 61–70; and Martha Crenshaw, "An Organizational Approach to the Analysis of Political Terrorism," *Orbis*, 29 (Fall 1985), pp. 465–489.

19. The term is borrowed from Newhouse, *op. cit.*, p. 46.

20. Buckley, *op. cit.* For a good survey of terrorist groups operating in different regions of the world, see Michael Stohl, ed., *The Politics of Terrorism*, 2nd ed. (New York: Marcel Dekker, 1983), pt 2.

21. See Aaron David Miller, *The PLO and the Politics of Survival* (Washington, D.C.: Center for Strategic and International Studies, 1983); and *The Middle East*, 6th ed. (Washington, D.C.: Congressional Quarterly, 1986), p. 14.

22. Evidence of Soviet and Libyan support for international terrorism is presented in Sterling, *op. cit.*; and Wilson, *op. cit.* "Dirty tricks" played by the U.S. Central Intelligence Agency are discussed in Philip Agee, *Inside the Company: CIA Diary* (New York: Stonehill, 1975).

23. See Garrigan and Lopez, *op. cit.*, pp. 14–15. On the problems associated with developing a legal regime for regulating terrorism, see Harry H. Almond, Jr., "The Legal Regulation of International Terrorism," *Conflict*, 3, no. 2 (1981), pp. 144–165.

24. Alona Evans, "Aerial Hijacking," in *International Terrorism and Political Crimes*, M. Cherif Bassionni, ed. (Springfield, Ill.: Charles C. Thomas, 1974), p. 247.

25. See Paul A. Tharp, Jr., "The Laws of War as a Potential Legal Regime for the Control of Terrorist Activities," *Journal of International Affairs*, 32 (Spring-Summer 1978), pp. 94–97; and Juliet Lodge, "The European Community and Terrorism: Establishing the Principle of Extradite or Try," in *Terrorism: A Challenge to the State*, Lodge, ed. (Oxford: Martin Robertson, 1981), pp. 164–194.

26. Stephen Sloan, "International Terrorism: Academic Quest, Operational Art and Policy Implications," *Journal of International Affairs*, 32 (Spring-Summer 1978), p. 3; and Abraham H. Miller, *Terrorism and Hostage Negotiations* (Boulder, Colo.: Westview Press, 1980).

27. Livingstone, *op. cit.*, p. 409.

Chapter 13.   The Promotion of Prosperity: Keeping the World Economy Running

1. The first term is attributed to Peter Drucker; cited in Richard J. Barnet and Ronald E. Müller, *Global Reach* (New York: Simon and Schuster, 1975), p. 14. The second term is attributed to the president of the IBM World Trade Corporation; cited in *ibid*.

2. *Newsweek*, May 10, 1982, p. 98.

3. Charles Lipson, "International Cooperation in Economic and Security Affairs," *World Politics*, 37 (October 1984), p. 12. A similar observation is made by Robert Jervis in "Security Regimes," *International Organization*, 36 (Spring 1982), pp. 357–378.

4. Statistics on postwar world economic trends can be found in Joan E. Spero, *The Politics of International Economic Relations*, 3rd ed. (New York: St. Martin's Press, 1985), pp. 117–118; John W. Sewell *et al.*, *U.S. Foreign Policy and the Third World, Agenda 1985–86* (New Brunswick, N.J.: Transaction Books, 1985), p. 181; the Brandt Commission, *Common Crisis— North-South: Cooperation for World Recovery* (London: Pan Books, 1983), p. 22; and Lester R. Brown *et al.*, *State of the World, 1985* (New York: W. W. Norton, 1985), pp. 7–8.

5. For one of the best statements of the mercantilist view, see Jacob Viner, "Power Versus Plenty as Objectives of Foreign Policy in the Seventeenth and Eighteenth Centuries," *World Politics*, 1 (October 1948), pp. 1–29.

6. One of the foremost proponents of the liberal internationalist school is Harry Johnson. See his *Economic Policies Toward Developed Countries* (Washington, D.C.: Brookings Institution, 1967) and "The Probable Effects of Freer Trade on Individual Countries," in *Toward a New World Policy: The Maidenhead Papers*, C. Fred Bergsten, ed. (Lexington, Mass.: D. C. Heath, 1975). Also representative of this school, but somewhat more sympathetic toward Third World concerns, are Richard Cooper and Roger Hansen. See Richard N. Cooper *et al.*, *Towards a Renovated International System* (New York: The Trilateral Commission, 1977); and Roger Hansen *et al.*, *Rich and Poor Nations in the World Economy* (New York: McGraw-Hill, 1978).

7. Representative of the *dependencia* school are Gabriel Kolko's *The Limits of Power* (New York: Harper and Row, 1972); Johan Galtung's "A Structural Theory of Imperialism," *Journal of Peace Research*, 8, no. 2 (1971), pp. 81–117; and Susanne Bodenheimer, "Dependency and Imperialism: The Root of Latin American Underdevelopment," in *Readings in U.S. Imperialism*, K. T. Fann and D. C. Hodges, eds. (Boston: Porter Sargent Publisher, 1971), pp. 155–182.

8. The world system approach can be found in Immanuel Wallerstein's *The Modern World-System II: Mercantilism and the Consolidation of the European World-Economy, 1600–1750* (New York: Academic Press of America, 1980) and *The Capitalist World-Economy* (Cambridge: Cambridge University Press, 1979). Also, see "World System Debates," a special issue of *International Studies Quarterly*, 25 (March 1981), devoted to discussion of the world system approach.

9. See Stephen Hymer, "The Multinational Corporation and the Law of Uneven Development," in *Economics and World Order: From the 1970s to the 1990s*, Jagdish N. Bhagwati, ed. (New York: Macmillan, 1972), pp. 113–140; and Christopher K. Chase-Dunn, "The System of World Cities," mimeo, Johns Hopkins University, Department of Social Relations, May 1981.

10. For a critique of both "global liberalism" and "dependencia" ideas from a realist perspective, see Stephen D. Krasner, *Structural Conflict: The Third World Against Global Liberalism* (Berkeley: University of California Press, 1985).

11. This framework follows that suggested by William D. Coplin in his *Introduction to International Politics: A Theoretical Overview* (Chicago: Markham, 1971), pp. 194–200.

12. For patterns of world trade, see *Atlas of United States Foreign Relations* (Washington, D.C.: U.S. State Department, 1985), p. 53; and David H. Blake and Robert S. Walters, *The Politics of Global Economic Relations*, 3rd ed. (Englewood Cliffs, N.J.: Prentice-Hall, 1987), ch. 2.

13. See Steven E. Sanderson, ed., *The Americas in the New International Division of Labor* (New York: Holmes and Meier, 1984); Sewell *et al.*, *op. cit.*, p. 191; and *World Development Report, 1983* (Washington, D.C.: World Bank, 1983).

14. Mark Gasiorowski, "The Structure of Third World Interdependence," paper delivered at the annual meeting of the International Studies Association, Cincinnati, Ohio, March 26, 1982, p. 39. GDP refers to the total value of goods and services produced during a given period of time by all factors of production that earn income within a particular country.

15. F. L. Rivera-Batiz and L. Rivera-Batiz, *International Finance and Open Economy Macroeconomics* (New York: Macmillan, 1985), p. 2.

16. Also, see Sewell, *op cit.*, pp. 188–189.

17. Sylvia Porter, comments in *New York Daily News*; cited in *World Development Newsletter*, 4 (March 4, 1981), p. 1.

18. Remarks by Sir Roy Denman, head of EEC Mission to U.S.; cited in *Washington Post National Weekly Edition*, September 22, 1986, p. 19.

19. See *Direction of Trade Statistics Yearbook, 1986* (Washington, D.C.: IMF, 1986), p. v; and Spero, *op. cit.*, p. 117.

20. Remarks made by Norman Krandell, Ford Motor Company executive, on a panel at the annual meeting of the International Studies Association, Cincinnati, Ohio, March 26, 1982.

21. See Benjamin J. Cohen, "A Brief History of International Monetary Relations," in Jeffry A. Frieden and David A. Lake, eds., *International Political Economy* (New York: St. Martin's Press, 1987), pp. 245–268.

22. Data are from Sewell, *op. cit.*, appendix D.

23. *Ibid.*

24. *Aid from OPEC Countries* (Paris: OECD, 1983), p. 15.

25. Blake and Walters, *op. cit.*, ch. 5.

26. Gasiorowski, *op. cit.*, p. 21.

27. *Atlas of U.S. Foreign Relations*, *op. cit.*, p. 66; Blake and Walters, *op. cit.*, p. 93.

28. For a discussion of foreign investment activity in the Soviet Union, based on a survey of U.S. firms doing business in the Soviet Union, see Alice Gorlin, "East-West Commercial Contacts

and Changes in Soviet Management," in D. Sheldon, ed., *Dimensions of Détente* (New York: Praeger, 1978).

29. J. W. Vaupel and J. P. Curhan, *The Making of Multinational Enterprise* (Boston: Harvard Business School, 1969).

30. The definition is attributed to David Lilienthal; cited in Yair Aharoni, "On the Definition of a Multinational Corporation," in *The Multinational Enterprise in Transition*, Ashok Kapur and Phillip D. Grub, eds. (Princeton, N.J.: Darwin Press, 1972).

31. Raymond Vernon, "Economic Sovereignty at Bay," *Foreign Affairs*, 47 (October 1968), p. 114.

32. An excellent discussion of definitional problems surrounding MNCs is provided by Aharoni, *op. cit.*

33. Historical background on the evolution of MNCs is furnished in ch. 1 of *The New Sovereigns*, Abdul A. Said and Luiz R. Simmons, eds. (Englewood Cliffs, N.J.: Prentice-Hall, 1975).

34. Duane Kujawa, "International Business Education and International Studies: A Multinational Enterprise Perspective on the Development of a Convergence Theorem," paper presented at the annual meeting of the International Studies Association, Cincinnati, Ohio, March 25, 1982.

35. The number varies with the definition used. One author notes a global register of transnational corporations that lists over 9000 firms having operations outside their home countries; see Harold K. Jacobson, *Networks of Interdependence*, 2nd ed. (New York: Knopf, 1984), p. 53. Another work counts 16,000 MNCs by 1980; see Frieden and Lake, *op. cit.*, p. 170.

36. For comparisons of American, European, and Japanese MNCs, see Said and Simmons, *op. cit.*, p. 9; George Modelski, "Multinational Business: A Global Perspective," *International Studies Quarterly*, 16 (December 1972) pp. 407–432; and Raymond Vernon, *Storm Over the Multinationals: The Real Issues* (Cambridge, Mass.: Harvard University Press, 1977).

37. On comparison of MNC annual sales with country GNPs, see UN Centre on Transnational Corporations, *Transnational Corporations in World Development: Third Survey* (New York: UN, 1983), p. 46.

38. Frieden and Lake, *op. cit.*, p. 170.

39. Barnet and Müller, *op. cit.*, p. 15.

40. Louis Turner, *Invisible Empires* (New York: Harcourt Brace Jovanovich, 1971).

41. Said and Simmons, *op. cit.*

42. Raymond Vernon, *Sovereignty at Bay: The Multinational Spread of U.S. Enterprise* (New York: Basic Books, 1971).

43. See Richard D. Robinson, *National Control of Multinational Corporations: A Fifteen Country Study* (New York: Praeger, 1976); and Edith Penrose, "The State and Multinational Enterprises in Less Developed Countries," in Frieden and Lake, *op. cit.*, pp. 218–230.

44. Spero, *op. cit.*, p. 271.

45. See Stephen J. Korbin, "Expropriation as an Attempt to Control Foreign Firms in LDCs: Trends from 1960 to 1979," *International Studies Quarterly*, 28 (September 1984), pp. 329–348.

46. K. J. Holsti, "Change in the International System: Interdependence, Integration, and Fragmentation," in *Change in the International Sytem*, Ole R. Holsti et al., eds. (Boulder, Colo.: Westview Press, 1980), p. 37.

47. Peter Kresl, "Canada–United States Investment Linkages," paper delivered at the annual meeting of the International Studies Association, Cincinnati, Ohio, March 26, 1982, p. 6.

48. "The Buying of America," featuring a hypothetical "For Sale" sign on the Statue of Liberty, was the cover story of the November 27, 1978, issue of *Newsweek*. See Earl H. Fry, *Financial Invasion of the U.S.A.* (New York: McGraw-Hill, 1980).

49. By 1985, the combination of a growing trade deficit along with increased funds owed to foreign investors had resulted in the U.S. becoming a "net debtor" nation for the first time since 1914.

50. On host government concerns, see Robert Kudrle, "The Several Faces of the Multinational Corporation: Political Reaction and Policy Response," in W. Ladd Hollist and F. Lamond

Tullis, eds., *An International Political Economy* (Boulder, Colo.: Westview Press, 1985), pp. 175–197.

51. For a discussion of these and other examples, see Jack N. Behrman, *National Interests and the Multinational Enterprise: Tensions Among the North Atlantic Countries* (Englewood Cliffs, N.J.: Prentice-Hall, 1970). For the role of ITT in Chile, see Richard W. Mansbach *et al., The Web of World Politics* (Englewood Cliffs, N.J.: Prentice-Hall, 1976), pp. 175–176.

52. Raymond Vernon, "The Multinationals: No Strings Attached," *Foreign Policy*, 33 (Winter 1978–79), p. 121.

53. See Barnet and Müller, *op. cit.*, pp. 77 and 87–89, for discussion of several such incidents.

54. Raymond Vernon, "The Role of U.S. Enterprise Abroad," *Daedalus*, 98 (Winter 1969), p. 129. Vernon has since had some second thoughts, however.

55. Cited in Barnet and Müller, *op. cit.*, p. 16.

56. *Ibid.*

Chapter 14. Economic Development: The Call for a New International Economic Order

1. *Daily Telegraph* (London), October 21, 1981, p. 6.

2. *St. Louis Post-Dispatch*, August 10, 1981, p. 7A.

3. Issues of the *New York Times*, July 13–21, 1985.

4. For views, both pro and con, about NIEO, see the Brandt Commission, *Common Crisis–North-South: Cooperation for World Recovery* (London: Pan, 1983); Jagdish N. Bhagwati, ed., *The New Economic Order: The North-South Debate* (Cambridge, Mass.: MIT Press, 1977); Richard N. Cooper, "A New International Economic Order for Mutual Gain," *Foreign Policy*, no. 26 (Spring 1977), pp. 66–120; Nathaniel H. Leff, "The New Economic Order—Bad Economics, Worse Politics," *Foreign Policy*, no. 24 (Fall 1976), pp. 202–217; and Craig N. Murphy, "What the Third World Wants: An Interpretation of the Development and Meaning of the New International Economic Order Ideology," *International Studies Quarterly*, 27 (March 1983), pp. 55–76.

5. *North-South: A Program for Survival. Report of the Independent Commission on International Development Issues* (Cambridge, Mass.: MIT Press, 1980), p. 32.

6. Even the figures for *current* world poverty levels are rough guesses, since an accurate census in poverty-stricken areas is extremely difficult to obtain. The figures quoted are from *St. Louis Post-Dispatch*, August 10, 1981, p. 7A. For the latest available figures, see *World Bank Atlas, 1986* (Washington, D.C.: World Bank, 1986). See the figures cited in Chapter 3 of this text, especially in Tables 3.2 and 3.3.

7. *North-South*, pp. 48–49. See ch. 2 of this report for a discussion of "dimensions of development."

8. Ian Guest, "Cong Dispute Expected on Merits of Private vs. Public Third World Aid," *International Herald Tribune*, October 27, 1981. See also David R. Francis, "One Billion New Jobs Needed to Keep the World Working," *Christian Science Monitor*, August 30, 1985, p. 1.

9. *North-South*, p. 34.

10. Ruth Leger Sivard, *World Military and Social Expenditures, 1985* (Washington, D.C.: World Priorities, 1985), p. 27; citing International Labor Organization (ILO) estimates.

11. Brandt Commission, *Common Crisis*, pp. 21–22.

12. See Jeffrey D. Sachs, "External Debt and Macro-economic Performance in Latin America and East Asia," *Brookings Papers on Economic Activity*, 2 (1985), pp. 523–573; Rudiger Dornbusch, "Policy and Performance Links Between LDC Debtors and Industrial Nations," *Brookings Papers*, 2 (1985), pp. 303–368; and Carlos F. Diaz-Alejandro, "Latin American Debt: I Don't Think We Are in Kansas Anymore," *Brookings Papers*, 2 (1984), pp. 335–403.

13. Morris David Morris, *Measuring the Condition of the World's Poor: The Physical Quality of Life Index* (New York: Pergamon Press, 1979), appendix A; and James A. Bill and Carl Leiden, *Politics in the Middle East*, 2nd ed. (Boston: Little, Brown, 1984), pp. 20–25.

14. Sivard, *op. cit.*, p. 27.

15. Lester R. Brown, "Reducing Hunger," in *State of the World 1985*, ed. by Brown *et al.* (New York: W. W. Norton, 1985), ch. 2; "Primary Health Care Is Not Curing Africa's Ills," *The Economist*, May 31, 1986, pp. 97–100; and Ward Sinclair, "World Food Production Is Belying the Doomsayers," *International Herald Tribune*, January 2, 1986.

16. Brown, "A False Sense of Security," in *State of the World 1985*, ch. 1.

17. Neal Spivack and Ann Florini, *Food on the Table* (New York: United Nations Association, 1986), p. 28.

18. *Interdependent*, 7 (July-August 1981).

19. Robert Holden, "The Hamburger Connection," *St. Louis Post-Dispatch*, November 18, 1981.

20. For details on the "green revolution," see Lester R. Brown, *By Bread Alone* (New York: Praeger, 1974), especially ch. 10.

21. *North-South*, p. 106.

22. Rafael M. Salas, "The Time to Tame Runaway Cities Is Now," *International Herald Tribune*, May 27, 1986, p. 4.

23. Roger D. Hansen, *Beyond the North-South Stalemate* (New York: McGraw-Hill, 1979), pp. 94 and 117.

24. Lester R. Brown *et al.*, *State of the World 1984* (New York: W. W. Norton, 1984), ch. 2.

25. U.S. Bureau of the Census, *Statistical Abstract of the United States: 1986*, 106th ed. (Washington, D.C.: U.S. Government Printing Office, 1986), p. 840.

26. "Primary Health Care," p. 97.

27. *Ibid.*, p. 100. See also Harry Clay Blaney III, *Global Challenges: A World at Risk* (New York: Franklin Watts, 1979), pp. 56–64; and Charles O. Pannenborg, *A New International Health Order: An Inquiry into the International Relations of World Health and Medical Care* (Alphen aan den Rijn, Netherlands: Sijthoff and Noordhoff, 1979), p. 333.

28. *North-South*, pp. 55 and 82; and "Primary Health Care," p. 98.

29. *Atlas of U.S. Foreign Affairs* (Washington, D.C.: U.S. State Department, December 1985), pp. 54–55.

30. Brandt Commission, *Common Crisis*, p. 19.

31. *Financial Times* (London), January 8, 1982, p. 3.

32. See the quotation in Karin Lissakers, "Dateline Wall Street: Faustian Finance," *Foreign Policy*, no. 51 (Summer 1983), p. 160. On international bank lending practices, see Anthony Sampson, *The Money Lenders: The People and Politics of the World Banking Crisis* (New York: Penguin, 1981). Note that non-U.S. banks, especially those in Europe and Japan, held two-thirds of the debt of the four largest Latin American debtors—Argentina, Brazil, Mexico, and Venezuela. See Steward Fleming, "Baker Banks on Non-U.S. Creditors," *Financial Times* (London), October 28, 1985, p. 3.

33. William H. Kester, "Bankers Relax a Bit on Debt Problem," *St. Louis Post-Dispatch*, September 23, 1984, p. 1E. Also, on the debt problem, see William Montalbano, "Latin Money Crisis Growing, Bank Says," *International Herald Tribune*, March 25, 1986, pp. 1 and 7; William A. Orme, Jr., "Latin American Debtors Resisting IMF Terms," *International Herald Tribune*, November 26, 1985, pp. 9–10; and Ron Scherer, "Debtor Nations Get on the Financial Track," *The Christian Science Monitor* (November 5, 1986), pp. 3–4.

34. UN Conference on Trade and Development, *The Least Developed Countries—1985* (Geneva: United Nations, 1986).

35. Brandt Commission, *Common Crisis*, pp. 82–83.

36. *Interdependent*, 7 (December 1981), p. 7.

37. Marshall R. Singer, *Weak States in a World of Powers* (New York: Free Press, 1972), p. 190.

38. Lester R. Brown, *The Twenty-Ninth Day* (New York: W. W. Norton, 1978).

39. Hansen, *op. cit.*, p. 216.

40. See Joan Edelman Spero, *The Politics of International Economic Relations*, 3rd ed. (New York: St. Martin's, 1985), p. 253.

41. For a review of the shifting tides of power in the North-South struggle, see Tony Smith, "Changing Configurations of Power in North-South Relations Since 1945," *International Organization*, 31 (Winter 1977), pp. 1–28; Michael W. Doyle, "Stalemate in the North-South Debate: Strategies and the NIEO," *World Politics*, 35 (April 1983), pp. 426–464; and Robert Ramsay, "UNCTAD's Failures: The Rich Get Richer," *International Organization*, 38 (Spring 1984), pp. 387–397.

42. Robert Rothstein, *Global Bargaining: UNCTAD and the Quest for a New International Economic Order* (Princeton, N.J.: Princeton University Press, 1979), pp. 23–24. The role of the developed Communist states in the NIEO debate, minimal as it is, is discussed in Robert M. Cutler, "East-South Relations at UNCTAD: Global Political Economy and the CMEA," *International Organization*, 31 (Winter 1983), pp. 121–142.

43. See Ernst Haas, "Why Collaborate? Issue-Linkage and International Regimes," *World Politics*, 32 (April 1980), pp. 364–365. If the international order is to be transformed, one author has argued it could go in one or more of four directions: (1) toward more "capitalist" economic and political power balancing, with East-West agreements on spheres of influence, and support for existing financial institutions such as the IMF; (2) toward Soviet "socialism," with single party states emphasizing economic rather than political rights and developing a centralized planned global economy; (3) toward "collective self-reliance," with individual states and regional groups of states negotiating and working for self-help, and less stress on global regimes and institutions; (4) toward "corporatist authoritarianism," based on right-wing authoritarian states out to keep "order" through a global anti-Marxist alliance. See Hayward R. Alker, "Dialectical Foundations of Global Disparities," *International Studies Quarterly*, 25 (March 1981), pp. 69–98.

44. See Hans-Henrik Holm, *The Game Is Up: The North-South Debate Seen Through Four Different Perspectives* (Aarhus, Denmark: Institute of Political Science, University of Aarhus, 1982); and Thomas Franck and Mark M. Munansangu, *The New Order: International Law in the Making* (New York: UNITAR, 1982).

45. Peter G. Brown and Henry Shue, eds., *Food Policy: The Responsibility of the United States in the Life and Death Choices* (New York: Free Press, 1977), p. 2.

46. Blaney, *op. cit.*, p. 50. See also Alan W. Horton, "The World Food Council Ten Years Later," *UFSI Reports*, no. 8 (Hanover, N.H.: University Field Staff International, 1984).

47. *The Economist*, December 26, 1981, pp. 79–80. For a discussion of the problems experienced by IGOs in the food area, see Blaney, *op. cit.*, pp. 50–51; Raymond F. Hopkins and Donald J. Puchala, "Perspectives on the International Relations of Food," *International Organization*, 32 (Summer 1978), pp. 581–616.

48. Quoted by William U. Chandler, "Investing in Children," *State of the World 1986*, ed. by Brown *et al.* (New York: W. W. Norton, 1986), pp. 173–174. See also Brown, "Stopping Population Growth," *State of the World 1985*, ch. 9.

49. "The Malthusian Time Bomb is Still Ticking," *New York Times*, July 29, 1984, p. E3.

50. Michael J. Berlin, "The Politics of Population," *Interdependent*, 12 (September-October 1986), p. 5; see also David K. Willis, "Population Growth: A Critical North-South Issue?" *Christian Science Monitor* (March 5, 1985), pp. 20–21.

51. See Parker G. Marden *et al.*, *Population in the Global Arena* (New York: Holt, Rinehart and Winston, 1982), ch. 2.

52. *Ibid.*, p. 44.

53. W. Dobson, "Proposed Global Targets Rejected as Solution to People Puzzle," *International Perspectives* (November-December 1974), pp. 43–48.

54. *The Economist* (December 26, 1981), pp. 79–80; and "UN Agency Faces Deficit As Refugee Cases Mount," *International Herald Tribune*, October 9, 1985, p. 2.

55. Ian Guest, "Nobel Award Raises Hope for 10m Refugees," *Manchester Guardian* (U.K.), November 1981.

56. *New York Times*, March 28, 1982, p. 4.

57. Linda Feldman, "UNICEF 'Revolution' in Child Survival," *Christian Science Monitor*, December 11, 1986, p. 15; see also Pannenborg, *op. cit.*, chs. 7 and 8.

58. William J. Broad, "Is Man Losing Battle with Mosquito?" *International Herald Tribune*, July 26, 1984.

59. For a general description of WHO activities, especially its administration of health conventions and regulations, see Moshe Y. Sachs, *Handbook on the United Nations* (New York: Wiley, 1977), pp. 149–161. WHO's success in getting acceptance of an International Code of Marketing of Breast-milk Substitutes by governments as well as MNCs (such as Nestlé) is discussed in Kathryn Sikkink, "Codes of Conduct for Transnational Corporations: The Case of the WHO/UNICEF Code," *International Organization*, 40 (Autumn 1986), pp. 815–840.

60. Blaney, *op. cit.*, pp. 59–64.

61. David R. Francis, "World Bank, IMF Take Action on Some Key Money Problems," *Christian Science Monitor*, September 28, 1984, pp. 19–20.

62. Christian Tyler, "Billion-dollar Boost for Third World," *Financial Times* (London), April 24, 1986.

63. Stefan Wagstyl, "The Crisis No One is Ready to Resolve," *Financial Times* (London), November 1, 1985; Andrew Gowers, "Gloom Over Cocoa Pact Prospects," *Financial Times*, July 2, 1986, p. 30.

64. Roger May, "Africans Agree to Respect Coffee-Export Requirements," *International Herald Tribune*, November 5, 1985, p. 11.

65. Robert L. Rothstein, "Regime-Creation by a Coalition of the Weak: Lessons from the NIEO and the Integrated Program for Commodities," *International Studies Quarterly*, 28 (September 1984), pp. 306–329. An excellent article on the recent history of the "international commodity regime" is Mark Zacher's "Trade Gaps, Analytical Gaps: Regime Analysis and International Commodity Trade Regulation," *International Organization*, 41 (Spring 1987), pp. 173–202.

66. *Financial Times* (London), January 11, 1982, p. 2.

67. David R. Francis, "US Stepping Up Push for Free Enterprise via Third World Aid," *Christian Science Monitor*, May 30, 1985, p. 19.

68. Brandt Commission, *Common Crisis*, p. 89.

69. Jimmy Burns, "Cartegena Group Meets to Discuss Baker Debt Plan," *Financial Times* (London), December 13, 1985; Clyde H. Farnsworth, "Behind Baker Plan: A Trade Deficit—and the Kremlin," and Juan de Onis, "At the Critical Point, Debtor Countries Look to a Political Solution," *International Herald Tribune*, January 27, 1986, pp. 9–10; and Hobart Rowen, "Conable's World Bank," *Washington Post National Weekly Edition*, July 14, 1986.

70. Some states, including Zaire and Peru, declared during the 1980s that they would pay no more than 10 percent of their export earnings in loan interest per year. Such threats caught the interest of the IMF and international bankers, and compromises were sought. Still, Peru, along with Liberia, Sudan, Guyana, and Vietnam, were declared ineligible for loans by the IMF because of nonrepayment. At some point, though, IGOs like the IMF risk undermining their own support with such declarations, especially if larger, more influential states become the target. See Barbara Bradley, "Model Zaire Joins Countries Asking for Debt Rescheduling," *Christian Science Monitor*, November 17, 1986, p. 10.

71. Robert M. Press, "Big Lenders Now Consider Ecology in Development," *Christian Science Monitor*, December 18, 1986, pp. 1 and 36.

Chapter 15.   The Management of Resources: Negotiating the World's Troubled Waters, Land, and Air

1. See Oscar Schachter, *Sharing the World's Resources* (New York: Columbia University Press, 1977), pp. 38–39.

2. See Donnella H. and Dennis Meadows *et al.*, *The Limits to Growth* (Washington, D.C.: Potomac Associates, 1972).

3. For an extremely optimistic view that rejects the doomsday perspective, see Julian Simon, *The Ultimate Resource* (Princeton, N.J.: Princeton University Press, 1981).

4. W. Jackson Davis, *The Seventh Year: Industrial Civilization in Transition* (New York: W. W. Norton, 1979), p. 109.

5. Walter Sullivan, "Ozone Depletion Called Faster than Expected," *International Herald Tribune*, November 14, 1985, p. 6; and Robert C. Cowen, "Geneva Meeting on Ozone Focuses Efforts to Set World Standards," *Christian Science Monitor*, December 5, 1986, p. 10.

6. Ian Davidson, "The World in 2000: A Planet Heading for Trouble," *Financial Times* (London), February 15, 1982, p. 19, citing *The Global 2000 Report to the President* (New York: Allen Land and Penguin, 1982).

7. Sandra Postel, "Managing Freshwater Supplies," in *State of the World 1985*, ed. by Lester R. Brown *et al.* (New York: W. W. Norton, 1985), p. 43.

8. André van Dam, "The Future of Waste," *International Studies Notes*, 4 (Winter 1977), p. 17.

9. Harry Clay Blaney III, *Global Challenges: A World at Risk* (New York: Franklin Watts, 1979), pp. 82–86.

10. Davis, *op. cit.*, p. 106.

11. Lester R. Brown, "Maintaining World Fisheries," in *State of the World 1985*, ch. 4.

12. Blaney, *op. cit.*, pp. 134–136.

13. William U. Chandler, "Increasing Energy Efficiency," and Christopher Flavin and Cynthia Pollock, "Harnessing Renewable Energy," in *State of the World 1985*, chs. 7 and 8.

14. Davis, *op. cit.*, p. 64.

15. Barry B. Hughes *et al.*, *Energy in the Global Arena* (Durham, N.C.: Duke University Press, 1985), p. 6.

16. Dennis Pirages, *The New Context for International Relations: Global Ecopolitics* (North Scituate, Mass.: Duxbury Press, 1978), pp. 115–118; Hughes *et al.*, *op. cit.*, ch. 5; and James E. Harf and B. Thomas Trout, *The Politics of Global Resources: Energy, Environment, Population, Food* (Durham, N.C.: Duke University Press, 1986), ch. 3.

17. Lester R. Brown, *The Twenty-ninth Day: Accommodating Human Needs and Numbers to the Earth's Resources* (New York: W. W. Norton, 1978), p. 126.

18. Joan Edelman Spero, *The Politics of International Economic Relations*, 3rd ed. (New York: St. Martin's Press, 1985), p. 333.

19. Pirages, *op. cit.*, ch. 5.

20. International Economic Studies Institute, *Raw Materials and Foreign Policy* (Boulder, Colo.: Westview Press, 1976), p. 73. See also Kenneth A. Dahlberg *et al.*, *Environment and the Global Arena: Actors, Values, Policies and Futures* (Durham, N.C.: Duke University Press, 1985), chs. 5 and 6.

21. Davis, *op. cit.*, pp. 134–136.

22. Donald L. Rheem, "Environmental Action: A Movement Comes of Age," *Christian Science Monitor*, January 15, 1987, p. 19.

23. UN General Assembly, 22nd Regular Session, Document A/16695 (August 17, 1967).

24. *The Law of the Sea* (New York: United Nations, 1973), pp. 2–5; and Pirages, *op. cit.*, p. 201.

25. David L. Larson, ed., *Major Issues of the Law of the Sea* (Durham, N.H.: University of New Hampshire, 1976), p. 10.

26. Finn Laursen, "The European Community at UNCLOS III," paper presented to the annual meeting of the International Studies Association, Cincinnati, Ohio, March 1982.

27. For debates over fishing, see Godfrey Brown, "Ministers Study Long-Term EEC Fish Proposals," *The Daily Telegraph* (London), June 16, 1982, p. 6.

28. Schachter, *op. cit.*, p. 43; see also Bernard D. Nossiter, "Sea Treaty Approved Despite U.S. 'No' Vote," *International Herald Tribune*, May 1, 1982; and Louis Wiznitzer, "Bonn to Sign New Law of Sea Treaty," *Christian Science Monitor*, November 5, 1984, p. 18.

29. See Schachter, *op. cit.*, pp. 43–50.

30. Seyom Brown, Nina W. Cornell, Larry L. Fabian, and Edith Brown Weiss, *Regimes for Ocean, Outer Space, and Weather* (Washington, D.C.: Brookings Institution, 1977), pp. 38–40; and

U.K. Foreign and Commonwealth Office, "Background Briefing: World Shipping Prospects" (London, December 1985).

31. Dahlberg *et al., op. cit.,* pp. 107–108.

32. See Thomas Busha and James Dawson, "A Safe Voyage to a New World," in *Ocean Yearbook I,* Elisabeth Mann Borgese and Norton Ginsburg, eds. (Chicago: University of Chicago Press, 1978), pp. 41–49.

33. *Ibid.,* pp. 50–62. The addition of Spain and Portugal to the EEC also complicated fishing disputes since EEC fishing capacities were doubled. See Tim Dickson, Paul Betts, and David White, "EEC Commission Tries to Defuse Fishing Disputes," *Financial Times* (London), July 12, 1986, p. 1.

34. See Blaney, *op. cit.,* pp. 80–81; and Schachter, *op. cit.,* p. 62. Similarly, efforts are underway to protect rare land animals from hunting and trading that nets butterfly and crocodile hunters hundreds of millions of dollars yearly. Countries participating in the Convention on International Trade in Endangered Species (CITES) have moved toward creation of international quotas on hunting and trading in ivory tusks, for example, although as with whales, enforcement of the rules remains difficult. See "Of Butterfly Ranchers and Crocodile Catchers," *The Economist,* March 1986, pp. 73–74.

35. Cited in *St. Louis Post-Dispatch,* September 16, 1982, p. 6A.

36. Brown *et al., op. cit.,* pp. 212–213.

37. Daniel Zwerdling, reporting on National Public Radio, December 26, 1986; and Michael Dobbs, "Nations Agree on Steps After Atomic Accidents," *International Herald Tribune,* May 23, 1986, p. 1.

38. Robert C. Cowen, "US Experts Urge Cooperation Among Africa Weather Services," *Christian Science Monitor,* March 5, 1985.

39. Sylvia Maureen Williams, "International Law Before and After the Moon Agreement," *International Relations* (London), 7 (November 1981), pp. 1170–1171.

40. Cited in *ibid.,* p. 1187.

41. Pirages, *op. cit.,* pp. 153–154.

42. Blaney, *op. cit.,* pp. 170–175.

43. Brown, *op. cit.,* p. 40.

44. Schachter, *op. cit.,* pp. 68–69.

45. Rheem, *op. cit.*

46. See Davis, *op. cit.,* pp. 276–283; and Gerald Foley, with Charlotte Nassim, *The Energy Question* (London: Penguin, 1976), ch. 17.

47. Cited in *The Interdependent,* 7 (January-February 1981), p. 2.

PART V. CONCLUSION

1. Robert G. Gilpin, *War and Change in World Politics* (Cambridge: Cambridge University Press, 1981), p. 227.

2. Remark by Governor Richard Lamm of Colorado, cited in *Christian Science Monitor,* April 24, 1985, p. 5.

Chapter 16.   Toward the Year 2000 and Beyond

1. This excerpt is from Burns H. Weston, Richard Falk, and Anthony D'Amato, *International Law and World Order: A Problem-Oriented Casebook* (St. Paul, Minn.: West, 1980), p. 1032; these international lawyers acknowledge that this view of the world is not widely shared and is open to serious question.

2. Hans J. Morgenthau, "The New Diplomacy of Movement," *Encounter,* 43 (August 1974), p. 57.

3. Arthur Koestler, "Janus: A Summing Up," *The Bulletin of the Atomic Scientists*, 35 (March 1979), p. 4.

4. For the WOMP point of view, see Richard A. Falk, *This Endangered Planet* (New York: Random House, 1972); Rajni Kothari, *Footsteps into the Future: Diagnosis of the Present World and a Design for an Alternative* (New York: Free Press, 1974); and Saul H. Mendlovitz, *On the Creation of a Just World Order: Preferred Worlds for the 1990s* (New York: Free Press, 1975).

5. The "unit veto system" and other variants of the state system are discussed in Morton A. Kaplan's *System and Process in International Politics* (New York: John Wiley, 1957), ch. 2.

6. Robert C. North, *The World That Could Be* (New York: W. W. Norton, 1976), p. 136.

7. Robert C. Johansen, *The National Interest and the Human Interest* (Princeton, N.J.: Princeton University Press, 1980), p. 29.

8. Joseph S. Nye, *Peace in Parts* (Boston: Little, Brown, 1971), p. 199. Nye is more skeptical about the possibility that regional organizations will lead to regional governments or a world government.

9. For a discussion of approaches to world government, see Louis René Beres and Harry R. Targ, *Reordering the Planet: Constructing Alternative Futures* (Boston: Allyn and Bacon, 1974), ch. 6.

10. See Karl W. Deutsch *et al.*, *Political Community and the North Atlantic Area* (Princeton, N.J.: Princeton University Press, 1957).

11. W. Jackson Davis, *The Seventh Year* (New York: W. W. Norton, 1979), p. 276.

12. Jonathan Schell, *The Fate of the Earth* (New York: Knopf, 1982).

13. Howard V. Perlmutter, "A View of the Future," in Abdul A. Said and Luiz R. Simmons, eds., *The New Sovereigns* (Englewood Cliffs, N.J.: Prentice-Hall, 1975), pp. 167–186; and "The Multinational Firm and the Future," *The Annals of the American Academy of Political and Social Science*, vol. 403 (September 1972).

14. Remarks in an interview by Rushworth M. Kidder, cited in *Christian Science Monitor*, December 16, 1986, p. 20.

15. As of 1983, there had been ten international launchings in the "Intercosmos" series bringing Soviet and foreign cosmonauts together in outer space. In June of 1982, French and Soviet cosmonauts dined on French "haute cuisine" in space, eating tube-fed creamed crab, pâté, and other items. *St. Louis Post-Dispatch*, June 25, 1982, p. 11A.

16. This line is taken from Robert Heilbroner's *An Inquiry into the Human Prospect* (New York: W. W. Norton, 1975), p. 169. Heilbroner paints an extremely gloomy picture of humanity's ability to come to grips with its problems.

Glossary

Alien. A person traveling or residing within a state who is either a citizen of another state or stateless.

Alliance. A formal agreement to provide mutual military assistance in time of war.

Alternative world order models. Alternative political systems into which human beings could conceivably organize themselves.

Ambassador. A high-level diplomatic official appointed as a representative by one government to another.

Anti-ballistic missile (ABM). A defensive missile system designed to stop an enemy nuclear attack by destroying incoming missiles before they hit their targets.

Apartheid. South Africa's anti-black policies.

Arms control. Agreements to limit the development, stockpiling, or use of certain types of weapons, or the deployment of weapons in certain areas.

Arms race. Competitive armament by two or more countries seeking security and protection against each other.

Arms transfers. Sales and gifts across national boundaries of weapons systems, support services, spare parts, and designs.

Autarky. National economic self-sufficiency.

Balance of payments. A financial statement of a country's economic transactions with the rest of the world, taking into account both outflows and inflows of money (e.g., foreign aid given and received, imports and exports, foreign investment funds spent abroad or received from abroad).

Balance of power. A basis for maintaining order among states, whereby aggressive-minded states are to be deterred by the prospect of coming up against a coalition of states having equal or superior power.

Balance of trade. A country's annual net trade surplus or deficit, based on the difference in the value of its total exports and imports.

Bargaining. A means of resolving differences over priorities between contestants through an exchange of proposals containing mutually acceptable terms.

Behavioralists. International relations theorists who use rigorous social science methods, such as collection and analysis of quantitative data, to develop and test theories explaining the behavior of international actors.

Bilateral. Pertaining to relations between pairs of countries.

Bilateral diplomacy. Diplomatic negotiations between two countries.

Bimultipolar system. An international system in which two major powers predominate but in which other powers have significant freedom of action. (Sometimes called a loose bipolar system.)

Biological weapons. Toxic substances that can create diseases and epidemics when launched against enemy troops or populations.

Biological Weapons Convention of 1972. An agreement forbidding not only the use of biological weapons but also their production and stockpiling.

Bipolar system. An international system in which countries align themselves into two cohesive blocs.

Boycott. The refusal of one country to purchase goods from another country.

Brain drain. The loss of native Third World technicians, engineers, and scientists to the more technically advanced countries.

Brezhnev Doctrine. A Soviet policy, established in 1968, stipulating that Communist countries can intervene in those states (such as Czechoslovakia) where "capitalist circles" threaten to topple an established Communist government.

Bureaucratic politics. The infighting between various agencies of a government which in the process of pursuing organizational interests often produce a foreign policy based more on domestic politics than on national interest or national security.

Capitalism. An economic system that stresses private property and the accumulation of private wealth, based on laissez-faire free enterprise principles (a market economy as opposed to an economy stressing a high level of central governmental planning and control).

Capital sector. In the international economy, the flow of foreign aid and foreign investment funds across national boundaries.

Charter of Economic Rights and Duties of States. A resolution passed by the UN General Assembly in 1974 recognizing the right of every state to exercise full permanent sovereignty over all its wealth, natural resources, and economic activities.

Chemical weapons. Gases, herbicides, and other chemical substances that can kill or paralyze enemy troops or populations.

Civil war. Sustained violent conflict between organized political forces within a state.

Collective goods. Goods that are jointly available and indivisible, which no one can be deprived of even if they did not contribute to the production of the goods.

Collective security. A system of world order in which the weight of the entire international community would be thrown against any state committing aggression, as provided for in the UN Charter.

Commerce. In the international economy, imports and exports of commodities and products that flow across national boundaries; international trade.

Commodity agreement. An agreement to raise and stabilize agricultural and raw materials prices and to create buffer stocks that could be released in controlled ways on the market.

Common market. A stage in economic integration, as envisioned in the European Community plan, in which not only goods and services but workers and capital are able to move freely across national boundaries.

Communism. A political ideology and movement which, since Lenin, has advocated the use of a single mass-based party vanguard leadership to bring about a workers' and peasants' revolution, leading to first a socialist society based on central government planning along with state ownership of property and ultimately to a stateless and classless society.

Comparative foreign policy analysis. A body of research that attempts to examine systematically the foreign policy behavior patterns that states exhibit and the determinants of these patterns.

Compellance. The attempt by one state to persuade another state to do something the latter generally does not wish to do.

Concert of Europe. Nineteenth-century system of "great power" consultation, created by Britain, Prussia, Russia, and other European powers at the 1815 Congress of Vienna, following the Napoleonic Wars; designed to resolve international problems whenever a dispute threatened to erupt into war.

Conference on the Human Environment. A 1972 UN-sponsored conference in Stockholm that was a landmark attempt to address environmental concerns at the global level.

Conference on the Law of the Sea. A UN conference convened in 1958 and in subsequent years to codify rules governing the oceans.

Congress of Vienna. The 1815 peace conference following the Napoleonic Wars, which created the Concert of Europe and produced one of the first sets of rules governing exchange of ambassadors and other diplomatic relations among states.

Containment. A major theme running through American foreign policy after World War II, involving the establishment of alliances by the United States to halt the expansion of communism.

Convention. See Treaty.

Conventional arms. Non-nuclear weapons.

Counterinsurgency. Tactics used to combat revolutionaries engaged in guerrilla warfare, stressing combat in rugged terrain, intelligence operations to identify and destroy guerrilla sanctuaries, and inducements to civilians to report guerrillas to government authorities.

Credibility. The extent to which one state's threats or promises are believed by another state.

Crisis decision. A foreign policy decision made in situations normally characterized by a sense of high threat and potential gravity, an element of surprise, a short time frame, and involvement of the highest level of the foreign policy establishment.

Cultural Revolution. The internal upheaval in the People's Republic of China that occurred in the late 1960s and early 1970s in which the regime of Chairman Mao Tse-tung undertook to rekindle revolutionary fervor in the masses and prevent a technologically elitist society.

Currency. Any form of money used as a medium of exchange in domestic and international economic transactions.

Customary rules. Those practices that have been widely accepted as legally binding by states over a period of time as evidenced by repeated usage.

Customs union. A stage in economic integration, as envisioned in the European Community plan, in which all member states impose a common external tariff on goods entering the union from nonmember states.

Democracy. An open, pluralistic governmental system, allowing for the free expression and flow of ideas and for rival political groupings.

***Dependencia* school.** An international economic perspective that sees the international economy as consisting of two sets of states: the dominant North and the dependent South, resulting in pervasive poverty in the South and great wealth in the North.

Détente. The relaxation of tensions between adversaries; applied in the 1970s to the United States and the Soviet Union.

Deterrence. The attempt by one state to dissuade another state from doing something, particularly an act of military aggression.

Devaluation. The lowering of the value of a country's currency relative to other national currencies.

Dictatorship. A closed, authoritarian governmental system in which the free expression and flow of ideas is severely curtailed and political opposition severely restricted.

Diplomacy. The formal practices and methods whereby states conduct their foreign relations, including the exchange of ambassadors; the general process whereby states seek to communicate, to influence each other, and to resolve conflicts through bargaining.

Diplomatic immunity. The freedom

from arrest or prosecution enjoyed by foreign diplomats in a host country, based on the Vienna Convention on Diplomatic Relations.

Disarmament. The decision by one or more states to destroy weapons in their possession and to acquire no others.

East-West conflict. The conflict between the two major competing blocs that had formed after World War II—the "First World" (the United States and the economically developed capitalist democracies of Western Europe, Japan, Canada, Australia, and New Zealand) and the "Second World" (the Soviet Union and its Communist allies in Eastern Europe and elsewhere).

Economic and monetary union. A stage in economic integration in which all member states harmonize their economic policies and introduce a common currency.

Economic and Social Council (ECO-SOC). The UN organ charged with offering recommendations, issuing reports, organizing conferences, and coordinating the activities of various UN agencies in the economic and social field.

Economic development. The improvement of techniques of production and distribution of goods and services, with less waste of resources or human energy, in order to establish conditions that enable the average person to attain a decent standard of living.

Embargo. The refusal of one country to sell goods to another country.

Embassy. A permanent mission established by a government in a foreign country to represent its interests in that country.

European Community. A regional body consisting of twelve Western European states collaborating in the European Coal and Steel Community (ECSC), the European Economic Community (EEC or Common Market), and the European Atomic Energy Community (EURA-TOM); created after World War II to promote economic efficiency, free trade, and prosperity among its members.

Exchange rate. The value of one country's currency in terms of another's, in trade and other transactions.

Export. To sell goods to another country in international trade.

Expropriation. Government seizure of foreign-owned property or assets.

Fascism. A political system, such as existed in Mussolini's Italy or Franco's Spain, with a single party dictatorship ruling and representing interests of the Church, large landholders, the military, and the wealthy industrial classes.

Food and Agriculture Organization (FAO). The UN Specialized Agency that engages in research, technical assistance, and financial support aimed at improving agricultural production and addressing the food needs of less developed countries.

Force without war. The use of armed force in some fashion short of war, e.g., border skirmishes, raids, interventions, and other acts of violence used in limited or low-intensity conflict situations.

Foreign aid. The transfer of resources between governments on generous terms, in the form of grants, loans, export credits, or technical and military assistance.

Foreign investment. The transfer of funds into a country, by a foreign government or by private parties, for the purchase of property, production facilities, or dividend-bearing securities in that country.

Foreign policy. A set of priorities and guides for action in certain circumstances that underlies a country's behavior toward other states and includes both the basic goals a national government seeks to pursue in the international arena and the instruments used to achieve those goals.

Foreign policy behavior. The specific actions states take toward each other.

Fourth World. Approximately twenty-eight of the world's poorest nation-states, designated by the United Nations as "least developed countries."

Free trade. The practice of encouraging as much international trade as possible by removing government-imposed tariff and nontariff barriers between states.

Free trade area. A stage in economic integration, as envisioned in the European Community plan, in which all tariff barriers are eliminated in trade among member states.

Functionalist school. A school of thought arguing that as states collaborate on specific noncontroversial or technical issues, their governments will learn habits of cooperation and will find reason to collaborate on politically more sensitive issues as well, leading gradually to surrender of sovereignty and ultimately a possible supranational community.

Game theory. A branch of social science analysis that uses game models to explain and predict human behavior, and bases those predictions on mathematical probabilities and the values people attach to various outcomes possible in the game.

General Agreement on Tariffs and Trade (GATT). An intergovernmental organization established in 1947 to serve as a global forum for multilateral negotiations aimed at reducing tariff and nontariff barriers to trade.

General Assembly. The main deliberative body of the United Nations, representing the entire UN membership and authorized by the Charter to deal with a broad range of political, economic, and social issues.

Geneva Protocol of 1925. An agreement prohibiting the first use of lethal biological and chemical weapons by the signatories against each other.

Global actors. States whose interests and activities are global in scope, manifested by widespread diplomatic, commercial, and other ties outside their region.

Globalist school. A major school of international relations, which argues that the struggle between national governments competing for power and security is only one aspect of world politics and that a fuller understanding of world politics requires one to look also at nonstate actors and at economic and nonsecurity issues in an interdependent world.

Great man theory. The belief that a single individual is capable of shaping great events.

Greenhouse effect. An overall rise in the earth's temperature resulting from the accumulation of carbon dioxide caused by the burning of coal and other fossil fuels.

Green revolution. The introduction of high-yielding "miracle" seeds, along with the heavy application of chemical fertilizer and extensive irrigation, in order to bring about higher agricultural production in less developed countries.

Group of 77. A group of more than 100 Third World countries which in the UN and other forums has sought to promote a New International Economic Order aimed at redistributing wealth from the North to the South.

Groupthink. A social-psychological phenomenon whereby the pressures for group conformity may lead individual members of a decision-making group to suppress any personal doubts they may have about the emerging group consensus.

Guerrilla warfare. "Hit-and-run" tactics used by small bands of irregular forces against an invading army or in rebellion against established authorities.

Hague Convention of 1970. A treaty requiring signatories to extradite or prosecute air hijackers in their custody.

High politics. Issues that involve the most crucial interests of states and are the most controversial in nature, such as national security issues.

High sea. Waters beyond the control or sovereignty of any state.

Home government. The government of the country in which a multinational corporation is headquartered.

Host government. The government of a country in which a foreign-based multinational corporation operates subsidiaries.

Human rights. The set of privileges supposedly enjoyed by all human beings, defined in various treaties and declarations, including the Universal Declaration of Human Rights.

Idealist school. A major school of international relations, focusing on the role of international law and international organization as well as morality in international affairs.

Ideology. A relatively inflexible set of beliefs regarding the nature of political, economic, and social relations.

Idiosyncratic factors. The characteristics of individual leaders and groups of decision makers, which can affect a state's foreign policy.

Image. An individual's view of the world that tends to color, and sometimes distort, perceptions of reality.

Imperialism. The policy of acquiring foreign territory through force; associated especially with the building of colonial empires during the nineteenth century.

Import. To purchase goods from another country in international trade.

Influence. The process whereby one political actor seeks to get another actor to conform to the former's preferences.

Integration theory. A theory explaining how political units tend to merge together and transfer loyalty to a larger community.

Inter-continental ballistic missiles (ICBMs). Electronically guided land-based rockets able to deliver nuclear payloads at distances of over 3,000 miles.

Interdependence. The interrelatedness of national societies, which are in varying degrees sensitive and vulnerable to each other's policies.

Intergovernmental organizations (IGOs). International organizations that have national governments as members and are created through treaties among states.

International Atomic Energy Agency (IAEA). The UN Specialized Agency responsible for maintaining safeguards on the use of nuclear fuels and disposal of wastes associated with the Non-Proliferation Treaty and other nuclear arms control agreements.

International Bank for Reconstruction and Development (IBRD). See World Bank.

International Civil Aviation Organization (ICAO). The UN Specialized Agency responsible for establishing uniform practices and standards of international air safety.

International Court of Justice. See World Court.

International Labor Organization (ILO). The UN Specialized Agency responsible for monitoring working conditions worldwide and improving the general standard of living of the world's workers through the drafting of an international labor code and other activities.

International law. The body of rules governing relations between states, derived mainly from custom and treaties.

International Maritime Organization (IMO). The UN Specialized Agency responsible for managing international maritime traffic.

International Monetary Fund (IMF). The UN Specialized Agency responsible for promoting international monetary cooperation, stabilizing exchange rates, and providing foreign exchange funds for needy states so that the maximum amount of world trade can occur.

International organizations. Intergovernmental and nongovernmental organizations, established on a regional or global basis in response to problems that transcend national boundaries.

International relations. The study of who gets what, when, and how in the international arena; primarily deals with relations between nation-states but includes nonstate actors also.

International Seabed Authority. An organization proposed by the Law of the Sea Conference in 1982, designed to regulate deep seabed mining and to distribute resultant revenues between private investors and developing countries.

International system. The general pattern of political, economic, social, geographical, and technological relationships in world affairs; the general setting in which international relations occur at any point in time.

International Telecommunication Union (ITU). The UN Specialized Agency responsible for managing the flow of telegraph, radio, and television communications across the globe.

Intervention. Military, economic, or diplomatic interference by one country in another country's territory or internal affairs.

Isolationism. A national policy advocating aloofness from political or economic entanglements with other countries.

Kellogg-Briand Pact. A multilateral treaty concluded in 1928 that attempted to outlaw war as a means of settling disputes between members of the international community.

Law of the Sea Treaty. The document drafted at the UN Conference on the Law of the Sea in 1982, aimed at establishing a single set of rules governing the use of territorial waters, economic zones, and all other parts of the oceans.

League of Nations Covenant. The charter establishing a global intergovernmental organization after World War I, the precursor of the United Nations.

Liberal internationalist school. An international economic perspective, widely held in developed capitalist societies, according to which consumers in all nations can expect to benefit from an international economy based on the most efficient allocation and use of resources, competition, and free trade among countries.

Limited war. Violent conflict involving the controlled use of military force, with participants refraining from using their entire arsenals.

Limits to growth school. A school of thought predicting imminent resource scarcities and environmental decay and arguing that economic growth will have to be halted in the late twentieth century if civilization is to survive.

Low politics. Issues that are relatively narrow, technical, and noncontroversial in nature.

Macro-decision. A foreign policy decision that involves relatively large, general concerns (e.g., the composition of the defense budget) and is designed to establish guidelines to be applied later to specific situations as they arise.

Marshall Plan. An American foreign aid program that helped to rebuild the wartorn economies of Western Europe following World War II.

Marxist school. A major school of thought that views international relations as a struggle between rich and poor classes rather than as a contest between national governments or nation-states.

Massive retaliation. A U.S. strategic doctrine enunciated during the Eisenhower administration, threatening large-scale nuclear retaliation for Soviet-sponsored aggression in Europe or other regions.

Mercantilism. An economic philosophy advocating the use of protective tariffs and other economic measures to be taken by a state to expand national power.

Micro-decision. A foreign policy decision involving concerns that are relatively narrow in scope, that are low threat in nature, and that tend to be handled at the lower levels of the government bureaucracy.

Military-industrial complex. A mutually supportive ongoing relationship between a nation's defense-related industries and its military forces.

Monroe Doctrine, A statement issued by President James Monroe in 1823 opposing European intervention in the Western Hemisphere and promising to refrain from intervention in Europe; the Doctrine has continued to be the basis for American opposition to foreign intervention in Latin America.

Montreal Convention of 1971. A treaty requiring signatories to prosecute or extradite anyone committing acts of sabotage against airports or aircraft on the ground, with the ICAO empowered to suspend air travel to states that fail to comply.

Most favored nation principle. The principle, adopted by GATT, that whenever one member state lowers tariffs on certain kinds of imports from another member state, all member states are entitled to the same favorable treatment with regard to their goods.

Multilateral. Involving several countries.

Multilateral diplomacy. Diplomatic negotiations between several countries.

Multinational corporation (MNC). A corporation having branch operations abroad that are connected with and subordinate to a headquarters office in another country.

Multipolar system. An international system characterized by multiple power centers and very flexible alignments.

Munich Pact. A 1938 pact whereby Britain and France abandoned their Czech allies and appeased Hitler's territorial demands; became a symbol after World War II of the need to "fight force with force" in order to deter aggression.

Municipal law. Law within a national political system (domestic law), as opposed to international law.

Mutually assured destruction (MAD). A strategic doctrine of deterrence under which each adversary preserves the capability to absorb a first nuclear attack by the other and still retaliate with devastating nuclear force—inflicting unacceptable damage on the attacker.

Nation. A cultural or social entity whose members have some sense of shared historical experience as well as shared destiny, based on common language or other ties.

National. A person owing permanent allegiance to a particular state, either through birth or through naturalization; a citizen.

National air space. The air above a country's land mass and its territorial sea in which that country exercises sovereignty and can exclude foreign aircraft.

National attribute factors. The demographic, economic, military, and governmental characteristics of a nation-state, which can affect the foreign policy of that state.

National interests. The fundamental interests, defined by the government, that a nation's foreign policy is geared to achieve, ordinarily including a nation's physical survival, economic well-being, and self-determination.

National Socialism. The political system in Germany from 1932 to 1945, commonly called "Naziism," with a single party dictatorship exercising total control of the society and economy based on racial superiority theories, anticommunism, anti-Semitism, and ultra-nationalism.

Nationalism. The determination of a group of people to establish or preserve themselves as a nation and to achieve or maintain statehood.

Nation-state. A national political unit; a term often used by scholars as a synonym for "state."

NATO. See North Atlantic Treaty Organization.

Negotiation. A form of diplomacy in which bargaining occurs through formal, direct discussion between parties.

Neocolonialism. The subtle domination of another country, through economic penetration rather than through outright takeover by force.

Neofunctionalist school. A branch of the functionalist school which identifies certain sectors of intergovernmental cooperation as more likely to lead to further cooperation, or "spillover," than others.

Neutrality. A stance of formal nonpartisanship in world affairs; a refusal to join alliances.

New International Economic Order (NIEO). A new set of trade, aid, and investment relationships demanded by Third World countries, intended to produce a more even distribution of wealth between the generally rich North and the generally impoverished South.

Nixon Doctrine. An American policy during the Nixon administration, stressing military self-help by Third World states, assisted by transfers of U.S. military equipment.

Nonalignment. A policy of asserting independence from and nonattachment to competing blocs of states, especially as regards the East-West conflict.

Nongovernmental organizations (NGOs). International organizations composed of private individuals or groups.

Nonrational behavior. The failure of a decision maker to specify goals clearly, to consider every possible alternative, and to choose that option calculated to maximize the achievement of goals.

Nonrenewable resources. Raw materials that are in finite supply and capable of being exhausted.

Nonstate actor. An actor other than a national government that has an impact on international relations (e.g., IGOs and NGOs).

North Atlantic Treaty Organization (NATO). A military alliance established in 1949 by fifteen countries in North America and Western Europe, in which the members pledge that an attack on one will be considered equivalent to an attack on all.

North-South conflict. The conflict between the largely well-to-do states of the Northern Hemisphere and the generally poverty-stricken states of the Southern Hemisphere.

Nuclear arms. High-explosive bombs, operating through atomic fusion reactions, that are capable of producing destructive force up to the equivalent of millions of tons of TNT.

Nuclear deterrence. A form of military dissuasion in which a nuclear-armed nation threatens to use nuclear weapons if an adversary initiates a nuclear strike or commits a conventional aggression.

Nuclear Non-Proliferation Treaty (NPT) of 1970. An agreement in which the signatory nuclear states are pledged not to transfer nuclear weapons to nuclear have-nots, while the have-nots are pledged not to attempt to acquire nuclear weapons.

Nuclear proliferation. The acquisition of nuclear weapons by states that formerly did not have them.

Nuremberg Trials. The trials following World War II of those leaders of Nazi Germany charged with committing war crimes and crimes against humanity.

Optional Clause. A clause in the International Court of Justice Statute giving the Court compulsory jurisdiction in certain kinds of disputes.

Organization for Economic Cooperation and Development (OECD). A key institution through which the industrialized democracies—the United States, Japan, Canada, and the Western European states—promote mutual economic cooperation and plan common strategies to address the demands of less developed countries.

Organization of Petroleum Exporting Countries (OPEC). An organization of thirteen less developed countries that together account for a major portion of the world's oil exports.

Outer Space Treaty of 1967. A treaty banning the placement of "mass destruction" weapons in orbit around the earth or on celestial bodies.

Pacta sunt servanda. The fundamental principle of international law stipulating that treaties are to be obeyed.

Paradigm. An intellectual framework that structures one's thinking about a set of phenomena.

Partial Test Ban Treaty of 1963. A treaty banning nuclear testing in the atmosphere by the signatories.

Peaceful settlement procedures. Procedures, such as mediation and adjudication, that are outlined in Chapter VI of the UN Charter and are designed to forestall the use of military force in disputes between states.

Peace of Westphalia. The treaty ending the Thirty Years' War in 1648, widely accepted as marking the origin of the nation-state system.

Polis. A human-scale community, modeled after the ancient Greek city-states.

Potency. The importance of a promise or a threat—in terms of either attraction or potential harm—as perceived by the other side; an essential ingredient in bargaining.

Power. The ability to get others to do something they would not otherwise do; in international relations, a country's existing strength or relative capabilities and the manner in which one state seeks

to control the behavior of another state.

Preventive diplomacy. A UN peacekeeping role, often involving multinational forces, whereby local conflicts are kept from escalating into larger conflagrations directly involving major powers.

Primary resources. The main elements—in land, air, and water—that sustain life on earth.

Private goods. Goods that can be possessed by individuals and can be divided and consumed, as opposed to collective goods.

Prominent solution. In international bargaining, an alternative that is so self-evidently better than others, even if not optimal, that all parties are inclined to settle on it.

Promise. In international bargaining, a statement of intent to reward acceptable or desired behavior.

Punishment. In international bargaining, a penalty imposed on actors whose behavior is considered unacceptable or undesired.

Quota. A method of protecting domestic producers from foreign competition by imposing a limit on the maximum volume of allowable imports.

Rational actor model. A model of decision making whereby one carefully defines the situation, specifies goals, weighs all conceivable alternatives, and selects that option most likely to achieve the goals.

Reagan Doctrine. A policy associated with the Reagan administration in the 1980s, declaring the intention of the United States not only to contain the further spread of communist governments around the world but also to "roll back" communism by supporting insurgency movements against Marxist regimes thought to be aligned too closely with the Soviet Union.

Realist school. A major school of international relations that views international relations as a struggle for power between nation-states whose ultimate goal is security in a hostile, anarchic environment.

Rebus sic stantibus. A legal basis for termination of a treaty obligation on the grounds that present conditions are so radically different from those existing at the outset of the treaty as to render it impossible to continue honoring the terms of the pact.

Regimes. Widely accepted practices, rules, and institutional arrangements governing relations between states in various issue-areas.

Regional actor. A state that interacts primarily with neighboring states in the same geographical area, except for interactions with global actors in economic and other affairs.

Regionalism. The growth of international organizations and other kinds of ties among countries at the regional level.

Renewable resources. Resources such as air and water that are in infinite supply or are constantly renewed by natural processes.

Reward. In international bargaining, a benefit afforded to actors whose behavior is considered acceptable or desirable.

Right of innocent passage. The right of foreign vessels to pass through a state's coastal waters as long as it is done peaceably.

SALT. See Strategic Arms Limitation agreements.

Scapegoat hypothesis. The assumption that governments experiencing domestic turmoil are especially likely to become involved in foreign conflict, attempting to unify the home population through aggressive behavior against external "scapegoats."

Secondary resources. Resources such as minerals, vegetables, and animals that are derived from primary resources.

Secretariat. The administrative arm of the United Nations.

Secretary-General. The chief administrative officer of the United Nations.

Security community. A group of states among which war is no longer a serious option for pursuing goals or resolving differences.

Security Council. The UN organ with primary responsibility in the area of peace and security, consisting of fifteen states, including five permanent members (China, France, Great Britain, the Soviet Union, and the United States).

Sensitivity. The degree of one country's concern about another country's actions.

Sovereignty. Supreme decision-making authority within the boundaries of a territorial unit and acknowledging no higher authority outside those boundaries.

Specialized Agencies. A group of intergovermental organizations that are affiliated with the UN but have their own memberships, budgets, secretariats, and decision-making machinery.

Spillover. The process whereby one type of international cooperation might lead to or create needs for other types of international cooperation.

State. A legal-political entity with a sovereign government exercising supreme authority over a relatively fixed population within well-defined territorial boundaries and acknowledging no higher authority outside those boundaries.

State-centric. A focus on nation-states and their national governments as the major actors in world politics.

Strategic Arms Limitation (SALT) agreements. Bilateral agreements between the United States and the Soviet Union during the 1970s setting limits on the number and types of strategic nuclear weapons (e.g., ICBMs) the two sides could possess.

Strategic weapons. Large-scale, long-range nuclear weapons.

Submarine-launched ballistic missiles

(SLBMs). Sea-based rockets able to deliver nuclear payloads at long or short distances.

Summitry. Direct, personal contact and negotiation between heads of state.

Supranational. A type of organization or community in which nation-states surrender sovereignty to a higher authority.

Systemic factors. External factors such as geography, international interactions and links, and international system structure, which affect a state's foreign policy.

Tacit diplomacy. Informal, indirect communication through words and actions designed to signal intentions or the importance one attaches to some issue.

Tariff. An import tax imposed on foreign products entering a country.

Territorial sea. Waters immediately adjacent to a country's coast, over which that country exercises sovereignty and can regulate navigation and other activities in its own interest.

Terrorism. The use or threat of violence for purposes of political extortion, coercion, or publicity for a political cause.

Tertiary resources. Secondary resources that have been processed by humans into other usable forms.

Theory of hegemonic stability. The theory that throughout history large-scale wars involving major powers have tended to produce among the victors one dominant state (a "hegemon") capable of maintaining a degree of world order, and that this order gradually tends to break down as the hegemon suffers decline due to the draining costs of maintaining large armed forces and extensive economic commitments, finally leading to the rise of new hegemonic challengers and a new cycle of war and postwar reconstruction of world order.

Third World. The less developed countries, mainly located in the Southern Hemisphere.

Threat. In international bargaining, a statement of intent to penalize unacceptable or undesired behavior.

Threat perception. One nation's estimate of another country's capability and intent to do harm.

Tokyo Convention of 1963. A treaty obligating signatory states to effect the safe release of hijacked aircraft, passengers, and crews entering their borders.

Trade dependence. The extent to which a country's economy requires external trade, reflected in the sum of a country's imports and exports as a percentage of its gross national product (or gross domestic product).

Traditionalists. International relations scholars who base their analysis not on scientific methods but on insights gained from first-hand participant observation and practical experience or second-hand immersion in the great works of diplomatic history, statesmen's memoirs, international law treatises, and philosophical writings.

Transnational relations. Interactions between private individuals and groups across national boundaries.

Treaty. A formal written agreement or convention between states that creates legal obligations for the governments that are parties to it.

Truman Doctrine. A 1947 declaration promising U.S. assistance against Soviet aggression in Greece and Turkey and in other parts of the world where Communist expansion threatened to occur.

Trusteeship Council. A UN organ charged with facilitating the dismantling of colonial empires.

United Nations (UN). A global intergovernmental organization formed in 1945 to promote peace and international security as well as cooperation in the economic and social field.

United Nations Charter. The document enumerating the powers of the United Nations and its various organs and specifying the rights and obligations of member states.

United Nations Conference on Trade and Development (UNCTAD). A UN General Assembly organization established in 1964 to supplement GATT as a world trade forum; relied on primarily by less developed countries.

United Nations Educational, Scientific and Cultural Organization (UNESCO). The UN Specialized Agency responsible for improving literacy rates in less developed countries, promoting scientific and cultural exchanges, and facilitating the dissemination of information by drafting universal copyright conventions and related rules.

UN Environmental Program (UNEP). The major global environmental agency, established after the 1972 Conference on the Human Environment.

Universal Postal Union (UPU). The UN Specialized Agency responsible for facilitating the flow of mail across national boundaries.

Variable-sum game. In game theory, a type of game in which both parties can simultaneously win something, even though one might benefit more than the other.

Vulnerability. The degree of harm or damage that one country might suffer from another country's actions.

War. Sustained armed combat between the organized military forces of at least two nation-states.

Warsaw Pact. An alliance formed in 1955 by the Soviet Union and Eastern European countries following West Germany's entry into NATO.

World Bank (International Bank for Reconstruction and Development). The UN Specialized Agency responsible for providing loans to less developed countries to finance the building of bridges, dams, roads, and other developmental needs.

World Court (International Court of Justice). A global institution for adjudicating international disputes, located in The Hague, Netherlands.

World Food Conference of 1974. A UN-sponsored conference in Rome whose purpose was to recommend ways to improve the supply and distribution of food in the world.

World government. A political system in which one central set of authoritative institutions would preside over all human beings and political units on the planet.

World Health Organization (WHO). The UN Specialized Agency responsible for controlling communicable diseases and promoting health education and public health services in less developed countries.

World Meteorological Organization (WMO). The UN Specialized Agency responsible for collecting and exchanging global weather forecasting data and monitoring conditions relating to the global environment and climatic change.

World Population Conference of 1974. A UN-sponsored conference in Bucharest, organized to address global population issues and resulting in a World Population Plan of Action.

World system school. Similar to the *dependencia* school, an international economic perspective that focuses on interactions between nonstate actors and argues that the international economy is driven by the interests of economic elites who compete with each other in accumulating wealth.

Zero-sum game. In game theory, a type of game in which whatever one party wins the other party automatically loses; in other words, conflict is total.

Index of Names

Subject Index